T0073419

Waves
and Wave
Interaction
in Plasmas

Recommended Titles in Related Topics

Waves and Instabilities in Plasmas
by Liu Chen
ISBN: 978-9971-5-0389-5
ISBN: 978-9971-5-0390-1 (pbk)

Interaction of Electromagnetic Waves with Electron Beams and Plasmas
by C S Liu and V K Tripathi
ISBN: 978-981-02-1577-4

Linear and Nonlinear Wave Propagation
by Spencer Kuo
ISBN: 978-981-123-163-6

Slowly Varying Oscillations and Waves: From Basics to Modernity
by Lev Ostrovsky
ISBN: 978-981-124-748-4

Waves and Wave Interaction in Plasmas

Prasanta Chatterjee
Visva Bharati University, India

Kaushik Roy
Beluti M K M High School, India

Uday Narayan Ghosh
K K M College (A Constituent Unit of Munger University), India

 **World Scientific**

NEW JERSEY · LONDON · SINGAPORE · BEIJING · SHANGHAI · HONG KONG · TAIPEI · CHENNAI · TOKYO

Published by

World Scientific Publishing Co. Pte. Ltd.

5 Toh Tuck Link, Singapore 596224

USA office: 27 Warren Street, Suite 401-402, Hackensack, NJ 07601

UK office: 57 Shelton Street, Covent Garden, London WC2H 9HE

Library of Congress Control Number: 2022052897

British Library Cataloguing-in-Publication Data
A catalogue record for this book is available from the British Library.

WAVES AND WAVE INTERACTION IN PLASMAS

ISBN 978-981-126-533-4 (hardcover)
ISBN 978-981-126-534-1 (ebook for institutions)
ISBN 978-981-126-535-8 (ebook for individuals)

For any available supplementary material, please visit
https://www.worldscientific.com/worldscibooks/10.1142/13114#t=suppl

Typeset by Stallion Press
Email: enquiries@stallionpress.com

Preface

Waves and wave interactions in plasmas is written in a lucid and systematic way to serve as a special book for advanced post graduate students and researchers in Applied Mathematics, Plasma Physics, Nonlinear differential equations, Nonlinear Optics, and other Engineering branches where nonlinear wave phenomena is studied. The first chapter deals with basic plasma with elementary definitions of magnetized and unmagnetized plasmas, plasma modeling, dusty plasma, and quantum plasma. In Chapter 2, we deal with linear and nonlinear waves, solitons and shocks, and other wave phenomena.

In Chapter 3, solution of some nonlinear wave equations is discussed by using some standard technique. Chapter 4 starts with elementary knowledge of perturbation and nonperturbation methods. Several evolution equations are obtained in different plasma situations and properties of solitons in those environments are discussed. In Chapter 5, Higher-order correction to those equations and the improvement of the solution is are discussed. In Chapter 6, evolution equations in nonplanar geometry are obtained and the wave solution for such equation is also obtained. In Chapter 7, different type collisions of solitons in a plasma environment is discussed. The phenomena of soliton turbulence are also discussed as a consequence of multi soliton interactions. In Chapter 8, the properties of large amplitude solitary waves are obtained by using a non perturbative approach called Sagdeev's Pseudopotential Approach. Speed and shape of solitons are also discussed in this chapter. Possible future developments of research in this area are explained in brief in Chapter 9.

Prasanta Chatterjee, Kaushik Roy

Uday Narayan Ghosh

India

April 2022

Acknowledgments

We are greatly delighted to publish a book on *Waves and Wave Interaction in Plasma*. During writing this book, we have got help from many of our seniors and friends. We are highly obliged by the guidance we have received from Prof. Rajkumar Roychoudhury, Emeritus Professor of ISI, Kolkata. Dr. Santo Banerjee and Dr. Amar Prasad Misra have supported and motivated us in our endeavor. We are also grateful to Dr. Malay Gorui, Dr. Asit Saha, Dr. Pankaj Kumar Mandal, Dr. Ganesh Mandal, Dr. Rustam Ali, and Laxmikanta Mandi. Last but not the least, we are thankful to Dr. Sriparna Chatterjee and Diya Chatterjee for helping us in improving the language of the book.

Contents

Chapter 1

Introduction to Plasmas

1.1 Introduction

The word "Plasma" has originated from the Greek word, which indicates anything formed or shaped. Sir William Crookes first identified it as a radiant matter in 1879. In 1897, Sir J. J. Thomson studied the nature of electron discharge in a cathode-ray tube and pointed the character of matter. In 1929, the word "Plasma" was first coined by two American Physicists Tonks and Langmuir to explain the inner zone of a luminous gas that is ionized and produced by electricity discharged in a tube. Besides the three states of matter, i.e., solid, liquid, and gas, there is also a fourth state called plasma. The transition of the state of matter from solid to liquid and then to gas takes place with the temperature rise. With a further increase in temperature, some or all of the atoms of neutral gas are ionized. The gas turns out to be completely or partially ionized. Eventually, a plasma state is formed. The electromagnetic forces predominate the behavior of plasma. It has a tendency to become electrically neutral. So roughly speaking, a volume of plasma is a group of an equal number of particles charged oppositely at least on a certain level.

Research shows that plasma constitutes 99% of the visible universe. We belong to the rest 1% of the matter on earth which is something different from plasma. Plasmas are found in and around the earth, in lightning channels of the ionosphere, in the aurora, and the earth's magnetosphere. Plasmas are found in the solar wind, in the magnetosphere, and in comets. Around Jupiter and Saturn, we have plasmas in the form of gigantic plasma toroids. The sun and the other stars are nothing but enormous plasma balls. Not only the stars but also the nebula within the galaxies is also composed of plasma and so on.

Plasmas consist of positively and negatively charged particles, so at a larger length scale, the number of positively charged particles and the number of negatively charged particles in plasmas are the same. But locally, they may be different. This is what we call quasineutrality. So plasma can be characterized as a gas that is quasineutral and which contains charged and neutral particles. Moreover, plasma can also display unified behavior. Here, unified behavior indicates the movements that depend upon not only topical circumstances but also the whole plasma. Usually, a single particle (neutral) at rest will move if it takes a blow. But the situation is different in the plasma world. Plasma comprises charged particles. When these charges start moving, they generate a local concentration of positive or negative charges, which give rise to electric fields. Motions of charges also generate electric currents and hence magnetic fields. Electromagnetic fields affect the movement of other charged particles even far away. The constituent parts of plasma wield a force among them even when the distance is large. One of the most exciting features of plasma is that the forces that arise from common local collisions can be ignored if the long-range electromagnetic forces are very large. Such plasmas are called "collision-less plasmas".

1.2 Saha Equation and Plasma Temperature

The thermal ionization rule was discovered by the Indian physicist M. N. Saha (1920). He showed that the quantity of ionization can be expected in a gas that is in thermal equilibrium by the following equation. This can be represented as

$$\frac{n_i}{n_0} \simeq 2.4 \times 10^{21} \frac{T^{3/2}}{n_i} exp(-V_i/K_B T) \tag{1.1}$$

where n_i, n_0, V_i, and T denote the ion density, the neutral density, the ionization energy of the gas, and the temperature (in degrees Kelvin), respectively. K_B is the Boltzmann constant and n_i/n_0 is a balance between the ionization rate (time-dependent) and the recombination rate (density-dependent). Equation (1.1) is the famous *Saha equation*.

Let it be explained in brief. Suppose the number of particles with energy level E_i under temperature T is given by the Boltzmann distribution as

$$n_i = g_i e^{-E_i/K_B T}$$

where g_i is the ion degeneracy state. The ratio of the particle number of similar species having energy level E_i and ground state E_0 is explained as

$$\frac{n_i}{n_0} = \frac{g_i}{g_0}e^{-E_{i0}/K_BT}, \quad E_{i0} = E_i - E_0.$$

The ionization potential $V_i[eV]$ is the energy difference of two states and the kinetic energy of the electron as $E_{i0} = eV_i + \frac{p^2}{2m_e}$, where $\vec{p}$ is the momentum and m_e is the electron mass. Then, the ratio of the densities of the charged and neutral particles in a weakly ionized gas can be obtained by the Saha equation

$$\frac{n_i}{n_0} = \frac{g_i}{g_0}\frac{2}{h^3 n_e} \int_{-\infty}^{\infty} e^{-(eV_i + \vec{p}^2/2m_e)/K_BT} d\vec{p}$$

$$= \frac{2g_i}{g_0}\frac{1}{n_e}\left(\frac{2\pi m_e K_BT}{h^2}\right)^{3/2} e^{-eV/K_BT} \simeq 2.4 \times 10^{21}\frac{T^{3/2}}{n_e}e^{-eV_i/K_BT}.$$

Consider $2g_i/g_0 \sim 1$ and n_i and n_e are the ion and electron densities, respectively. If an ion is charged when it comes in contact with an electron, then $n_i \propto \frac{1}{n_e}$. This is because it is in an equilibrium state where the combination rate is proportional to the density of the electron.

Now, the ionization ratio $r_i = \frac{n_i}{n_0} \simeq \frac{n_e}{n_0}$ and the degree of ionization $\alpha = \frac{n_i}{n_0 + n_i} = \frac{r_i}{1+r_i}$. As $r_i \ll 1$, so

$$\alpha^2 \simeq r_i^2 = \frac{2.4}{n_0} \times 10^{21}T^{3/2} exp[-eV_i/K_BT].$$

The degree of ionization and temperature are proportional. But the degree of ionization is inversely proportional to the neutral density and ionization potential.

At thermal equilibrium, the distribution of particle velocity of a gas is given by

$$f(\vec{v}) = \left(\frac{m}{2\pi K_BT}\right)^{3/2} n\, exp\left(-\frac{mv^2}{2K_BT}\right).$$

The following relation will give the average kinetic energy:

$$E = \frac{1}{n}\int_{-\infty}^{\infty} \frac{1}{2}mv^2 f(\vec{v})d\vec{v} = \frac{3}{2}K_BT.$$

In plasma physics, temperatures are given in units of energy. Now, $1\,eV = 1.6 \times 10^{-19}\,J = K_BT$, so $T = \frac{1.6\times10^{-19}}{1.38\times10^{-23}} = 11600\,K$.

1.3 Basic Concepts of Plasma

1.3.1 *Basic dimensionless parameters*

The criteria for analysis without dimension are time t and length l. Let us look at the following three important parameters related to our criteria:

$$p_1 = n = \text{particle number density} \sim l^{-3}$$

$$p_2 = v_{th} = \text{particle thermal velocity} \sim lt^{-1}$$

$$p_3 = \frac{e^2}{m\epsilon_0} = \text{interaction strength} \sim l^3 t^{-2}.$$

Note that the final quantity contains only l and t and measures the strength of the coulomb interaction between the free particles charged in the plasma. We are now combining the three physical quantities to obtain a dimensionless parameter that characterizes the creature

$$P = p_1^\alpha p_2^\beta p_3^\gamma \sim l^{3(\gamma - \alpha) + \beta} t^{(-2\gamma - \beta)}.$$

Now, $-2\gamma - \beta = 0$ and $\gamma - 3\alpha = 0$. So, $\beta = -2\gamma$ and $\gamma = 3\alpha$, where α is an arbitrary constant. If we consider $\alpha = 1$, we get the dimensionless quantity as

$$P_0 \sim \frac{p_1 p_3^3}{p_2^6} \equiv \frac{1}{\Lambda^2}$$

where $\Lambda = n \left[\frac{v_{th}}{(\frac{ne^2}{m\epsilon_0})^{1/2}} \right]^3$ and $m = m_i$ or $m = m_e$. Choosing a different value of α would result in a power of P_0 which would nevertheless remain dimensionless.

Λ is used to measure plasma parameters. This is dimensionless and consists of unmagnetized plasma systems. For strongly coupled plasma, the value of $\Lambda \ll 1$. On the other hand, for weakly coupled plasma, $\Lambda \gg 1$. In the former case, the potential energy of the interacting particles is more important than their kinetic motions. Also, for the latter case, the particle thermal motions are more significant.

1.3.2 *Debye length and Debye shielding*

The Debye length is a basic unit of length measurement in plasma physics. This unit of length appeared in the electrolyte theory developed by P. Debye and was, therefore, given the name Debye length. Debye and Huckel (1923) have shown, using the equations from Boltzmann and Poisson, that under equilibrium conditions in plasma, the average potential in the vicinity of a charged plane varies according to the law

$$\phi = \phi_0 \, exp(-x/\lambda_D).$$

Here, x is the distance from the plane and λ_D is represented by

$$\lambda_D = \left(\frac{KT}{4\pi n q^2} \right)^{1/2}.$$

Here, n is the number density of the particle per cubic centimeter, each carrying an identical charge q. The particles have a thermal movement characterized by a temperature T. If we consider a charged particle emerge in a plasma volume, it attracts oppositely charged particles, and a charge cloud around the test charge builds up. If we assume that the plasma is cold, then there is no thermal movement, and the shielding is perfect, and the number of negative charges is equal to the number of positive charges in the cloud. However, when the temperature is finite, the charged particles at the edge of the cloud (where the electric field is weak) have enough thermal energy to escape from the static potential wall of the electron. Then, the edge of the cloud appears at the radius where the potential energy is equal to the thermal energy. This radius is the *Debye length* and the spherical cloud is called the *Debye sphere*.

To find the expression of Debye length, and to understand Debye shielding, consider a plasma of a uniform density (n_0) of both electrons and ions. Initially, there is no net charge density and no electric field. If we consider a positive test charge $+q$ that is introduced into the plasma, which is at the origin of a spherical polar coordinate system, then the positive charge attracts negatively charged electrons and repels positively charged ions. In the steady state, the number densities of the electrons $n_e(\vec{r})$ and the ions $n_i(\vec{r})$ differ slightly in the vicinity of the test charge, but they are the same at a large distance, i.e, $n_e(\infty) = n_i(\infty) = n_0$. When the plasma reaches a thermodynamic equilibrium, the charged particles are distributed according to the Boltzmann law. The number density of the electrons and ions can thus be written as follows:

$$n_e(\vec{r}) = n_0 \, exp(e\phi(r)/K_B T_e) \tag{1.2}$$

$$n_i(\vec{r}) = n_0 \, exp(-e\phi(r)/K_B T_i) \tag{1.3}$$

where e, T_i, T_e, and K_B are the electron charge, ion temperature, electron temperature, and the Boltzmann constant, respectively. The total charge density $\rho(\vec{r})$ with the test charge can be given as

$$\rho(\vec{r}) = e[n_i(\vec{r}) - n_e(\vec{r})] + q\delta(\vec{r}) \qquad (1.4)$$

where $\delta(\vec{r})$ is the Dirac delta function.

Now from Poisson's equation with the help of Equations (1.2)–(1.3), we get

$$\nabla^2\phi = -\frac{\rho(\vec{r})}{\epsilon_0} = \frac{en_0}{\epsilon_0}\left[exp\left(\frac{e\phi}{K_BT_e}\right) - exp\left(-\frac{e\phi}{K_BT_i}\right)\right] - \frac{q}{\epsilon_0}\delta(\vec{r}) \quad (1.5)$$

where ϵ_0 is the absolute permittivity for free space. We also assume the disturbed electrostatic potential is weak so that the electrostatic dynamic energy is much less than the average thermal energy, i.e.,

$$e\phi \ll K_BT_e \ll K_BT_i. \qquad (1.6)$$

Using (1.6) in (1.5) and considering terms up to $O(\phi)$, we get

$$\nabla^2\phi = \frac{n_0e^2}{\epsilon_0 K_B}\left(\frac{1}{T_e} + \frac{1}{T_i}\right)\phi - \frac{q}{\epsilon_0}\delta(\vec{r}).$$

Assuming ϕ is spherically symmetric around the test charge, we get

$$\nabla^2\phi = \frac{1}{r^2}\frac{d}{dr}\left(r^2\frac{d\phi}{dr}\right) = \frac{1}{r}\frac{d^2}{dr^2}(r\phi).$$

So, for $r \neq 0$,

$$\frac{d^2}{dr^2}(r\phi) - \frac{1}{\lambda_D^2}(r\phi) = 0 \qquad (1.7)$$

where

$$\frac{1}{\lambda_D^2} = \frac{n_0e^2}{\epsilon_0 K_B}\left(\frac{1}{T_e} + \frac{1}{T_i}\right).$$

Solution of Equation (1.7) that remains finite at $r \to \infty$, i.e.,

$$\phi = \frac{A}{r}exp\left(-\frac{r}{\lambda_D}\right) \qquad (1.8)$$

where A is a constant. Near the test charge, the electrostatic potential should be the same as it is generated by an isolated test charge q in free space. Then, the initial condition will be $\phi \to \frac{1}{4\pi\epsilon_0}\frac{q}{r}$ as $r \to 0$. Using this condition in (1.8), we get $A = \frac{q}{4\pi\epsilon_0}$. Thus,

$$\phi = \frac{q}{4\pi\epsilon_0 r} exp\left(-\frac{r}{\lambda_D}\right). \tag{1.9}$$

This $\phi(r)$ is commonly known as *Debye potential*. It shows that if $r \ll \lambda_D$, then $\phi \to \frac{q}{4\pi\epsilon_0 r}$. So, the effective potential is almost the same as the bare Coulomb potential of the test charge. While at points $r \gg \lambda_D$, the potential decreases exponentially (not as $1/r$) due to the shielding effect of surrounding charges. Obviously, in free space, $n_0 \to 0$, $\lambda_D \to \infty$, and ϕ fall off as $1/r$.

Roughly, the test charge is shielded by the plasma particles, located in a sphere with the radius λ_D. The test charge only interacts with these particles and has a negligible influence on particles at intervals $r > \lambda_D$. λ_D gives a rough measure of the distance above which the electron density can differ significantly from the ion density. The length λ_D as defined by Equation (1.8) is known as *Debye length*, and the sphere of radius λ_D is called *Debye sphere*.

1.3.3 *Quasineutrality*

Quasineutrality is a fundamental concept of plasma. It means that it creates an equilibrium between both positive and negative charges in the microscopic volume element. In the plasma production process, it is evident that the number of positive and negative charges must be the same. Since the velocities of electrons and ions are different, the former is more likely to leave the regions in which they occurred. So, the number of charges of one or the other sign is initially the same. It is because the electrons are faster than the ions, and they move much more quickly towards the walls of the tube consisting of discharge and leftover ions. With the loss of electrons, there will be an excessive charge of opposite sign, which will tend to equalize the current of electrons and ions and reduce the concentration of particles of opposite sign. This tendency is called the quasineutrality of plasma.

1.3.4 *Response time*

An example of the collective behavior of plasma is the timescale according to which the electrons establish a shielded equilibrium. The ions need much longer time than electrons to reach their equilibrium position. If we have

$|e\phi| \ll K_B T_e$, where K_B is the Boltzmann constant, the electron energy does not change significantly from its thermal value. Therefore, the electron velocity remains close to a thermal velocity $V_e = \sqrt{K_B T_e/m_e}$. To establish the new balance, the electron must reach its unique position at a typical distance λ_D. This time can be estimated as $\tau = \lambda_{D_e}/V_e$ and known as *response time*. The reciprocal of this response time is called *plasma frequency*.

1.3.5 *Plasma frequency*

In the Debye screening analysis, the plasma is assumed to be at equilibrium, i.e., the plasma charges do not move. Screening is, therefore, an example of static collective behavior. We will now give an example of dynamic collective behavior. Suppose the plasma comprises electrons moving freely in an immobile neutralization background where the charge of the electron is q, the density is n, and the mass is m. Let the electrons move a distance d to the right and leave a background of charge density $\rho = -nq$ and width d. Hence, the electric field produced on the edges is $E = 2\pi\rho d = -2\pi nqd$ (for the right edge) and $E = 2\pi\rho d = 2\pi nqd$ (for the left edge). So, the total force acted on the electrons is $F = qE = -2\pi nq^2 d$, which accelerates the right electron towards the left and vice versa. The relative acceleration of the edges of the electrons would be $a = 2(qE/m) = -4\pi nq^2 d/m$. As $a = \ddot{d}$, one gets

$$\ddot{d} = -\omega_p^2 d$$

where $\omega_p^2 = 4\pi nq^2/m$. It shows that the oscillation occurs with the frequency ω_p, known as *Plasma frequency*. These periods of oscillation must be much smaller than the typical lifetime of the system. From the fundamental length λ_D and the basic velocity of the particles $v = (K_B T/m)^{1/2}$, we have

$$\omega_p = \frac{v}{\lambda_D} = \left(\frac{4\pi nq^2}{m}\right)^{1/2} \; rad/s$$

where ω_p is the characteristic oscillation rate for electrostatic disturbances in plasmas. For electron oscillations, the numerical value of ω_p can be given by

$$f_p \equiv \omega_p \approx 9000\sqrt{n_e} \; Hz.$$

1.3.6 *Collisions and coupling limit*

The concept of weakly coupled plasma comes from the requirement of many electrons inside the electron-Debye sphere. Let us define the number of electrons inside the electron-Debye sphere by

$$N_{D_e} = \frac{4\pi}{3}\lambda_{D_e}^3 n_e.$$

The borderline between weakly and strongly coupled plasma is defined earlier. Also, $N_{D_e} = 1 \Rightarrow \frac{4\pi}{3}\lambda_{D_e}^3 n_3 = 1 \Rightarrow n_e = \frac{3}{4\pi}\cdot\frac{1}{\lambda_D^3} = (\frac{4\pi\epsilon_0}{3e^2})^2 T_e^3$. Due to the occurrence of different temperatures of electrons and ions, different coupling space occurs. For $N_{D_e} \neq N_{D_i}$, $\Gamma_i = \frac{1}{3}N_{D_i}^{2/3}$.

Due to the long range of the Coulomb force, collisions between charged particles in a plasma differ from the collisions of molecules in a neutral gas. However, collisions in weakly coupled plasmas are present due to the collective effects of the many-particle processes of Debye shielding.

However, collision frequencies are estimated qualitatively as follows. An impact parameter b is set by equating kinetic energy equal to potential energy as

$$\frac{e^2}{b} \sim \frac{T}{2}.$$

The collision cross-section is obtained by

$$\sigma \sim \pi b^2 \sim \frac{4\pi e^4}{T^2}$$

and so the collision time τ is estimated by

$$\frac{1}{\tau} \sim n\sigma v \sim nm\sigma\sqrt{T} \sim \frac{1}{4\pi}\frac{\omega_p}{n\lambda_D^3}$$

where λ_D is the Debye length and ω_p is the plasma frequency. For high-temperature plasmas $n\lambda_D^3 \gg 1$, which indicates that plasma is collisionless if $\omega_p\tau \gg 1$. Collision frequency $1/\tau_{\alpha\beta}$ of a charged particle of species α against a particle of β is approximately given by

$$\frac{1}{\tau_{ei}} \sim \frac{\omega_{pe}}{n\lambda_D^3}, \quad \frac{1}{\tau_{ee}} \sim \frac{1}{\tau_{ei}}, \quad \frac{1}{\tau_{ii}} \sim \sqrt{\frac{m_e}{m_i}}\frac{1}{\tau_{ee}}, \quad \frac{1}{\tau_{ie}} \sim \frac{m_e}{m_i}\frac{1}{\tau_{ei}}.$$

The ratio of the magnitude of the collision frequencies is given by

$$\frac{1}{\tau_{ee}} : \frac{1}{\tau_{ii}} : \frac{1}{\tau_{ie}} = 1 : \sqrt{\frac{m_e}{m_i}} : \frac{m_e}{m_i}.$$

When the plasma reaches the thermal equilibrium, the thermal equilibrium of the electrons arises first, followed by the ions in between, and finally, the thermal balance between the electrons and ions gets completed. Thus, a two-temperature state occurs long before the thermal equilibrium is reached. So, the plasma may have several temperatures at the same time. The electrons and ions may have different temperatures even when both are Boltzmann distributed.

1.4 Criteria for Plasma

An ionized gas becomes plasma if it satisfies the following conditions:

(i) the Debye length λ_D is much smaller than the dimensions L of the system, i.e., $\lambda_D \ll L$,

(ii) the number of particles within the Debye sphere is more than 1, i.e., $N_D \gg 1$,

(iii) $\omega\tau > 1$, then neutral gas becomes plasma where ω is the normal plasma oscillations frequency and τ represents the mean time between collisions with neutral atoms.

1.5 High-Temperature Plasmas

The condition for the existence of plasma is that the average electron kinetic energy should be larger than the Coulomb potential, that is, $T \gg \frac{e^2}{\langle r \rangle}$, where $\langle r \rangle$ is the average particle distance and is obtained by

$$\frac{4}{3}\pi \langle r \rangle^3 n = 1.$$

A high-temperature plasma is characterized by the smallness of the ratio of the average potential energy to the electron kinetic energy

$$\Gamma = \frac{e^2/\langle r \rangle}{T} = \frac{1}{3}\left(\frac{4\pi}{3}n\lambda_D^3\right)^{-2/3} \ll 1.$$

In a high-temperature plasma, the number of particles in the Debye sphere is much greater than one, i.e., $n\lambda_D^3 \gg 1$. It indicates that the total number of charged particles in the Debye sphere is enough to be an effective shield.

1.6 Mathematical Description

To explain the state of a plasma mathematically, we have to write down all particles' positions and velocities to describe the electromagnetic field acting in the plasma. It is, however, neither practical nor necessary to trace all the particles in a plasma. Therefore, plasma physicists typically use less detailed descriptions known as plasma models. There are two main types of models: (a) kinetic model and (b) fluid model. Sometimes, the motion of individual particles under electromagnetic force can also provide us important information.

The fluid model of plasma consists of smoothed quantities such as density and average speed around each position. In the simple fluid model, a single charged species follows the basic fluid equation in an electromagnetic field, and the motion is controlled by Maxwell's equations, Lorentz force, and other forces that may occur. A more general description is the two-fluid model, in which the ions and electrons are described separately. Fluid models are more accurate if the collision is high enough to keep the plasma velocity distribution close to a Maxwell–Boltzmann distribution. As the fluid models usually describe the plasma as a single flow at a specific temperature in any spatial location, it fails to give an accurate result for velocity space structures, such as beams or double layers, or can they resolve wave–particle effects. But a kinetic model describes the particle velocity distribution function at every point in the plasma. Therefore, it does not have to assume a Maxwell–Boltzmann distribution. Generally, there are two common approaches to the kinetic description of a plasma: one is based on the representation of the smoothed distribution function on a grid in speed and position and the other technique is known as particle-in-cell (PIC) technology. It contains kinetic information by following the trajectories of a large number of individual particles. Kinetic models are usually more computationally intensive than fluid models. The Vlasov equation can be used to describe the dynamics of a system of modified particles that interact with an electromagnetic field.

1.7 Magnetized Plasmas

A plasma in which the magnetic field is strong enough to influence the movement of the charged particles is called *magnetized plasmas*. A general quantitative criterion is that an average particle completes at least one gyration around the magnetic field before it collides (i.e., $\omega_{ce}/\nu_{coll} \geq 1$, where ω_{ce} is the electron gyrofrequency and ν_{coll} is the electron collision rate). It is often the case that the electrons are magnetized while the ions are not. Magnetized plasmas are anisotropic, meaning their properties in the direction parallel to the magnetic field differ from those perpendicular to them. While the electric field in plasmas is usually small due to its high conductivity, the electric field associated with a plasma moving in a magnetic field is given by $\vec{E} = -\vec{v} \times \vec{B}$ (where $\vec{E}$ is the electric field, $\vec{v}$ is the speed, and $\vec{B}$ is the magnetic field) and is not affected by the Debye shield.

Lorentz Force: The amalgamation of the electric force and magnetic force on a point charge produces electromagnetic force, which is also known as Lorentz force. It happens because of the electromagnetic field. The equation of motion is

$$m\frac{d\vec{v}}{dt} = \vec{F} = (\vec{E} + \vec{v} \times \vec{B})q \tag{1.10}$$

where $q, m, \vec{v}, \vec{E}$, and $\vec{B}$ are the charge of the particle, particle mass, velocity, electric field, and magnetic field, respectively.

Gyrofrequency and Gyroradius: Let us consider that particle is moving in a homogeneous and stationary magnetic field which is working along the z-axis. Let $\vec{E} = 0$ and $\vec{B} = (0, 0, B_z)$. From (1.10), we get

$$m\frac{d\vec{v}}{dt} = q(\vec{v} \times \vec{B}) = (\vec{i}v_y - \vec{j}v_x)B_z. \tag{1.11}$$

Therefore,

$$\frac{dv_x}{dt} = \frac{q}{m}v_y B_z, \tag{1.12}$$

$$\frac{dv_y}{dt} = -\frac{q}{m}v_x B_z, \tag{1.13}$$

$$\frac{dv_z}{dt} = 0. \tag{1.14}$$

Integrating Equation (1.14), we obtain $v_z = $ constant. The velocity component along the z-axis remains constant. So, it is not affected by $\vec{B}$.

Differentiating Equation (1.12), we get

$$\frac{d^2v_x}{dt^2} = \frac{qB_z}{m}\frac{dv_y}{dt} = -\left(\frac{qB_z}{m}\right)^2 v_x$$

$$= -\omega_c^2 v_x. \tag{1.15}$$

Similarly, from Equation (1.13), we get

$$\frac{d^2v_y}{dt^2} = -\omega_c^2 v_y \tag{1.16}$$

where $\omega_c = \frac{|q|B_z}{m}$ is known as *cyclotron frequency* or *gyrofrequency* which is always positive. Equations (1.15) and (1.16) represent the simple harmonic motion of the charged particle separately.

Solving Equations (1.15) and (1.16), we have

$$v_x = A\sin(\omega_c t + \phi_0) \tag{1.17}$$

$$v_y = A\cos(\omega_c t + \phi_0) \tag{1.18}$$

where A and ϕ_0 are integrating constants. Consider

$$\vec{v} = \vec{v}_\parallel + \vec{v}_\perp \tag{1.19}$$

where $\vec{v}_\parallel$ and $\vec{v}_\perp$ are the components of $\vec{v}$ parallel and perpendicular to $\vec{B}$, respectively. Since $|\vec{v}_\parallel|$ and $|\vec{v}|$ are constants, so $|\vec{v}_\perp|$ is also constant. From Equations (1.18) and (1.19), we get

$$v_\perp^2 = v_{x_0}^2 + v_{y_0}^2 = A^2$$

$$\Rightarrow A = v_\perp$$

and

$$\frac{v_{x_0}}{v_{y_0}} = \tan(\phi_0) \Rightarrow \phi_0 = \tan^{-1}\left(\frac{v_{x_0}}{v_{y_0}}\right)$$

where v_{x_0} and v_{y_0} are initial velocity components. Integrating Equations (1.17) and (1.18) and using the initial conditions, we get

$$x - x_0 = -\frac{v_\perp}{\omega_c}\cos(\omega_c t + \phi_0) + \frac{v_\perp}{\omega_c}\cos(\phi_0) \tag{1.20}$$

$$y - y_0 = \frac{v_\perp}{\omega_c}\sin(\omega_c t + \phi_0) - \frac{v_\perp}{\omega_c}\sin(\phi_0) \tag{1.21}$$

where (x_0, y_0, z_0) is the initial position of the particle. Equations (1.17) and (1.18) represent the trajectory of the charged particles.

Squaring and adding Equations (1.20) and (1.21), we get

$$(x - x_1)^2 + (y - y_1)^2 = \left(\frac{v_\perp}{\omega_c}\right)^2 \tag{1.22}$$

where $x_1 = x_0 + \frac{v_\perp}{\omega_c}\cos(\phi_0)$ and $y_1 = y_0 - \frac{v_\perp}{\omega_c}\sin(\phi_0)$.

Case 1: If $v_\parallel = 0$, the particle describes a circular orbit with radius r_L such that $r_L = \frac{v_\perp}{\omega_c} = \frac{mv_\perp}{|q|B}$ in XY plane perpendicular to $\vec{B}$. The center (x_1, y_1) of the circular orbit is fixed. The center and radius of the circular orbit are known as *guiding center* and *gyroradius or cyclotron radius*, respectively.

The time period of rotation is $T = \frac{2\pi}{\omega_c} = \frac{2\pi m}{qB}$ which is independent of speed for nonrelativistic motion.

Case 2: If $v_\parallel \neq 0$, then the particle advances along or opposite to $\vec{B}$ with a constant speed $v_\parallel$, and at the same time, it gyrates about $\vec{B}$. The orbit will be a helix with $\vec{B}$ as an axis. The pitch angle ϕ of the helix will be given by

$$\tan\phi = \frac{v_\parallel T}{v_\perp T} = \frac{v_\parallel}{v_\perp}. \tag{1.23}$$

1.8   Single Particle Motion in Uniform Electric and Magnetic Field

Let us consider that the charged particle moves in an electromagnetic field where $\vec{E} = (E_x, 0, E_z)$ and $\vec{B} = (0, 0, B_z)$. Now,

$$\frac{d\vec{v}}{dt} = \frac{q}{m}(\vec{E} + \vec{v} \times \vec{B}) = \frac{q}{m}(E_x + v_y B_z)\vec{i} - v_x B_z \vec{j} + E_z \vec{k}. \tag{1.24}$$

Therefore, from (1.24), we get

$$\frac{dv_x}{dt} = \frac{q}{m}(E_x + v_y B_z), \tag{1.25}$$

$$\frac{dv_y}{dt} = -\frac{q}{m}v_x B_z, \tag{1.26}$$

$$\frac{dv_z}{dt} = \frac{q}{m}E_z. \tag{1.27}$$

Differentiating Equation (1.25) with respect to t and using Equation (1.26), we get

$$\frac{d^2 v_x}{dt^2} = \frac{qB_z}{m}\frac{dv_y}{dt} = -\left(\frac{q}{m}B_z\right)^2 v_x = -\omega_c^2 v_x \tag{1.28}$$

where $\omega_c = \frac{|q|B_z}{m}$. Similarly, from (1.26), we obtain

$$\frac{d^2 v_y}{dt^2} = -\frac{qB_z}{m}\frac{q}{m}(E_x + v_y B_z) = -\omega_c^2\left(v_y + \frac{E_x}{B_z}\right). \tag{1.29}$$

A harmonic oscillation occurs in the x-direction with frequency ω_c. Let us consider a linear transformation $\bar{v}_y = \left(v_y + \frac{E_x}{B_z}\right)$, which means the frame is moving with a constant velocity $\left(-\frac{E_x}{B_z}\right)$ in the $-y$ direction. Thus, the motion can be considered as the superposition of a circular orbit, and a constant motion is called $\vec{E} \times \vec{B}$ drift. Solving (1.28) and (1.29), we get

$$v_x = A \cos \omega_c t + B \sin \omega_c t \tag{1.30}$$

$$v_y = C \cos \omega_c t + D \sin \omega_c t + \left(-\frac{E_x}{B_z} \right) \tag{1.31}$$

where A, B, C, and D are the integration constants.

If initially the particle is at rest at origin and the particle has a constant acceleration $\frac{E_x}{B_z}\omega_c$, the initial conditions are $x = y = 0$, $\frac{dx}{dt} = \frac{dy}{dt} = 0$, and $\frac{d^2x}{dt^2} = \frac{E_x}{B_z}\omega_c$ at $t = 0$.

Using the initial conditions, from (1.30), we get $A = 0$ and $B = \frac{E_x}{B_z}$. Thus,

$$v_x = \frac{dx}{dt} = \frac{E_x}{B_z} \sin(\omega_c t). \tag{1.32}$$

On integration, we get

$$x = -\frac{E_x}{B_z\omega_c} \cos \omega_c t + C_1 \tag{1.33}$$

where C_1 is the integration constant. Using the same set of initial conditions, we get $C_1 = \frac{E_x}{B_z\omega_c}$. Thus,

$$x = \frac{E_x}{B_z\omega_c}(1 - \cos \omega_c t). \tag{1.34}$$

Similarly, we obtain

$$y = \frac{E_x}{B_z\omega_c}(\sin \omega_c t - \omega_c t). \tag{1.35}$$

Hence, (1.34) and (1.35) are the required trajectories of the charged particles.

1.9 Fluid Approach

Plasma is characterized by a huge number of particles. As observed, the single-particle approach is unnecessarily complex. As it is difficult to keep track of each particle, a comprehensive statistical approach is required. The fluid model is extremely helpful in explaining the majority of the plasma phenomena because the movement of fluid elements is only considered and the uniqueness of single particles is ignored. Electric charges characterize plasma fluid. For any random fluid, the recurrent collisions between particles maintain the fluid component in continuous motion. But the presence of a magnetic field in plasma prevents frequent collisions. The fluid description method is advantageous because it is simple to use and results in seven-dimensional phase space instead of three spatial dimensions and time. However, the velocity dependence effect like Landau damping cannot be explained by this method.

(i) Continuity equations

The equation of continuity is born from the conservation of mass. The conservation of matter requires that the rate of decrease of the number of particles in a volume V must be equal to that leaves the volume V per unit time through the surface S bounding the volume V. Therefore,

$$\frac{\partial N}{\partial t} = \int_V \frac{\partial n}{\partial t} dV = - \oint nu.dS = - \int_V \nabla.(nu) dV \qquad (1.36)$$

where N is the total number of particles in a volume V and $\vec{u}$ is the fluid velocity. Using divergence theory, we get

$$\frac{\partial n}{\partial t} + \nabla.(nu) = 0. \qquad (1.37)$$

This is the equation of continuity.

(ii) Equation of motion

Let us consider the equation of motion for a single particle with velocity $\vec{v}$

$$m\frac{d\vec{v}}{dt} = \vec{F} = q(\vec{E} + \vec{v} \times \vec{B}) \qquad (1.38)$$

where $\vec{F}$ is the Lorentz force. If all the particle fluid elements will move together with average velocity $\vec{u}$ and we neglect collisions and thermal effect, the equation is

$$nm\frac{d\vec{u}}{dt} = qn(\vec{E} + \vec{u} \times \vec{B}). \qquad (1.39)$$

In the above equation, the time derivative is with respect to a reference frame moving with the average velocity $\vec{u}$. Therefore, the time derivative operator is written as

$$\frac{d}{dt} = \frac{\partial}{\partial t} + \vec{u} \cdot \vec{\nabla} \qquad (1.40)$$

where $\frac{\partial}{\partial t}$ is the time derivative in a fixed frame and the term $\vec{u} \cdot \vec{\nabla}$ corresponds to change as the observer moves with the fluid. Hence, the convective derivative is

$$\frac{d\vec{u}}{dt} = \frac{\partial \vec{u}}{\partial t} + (\vec{u} \cdot \vec{\nabla})\vec{u}. \tag{1.41}$$

Therefore, from Equation (1.39), we get

$$mn\left[\frac{\partial \vec{u}}{\partial t} + (\vec{u} \cdot \vec{\nabla})\vec{u}\right] = qn(\vec{E} + \vec{u} \times \vec{B}). \tag{1.42}$$

When the thermal motion of the particle is considered, an additional force of pressure gradient is added to the right-hand side of Equation (1.42). This force arises due to the random motion of particles in and out of a fluid element. This pressure gradient force per unit volume may be calculated as $-\vec{\nabla}p$, where p is the scalar kinetic pressure. So, the fluid equation of motion is written as

$$mn\left[\frac{\partial \vec{u}}{\partial t} + (\vec{u} \cdot \vec{\nabla})\vec{u}\right] = qn(\vec{E} + \vec{u} \times \vec{B}) - \vec{\nabla}p. \tag{1.43}$$

For generalization (like anisotropic distribution and shearing forces), the effect of viscosity $-\vec{\nabla}p$ is replaced by $-\vec{\nabla} \cdot \vec{P}$, where $\vec{P}$ is the pressure tensor.

(iii) Pressure equations

Let us consider the thermodynamic equation of state

$$p = C\rho^{\gamma} \tag{1.44}$$

where C is a constant and γ is the ratio of specific heats C_p/C_v. Therefore,

$$\nabla p = C\gamma\rho^{\gamma-1}\nabla\rho = \gamma p\frac{\nabla\rho}{\rho}$$

$$\Rightarrow \frac{\nabla p}{p} = \gamma\frac{\nabla n}{n} \quad (as\ \rho = mn). \tag{1.45}$$

Now, (i) for isothermal compression, $\nabla p = \nabla(nkT) = kT\nabla n$, so $\gamma = 1$, and (ii) for adiabatic compression, $\frac{\nabla n}{n} + \frac{\nabla T}{T} = \gamma\frac{\nabla n}{n}$, so $\frac{\nabla T}{T} = (\gamma - 1)\frac{\nabla n}{n}$. Generally,

$$\gamma = (2 + d)/d \tag{1.46}$$

where d is the number of degrees of freedom. It is valid only for negligible heat flow, i.e., for low thermal conductivity.

1.10 Maxwell's Equations

Maxwell's equations are considered one of the fundamental equations of electromagnetism. It is a combination of four basic equations such as Gauss's law in electrostatics, Gauss's law in magnetostatics, Faraday's law of electromagnetic induction, and Ampere's law with Maxwell's modification.

Differential Form: Maxwell's equations can be expressed in differential form as

$$\vec{\nabla} \cdot \vec{D} = \rho \ or \ \vec{\nabla} \cdot \vec{E} = \frac{\rho}{\epsilon_0} \quad \text{(Gauss's law in electrostatic)}, \qquad (1.47)$$

$$\vec{\nabla} \cdot \vec{B} = 0 \quad \text{(Gauss's law in magnetostatics)}, \qquad (1.48)$$

$$\vec{\nabla} \times \vec{E} = -\frac{\partial \vec{B}}{\partial t} \quad \text{(Faraday's law of electromagnetic induction)},$$

$$(1.49)$$

$$\vec{\nabla} \times \vec{H} = \vec{J} + \frac{\partial \vec{D}}{\partial t} \quad \text{(Ampere's law with Maxwell's modification)}$$

$$(1.50)$$

where $\vec{D}$, ρ, $\vec{B}$, $\vec{E}$, and $\vec{H}$ are electric displacement vector (coulomb/m^2), charge density (coulomb/m^3), magnetic induction (weber/m^2), electric field intensity (volt/m), and magnetic field intensity (amp/m-turn), respectively. Equation (1.47) is derived from Coulomb's law. Equation (1.48) means that the magnetic monopole does not exist in our physical world. Maxwell's equations represent the mathematical expression of certain experimental results. These equations cannot be checked directly. However, their application to any situation can be checked. Due to extensive experimental work, Maxwell's equations are now considered one of the guiding principles such as the conservation of momentum and energy.

Integral form:

(i) Gauss's law in electrostatics is

$$\vec{\nabla} \cdot \vec{D} = \rho.$$

Integrating over volume space V,

$$\int_V \vec{\nabla} \cdot \vec{D} d\vec{V} = \int_V \rho d\vec{V}.$$

Using Gauss divergence theorem, we get

$$\int_S \vec{D}d\vec{S} = \int_V \rho d\vec{V} \tag{1.51}$$

where the surface S bounds the volume V. Since $\int_V \rho d\vec{V} = q$, the net charge is contained in V. The physical significance of Equation (1.51) is that the total flux of electric displacement vector through the surface enclosed by the volume is equal to the total charge contained within that volume.

(ii) Gauss's law in magnetostatics is

$$\vec{\nabla} \cdot \vec{B} = 0.$$

Integrating over volume V,

$$\int_V \vec{\nabla} \cdot \vec{B}d\vec{V} = 0.$$

Using Gauss divergence theorem, we get

$$\int_S \vec{B}d\vec{S} = 0. \tag{1.52}$$

The signification of the equation is that the total outward flux of magnetic induction through any closed surface is equal to zero, i.e., a magnetic monopole does not exist.

(iii) Faraday's law of electromagnetic induction equation is

$$\vec{\nabla} \times \vec{E} = -\frac{\partial \vec{B}}{\partial t}.$$

Integrating the equation over a surface S bounded by a curve C, we get

$$\int_S \vec{\nabla} \times \vec{E}d\vec{S} = -\int_S \frac{\partial \vec{B}}{\partial t}d\vec{S}.$$

Using Stokes' theorem, we get

$$\int_C \vec{E}d\vec{l} = -\int_S \frac{\partial \vec{B}}{\partial t}d\vec{S}. \tag{1.53}$$

The electromagnetic force is $\int_C \vec{E}d\vec{l}$ and the magnetic flux is $\phi = \int_S \vec{B}d\vec{S}$. Equation (1.53) states that the e.m.f around a closed path is equal to the negative rate of change of magnetic flux linked with the path.

(iv) Ampere's law with Maxwell's modification equation is

$$\vec{\nabla} \times \vec{H} = \vec{J} + \frac{\partial \vec{D}}{\partial t}.$$

Integrating the above equation, we get

$$\int_S \vec{\nabla} \times \vec{H} d\vec{S} = \int_S \left(\vec{J} + \frac{\partial \vec{D}}{\partial t} \right) d\vec{S}.$$

Using stokes' theorem, we get

$$\int_C \vec{H} d\vec{l} = \int_S \left(\vec{J} + \frac{\partial \vec{D}}{\partial t} \right) d\vec{S}. \tag{1.54}$$

This equation states that the magnetomotive force $\left(= \int_C \vec{H} d\vec{l} \right)$ around a closed path is equal to the conduction current plus displacement current through any surface bounded by the path.

1.11 Electromagnetic Wave Equation in Free Space

In free space, the volume charge density $\rho = 0$ and current density $J = 0$, hence Maxwell's equations become

$$\vec{\nabla} \cdot \vec{D} = 0, \tag{1.55}$$

$$\vec{\nabla} \cdot \vec{B} = 0, \tag{1.56}$$

$$\vec{\nabla} \times \vec{E} = -\frac{\partial \vec{B}}{\partial t}, \tag{1.57}$$

$$\vec{\nabla} \times \vec{H} = \frac{\partial \vec{D}}{\partial t} \tag{1.58}$$

with $\vec{D} = \epsilon_0 \vec{E}$ and $\vec{B} = \mu_0 \vec{H}$, and ϵ_0 and $\vec{\mu}_0$ are the absolute permittivity and permeability of the free space, respectively.

From (1.57), we get

$$\vec{\nabla} \times (\vec{\nabla} \times \vec{E}) = -\frac{\partial}{\partial t}(\vec{\nabla} \times \vec{B})$$

$$\Rightarrow \vec{\nabla}(\vec{\nabla} \cdot \vec{E}) - \vec{\nabla}^2 \vec{E} = \frac{\partial}{\partial t}(\vec{\nabla} \times \mu_0 \vec{H})$$

$$\Rightarrow \vec{\nabla}^2 \vec{E} = \mu_0 \frac{\partial}{\partial t}(\vec{\nabla} \times \vec{H}) \quad (using\ (1.55))$$

$$\Rightarrow \vec{\nabla}^2 \vec{E} = \mu_0 \frac{\partial}{\partial t}\left(\frac{\partial \vec{D}}{\partial t}\right) \quad (using\ (1.56))$$

$$\Rightarrow \vec{\nabla}^2 \vec{E} = \mu_0 \epsilon_0 \frac{\partial^2 \vec{E}}{\partial t^2}. \tag{1.59}$$

Similarly,

$$\vec{\nabla} \times (\vec{\nabla} \times \vec{H}) = \frac{\partial}{\partial t}(\vec{\nabla} \times \vec{D})$$

$$\Rightarrow \vec{\nabla}(\vec{\nabla} \cdot \vec{H}) - \vec{\nabla}^2 \vec{H} = \frac{\partial}{\partial t}(\vec{\nabla} \times \epsilon_0 \vec{E})$$

$$\Rightarrow \vec{\nabla}^2 \vec{H} = \epsilon_0 \frac{\partial^2 \vec{B}}{\partial t^2} \quad (using\ (1.56))$$

$$\Rightarrow \vec{\nabla}^2 \vec{H} = \mu_0 \epsilon_0 \frac{\partial^2 \vec{H}}{\partial t^2}. \tag{1.60}$$

Equations (1.59) and (1.60) are called electromagnetic wave equations in free space.

1.12 Plasma Kinetic Theory

1.12.1 *Distribution function*

In plasma kinetic theory, distribution functions are used extensively. Suppose $f(\vec{r}, \vec{v}, t)$ is the distribution function[1] in a six-dimensional phase space $(\vec{r}, \vec{v})$. Here, $\vec{r}$ and $\vec{v}$ represent the position vector and velocity vector in phase space. The particle position in phase space is defined by the coordinates $(\vec{r}, \vec{v})$. $f(\vec{r}, \vec{v}, t)$ is a function of seven independent variables: 3 for the position, 3 for velocity, and the last is time. Let $\vec{r} = x\vec{i} + y\vec{j} + z\vec{k}$ and $\vec{v} = v_x\vec{i} + v_y\vec{j} + v_z\vec{k}$. Volume element in phase space is $d\vec{V} = d\vec{v}d\vec{r}$, $d\vec{r} = d^3r = dxdydz$, and $d\vec{v} = d^3v = dv_xdv_ydv_z$. Accordingly, $f(\vec{r}, \vec{v}, t)d\vec{r}d\vec{v}$ is the number of particle in a volume element $d\vec{V}(= d\vec{r}d\vec{v})$ in phase space. It means $f(\vec{r}, \vec{v}, t)$ is space particle number density in phase space at time t.

---

[1]If $f(\vec{r}, \vec{v}, t)$ depends on $\vec{r}$, the distribution is inhomogeneous and $f(\vec{r}, \vec{v}, t)$ is homogeneous if it is vice versa. Again, if $f(\vec{r}, \vec{v}, t)$ depends on the direction of $\vec{v}$, then $f(\vec{r}, \vec{v}, t)$ is anisotropic, and the distribution is isotropic if it is vice versa.

1.12.2 *Macroscopic variables*

Macroscopic parameters like density, average velocity, and pressure are used.

(a) **Density:** The density $n(\vec{r}, t)$ is obtained as

$$n(\vec{r},t) = \int_{-\infty}^{\infty}\int_{-\infty}^{\infty}\int_{-\infty}^{\infty} f(\vec{r},\vec{v},t) dv_x dy dv_z = \int_{-\infty}^{\infty} f(\vec{r},\vec{v},t) d\vec{v}.$$

If $\hat{f}(\vec{r}, \vec{v}, t)$ is the normalization of $f(\vec{r}, \vec{v}, t)$, then it means $\int_{-\infty}^{\infty} \hat{f}(\vec{r}, \vec{v}, t) dv = 1$. Thus, $\hat{f}(\vec{r}, \vec{v}, t) d\vec{v} d\vec{r}$ is the probability of finding a particle in a volume element $d\vec{V} = d\vec{v}d\vec{r}$. So, $\hat{f}(\vec{r}, \vec{v}, t)$ is the probability per unit volume of phase space. Therefore, $\hat{f}(\vec{r}, \vec{v}, t) n(\vec{r}, t) = f(\vec{r}, \vec{v}, t)$.

(b) **Average velocity:** The probability of finding a particle at $\vec{r}$ and time t with velocity $\vec{v}$ and $\vec{v} + d\vec{v}$ is $\hat{f}(\vec{r}, \vec{v}, t) d\vec{v}$. So, an average velocity can be obtained from the relation

$$\vec{u}(\vec{r},t) = \int_{-\infty}^{\infty} \hat{f}(\vec{r},\vec{v},t)\vec{v}d\vec{v}$$

or

$$\vec{u}(r,t) = \frac{1}{n(\vec{r},t)} \int_{-\infty}^{\infty} f(\vec{r},\vec{v},t)\vec{v}dv.$$

(c) **Average random kinetic energy:** Average random kinetic energy is defined as

$$E_{av} = \frac{1}{n(\vec{r},t)} \int_{-\infty}^{\infty} \frac{1}{2}m\vec{v}^2 f(\vec{r},\vec{v},t)\vec{v}dv.$$

(d) **Pressure tensor:** Pressure tensor is defined as

$$\vec{P}(\vec{r},t) = m\int_{-\infty}^{\infty} (\vec{v}-\vec{u})(\vec{v}-\vec{u})f(\vec{r},\vec{v},t)d\vec{v}.$$

1.12.3 *Maxwellian distribution function*

A particularly important distribution function is the Maxwellian function

$$f_m(\vec{v}) = n\left(\frac{m}{2\pi K_B T}\right)^{3/2} exp\left(-v^2/v_{th}^2\right)$$

where $v^2 = v_x^2 + v_y^2 + v_z^2$, $v_{th} = (2K_B T/m)^{1/2}$, and K_B is the Boltzmann constant.

To show Maxwellian distribution as a distribution function, we need the values of three necessary integrals, as follows:

(i) $\int_{-\infty}^{\infty} e^{-\alpha v^2} dv = \frac{\sqrt{\pi}}{\sqrt{\alpha}}$

(ii) $I = \int_{-\infty}^{\infty} v^2 e^{-\alpha v^2} dv = \frac{\sqrt{\pi}}{2\alpha^{3/2}}$

(iii) $I = \int_{\infty}^{\infty} v e^{-\alpha v^2} dv = 0$.

Using the results of (i), (ii), and (iii), we get the result of $f_m(\vec{v}) = n\left(\frac{m}{2\pi K_B T}\right)^{\frac{3}{2}} e^{-v^2/v_{th}^2}$ where $v^2 = v_x^2 + v_y^2 + v_z^2$ and $v_{th}^2 = 2K_B T/m$, then $\int_{-\infty}^{\infty} \bar{f}_m(v) dv = 1$.

1.12.4 *Non-Maxwellian distribution in plasmas*

It has been observed that in space and astrophysical plasmas, the charged particles do not follow the Maxwellian distribution. The distribution functions have a non-Maxwellian high-energy tail. In a uniform magnetic field, the particle trajectories are altered. The power-law tails are produced. It is known from Boltzmann's theory that the velocity distributions are Maxwellian due to random collision. But the rapid fall off of the collision cross-section with particle speed shows that the high-energy particles in the tail can deviate strongly from Maxwellian. Then, the distribution of tail particles can be metastable and becomes non-Maxwellian. Maxwell distribution describes the long-range interactions in collisionless unmagnetized plasma, where the nonequilibrium stationary state exists. But from space plasma experiments, it is seen that ion and electron populations are far away from their thermodynamic equilibrium, so a non-Maxwellian distribution is adopted.

1.12.5 *Nonthermal distribution*

Space plasma research suggests that in many situations, electron and ion populations are not in thermodynamic equilibrium. Various research clearly shows the presence of energetic electrons in astrophysical plasma environments like Earth's bow shock and foreshock, the upper Martian ionosphere, and the vicinity of the moon. The distribution functions are considered nonthermal [1]. An energetic electron distribution is also observed in different regions of the magnetosphere. Accordingly, the nonthermal electron–ion distribution is proved to be very widespread and characteristic of space plasmas, in which coherent nonlinear waves and structures [2, 3] are expected to play a crucial role. Cairnes *et al.* [4] used the nonthermal distribution of electrons to examine the ion-acoustic single structures observed by the FREJA satellite. It has been observed that solitons with both positive and negative density disturbances could exist. The nonthermal distribution [4] for electrons is given by

$$f_e(v) = \frac{n_{e0}}{(3\alpha + 1)\sqrt{2\pi v_e^2}}\left(1 + \frac{\alpha v^4}{v_e^4}\right) exp\left(-\frac{v^2}{2v_e^2}\right) \qquad (1.61)$$

where n_{e0} is the electron density at equilibrium, v_e is the thermal speed of the electron, and α is a parameter that determines the population of energetic nonthermal electrons. Here, assume that the speed of the structure is low compared to the thermal speed of the electrons. Therefore, one can neglect the effect of the flow velocity on the electrons since the electron distribution in the steady state is a function of the electron energy. The distribution of electrons in the presence of nonzero potential can be determined by replacing $\frac{v^2}{v_e^2}$ by $\left(\frac{v^2}{v_e^2} - 2\Phi\right)$, where dimensionless potential $\Phi = \frac{e\phi}{m_e v_e^2}$. ϕ, e, and m_e are the electrostatic potential of the wave or structure, electron charge, and electron mass, respectively.

Thus, integration over the resulting distribution function results in the following expression for the electron density:

$$n_e = n_{e0}(1 - \beta\Phi + \beta\Phi^2)\, exp(\Phi) \qquad (1.62)$$

where $\beta = \frac{4\alpha}{1+3\alpha}$. It is clear that $\beta \to 4/3$ for very large α.

1.12.6 *Superthermal distribution*

Plasmas can hold a considerable amount of high-energy particles both in space and in laboratories. Known as superthermal particles, these high-energy particles may spring up from external forces on the natural space environment plasmas or wave–particle interactions. A long tail is found in the region with high energy in the plasmas with a surplus of superthermal electrons. To model such plasmas, which is a generalized Lorentzian [5] distribution, appropriate particle distribution is used. It is popularly known as *Kappa Distribution*. The speed of resonant energy transmission between particles and plasma waves can notably vary if a significantly bigger number of superthermal particles is present. This fact differentiates kappa distribution from Maxwellian distribution. For the macroscopic ergodic equilibrium condition, Maxwell distribution is taken to be suitable. But in the case of long-range interactions in unmagnetized collisionless plasma where the nonequilibrium stationary condition is present, Maxwell distribution may fail to explain. Thus, in this situation, the kappa distribution can be a better option, which has been introduced by the distribution function as

$$f_e(x, v_x) = C_e \left(1 - \frac{e\phi}{km_e\theta_{the}^2} + \frac{v_x}{2k\theta_{the}^2}\right)^{-k-1}, \qquad (1.63)$$

where the normalization is given for any value of the spectral index $k > 1/2$ by

$$C_e = \frac{n_{e0}}{\left(2\pi k\theta_{the}^2\right)^{1/2}} \frac{\Gamma(k+1)}{\Gamma(k+1/2)}.$$

Here, k forms mainly the superthermal tail of the distribution, the quantity Γ signifies for the gamma function, and

$$\theta_{the} = \left(\frac{k-1/2}{k} \frac{T_e}{m_e}\right)^{1/2}.$$

In the limit $k \to \infty$, distribution (1.63), we get Maxwell–Boltzmann velocity distribution. Hence,

$$f_e(x, v_x) = \frac{n_{e0}}{(2\pi K v_{the}^2)^{1/2}} exp\left(1 - \frac{v_x^2 - 2e\phi/m_e}{2v_{the}^2}\right) \qquad (1.64)$$

where $v_{the} = (T_e/m_e)^{1/2}$. Integrating $f_e(v_x)$ over all velocity space, we get

$$n_e(\phi) = n_{e0}\left(1 - \frac{1}{k-1/2}\frac{e\phi}{T_e}\right)^{-k-1/2}. \qquad (1.65)$$

The kappa distribution function $f_e(v)$ against v for various values of κ is given in Figure 1.1. It is visible from this figure that the height and shape of the distribution differ considerably with a variation of κ. It also proves that the height decreases along with the increase in the parameter κ. It leans to the Maxwell (solid line) distribution.

1.12.7 *q-nonextensive distribution*

Tsallis statistics or nonextensive statistics is a new advance towards statistics, and this is rooted in Boltzmann–Gibbs–Shannon (BGS) entropic measure. This new statistical approach studies the cases where Maxwell distribution fails. Renyi [6] first gave recognition to this, and later Tsallis [7] propounded this in cases where entropic index q describes the degree of

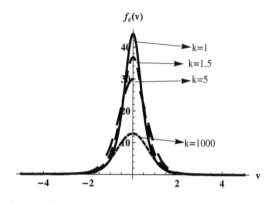

Fig. 1.1: Plot of kappa distribution function $f_e(v)$ vs. v for several values of $k = 1.0$, 1.5, 5.0, and 1000.0.

nonextensivity of the above approach. The stricture q that supports the generalized entropy of Tsallis is connected to the fundamental dynamics of the system. It determines the quantity of its nonextensivity. The quality of nonextensivity marks the systems in both statistical mechanics and thermodynamics. Even the entropy of the whole is dissimilar to the total of the entropies of the individual parts. If $q < 1$ (superextensivity), the generalized entropy of the whole is bigger than the total of the entropies of the parts. If $q > 1$ (subextensivity), the generalized entropy of the method is lesser than the sum of the entropies of the parts. Thus, accordingly, q-entropy may offer a suitable structure for the study of numerous astrophysical scenarios [8]. For example, stellar polytropes, solar neutrino problem, and velocity distribution of galaxy clusters. The q distribution function, which is a one-dimensional equilibrium in nature, establishes the electron nonextensivity.

This is shown by

$$f_e(v) = C_q\{1 - (q-1)[(m_e v_x^2)/(2T_e) - (e\phi)/T_e]\}^{1/(q-1)} \qquad (1.66)$$

where normalization is

$$
\left.
\begin{aligned}
C_q &= n_{e0} \frac{\Gamma\left(\frac{1}{1-q}\right)}{\Gamma\left(\frac{1}{1-q} - \frac{1}{2}\right)} \sqrt{\frac{m_e(1-q)}{2\pi T_e}} & \quad for\ -1 < q < 1 \\[2em]
C_q &= n_{e0} \left(\frac{1+q}{2}\right) \frac{\Gamma\left(\frac{1}{q-1} + \frac{1}{2}\right)}{\Gamma\left(\frac{1}{q-1}\right)} \sqrt{\frac{m_e(q-1)}{2\pi T_e}} & \quad for\ q > 1.
\end{aligned}
\right\}
$$

For $q < -1$, the q distribution cannot be normalized, and if $q \to 1$, the distribution diminishes to Maxwell–Boltzmann velocity distribution. For $-1 < q < 1$, high-energy states are more likely than in the extensive Maxwell case. High-energy states are less likely for $q > 1$ than in the extensive Maxwell case, and q distribution function shows a thermal shutdown of the extreme value v_{max} for the speed of the particles as

$$v_{max} = \sqrt{\frac{2T_e}{m_e(q-1)} - \frac{2e\phi}{m_e}}.$$

We get

$$\left.\begin{array}{l} n_e(\phi) = \displaystyle\int_{\infty}^{\infty} f_e(v_x)dv_x \qquad for \ -1 < q < 1 \\[3mm] n_e(\phi) = \displaystyle\int_{-v_{max}}^{v_{max}} f_e(v_x)dv_x \quad for \ q > 1. \end{array}\right\}$$

So,

$$n_e(\phi) = n_{e0}\left[1 + (q-1)\frac{e\phi}{KT_e}\right]^{\frac{(q+1)}{2(q-1)}}. \tag{1.67}$$

Figure 1.2 shows the q distribution function $f_e(v)$ against v for different values of $q = -0.5, 1.0, 1.5$. From this figure, it is seen that the amplitude and width of the distributions change remarkably as q increases. It means that the nonextensive character of the plasma has become essential. It is

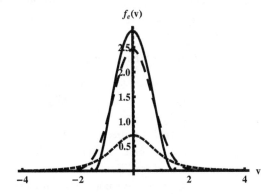

Fig. 1.2: Plot of $f(v)$ vs. v for $q \to 1$ (dashed line), $q = -0.5$ (dotted line), and 1.5 (solid line).

also clear that the amplitude increases along with the rise of the parameter q and tends to the Maxwell distribution (dashed line) when $q \to 1$.

Boltzmann equation: Ludwig Boltzmann (1844–1906) used an equation in his works and it has come to be known as the Boltzmann equation. It explained the statistical character of a thermodynamic system that is not in an equilibrium state. Let $f(\vec{r}, \vec{v}, t)$ be a distribution function and satisfy the Boltzmann equation in the six-dimensional phase space $(\vec{r}, \vec{v})$

$$\frac{\partial f}{\partial t} + \vec{v} \cdot \vec{\nabla} f + \frac{\vec{F}}{m} \cdot \frac{\partial f}{\partial \vec{v}} = \left(\frac{\partial f}{\partial t} \right)_{coll} \tag{1.68}$$

where F is the external force acting on the particle. The term $\left(\frac{\partial f}{\partial t} \right)_{coll}$ explains the rate of change of f due to collisions. If $\left(\frac{\partial f}{\partial t} \right)_{coll} = 0$, then the particle does not clash. Collisionless Boltzmann equation, where self-clash long-range interactions are neglected, is known as Vlasov equation.

Vlasov equation: The Vlasov equation explained the time progression of the distribution function $f(\vec{r}, \vec{v}, t)$ in the phase space $(\vec{r}, \vec{v})$. This equation can be found from the collisionless Boltzmann equation. Moreover, the self-consistent electromagnetic fields can be produced by the existence and movement of all the charged plasma particles.

$$\frac{\partial f}{\partial t} + \vec{v} \cdot \vec{\nabla} f + \frac{q}{m} (\vec{E} + \vec{v} \times \vec{B}) \cdot \frac{\partial f}{\partial \vec{v}} = 0 \tag{1.69}$$

where $q, m, \vec{E}$, and $\vec{B}$ are the charge of the particle, the mass of the particle, and the self-consistent electric field and magnetic field, respectively.

1.13 Closure Form of Moment Equation

The continuity equation arises from the zeroth velocity moment of the Boltzmann equation, which links the number density with the flow velocity. Two independent equations are needed to verify these two variables. The equation of motion connecting number density, flow velocity, and pressure tensor results from the first velocity moment of the Boltzmann equation, and these need to be reflected on. Thus, three variables are connected by two transport equations. Commonly, an equation for nth-order velocity moment of f has $(n+1)$th-order velocity moment of f. By considering various moments of the Boltzmann equation, the groups of equations derived fail to structure a closed set because they constantly embrace extra variables than the number of equations. But a closed group of equations can be obtained by producing some suppositions for the maximum moment of the distribution function emerging in the system.

If the distribution function $f(\vec{r}, \vec{v}, t)$ is known, plasma macroscopic variables, such as number density $n(\vec{r}, t)$, average velocity $\vec{u}(\vec{r}, t)$, and temperature, can be obtained by taking appropriate velocity moments of the distribution function.

Taking the zeroth velocity moment of $f(\vec{r}, \vec{v}, t)$, we get number density as

$$n(\vec{r}, t) = \int_v f d^3 v. \tag{1.70}$$

The first velocity moment of $f(\vec{r}, \vec{v}, t)$ gives the average velocity as

$$\vec{u}(\vec{r}, t) = \frac{1}{n} \int_v \vec{v} f d^3 v. \tag{1.71}$$

The secocnd velocity moment of $f(r, v, t)$ gives the pressure tensor as

$$\vec{P}(\vec{r}, t) = m \int_v (\vec{v} - \vec{u})(\vec{v} - \vec{u}) f d^3 v. \tag{1.72}$$

The transport equations satisfied by these variables can be obtained by taking various moments of the Boltzmann equation.

1.13.1 *Equation of continuity*

To derive the equation of continuity, we consider the Boltzmann equation as

$$\frac{\partial f}{\partial t} + \vec{v} \cdot \vec{\nabla} f + \frac{\vec{F}}{m} \cdot \frac{\partial f}{\partial \vec{v}} = \left(\frac{\partial f}{\partial t} \right)_{coll} \tag{1.73}$$

where $\vec{F} = \vec{E} + \vec{v} \times \vec{B}$ is the Lorentz force.

Integrating Equation (1.73) over velocity space, we get

$$\int_v \frac{\partial f}{\partial t} d\vec{v} + \int_v \vec{v} \cdot \vec{\nabla} f d\vec{v} + \int_v \frac{q}{m}(\vec{E} + \vec{v} \times \vec{B}) \cdot \frac{\partial f}{\partial \vec{v}} d\vec{v} = \int_v \left(\frac{\partial f}{\partial t} \right)_{coll} d\vec{v}. \tag{1.74}$$

Now,

$$\int_v \frac{\partial f}{\partial t} d\vec{v} = \frac{\partial}{\partial t} \int_v f d\vec{v} = \frac{\partial n}{\partial t}, \tag{1.75}$$

since $\vec{v}$ is an independent variable.

$$\int_v \vec{v} \cdot \vec{\nabla} f d\vec{v} = \vec{\nabla} \cdot \int_v \vec{v} f d\vec{v} = \vec{\nabla} \cdot (n\vec{u}) \quad \text{(using Equation (1.71))}. \quad (1.76)$$

Also,

$$\int_v \vec{E} \cdot \frac{\partial f}{\partial \vec{v}} d\vec{v} = \int_v \frac{\partial}{\partial \vec{v}} \cdot (f\vec{E}) d\vec{v} = \int_{S_\infty} f\vec{E}.d\vec{s} = 0. \quad (1.77)$$

Here, S_∞ is the v-space at $\vec{v} \to \infty$. Since $f \to 0$ faster than v^{-2} as $v \to \infty$, for any distribution with finite energy,

$$\int_v (\vec{v} \times \vec{B}) \cdot \frac{\partial f}{\partial \vec{v}} d\vec{v} = \int_v \frac{\partial}{\partial \vec{v}} \cdot (f\vec{v} \times \vec{B}) d\vec{v} - \int_v f \frac{\partial}{\partial \vec{v}} \times (\vec{v} \times \vec{B}) d\vec{v}$$

$$= 0. \quad \left[Since \ \left(\vec{v} \times \vec{B} \right) \perp \left(\frac{\partial}{\partial \vec{v}} \right) \right]. \quad (1.78)$$

The collision cannot change the net amount of the number of particles. Therefore,

$$\int_v \left(\frac{\partial f}{\partial t} \right)_{coll} d\vec{v} = 0. \quad (1.79)$$

Using results (1.75)–(1.79) in Equation (1.74), we obtain

$$\frac{\partial n}{\partial t} + \vec{\nabla}.(n\vec{u}) = 0. \quad (1.80)$$

This is the required *equation of continuity*.

1.13.2   *Equation of motion*

To obtain the equation of motion, we multiply Equation (1.73) by $m\vec{v}$ and integrating the resulting equation over the velocity space, we get

$$\int_v mv \frac{\partial f}{\partial t} d\vec{v} + \int_v m\vec{v}(\vec{v} \cdot \vec{\nabla}) f d\vec{v} + \int_v q(\vec{E} + \vec{v} \times \vec{B}) \cdot \frac{\partial f}{\partial \vec{v}} d\vec{v}$$

$$= \int_v mv \left(\frac{\partial f}{\partial t} \right)_{coll} d^3v. \quad (1.81)$$

Now,

$$\int_v m\vec{v} \frac{\partial f}{\partial t} d\vec{v} = m \frac{\partial}{\partial t} \int_v \vec{v} f d\vec{v} = m \frac{\partial}{\partial t} (n\vec{u}) \quad \text{[using Equation (1.71)]}. \quad (1.82)$$

Since $\vec{v}$ is an independent variables. So,

$$\int_v m\vec{v}(\vec{v}\cdot\vec{\nabla})f d\vec{v} = m\vec{\nabla}\cdot\int_v \vec{v}\vec{v}f d\vec{v} = m(\vec{\nabla}\cdot n\langle\vec{v}\vec{v}\rangle). \qquad (1.83)$$

Let us write $\vec{v} = \vec{u}+\vec{U}$, where $\vec{u}$ is the average velocity and $\vec{U}$ is the thermal velocity.

$$m\vec{\nabla}\cdot n(\vec{v}\vec{v}) = m\vec{\nabla}\cdot(n\vec{u}\vec{u}) + m\vec{\nabla}\cdot(n\langle\vec{U}\vec{U}\rangle) + 2m\vec{\nabla}\cdot(n\vec{u}\langle\vec{U}\rangle). \qquad (1.84)$$

Here, the average $\langle\vec{U}\rangle$ is obviously zero and the quantity $mn\langle\vec{U}\vec{U}\rangle$ is the kinetic pressure tensor $\vec{P}$. Also, $\vec{\nabla}\cdot(n\vec{u}\vec{u}) = m\vec{u}\vec{\nabla}\cdot(n\vec{u})+n(\vec{u}\cdot\vec{\nabla})\vec{u}$. Therefore,

$$\int_v m\vec{v}(\vec{v}\cdot\vec{\nabla})f d\vec{v} = m\vec{u}\vec{\nabla}\cdot(n\vec{u}) + mn(\vec{u}\cdot\vec{\nabla})\vec{u} + \vec{\nabla}\cdot\vec{P}. \qquad (1.85)$$

Again,

$$\int_v \vec{v}(\vec{E}+\vec{v}\times\vec{B})\cdot\frac{\partial f}{\partial\vec{v}}d\vec{v} = \int_v \frac{\partial}{\partial\vec{v}}\cdot[f\vec{v}(\vec{E}+\vec{v}\times\vec{B})]d\vec{v}$$

$$- \int_v f\vec{v}\cdot(\vec{E}+\vec{v}\times\vec{B})d\vec{v} - \int_v f(\vec{E}+\vec{v}\times\vec{B})\cdot\frac{\partial}{\partial\vec{v}}\vec{v}d\vec{v}$$

$$= -\int_v (\vec{E}+\vec{v}\times\vec{B})f d\vec{v}$$

$$= -n(\vec{E}+\vec{v}\times\vec{B}). \qquad (1.86)$$

Here, $\int_v \frac{\partial}{\partial\vec{v}}\cdot[f\vec{v}(\vec{E}+\vec{v}\times\vec{B})]d\vec{v} = \int_{S_\infty}[f\vec{v}(\vec{E}+\vec{v}\times\vec{B})]d\vec{S} = 0$ as the quantity $[f\vec{v}(\vec{E}+\vec{v}\times\vec{B})]$ tends to zero faster than $\vec{v}^{-2}$ as $v\to\infty$. Also, $\int_v f\vec{v}\cdot(\vec{E}+\vec{v}\times\vec{B})d\vec{v} = 0$ because both forces $\vec{E}$ and $\vec{B}$ are independent of the velocity component. Now, $\int_v m\vec{v}\left(\frac{\partial f}{\partial t}\right)_{coll}d\vec{v}$ is the change of momentum due to collisions and is denoted by $\vec{P}_c$. Using results (1.82)–(1.86) in Equation (1.81), we get

$$mn\left[\frac{\partial\vec{u}}{\partial t} + (\vec{\nabla}\cdot\vec{u})\vec{u}\right] = qn(\vec{E}+\vec{u}\times\vec{B}) - \vec{\nabla}\cdot\vec{P} + \vec{P}_c. \qquad (1.87)$$

Equation (1.87) is *the equation of motion*. When collision is neglected, then Equation (1.86) can be written as

$$mn\left[\frac{\partial\vec{u}}{\partial t} + (\vec{\nabla}\cdot\vec{u})\vec{u}\right] = qn(\vec{E}+\vec{u}\times\vec{B}) - \vec{\nabla}\cdot\vec{P}. \qquad (1.88)$$

The physical significance of Equation (1.87) is that the time rate of change of mean momentum in each fluid element is due to externally applied forces, plus the pressure forces of the fluid itself, and the forces are also associated with collisional interactions.

1.13.3 *Equation of energy*

To derive the energy equation, we multiply Equation (1.73) by $m\bar{v}^2/2$ and integrate it. The resulting energy equation is obtained. If we neglect the effects of velocity, the effects of the collision, and thermal conductivity, then we find an adiabatic equation of state as

$$P = C\rho^\gamma \tag{1.89}$$

where C is a constant and $\gamma = C_p/C_v$. So, $\frac{\nabla P}{P} = \gamma\frac{\nabla}{n}$. For isothermal process, $\gamma = 1$ ($\nabla p = \nabla(nT) = T\nabla n$), and for the adiabatic process, $\gamma = (2 + D)/D$, where D is the degree of the freedom.

1.14 Dusty Plasma

The interaction of plasmas and charged dust particles have opened a new and fascinating research area called *dusty plasma*. Dusty plasmas are a special form of plasmas that originated from completely or partially ionized gases, which consist of electrons, ions, and extremely massive charged dust particles in the micrometer size. It is a normal electron–ion plasma with an additional charge component of macroparticles. The different characteristic lengths in dusty plasmas are (i) dust grain size length "a", (ii) Debye length "λ_D", and (iii) the average interparticle distance "d" (where $n_d d^3 \sim 1$); n_d is the dust number density. A plasma with dust particles or grains can either be called "dust in a plasma" or "dusty plasma". If $a \ll \lambda_D < d$, the plasma is called "dust in a plasma", and the situation $a \ll d < \lambda_D$ corresponds to "a dusty plasma".

   Electron–ion plasma and dusty plasma are dissimilar to each other as the dust particle's charge to mass ratio is relatively small for the latter compared to the former. Moreover, the frequencies of the dust particles are lesser compared to electrons and ions. There are differences between usually electron–ion (e-i) plasma and dusty plasma.

(i) **Neutrality**: Like *e-i* plasma, a dusty plasma is also globally neutral. So, at equilibrium, the charge neutrality condition becomes $q_i n_{i0} = en_{e0} - q_d n_{d0}$, where n_{s0} are unperturbed number density of the plasma species s ($s = e, i, d$ for electrons, ions, and dust, respectively) and $q_i = Z_i e$. $q_d = Z_d e$ ($-Z_d e$) is the dust particle charge when the grains are positively (negatively) charged, where $Z_i = 1$, and Z_d is the number of charges residing on the dust grain surface.

(ii) **Debye shielding**: Considering the ions and electrons obey Boltzmann distribution, i.e., $n_e = n_{e0} exp\left(\frac{e\phi_s}{K_B T_e}\right)$ and $n_i = n_{i0}$ $exp\left(-\frac{e\phi_s}{K_B T_i}\right)$, and also considering Poisson's equation as $\nabla^2 \phi_s = 4\pi(en_e - n_i - q_d n_d)$ and calculating the same as before, one can early obtain the dusty plasma Debye length λ_D as $\lambda_D = (\lambda_{De}\lambda_{Di})/\sqrt{\lambda_{De}^2 + \lambda_{Di}^2}$, where $\lambda_{De} = \sqrt{(K_B T_e)/(4\pi n_{e0} e^2)}$ and $\lambda_{Di} = \sqrt{(K_B T_i)/(4\pi n_{i0} e^2)}$ are electron and ion Debye length.

(iii) **Plasma frequency**: In plasma, the collective motion is characterized by plasma frequency ω_p. In dusty plasma also the same situation arises, if we treat the same as that in e-i plasma. In plasmas, electrons oscillate around ions with the electron plasma frequency $\omega_{pe} = \sqrt{4\pi n_{e0} e^2 / m_e}$, and here the ions also oscillate around dusts with the ion plasma frequency $\omega_{pi} = \sqrt{4\pi n_{i0} e^2 / m_i}$, and the dust particles also oscillate around their equilibrium position with the dust plasma frequency $\omega_{pd} = \sqrt{4\pi n_{d0} e^2 / m_d}$. In dusty plasma, the formation of dusty plasma crystal is another critical phenomenon and it is characterized by Coulombs coupling parameter Γ_c. It is defined as the ratio of dust potential energy to dust thermal energy. If the dust potential energy $\Sigma_c = \frac{q_d^2}{a} exp(-\frac{a}{\lambda_D})$ and dust thermal energy is $K_B T_d$, then $\Gamma_c = \frac{Z_d^2 e^2}{a K_B T_d} exp(-\frac{a}{\lambda_D})$. A dusty plasma is called weakly coupled if $\Gamma_c \ll 1$ and strongly coupled if $\Gamma_c \gg 1$.

Charged dust grains demonstrate a group behavior and are significant from the standpoint of wave dynamics. In dusty plasma, the ion numbers and electron numbers are asymmetrical.

Charge process: The crux of the dusty plasma research is to understand the charging of dust grains in plasma. It depends on the environment of the dust grains. The charging process causes the interaction of dust grains with gaseous plasma, with charged particles, or with photons. When dust particles are immersed in an electron–ion plasma, electrons reach the dust grain surface more rapidly than the ions as the electron thermal speed is higher than the ion thermal speed. As a result, the surface potential becomes negative. Then, eventually, the electrons are repelled, and the ions are attracted. On the other hand, if the surface potential becomes positive, it attracts electrons and repelled ions. Assuming the maxwell velocity distribution for plasma species $f_j(v_j) = n_j \left(\frac{m_j}{2\pi K_B T_j} \right)^{3/2} exp\left(-\frac{m_j v_j^2}{2K_B T_j} \right)$, one can obtain the charging current I_j for attractive ($q_j \phi_d < 0$) and repulsive ($q_j \phi_d > 0$) potentials as

$$I_j = 4\pi r_d^2 n_j q_j \left(\frac{K_B T_j}{2\pi m_j} \right)^{1/2} \left(1 - \frac{q_j \phi_d}{K_B T_j} \right) \quad \text{for } q_j \phi_d < 0$$

and

$$I_j = 4\pi r_d^2 n_j q_j \left(\frac{K_B T_j}{2\pi m_j} \right)^{1/2} exp\left(-\frac{q_j \phi_d}{K_B T_j} \right) \quad \text{for } q_j \phi_d > 0.$$

Accordingly, one can obtain the electron current I_e and ion current I_i as

$$I_e = -4\pi r_d^2 n_e e \left(\frac{K_B T_e}{2\pi m_e} \right)^{1/2} exp\left(\frac{e\phi_d}{K_B T_e} \right)$$

and

$$I_i = 4\pi r_d^2 n_i e \left(\frac{K_B T_i}{2\pi m_i} \right)^{1/2} \left(1 - \frac{e\phi_d}{K_B T_i} \right).$$

The time evolution of the charge on a dust grain in plasma can be written as

$$\frac{dq_d}{dt} = I_e + I_i$$

$$\text{or} \quad \frac{dZ_d}{dt} = -\frac{I_e + I_i}{e}.$$

Fluid equation: Like electron–ion plasma, the fluid equations for dusty plasma can also be written in the equation of continuity, equation of motion, and Poisson's equation. The equation of continuity is

$$\frac{\partial n_d}{\partial t} + \nabla \cdot (n_d u_d) = S_d$$

where the source or sink term S_d may arise in dust–ion collision and vanish in equilibrium. In general, dust number density is not affected by dust losing or picking up some charge, so generally, S_d is considered zero. The equation of momentum is

$$\left(\frac{\partial}{\partial t} + u_d \cdot \nabla\right) n_d + \frac{1}{n_d m_d} \nabla \cdot P_d = \frac{q_d}{m_d}(E + u_d \times B) - \nabla\phi + n_d,$$

and Poisson's equation is

$$\nabla^2 \phi = 4\pi \sum_\alpha m_\alpha n_\alpha,$$

and charge fluctuation is

$$\frac{dI}{dt} = I_e + I_i.$$

The reason behind this is that the dust particles are charged and get their electric charge by (i) electron emission, (ii) electron and ion capture, and (iii) other charging procedures. The significant basic dust grain charging procedures are (i) interaction of dust grains with gaseous plasma particles, (ii) interaction of dust grains with energetic particles (electrons and ions), and (iii) interaction of dust grains with photons. Quasineutrality condition of the plasma $\sum_p (q_p n_{p0} + Q_0 n_{d0}) = 0$. Here, $Q_0 = \epsilon e Z_d$ is the dust charge at equilibrium position and $\epsilon = 1$ or -1 according to positive and negative dust charge, respectively. As the electric potential of the adjacent plasma environments resolves the electric charge of dust grains, the electric charge of the dust particle is irregular. Thus, if a wave controls this potential, the electric charge of dust particles is influenced. As there is a variation of time in the dust charge, it is suitable to illustrate the plasma as $f_d = f_d(r, p, t, q)$. Here, q is the electric charge of the grains. As in the dusty plasma, the shielding of the electric charge of dust particles by the other plasma particles is not exponential; the Debye shielding in dusty plasma is somewhat dissimilar from that in electron–ion plasma. The dust grain charge q is established by $\frac{dq}{dt} = I$, where I is the sum of charging currents that are attained by the grain surface. This total charge results from two parts: an external current I_1 and another part I_p with $p = e, i$. I_p are the currents by the electrons and ions from the plasma. Thus, $I = I_1 + \sum_{p=e,i} I_p$. The external current can be obtained from various processes like photo emission by the incident UV radiation, secondary electron emission by the impact of the energetic particles, thermionic emission, and radioactive rays. Since the electrons move faster than the ions, the dust grains mainly attain their negative charge by the dust grains while considering I_p with $p = e, i$. The total current that flows on the surface of the dust grains in an equilibrium state is zero.

1.15 Quantum Plasma

Quantum mechanics was born and claimed to describe physics in the first quarter of the 20th century in a completely new way. The interpretation of quantum theory seems confusing but has a wide range of applications in astrophysics, microelectronics, and nanotechnology. Many bodily systems must be described by a so-called density matrix, which has no counterpart in classical theory. Many scientists like Max Planck, A. Einstein, N. Bohr, W. Heisenberg, E. Schrodinger, and P. Dirac have made enormous efforts to develop the subject. The development was done in two stages. On December 14, 1900, Max Plank made a presentation at a meeting of the German Physical Society. He stated that radiation is emitted or observed by matter in discrete or quanta packets of energy $h\nu$, where h is the frequency of the radiation and ν is Planck's constant. The first step started with Max Planck's hypothesis, which is a combination of classical and nonclassical theory. The second stage of quantum mechanics began in 1925, where Werner Heisenberg introduced a special form of quantum mechanics, also called matrix mechanics. Next year, Erwin Schrodinger introduced another mathematical form of quantum mechanics and is called wave mechanics. This mechanics combines the theory of classical waves and the relation of wave particles by Louis de Broglie. Mathematically, the ideas of wave mechanics and matrix mechanics are different. But they are identified according to the concept of physics. A classical charged particle system can be called plasma if it is almost neutral and if collective effects play a vital role in the dynamics. Traditional plasma physics has intensely focused on regimes characterized by high temperatures and low densities for which the effects of quantum mechanics have practically no impact. However, with the advancement of recent technology in semiconductors, it has become possible to imagine practical applications of plasma physics. It is here that the quantum nature of particles has a vital role to play. The quantum causes cannot be disregarded both at standard metal densities and room temperature. To examine the active characteristics of quantum plasma, electron gas is considered quantum fluid. But while reviewing particular astrophysical objects under severe density and temperature like the neutron stars and the white dwarf stars where the density is almost 10 times magnitudes bigger than ordinary solids, the quantum aspect must be considered along with plasma. In the 1960s, Pines first examined quantum plasmas consisting of electrons, ions, positrons, and holes. The concept of the quantum plasma was developed with the help of the well-known mathematical model, namely (i) Schrodinger–Poisson model, (ii) Winger–Poisson model, and (iii) quantum hydrodynamics model. If the macroscopic properties are considerably influenced by the quantum nature of plasma particles, it can be taken as quantum plasma. The quantum plasma differs significantly from classical plasmas in the following ways: (a) For classical plasmas, the system temperature is much higher than the Fermi temperature because it is fully quantum or fully degenerate. (b) When we consider the quantum effects on plasmas, the density is extremely high, and the temperature is comparatively low. In contrast to traditional plasmas, these have a high temperature and a low density. Plasmas exist on the sun's surface, in the earth's magnetosphere, and the interplanetary and interstellar media. Both fusion and space plasmas are characterized by high-temperature and low-density regimes, for which quantum effects are entirely negligible. However, physical systems in which both plasmas and quantum effects coexist occur in nature, the most obvious example being the electron gas in a common metal. Quantum plasma also occurs in some astrophysical objects such as white dwarf stars and neutron stars, where the density is greater than that of regular solids. The interaction and the quantum effects are also crucial in dense plasmas, which are relevant for intensive plasma experiments with a fixed laser density. For microscale and nanoscale objects such as quantum diodes, quantum-free electron lasers, quantum dots and nanowires, nanophotonics, and ultra-small electronic devices, for microplasmas and semiconductors, quantum correction to plasma is essential.

The thermal de Broglie wavelength (λ_B) of the particles comprising plasma can be used to measure the quantum effects and is defined as

$$\lambda_B = \frac{\hbar}{m v_T}.$$

Here, $\hbar$ is the Planck constant divided by 2π, m is the mass of the charged species, and $v_T = \sqrt{\frac{K_B T}{m}}$. The thermal de Broglie wavelength is so small that the charged particles can be compared to the shape of a point for classical plasmas. However, when de Broglie wavelength is equal to or bigger than the average interparticle distance $d = n^{-1/3}$, then both wave functions and quantum interference overlap with each other. The quantum effects can be considered when $n\lambda_B^3 \geq 1$. Similarly, the system is notably influenced by the quantum features of the charged species when the system temperature is lower than the Fermi temperature T_F of the species, where T_F is defined as

$$T_F = \frac{E_F}{K_B}$$

where E_F is the Fermi energy of the charged species and is explained as $E_F = \frac{p_F^2}{2m} = \frac{\hbar^2}{2m}(3\pi^2)^{2/3}n^{2/3}$. p_F is called the Fermi momentum and is defined by $p_F = \hbar(3\pi^2 n)^{1/3}$. When the system temperature $T \to T_F$ of the species, then the proper distribution functions of the species transform from the Maxwell–Boltzmann distribution to the Fermi–Dirac distribution.

Now,

$$\chi = \frac{T_F}{T} = \frac{1}{2}(3\pi^2)^{2/3}(n\lambda_B^3)^{2/3}.$$

Thus, plasma can be called a classical plasma when $\chi \ll 1$, i.e., $T \gg T_F$. On the other hand, plasma can be defined as a quantum plasma if $\chi \gg 1$, i.e., if $T \ll T_F$. In a quantum system, the thermal speed (v_T) can be changed by the Fermi velocity (v_F) because v_T is pointless in extremely low temperatures. The Fermi velocity is explained as

$$v_F = \left(\frac{2E_F}{m}\right)^{1/2} = \frac{\hbar}{m}\left(3\pi^2 n\right)^{1/3}.$$

Now, the quantum analog of the Debye length is indicated by the symbol λ_F. So,

$$\lambda_F = \frac{v_F}{\omega_p}.$$

Thus, λ_F is the Fermi screening length for quantum plasmas. g_Q is the quantum coupling parameter and can be defined as the ratio of interaction

Table 1.1: Comparison between classical plasmas and quantum plasmas.

	Classical Plasma	Quantum Plasma
(i) Debye Length	$\lambda_D = \frac{v_T}{\omega_p} = \left(\frac{\epsilon_0 K_B T}{ne^2}\right)^{1/2}$	$\lambda_B = \frac{\hbar}{mv_T}$
(ii) Velocity	$v_T = \left(\frac{K_B T}{m}\right)^{1/2}$	$v_F = \frac{\hbar}{m}(3\pi^2 n)^{1/3}$
(iii) Temperature	T	T_F
(iv) Coupling Parameter	$g_c = \left(\frac{1}{n\lambda_D^3}\right)^{2/3}$	$g_Q = \left(\frac{1}{n\lambda_F^3}\right)^{2/3}$

energy E_{ie} to the Fermi energy E_F.

$$g_Q = \frac{E_{ie}}{E_F} = \frac{2e^2 m}{\hbar^2 \epsilon_0 n^{1/3} (3\pi^2)^{2/3}} \sim \left(\frac{1}{n\lambda_F^3} \right)^{2/3} \sim \left(\frac{\hbar \omega_p}{E_F} \right)^2 \equiv H^2.$$

Thus, it is obvious that g_Q and g_C are equivalent when $\lambda_F \mapsto \lambda_D$. g_Q has no classical counterpart, and it represents the ratio between the plasmon energy $\hbar \omega_p$ with the Fermi energy E_F.

1.16 Quantum Plasma Models

The important problem of macroscopic observability of quantum phenomena in plasmas is connected with the question of when and which quantum phenomena are important in quantum plasmas. The answer to this question, of course, depends upon the models and approximations used to describe the quantum plasma. The complete description of quantum plasma as a system of many particles is a hopeless task because it is impossible to solve the Schrodinger equation for the N particle wave function of the system. This problem can be simplified by assuming that plasma is nearly ideal, i.e., two and higher-order correlations between the particles are neglected. In this view, plasma is considered as a collection of quantum particles that interact only with the collective field.

Let us consider the Schrodinger equation for the N-particle wave function ψ as a function of $q_1, q_2, \ldots, q_n$, where $q_j(r_j, s_j)$ is the coordinate (space, spin) of the j particle, and it gives the dynamics of the N-body problem. Let the jth particle have energy E_j. We also neglect the correlation particles, and so the wave function can be written as a product of a single particle wave function. Let the particle be identical, and so each wave function satisfies the Schrodinger equation.

Let us consider a one-dimensional quantum plasma, where the electrons are described by a statistical mixture of M pure states, each with a wave function $\psi_j, j = 1, \ldots, M$ obeying the Schrodinger–Poisson system

$$i\hbar \frac{\partial \psi_j}{\partial t} + \frac{\hbar^2}{2m_e} \nabla^2 \psi_j + e\phi \psi_j = 0 \tag{1.90}$$

$$\nabla^2 \phi = 4\pi e \left(\sum_{j=1}^{N} |\psi_j|^2 - Z_i n_i \right) \tag{1.91}$$

where $\phi(x,t)$ is the electrostatic potential, m is the electron mass, and $-e$ is the electron charge. Electrons are globally neutralized by a fixed ion background with density n_0. We assume periodic boundary conditions, with spatial period L. Finally, in the context of this chapter, it is convenient to adopt the normalization

$$\int dx |\psi_j|^2 = N/M \tag{1.92}$$

where N is the number of particles in a length L so that $n_0 = N/L$ and global charge neutrality is assured. Let us introduced the amplitude $A_j = A_j(x,t)$ and the phase $S_j = S_j(x,t)$ associated with the pure state $psi_j = \psi_j(x,t)$ according to

$$\psi_j = A_j \, exp(iS_j/\hbar). \tag{1.93}$$

Both A_j and S_j are defined as real quantities. The density n_j and the velocity u_j of the jth stream of the plasma are given by

$$n_j = A_j^2, \quad u_j = \frac{1}{m}\frac{\partial S_j}{\partial x}. \tag{1.94}$$

Introducing (1.93) and (1.94) into (1.90) and (1.91) and separating the real and imaginary parts of the equation, we find

$$\frac{\partial n_j}{\partial t} + \frac{\partial}{\partial x}(n_j u_j) = 0 \tag{1.95}$$

$$\frac{\partial u_j}{\partial t} + u_j \frac{\partial u_j}{\partial x} = \frac{e}{m}\frac{\partial \phi}{\partial x} + \frac{\hbar^2}{2m^2}\frac{\partial}{\partial x}\left(\frac{\partial^2(\sqrt{n_j})/\partial x^2}{\sqrt{n_j}}\right) \tag{1.96}$$

$$\frac{\partial^2 \phi}{\partial x^2} = \frac{e}{\epsilon_0}\left(\sum_{j=1}^{M} n_j - n_0\right) \tag{1.97}$$

where $\frac{\hbar^2}{2m^2}\frac{\partial}{\partial x}\left(\frac{\partial^2(\sqrt{n_j})/\partial x^2}{\sqrt{n_j}}\right)$ is called the Bohm potential. The continuity equation (1.95) and the quantum Euler equation (1.96) are the fluid dynamic representation of the Schrodinger equation. In this context, (1.93) can be termed the Madelung decomposition of the wave function. In the resulting set of equations, quantum effects are contained in the pressure like, $\hbar$-dependent term in (1.96). If $\hbar = 0$, we simply obtain the result of the classical multistream model. Therefore, we shall refer to (1.95)–(1.97) as the quantum multistream or quantum Dawson model.

The classical analog of this system is the "cold plasma" model because there is no pressure term in the momentum equation. However, in the quantum plasma, the Bohm potential term plays a role similar to the pressure. It does not correspond to the gradient of a function of the density only. Although it arises directly from the Schrodinger equation and is responsible for typical quantum-like behavior involving tunneling and wave packet spreading, it also contributes to extra dispersion of the small wavelengths and is relevant when we compare the propagation of nonlinear waves in the classical and quantum cases.

References

[1] M. V. Goldman, M. M. Oppenheim, and D. L. Newman, *Nonlinear Proc. Geophys.* 6, 221 (1999).
[2] R. C. Davidson, *Methods in Nonlinear Plasma Theory.* New York: Academic (1972).
[3] M. Tribeche, R. Amour, and P. K. Shukla, *Phys. Rev. E* 85, 037401 (2012).
[4] R. A. Cairns, A. A. Mamum, R. Bingham, R. Bostrom, R. O. Dendy, C. M. C. Nairn, and P. K. Shukla, *Geophys. Res. Lett.* 20, 2702 (1995).
[5] V. M. Vasyliunas, *J. Geophys. Res.* 73, 2839 (1968).
[6] A. Renyi, *Acta. Math. Hung* 6, 285 (1955).
[7] C. J. Tsallis, *Stat. Phys.* 52, 479 (1988).
[8] J. A. S. Lima, R. Silva, Jr. Santos, and J. Santos, *Phys. Plasmas* 19, 104502 (2010).

Chapter 2

Introduction to Waves in Plasma

2.1 Introduction

A wave can be defined as a disturbance that traverses a medium by transferring the energy of a particle or a point to another devoid of any permanent dislocation of the medium. Certain waves do not need the medium to move. Waves can be found in the environment in various forms and can be treated as carriers of energy and information from one place to another. Linear waves propagate with an unchanging form at a constant speed. With absorption, the waves will decrease in size as it moves. But in the presence of a dispersive medium, various frequencies travel at a different speed, in two or three dimensions. As the waves spread, their amplitude also decreases. Studying nonlinear waves and oscillations in various fields is important since wave phenomena always maintain a close relationship between theories and experiments. In nature, waves exist in different forms: waves on the ocean surface, acoustic waves from a beautiful piece of music that reaches our ears, ancient electromagnetic waves from a distant star, etc. If a wave propagates through a continuous medium, it is called a mechanical wave. Here, the medium could be air, water, a spring, the earth, or even people. Sound, water waves, a pulse that travels in the spring, and earthquakes are all mechanical waves. A wave of people in a soccer stadium like "Mexican Wave" is also a mechanical wave. The particles in the medium can travel either perpendicularly towards the wave or parallel to the path of the wave. If the medium oscillates at right angles to the direction of the waves, it is called the transverse wave. Again, if the medium shifts backward and forward in the same direction, the wave is called the longitudinal wave. The sound wave is an example of a longitudinal wave. A combination of the two is known as a surface wave. The movement of the particles is generally circular or elliptical on the surface of the medium. Seismic waves can be defined as waves that either move through the interior of the earth or near the surface of the earth. Seismic waves are the result of an earthquake, explosion, or volcano that emits low-frequency acoustic energy. Although there are many different seismic waves in nature, there are four types of basic waves: (i) primary wave (P-type), (ii) secondary wave (S-type), (iii) love wave, and (iv) Rayleigh wave. The electromagnetic waves can propagate without a medium. These waves occur due to the vibration of the electromagnetic field. Light is an electromagnetic wave, and, therefore, light can travel without a medium. Matter wave and gravitational wave are also important in today's science. Matter wave is generally used to denote particles like electrons that have wavy properties. These waves are a part of quantum mechanics. A gravitational wave is a ripple in the fabric of space–time itself. Mathematically, the energy of a wave is proportional to the square of its amplitude, i.e., $E = CA^2$, where E and A are the energy and amplitude of the wave, respectively. The constant C is dependent on the medium.

2.2 Mathematical Description of Waves

Suppose a progressive wave is moving along the x-axis. Its motion and all other similar kinds of wave motions can be explained quantitatively through the famous wave equation

$$\frac{\partial^2 u}{\partial t^2} = c^2 \frac{\partial^2 u}{\partial x^2} \tag{2.1}$$

where u is the amplitude function and is a measurement of the variation of displacement along the y-axis at a particular distance x along the x axis, c is the *wave speed* or *phase speed* with which the wave is traveling, and t is the time. This is a linear second-order partial differential equation. This equation can be rewritten as

$$\left(\frac{\partial}{\partial t} - c \frac{\partial}{\partial x} \right) \left(\frac{\partial}{\partial t} + c \frac{\partial}{\partial x} \right) u = 0.$$

Introducing the new variable $v = \frac{\partial u}{\partial t} + c \frac{\partial u}{\partial x}$, we therefore obtain the two equations

$$\frac{\partial u}{\partial t} + c \frac{\partial u}{\partial x} = v, \quad \frac{\partial v}{\partial t} - c \frac{\partial v}{\partial x} = 0.$$

$\left(\frac{\partial v}{\partial t} - c\frac{\partial v}{\partial x}\right)$ is the directional derivative of the function v in the direction $(-c, 1)$. Also, $\left(\frac{\partial v}{\partial t} - c\frac{\partial v}{\partial x}\right)$ express that v is constant on the lines $x + ct =$ constant. In other words, $v(x, t) = f(x + ct)$. Then, the first equation now becomes

$$\frac{\partial u}{\partial t} + c\frac{\partial u}{\partial x} = f(x + ct).$$

After some calculation, we can easily obtain the solution as

$$u(x, t) = F(x + ct) + G(x - ct).$$

This solution is the general solution of the sum of a wave moving to the left, $F(x + ct)$, and a wave moving to the right, $G(x - ct)$, with velocity c. It has many solutions, one of which in terms of the sine function is

$$u = A \sin 2\pi(x/\lambda - \omega t)$$

where λ, ω, and A are the wavelength, the frequency, and the amplitude of the wave, respectively. So, a linear wave in mathematical theory is usually with sine (or cosine) wave of the form

$$u(x, t) = a \sin(kx \pm \omega t). \tag{2.2}$$

Here, x is the space and t is the time, while a, k, and ω are positive parameters. a, k, and ω are the amplitude of the waves, wavenumber, and angular frequency, respectively. Moreover, u is periodic in both space and time with periods $\lambda = \frac{2\pi}{k}$ and $T = \frac{2\pi}{\omega}$. λ is called the wavelength and T the periods. The wave has crests (local maxima) when $kx \pm \omega t$ is an even multiple of π and troughs (local minima) when it is an odd multiple of π. We see that as t changes, the fixed shape $X \to \sin(kX)$ changes at constant speed c along the x-axis, and $X = x \pm ct$ is obtained as a phase. The number $c = \omega/k$ is called the speed of the wave phase or phase speed. If the sign is positive, the waves move to the left and vice versa if the sign is negative. A wave of permanent shape moving at constant speed is called a *traveling wave* or sometimes a *steady wave*. For linear waves, if two waves u_1 and u_2 cross each other, then the resultant amplitude is the sum of the amplitudes of each separate wave at the point of crossing. The resultant amplitude function U is equal to the linear combinations of two separate amplitude functions u_1 and u_2.

$$U = a_1 u_1 + a_2 u_2$$

where a_1 and a_2 are arbitrary constants, called mixing coefficients.

If we consider two equivalent waves one traveling along the $+x$ axis and the other traveling exactly in the opposite direction, i.e., along the $-x$ axis, then

$$u_1 = A \sin 2\pi(x/\lambda - \omega t)$$

$$u_2 = A \sin 2\pi(x/\lambda + \omega t)$$

and also $u_1 = u_2$ and $a_1 = a_2 = 1$. We have the linear combination of two waves whose resultant amplitude function will be

$$U_1 = A \sin 2\pi(x/\lambda - \omega t) + A \sin 2\pi(x/\lambda + \omega t).$$

The new resultant wave, which does not move either forward or backward, is known as a *standing wave or stationary wave*.

As per the example, the linearized Korteweg–de Vries equation

$$\frac{\partial u}{\partial t} + \frac{\partial^3 u}{\partial x^3} = 0$$

appears as a model for water waves with a small amplitude and long wavelength. The equations are sometimes referred to as *Airy's equation* although this name is also used for the closely related ordinary differential equation $y'' - xy = 0$. Substituting $u(x,t) = e^{i(kx - \omega(k)t)}$ into the equation, we find $\omega(k) = -k^3$ and hence $c(k) = -k^2$. Here, c is negative means that the wave travels to the left.

2.3   Dispersion Relation

The relationship between the energy of a system and its momentum is known as a *dispersion relation*. Equation $\omega = ck$ is an example of a dispersion relation as energy in waves is proportional to frequency ω and the wavenumber k is proportional to momentum. This relationship is important while studying how quickly a particular kind of Fourier components in the initial profile of wave travel and how quick energy dissipates for a certain system. To differentiate between these concepts, two types of velocities are used: phase velocity and group velocity.

Phase velocity: Let us assume a one-dimensional wave $u(x,t) = f(kx - \omega t)$, where k and ω are constants. While we observe a peak of the wave, we find that at a certain point in time t_0 and in space x_0, the wave has a height $H = u(x_0, t_0) = f(C_0)$ where $C_0 = kx_0 - \omega t_0$. Following this, it is seen that after time Δt the point H has traveled a small distance Δx so that $u(x_0 + \Delta x, t_0 + \Delta t) = H$. For Δt and Δx small, this can only be the case if $kx_0 - \omega t_0 = C_0 = k(x_0 + \Delta x) - \omega(t_0 + \Delta t)$, e.g., the point that gets mapped to H is the same after the wave has traveled a small distance. It will happen if

$$k\Delta x = \omega \Delta t \Rightarrow \frac{\Delta x}{\Delta t} = \frac{\omega}{k}.$$

This is known as the *phase velocity* of the wave. So for a wave of the form $u(x, t) = f(kx - \omega t) = e^{(kx - \omega t)}$ where k and ω are constants, the phase velocity V_p is defined as the constant

$$V_p = \frac{\omega}{k}. \tag{2.3}$$

Although the phase velocity can also be defined more generally, where V_p determines the speed at which anyone frequency component travels, in three dimensions, the exponent $(k.r - \omega t)$ is called the *phase* of the disturbance. The temporal derivative of the phase is given by the frequency ω and the spatial derivative of phase is given by the wave vector $\vec{k}$ that specifies the direction of propagation. A surface of a constant phase is called a *wave surface*. The velocity of the constant phase is called phase velocity which can be determined from

$$\frac{d}{dt}(k.r - \omega t) = 0 \Rightarrow v_p = \frac{\omega}{k}.$$

It can be noted that phase velocity may exceed the speed of light.

Group velocity: The propagation of energy in a system is given by the velocity of wave packets, known as the *group velocity*. The modulation information does not travel at the phase velocity but at the group velocity, which is always less than the velocity of light c. Let us consider two waves of nearly equal frequencies whose equations are given as follows:

$$E_1 = E_0 \cos[(k + \Delta k)x - (\omega + \Delta\omega)t]$$
$$E_2 = E_0 \cos[(k - \Delta k)x - (\omega - \Delta\omega)t].$$

E_1 and E_2 differ in frequency by $2\Delta\omega$. Since each wave must have the phase velocity ω/k appropriate to the medium in which they propagate, one must allow for a difference $2\Delta k$ in propagation constant.

$$E_1 + E_2 = 2E_0 \cos[(\Delta k)x - (\Delta\omega)t] \cos(kx - \omega t).$$

This represents a sinusoidally modulated wave. The envelope of the wave, given by $\cos[(\Delta k)x - (\Delta\omega)t]$, carries information; it travels at the velocity $\frac{\Delta\omega}{\Delta k}$. Taking the limit $\Delta\omega \to 0$, we obtain the group velocity as

$$V_g = \frac{d\omega}{dk}. \qquad (2.4)$$

In the case of right-traveling waves $f(x - ct)$, we determined the linear dispersion relation $\omega = ck$. Applying the definitions for the group and phase velocities, we see that in this instance

$$V_p = \frac{\omega}{k} = \frac{ck}{k} = c = \frac{d\omega}{dk} = V_g.$$

It does not contradict the theory of relativity because an indefinite long wave train cannot carry information. Information can be carried by a modulated wave, on which variation in frequency or amplitude is superimposed. We can regard each beat of information in this modulated signal as a wave packet that moves with a velocity called group velocity,

$$V_g = \frac{d\omega}{dk}.$$

We get the group velocity by the slope of the dispersion relation where V_g is less than the velocity of light, and it determines the velocity with which the energy of the wave is transmitted.

Classification: Propagation of any disturbance is classified by the dispersion function $D(\omega, k) = 0$ relating the frequency ω with the wave vector $\vec{k}$. This relation helps us to determine phase velocity and group velocity. If $\frac{\partial\omega}{\partial k} \to 0$, then there is a resonance at this frequency, the wave will not propagate, and the wave energy is used for stationary oscillation. A linear dispersion relation dominates a nondispersive wave. For linear equations, the differentiation of ω produces the coefficient of k, which is attained likewise by division. A linear relation thus entails the equality of V_p and V_g. On the other hand, let us imagine that the relation holds $V_p = V_g$. Now, if we take ω as a function only of k, we can segregate variables and solve the differential equation as follows:

$$\frac{d\omega}{dk} = \frac{\omega}{k} \Rightarrow \frac{d\omega}{\omega} = \frac{dk}{k}.$$

On integration, we get

$$\log\omega = \log k + c.$$

The linear dispersion relation is $\omega = Ck$ where $C = e^c$. Dispersive waves consist of unequal phase and group velocities, while nondispersive waves contain equal phase and group velocities.

Let $L(\phi) = 0$ be the partial differential equation and the dispersion relation is given by $D(\omega, k, A_i) = 0$ which can be expressed as

$$\omega = \omega(k; A_i). \tag{2.5}$$

Each root of this equation is called *mode* and each mode generates different waves.

For each mode, the phase velocity $V_p = \frac{\omega}{k}$ is the characteristic velocity for the mode. If an observer moves with that velocity, he can see the mode as a static disturbance. In a dispersive medium, the group velocity V_g has more importance due to this velocity of transfer of energy being through the medium.

Let

$$\phi(x) \propto e^{i(kx - \omega(k)t)}, \tag{2.6}$$

and the temporal evaluation of ϕ depends on the nature of $\omega(k)$.

(i) If $\omega(k)$ is real, then $\phi(x)$ represents a harmonic wave.

(ii) If $\omega(k)$ is purely imaginary $= i\omega_2(k)$, then $\phi(x,t) = e^{ikx}.e^{\omega_2(k)t}$. It represents a nonpropagating standing wave.

(iii) Also, if $\omega(k) = \omega_1(k) + i\omega_2(k)$, then $\phi(x) \propto e^{i(kx - \omega_1(k)t)}.e^{\omega_2(k)t}$. In that case, two cases arise, namely (a) if $\omega_2(k) > 0$, the solution is unstable and (b) if $\omega_2(k) < 0$, the solution is stable.

The wave is called diffusive and nondiffusive according to the value of $\omega = \omega(k)$ and is complex and real, respectively. A wave will be dispersive and nondispersive depending on the value of $\frac{\partial^2 \omega}{\partial k^2}$. If $\frac{\partial^2 \omega}{\partial k^2} \neq 0$, then the wave is dispersive. On the other hand, if $\frac{\partial^2 \omega}{\partial k^2} = 0$, then the wave is nondispersive. In the case of dispersive wave, $v_g \neq v_p$ and v_g depends on k. So, various wavelength waves travel with various group velocities, and after a certain time, the disturbance spreads over a certain length. Here, we can assume that the wave undergoes dispersion. The nondispersive wave, v_g, coincides with v_p, and there is no dispersion. The energy in a dispersive wave moves with the group velocity. A wave initially is propagating with phase velocity ω and after a sufficiently large time it will propagate with group velocity and satisfy the equation $k_t + \omega_x(k) = 0 \Rightarrow \frac{\partial k}{\partial t} + \omega'(k)\frac{\partial k}{\partial x} = 0$, i.e., along with the characteristic $\frac{dx}{dt} = \omega'(k)$, where k is constant. So, an observer moving with group velocity $\frac{dx}{dt} = \omega'(k) = V_g(k)$ will always be with a wave of wavenumber k.

2.4 Linear Waves in Plasmas

The fluid model is used to elucidate 80% and more plasma phenomena. Here, we neglect the individual identity of a particle, and we only consider the fluid element motions. Electric charges characterize the fluid in plasma. In any random fluids, the constant collisions between particles aid the fluids' elements to progress together. However, the same model in plasma functions as magnetic fields is present and not due to collisions.

In 1928, Langmuir first explained the electron oscillations in plasma. Two types of oscillations are possible: (i) oscillations of electrons which are very fast so the ions cannot follow them and (ii) oscillations of ions which are so slow that the electrons may satisfy the Boltzmann law. In plasma, electron oscillations arise, as the plasma wants to remain neutral. When electrons are shifted in a background of ions that are uniform in nature, it gives rise to electric fields. It, in turn, pulls back and reinstates plasma in a neutral state by putting back the electrons to their original position. The electrons exceed and oscillate around the stable position with a characteristic frequency, defined as the plasma frequency due to their inertia. The charged particles move haphazardly. The charged particles in a plasma move haphazardly, intermingle with each other with the help of their own electromagnetic forces and even reciprocate to perturbations that are externally applied. This consistent movement of plasma particles gives birth to different kinds of collective wave phenomena. Both longitudinal and transverse waves are supported by electron–ion plasma. Langmuir waves and ion acoustic waves evolve due to density and potential fluctuations. In an unmagnetized plasma, traverse waves are electromagnetic and do not go with density fluctuations. The existence of an external magnetic field in plasma affords the possibility of such a variety of longitudinal and transverse waves. When neutral dust grains are placed in electron–ion plasma, they are charged due to various processes. The wave propagation can be dominated or even changed in the presence of dust grains that are charged. The wave phenomena occur due to the inhomogeneity related to an arbitrary distribution of the charged particles and the digression from the traditional quasineutrality state in electron–ion plasma. It is because of charged dust grains, and the importance of the dust particle dynamics is present. Primarily, the fluid equations in various states are linearized to obtain linear waves. After that, the perturbation quantity is proportional to $e^{i(kx-\omega t)}$, and the relation between ω and k is derived. It is known as a dispersion relation. We get different waves from the dispersion relation.

The steps that we follow to obtain the dispersion relation are

(i) finding linearized fluid equations using the restriction for each wave to exist,

(ii) using Maxwell's equations as and where needed, and

(iii) considering the dependent variable of the partial differential equations for $e^{i(kx-\omega t)}$. Replace partial equation to algebraic equation by replacing $\frac{\partial}{\partial x} \to ik$ and $\frac{\partial}{\partial t} \to i\omega$.

2.5 Plasma Oscillation

If the electrons are dislocated from the equilibrium position, an electric field is created, and in time, it wants to withdraw the electron at the point of equilibrium for neutrality. But for the inertia of the electrons, this will exceed and oscillate around the equilibrium position, and oscillations will occur. This is called *plasma oscillation*.

Let us neglect the magnetic field and the thermal movement for the expression of the plasma oscillation and assume that the electron movement takes place only in the x direction, the ions are fixed uniformly in space, and the plasmas are homogeneous and infinitely extended. The fluid equations are

$$
\left.
\begin{aligned}
m_e n_e \left(\frac{\partial \vec{v}_e}{\partial t} + \vec{v}_e \frac{\partial \vec{v}_e}{\partial x} \right) &= -e n_e \vec{E} \\[2mm]
\frac{\partial n_e}{\partial t} + \frac{\partial (n_e \vec{v}_e)}{\partial x} &= 0 \\[2mm]
\epsilon_0 \frac{\partial \vec{E}}{\partial x} &= e(n_i - n_e)
\end{aligned}
\right\}
\tag{2.7}
$$

where n_e, n_i, $\vec{v}_e$, and $\vec{E}$ are electron number density, ion number density, electron velocity, and electric field, respectively. In equilibrium, let $n_i = n_e = n_0$, $\vec{v}_e = \vec{v}_0$, and $\vec{E} = \vec{E}_0$ and there is no oscillation. To linearize Equation (2.7), we separated the dependent variable into two parts, equilibrium part and perturbation part, and write $n_e = n_0 + n_1$, $\vec{v}_e = \vec{v}_0 + \vec{v}_1$, and $\vec{E} = \vec{E}_0 + \vec{E}_1$, where the subscript is '0' for equilibrium part and '1' for perturbation part. The equilibrium quantities convey the state of plasma without oscillation. Hence, $\frac{\partial n_0}{\partial x} = 0 = v_0 = E_0$. So, $\frac{\partial n_0}{\partial t} = \frac{\partial v_0}{\partial t} = \frac{\partial E_0}{\partial t} = 0$.

From (2.7), we get

$$m_e \frac{\partial \vec{v}_1}{\partial t} = -e\vec{E}_1, \quad \frac{\partial n_1}{\partial t} + n_0 \frac{\partial \vec{v}_1}{\partial x} = 0, \quad \epsilon_0 \frac{\partial \vec{E}_1}{\partial x} = -en_1. \tag{2.8}$$

Let us assume that the oscillating quantity behaves sinusoidally. Hence, $\vec{v}_1 = v_1 e^{i(kx-\omega t)}\hat{x}$, $n_1 = n_1 e^{i(kx-\omega t)}$, $\vec{E}_1 = E_1 e^{i(kx-\omega t)}\hat{x}$, and so $\frac{\partial \vec{v}_1}{\partial t} = -i\omega\vec{v}_1$, $\frac{\partial \vec{v}_1}{\partial x} = -ik\vec{v}_1$. So, $\frac{\partial}{\partial t}$ may be replaced by $-i\omega$ and $\frac{\partial}{\partial x}$ is replaced by ik.

From (2.8), we get

$$im_e\omega v_1 = eE_1, \quad n_1\omega = n_0 k v_1, \quad \epsilon_0 ik E_1 = -en_1. \tag{2.9}$$

From (2.9), we get

$$\left(\omega^2 - \frac{e^2 n_0}{\epsilon_0 m_e}\right) v_1 = 0. \tag{2.10}$$

Since $v_1 \neq 0$ for all space and time, so

$$\omega = \sqrt{\frac{e^2 n_0}{\epsilon_0 m_e}} = \omega_p \ \ (say). \tag{2.11}$$

$\omega_p = \sqrt{(e^2 n_0)/(\epsilon_0 m_e)}$ rad/sec is called *Plasma frequency*. The plasma frequency depends on n_0, i.e., $\omega_p \propto \sqrt{n_0}$. It is seen that ω does not depend upon k, then $\frac{\partial \omega}{\partial k} = 0$. So, there is no group velocity and it has only oscillation. Thus, the disturbance does not propagate and there is no wave.

2.6   Electromagnetic Waves

The electromagnetic fields in plasmas can have two parts: (i) static or undisturbed part and (ii) oscillating part. Generally, the static part (or equilibrium part) is written with suffix 0 and the oscillating part (or perturbed part) with suffix 1 (for example, $\vec{B} = \vec{B}_0 + \vec{B}_1$ and $\vec{E} = \vec{E}_0 + \vec{E}_1$ where $\vec{B}_0$, $\vec{B}_1$, $\vec{E}_0$, and $\vec{E}_1$ are undisturbed magnetic field, oscillating magnetic field, undisturbed electric field, and oscillating electric field, respectively). All the oscillatory quantity varies sinusoidally, i.e., $\propto e^{i(kx-\omega t)}$, so $\frac{\partial}{\partial x} \to ik$ and $\frac{\partial}{\partial t} \to -i\omega$. The presence of an oscillating magnetic field determines the classification of plasma waves. In the existence of oscillating magnetic fields, plasma waves are referred to electromagnetic waves, and when there are no oscillating magnetic fields, electrostatic waves are generated. Plasma waves are also classified as follows:

Parallel wave: If the direction of wave vector $\vec{k}$ is parallel to the undisturbed magnetic field $\vec{B}_0$, then the wave is called a *parallel wave*.

Perpendicular wave: If the direction of wave vector $\vec{k}$ is the perpendicular undisturbed magnetic field $\vec{B}_0$, i.e., if $\vec{B}_0$ is along the direction of z, then $\vec{k}$ will be either in the direction of y or x, then the wave is called a *perpendicular wave*.

Longitudinal wave: If the direction of wave vector $\vec{k}$ is parallel to the oscillatory electric field $\vec{E}_1$ with no oscillatory magnetic field, then a wave that exists is called a *longitudinal wave*.

Transverse wave: If the direction of $\vec{k}$ is perpendicular to $\vec{E}_1$, then the wave is a *transverse wave*. For the transverse wave, $\vec{B}_1$ is finite, and the wave is electromagnetic.

2.7 Upper Hybrid Frequency

In a magnetized plasma, different modes of oscillations and waves are possible. Let us consider that the electrons oscillate perpendicular to $\vec{B}_0$, the ions are static in the uniform background of positive charge, and the thermal motions of the electrons are neglected (i.e., $K_B T_e = 0$). The equilibrium states are n_0, $\vec{B}_0$, $\vec{E}_0$, and $\vec{v}_0$, where $\vec{E}_0 = \vec{v}_0 = 0$. Again, if we consider longitudinal waves only, i.e., $\vec{k} \parallel \vec{E}_1$, then the oscillation occurring in the plane is called *upper hybrid oscillation*. On the other hand, if the ion acoustic wave considers, then $\vec{k}$ is perpendicular to $\vec{B}_0$, i.e., $\vec{k} \cdot \vec{B}_0 = 0$, the oscillation is called the *lower hybrid frequency*. The basic fluid equations are

$$\frac{\partial n_e}{\partial t} + \vec{\nabla} \cdot [n_e \vec{v}_e] = 0 \qquad (2.12)$$

$$m_e n_e \left(\frac{\partial}{\partial t} + \vec{v}_e \cdot \vec{\nabla} \right) \vec{v}_e = -e n_e [\vec{E} + \vec{v}_e \times \vec{B}] \qquad (2.13)$$

$$\epsilon_0 \vec{\nabla} \cdot \vec{E} = e(n_i - n_e) \qquad (2.14)$$

where m_e, $\vec{v}_e$, $\vec{E}$, e, and n_e are the electron mass, electron velocity, electric field, electron charge, and electron number density, respectively. If there is no thermal motion of electrons, $K_B T_e = 0$. We assume at equilibrium the density of plasma is a constant, and static electric field, static magnetic field, and oscillation magnetic field velocity at equilibrium are all zero. Accordingly, $n = n_0 + n_{e_1}$, $\vec{B} = \vec{B}_0 + \vec{B}_1$, $\vec{v} = \vec{v}_{e_1}$, and $\vec{E} = \vec{E}_1$.

So, the linearized equations are

$$\frac{\partial n_{e_1}}{\partial t} + n_0 \vec{\nabla} \cdot v_{e_1} = 0 \tag{2.15}$$

$$m_e \frac{\partial \vec{v}_{e_1}}{\partial t} = -e[\vec{E}_1 + \vec{v}_{e_1} \times \vec{B}_0] \tag{2.16}$$

$$\epsilon_0 \vec{\nabla} \cdot \vec{E}_1 = -e n_{e_1}. \tag{2.17}$$

Let us consider only longitudinal wave, i.e., $\vec{k} \parallel \vec{E}_1$. Without loss of generality, we take $\vec{k}$ and $\vec{E}_1$ in the direction of the x-axis and $\vec{B}_0$ is in the z-direction, i.e., $\vec{k} = (k_x, 0, 0)$, $\vec{E} = (E_x, 0, 0)$, $\vec{v}_{e_1} = (v_x, v_y, v_z)$, and $\vec{B} = (0, 0, B_0)$. We also assume that the oscillating quantities behave sinusoidally and hence replacing $\frac{\partial}{\partial x}$ by ik and $\frac{\partial}{\partial t}$ by $-i\omega$, we obtain from Equations (2.15)–(2.17)

$$-i\omega n_{e_1} + i n_0 k v_x = 0 \Rightarrow n_1 = \frac{k}{\omega} n_0 v_x \tag{2.18}$$

$$-i\omega m_e \vec{v}_{e_1} = -e\left(\vec{E}_1 + \vec{v}_{e_1} \times \vec{B}_0\right) \tag{2.19}$$

$$\epsilon_0 i k E_x = -e n_{e_1}. \tag{2.20}$$

Equation (2.19) can be written into the component forms

$$-i\omega m_e v_x = -e E_x - e v_y B_0 \tag{2.21}$$

$$-i\omega m_e v_y = e v_x B_0 \tag{2.22}$$

$$-i\omega m_e v_z = 0. \tag{2.23}$$

From Equations (2.22) and (2.23), we get

$$v_x = \frac{\frac{eE_x}{im\omega}}{\left(1 - \frac{\omega_c^2}{\omega^2}\right)} \tag{2.24}$$

where $\omega_c = \sqrt{eB_0/m}$ is the *cyclotron frequency*.

Again, from Equations (2.18), (2.20), and (2.24), we get

$$\left(1 - \frac{\omega_c^2}{\omega^2}\right) E_x = \frac{\omega_p^2}{\omega^2} E_x \tag{2.25}$$

where $\omega_p = \frac{e^2 n_0}{\epsilon_0 m}$ is the plasma frequency. Thus,

$$\omega = \sqrt{\omega_c^2 + \omega_p^2}. \tag{2.26}$$

This ω is called *higher hybrid frequency*. The frequency of this oscillation is higher than the plasma frequency ω_p. The reason behind this here is that two restoring forces are acting on the electrons, namely the electrostatic force and the Lorentz force. If $\omega_c = 0$, then $\omega = \omega_p$. Thus, the higher hybrid frequency is equal to the plasma frequency if the cyclotron frequency is zero.

2.8 Electrostatic Ion Cyclotron Waves

Electrostatic ion cyclotron waves are longitudinal waves of the ions and electrons in magnetized plasma which propagate perpendicular to the magnetic field. Suppose the electrostatic ion waves are propagating perpendicular to the magnetic field $\vec{B}$. The fluid equations are

$$M\frac{\partial \vec{v_i}}{\partial t} = e[\vec{E} + \vec{v_i} \times \vec{B}] \tag{2.27}$$

$$\frac{\partial n_i}{\partial t} + \frac{\partial}{\partial x}(n_i v_i) = 0 \tag{2.28}$$

where M is the mass of ions. To linearize Equations (2.27) and (2.28), as usual, we separate the dependent variable into an equilibrium part and a perturbation part and write $\vec{v_i} = \vec{v_0} + \vec{v_1} = \vec{v_1}$, $\vec{E} = -\vec{\nabla}\phi$, $\vec{B} = \vec{B_0} + \vec{B_1}$, $\phi = \phi_0 + \phi_1 = \phi_1$, and $n_i = n_0 + n_1$. Assume $v_0 = 0$ and $\phi_0 = 0$. Then, the linearized equations are

$$M\frac{\partial \vec{v_1}}{\partial t} = -e\vec{\nabla}\phi_1 + e\vec{v_1} \times \vec{B_0} \tag{2.29}$$

$$\frac{\partial n_1}{\partial t} + n_0\frac{\partial v_1}{\partial x} = 0. \tag{2.30}$$

Now assuming $v_1 = (v_x, v_y, v_z)$ and $B_0 = (0, 0, B_z)$, Equation (2.29) can be written as

$$M\dot{\vec{v}}_x = -e\frac{\partial \phi_1}{\partial x} + ev_y B_0 \tag{2.31}$$

$$M\dot{\vec{v}}_y = ev_x B_0. \tag{2.32}$$

Assuming all perturbed terms are proportional to $e^{-i(kx-\omega t)}$ and replacing $\partial/\partial x$ by ik and $\partial/\partial t$ by $-i\omega$, from (2.31) and (2.32), we have

$$-Mi\omega v_x = -eik\phi_1 + ev_y B_0 \tag{2.33}$$

$$-i\omega M v_y = -ev_x B_0. \tag{2.34}$$

Eliminating v_y from Equations (2.33) and (2.34), we get

$$v_x = \frac{ek\phi_1}{\omega M}\left(1 - \frac{\Omega_c^2}{\omega^2}\right)^{-1} \tag{2.35}$$

where $\Omega_c = eB_0/M$. Also from Equation (2.30), we get

$$n_1 = \frac{n_0 k v_0}{\omega}. \tag{2.36}$$

We have already assumed that electrons can move along $\vec{B}_0$ and therefore, it is assumed that the electrons obey the Boltzmann distribution.

$$n_e = n_0 e^{\frac{e\phi_1}{K_B T_e}}$$

$$or. \ n_0 + n_{e_1} = n_0\left[1 + \frac{e\phi_1}{K_B T_e} + O(\phi t)\right]$$

$$\Rightarrow n_{e_1} = \frac{n_0 e\phi_1}{K_B T_e}. \tag{2.37}$$

Assuming the neutrality $n_1 = n_{e_1}$, we have from (2.36)–(2.37)

$$\omega^2 = \Omega_c^2 + k^2 v_s^2 \tag{2.38}$$

(2.38) is called the dispersion relation for electrostatic cyclotron waves, where $v_s = \sqrt{K_B T_e/M}$ is the ion acoustic speed. If $v_s = 0$, then $\omega = \Omega_c$, then cyclotron waves become cyclotron frequency.

2.9 Lower Hybrid Frequency

A longitudinal oscillation of ions and electrons in a magnetized plasma is known as lower hybrid oscillation. Let us consider the propagation angle θ between $\vec{k}$ and $\vec{B}_0$ to be $\frac{\pi}{2}$. So, electrons obey the fluid equations of motion. We also consider the electron temperature $T_e = 0$ and consequently pressure gradient becomes zero, i.e., $\nabla p_e = 0$.

Like previous case we shall get (2.35)

$$v_{ix} = \frac{ek}{M\omega}\phi_1\left(1 - \frac{\Omega_c^2}{\omega^2}\right)^{-1}. \tag{2.39}$$

As electrons are also considered mobile, similarly we have,

$$v_{ex} = -\frac{ek\phi_1}{m\omega}\left(1 - \frac{\omega_c^2}{\omega^2}\right)^{-1} \tag{2.40}$$

where Ω_c and ω_c are the ion cyclotron frequency and the electron cyclotron frequency, respectively. The equation of continuity for ions is

$$\frac{\partial n_i}{\partial t} + \frac{\partial}{\partial x}(n_i v_i) = 0. \tag{2.41}$$

To linearize (2.41), we use $n_i = n_0 + n_i$ and $v_i = 0 + v_{i1}$ and get the linearized equation as

$$\frac{\partial n_{i1}}{\partial t} + n_0 \frac{\partial v_{i1}}{\partial x} = 0. \tag{2.42}$$

As all perturbed components n_{i1} and v_{i1} are proportional to $e^{i(kx-\omega t)}$, Equation (2.42) becomes

$$(-i\omega)n_{i1} + n_0(ik)v_{i1} = 0$$

$$or. \ n_{i1} = n_0\frac{k}{\omega}v_{i1}. \tag{2.43}$$

Similarly, the equation of continuity of electrons gives

$$n_{e1} = n_0\frac{k}{\omega}v_{e1}. \tag{2.44}$$

At equilibrium, $n_i = n_e$ or. $n_{i1} = n_{e1}$, or. $v_{i1} = v_{e1}$ or. $v_{ix} = v_{ex}$. Therefore,

$$\frac{ek\phi_1}{M\omega}\left(1 - \frac{\Omega_c^2}{\omega^2}\right)^{-1} = -\frac{ek\phi_1}{m\omega}\left(1 - \frac{\omega_c^2}{\omega^2}\right)^{-1}$$

$$\Rightarrow M\left(1 - \frac{\Omega_c^2}{\omega^2}\right) + m\left(1 - \frac{\omega_c^2}{\omega^2}\right) = 0$$

$$\Rightarrow \omega^2 = \Omega_c\omega_c$$

$$\Rightarrow \omega = (\Omega_c\omega_c)^{\frac{1}{2}} = \omega_l \ (say) \tag{2.45}$$

where ω_l is called *Lower hybrid frequency*. Lower hybrid frequency is the geometric mean of ion cyclotron frequency and electron cyclotron frequency, i.e., $\omega_l = \sqrt{\Omega_c\omega_c}$.

2.10 Electromagnetic Waves with $\vec{B}_0 = 0$

Let us consider $\vec{B}_1 \neq 0$. We also assume electromagnetic waves with $\vec{B}_0 = 0$, i.e., $\vec{B} = \vec{B}_0 + \vec{B}_1 = \vec{B}_1$. The relevant Maxwell's equations are

$$\vec{\nabla} \cdot \vec{E}_1 = \frac{\rho}{\epsilon_0} \tag{2.46}$$

$$\vec{\nabla} \times \vec{E}_1 = -\frac{\partial \vec{B}_1}{\partial t} \tag{2.47}$$

$$c^2 \vec{\nabla} \times \vec{B}_1 = \frac{\partial \vec{E}_1}{\partial t} + \frac{J}{\epsilon_0} \tag{2.48}$$

where $c^2 = (\mu_0 \epsilon_0)^{-1}$ and μ_0 and ϵ_0 are the permittivity in free space. In free space, $\vec{J} = 0$, and the density ρ must be equal to zero.

$$\vec{\nabla} \cdot \vec{E}_1 = 0 \tag{2.49}$$

$$\vec{\nabla} \times \vec{E}_1 = -\frac{\partial \vec{B}_1}{\partial t} \tag{2.50}$$

$$c^2 \vec{\nabla} \times \vec{B}_1 = \frac{\partial \vec{E}_1}{\partial t}. \tag{2.51}$$

From (2.51) and using (2.50), we get

$$c^2 \vec{\nabla} \times \frac{\partial \vec{B}_1}{\partial t} = \frac{\partial^2 \vec{E}_1}{\partial t^2}$$

$$\Rightarrow \left(\frac{\partial^2}{\partial t^2} - c^2 \frac{\partial^2}{\partial x^2} \right) \vec{E}_1 = 0. \tag{2.52}$$

When $J \neq 0$ is considered in plasma, it includes a term $\frac{J_1}{\epsilon_0}$ to account for current. This is because of first-order charged particle motion. Let $J \neq 0$ and $J = J_0 + J_1$ (J_0 is the equilibrium part and J_1 is the perturbed part). Then, Maxwell's equations of motion are

$$\vec{\nabla} \times \vec{E}_1 = -\frac{\partial \vec{B}_1}{\partial t}$$

$$c^2 \vec{\nabla} \times \vec{B}_1 = \frac{\partial \vec{E}_1}{\partial t} + \frac{\vec{J}_1}{\epsilon_0}$$

$$\Rightarrow c^2 \vec{\nabla} \times \frac{\partial \vec{B}_1}{\partial t} = \frac{\partial^2 \vec{E}_1}{\partial t^2} + \frac{1}{\epsilon_0} \frac{\partial \vec{J}_1}{\partial t}$$

$$\Rightarrow -c^2 \vec{\nabla} \times (\vec{\nabla} \times \vec{E}_1) = \frac{\partial^2 \vec{E}_1}{\partial t^2} + \frac{1}{\epsilon_0} \frac{\partial \vec{J}_1}{\partial t}. \tag{2.53}$$

Assuming the oscillating quantity behaves sinusoidally and replacing $\vec{\nabla}$ by ik and $\partial/\partial t$ by $-i\omega$, we get

$$c^2\vec{k}(\vec{k} \cdot \vec{E}_1) - c^2\vec{k}^2\vec{E}_1 = -\omega^2\vec{E}_1 - \frac{1}{\epsilon_0}\vec{J}_1 i\omega. \tag{2.54}$$

Since the wave is transverse, $\vec{k}.\vec{E}_1 = 0$, hence

$$(\omega^2 - c^2\vec{k}^2)\vec{E}_1 = -\frac{1}{\epsilon_0}i\omega\vec{J}_1 \tag{2.55}$$

$$\left(\frac{\partial^2}{\partial t^2} - c^2\frac{\partial^2}{\partial x^2}\right)\vec{E}_1 = -\frac{i\omega\vec{J}_1}{\epsilon_0}. \tag{2.56}$$

If we consider equivalently high-frequency waves, like light waves or microwaves, the ions are considered to be fixed. Now, from electron motion, we have $\vec{J} = en(\vec{v}_i - \vec{v}_e)$. For linearization, we write $\vec{J} = \vec{J}_0 + \vec{J}_1 = \vec{J}_1$, $n = n_0 + n_1$, $\vec{v}_i = \vec{v}_{i0} + \vec{v}_{i1}$, and $\vec{v}_e = \vec{v}_{e0} + \vec{v}_{e1}$ ($\vec{J}_0 = 0 = \vec{v}_{i0} = \vec{v}_{e0}$). Thus, we get

$$\vec{J}_1 = e(n_0 + n_1)(\vec{v}_{i1} - \vec{v}_{e1}).$$

Assuming $\vec{v}_{i1} = 0$ and deleting the nonlinear term, we get $\vec{J}_1 = -en_0\vec{v}_{e1}$. So,

$$\vec{v}_{e1} = -\frac{\vec{J}_1}{en_0}. \tag{2.57}$$

The electron motion equation is

$$m\frac{\partial\vec{v}_e}{\partial t} = -e[\vec{E} + \vec{v} \times \vec{B}]. \tag{2.58}$$

For linearization at one place $\vec{v}_e = \vec{v}_{e0} + \vec{v}_{e1}$, $\vec{E} = \vec{E}_0 + \vec{E}_1$, $\vec{B} = \vec{B}_0 + \vec{B}_1$, and $\vec{v} = \vec{v}_0 + \vec{v}_1$ ($\vec{B}_0 = \vec{v}_0 = \vec{E}_0 = \vec{v}_{e0} = 0$), and neglecting the nonlinear term and replacing $\frac{\partial}{\partial t}$ by $-i\omega$, we obtain

$$im\omega\vec{v}_{e1} = e\vec{E}_1. \tag{2.59}$$

Now, from (2.55),

$$(\omega^2 - c^2\vec{k}^2)\vec{E}_1 = -\frac{i\omega}{\epsilon_0}\vec{J}_1 = \omega_p^2\vec{E}_1 \tag{2.60}$$

where $\omega_p = (e^2n_0)/(\epsilon_0 m)$. It is known as the plasma frequency. Therefore,

$$\omega^2 = \omega_p^2 + c^2\vec{k}^2. \tag{2.61}$$

Equation (2.61) is the dispersion relation for electromagnetic waves. The phase velocity $= v_\phi^2 = \frac{\omega^2}{k^2} = c^2 + \omega_p^2/k^2 > c^2$ and the group velocity is v_g. Now,

$$2\omega \frac{d\omega}{d\vec{k}} = 2c^2 \vec{k} \Rightarrow v_g = \frac{c^2}{v_\phi}.$$

2.11 Electromagnetic Waves Perpendicular to B_0

Let us now consider the electromagnetic waves. When the unperturbed magnetic field $\vec{B}_0$ is present, then the waves are called electromagnetic. At first, we consider the direction of $\vec{k}$ is perpendicular to $\vec{B}_0$, i.e., $\vec{k} \perp \vec{B}_0$. If we take transverse waves with $\vec{k} \perp \vec{E}_1$, then two cases arise: either $\vec{E}_1 \parallel \vec{B}_0$ or $\vec{E}_1 \perp \vec{B}_0$. In the first case, the waves are called ordinary waves, and in the second case, it is called extraordinary waves. Now, we evaluate the dispersion relation of ordinary waves and extraordinary waves.

2.11.1 *Ordinary wave*

When $\vec{E}_1$ is parallel to $\vec{B}_0$, we choose $\vec{B}_0 = B_0 \hat{z}$, $\vec{E}_1 = E_1 \hat{z}$, and $\vec{k} = k\hat{x}$. From (2.54), we get

$$\left(\vec{k}^2 - \frac{\omega^2}{c^2} \right) \vec{E}_1 = \frac{i\omega}{\epsilon_0 c^2} (-n_0 e \vec{v}_{e_1})$$

where $\vec{J}_1 = -n_0 e \vec{v}_{e_1}$ and $\vec{k} \cdot \vec{E}_1 = 0$. Since $\vec{E}_1 = E_1 \hat{z}$, we only need the component v_{ez}. The equation of motion is

$$m \frac{\partial \vec{v}_e}{\partial t} = -e[\vec{E} + \vec{v}_e \times \vec{B}]$$

$$\Rightarrow v_{ez} = \frac{e}{im\omega} E_1.$$

Taking perturbation $\vec{v}_{ez} = \vec{v}_{e0} + \vec{v}_{e1}$, $\vec{B} = \vec{B}_0 + \vec{B}_1$, and $\vec{E} = \vec{E}_0 + \vec{E}_1$ and using the same way, we have

$$\omega^2 = \omega_p^2 + c^2 \vec{k}^2.$$

The above relation is the dispersion relation for ordinary waves. In the absence of ck, $\omega = \omega_p$, and if $\omega_p = 0$, then $\omega = \pm ck$.

2.11.2 *Extraordinary wave*

Extraordinary wave is an electromagnetic wave which is partially longitudinal and partially transverse. This wave propagates perpendicularly to $\vec{B}_0$ with $\vec{E}_1 \perp \vec{B}_0$. So, we consider $\vec{E}_1 \perp \vec{B}_0$. Let $\vec{E}_1 = E_x \hat{x} + E_y \hat{y}$, $\vec{B}_0 = B_0 \hat{z}$, and $\vec{k} = k\hat{x}$. However, it turns out that waves with $\vec{E}_1 \perp \vec{B}_0$ tend to be elliptically polarized instead of being plane polarized. While propagating into a plasma, the wave develops a component E_x along $\vec{k}$. Thus, becoming partly longitudinal and partly transverse. The equation of motion of electrons is

$$m\frac{\partial \vec{v}_e}{\partial t} = -e[\vec{E} + \vec{v}_e \times \vec{B}]. \tag{2.62}$$

To get the linearized form, we write $\vec{v}_e = \vec{v}_{e0} + \vec{v}_{e1}$ and $\vec{B} = \vec{B}_0$, where $\vec{v}_{e1} = (v_x, v_y, v_z)$ and $\vec{B}_0 = (0, 0, B_0)$. So, we have a set of linearized equations of motion in x and y directions, and solving it we get

$$v_x = -\frac{ie}{m\omega}(E_x + v_y B_0), \quad v_y = -\frac{ie}{m\omega}(E_y - v_x B_0).$$

Thus,

$$v_x = \frac{e}{m\omega}\left[-iE_x - \frac{\omega_c}{\omega}E_y\right]\left(1 - \frac{\omega_c^2}{\omega^2}\right)^{-1} \tag{2.63}$$

$$v_y = \frac{e}{m\omega}\left[-iE_y + \frac{\omega_c}{\omega}E_x\right]\left(1 - \frac{\omega_c^2}{\omega^2}\right)^{-1}. \tag{2.64}$$

The wave equation is given by (2.54)

$$-\vec{k}(\vec{k} \cdot \vec{E}_1) + \vec{k}^2 \vec{E}_1 = \frac{i\omega}{\epsilon_0 c^2}\vec{J}_1 + \frac{\omega^2}{c^2}\vec{E}_1. \tag{2.65}$$

For longitudinal wave, $\vec{k} \cdot \vec{E}_1 = kE_x$, and using this relation in Equation (2.65), we get

$$(\omega^2 - c^2\vec{k}^2)\vec{E}_1 + \vec{k}c^2 kE_x = \frac{i\omega n_0 e \vec{v}_{e1}}{\epsilon_0}.$$

The above equation can be written into the component forms, and then using (2.63) and (2.64), we get

$$\omega^2 E_x = \frac{i\omega n_0 e}{\epsilon_0}v_x$$

$$\Rightarrow \omega^2 E_x = -\frac{i\omega n_0 e}{\epsilon_0}\frac{e}{m\omega}\left[iE_x + \frac{\omega_c}{\omega}E_y\right]\left(1 - \frac{\omega_c^2}{\omega^2}\right)^{-1} \tag{2.66}$$

$$(\omega^2 - c^2 k^2) E_y = \frac{i\omega n_0 e}{\epsilon_0} v_y$$

$$\Rightarrow (\omega^2 - c^2 k^2) E_y = -\frac{i\omega n_0 e}{\epsilon_0} \frac{e}{m\omega} \left[i E_y - \frac{\omega_c}{\omega} E_x \right] \left(1 - \frac{\omega_c^2}{\omega^2} \right)^{-1}.$$

$$(2.67)$$

In (2.66), using $\omega_p^2 = n_0 e^2 / \epsilon_0 m$ we get

$$\left[\omega^2 \left(1 - \frac{\omega_c^2}{\omega^2} \right) - \omega_p^2 \right] E_x + i \frac{\omega_p^2 \omega_c}{\omega} E_y = A E_x + i B E_y = 0$$

where $A = (\omega^2 (1 - \frac{\omega_c^2}{\omega^2}) - \omega_p^2)$ and $B = \omega_p^2 \omega_c / \omega$.

Similarly, from (2.67), we get

$$\left[(\omega^2 - c^2 k^2) \left(1 - \frac{\omega_c^2}{\omega^2} \right) - \omega_p^2 \right] E_y - i \frac{\omega_p^2 \omega_c}{\omega} E_x = C E_x + i D E_y = 0$$

where $C = \omega_p^2 \omega_c / \omega$ and $D = [(\omega^2 - c^2 k^2)(1 - \frac{\omega_c^2}{\omega^2}) - \omega_p^2]$, which is of the form

$$A E_x + i B E_y = 0$$

$$C E_x + i D E_y = 0.$$

For nontrivial solution,

$$\det \begin{pmatrix} A & B \\ C & D \end{pmatrix} = 0$$

$$\Rightarrow AD = BC.$$

Now using $\omega_h^2 = \omega_c^2 + \omega_p^2$, where ω_h is the upper hybrid frequency, then the condition $AD = BC$ can be written as

$$\frac{c^2 k^2}{\omega^2} = \frac{\omega^2 - \omega_h^2 - \frac{\left(\frac{\omega_p^2 \omega_c}{\omega} \right)^2}{(\omega^2 - \omega_h^2)}}{\omega^2 - \omega_c^2}.$$

$$(2.68)$$

With the help of a few algebraic calculations, this can be made simple. In Equation (2.68), substituting ω_h^2 in place of $\omega_c^2 + \omega_p^2$ and multiplying through by $\omega^2 - \omega_h^2$, we have

$$\frac{c^2 k^2}{\omega^2} = \frac{\omega^2 - \omega_c^2 - \omega_p^2 - \frac{\left(\frac{\omega_p^2 \omega_c}{\omega}\right)^2}{(\omega^2 - \omega_h^2)}}{\omega^2 - \omega_c^2} = 1 - \frac{\omega_p^2}{\omega_c^2} \frac{\omega^2 - \omega_p^2}{\omega^2 - \omega_h^2}.$$

Thus,

$$\frac{c^2 k^2}{\omega^2} = \frac{c^2}{v_\phi^2} = 1 - \frac{\omega_p^2}{\omega_c^2} \frac{\omega^2 - \omega_p^2}{\omega^2 - \omega_h^2}. \tag{2.69}$$

This is the dispersion relation.

2.12 Electromagnetic Waves Parallel to $\vec{B}_0$

To consider the electromagnetic waves parallel to $\vec{B}_0$, let $\vec{k}$ lie along the z-axis and let $\vec{E}_1$ have both transverse components E_x and E_y, i.e., $\vec{k} = k\hat{z}$ and $\vec{E}_1 = E_x \hat{x} + E_y \hat{y}$.

Now, we consider the equation of motion

$$m\frac{d\vec{v}}{dt} = -e[\vec{E} + \vec{v} \times \vec{B}]. \tag{2.70}$$

We shall linearize the equation such that the dependent variables can be written into two parts: the equilibrium part and the perturbation part, i.e., $\vec{v} = \vec{v}_0 + \vec{v}_1$, $\vec{E} = \vec{E}_0 + \vec{E}_1$ and $\vec{B} = \vec{B}_0$, where $\vec{v}_0 = \vec{E}_0 = 0$. From Equation (2.70), we get

$$m\frac{d\vec{v}_1}{dt} = -e(\vec{E}_1 + \vec{v}_1 \times \vec{B}_0).$$

So, $\vec{v}_1 \times \vec{B}_0 = v_y B_0 \hat{i} - v_x B_0 \hat{j}$. Now, equating along the component wise, we get

$$m\dot{v}_x = -e[E_x + v_y B_0] \tag{2.71}$$

$$m\dot{v}_y = -e[E_y - v_x B_0] \tag{2.72}$$

$$m\dot{v}_z = 0. \tag{2.73}$$

From (2.71), we have

$$-i\omega m v_x = -e(E_x + v_y B_0) \quad or \quad v_x = \frac{e}{im\omega}(E_x + v_y B_0). \tag{2.74}$$

Similarly, from (2.72), we obtain

$$v_y = \frac{e}{im\omega}[E_y - v_x B_0].$$ (2.75)

From (2.74)–(2.75), we have

$$v_x = \frac{e}{m\omega}\left(-iE_x - \frac{\omega_c}{\omega}E_y\right)\left(1 - \frac{\omega_c^2}{\omega^2}\right)^{-1}$$ (2.76)

$$v_y = \frac{e}{m\omega}\left(-iE_y + \frac{\omega_c}{\omega}E_x\right)\left(1 - \frac{\omega_c^2}{\omega^2}\right)^{-1}$$ (2.77)

where $\omega_c = B_0 e/m$. From Maxwell's equations, we have

$$\vec{\nabla} \times \vec{B}_0 = \mu\left(\epsilon_0 \frac{\partial \vec{E}_1}{\partial t} + \vec{J}_1\right)$$ (2.78)

and

$$\vec{\nabla} \times \vec{E}_1 = -\frac{\partial \vec{B}_0}{\partial t}.$$ (2.79)

Differentiating (2.78) with respect to t, we get

$$\vec{\nabla} \times \frac{\partial \vec{B}_0}{\partial t} = \mu\left(\epsilon_0 \frac{\partial^2 \vec{E}_1}{\partial t^2} + \frac{\partial \vec{J}_1}{\partial t}\right).$$

Substituting (2.79), we get

$$-\vec{\nabla}(\vec{\nabla} \cdot \vec{E}_1) + \vec{\nabla}^2 \vec{E}_1 = \mu\left(\epsilon_0 \frac{\partial^2 \vec{E}_1}{\partial t^2} + \frac{\partial \vec{J}_1}{\partial t}\right).$$

$\vec{E}_1$ and $\vec{J}_1$ oscillate sinusoidally and replace $\vec{\nabla} \to ik$ and $\partial/\partial t \to -i\omega$, and thus we have

$$-ik(i\vec{k} \cdot \vec{E}_1) + (ik)^2 \vec{E}_1 = \mu_0[\epsilon_0(-i\omega)^2 E_1 + (-i\omega)J_1].$$

Since, $\vec{E}_1$ and $\widehat{k}$ are perpendicular, so $\vec{E}_1 \cdot \vec{k} = 0$. Therefore,

$$(\omega^2 - c^2 k^2)\vec{E}_1 = \frac{i\omega e n_0}{\epsilon_0}\vec{v}_1.$$

After this equating along the x and y axis, we get

$$(\omega^2 - c^2 k^2)E_x = \frac{i\omega e n_0}{\epsilon_0}v_x$$ (2.80)

$$(\omega^2 - c^2 k^2)E_y = \frac{i\omega e n_0}{\epsilon_0}v_y.$$ (2.81)

From (2.80) and (2.76), we get

$$\left(\omega^2 - c^2 k^2\right) E_x = \frac{i\omega e n_0}{\epsilon_0} \frac{e}{m\omega} \left(-iE_x - \frac{\omega_c}{\omega} E_y\right) \left(1 - \frac{\omega_c^2}{\omega^2}\right)^{-1}$$

$$= \frac{\omega_p^2}{\left(1 - \frac{\omega_c^2}{\omega^2}\right)} \left(E_x - i\frac{\omega_c}{\omega} E_y\right) \tag{2.82}$$

where $\omega_p^2 = e^2 n_0/(\epsilon_0 m)$. Similarly, from (2.81) and (2.77), we have

$$(\omega^2 - c^2 k^2) E_y = \frac{\omega_p^2}{\left(1 - \frac{\omega_c^2}{\omega^2}\right)} \left(E_y + i\frac{\omega_c}{\omega} E_x\right). \tag{2.83}$$

Let $\alpha = \omega_p^2/(1 - \omega_c^2/\omega^2)$. Thus, from (2.82) and (2.83), we obtain

$$(\omega^2 - c^2 k^2 - \alpha) E_x + i\alpha \frac{\omega_c}{\omega} E_y = 0 \tag{2.84}$$

$$(\omega^2 - c^2 k^2 - \alpha) E_y - i\alpha \frac{\omega_c}{\omega} E_x = 0. \tag{2.85}$$

For a nontrivial solution of E_x and E_y, we have

$$\omega^2 - c^2 k^2 = \frac{\omega_p^2}{\left(1 \mp \frac{\omega_c}{\omega}\right)}. \tag{2.86}$$

The sign $\pm$ means that there are two possible solutions to Equations (2.84) and (2.85). They can propagate along $\vec{B}_0$.

$$\tilde{n}^2 = (ck/\omega)^2 = 1 - \frac{(\omega_p^2/\omega^2)}{(1 - \omega_c/\omega)}.$$

The above relation is dispersion relation for the R-wave.

$$\tilde{n}^2 = (ck/\omega)^2 = 1 - \frac{(\omega_p^2/\omega^2)}{(1 + \omega_c/\omega)}.$$

The above relation is the dispersion relation for the L-wave. The R and L waves turn out to be circularly polarized. The designations R and L mean right-hand circular polarization and left-hand circular polarization, respectively. The electric field vector for the R-wave rotates clockwise in time as viewed along the direction of $\vec{B}_0$ and vice versa for the L-waves.

2.13 Hydromagnetic Waves

Hydromagnetic waves are electromagnetic ion waves when undisturbed magnetic field $\vec{B}_0$ and oscillating magnetic field $\vec{B}_1$ are both nonzero, then this wave exists. When $\vec{k} \parallel \vec{B}_0$, then it is called *Alfven wave* and when $\vec{k} \perp \vec{B}_0$, then it is called *Magnetosonic wave*.

2.13.1 *Alfven wave*

An Alfven wave, named after Hannes Alfven, is a low-frequency magneto-hydrodynamic wave (compare to the ion cyclotron frequency) where ions oscillate due to the tension of the magnetic field. The ion mass density and the magnetic field line tension provide the inertia and the restoring force, respectively. The motion of the ions and the oscillating magnetic field act in the same direction and transverse to the direction of propagation.

To find the dispersion relation of the Alfven waves in plane geometry, let us assume $\vec{k}$ acts along with $\vec{B}_0$, $\vec{E}_1$, and $\vec{J}_1$ perpendicular to $\vec{B}_0$, $\vec{B}_1$, and $\vec{v}_1$ perpendicular to both $\vec{B}_0$ and $\vec{E}_1$.

In electromagnetic waves, $\vec{B}_1 \neq 0$ and $\vec{B}_0 = 0$ in a vacuum $\vec{J} = 0$ and $\epsilon_0 \mu_0 = c^{-2}$, so the relevant Maxwell's equations are

$$\vec{\nabla} \times \vec{E}_1 = -\dot{\vec{B}}_1 \tag{2.87}$$

$$c^2 \vec{\nabla} \times \vec{B}_1 = \vec{\nabla} \times \vec{E}_1. \tag{2.88}$$

Taking the curl of Equation (2.87) and substituting into the time derivative of Equation (2.88), we have

$$c^2 \vec{\nabla} \times (\vec{\nabla} \times \vec{B}_1) = \vec{\nabla} \times \dot{\vec{E}}_1 = -\ddot{\vec{B}}_1. \tag{2.89}$$

Assuming plane waves varying as $e^{i(kx - \omega t)}$ and accordingly $\vec{\nabla}$ is replaced by ik and $\partial/\partial t$ is replaced by $-i\omega$. From (2.89), we get

$$\omega^2 \vec{B}_1 = -c^2 [k(\vec{k} \cdot \vec{B}_1) - k^2 \vec{B}_1].$$

Also, $\vec{\nabla} \cdot \vec{B} = 0$ gives $\omega^2 = k^2 c^2$ and c is the phase velocity ω/k of light waves.

In plasma, if we consider $\vec{B}_0 = 0$, Equation (2.87) is unchanged. But we add a term J_1/ϵ_0 to the right-hand side of Equation (2.88) to account for current due to first-order charged particle motions. Hence, (2.88) becomes

$$c^2 \vec{\nabla} \times \vec{B}_1 = \frac{\vec{J}_1}{\epsilon_0} + \dot{\vec{E}}_1. \tag{2.90}$$

Taking time derivative of this, we get

$$c^2 \vec{\nabla} \times \dot{\vec{B}}_1 = \frac{1}{\epsilon_0} \frac{\partial \dot{\vec{J}}_1}{\partial t} + \ddot{\vec{E}}_1.$$

Taking curl of Equation (2.87), we have

$$\vec{\nabla}(\vec{\nabla} \cdot \vec{E}_1) - \vec{\nabla}^2 \vec{E}_1 = -\vec{\nabla} \times \dot{\vec{B}}_1.$$

Eliminating $\vec{\nabla} \times \dot{\vec{B}}_1$ and assuming an $exp[i(k \cdot r - \omega t)]$ dependence, we have

$$-\vec{k}(\vec{k} \cdot \vec{E}_1) + \vec{k}^2 \vec{E}_1 = \frac{i\omega}{\epsilon_0 c^2} \vec{J}_1 + \frac{\omega^2}{c^2} \vec{E}_1. \tag{2.91}$$

Since $\vec{k} = k\hat{z}$ and $\vec{E}_1 = E_1 \hat{x}$ by assumption, only the x-component of this equation is nontrivial. The current $\vec{J}_1$ is contributed from both ions and electrons. So, $J_1 = n_0(v_{ex} - v_{ix})$. Since we are considering low frequencies and $\vec{k} \cdot \vec{E}_1 = 0$, the x-component of Equation (2.91) becomes

$$k^2 E_1 = \epsilon_0(\omega^2 - c^2 k^2)E_1 = -i\omega n_0 e(v_{ix} - v_{ex}). \tag{2.92}$$

The ion equation of motion is

$$M\frac{\partial \vec{v}_{i1}}{\partial t} = -e\nabla \phi_1 + e v_{i1} \times B_0.$$

Assuming that the wave is propagating in the x-direction and separating into components, we get

$$-i\omega M v_{ix} = -eik\phi_1 + e v_{iy}B_0, \quad -i\omega M v_{iy} = -e v_{ix}B_0.$$

Thus, after some calculations, we get

$$v_{ix} = \frac{ek}{M\omega}\left(1 - \frac{\Omega_c^2}{\omega^2}\right)^{-1}\phi_1. \tag{2.93}$$

Here, we neglect the thermal motion for this wave, i.e., the solution of the ion equation of the motion is considered with $T_i = 0$. For completeness, we also include the component v_{iy} and

$$v_{ix} = \frac{ie}{M\omega}\left(1 - \frac{\Omega_c^2}{\omega^2}\right)^{-1}E_1 \tag{2.94}$$

$$v_{iy} = \frac{e}{M\omega}\frac{\Omega_c}{\omega}\left(1 - \frac{\Omega_c^2}{\omega^2}\right)^{-1}E_1. \tag{2.95}$$

Similarly, the components of velocity of electrons are found by considering $M \to m$, $e \to -e$ and $\Omega_c \to -\omega_c$ and taking the limit $\omega_c^2 \gg \omega^2$, we get

$$v_{ex} = -\frac{ie}{m\omega}\frac{E_1\omega^2}{\omega^2 - \omega_c^2} = \frac{ie}{m\omega}\frac{\omega^2}{\omega_c^2}E_1 \to 0$$

$$v_{ey} = -\frac{e}{m\omega}\frac{-\omega_c}{\omega}\frac{E_1\omega^2}{\omega^2 - \omega_c^2} = -\frac{e}{m}\frac{\omega_c}{\omega^2}\frac{\omega^2}{\omega_c^2}E_1 = -\frac{E_1}{B_0}.$$

Hence, the Larmor gyrations of the electrons are neglected, and the electrons have an $\vec{E} \times \vec{B}$ drift in the y-direction. Now, from (2.92), we get

$$\epsilon_0(\omega^2 - c^2k^2)E_1 = -i\omega n_0 e\frac{ie}{M\omega}\left(1 - \frac{\Omega_c^2}{\omega^2}\right)^{-1}E_1$$

$$\omega^2 - c^2k^2 = \Omega_p^2\left(1 - \frac{\Omega_c^2}{\omega^2}\right)^{-1} \tag{2.96}$$

where Ω_p is the ion plasma frequency. Also, assuming $\omega^2 \ll \Omega_c^2$, we get

$$\omega^2 - c^2k^2 = \Omega_p^2\frac{\omega^2}{\omega^2 - \Omega_c^2} = -\omega^2\frac{\Omega_p^2}{\Omega_c^2} = -\omega^2\frac{Mn_0}{\epsilon_0 B_0^2} = -\omega^2\frac{\rho}{\epsilon_0 \vec{B}_0^2}$$

$$or. \quad \frac{\omega^2}{k^2} = \frac{c^2}{1 + \frac{\rho}{\epsilon_0 \vec{B}_0^2}} = \frac{c^2}{1 + \frac{\rho\mu_0 c^2}{\vec{B}_0^2}} \tag{2.97}$$

where $\mu_0\epsilon_0 = \frac{1}{c^2}$ and ρ is the mass density. The denominator is the relative dielectric constant for low frequency perpendicular motions and can be written as

$$\epsilon_R = 1 + \frac{\mu_0\rho c^2}{\vec{B}_0^2}.$$

The phase velocity for an electromagnetic wave in a dielectric medium is

$$\frac{\omega}{k} = \frac{c}{\sqrt{\epsilon_R}}$$

(as $\mu_R = 1$). As for most laboratory plasmas, $\epsilon \gg 1$, then $\epsilon_R = \frac{\rho\mu_0 c^2}{B_0^2}$ and hence,

$$\frac{\omega}{k} = v_\phi = \frac{\vec{B}_0}{\sqrt{\mu_0\rho}}.$$

These hydromagnetic waves travel along $\vec{B}_0$ at a constant velocity v_A called the *Alfven velocity*. This is written as

$$v_A = \frac{\vec{B}}{\sqrt{\mu_0\rho}}.$$

2.13.2 *Magnetosonic wave*

In magnetized plasma, magnetosonic waves are longitudinal waves that propagate perpendicular to the undisturbed magnetic field $\vec{B}_0$. It is driven both by pressure and magnetic tension and are observed recently in solar corona. Let us consider low-frequency electromagnetic waves propagating across $\vec{B}_0 = B_0\hat{z}$ and released in the course of oscillation. Here, we consider the $\vec{\nabla}p$ term in the equation of motion.

For the ions, the equation of motion is

$$Mn_0\frac{\partial \vec{v}_{i1}}{\partial t} = en_0(\vec{E}_1 + \vec{v}_{i1} \times \vec{B}_0) - \gamma_i K_B T_i \vec{\nabla} n_1. \tag{2.98}$$

Now, $\vec{E}_1 = (E_x, 0, 0)$, $\vec{v}_{i1} = (v_{ix}, v_{iy}, v_{iz})$, $\vec{B}_0 = (0, 0, B_0)$, and $\partial/\partial t$ is replaced by $-i\omega$, then along the component wise,

$$-Mn_0 i\omega v_{ix} = en_0(E_x + v_{iy}\vec{B}_0)$$

$$\Rightarrow v_{ix} = \frac{ie}{M\omega}(E_x + v_{iy}\vec{B}_0). \tag{2.99}$$

Similarly, we have

$$v_{iy} = \frac{ie}{M\omega}(-v_{ix}\vec{B}_0) + \frac{k}{\omega}\frac{\gamma_i K_B T_i}{M}\frac{n_1}{n_0}. \tag{2.100}$$

The equation of continuity yields

$$\frac{\partial n_i}{\partial t} + \frac{\partial}{\partial x}(n_i\vec{v}_{i1}) = 0$$

$$\Rightarrow \frac{n_1}{n_0} = \frac{k}{\omega}v_{iy}. \tag{2.101}$$

So, $v_{iy} = -\frac{ie}{M\omega}v_{ix}\vec{B}_0 + \frac{k^2}{\omega^2}\frac{\gamma_i K_B T_i}{M}v_{iy}$. Assuming $A = \frac{k^2}{\omega^2}\frac{\gamma_i K_B T_i}{M}$, we get

$$v_{iy}(1 - A) = -\frac{i\Omega_c}{\omega}v_{ix} \tag{2.102}$$

where $\Omega_c = e\vec{B}_0/M$. Using (2.102) in (2.99), we get

$$v_{ix} = \frac{ie}{M\omega}E_x. \tag{2.103}$$

This is the only component of $\vec{v}_{i1}$. The only nontrivial component of the wave equation is

$$\epsilon_0(\omega^2 - c^2 k^2)E_x = -i\omega n_0 e(v_{ix} - v_{ex}). \tag{2.104}$$

To obtain v_{ex}, we have to take the limit of small electron mass so that $\omega^2 \ll \omega_c^2$ and $\omega^2 \ll k^2 v_{th}^2$. So,

$$v_{ex} = \frac{ie}{m\omega}\frac{\omega^2}{\omega_c^2}\left(1 - \frac{k^2}{\omega^2}\frac{\gamma_e K_B T_e}{m}\right)E_x \to -\frac{ik^2}{\omega\vec{B}_0^2}\frac{\gamma_e K_B T_e}{e}E_x. \tag{2.105}$$

Now, (2.103)–(2.105) together give

$$\epsilon_0(\omega^2 - c^2 k^2)E_x$$
$$= -i\omega n_0 e\left[\frac{ie}{m\omega}E_x\left(\frac{1 - A}{1 - A - \frac{\Omega_c^2}{\omega^2}}\right) + \frac{ik^2 M}{\omega\vec{B}_0^2}\frac{\gamma_e K_B T_e}{eM}E_x\right]. \tag{2.106}$$

We shall again assume $\omega^2 \ll \Omega_c^2$ so that $(1 - A)$ can be neglected relatively to Ω_c^2/ω^2. With the help of the definition of Ω_p and Alfven velocity v_A, we have

$$(\omega^2 - c^2 k^2) = \frac{\Omega_p^2}{\Omega_c^2}\omega^2(1 - A) + \frac{K^2 c^2}{v_A^2}\frac{\gamma_e K_B T_e}{M}$$

$$\Rightarrow \omega^2 - c^2 k^2\left(1 + \frac{\gamma_e K T_e}{M v_A^2}\right) + \frac{\Omega_p^2}{\omega_c^2}\left(\omega^2 - k^2\frac{\gamma_i K_B T_i}{M}\right) = 0. \tag{2.107}$$

Since $\Omega_p^2/\omega_c^2 = c^2/v_A^2$, Equation (2.107) becomes

$$\omega^2\left(1 + \frac{c^2}{v_A^2}\right) = c^2 k^2\left(1 + \frac{\gamma_e K_B T_e + \gamma_i K_B T_i}{M v_A^2}\right)$$

$$\omega^2\left(1 + \frac{c^2}{v_A^2}\right) = c^2 k^2\left(1 + \frac{v_s^2}{v_A^2}\right).$$

Table 2.1: Summary of elementary electrostatic wave.

Initial Condition	Oscillating Species	Dispersion Relation	Name
$\vec{B}_0 = 0$ or $\vec{k} \parallel \vec{B}_0$	Electrons	$\omega^2 = \omega_p^2 + \frac{3}{2}k^2 v_{th}^2$	Plasma oscillations
$\vec{k} \perp \vec{B}_0$	Electrons	$\omega^2 = \omega_p^2 + \omega_c^2 = \omega_h^2$	Upper hybrid oscillations
$\vec{B}_0$ or $\vec{k} \parallel \vec{B}_0$	Ions	$\omega^2 = k^2 v_s^2$ $= k^2 \frac{\gamma_e K_b T_e + \gamma_i K_B T_i}{M}$	Ion acoustic waves
$\vec{k} \perp \vec{B}_0$ (nearly)	Ions	$\omega^2 = \Omega^2 + k^2 v_s^2$	Electrostatics ion cyclotron waves
$\vec{k} \perp \vec{B}_0$	Ions	$\omega^2 = \Omega^2 \omega_c = \omega_l^2$	Lower hybrid oscillations

Table 2.2: Summary of elementary electromagnetic wave.

Initial Condition	Oscillating Species	Dispersion Relation	Name
$\vec{B}_0 = 0$	Electrons	$\omega^2 = \omega_p^2 + k^2 c^2$	Light waves
$\vec{k} \parallel \vec{B}_0$	Electrons	$\frac{c^2 k^2}{\omega^2} = 1 - \frac{\frac{\omega_p^2}{\omega^2}}{1 - \frac{\omega_c}{\omega}}$	R wave
$\vec{k} \parallel \vec{B}_0$	Electrons	$\frac{c^2 k^2}{\omega^2} = 1 - \frac{\frac{\omega_p^2}{\omega^2}}{1 + \frac{\omega_c}{\omega}}$	L wave
$\vec{k} \perp \vec{B}_0,\ \vec{E}_1 \parallel \vec{B}_0$	Electrons	$\frac{c^2 k^2}{\omega^2} = 1 - \frac{\omega_p^2}{\omega^2}$	O wave
$\vec{k} \perp \vec{B}_0,\ \vec{E}_1 \perp \vec{B}_0$	Electrons	$\frac{c^2 k^2}{\omega^2} = 1 - \frac{\omega_p^2}{\omega^2} \frac{\omega^2 - \omega_p^2}{\omega^2 - \omega_h^2}$	X wave
$\vec{B}_0 = 0$	Ions		Waves does not exist
$\vec{k} \parallel \vec{B}_0$	Ions	$\omega^2 = k^2 v^2$	Alfven wave
$\vec{k} \perp \vec{B}_0$	Ions	$\frac{\omega^2}{k^2} = c^2 \frac{v_s^2 + V_A^2}{c^2 + v_A^2}$	Magnetosonic wave

Here, v_s denotes the acoustic speed. Finally, we get the dispersion relation as

$$\frac{\omega^2}{k^2} = c^2 \frac{v_s^2 + v_A^2}{c^2 + v_A^2}.$$

2.14 Some Acoustic Type of Waves in Plasmas

In a plasma, the particles move randomly and interact among themselves under electromagnetic forces. They also respond to the externally applied perturbations. As a result, we have a great variety of waves in plasma.

The existence of different types of waves in plasma is important in plasma research. This is because, on the one hand, they are easy to observe, and on the other hand, their theoretical background is also well established. A brief discussion on different types of waves in plasmas is given in the following:

2.14.1   Electron plasma waves

In cold plasmas, there is no thermal movement of the particles. If thermal movements are taken into account, the plasmas can be treated as classical plasma consisting of electrons and ions. The thermal movement of the electron can cause the plasma oscillation to propagate. Electrons that flow into an adjacent plasma layer with their thermal velocity carry information about what is happening in the plasma region. The plasma oscillation is then called the plasma wave. Now, the electron motion is described by the following equations:

$$\frac{\partial n_e}{\partial t} + \vec{\nabla} \cdot (n_e \vec{v_e}) = 0 \tag{2.108}$$

$$m_e n_e \left(\frac{\partial}{\partial t} + \vec{v_e} \cdot \vec{\nabla} \right) \vec{v_e} = -n_e \vec{E} - \vec{\nabla} p \tag{2.109}$$

$$\epsilon_0 (\vec{\nabla} \cdot \vec{E}) = e(n_i - n_e). \tag{2.110}$$

The equation of state is

$$p = C \rho_m^\gamma$$

where C is a constant, ρ_m is the mass density, and $\gamma = C_p/C_v$. As

$$p = n_e K_B T_e, \quad \vec{\nabla} p = \gamma K_B T_e \vec{\nabla} n_e$$

and considering one dimension motion, we get $\gamma = 3$. Let us assume all the gradients in the above equations become derivatives with respect to x only. Here, considering small amplitude waves, we separate the dependent variable into two parts: the equilibrium part and the perturbation part. Let $n_e = n_0 + n_e^{(1)}$, $\vec{v_e} = \vec{v_0} + \vec{v_e}^{(1)}$, and $\vec{E} = \vec{E_0} + \vec{E_1}$, where n_0, $\vec{v_0}$, and $\vec{E_0}$ are the equilibrium part and $n_e^{(1)}$, $\vec{v_e}^{(1)}$, and $\vec{E_1}$ are the perturbation part. At equilibrium state, $\vec{\nabla} n_0 = \vec{v_0} = E_0 = 0$ and $\frac{\partial n_0}{\partial t} = \frac{\partial \vec{v_0}}{\partial t} = \frac{\partial \vec{E_0}}{\partial t} = 0$. The pressure term will be

$$\vec{\nabla} p_e = 3 K_B T_e \frac{\partial n_e^{(1)}}{\partial x} \widehat{x}. \tag{2.111}$$

Hence, Equations (2.108)–(2.110) become

$$m_e n_0 \frac{\partial \vec{v}_e^{(1)}}{\partial t} = -e n_0 \vec{E}_1 - 3 K_B T_e \vec{\nabla} n_e^{(1)} \tag{2.112}$$

$$\frac{\partial n_e^{(1)}}{\partial t} + n_0 \vec{\nabla} \cdot \vec{v}_e^{(1)} = 0 \tag{2.113}$$

$$\epsilon_0 \vec{\nabla} \cdot \vec{E}_1 = e(n_0 - n_0 - n_e^{(1)}) = -e n_e^{(1)}. \tag{2.114}$$

Let all the perturbation quantities be proportional to $exp[i(kx-\omega t)]$. Then, replacing $(\partial/\partial x) \to ik$ and $(\partial/\partial t) \to -i\omega$ and using the same procedure discussed above, we obtain

$$\omega^2 = \omega_p^2 + \frac{3}{2} v_{th}^2 k^2 \tag{2.115}$$

where $\omega_p^2 \left(= \frac{e^2 n_0}{\epsilon_0 m} \right)$. It is known as plasma frequency and $v_{th}^2 = \frac{2KT_e}{m}$ is the thermal velocity. Therefore,

$$v_g = \frac{3}{2} \frac{v_{th}^2}{v_p} \tag{2.116}$$

where $v_p (= \omega/k)$ is the phase velocity and v_g is the group velocity. Here, $v_g = \frac{3}{2} v_{th}^2 \frac{1}{v_p} = \sqrt{\frac{3}{2}} v_{th} \frac{\sqrt{\omega^2 - \omega_p^2}}{\omega}$. It is clear that at large k, $\omega^2 \gg \omega_p^2$, then we get $v_g \approx \sqrt{\frac{3}{2}} v_{th}$. But at small k, $v_g < v_{th}$. For large λ_d, density gradient is small and the thermal motions carry very little information into adjacent layers.

As $\omega < \omega_p$, there is no real solution for v_g. This means that the wave cannot propagate. This situation is called a cut-off in the dispersion relation. Physically, the wave is reflected at the point at which $\omega = \omega_p$.

2.14.2 *Ion acoustic waves*

In ordinary air, the sound wave propagates from one layer to the next by collisions of the air molecules. In the absence of collisions, ordinary sound waves would not occur. But in plasma, one can observe such waves without collisions. Ions can transmit vibrations to each other because of their charge and acoustic type waves can occur in plasma. Since the motion of massive ions is involved, these are low-frequency oscillations.

To obtain the dispersion relation for the ion acoustic waves, we consider two fluid models. For electrostatic oscillations, the two fluid models are as follows:

For electron,

$$\frac{\partial n_e}{\partial t} + \vec{\nabla} \cdot (n_e \vec{v}_e) = 0 \tag{2.117}$$

$$m_e n_e \left[\frac{\partial \vec{v}_e}{\partial t} + (\vec{v}_e \cdot \vec{\nabla})\vec{v}_e \right] = -e n_e \vec{E} - \gamma_e K_B T_e \vec{\nabla} n_e. \tag{2.118}$$

For ions,

$$\frac{\partial n_i}{\partial t} + \vec{\nabla} \cdot (n_i \vec{v}_i) = 0 \tag{2.119}$$

$$m_i n_i \left[\frac{\partial \vec{v}_i}{\partial t} + (\vec{v}_i \cdot \vec{\nabla})\vec{v}_i \right] = e n_i \vec{E} - \gamma_i K_B T_i \vec{\nabla} n_i. \tag{2.120}$$

The electric field couples these two motions: $\vec{\nabla}\vec{E} = 4\pi e(n_i - n_e)$ and $\vec{E} = -\vec{\nabla}\phi$. The electrons can move much faster than the heavier ions. Here, we are considering low-frequency waves and so the electron inertia is neglected. Using $m_e = 0$ in (2.118), we get

$$e n_e \vec{\nabla}\phi - \gamma_e K_B T_e \vec{\nabla} n_e = 0. \tag{2.121}$$

For slow ion waves, the electrons move so fast that they have enough time to equalize their temperature everywhere. So, the electrons are considered isothermal and we can take $\gamma_e = 1$. Therefore, Equation (2.121) can be written in one dimension as

$$e\frac{d\phi}{dx} = \frac{K_B T_e}{n_e}\frac{dn_e}{dx}.$$

On integration, we have

$$\phi = \left(\frac{K_B T_e}{e}\right)\log n_e + C_1.$$

In equilibrium state $n_e = n_0$ and $\phi = 0$, we get $C_1 = -K_B T_e \log n_0$. Therefore,

$$\phi = \left(\frac{K_B T_e}{e}\right)\log\left(\frac{n_e}{n_0}\right). \tag{2.122}$$

Hence,

$$n_e = n_0 exp\left(\frac{e\phi}{K_B T_e}\right). \tag{2.123}$$

This shows that the electrons are Boltzmann distributed. We assume the perturbation to be small relative to the thermal energy, i.e., $\phi \ll K_B T_e$.

Therefore, from (2.124), we have

$$n_e \approx n_0 \left[1 + \frac{e\phi}{K_B T_e} \right]. \tag{2.124}$$

We assume small-amplitude waves and so the perturbations in plasma parameters are small as compared to their equilibrium value. Let $n_j = n_0 + n_{j1}$, $\vec{v}_j = \vec{v}_{j0} + \vec{v}_{j1}$, and $\phi = \phi_0 + \phi_1$. Again, let $j = e$, and i, which stands for electrons, and ions, respectively. The subscript 0 refers to equilibrium values, and the subscript 1 refers to the perturbed part. For a uniform neutral plasma at rest in the equilibrium state, $\vec{v}_{j0} = \phi_0 = 0$; $\frac{\partial n_0}{\partial t} = \frac{\partial \vec{v}_{j0}}{\partial t} = \frac{\partial \phi_0}{\partial t} = 0$.

So, from (2.124), the perturbation in electron density is $n_{e1} = n_e - n_0 = \frac{e\phi n_0}{K_B T_e}$. Therefore, the perturbation of ion density $n_{i1} = \frac{e\phi n_0}{K_B T_e}$.

Substituting the perturbation expression in equations for ions (2.119) and (2.120), we have

$$\frac{\partial n_{i1}}{\partial t} + n_0 \vec{\nabla}.\vec{v}_{i1} = 0 \tag{2.125}$$

$$m_i n_0 \frac{\partial \vec{v}_{i1}}{\partial t} = -e n_0 \vec{\nabla}\phi_1 - \gamma_i K_B T_i \vec{\nabla} n_{i1}, \tag{2.126}$$

where we have assumed the changes n_{j1}, v_{j1}, and ϕ_1. It is due to perturbations of small quantities of the first order. We also neglected the higher-order smaller terms.

Now, considering the one-dimensional case and assuming that all the perturbation quantities vary as $exp[i(kx - \omega t)]$, we get from Equations (2.125) and (2.126)

$$-i\omega n_{i1} + n_0 i k v_{i1} = 0 \tag{2.127}$$

$$-i\omega m_i n_0 v_{i1} = -iken_0\phi_1 - ik\gamma_i K_B T_i n_{i1}. \tag{2.128}$$

Eliminating v_{i1} from these two equations and then using the relation $n_{e1} = n_{i1}$, we get for nonzero solutions

$$\omega^2 = k^2 \cdot \frac{K_B T_e + \gamma_i K_B T_i}{m_i} \tag{2.129}$$

$$\Rightarrow \frac{\omega}{k} = \left(\frac{K_B T_e + \gamma_i K_B T_i}{m_i} \right)^{1/2} = v_s(say). \tag{2.130}$$

This is the dispersion relation for ion acoustic waves and v_s is the sound speed in a plasma. The dispersion curve for ion waves has a fundamentally different character from that for electron waves. Plasma oscillations are constant frequency waves, with a correction due to thermal motions. Ion waves are constant velocity waves and exist only when there are thermal motions. The reasons for this difference can be seen from the following description of the physical mechanisms involved. Ion electron plasma oscillations, the other species (ions) remain essentially fixed. In ion acoustic waves, the other species (electrons) is far from fixed; in fact, electrons are pulled along with the ions and tend to shield out electric field arising from the bunching of ions.

2.14.3 *Dust acoustic waves*

The propagation of IAWs in a spatial inhomogeneity is created by a distribution of immobile dust particles. The low-frequency behavior of a dusty plasma is very similar to that of a plasma consisting of negative ions. In fact, for the case in which the wavelength and the inter-particle distance are much larger than the grain size, the dust grains can be treated as negatively charged point masses (like negative ions). However, here the charge to mass ratio of a dust particle can take on any value. Thus, with minor corrections, many results from the theory of negative ion plasmas can be adapted to dusty plasma. The long-wavelength low-frequency collective oscillations can exist in dusty plasma. We shall consider modes so that the dust particle dynamics is crucial rather than the modes affected by the dust. In particular, we study the collective motion of the negatively charged dust in thermodynamics equilibrium. We find that new types of sound waves, namely dust acoustic waves, can appear. These waves are usually of low frequency. But in some cases, the latter can be compared with that of the ion acoustic wave.

It is a very low-frequency acoustic mode. Here, the dust grains participate directly in the wave dynamics. The DA waves have been theoretically predicted by Rao *et al.* [1], in a multicomponent collisionless dusty plasma consisting of electrons, ions, and negatively charged dust grains. The phase velocity of the DA waves is smaller than the electron and ion thermal speeds. Hence, the inertialess electrons and ions establish equilibrium in the DA wave potential ϕ. Dust inertia is significant here. In the DA waves, the pressures of the electrons and ions provide the restoring force, while the inertia comes from the dust mass. Thus, the DA waves are very low-frequency waves. The relation is given by

$$\omega^2 = 3k^2 V_{Td}^2 + \frac{k^2 C_D^2}{1 + k^2 \lambda_D^2} \qquad (2.131)$$

where V_{Td} is the dust thermal speed and $C_D = \omega_{pd}\lambda_D$ is the DA speed. Since $\omega \gg kV_{Td}$, the DA wave frequency is

$$\omega = \frac{kC_D}{(1 + k^2\lambda_D^2)^{1/2}}. \qquad (2.132)$$

In the long-wavelength limit (namely $k^2\lambda_D^2 \ll 1$), it reduces to

$$\omega = kZ_{d0} \left(\frac{n_{d0}}{n_{i0}}\right)^{1/2} \left(\frac{k_BT_i}{m_d}\right)^{1/2} \left[1 + \frac{T_i}{T_e}\left(1 - \frac{Z_{d0}n_{d0}}{n_{i0}}\right)\right]^{-1/2}, \qquad (2.133)$$

which shows that the restoring force in the DA waves comes from the pressures of the inertialess electrons and ions, while the dust mass provides the inertia to support the waves. The frequency of the DA waves is much smaller than the dust plasma frequency. The DA waves have been observed in several laboratory experiments (e.g., Barkan *et al.* [2], Pieper and Goree [3]). The observed DA wave frequencies are of the order of 10–20 Hz. Video images of the DA wavefronts are possible, and they can be viewed with the naked eye.

2.14.4 *Dust ion acoustic waves*

The DIA waves were predicted by Shukla and Silin [4]. For DIA waves, the phase velocity is much smaller (larger) than the electron thermal speed (ion and dust thermal speeds). In this case, the electron number density perturbation is related to the DIA waves, while the ion number density perturbation is determined from the ion continuity equation. Assuming $\omega \gg kV_{Ti}, kV_{Td}$, the dispersion relation is written as

$$1 - \frac{k_{De}^2}{k^2} - \frac{\omega_{pi}^2 + \omega_{pd}^2}{\omega^2} = 0. \qquad (2.134)$$

As the dust grains have a large mass, the ion plasma frequency ω_{pi} is much larger than the dust plasma frequency ω_{pd}. Thus, we have

$$\omega^2 = \frac{k^2C_S^2}{1 + k^2\lambda_{De}^2} \qquad (2.135)$$

where $C_S = \omega_{pi}\lambda_{De}$. In the long-wavelength limit, i.e., when $k^2\lambda_{De}^2 \ll 1$, then

$$\omega = k\omega_{pi}\lambda_{De}. \qquad (2.136)$$

It shows that the phase velocity of the DIA waves in a dusty plasma is larger than $c_s = (k_B T_e/m_i)^{1/2}$. The DIA waves have also been observed in laboratory experiments (Barkan *et al.* [5], Nakamura *et al.* [6]). The frequencies of the DIA waves for laboratory plasma parameters are in the order of kHz. At low frequencies, a new ultra low-frequency mode arises from ion oscillations in static dust distribution.

2.15 Nonlinear Wave

Let us consider a linear hyperbolic equation in one dimension as

$$\frac{\partial u}{\partial x} + c\frac{\partial u}{\partial x} = 0 \tag{2.137}$$

where c is a constant.

The physical meaning of Equation (2.137) is that the magnitude of u at every point is carried with constant velocity c so that the disturbance of u moves with the velocity c without distortion. The general solution of (2.137) is

$$u = f(x - ct) \tag{2.138}$$

where f is an arbitrary function and can be determined by an initial or a boundary condition. If the velocity c is constant, then the wave is called progressive. Here, $\xi = x - ct$ is called the phase. The phase ξ is invariant along the characteristic curve. Hence, u is constant along the line $\xi = $ constant. The above expression can be written in the form of

$$u = f(x - ct) = r(\xi) \tag{2.139}$$

where $r(\xi)$ is the Riemann invariant.

Now, we consider the second-order linear wave equation as

$$\frac{\partial^2 u}{\partial x^2} - \frac{1}{c^2}\frac{\partial^2 u}{\partial t^2} = 0. \tag{2.140}$$

The general solution of (2.140) is

$$u = f(x - ct) + g(x + ct). \tag{2.141}$$

Equation (2.141) represents the superposition of two arbitrary progressive waves moving to the left and the right, respectively.

If the initial disturbance is localized within a certain domain so that $u(x,0) = 0$ and $\frac{\partial u(x,0)}{\partial t} = 0$ for $|x| > d$, then we can write

$$f(x) = 0 = g(x), \quad for \ |x| > d. \tag{2.142}$$

Consequently,

$$\left. \begin{array}{l} f(x - t) = 0, \quad for \ |x - t| > d \\ g(x + t) = 0, \quad for \ |x + t| > d. \end{array} \right\} \tag{2.143}$$

It means that after the time t, only the rightward or the leftward progressive wave is observed, whenever it is at a place sufficiently far from the origin.

If we consider a nonlinear hyperbolic equation

$$\frac{\partial^2 u}{\partial x^2} + \frac{1}{c(u)} \frac{\partial^2 u}{\partial t^2} = 0, \tag{2.144}$$

and a solution of Equation (2.144) as

$$u = f(x - ct) \tag{2.145}$$

where c is the local phase velocity and is written as

$$\frac{\frac{\partial u}{\partial t}}{\frac{\partial u}{\partial x}} = -c. \tag{2.146}$$

If c is constant, Equation (2.145) reduces to Equation (2.138). In the nonlinear Equation (2.144), the phase velocity of the wave is not constant and so the wave distorts as it propagates. A wave with a single phase as given by Equation (2.145) is called a *simple wave*. The progressive wave is a special case of a simple wave. Along with the equiphase line $u = $ constant, i.e., along with each characteristic, the velocity is given by the following equation:

$$\frac{dx}{dt} = c. \tag{2.147}$$

u is constant, i.e., $u = r(\xi)$, so that Equation (2.144) can be integrated to give a family of straight lines but each with a different slope,

$$x - c(\xi, 0)t = \xi. \tag{2.148}$$

Here, ξ is the parameter specifying the characteristic issuing out of the point $x = \xi$ at $t = 0$. Since, u is constant along each characteristic, and if "c" decreases with ξ, then the characteristics intersect for $t > 0$. At the intersection, we have two different values of u so that this can be interpreted physically as the breaking of a wave. The process leading up to this corresponds to steepening of the wave. Hence, in general, a solution does not exist for all time.

The inviscid Burgers' equation is a conservation equation, more generally a first-order quasilinear equation. The solution to the equation and along with initial condition is written as

$$\frac{\partial u}{\partial t} + u\frac{\partial u}{\partial x} = 0, \ u(x,0) = f(x). \tag{2.149}$$

Consider the function u at each point of the (x,t) plane and let $u_t + uu_x$ be the total derivative of u along with the curve which has slop $\frac{dx}{dt} = u$ at every point of it.

For any curve ψ in (x,t) plane, assume x and u to be function of t, and total derivative of u is $\frac{du}{dt} = \frac{\partial u}{\partial t} + \frac{dx}{dt}\frac{\partial u}{\partial x}$. Now, on the curve ψ in (x,t) plane, the characteristic equations are

$$\frac{du}{dt} = 0, \tag{2.150}$$

$$\frac{dx}{dt} = u. \tag{2.151}$$

So, u is constant (c) along with the characteristic and $x = ct + c_1$ where $c_1 =$ constant.

Let $x = \xi$, at $t = 0$, then $x = ct + \xi$ is a straight line where ξ is a point on the $x - axis(t = 0)$ of the $x - t$ plane and ξ is the implicit function of x and t.

Now, from the initial condition, assume $u(\xi,0) = f(\xi)$. So, writing $u = f(\xi)$ on that characteristic, the characteristic is

$$x = f(\xi)t + \xi. \tag{2.152}$$

Thus, the solution is given by $u(x,t) = f(\xi) = f(x-ut)$ where $\xi = x-ut$. It is an implicit relation that determines the solution of the inviscid Burgers' equation, provided the characteristic does not intersect.

Now,

$$\frac{\partial u}{\partial t} = f'(\xi)\frac{\partial \xi}{\partial t} \tag{2.153}$$

$$\frac{\partial u}{\partial x} = f'(\xi)\frac{\partial \xi}{\partial x}. \tag{2.154}$$

Differentiating Equation (2.152) with respect to t, we get

$$0 = \frac{\partial \xi}{\partial t} + f(\xi) + f'(\xi)t\frac{\partial \xi}{\partial t} \tag{2.155}$$

$$1 = \frac{\partial \xi}{\partial x} + f'(\xi)t\frac{\partial \xi}{\partial x}. \tag{2.156}$$

From Equations (2.153)–(2.156), we get $\frac{\partial u}{\partial t} = -\frac{f'(\xi)f(\xi)}{1+f'(\xi)t}$ and $\frac{\partial u}{\partial x} = \frac{f'(\xi)}{1+f'(\xi)t}$. So,

$$\frac{\partial u}{\partial t} + u\frac{\partial u}{\partial x} = 0$$

where $1 + f'(\xi)t \neq 0$. The initial condition $u = f(\xi)$ is satisfied as $\xi = x$ when $t = 0$.

On any characteristic for which $f'(\xi) < 0$, $1 + tf'(\xi) \to 0$, a classical solution to the partial differential equation does not exist and it leads to the formation of a shock wave. The breaking time before a shock wave can be formed and is given by $1 + f'(\xi)t_b = 0$, i.e., $t_b = \frac{-1}{f'(\xi)}$.

For nonlinear waves, as the wave speed depends on c and u, a gradual nonlinear distortion of the wave is produced. It propagates in the medium. It indicates that some parts of the wave travel faster than others. When $c'(u) > 0$, $c(u)$ is an increasing function of u, and so the higher values of u propagate faster than the lower value of u. Similarly, when $c'(u) < 0$, higher values of u travel slower than the lower ones. So, the wave profile progressively distorts itself, leading to a vertical slope, and hence, it breaks.

As for the compressive part, the wave speed is a decreasing function of x, the wave profile distorts and it ultimately breaks. The solution of the nonlinear initial-value problem exists if $1 + tf'(\xi) \neq 0$. This condition is always satisfied even for a small-time t. Also, u_x and u_t tend to infinity as $1 + tf'(\xi) \to 0$. So, the solution develops a discontinuity (singularity) when $1 + tf'(\xi) = 0$. Thus, on any characteristic for which $f'(\xi) < 0$, a discontinuity occurs at a time $t = -\frac{1}{f'(\xi)}$. Hence, $f'(\xi) = c'(f)f'(\xi) < 0$. Let $t = \tau$ be the time when the solution first develops a singularity for some value of ξ. Then,

$$\tau = -\frac{1}{\min_{-\infty < \xi < \infty} c'(f)f'(\xi)} > 0.$$

Therefore, the solution breaks down when $f'(\xi) < 0$ for some ξ, and such breaking is a strikingly nonlinear phenomenon. In the linear theory, such breaking will never occur.

More precisely, the development of a discontinuity in the solution for $t \geq \tau$ can also be seen in the (x, t) plane. Finally, we conclude the above discussion by stating the remarkable fact that both the distortion of the wave profile and the development of a discontinuity or a shock is typical nonlinear phenomena.

Therefore, when $1 + tf'(\xi) = 0$, the solution develops a discontinuity known as shock. The analysis of a shock involves an extension of a solution to allow for discontinuity.

2.16   Solitary Waves and Solitons

Solitary waves are localized waves that propagate in a well-formed shape along a single spatial direction. However, the soliton is a localized wave that propagates without changing its properties such as shape and speed. The solitons are stable against mutual collisions and retain their identities. Therefore, they are dynamic structures as they move with constant speed and shape. Solitons form in a medium when the effects of dispersion and nonlinearity are balanced. In the absence of nonlinearity, any dispersion can destroy a solitary wave as the various components of the wave propagate at different speed. The introduction of nonlinearity without dispersion rules out the possibility of solitary waves because the pulse energy is continuously injected in a high-frequency mode and the wave is destroyed. But both with dispersion and with nonlinearity, the current formation of solitons is possible.

2.16.1   *History of solitary waves and solitons*

The history behind the discovery of solitons is really interesting. In 1834, a Scottish scientist and engineer John Scott Russell first noticed the presence of solitary water waves on the Edinburgh and Glasgow Union Canal. In 1844, in his Report on waves, he accounted his experience to the British Association. He wrote, "I was observing the motion of a boat which was rapidly drawn along a narrow channel by a pair of horses when the boat suddenly stopped not so the mass of water in the channel which it had put in motion; it accumulated around the prow of the vessel in a state of violent agitation, then suddenly leaving it behind, rolled forward with great velocity, assuming the form of a large solitary elevation, a rounded, smooth and well defined heap of water, which continued its course along the channel apparently without change of form or diminution of speed. I followed it on horseback and overtook it still rolling on at a rate of some eight or nine miles an hour, preserving its original figure some thirty feet long and a foot to a foot and a half in height. Its height gradually diminished and after a chase of one or two miles, I lost it in the windings of the channel. Such in August 1834 was my first chance interview with that singular and beautiful phenomenon which I have called the Wave of Translation". Scott Russell coined the term 'solitary wave'. It is so named because the waves are localized and appear as a single unit. Thorough observations and widespread wave tank experiments resulted in the finding of some important characteristics of solitary waves. First, the bell structured localized waves move with stable velocity and form. The velocity of these waves is described as $c^2 = g(h + a)$, where g, a, and h are the acceleration of the gravity, amplitude of the wave, and the unaffected depth of the water. Second, crossing each other minus change is the other characteristic of solitary waves. These examinations of John Scott Russell created a stir in the scientific community as it generated a debate with the knowledge prevailing in the wave theory. Russell's observations disagreed with erstwhile knowledge of waves. He noticed that only in deep water a periodic wave of finite amplitude and permanent form is feasible. Unlike Russell's observations, recent studies have noted a permanent profile even in shallow water. Finally, the scientific community acknowledged the permanent structure of solitary waves that was explained with the help of nonlinearity and dispersion. Nonlinearity and dispersion can generate such waves in an ideal equilibrium state.

A Dutch professor Diederik Johannes Korteweg and his Ph.D. student Gustav de Vries in 1895 developed a model equation that explained the one-way propagation of waves that are long in comparatively shallow water. The shallow water waves are explained by this equation in the places where the presence of solitary waves is mathematically proven. This equation came to be known as the Korteweg–de Vries equation or KdV equation. It is one of the most important equations of soliton theory as it explains the elementary concepts beyond soliton theory. A significant characteristic of solitons is that even during the collision of two or more solitons, it remains unscattered and also evolves with identical velocity and shape. It is for this property of solitons that Zabusky and Kruskal named it so. In 1967, Garner *et al.* [7] found the solution of N-soliton of the KdV equation. The solution of a single soliton of the KdV equation is a solitary wave. But in the presence of more than one solution, they are known as multisolitons. In 1971, a method was developed by Ryogo Hirota [8] to find the exact solution of multisolitons from the KdV equation. This method came to be known as the Hirota direct method. Other methods like Darboux transformation, Backlund transformation, and inverse scattering transformation are also used to find the multisoliton solution of the nonlinear evolution equation.

2.17 Properties of Solitons

Solitons are solitary waves with the remarkable property of preserving the form asymptotically even when undergoing a collision. The fundamental "microscopic" properties of the soliton interaction are as follows: (i) the interaction does not change the soliton amplitudes, (ii) after the interaction, each soliton gets an additional phase shift, and (iii) the total phase shift of a soliton acquired during a certain time interval can be calculated as a sum of the elementary phase shifts in pairwise collisions of this soliton with other solitons during this time interval is of importance. An arbitrary initial profile will evolve into two waves that then move apart and progressively approach individual solitary waves as time tends to infinity. At first, the larger soliton moves faster, then approaches the smaller ones, and finally, after overtaking collision, both of them resume their original shape and speed. These are nonlinear waves, and they do not satisfy the linear superposition principle.

Soliton propagates with a regular speed and shape. Mathematically, two types of solitons are defined: one is topological and the another is nontopological. When two sides of the state of the medium of the soliton are different, they are called topological soliton. On the other hand, when both sides of the state of the medium of the soliton are the same, they are called nontopological soliton. Topological soliton can exist at rest, whereas nontopological soliton never exists at rest. The sine-Gordon equation and the KdV equation have soliton solutions that are examples of topological and nontopological soliton, respectively. Nontopological solitons (KdV type) have many applications in plasma physics. Applications in solitons in fiber optics, optical computers, etc., create a sensation even in today's scientific community. Traditional signal processing relies on the linear system and linear techniques. Moreover, here nonlinear systems produce more efficient algorithms. Hence, the properties of solitons are useful in optical fiber communication systems. Experimentally it is known that blood pressure pulses propagated along the major arteries with characteristic shape changes.

References

[1] N. N. Rao, P. K. Shukla, and M. Y. Yu, *Planet Space Sci.* 38, 543 (1990).

[2] A. Barken, R. L. Merlino, and N. D'Angelo, *Phys. Plasmas*, 2, 3563 (1995).

[3] J. B. Pieper and J. Gorce, *Phys. Rev. Lett.* 77, 3137 (1996).

[4] P. K. Shukla and V. P. Silin, *Phys. Scripta* 45, 508 (1992).

[5] A. Barken, N. D'Angelo, and R. L. Merlino, *Planet Space Sci.* 44, 239 (1996).

[6] Y. Nakamura, H. Bailung, and P. K. Shukla, *Phys. Rev. Lett.* 83, 1602 (1999).

[7] C. S. Gardner, J. M. Greene, M. D. Kruskal, and R. M. Miura, *Phys. Rev. Lett.* 19, 1095 (1967).

[8] R. Hirota, *Phys. Rev. Lett.* 27, 1192 (1971).

Chapter 3

Solution of Nonlinear Wave Equations

3.1 Nonlinear Waves

Nonlinear waves described by the nonlinear partial differential equation are difficult to analyze mathematically. In general, the principle of superimposition does not apply to such waves or can they be used to obtain their solutions. The solution to the nonlinear wave equation cannot be derived by any general procedure. Therefore, each wave equation requires individual treatment. Important examples of nonlinear equations in plasma physics are the KdV equation and the modified form of these equations. Some advanced methods that have been used successfully to obtain closed-form solutions are as follows: Exp function method, Factorization method, Tanh method, Hirota bilinear method, Generalized separation of variables method, Differential constraints method, Inverse scattering transformation method, etc. However, this chapter discusses some of the methods commonly used in plasma dynamics.

3.2 Direct Method

To solve the nonlinear wave equation, one needs to study dispersive effects, diffusion, and convection on the nonlinear wave evolution equation. The traveling wave solution of the nonlinear wave equation can be found easily. Initially, the partial differential equation converts into the ordinary differential equation. In a conservative system, solutions of the nonlinear differential equation are obtained by different steps like direct integration, appropriate transformation, or substitution.

3.2.1 *Korteweg–de Vries (KdV) equation*

The solitary wave in shallow water was first observed by John Scott Russel [1] and ultimately, it was modeled by Korteweg and de Vries. Although this equation was first introduced by Boussinesq [2] in 1877, the study of the KdV equation became popular after the famous discovery of Zabusky and Kruskal [3] in 1965. They have shown that those waves are almost unaffected in shape by passing through each other, and accordingly, the term "Soliton" is coined for such waves. This remarkable feature initiated the study of several KdV equations not only in shallow water waves but also in long internal waves in a notion, acoustic waves in plasma, and acoustic on crystal tails. Several interesting properties of this equation have also been exposed by several investigations. In 1968, Miura [4] found conservation laws for the KdV equation, and in 1989, Tabor [5] has shown that an infinite number of conserved quantities may exist for the KdV equation. It indicates the permanent shape of a nonlinear wave. In 1968, P. Lax [6] has shown that the KdV equation is equivalent to the isospectral integrability condition for pair at linear operators and so on.

Let us consider the KdV equation as

$$\frac{\partial \phi}{\partial t} + a\phi \frac{\partial \phi}{\partial x} + b\frac{\partial^3 \phi}{\partial x^3} = 0. \tag{3.1}$$

The KdV equation is a useful approximation in the modeling of many physical systems. Let x and t be the two independent variables, a and b be two nonzero constants. Equation (3.1) is nonlinear to the convective term $\phi \frac{\partial \phi}{\partial x}$ and dispersive term $\frac{\partial^3 \phi}{\partial x^3}$.

To scale Equation (3.1), let us recall x by $\bar{x}a^{m_1}b^{n_1}$, ϕ by $\bar{\phi}a^{m_2}b^{n_2}$, and t by $\bar{t}$. Then Equation (3.1) can be reduced to the equation

$$\frac{\partial \bar{\phi}}{\partial \bar{t}} + a^{1+m_2-m_1}b^{n_2-n_1}\bar{\phi}\frac{\partial \bar{\phi}}{\partial \bar{x}} + a^{-3m_1}b^{-3n_1+1}\frac{\partial^3 \bar{\phi}}{\partial \bar{x}^3} = 0.$$

Now, putting

$$m_1 - m_2 = -1, n_2 = n_1, 3m_1 = 0, -3n_1 + 1 = 0 \tag{3.2}$$

or

$$m_1 = 0, \ m_2 = -1, \ n_1 = n_2 = 1/3,$$

we get $x = \bar{x}b^{1/3}$ and $\phi = \bar{\phi}a^{-1}b^{1/3}$. Hence, Equation (3.1) transforms to

$$\frac{\partial \bar{\phi}}{\partial \bar{t}} + \bar{\phi}\frac{\partial \bar{\phi}}{\partial \bar{x}} + \frac{\partial^3 \bar{\phi}}{\partial \bar{x}^3} = 0.$$

Omitting the bar, the above equation is written as

$$\frac{\partial \phi}{\partial t} + \phi \frac{\partial \phi}{\partial x} + \frac{\partial^3 \phi}{\partial x^3} = 0. \tag{3.3}$$

To discuss the wave solution of Equation (3.3), we introduce a traveling wave solution $\phi = \phi(\xi)$, $\xi = x - vt$, which is dependent on x and t through the time variable and v is a constant. So, Equation (3.3) is reduced to the given equation

$$-v \frac{d\phi}{d\xi} + \phi \frac{d\phi}{d\xi} + \frac{d^3 \phi}{d\xi^3} = 0.$$

Integrating the above equation and then using the boundary condition $\phi \to 0$, $\frac{d^2 \phi}{d\xi^2} \to 0$ at $\xi \to \pm\infty$, we get

$$\frac{d^2 \phi}{d\xi^2} + \left(\frac{\phi}{2} - v \right) \phi = 0.$$

Multiplying by $2\frac{d\phi}{d\xi}$ the above equation and integrating, we get

$$\left(\frac{d\phi}{d\xi} \right)^2 + \left(\frac{\phi}{3} - v \right) \phi^2 = C_1.$$

Again, using the boundary condition $\phi \to 0$, $\frac{d\phi}{d\xi} \to 0$ as $\xi \to \pm\infty$, then $C_1 = 0$. So, for $v > 0$,

$$\frac{d\phi}{d\xi} = \pm \frac{1}{\sqrt{3}} \phi \sqrt{3v - \phi}.$$

On integration we get

$$\int \frac{d\phi}{\phi \sqrt{3v - \phi}} = \pm \int \frac{1}{\sqrt{3}} d\xi. \tag{3.4}$$

Putting $\phi = 3v \operatorname{sech}^2 \theta$ in Equation (3.4) and integrating, we get

$$\theta = \mp \frac{\sqrt{v}}{2} \xi + \theta_0$$

where θ_0 is a constant of integration.

Therefore,

$$\phi = 3v \operatorname{sech}^2 \left(\frac{\sqrt{v}}{2} \xi \mp \theta_0 \right).$$

If we choose the origin of the coordinates ξ in such a way that ϕ attains a maximum at $\xi = 0$, then $\theta_0 = 0$. Hence, the *solitary wave solution* is

$$\phi(\xi) = 3v sech^2\left(\frac{\xi\sqrt{v}}{2}\right)$$

$$= A sech^2\left(\frac{\xi}{W}\right) \tag{3.5}$$

where $A = 3v$ and $W = \frac{2}{\sqrt{v}}$ are the amplitude and the width of the wave respectively and they are related by $A = \frac{12}{W^2}$, i.e., $A \propto \frac{1}{W^2}$. So, we conclude that the amplitude is inversely proportional to the square of the width of the wave.

3.2.2 *Cnoidal waves*

KdV equation gives not only solitary wave solution but also another type of periodic solution known as cnoidal wave. A cnoidal wave is a nonlinear wave and exact periodic wave solution that may be obtained from the KdV equation or similar equations. Now, we are going to obtain the cnoidal wave from the KdV equation. These solutions are obtained in terms of the Jacobi elliptic function c_n. It is the reason for which they are termed as "cnoidal waves". In 1895, Korteweg and de Vries [7] derived the cnoidal wave solution in one of their papers. They suggested a dispersive long wave equation known as the KdV equation. In the limit of infinite wavelength, the cnoidal wave transforms into a solitary wave. A cnoidal wave is an exact periodic traveling wave solution of the KdV equation, and such a wave describes surface waves whose wavelength is larger compared to the water depth. Cnoidal wave solutions can appear in surface gravity waves and can be used to describe ion acoustic waves in plasma physics.

Let us look for the elementary wave solution of (3.3) in the form

$$u = f(x - ct) = f(\xi) \tag{3.6}$$

where f is an arbitrary function and $\xi = x - ct$.

Therefore, (3.3) can be reduced to an ordinary differential equation

$$-c\frac{\partial f}{\partial \xi} + f\frac{\partial f}{\partial \xi} + \frac{\partial^3 f}{\partial \xi^3} = 0. \tag{3.7}$$

Integrating the equation, we get

$$\frac{\partial^2 f}{\partial \xi^2} + \frac{1}{2}f^2 - cf = C_1 \tag{3.8}$$

where C_1 is the integration constant. Multiplying (3.8) by $\frac{\partial f}{\partial \xi}$ and then integrating, we obtain

$$\frac{1}{2}\left(\frac{\partial f}{\partial \xi}\right)^2 + \frac{1}{6}f^3 - \frac{c}{2}f^2 = C_1 f + C_2 \qquad (3.9)$$

where C_2 is the integration constant.

Cnoidal wave solution: When $C_1, C_2 \neq 0$, then Equation (3.9) admits Jacobi elliptic function as solution which corresponds to the cnoidal waves. For $C_1, C_2 \neq 0$, Equation (3.9) can be described as

$$\sqrt{3}\frac{\partial f}{\partial \xi} = \sqrt{-f^3 + 3cf^2 + 6C_1 f + 6C_2} \qquad (3.10)$$

or

$$\frac{\sqrt{3}df}{\sqrt{-f^3 + 3cf^2 + 6C_1 f + 6C_2}} = d\xi. \qquad (3.11)$$

If α_1, α_2, and α_3 are the three real root of the algebraic equation

$$f^3 - 3cf^2 - 6C_1 f - 6C_2 = 0,$$

then we can write Equation (3.11) as

$$\frac{\sqrt{3}df}{\sqrt{(\alpha_1 - f)(f - \alpha_2)(f - \alpha_3)}} = d\xi. \qquad (3.12)$$

Let $f = \alpha_1 + (\alpha_2 - \alpha_1)\sin^2 \phi$, then $df = 2(\alpha_2 - \alpha_1)\sin\phi \, \cos\phi d\phi$. Therefore, Equation (3.12) becomes

$$\frac{2\sqrt{3}d\phi}{\sqrt{\alpha_1 - \alpha_3}\sqrt{1 - \frac{(\alpha_2 - \alpha_1)}{\alpha_1 - \alpha_3}\sin^2 \phi}} = d\xi. \qquad (3.13)$$

Hence, in terms of Jacobi elliptic function, the above equation is written as

$$sn\left(\frac{\sqrt{\alpha_1 - \alpha_3}\xi}{2\sqrt{3}}, k\right) = \sin\phi$$

or

$$\sin^2 \phi = sn^2\left(\frac{\sqrt{\alpha_1 - \alpha_3}\xi}{2\sqrt{3}}, k\right)$$

or

$$\frac{f - \alpha_1}{\alpha_2 - \alpha_1} = sn^2\left(\frac{\sqrt{\alpha_1 - \alpha_3}\,\xi}{2\sqrt{3}}, k\right)$$

which gives

$$u(x,t) = (\alpha_2 - \alpha_1)cn^2\left(\frac{\sqrt{\alpha_1 - \alpha_3}\,\xi}{2\sqrt{3}}, k\right) + \alpha_2$$

or

$$u(x,t) = (\alpha_2 - \alpha_1)cn^2\left(\frac{\sqrt{\alpha_1 - \alpha_3}\,(x - ct)}{2\sqrt{3}}, k\right) + \alpha_2.$$

Soliton solution can be obtained as a limiting case of cnoidal wave solution when $k = 1$, i.e., $\alpha_1 - \alpha_3 = \alpha_2 - \alpha_1$. In that case, $cn(t, 1) = secht$, which gives the soliton solution

$$u(x,t) = (\alpha_1 - \alpha_3)sech^2\left(\frac{\sqrt{\alpha_1 - \alpha_3}\,(x - ct)}{2\sqrt{3}}\right) + \alpha_2.$$

Soliton solution: We get the soliton solution from Equation (3.7) itself when $C_1, C_2 = 0$. Equation (3.7) is then written as integrating, and we obtain

$$\left(\frac{\partial f}{\partial \xi}\right)^2 = cf^2 - \frac{1}{3}f^3. \tag{3.14}$$

Therefore,

$$\left(\frac{df}{f\sqrt{c - \frac{1}{3}f}}\right)^2 = \pm d\xi. \tag{3.15}$$

Integrating the equation, we get

$$u(x - ct) = 3csech^2\left(\pm\frac{\sqrt{c}}{2}(x - ct) + \theta\right) \tag{3.16}$$

where θ is the phase of the system. This is the famous soliton solution.

If in addition $c = 0$, then Equation (3.9) becomes

$$\left(\frac{\partial f}{\partial \xi}\right)^2 = -\frac{1}{3}f^3. \tag{3.17}$$

The solution of this equation is readily obtained as $f(\xi) = \frac{-12}{(\xi + \theta)^2}$ or $u(x,t) = \frac{-12}{x + \theta}$, singular stationary solution.

3.2.3 *Modified KdV (MKdV) equation*

The modified KdV equation is popular for its special solution behavior, i.e., breathers. The coefficient KdV equation depends on the parameter on the medium on which it appears. If the coefficient of the nonlinear term vanishes, the equation no longer contains the nonlinearity of the medium. Here, the researchers try instead to find an equivalent equation with a cubic nonlinearity in place of quadratic nonlinearity. Such an equation is called a modified KdV (MKdV) equation. This equation is applied in electrodynamics, nonlinear optics, and other areas. Let us consider an MKdV equation as

$$\frac{\partial \phi}{\partial t} + a\phi^2 \frac{\partial \phi}{\partial x} + b\frac{\partial^3 \phi}{\partial x^3} = 0. \tag{3.18}$$

Using transformation and omitting the bar, Equation (3.18) reduces to

$$\frac{\partial \phi}{\partial t} + \phi^2 \frac{\partial \phi}{\partial x} + \frac{\partial^3 \phi}{\partial x^3} = 0. \tag{3.19}$$

To obtain the solution of Equation (3.19) by using the transformation $\xi = x - vt$ and $t = t$ where v is a constant speed, we get

$$-v\frac{d\phi}{d\xi} + \phi^2 \frac{d\phi}{d\xi} + \frac{d^3 \phi}{d\xi^3} = 0.$$

Integrating the above equation and using the boundary condition $\phi \rightarrow 0$, $\frac{d\phi}{d\xi} \rightarrow 0$, $\frac{d^2\phi}{d\xi^2} \rightarrow 0$ at $\xi \rightarrow \pm\infty$, we get

$$\frac{d^2 \phi}{d\xi^2} + \left(\frac{\phi}{3} - v\right)\phi = 0.$$

Multiplying the above equation by $2\frac{d\phi}{d\xi}$ and then integrating and imposing the condition $\phi \rightarrow 0$, $\frac{d\phi}{d\xi} \rightarrow 0$, we get for $v > 0$

$$\frac{d\phi}{d\xi} = \frac{1}{\sqrt{6}}\phi\sqrt{6v - \phi^2}.$$

Again, integrating the above equation, we get the solitary wave solution as

$$\phi(\xi) = A\text{sech}\left(\frac{\xi}{W}\right) \tag{3.20}$$

where $A = \sqrt{6v}$ is the amplitude and $W = \frac{1}{\sqrt{v}}$ is the the width of the wave. They are related by $A = \frac{\sqrt{6}}{W}$, i.e., $A \propto \frac{1}{W}$. So, we conclude that the amplitude is inversely proportional to the width of the wave.

3.2.4 *Schamel-type KdV (S-KdV) equation*

To investigate the propagation of acoustic type waves in the presence of trapped charged particles, H. Schamel [8] considered a non-Maxwellian distribution for trapped particles that are known as Schamel distribution. Accordingly, a KdV like equation was derived from the model, and such equation is called Schamel-type KdV (S-KdV) equation. The S-KdV equation contains a square root nonlinearity and can be derived from a plasma model, where trapped electrons/ions are considered. We obtain exact traveling wave solutions of the S-KdV equation by employing the direct method. The S-KdV equation is

$$\frac{\partial \phi}{\partial t} + a\sqrt{\bar{\phi}}\frac{\partial \phi}{\partial x} + b\frac{\partial^3 \phi}{\partial x^3} = 0. \tag{3.21}$$

Using transformation and omitting the bar, Equation (3.21) reduces to

$$\frac{\partial \phi}{\partial t} + \sqrt{\bar{\phi}}\frac{\partial \phi}{\partial x} + \frac{\partial^3 \phi}{\partial x^3} = 0. \tag{3.22}$$

To obtain the solution of Equation (3.22) by using the transformation $\xi = x - vt$, where v is a constant speed, we get

$$-v\frac{d\phi}{d\xi} + \sqrt{\bar{\phi}}\frac{d\phi}{d\xi} + \frac{d^3 \phi}{d\xi^3} = 0.$$

Integrating the above equation and imposing the condition $\phi \to 0$, $\frac{d^2\phi}{d\xi^2} \to 0$ at $\xi \to \pm\infty$, we get

$$\frac{d^2 \phi}{d\xi^2} = \left(v\phi - \frac{2}{3}\phi^{3/2}\right).$$

Multiplying the above equation by $2\frac{d\phi}{d\xi}$ and then integrating and using the boundary condition $\phi \to 0$, $\frac{d\phi}{d\xi} \to 0$ at $\xi \to \pm\infty$, we get

$$\frac{d\phi}{d\xi} = \frac{1}{\sqrt{15}}\phi\sqrt{15v - 8\sqrt{\phi}}.$$

Again, integrating the above equation, we get the solitary wave solution as

$$\phi = A\text{sech}^4\left(\frac{\xi}{W}\right) \tag{3.23}$$

where $A = \frac{225v^2}{64}$ is the amplitude and $W = \frac{4}{\sqrt{v}}$ is the the width of the wave and they are related by $A = \frac{900}{W^4}$, i.e., $A \propto \frac{1}{W^4}$.

3.2.5 Burgers' equation

Burgers' equation or Bateman–Burgers equation occurs in various areas at applied mathematics and physics. This equation models the shock waves in fluid mechanics, nonlinear acoustic, gas dynamic, and traffic flow. In 1915, Harry Bateman [9] introduced a nonlinear partial differential equation where dissipation was considered with nonlinearity. After 1948, this nonlinear equation was analyzed by Johannes Martinus Burgers [10]. This equation is known as Burgers' equation. Burgers' equation is the simplest nonlinear differential equation for diffusive waves in fluid dynamics. This equation can also be taken as a modified form of the Navier–Stokes equation because of the nonlinear convection term and the presence of the viscosity term. Burgers' equation also appears in many physical problems like acoustic, dispersive water, shock waves, and turbulence. Few nonlinear partial differential equations can be solved exactly like this. Now, in this section, Burgers' equation will be solved by the direct method. Burgers' equation is given by

$$\frac{\partial \phi}{\partial t} + \phi \frac{\partial \phi}{\partial x} - \frac{\partial^2 \phi}{\partial x^2} = 0. \tag{3.24}$$

Let us consider the wave moves with velocity v. Now, considering the traveling wave transformation $\xi = x - vt$, where $x - vt$ is the phase, Equation (3.24) is converted to

$$-v\frac{d\phi}{d\xi} + \phi\frac{d\phi}{d\xi} - \frac{d^2\phi}{d\xi^2} = 0. \tag{3.25}$$

Integrating and using the conditions $\phi \to 0$, $\frac{d\phi}{d\xi} \to 0$ at $\xi \to \pm\infty$, we get

$$\frac{d\phi}{v^2 - (\phi - v)^2} = -\frac{1}{2}d\xi.$$

On integration and using the boundary condition $\phi \to 0$ at $\xi \to \infty$, we get the solitary wave solution as

$$\phi(\xi) = \phi_0 \left[1 + tanh\left(\frac{\xi}{\delta}\right) \right] \tag{3.26}$$

where $\phi_0 = v$ is the amplitude and $\delta = -2/v$ is the width of the shock wave.

3.2.6 *KP equation*

The Kadomtsev–Petviashvili (KP) equation is a nonlinear partial differential equation with a dimension (2+1) that describes the wave phenomena in different nonlinear mediums. This equation can also be termed as the (2+1) dimensional KdV equation. Two Soviet physicists Boris Kadomtsev and Vladimir Petviashvili [11] introduced this equation in 1970. Like the KdV equation, this equation is also modeled as acoustic waves in plasma under the influences of dissipation at long transverse perturbation. So, this is a natural extension of the KdV equation to two special dimensions. It is also applicable in nonlinear optics and other relative fields. To obtain the solution of the KP equation by the direct method, let us consider a KP equation as

$$\frac{\partial}{\partial \xi}\left(\frac{\partial \phi}{\partial \tau} + A\phi\frac{\partial \phi}{\partial \xi} + B\frac{\partial^3 \phi}{\partial \xi^3}\right) + C\frac{\partial^2 \phi}{\partial \eta^2} = 0. \tag{3.27}$$

To obtain the soliton solution of the equation by using the transformation $\chi = l\xi + m\eta - u\tau$ in Equation (3.27) then integrating the transformed equation with the help of boundary condition $\phi \to 0$, $\frac{d\phi}{d\chi} \to 0$, $\frac{d^2\phi}{d\chi^2} \to 0$ at $\chi \to \pm\infty$, we get

$$(Cm^2 - lu)\frac{d\phi}{d\chi} + Al^2\phi\frac{d\phi}{d\chi} + Bl^4\frac{d^3\phi}{d\chi^3} = 0.$$

Again, integrating the above equation and imposing the boundary condition $\phi \to 0$, $\frac{d\phi}{d\chi} \to 0$, $\frac{d^2\phi}{d\chi^2} \to 0$ at $\chi \to \pm\infty$, we get

$$\frac{d^2\phi}{d\chi^2} = \frac{lu - Cm^2}{Bl^4}\phi - \frac{A}{2Bl^2}\phi^2.$$

Multiplying both sides by $2\frac{d\phi}{d\chi}$ and then integrating with the help of the boundary condition $\phi \to 0$, $\frac{d\phi}{d\chi} \to 0$ at $\chi \to \pm\infty$, we get

$$\frac{d\phi}{\phi\sqrt{A_1 - B_1\phi}} = d\chi$$

where $A_1 = \frac{lu - Cm^2}{Bl^4}$, $B_1 = \frac{A}{3Bl^2}$.

Integrating the above equation and finally, we get the soliton solution as

$$\phi = \frac{A_1}{B_1}sech^2\left(\frac{\sqrt{A_1}\chi}{2}\right) = \phi_0 sech^2\left(\frac{\chi}{W}\right) \tag{3.28}$$

where $\phi_0 = \frac{3(lu - Cm^2)}{l^2 A}$ is the amplitude and $W = 2\sqrt{\frac{l^4}{lu - Cm^2}}$ is the width of the wave.

3.2.7 *Modified KP equation*

Grimshaw and Melville [12] derived a modified KP equation to describe long surface or initial waves in the existence of rotation. This equation is the appropriate extension of the KdV equation that provides a correct asymptotic explanation of the waves traveling to the right. In general, it cannot be assumed that the solutions are locally confined. Hence, we are going to obtain the wave solution from the modified KP equation. Let us consider the modified KP equation as

$$\frac{\partial}{\partial \xi}\left(\frac{\partial \phi}{\partial \tau} + A\phi^2 \frac{\partial \phi}{\partial \xi} + B\frac{\partial^3 \phi}{\partial \xi^3}\right) + C\frac{\partial^2 \phi}{\partial \eta^2} = 0. \tag{3.29}$$

To obtain the solution of Equation (3.29) by using the transformation $\chi = l\xi + m\eta - u\tau$ in Equation (3.27) and then integrating the transformed equation with the help of the boundary condition $\phi \to 0$, $\frac{d\phi}{d\chi} \to 0$, $\frac{d^2\phi}{d\chi^2} \to 0$ at $\chi \to \infty$, we get

$$(Cm^2 - lu)\frac{d\phi}{d\chi} + Al^2\phi^2\frac{d\phi}{d\chi} + Bl^4\frac{d^3\phi}{d\chi^3} = 0.$$

Again, integrating the above equation and imposing the boundary condition $\phi \to 0$, $\frac{d\phi}{d\chi} \to 0$, $\frac{d^2\phi}{d\chi^2} \to 0$ as $\chi \to \infty$, we get

$$\frac{d^2\phi}{d\chi^2} = \frac{(lu - Cm^2)}{Bl^4}\phi - \frac{A}{3Bl^2}\phi^3.$$

Multiplying both sides by $2\frac{d\phi}{d\chi}$ and then integrating the equation and using the boundary condition, we get

$$\frac{d\phi}{\phi\sqrt{A - B\phi^2}} = d\chi$$

where $A_1 = \frac{(lu - Cm^2)}{Bl^4}$ and $B_1 = \frac{A}{6Bl^2}$.

Integrating the above equation and finally, we get the solution as

$$\phi = \sqrt{\frac{A_1}{B_1}}sech\left(\sqrt{A}\chi\right) = \phi_0 sech\left(\frac{\chi}{W_c}\right) \tag{3.30}$$

where $\phi_0 = \sqrt{\frac{6(lu - Cm^2)}{l^2 A}}$ is the amplitude and $W_c = \sqrt{\frac{l^4 B}{lu - Cm^2}}$ is the width of the wave.

3.3 Hyperbolic Tangent Method

Solving the majority of the partial differential equation is not easy. To handle this, Malfliet [13] introduced a popular technique to find a traveling wave solution of the nonlinear partial differential equations. This technique is called the *hyperbolic tangent or tanh method*. To avoid algebraic complications, this method uses tanh as a new variable because all derivatives of tanh are represented also by the tanh function. So, this method is a bit simpler, and we can use this method to solve nonlinear evolution equations. The starting point is a nonlinear evolution equation, which describes the dynamical evolution of the waveform $u(x, t)$. The following are the steps:

Step 1

A traveling wave solution needs a single coordinate $\xi = c(x - vt)$ and $u(x, t) = u(\xi)$, where $u(\xi)$ represents the wave solution, which travels with speed v. Without loss of generality, we define $c > 0$ and accordingly as a consequence, the derivatives are changed into

$$\frac{\partial}{\partial t} \to -cv\frac{d}{dv}, \quad \frac{\partial}{\partial x} \to c\frac{d}{dv}. \tag{3.31}$$

Step 2

Using (3.31), then the partial differential equation becomes an ordinary differential equation.

Step 3

In the next step, the ordinary differential equation is integrated as all terms contain derivatives. One should continue this procedure unless one of the terms contains no derivatives. The integration constants are associated with the problem and are taken to be zero.

Step 4

This step is the most important step. In this step, we introduce $Y = \tanh(\xi)$ as a new independent variable. The corresponding derivatives are changed to

$$\frac{d}{d\xi} = \frac{\partial Y}{\partial \xi}\frac{d}{dY} = sech^2(\xi)\frac{d}{dY} = (1 - Y^2)\frac{d}{dY}.$$

Therefore,

$$\frac{d}{d\xi} = (1 - Y^2)\frac{d}{dY} \tag{3.32}$$

$$\frac{d^2}{d\xi^2} = (1 - Y^2)\left[-2Y\frac{d}{dY} + (1 - Y^2)\frac{d^2}{dY^2}\right] \tag{3.33}$$

$$\frac{d^3}{d\xi^3} = -2Y(1 - Y^2)\left[-2Y\frac{d}{dY} + (1 - Y^2)\frac{d^2}{dY^2}\right] + (1 - Y^2)^2\left[-2Y\frac{d}{dY}\right.$$

$$\left. - 2Y\frac{d^2}{dY^2} + (1 - Y^2)\frac{d^2}{dY^2}\right]. \tag{3.34}$$

Higher-order derivatives can also be found accordingly.

Step 5

The solutions we are looking for will come in power series of Y. Although no general procedure exists at this final stage, the series expansion of the dependent variable is most preferred.

$$S(Y) = \sum_{m=0}^{M} a_m Y^m. \tag{3.35}$$

Detection of the parameter M is the crux of the idea of finding the solution. M will be found by balancing the linear term(s) of the highest order with the nonlinear term(s). To carry out the balance method, the highest exponents for the function u and its derivatives are as follows:

$$\left.\begin{array}{l} u \to M \\ u^n \to nM \\ u' \to M + 1 \\ u'' \to M + 2 \\ u^{(r)} \to M + r. \end{array}\right\} \tag{3.36}$$

The linear term of the highest order is contained in the highest derivative of the equation. This can be easily obtained by using the set of relations (3.32), (3.33), and (3.34) in the equation. The Y^2 component of Equation (3.32) leads to the order $(2 + M - 1) = M + 1$ and similarly for Y^3 and

Y^4. On the other hand, the nonlinear terms yield a multiple of the result. In this way, the value of M can be determined. Normally, M will be a positive integer so that a closed analytical solution can be obtained. In principle, a negative or an infinite value for M is also allowed. But it can be used in those cases where a finite value of M does not lead to a solution, and such cases are not treated here. Finally, the series expansion (3.35) is substituted into the relevant equation, and recursion relations appear. Then, the coefficients a_m $(m = 0, 1, 2, \ldots, M)$ are evaluated.

3.3.1 *KdV equation*

Now, we are going to solve the KdV equation by tanh method.

$$\frac{\partial u}{\partial t} + 6u\frac{\partial u}{\partial x} + \frac{\partial^3 u}{\partial x^3} = 0. \tag{3.37}$$

Using the transformation $\xi = c(x - vt)$ and then integrating the transformed equation, we get

$$-cvu(\xi) + 3cu^2(\xi) + c^3\frac{du(\xi)}{d\xi^2} = 0. \tag{3.38}$$

Now, we introduce a new variable $Y = \tanh(\xi)$, and we get

$$-vS(Y) + 3s^2(Y) + c^2(1 - Y^2)\left[-2Y\frac{dS(Y)}{dY} + (1 - Y^2)\frac{d^2S(Y)}{dY^2}\right] = 0. \tag{3.39}$$

The highest power of S is Y^M, $\frac{dS}{dY}$ is Y^{M-1}, and $\frac{d^2S}{dY^2}$ is Y^{M-2}. The power of $S^2(Y)$ is $2M$, $Y^3\frac{dS}{dY}$ is $3 + M - 1$, and $Y^4\frac{d^2S}{dY^2}$ is $4 + M - 2$. Hence, balancing the highest order of linear and nonlinear term, we get

$$2M = 3 + M - 1 = 4 + M - 2.$$

So, $M = 2$. We are now able to proceed as before. However, from the fact that $M = 2$, we observe from the structure of Equation (3.38) that $S(Y)$ should be proportional to $(1 - Y^2)$. So, we can introduce $S(Y) = \nu(1 - Y^2)$. Dividing Equation (3.38) by $\nu(1 - Y^2)$, we obtain

$$-v + 3\nu(1 - Y^2) + c^2\left[-2Y\frac{d(1 - Y^2)}{dY} + (1 - Y^2)\frac{d^2(1 - Y^2)}{dY^2}\right] = 0.$$

Only terms proportional to Y^2 and Y^0 are left.

Thus, Y^0 coefficient:

$$-v + 3\nu - 2c^2 = 0$$

Y^2 coefficient:

$$-3\nu + 4c^2 + 2c^2 = 0.$$

We have three unknowns (v, ν, c) and two equations and we may choose c as a free parameter. The other variables are then found to be

$$\nu = 2c^2, v = 4c^2.$$

Finally, we obtain the solitary wave solution as

$$u(x, t) = 2c^2(1 - \tanh^2[c(x - 4c^2t)]) = 2c^2 \operatorname{sech}^2[c(x - 4c^2t)]. \quad (3.40)$$

3.3.2 *Modified KdV equation*

Now, we are going to solve the MKdV equation by the tanh method. Let us consider the MKdV equation as

$$\frac{\partial u}{\partial t} + 6u^2\frac{\partial u}{\partial x} + \frac{\partial^3 u}{\partial x^3} = 0. \quad (3.41)$$

A traveling wave solution needs a single coordinate $\xi = c(x - vt)$, where $c > 0$ and v is the velocity of the wave. So, $u(x, t) = u(\xi)$, where $u(\xi)$ represents the wave solution, which travels with speed v. Using the transformation and then integrating the transformed equation, we get

$$-cvu(\xi) + 2cu^2(\xi) + c^3\frac{du(\xi)}{d\xi^2} = 0. \quad (3.42)$$

Introducing the new variable $Y = \tanh(\xi)$, then Equation (3.42) becomes

$$-vS(Y) + 2s^2(Y) + c^2(1 - Y^2)\left[-2Y\frac{dS(Y)}{dY} + (1 - Y^2)\frac{d^2S(Y)}{dY^2}\right] = 0. \quad (3.43)$$

Following the previous procedure, we get $M = 1$. It is seen that for $M = 1$ the series expansion (3.35) does not yield a solution unless it is a trivial one ($u = $ constant). Here, we get two options as follows: (i) let us consider a series expansion with $M = \infty$ and we get recursion relation between $c, v,$ and $a_i(i \geq 1)$. However, it is unnecessary to discuss the unknowns in this chapter. (ii) We can also use $S(Y) = \nu(1 - Y^2)^{1/2}$ in Equation (3.43) and get

$$-v\nu + 2\nu^2(1 - Y^2) + c^2(1 - Y^2)^{1/2}$$
$$\times \left[-2Y\frac{dS(1 - Y^2)^{1/2}}{dY} + (1 - Y^2)\frac{d^2(1 - Y^2)^{1/2}}{dY^2} \right] = 0.$$

Eventually, we arrive at the following relations:

Y^0 coefficient:

$$-v + 2\nu^2 - 2c^2 = 0$$

Y^2 coefficient:

$$-2\nu^2 + 2c^2 = 0.$$

We have three unknowns (v, ν, c) and two equations and we may choose c as a free parameter. The other variables are then found to be $\nu = c$ and $v = c^2$. Finally, we obtain the solitary wave solution as

$$u(x, t) = c(1 - \tanh^2[c(x - c^2t)])^{1/2} = c\,\mathrm{sech}^2[c(x - c^2t)]. \quad (3.44)$$

3.3.3 *Burgers' equation*

Burgers' equation is given by

$$\frac{\partial u}{\partial t} + u\frac{\partial u}{\partial x} - \frac{\partial^2 u}{\partial x^2} = 0. \quad (3.45)$$

A traveling wave solution needs to single coordinate $\xi = c(x - vt)$, where $c > 0$ and v is the velocity of the wave. So, $u(x, t) = u(\xi)$, where $u(\xi)$ represents the wave solution, which travels with speed v. Using the transformation and then integrating the transformed equation, we get

$$-vu(\xi) + \frac{1}{2}u^2(\xi) - c\frac{du(\xi)}{d\xi} = 0. \quad (3.46)$$

Introducing the new variable $Y = \tanh(\xi)$ in Equation (3.46), we get

$$-vS(Y) + \frac{1}{2}S^2(Y) - c(1 - Y^2)\frac{dS(Y)}{dY} = 0. \quad (3.47)$$

Following the same procedure, we get $M = 1$. Therefore, the solution has the form

$$S(Y) = a_0 + a_1 Y. \tag{3.48}$$

Substituting (3.48) in (3.47), we get

$$-v(a_0 + a_1 Y) + \frac{1}{2}(a_0 + a_1 Y)^2 - c(1 - Y^2)a_1 Y = 0. \tag{3.49}$$

Each coefficient of power of Y has to vanish. So, we arrive at the following:

Y^2 coefficient:

$$\frac{1}{2}a_1^2 + a_1 c = 0 \Rightarrow a_1 = -2c. \tag{3.50}$$

Y^1 coefficient:

$$-v a_1 + a_0 a_1 = 0 \Rightarrow a_0 = v. \tag{3.51}$$

Y^0 coefficient:

$$-v a_0 + \frac{1}{2}a_0^2 - a_1 c = 0, \Rightarrow v^2 = 4c^2. \tag{3.52}$$

These three Equations ((3.50)–(3.52)) have four unknowns (a_0, a_1, c, v). We choose v as a free parameter. So, $a_0 = v$, $a_1 = -v$, and $c = \frac{v}{2}$. Finally, we obtain the shock wave solution as

$$u(x,t) = u(\xi) = v\left[1 - \tanh\left\{\frac{v}{2}\left(x - vt\right)\right\}\right]. \tag{3.53}$$

3.3.4 *KdV Burgers' equation*

We consider the KdVB equation

$$\frac{\partial \phi}{\partial t} - b\frac{\partial^2 \phi}{\partial x^2} + c\phi\frac{\partial \phi}{\partial x} + d\frac{\partial^3 \phi}{\partial x^3} = 0 \tag{3.54}$$

where a, b, c, and d are real constants. Assume Equation (3.54) has traveling wave solution in the form of $\phi(x,t) = u(\xi)$, where $\xi = x - vt$. Substituting $\xi = x - vt$ into Equation (3.54) and integrating the transformed equation, we get

$$d\frac{d^2u}{d\xi^2} - b\frac{du}{d\xi} + c\frac{u^2}{2} - vu = c_1 \tag{3.55}$$

where c_1 is an arbitrary constant, whose value depends on the initial conditions.

We now introduce the new independent variable $Y = \tanh\xi$ and $W(Y) = u(\xi)$, due to which Equation (3.55) transforms to

$$d(1 - Y^2)^2\frac{d^2W}{dY^2} - \{2dY(1 - Y^2) + b(1 - Y^2)\}\frac{dW}{dY} + \frac{c}{2}W^2 - vW = c_1. \tag{3.56}$$

Following the same procedure, we get $M = 2$. Thus,

$$W(Y) = a_0 + a_1Y + a_2Y^2. \tag{3.57}$$

Using (3.57), we get from Equation (3.56), the following system of equations:

$$2a_2d - ba_1 + \frac{1}{2}ca_0^2 - va_0 - c_1 = 0 \tag{3.58}$$

$$2a_1d + 2ba_2 - ca_0a_1 + va_1 = 0 \tag{3.59}$$

$$ba_1 - 8a_2d + \frac{1}{2}ca_1^2 + ca_0a_2 - va_2 = 0 \tag{3.60}$$

$$2a_1d + 2ba_2 + ca_1a_2 = 0 \tag{3.61}$$

$$6a_2d + \frac{1}{2}ca_2^2 = 0. \tag{3.62}$$

From these equations, the unknowns are determined as

$$a_0 = \frac{1}{c}(v + 12d), \quad a_1 = -\frac{12b}{5c}, \quad a_2 - \frac{12d}{c}$$

together with a relation between b and d as $b^2 = 100d^2$. Equation (3.58) determines v in terms of a_0, a_1, a_2, and c_1. Finally, we obtain the solution of KdV–Burgers' equation as

$$\phi(x, t) = a_0 + a_1\tanh(x - vt) + a_2\tanh^2(x - vt) \tag{3.63}$$

where a_0, a_1, and a_2 are given above together with the relation $b^2 = 100d^2$.

3.3.5 KP equation

Let us consider the KP equation

$$\frac{\partial}{\partial \xi}\left(\frac{\partial \phi}{\partial \tau} + A\phi\frac{\partial \phi}{\partial \xi} + B\frac{\partial^3 \phi}{\partial \xi^3}\right) + C\frac{\partial^2 \phi}{\partial \eta^2} = 0. \tag{3.64}$$

To obtain the traveling wave solution, we need the transformation $\zeta = \xi + \eta - u\tau$, and using the boundary conditions, i.e., $\phi \to 0$, $\frac{\partial \phi}{\partial \zeta} \to 0$, $\frac{\partial^2 \phi}{\partial \zeta^2} \to 0$, $\frac{\partial^3 \phi}{\partial \zeta^3} \to 0$, we have

$$-(u - C)\frac{\partial \phi}{\partial \zeta} + A\phi\frac{\partial \phi}{\partial \zeta} + B\frac{\partial^3 \phi}{\partial \zeta^3} = 0. \tag{3.65}$$

Following the same procedure, finally, we get the solution of the KP equation as

$$\phi(\zeta) = \frac{8B}{A} + \frac{(u - C)}{A} - \frac{12B}{A}\tanh^2(\xi + \eta - u\tau). \tag{3.66}$$

By the same procedure, one can easily obtain the solution of the modified KP and ZK equations.

3.4 Tanh–Coth Method

Let us consider a nonlinear differential equation

$$P(u, u_t, u_x, u_{xx}, u_{xxx}, \ldots) = 0. \tag{3.67}$$

To find the traveling wave solution of Equation (3.67), the wave variable $\xi = x - ct$ and then the partial differential Equation (3.67) converts to an ordinary differential equation

$$Q(u, u', u'', u''', \ldots) = 0. \tag{3.68}$$

Equation (3.68) is integrated as long as all terms contain derivatives and integration constants are zero. The standard tanh method is developed by Malfliet [13] where the tanh is used as a new variable. A new independent variable $Y = \tanh(\mu\xi)$, $\xi = x - ct$, where μ is the wavenumber, is introduced that leads to the following change of derivatives:

$$
\left.\begin{aligned}
\frac{d}{d\xi} &= \mu(1 - Y^2)\frac{d}{dY}\\[6pt]
\frac{d^2}{d\xi^2} &= 2\mu^2 Y(1 - Y^2)\frac{d}{dY} + \mu^2(1 - Y^2)\frac{d^2}{dY^2}\\[6pt]
\frac{d^3}{d\xi^3} &= 2\mu^3(1 - Y^2)(3Y^2 - 1)\frac{d}{dY} - 6\mu^3 Y(1 - Y^2)^2\frac{d^2}{dY^2}\\[6pt]
&\quad + \mu^3(1 - Y^2)^3\frac{d^3}{dY^3}\\[6pt]
\frac{d^4}{d\xi^4} &= -8\mu^4 Y(1 - Y^2)(3Y^2 - 1)\frac{d}{dY} + 4\mu^4(1 - Y^2)^2\\[6pt]
&\quad \times (9Y^2 - 2)\frac{d^2}{dY^2} - 12\mu^4 Y(1 - Y^2)^3\frac{d^3}{dY^3} + \mu^4(1 - Y^2)^4\frac{d^4}{dY^4}.
\end{aligned}\right\}
$$

$$(3.69)$$

In the tanh method, the positive integer value of M is considered, whereas in the tanh–coth method, we consider both positive and negative integer values of M. Hence, the finite expansion will be written as

$$
u(\mu, \xi) = S(Y) = \sum_{m=0}^{M} a_K Y^K + \sum_{m=0}^{M} b_K Y^{-K} \tag{3.70}
$$

where M is a positive integer, in most cases, that will be determined. For noninteger M, a transformation formula is used to overcome this difficulty and it reduces to the standard tanh method $b_k = 0, 1 \leq k \leq M$. Substituting (3.67) into the reduced ordinary differential equation results in an algebraic equation to the power of Y.

Following the same procedure, we determine the value of M and then collect all coefficients of power of Y in the resulting equation where these coefficients are zero. It will give a system of algebraic equations involving the parameters a_k, b_k, μ, and c. Having determined these parameters, we obtain solitons in terms of $sech^2$ or kinks in terms of tanh. However, this method may give periodic solutions.

3.4.1 *KdV equation*

The KdV equation is

$$
u_t + auu_x + u_{xxx} = 0. \tag{3.71}
$$

Substitute the wave variable $\xi = x - ct$ in Equation (3.71), where c is the wave speed. Now, integrating the transformed equation, we get

$$-cu + \frac{a}{2}u^2 + u'' = 0. \tag{3.72}$$

We first balance the terms u^2 with u''. This means that the highest power of u^2 is $2M$ and for u'' is $M+2$. This is obtained by using the scheme for the balancing process presented in the previous section. Using the balancing process leads to $2M = M + 2 \Rightarrow M = 3$. The tanh–coth method allows us to use the substitution

$$u(x,t) = S(Y) = \sum_{j=0}^{2} a_j Y^j + \sum_{i=1}^{2} b_j Y^{-1}. \tag{3.73}$$

Substituting (3.73) into (3.72), collecting the coefficient of each power of Y^r, $0 \leq r \leq 8$, setting each coefficient to zero, and solving the resulting system of algebraic equations, we find the following sets of solutions:

(i)

$$a_0 = \frac{3c}{2}, \; a_1 = a_2 = b_1 = 0, \; b_2 = -\frac{3c}{a}, \; \mu = \frac{1}{2}\sqrt{c}, \; c > 0 \tag{3.74}$$

(ii)

$$a_0 = -\frac{c}{a}, \; a_1 = a_2 = b_1 = 0, \; b_2 = \frac{3c}{a}, \; \mu = \frac{1}{2}\sqrt{-c}, \; c < 0 \tag{3.75}$$

(iii)

$$a_0 = \frac{3c}{a}, \; a_1 = a_2 = b_1 = 0, \; b_2 = \frac{3c}{a}, \; \mu = \frac{1}{2}\sqrt{c}, \; c > 0 \tag{3.76}$$

(iv)

$$a_0 = -\frac{c}{2}, \; a_1 = a_2 = b_1 = 0, \; b_2 = \frac{3c}{a}, \; \mu = \frac{1}{2}\sqrt{-c}, \; c < 0. \tag{3.77}$$

Consequently, we obtain the following soliton solutions and shocks:

$$\left. \begin{aligned} u_1(x,t) &= \frac{3c}{a}\operatorname{sech}^2\left[\frac{1}{2}\sqrt{c}(x - ct)\right], \; c > 0 \\ u_2(x,t) &= -\frac{c}{a}\left(1 - 3\tanh^2\left[\frac{1}{2}\sqrt{-c}(x - ct)\right]\right), \; C < 0. \end{aligned} \right\} \tag{3.78}$$

Moreover, the singular solitons and shocks are

$$
\left.
\begin{aligned}
u_3(x,t) &= -\frac{3c}{a}\operatorname{cosech}^2\left[\frac{1}{2}\sqrt{c}(x-ct)\right], \quad c > 0 \\
u_4(x,t) &= -\frac{c}{a}\left(1 - 3\coth^2\left[\frac{1}{2}\sqrt{-c}(x-ct)\right]\right), \quad c < 0.
\end{aligned}
\right\}
\tag{3.79}
$$

We obtain the following plane periodic solutions

$$
\left.
\begin{aligned}
u_5(x,t) &= \frac{3c}{a}c\left(\operatorname{cosech}^2\left[\frac{1}{2}\sqrt{-c}(x-ct)\right], \quad c < 0\right. \\
u_6(x,t) &= -\frac{c}{a}\left(1 - 3\coth^2\left[\frac{1}{2}\sqrt{c}(x-ct)\right]\right), \quad c > 0 \\
u_7(x,t) &= \frac{3c}{a}c\left(\operatorname{sech}^2\left[\frac{1}{2}\sqrt{-c}(x-ct)\right], \quad c < 0\right. \\
u_8(x,t) &= -\frac{c}{a}\left(1 + 3\tanh^2\left[\frac{1}{2}\sqrt{c}(x-ct)\right]\right), \quad c > 0.
\end{aligned}
\right\}
\tag{3.80}
$$

Similarly, we can obtain the solution of other KdV type equation. The modified KdV equation is

$$
u_t + au^2 u_x + u_{xxx} = 0.
\tag{3.81}
$$

We first substitute the wave variable $\xi = x - ct$, where c is the wave speed, into the MKdV equation and the following procedure as above, one can easily obtain the solution of MKdV equation.

The following solution and kink solutions are

$$
\left.
\begin{aligned}
u_1(x,t) &= \sqrt{\frac{3c}{a}}\operatorname{sech}\left[\sqrt{c}(x-ct)\right], \quad c > 0,\ a > 0 \\
u_2(x,t) &= \sqrt{\frac{3c}{a}}\left(\tanh\left[\sqrt{-\frac{1}{2}c}(x-ct)\right]\right), \quad c < 0,\ a < 0
\end{aligned}
\right\}
\tag{3.82}
$$

respectively obtained. Moreover, the following traveling wave periodic solutions (shocks and singular solitons) are derived

$$
\left.
\begin{aligned}
u_3(x,t) &= \sqrt{\frac{3c}{a}}\left(\coth\left[\sqrt{-\frac{1}{2}c}(x-ct)\right]\right), \quad c < 0,\ a < 0 \\
u_4(x,t) &= \sqrt{\frac{6c}{a}}\operatorname{sech}\left[\sqrt{-c}(x-ct)\right], \quad c < 0,\ a < 0 \\
u_4(x,t) &= \sqrt{\frac{-6c}{a}}\operatorname{cosech}\left[\sqrt{c}(x-ct)\right], \quad c > 0,\ a < 0.
\end{aligned}
\right\}
\tag{3.83}
$$

It can also be derived by using the sign of the wave speed c and the parameter a.

3.4.2 Burgers' equation

Burgers' equation is given by

$$\frac{\partial u}{\partial t} + u\frac{\partial u}{\partial x} - \frac{\partial^2 u}{\partial x^2} = 0. \tag{3.84}$$

Let $\xi = x - ct$ and $u(x,t) = u(\xi)$. Using the transformation and integrating the transformed equation with the help of initial condition $u(\xi) \to 0$, $\frac{du(\xi)}{d\xi} \to 0$ at $\xi \to \pm\infty$, we get

$$-cu(\xi) + \frac{1}{2}u^2(\xi) - \frac{du(\xi)}{d\xi} = 0. \tag{3.85}$$

Next, we transform to the new variable $Y = \tanh(\mu\xi)$ such that $U(\xi) = S(Y) = \Sigma_{m=0}^{M} a_m Y^M + \Sigma_{m=1}^{M} b_m Y^{-M}$. The parameter M will be found by balancing the linear terms of the highest order with nonlinear terms. So, $\frac{d}{d\xi} = \mu(1 - Y^2)\frac{d}{dY}$. Form (3.85), we have

$$-cS(Y) + \frac{1}{2}S^2(Y) - \mu(1 - Y^2)\frac{dS(Y)}{dY} = 0. \tag{3.86}$$

Following the same procedure, we get $M = 1$. Thus,

$$S(Y) = a_0 + a_1 Y + b_1 Y^{-1}. \tag{3.87}$$

Following the same procedure, we finally obtain the solution of Burgers' equation as

$$\left.\begin{aligned}
S(Y) &= c - \frac{c}{2}\left[\tanh\left[\frac{c}{4}(x - ct)\right] + \coth\left[\frac{c}{4}(x - ct)\right]\right], \quad c > 0, \\
S(Y) &= c + \frac{c}{2}\left[\tanh\left[-\frac{c}{4}(x - ct)\right] + \coth\left[-\frac{c}{4}(x - ct)\right]\right], \quad c < 0.
\end{aligned}\right\} \tag{3.88}$$

3.5 Solution of KP Burger Equation

We know that certain nonlinear second-order ordinary differential equations can be factorized under some conditions that coincide with those of integrability obtained from a Painleve analysis. These kinds of equations frequently appear when looking for traveling wave solutions of interesting nonlinear physical equations. We also know that the factorizations are directly related to the first integrals of the equation that are a kind of Bohlin's first integrals. Now, we are going to solve the KP equation. At first, find the Abel equation, and then we shall obtain the solution of that equation. Now, let us consider the KPB equation

$$\frac{\partial}{\partial \zeta} + \left(\frac{\partial \phi}{\partial \tau} + A\phi\frac{\partial \phi}{\partial \zeta} + B\frac{\partial^3 \phi}{\partial \zeta^3} - C\frac{\partial^2 \phi}{\partial \zeta^2} \right) + D\frac{\partial^2 \phi}{\partial \chi^2} = 0. \tag{3.89}$$

Since the KPB equation possesses the conditionally Painleve property, it can be solved if a specific method is developed. We want to solve this equation by the factorization method. Let the exact solution of the above equation in the form of a traveling wave be

$$\phi(\zeta, \chi, \tau) = \phi(\xi); \quad \xi = h\zeta + l\chi - \omega\tau \tag{3.90}$$

where the constant $h, l,$ and ω are to be determined. Then Equation (3.89) takes the form

$$-\omega h\frac{\partial^2 \phi}{\partial \xi^2} + h^2 A\frac{\partial}{\partial \xi}\left(\phi\frac{\partial \phi}{\partial \xi} \right) + Bh^4\frac{\partial^4 \phi}{\partial \xi^4} - Ch^3\frac{\partial^3 \phi}{\partial \xi^3} + Dl^2\frac{\partial^2 \phi}{\partial \xi^2} = 0. \tag{3.91}$$

Integrating twice with respect to ξ, we get

$$(Dl^2 - \omega h)\phi + h^2 A\left(\frac{\phi^2}{2} \right) + Bh^4\frac{\partial^2 \phi}{\partial \xi^2} - Ch^3\frac{\partial \phi}{\partial \xi} = R_1\xi + R_2 \tag{3.92}$$

where R_1 and R_2 are two integration constants. Then, we make a linear transformation as $\xi = -hB\theta$; $\phi(\xi) = -(2/AB)W(\theta)$ and substituting these we get

$$\frac{\partial^2 W}{\partial \theta^2} + C\frac{\partial W}{\partial \theta} - W^2 + KW = d_1\theta + d_2. \tag{3.93}$$

This is the required *Abel equation*, where $K = \frac{Dl^2 - \omega h}{h^2}B$; $d_1 = \frac{AB^3}{2h}R_1$, $d_2 = \frac{AB^2}{2h^2}R_2$.

If we consider $C = 0$, then the equation will be

$$\frac{\partial^2 W}{\partial \theta^2} - W^2 + KW = d_1\theta + d_2 \tag{3.94}$$

which is the Abel equation corresponding to the KP equation.

To solve Equation (3.93) by the factorization method, we first consider the integration constant $R_1 = 0$. Again, the nontrivial factorization is obtained only when $d_2 = 0$, which is a restrictive condition. To overcome this constraint, we apply a displacement on the unknown function, $W(\theta) = U(\theta) + \delta$, where δ is a solution of Equation (3.93) so that

$d_2 = k\delta - \delta^2$. To get real values of δ, $k^2 > 4\delta_2$. Again, $2\delta = k - \sqrt{k^2 - 4\delta_2}$ and therefore, $k - 2\delta > 0$.

Thus, Equation (3.93) takes the form

$$\frac{\partial U}{\partial \theta^2} + C\frac{\partial U}{\partial \theta} - U^2(\theta) + K - 2\delta)U(\theta) = 0. \tag{3.95}$$

Then, comparing the above equation with the factorization method, where f_1 and f_2 are two unknown functions, which may depend on U and θ, we get

$$C = -\left(f_2 + U\frac{\partial f_1}{\partial U}\right), \quad f_1 f_2 = \left(K - 2\delta - U(\theta) + \frac{\partial f_1}{\partial \theta}\right). \tag{3.96}$$

Here, we find a particular solution of the above equation in which f_1 and f_2 do not depend explicitly on θ. Using the ansatz

$$f_1 = XU^p + Y \tag{3.97}$$

where X and Y are constants.

$$f_2 = -C - (p+1)XU^p - Y. \tag{3.98}$$

Then taking the value $p = 1/2$, $X^2 2/3$, $Y = -(2C/5)$, we get $K - 2\delta = \frac{6C^2}{25} \Rightarrow d_2 = -(1/4)(k - 2\delta)^2 + \frac{K^2}{4} = \frac{K^2}{4} - \frac{9C^4}{625}$.

Then for the particular solution

$$\frac{dU}{d\theta} = \pm\sqrt{\frac{2}{3}}U^{3/2} - \frac{2C}{5}U \tag{3.99}$$

whose general solution is given by

$$U^{\pm}(\theta) = \frac{6C^2}{25}\frac{1}{[1 \mp e^{\frac{C}{5}(\theta-\theta_0)}]^2}. \tag{3.100}$$

We can write the solution of the KPB equation as

$$\phi(\zeta, \chi, \tau) = -\frac{2}{AB}(U(\theta) + \delta) \tag{3.101}$$

and substituting the value of $U(\theta)$ and δ, we get

$$\phi(\zeta, \chi, \tau) = -\frac{12C^2}{25AB}\frac{1}{[1 + z_0 e^{\frac{-C}{5hB}(h\xi + l\chi - \omega\tau)}]^2} - \frac{1}{AB}\left[\frac{Dl^2 - \omega h}{h^2}B + \frac{6C^2}{25}\right] \tag{3.102}$$

where $z_0 = e^{\frac{-C}{5}\theta_0)}$ is an arbitrary constant, which is the required particular traveling solitary wave solution.

3.6 Conservation Laws and Integrals of the Motions

A special significance of the KdV equation is the existence of an infinite number of conservation laws. By conservation law, we mean an equation of the form

$$T_t + X_x = 0, \tag{3.103}$$

where T, the conserved density, and X, the flux, are functions of x, t, u and higher-order x-derivatives of u. We only discuss conservation laws where T and X are polynomials in u and x-derivatives of u alone. A conserved density T is called trivial if T is an x-derivative for all u and if $T = F_x$, then we automatically have a conservation law

$$(F_x)_t + (-F_t)_x = 0$$

where the t-derivatives in the flux are eliminated by the repeated use of the evolution equation. The existence of conservation laws for the KdV equation and a conjectured connection to the conservation laws for a related equation motivated the inverse scattering method of the solution developed. Conservation laws can be used to obtain integrals of the motion. For example, if the flux X is zero as $|X| \to \infty$, then $\int_{-\infty}^{\infty} T dx = constant$.

Let the flux X be zero as $|X| \to \infty$, then from conservation law, we have

$$T_t + X_x = 0.$$

Integrating both sides with respect to x, we have

$$\int_{-\infty}^{\infty} T_t dx + \int_{-\infty}^{\infty} X_x dx = 0,$$

$$\Rightarrow \int_{-\infty}^{\infty} T_t dx + \int_{-\infty}^{\infty} dX = 0,$$

$$\Rightarrow \int_{-\infty}^{\infty} \frac{\partial T}{\partial t} dx + [X]_{-\infty}^{\infty} = 0,$$

$$\Rightarrow \frac{d}{dt} \int_{-\infty}^{\infty} T dx = 0,$$

$$\Rightarrow \int_{-\infty}^{\infty} T dx = c \quad (c \text{ is a constant}). \tag{3.104}$$

Furthermore, the existence of infinitely many conservation laws indicates that the KdV equation is a special equation of physical interest. Here, we explain the first three conservation laws for the KdV equation.

Law 1: Let us consider the KdV equation

$$u_t - 6uu_x + u_{xxx} = 0. \tag{3.105}$$

Equation (3.105) can be rewritten as

$$(u)_t + (-3u^2 + u_{xx})_x = 0.$$

Here, $T = u$, $X = -3u^2 + u_{xx}$ and accordingly $\int_{-\infty}^{\infty} T dx =$ constant. So, the first conservation law for KdV equation is $\int_{-\infty}^{\infty} u dx =$ constant.

Equation (3.104) must be true for all solutions of the KdV equation . However, not all solutions of the KdV equation satisfy the asymptotic relations. For example, the conservation laws do not apply to periodic solutions of the KdV equation.

Law 2: Multiplying Equation (3.105) by $2u$ and rewriting the equation, we get

$$(u^2)_t + (-4u^3 + 2uu_{xx} - (u_x)^2)_x = 0.$$

Here, $T = u^2$, $X = -4u^3 + 2uu_{xx} - (u_x)^2$ and the second conservation law is $\int_{-\infty}^{\infty} u^2 dx =$ constant.

Law 3: Again, multiplying Equation (3.105) by $(3u^2 - u_{xx})$ and rewriting the equation, we obtain

$$\left(u^3 + \frac{1}{2}(u_x)^2\right)_t + \left(-\frac{9}{2}u^4 + 3u^2 u_{xx} - 6u(u_x)^2 + u_x u_{xxx} - \frac{1}{2}(u_{xx})^2\right)_x = 0.$$

Here, $T = u^3 + \frac{1}{2}(u_x)^2$, $X = -\frac{9}{2}u^4 + 3u^2 u_{xx} - 6u(u_x)^2 + u_x u_{xxx} - \frac{1}{2}(u_{xx})^2$, and the third conservation law is $\int_{-\infty}^{\infty} (u^3)_t + \frac{1}{2}((u_x)^2) dx =$ constant.

Note: These conserved densities can be interpreted as mass, momentum, and energy for some physical systems. Due to the existence of so many conservation laws, the KdV equation plays a distinguished role, especially those of physical interest. But several other nonlinear partial differential equations also satisfy conservation laws and people are interested about the equations which has some physical applications.

Let us consider a more general equation

$$u_t - 6u^p u_x + u_{xxx} = 0, \quad p = 1, 2, \ldots \tag{3.106}$$

If $p = 1$, then Equation (3.106) is a KdV equation, and if $p = 2$, then Equation (3.106) is an MKdV equation.

Let us consider an MKdV equation as

$$u_t - 6u^2 u_x + u_{xxx} = 0. \tag{3.107}$$

This equation also possesses many polynomial conservation laws of which the first three conservation forms are given in the following:

Law 1: From Equation (3.107), we have

$$(u)_t + (-2u^3 + u_{xx})_x = 0.$$

Here, $T = u$, $X = -2u^3 + u_{xx}$, and the first conservation law for the MKdV equation is $\int_{-\infty}^{\infty} u \, dx = $ constant.

Law 2: Multiplying Equation (3.107) by $2v$ and rewriting the equation, we obtain

$$(u^2)_t + (-3u^4 + 2uu_{xx} - (u_x)^2)_x = 0.$$

Here, $T = u^2$, $X = -3u^4 + 2uu_{xx} - (u_x)^2$, and the second conservation law is $\int_{-\infty}^{\infty} u^2 \, dx = $ constant.

Law 3: Multiplying Equation (3.107) by $(4v^3 - 2v_{xx})$ and rewriting the equation, we get

$$(u^4 + (u_x)^2)_t + (-4u^6 + 4u^3 u_{xx} - 2u_x(6u^2 u_x - u_{xxx}) - (u_{xx})^2)_x = 0.$$

Here, $T = u^4 + (u_x)^2$, $X = -4u^6 + 4u^3 u_{xx} - 2u_x(6u^2 u_x - u_{xxx}) - (u_{xx})^2$, and the third conservation law is $\int_{-\infty}^{\infty} (u^4 + (u_x)^2) dx = $ constant.

However, a study of Equation (3.106) with $p \geq 3$ leads to the discovery of only three polynomial conservation laws. This apparent distinguished role is played by both the KdV equation and the modified KdV equation.

Miura transformation: If v is a solution of $Qv \equiv v_t - 6v^2 v_x + v_{xxx} = 0$. Then $u = v^2 + v_x$ is a solution of $Pu \equiv u_t - 6uu_x + u_{xxx} = 0$.

Let us put $u = v^2 + v_x$ in the equation $Pu \equiv u_t - 6uu_x + u_{xxx} = 0$ and we have

$$Pu = (v^2 + v_x)_t - 6(v^2 + v_x)(v^2 + v_x)_x + (v^2 + v_x)_{xxx},$$

$$\Rightarrow Pu = 2vv_t + v_{xt} - 12v^3v_x - 6v^2v_{xx} - 12v(v_x)^2 - 6v_xv_{xx}$$

$$+ 6v_xv_{xx} + 2vv_{xxx} + v_{xxxx},$$

$$\Rightarrow Pu = 2v(v_t - 6v^2v_x + v_{xxx}) + \frac{\partial}{\partial x}(v_t - 6v^2v_x + v_{xxx}),$$

$$\Rightarrow Pu = \left(2v + \frac{\partial}{\partial x}\right)(v_t - 6v^2v_x + v_{xxx}),$$

$$\Rightarrow Pu = \left(2v + \frac{\partial}{\partial x}\right)(Qv).$$

So, if $Qv = 0$, then u satisfies the KdV equation $Pu \equiv u_t - 6uu_x + u_{xxx} = 0$, provided $u = u_x + v^2$.

Gardner's generalization: One being with Gardner's generalization we know that the KdV equation is Galilean invariant and so introducing the following transformation $t' \equiv t$, $x' \equiv x + \frac{3}{2\epsilon^2 t}$, $u(x,t) \equiv u'(x', t') + \frac{1}{4\epsilon^2}$, $v(x,t) \equiv \epsilon\omega(x', t') + \frac{1}{2\epsilon}$, where the specific dependence on the formal parameter ϵ has been chosen to get the following desired results.

Now, $pu = 0 \Rightarrow u_t - 6uu_x + u_{xxx} = \left(2v + \frac{\partial}{\partial x}\right)(v_t - 6v^2v_x + v_{xxx}) = 0$. Putting $v = \epsilon\omega + \frac{1}{2\epsilon}$, we get $pu \equiv (2(\epsilon\omega + \frac{1}{2\epsilon}) + \frac{\partial}{\partial x})((\epsilon\omega + \frac{1}{2\epsilon})_t - 6(\epsilon\omega + \frac{1}{2\epsilon})^2(\epsilon\omega + \frac{1}{2\epsilon})_x + (\epsilon\omega + \frac{1}{2\epsilon})_{xxx}) = 0 \Rightarrow (1 + \epsilon\frac{\partial}{\partial x} + 2\epsilon^2\omega)(\omega_t - 6(\omega + \epsilon^2\omega^2)\omega_x + \omega_{xxx}) = 0$ [neglecting $\frac{1}{4\epsilon^2}$].

Also where we have dropped all primes and the Galilean transformation leaves the KdV equation invariant.

Now,

$$u = v^2 + v_x = \omega + \epsilon\omega_x + \epsilon^2\omega^2, \tag{3.108}$$

which is Gardner's generalization of u. Here, u is a function of x and t and ω is a function of x, t, and ϵ.

Now, let ω be a power series in ϵ with coefficients which are functions of u and x-derivatives of u, then ω can be written as

$$\omega(x, t; \epsilon) = \omega_0 + \epsilon\omega_1 + \epsilon^2\omega_2 + \cdots \tag{3.109}$$

or

$$\omega_x = \omega_{0x} + \epsilon\omega_{1x} + \epsilon^2\omega_{2x} + \cdots \tag{3.110}$$

and

$$\omega^2 = \omega_0^2 + \epsilon^2 \omega_1^2 + 2\epsilon\omega_0\omega_1 + \cdots. \qquad (3.111)$$

Now, using Equations (3.109)–(3.111) in (3.108), we get

$$u = \omega_0 + \epsilon(\omega_1 + \omega_{0x}) + \epsilon^2(\omega_2 + \omega_{1x} + \omega_0^2) + \cdots.$$

Comparing the coefficient of $\epsilon^0, \epsilon^1, \epsilon^2$ respectively we get $\omega_0 = u$, $\omega_1 = -\omega_{0x} = -u_x$, $\omega_2 = -\omega_{1x} - \omega_0^2 = u_{xx} - u^2$, etc. Using the above relation in (3.109), we get

$$\omega(x, t; \epsilon) = u - \epsilon u_x - \epsilon^2(u^2 - u_{xx}) + \cdots. \qquad (3.112)$$

So,

$$\left(1 + \epsilon\left(\frac{\partial}{\partial x} + 2\epsilon\omega\right)\right)[J\omega] = 0 \Rightarrow (1 + \epsilon M)[J\omega] = 0$$

where $\frac{\partial}{\partial x} + 2\epsilon\omega = M$ and $J\omega = \omega_t + (-3\omega^2 - 2\epsilon^2\omega^3 + \omega_{xx})_x = 0$.
Now,

$$J\omega = \omega_t + (-3\omega^2 - 2\epsilon^2\omega^3 + \omega_{xx})_x = 0 \qquad (3.113)$$

is called Gardner's equation. But in the form of (3.113), the coefficient of each power of ϵ is a conservation law for the KdV equation and there are infinitely many of them.

3.6.1   *Conserved quantity of KdV equation*

Let us consider the KdV equation

$$\frac{\partial\phi}{\partial\tau} + A\phi\frac{\partial\phi}{\partial\xi} + B\frac{\partial^3\phi}{\partial\xi^3} = 0. \qquad (3.114)$$

Let

$$I = \int_{-\infty}^{\infty} \phi^2 d\xi. \qquad (3.115)$$

Now, differentiating (3.115) under integration sign with respect to τ, we get

$$\frac{dI}{d\tau} = \int_{-\infty}^{\infty} 2\phi \frac{\partial \phi}{\partial \tau} d\xi$$

$$= 2 \int_{-\infty}^{\infty} \phi \left(-A\phi \frac{\partial \phi}{\partial \xi} - B \frac{\partial^3 \phi}{\partial \xi^3} \right) d\xi \quad \text{[from Equation (3.114)]}$$

$$= \left[-2A \frac{\phi^3}{3} \right]_{-\infty}^{\infty} - 2B \left[\left(\phi \frac{\partial^2 \phi}{\partial \xi^2} \right)_{-\infty}^{\infty} - \frac{1}{2} \int_{-\infty}^{\infty} \frac{d}{d\xi} \left(\frac{\partial \phi}{\partial \xi} \right)^2 d\xi \right].$$

$$= 0 \tag{3.116}$$

Since $\phi \to 0$, $\frac{\partial \phi}{\partial \xi} \to 0$ at $\xi \to \pm\infty$. Therefore, from (3.116), we get $\frac{dI}{d\tau} = 0$, i.e., $I = $ constant. There exists an infinite number of such conserved quantities like I.

3.7 Approximate Analytical Solutions

For a small perturbation, we expect that the solution will remain close to the soliton for some time. Therefore, the solution we seek will be roughly a soliton with a slowly changing shape and location plus a correction.

3.7.1 *Damped KdV equation*

Let us consider the KdV equation with damping term $c\phi$ when the constant c is small,

$$\frac{\partial \phi}{\partial \tau} + A\phi \frac{\partial \phi}{\partial \xi} + B \frac{\partial^3 \phi}{\partial \xi^3} + c\phi = 0. \tag{3.117}$$

Now,

$$\frac{dI}{d\tau} = \int_{-\infty}^{\infty} 2\phi \frac{\partial \phi}{\partial \tau} d\xi$$

$$= -2 \int_{-\infty}^{\infty} \phi \left(A\phi \frac{\partial \phi}{\partial \xi} + B \frac{\partial^3 \phi}{\partial \xi^3} + c\phi \right) d\xi$$

$$= -2c \int_{-\infty}^{\infty} \phi^2 d\xi \quad \text{[using Equation (3.116)]}$$

$$= -2cI. \tag{3.118}$$

The solution of Equation (3.118) is

$$I = I_0 e^{-2c(\tau - \tau_0)} \quad [I = I_0 \text{ at } \tau = \tau_0]. \tag{3.119}$$

Since $\phi = \phi_m(\tau) \text{sech}^2 \left(\frac{\xi - M(\tau)\tau}{\omega(\tau)} \right)$ is a solution of (3.117), where $\phi_m(\tau) = \frac{3M(\tau)}{A}$, $\omega(\tau) = \sqrt{\frac{4B}{M(\tau)}}$. So,

$$I = \int_{-\infty}^{\infty} \phi^2 d\xi = \int_{-\infty}^{\infty} \phi_m^2(\tau) \text{sech}^4 \left(\frac{\xi - M(\tau)\tau}{\omega(\tau)} \right) d\xi$$

$$= 2\phi_m^2 \omega(\tau) \int_0^1 (1 - t^2) dt \quad \left[\text{putting } t = \tanh \left(\frac{\xi - M(\tau)\tau}{\omega(\tau)} \right) \right]$$

$$= \frac{4}{3} \phi_m^2 \omega(\tau).$$

Hence,

$$I = \frac{4}{3} \phi_m^2(\tau_0) \omega(\tau_0) e^{-2c(\tau - \tau_0)}$$

where $\phi_m(\tau_0) = \frac{3M_0}{A}$, $\omega(\tau_0) = \sqrt{\frac{4B}{M_0}}$.

Hence, the solution of (3.117) is

$$\phi = \phi_m(\tau) \text{sech}^2 \left(\frac{\xi - M(\tau)\tau}{\omega(\tau)} \right) \tag{3.120}$$

where $\phi_m(\tau) = \frac{3M(\tau)}{A}$, $\omega(\tau) = \sqrt{\frac{4B}{M(\tau)}}$, and $M = M_0 e^{-\frac{4}{3}c(\tau - \tau_0)}$.

3.7.2 Force KdV equation

Let us consider the KdV equation with an external force $f_0 \cos(\omega\tau)$

$$\frac{\partial \phi}{\partial \tau} + A\phi \frac{\partial \phi}{\partial \xi} + B \frac{\partial^3 \phi}{\partial \xi^3} = f_0 \cos(\omega\tau). \tag{3.121}$$

Let the solution of (3.121) be

$$\phi = \phi_m(\tau) \text{sech}^2 \left(\frac{\xi - M(\tau)\tau}{\omega(\tau)} \right) \tag{3.122}$$

where $\phi_m(\tau) = \frac{3M(\tau)}{A}$ and $\omega(\tau) = \sqrt{\frac{4B}{M(\tau)}}$.

Therefore,

$$
\begin{aligned}
I &= \int_{-\infty}^{\infty} \phi^2 d\xi \\
&= \int_{-\infty}^{\infty} \phi_m^2(\tau) sech^4 \left(\frac{\xi - M(\tau)\tau}{w(\tau)} \right) d\xi \quad [from\ (3.122)] \\
&= \frac{24}{A^2} \sqrt{B} M^{\frac{3}{2}}(\tau).
\end{aligned}
$$

Again,

$$
\begin{aligned}
\frac{dI}{d\tau} &= 2f_0 \int_{-\infty}^{\infty} \cos(\omega\tau)\phi d\xi \quad [using\ (3.121)\ and\ (3.116)] \\
&= 2f_0 \cos(\omega\tau) \int_{-\infty}^{\infty} \phi_m(\tau) sech^2 \left(\frac{\xi - M(\tau)\tau}{w(\tau)} \right) d\xi \\
&= 4f_0 \cos(\omega\tau)\phi_m(\tau)w(\tau).
\end{aligned}
$$

After some elementary calculation, we get

$$
\frac{dM(\tau)}{d\tau} = \frac{2}{3} f_0 A \cos(\omega\tau).
$$

Integrating the above relation with respect to τ and using the initial condition $M(\tau) = M_0$ at $\tau = 0$, we get

$$
M(\tau) = \frac{2}{3w} f_0 A \sin(\omega\tau) + M_0. \tag{3.123}
$$

So, the solution of (3.121) is

$$
\phi = \phi_m(\tau) sech^2 \left(\frac{\xi - M(\tau)\tau}{w(\tau)} \right) \tag{3.124}
$$

where $\phi_m(\tau) = \frac{3M(\tau)}{A}$ and $w(\tau) = \sqrt{\frac{4B}{M(\tau)}}$.

3.7.3 *Damped-force KdV equation*

Let us consider the KdV equation with an external force $f_0 cos(\omega\tau)$ and a damped force c

$$
\frac{\partial\phi}{\partial\tau} + A\phi\frac{\partial\phi}{\partial\xi} + B\frac{\partial^3\phi}{\partial\xi^3} + c\phi = f_0 \cos(\omega\tau). \tag{3.125}
$$

Let the solution of (3.125) be

$$\phi = \phi_m(\tau) sech^2 \left(\frac{\xi - M(\tau)\tau}{\omega(\tau)} \right) \tag{3.126}$$

where $\phi_m(\tau) = \frac{3M(\tau)}{A}$ and $\omega(\tau) = \sqrt{\frac{4B}{M(\tau)}}$.

Therefore,

$$I = \int_{-\infty}^{\infty} \phi_m^2(\tau) sech^4 \left(\frac{\xi - M(\tau)\tau}{\omega(\tau)} \right) d\xi \quad [from \ (3.126)]$$

$$= \frac{24}{A^2} \sqrt{B} M^{\frac{3}{2}}(\tau).$$

Similarly, we get

$$\frac{dI}{d\tau} = -2c \int_{-\infty}^{\infty} \phi^2 d\xi + 2f_0 \int_{-\infty}^{\infty} \cos(\omega\tau)\phi d\xi.$$

So,

$$\frac{dI}{d\tau} + 2cI = 4f_0 \cos(\omega\tau)\phi_m(\tau)\omega(\tau).$$

After some elementary calculation, we get

$$\frac{dM(\tau)}{d\tau} + \frac{4}{3}cM(\tau) = \frac{2}{3}f_0 A \cos(\omega\tau).$$

Integrating the above relation with respect to τ and using the initial condition $M(\tau) = M_0$ at $\tau = 0$, we get

$$M(\tau) = M_0 e^{\frac{-4}{3}D\tau} + \frac{2f_0 A}{9\omega^2} \left[1 + \left(\frac{4D}{3\omega} \right)^2 \right]^{-1}$$

$$\times \left[3\omega \sin(\omega\tau) + 4D \cos(\omega\tau) - 4D e^{\frac{-4}{3}D\tau} \right]. \tag{3.127}$$

So, the solution of (3.125) is

$$\phi = \phi_m(\tau) sech^2 \left(\frac{\xi - M(\tau)\tau}{\omega(\tau)} \right) \tag{3.128}$$

where $\phi_m(\tau) = \frac{3M(\tau)}{A}$ and $\omega(\tau) = \sqrt{\frac{4B}{M(\tau)}}$.

Similarly, one can easily obtain the approximate analytical solution of the damped and or the forced KP/ZK equation.

3.8 Multisoliton and Hirota's Direct Method

In 1971, Ryogo Hirota [14] established a new method called "the Hirota direct method" to find the exact solution of the KdV equation for multiple collisions of solitons. This method can also be applicable for other nonlinear evolution equations such as the MKdV, sine-Gordon (SG), nonlinear Schrodinger (NLS), and Toda lattice (TL) equations.

Here, in the first step, nonlinear partial differential equations are converted to a quadratic form of dependent variables using suitable transformations.

In the second step, a special differential operator called Hirota D-operator is introduced to write the bilinear form of the equation as a polynomial of D-operator. It is called the Hirota bilinear form. There is no systematic way to construct the Hirota bilinear form for given nonlinear partial differential equations. In principle, all completely integrable nonlinear partial differential equations and difference equations can be put into the Hirota bilinear form. But the converse is not necessarily true, i.e., there exist some equations which are not integrable but have Hirota bilinear forms.

Finally, the Hirota method will use the perturbation expansion, in the Hirota bilinear form, considering the coefficients of the perturbation parameter and its powers separately. After that, we reach multisoliton solutions of the said equation. The Hirota direct method has taken a significant role in the study of integrable systems. Equations having Hirota bilinear form possess multisoliton solutions.

Hirota's direct method constructs multisoliton solutions to nonlinear evolution equations that are integrable. The idea was to transform new variables to enable new variable multisoliton solutions to appear in a simple form. The method turned out to be very effective and was quickly shown to give N-soliton solutions to the KdV, MKdV, SG, and NLS equations. It is also useful in constructing their Bäcklund transformations. The advantage of Hirota's method over the others is that it is algebraic rather than analytic. Accordingly, if one wants to find soliton solutions, Hirota's method is the fastest in producing results.

3.8.1 *Hirota's method*

If a function $f(x)$ is $(m + n)$ times differentiable, the Pade approximation of $f(x)$ of order (m, n) is the rational function

$$R(x) = \frac{p_0 + p_1 x + p_2 x^2 + \cdots + p_m x^m}{q_0 + q_1 x + q_2 x^2 + \cdots + q_n x^n} = \frac{G[x]}{F[x]}$$

which agrees with $f(x)$ to the highest possible order, i.e.,

$$f(0) = R(0)$$
$$f'(x) = R'(x)$$
$$\cdots$$
$$\cdots$$
$$f^{m+n}(0) = R^{m+n}(0).$$

From the Pade approximation, we can write $u = \frac{G(exp(kx-\omega t))}{F(exp(kx-\omega t))}$. Then,

$$u = \frac{G}{F}, \quad u_t = \frac{G_t F - G F_t}{F^2}, \quad u_x = \frac{G_x F - G F_x}{F^2},$$

$$u_{xx} = \frac{G_{xx} F^3 - G F^2 F_{xx} - 2 F^2 F_x G_x + 2 F F_x^2 G}{F^4}$$

$$u_{xxx} = \frac{G_{xxx}}{F} - \frac{3 G_{xx} F_x + 3 G_x F_{xx} + G F_{xxx}}{F^2}$$

$$+ 6 \frac{G_x F_x^2 + G F_{xx} F_x}{F^3} - \frac{G F_x^3}{F^4}.$$

Substitute these above terms in the KdV equation

$$u_x + 6 u u_x + U_{xxx} = 0 \tag{3.129}$$

$$\Rightarrow \frac{G_x F - G F_x}{F^2} + 6 \frac{G}{F} \frac{G_x F - G F_x}{F^2} - \frac{3 G_{xx} F_x + 3 G_x F_{xx} + G F_{xxx}}{F^2}$$

$$+ \frac{G_{xxx}}{F} + 6 \frac{G_x F_x^2 + G F_{xx} F_x}{F^3} - \frac{G F_x^3}{F^4} = 0. \tag{3.130}$$

Initially, Equation (3.129) might look more complicated. After some algebraic calculation, we get

$$G_t F - G F_t + G_{xxx} F - 3 G_{xx} F_x - 3 G_x F_{xx} - G F_{xxx} = 0$$

and

$$G G_x F^2 - G^2 F F_x + F G_x F_x^2 + F G F_{xx} F_x - G F_x^3 = 0.$$

So, a great deal of work is done. We introduce a new bilinear differentiation operator, the Hirota D-operator. The Hirota D-operator is for n-times differentiable function of f and g is defined by $D_x^n f \cdot g = (\partial_{x1} - \partial_{x2})^n f(x_1) g(x_2)|_{x_1 = x_2 = x}$.

3.8.2 *Multisoliton solution of the KdV equation*

We are going to obtain the multisoliton solution of the KdV equation by using the Hirota direct method. Let us assume a standard KdV equation as

$$u_t - 6uu_x + u_{xxx} = 0. \tag{3.131}$$

At first, we introduce the transformation $u(x,t) = -2\frac{\partial^2}{\partial x^2}(\log f) = 2\frac{\partial}{\partial x}\left(\frac{f'}{f}\right) = -2\frac{ff''-f^2}{f^2}\left[= \frac{G}{H}\right.$ form of the Pade approximation $\left.\right]$. Using this transformation in Equation (3.131), we get

$$ff_{xt} - f_xf_t + ff_{xxxx} - 4f_xf_{xxx} + 3f_{xx}^2 = 0. \tag{3.132}$$

This is the bilinear KdV form. Using the Hirota D-operator in Equation (3.132).

Now,

$$D_tD_x\{f \cdot f\} = \left(\frac{\partial}{\partial t} - \frac{\partial}{\partial \acute{t}}\right)\left(\frac{\partial}{\partial x} - \frac{\partial}{\partial \acute{x}}\right)\{f(x,t) \cdot f(\acute{x},\acute{t})\}|_{\acute{x}=x,\acute{t}=t}$$

$$= f_{xt}f + ff_{xt} - f_tf_x - f_xf_t$$

$$= 2(f_{xt}f - f_tf_x) \tag{3.133}$$

and

$$D_x^4\{f \cdot f\} = \left(\frac{\partial}{\partial x} - \frac{\partial}{\partial \acute{x}}\right)^4\{f(x,t) \cdot f(\acute{x},\acute{t})\}|_{\acute{x}=x,\acute{t}=t}$$

$$= f_{xxxx}f - 4f_{xxx}f_x + 6f_{xx}f_{xx} - 4f_xf_{xxx} + ff_{xxxx}$$

$$= 2(f_{xxxx}f - 4f_{xxx}f_x + 3f_{xx}^2). \tag{3.134}$$

Using relations (3.133) and (3.134) in (3.132), we get the Hirota bilinear form as

$$P(D)\{f \cdot f\} = (D_xD_t + D_x^4)\{f \cdot f\} = 0. \tag{3.135}$$

Finally, putting $f = 1 + \epsilon f_1 + \epsilon^2 f_2 + \cdots$ into Equation (3.135), we obtain

$$P(D)\{f \cdot f\} = P(D)\{1 \cdot 1\} + \epsilon P(D)\{f_1 \cdot 1 + 1 \cdot f_1\}$$

$$+ \epsilon^2 P(D)\{f_2 \cdot 1 + f_1 \cdot f_1 + 1 \cdot f_2\}$$

$$+ \epsilon^3 P(D)\{f_3 \cdot 1 + f_2 \cdot f_1 + f_1 \cdot f_2 + 1 \cdot f_3\} + \cdots = 0. \tag{3.136}$$

One-soliton solution: To obtain the one soliton solution of the KdV equation, we consider $f = 1 + \epsilon f_1$, where $f_1 = e^{\theta_1}$ and $\theta_1 = k_1 x + \omega_1 t + \alpha_1$. Also, $f_j = 0$ for all $j \geq 2$. Putting $f = 1 + \epsilon f_1$ into Equation (3.136). We need to equate the coefficients of ϵ^0, ϵ, and ϵ^2 to make them zero.

The coefficient of ϵ^0 is $P(D)\{1 \cdot 1\} = 0$ (since $P(0,0)\{1\} = 0$).

The coefficient of ϵ is

$$P(D)\{1 \cdot f_1 + f_1 \cdot 1\} = P(\partial)e^{\theta_1} + P(-\partial)e^{\theta_1} = 2P(p_1)e^{\theta_1} = 0.$$

We have the dispersion relation $P(p_1) = 0$ which implies $\omega_1 = -k_1^3$. The coefficient of ϵ^2 vanishes trivially since

$$P(D)\{f_1 \cdot f_1\} = P(D)\{e^{\theta_1} \cdot e^{\theta_1}\} = P(p_1 - p_1)e^{2\theta_1} = 0.$$

Finally, without loss of generality, we may set $\epsilon = 1$ so $f = 1 + e^{\theta_1}$ and the one-soliton solution of the KdV Equation (3.131) is

$$u(x,t) = -\frac{k_1^2}{2}sech^2\left(\frac{\theta_1}{2}\right) \tag{3.137}$$

where $\theta_1 = k_1 x - k_1^3 t + \alpha_1$.

Two-soliton solution: To obtain the two-soliton solution of the KdV equation, we consider $f = 1 + \epsilon f_1 + \epsilon^2 f_2$, where $f_1 = e^{\theta_1} + e^{\theta_2}$ and $\theta_i = k_i x + \omega_i t + \alpha_i$ for $i = 1, 2$. Also, $f_j = 0$ for all $j \geq 3$. Putting $f = 1 + \epsilon f_1 + \epsilon^2 f_2$ into Equation (3.136). Equating the coefficients of ϵ^0, ϵ, ϵ^2, ϵ^3, and ϵ^4 and making them to zero, the coefficient of ϵ^0 is $P(D)\{1 \cdot 1\} = P(0,0)\{1\} = 0$.

The coefficient of ϵ is

$$P(D)\{1 \cdot f_1 + f_1 \cdot 1\} = 2P(\partial)\{e^{\theta_1} + e^{\theta_2}\} = 2[P(\partial)e^{\theta_1} + P(\partial)e^{\theta_2}] = 0,$$

which implies $P(p_i) = k_i^4 + k_i \omega_i = 0$, i.e., $\omega_i = -k_i^3$ for $i = 1, 2$.

The coefficient of ϵ^2 becomes

$$P(D)\{1 \cdot f_2 + f_2 \cdot 1\} + P(D)\{f_1 \cdot f_1\}$$
$$= 2P(\partial)f_2 + P(D)\{(e^{\theta_1} + e^{\theta_2}) \cdot (e^{\theta_1} + e^{\theta_2})\}$$
$$= 2[P(\partial)f_2 + P(D)\{e^{\theta_1}e^{\theta_2}\}]$$
$$= 2[P(\partial)f_2 + P(p_1 - p_2)e^{\theta_1+\theta_2}]$$
$$= 0.$$

This makes f_2 to have the form $f_2 = A(1,2)e^{\theta_1+\theta_2}$. If we put f_2 in the above equation, we obtain $A(1,2)$ as

$$A(1,2) = -\frac{P(p_1 - p_2)}{P(p_1 + p_2)} = \frac{(k_1 - k_2)^2}{(k_1 + k_2)^2}. \tag{3.138}$$

Since $f_3 = 0$, the coefficient of ϵ^3 turns out to be

$$P(D)\{f_1 \cdot f_2 + f_2 \cdot f_1\}$$
$$= 2A(1,2)[P(D)\{(e^{\theta_1})(e^{\theta_1+\theta_2})\} + P(D)\{(e^{\theta_2})(e^{\theta_1+\theta_2})\}]$$
$$= 2A(1,2)[P(p_2)e^{2\theta_1+\theta_2} + P(p_1)e^{\theta_1+2\theta_2}]$$

and this is already zero since $P(p_i) = 0$, $i = 1, 2$. The coefficient of ϵ^4 also vanishes trivially. At last, we may set $\epsilon = 1$, thus $f = 1 + e^{\theta_1} + e^{\theta_2} + A(1,2)e^{\theta_1+\theta_2}$ and the two-soliton solution of the KdV Equation (3.131) is given by

$$u(x,t)$$
$$= -2\frac{\{k_1^2 e^{\theta_1} + k_2^2 e^{\theta_2} + A(1,2)(k_2^2 e^{\theta_1} + k_1^2 e^{\theta_2})e^{\theta_1+\theta_2} + 2(k_1 - k_2)^2 e^{\theta_1+\theta_2}\}}{(1 + e^{\theta_1} + e^{\theta_2} + A(1,2)e^{\theta_1+\theta_2})^2}$$
$$\tag{3.139}$$

where $\theta_i = k_i x - k_i^3 t + \alpha_i$, $i = 1, 2$, and $A(1,2) = \frac{(k_1 - k_2)^2}{(k_1 + k_2)^2}$.

Three-soliton solution: To obtain the three-soliton solution of the KdV equation, we consider $f = 1 + \epsilon f_1 + \epsilon^2 f_2 + \epsilon^3 f_3$, where $f_1 = e^{\theta_1} + e^{\theta_2} + e^{\theta_3}$ and $\theta_i = k_i x + \omega_i t + \alpha_i$ for $i = 1, 2, 3$. Also, $f_j = 0$ for all $j \geq 4$. Putting $f = 1 + \epsilon f_1 + \epsilon^2 f_2 + \epsilon^3 f_3$ into Equation (3.136) and equating the coefficients of ϵ^m, $m = 0, 1, 2, 3, 4, 5, 6$, and making them to zero. The coefficient of ϵ^0 is identically zero. By the coefficient of ϵ^1, we have

$$P(D)\{1 \cdot f_1 + f_1 \cdot 1\} = 2P(\partial)\{e^{\theta_1} + e^{\theta_2} + e^{\theta_3}\} = 0,$$

which implies $P(p_i)0$, i.e., $\omega_i = -k_i^3$ for $i = 1, 2, 3$. From the coefficient of ϵ^2, we get

$$-P(\partial)f_2 = [(k_1 - k_2)(\omega_1 - \omega_2) + (k_1 - k_2)^4]e^{\theta_1+\theta_2}$$
$$+ [(k_1 - k_3)(\omega_1 - \omega_3) + (k_1 - k_3)^4]e^{\theta_1+\theta_3}$$
$$+ [(k_2 - k_3)(\omega_2 - \omega_3) + (k_2 - k_3)^4]e^{\theta_2+\theta_3}.$$

This makes f_2 to have the form $f_2 = A(1,2)e^{\theta_1+\theta_2} + A(1,3)e^{\theta_1+\theta_3} + A(2,3)e^{\theta_2+\theta_3}$. If we put f_2 in the above equation, we obtain $A(i,j)$ as

$$A(i,j) = -\frac{P(p_i - p_j)}{P(p_i + p_j)} = \frac{(k_i - k_j)^2}{(k_i + k_j)^2}. \tag{3.140}$$

Here, $i,j = 1,2,3, i < j$. The coefficient of ϵ^3 becomes

$$-P(\partial)f_3 = e^{\theta_1+\theta_2+\theta_3}\{A(1,2)P(p_3 - p_2 - p_1) + A(1,3)P(p_2 - p_1 - p_3)$$
$$+ A(2,3)P(p_1 - p_2 - p_3)\}.$$

Hence, f_3 should be in the form of $f_3 = Be^{\theta_1+\theta_2+\theta_3}$. So, the above equation gives

$$B = -[A(1,2)P(p_3 - p_2 - p_1) + A(1,3)P(p_2 - p_1 - p_3)$$
$$+ A(2,3)P(p_1 - p_2 - p_3)]/[P(p_1 + p_2 + p_3)].$$

If we make all the simplifications by using $\omega_i = -k_i^3$ for $i = 1,2,3$, we see that the above expression is equivalent to $B = A(1,2)A(1,3)A(2,3)$. Since $f_4 = 0$, from the coefficient of ϵ^4, we have

$$P(D)\{f_1 \cdot f_3 + f_3 \cdot f_1 + f_2 \cdot f_2\} = 0.$$

After some calculations, the above equation becomes

$$e^{2\theta_1+\theta_2+\theta_3}[BP(p_2 + p_3) + A(1,2)A(1,3)P(p_2 - p_3)]$$
$$+ e^{\theta_1+2\theta_2+\theta_3}[BP(p_1 + p_3) + A(1,2)A(2,3)P(p_1 - p_3)]$$
$$+ e^{\theta_1+\theta_2+2\theta_3}[BP(p_1 + p_2) + A(1,3)A(2,3)P(p_1 - p_2)] = 0.$$

This is satisfied by $B = A(1,2)A(1,3)A(2,3)$. Finally, the coefficient of ϵ^5 and ϵ^6 also vanishes automatically. We set $\epsilon = 1$, therefore, $f = 1 + e^{\theta_1} + e^{\theta_2} + e^{\theta_3} + A(1,2)e^{\theta_1+\theta_2} + A(1,3)e^{\theta_1+\theta_3} + A(2,3)e^{\theta_2+\theta_3} + Be^{\theta_1+\theta_2+\theta_3}$. So, the three-soliton solution of the KdV Equation (3.131) is

$$u(x,t) = -2\frac{L(x,t)}{M(x,t)} \tag{3.141}$$

where

$$L(x,t) = e^{\theta_1+\theta_2}[2(k_1 - k_2)^2 + 2(k_1 - k_2)^2 A(1,3)A(2,3)e^{2\theta_3}$$
$$+ A(1,2)k_1^2 e^{\theta_2} + A(1,2)k_2^2 e^{\theta_1}]$$
$$+ e^{\theta_1+\theta_3}[2(k_1 - k_3)^2 + 2(k_1 - k_3)^2 A(1,2)A(2,3)e^{2\theta_2}$$
$$+ A(1,3)k_1^2 e^{\theta_3} + A(1,3)k_3^2 e^{\theta_1}]$$
$$+ e^{\theta_2+\theta_3}[2(k_2 - k_3)^2 + 2(k_2 - k_3)^2 A(1,2)A(1,3)e^{2\theta_1}$$
$$+ A(2,3)k_2^2 e^{\theta_3} + A(2,3)k_3^2 e^{\theta_2}] + k_1^2 e^{\theta_1} + k_2^2 e^{\theta_2} + k_3^2 e^{\theta_3}$$
$$+ Be^{\theta_1+\theta_2+\theta_3}[A(1,2)k_3^2 e^{\theta_1+\theta_2} + A(1,3)k_2^2 e^{\theta_1+\theta_3} + A(2,3)k_1^2 e^{\theta_2+\theta_3}]$$
$$+ e^{\theta_1+\theta_2+\theta_3}[A(1,2)(k_1^2 + k_2^2 + k_3^2 + 2k_1k_2 - 2k_1k_3 - 2k_2k_3)$$
$$+ A(1,3)(k_1^2 + k_2^2 + k_3^2 + 2k_1k_3 - 2k_1k_2 - 2k_2k_3)$$
$$+ A(2,3)(k_1^2 + k_2^2 + k_3^2 + 2k_2k_3 - 2k_1k_2 - 2k_1k_3)$$
$$+ B(k_1^2 + k_2^2 + k_3^2 + 2k_1k_2 + 2k_1k_3 + 2k_2k_3) \tag{3.142}$$

and

$$M(x,t) = [1 + e^{\theta_1} + e^{\theta_2} + e^{\theta_3} + A(1,2)e^{\theta_1+\theta_2} + A(1,3)e^{\theta_1+\theta_3}$$
$$+ A(2,3)e^{\theta_2+\theta_3} + Be^{\theta_1+\theta_2+\theta_3}]^2 \tag{3.143}$$

for $\theta_i = k_i x - k_i^3 t + \alpha_i$, $A(i,j) = \frac{(k_i-k_j)^2}{(k_i+k_j)^2}$ for $i,j = 1,2,3, i < j$, and $B = A(1,2)A(1,3)A(2,3)$.

3.8.3 *Multisoliton solution of the KP equation*

To obtain the multisoliton solution for the KP equation by using the Hirota direct method, let us assume the KP equation as

$$(u_t - 6uu_x + u_{xxx})_x + 3u_{yy} = 0. \tag{3.144}$$

At first, we introduce the transformation $u(x,t) = -2\frac{\partial^2}{\partial x^2}(\log f) = 2\frac{\partial}{\partial x}\left(\frac{f'}{f}\right) = -2\frac{ff''-f^2}{f^2}$. Using this transformation in Equation (3.144), we get

$$ff_{xt} - f_x f_t + ff_{xxxx} - 4f_x f_{xxx} + 3f_{xx}^2 + 3f_{yy} - 3f_y^2 = 0. \tag{3.145}$$

This is the bilinear KP form. After that, we use the Hirota D-operator in Equation (3.145) and we get the Hirota bilinear form as

$$P(D)\{f \cdot f\} = (D_x D_t + D_x^4 + 3D_y^2)\{f \cdot f\} = 0. \tag{3.146}$$

Finally, putting $f = 1 + \epsilon f_1 + \epsilon^2 f_2 + \cdots$ into Equation (3.146), we obtain

$$P(D)\{f \cdot f\} = P(D)\{1 \cdot 1\} + \epsilon P(D)\{f_1 \cdot 1 + 1 \cdot f_1\}$$
$$+ \epsilon^2 P(D)\{f_2 \cdot 1 + f_1 \cdot f_1 + 1 \cdot f_2\}$$
$$+ \epsilon^3 P(D)\{f_3 \cdot 1 + f_2 \cdot f_1 + f_1 \cdot f_2 + 1 \cdot f_3\} + \cdots = 0. \tag{3.147}$$

One-soliton solution: To obtain one-soliton solution of the KP equation, we consider $f = 1 + \epsilon f_1$ where $f_1 = e^{\theta_1}$ and $\theta_1 = k_1 x + l_1 y + w_1 t + \alpha_1$. Also, $f_j = 0$ for all $j \geq 2$. We put $f = 1 + \epsilon f_1$ into Equation (3.147) and then equate the coefficients of ϵ^0, ϵ, and ϵ^2 and make them zero. The coefficient of ϵ^0 is $P(D)\{1 \cdot 1\} = 0$ (since $P(0,0)\{1\} = 0$). By the coefficient of ϵ,

$$P(D)\{1 \cdot f_1 + f_1 \cdot 1\} = P(\partial)e^{\theta_1} + P(-\partial)e^{\theta_1} = 2P(p_1)e^{\theta_1} = 0.$$

We have the dispersion relation $P(p_1) = 0$ which implies $w_1 = -\frac{k_1^4 + 3l_1^2}{k_1}$.

Finally, without loss of generality, we may set $\epsilon = 1$ so $f = 1 + e^{\theta_1}$ and one-soliton solution of the KP equation (3.144) is

$$u(x, y, t) = -\frac{k_1^2}{2} \operatorname{sech}^2 \left(\frac{\theta_1}{2} \right) \tag{3.148}$$

where $\theta_1 = k_1 x - \left(\frac{k_1^4 + 3l_1^2}{k_1} \right) t + l_1 y + \alpha_1$.

Two-soliton solution: To obtain two-soliton solution of the KP equation, we consider $f = 1 + \epsilon f_1 + \epsilon^2 f_2$ where $f_1 = e^{\theta_1} + e^{\theta_2}$ and $\theta_i = k_i x + w_i t + l_i y + \alpha_i$ (for $i = 1, 2$). Also, $f_j = 0$ for all $j \geq 3$. We put $f = 1 + \epsilon f_1 + \epsilon^2 f_2$ into Equation (3.147) and then equate the coefficient of ϵ^0, ϵ, ϵ^2, ϵ^3, and ϵ^4 and make them zero. We shall only examine the nontrivial ones which are the coefficients of ϵ^1 and ϵ^2. From the coefficient of ϵ^1, we have

$$P(D)\{1 \cdot f_1 + f_1 \cdot 1\} = 2P(\partial)\{e^{\theta_1} + e^{\theta_2}\} = 0$$

which implies $P(p_i) = k_i^4 + k_i\omega_i + 3l_i^2 = 0$, i.e., $\omega_i = -\frac{k_i^4 + 3l_i^2}{k_i}$ for $i = 1, 2$. The coefficient of ϵ^2 becomes

$$P(D)\{1 \cdot f_2 + f_2 \cdot 1\} + P(D)\{f_1 \cdot f_1\}$$
$$= 2P(\partial)f_2 + P(D)\{(e^{\theta_1} \cdot e^{\theta_2}) + (e^{\theta_2} \cdot e^{\theta_1})\}$$
$$= 2[P(\partial)f_2 + P(p_1 - p_2)e^{\theta_1+\theta_2}] = 0.$$

This makes f_2 to have the form $f_2 = A(1,2)e^{\theta_1+\theta_2}$. If we put f_2 in the above equation, we obtain $A(1,2)$ as

$$A(1,2) = -\frac{P(p_1 - p_2)}{P(p_1 + p_2)}$$
$$= \frac{k_1\omega_2 + k_2\omega_1 + 4k_1^3k_2 - 6k_1^2k_2^2 + 4k_1k_2^3 + 6l_1l_2}{k_1\omega_2 + k_2\omega_1 + 4k_1^3k_2 + 6k_1^2k_2^2 + 4k_1k_2^3 + 6l_1l_2}. \quad (3.149)$$

At last, we may set $\epsilon = 1$, thus $f = 1 + e^{\theta_1} + e^{\theta_2} + A(1,2)e^{\theta_1+\theta_2}$ and the two-soliton solution of the KP equation is given by

$$u = -2 \times [\{k_1^2 e^{\theta_1} + k_2^2 e^{\theta_2} + [(k_1 - k_2)^2 + A(1,2)((k_1 + k_2)^2 + k_2^2 e^{\theta_1}$$
$$+ k_1^2 e^{\theta_2})]e^{\theta_1+\theta_2}\}]/[(1 + e^{\theta_1} + e^{\theta_2} + A(1,2)e^{\theta_1+\theta_2})^2] \quad (3.150)$$

where $\theta_i = k_i x - \left(\frac{k_i^4 + 3l_i^2}{k_i}\right)t + l_i y + \alpha_i$, $i = 1, 2$, and $A(1,2)$ is as given in (3.149).

References

[1] J. S. Russell, *Report of the 14th Meeting of the British Association for the Advancement of Science.* London: John Murray (1844), pp. 311–390.
[2] J. Boussinesq, *Memoires presentes par divers savants. l'Acad. des Sci. Inst. Nat. France* XXIII, 1–680 (1877).
[3] N. J. Zabusky and M. D. Kruskal, *Phys. Rev. Lett.* 15, 240–243 (1965).
[4] R. M. Miura, C. S. Gardner, and M. D. Kruskal, *J. Math. Phys.* 9, 1204–1209 (1968).
[5] M. Tabor, *Ch. 7 in Chaos and Integrability in Nonlinear Dynamics: An Introduction.* New York: Wiley (1989), pp. 278–321.
[6] P. Lax, *Comm. Pure Appl. Math.* 21, 467–490 (1968).
[7] D. J. Korteweg and G. de Vries, *Philos. Mag. Ser.* 5(39), 422–443 (1985).
[8] H. Schamel, *J. Plasma Phys.* 9, 377 (1973).
[9] H. Bateman, *Mon. Weather Rev.* 43(4), 163–170 (1915).

[10] J. M. Burgers, *In Advances in Applied Mechanics*, Vol. 1, pp. 171–199 (1948).

[11] B. B. Kadomtsev and V. I. Petviashvili, *Sov. Phys. Dokl.* 15, 539–541 (1970)

[12] R. Grimshaw and W. K. Melville, *Stud. Appl. Math.* 80, 3 (1989).

[13] W. Malfliet, *Math. Meth. Appl. Sci.* 28, 2031 (2005).

[14] R. Hirota, *Phys. Rev. Lett.* 27, 1192 (1971).

Chapter 4

RPT and Some Evolution Equations

4.1 Perturbation Technique

The perturbation technique is a special technique of applied mathematics to find the approximate solution of a complex problem by starting from the exact solution of a relatively simple problem. The methods rely on a small dimensionless parameter, called perturbation parameter, denoted by ϵ that indicates the strength of the complexity of the problem. In this method, we break the main problem into two parts: the solvable part and the perturbation part. After finding the exact solution of the solvable part, the approximate solution of the main problem is obtained as a power series of the small perturbation parameter ϵ. The solution ultimately comes as a series of ϵ that satisfy the problem up to a certain order of ϵ [1]. In the perturbation method, we solve the simplified form of the original problem and then add corrections to improve the solution. Initially, we consider the solution as an infinite series in terms of perturbation parameter ϵ. The infinite perturbation series can be written as $y(x) = y_0(x) + \epsilon y_1(x) + \epsilon^2 y_2(x) + \cdots$, where ϵ is the perturbation parameter and y_0 is the exact solution of the solvable part. The terms $y_1(x), y_2(x), \ldots$ are higher-order terms improving the solution.

If a slight change in perturbation parameter induces a small change in solution, then the problem is called *regular perturbation problem*. On the contrary, if small changes in perturbation parameter induce a huge change in the solution, the problem is called *singular perturbation problem*.

In general, the exact solutions to the problems of fluid mechanics, solid mechanics, classical mechanics, and physics cannot be obtained because of the nonlinearity, inhomogeneities, and general boundary conditions that arise in these problems. Only approximate solutions for such problems exist, and hence people use the perturbation technique. The beauty of the technique is that it is an analytical technique. This technique involves keeping certain elements, neglecting some, and approximating the rest. To do this, the order of magnitude of the different elements should be taken care of by comparing those with each other and with the basic elements of the system. This process is called non-dimensionalization, where we make the variable dimensionless. The variables are made dimensionless before attempting to make any approximations.

Let us consider the motion of a particle of mass m is in simple harmonic motion having the constant k and a viscous damper having the coefficient ν. So, the equation of motion is

$$m\frac{d^2u}{dt^2} + \nu\frac{du}{dt} + ku = 0 \tag{4.1}$$

where u is the displacement of the particle and t is the time. If the particle was released from rest from the position u_0, the initial conditions are

$$u(0) = u_0; \frac{du}{dt}(0) = 0. \tag{4.2}$$

Here, u is the dependent variable and t is the independent variable. Now, the variables need to be dimensionless by using proper characteristic distance and a proper characteristic time of the system. The displacement u can be made dimensionless by using the initial displacement u_0 and the time t can be made dimensionless by using the inverse of the system's natural frequency $\omega_0 = \sqrt{k/m}$. Thus, by putting $u^* = \frac{u}{u_0}$ and $t^* = \omega_0 t$ where an asterisk denotes dimensionless quantities, we have (from 4.1)

$$m\omega_0^2 u_0\frac{d^2u^*}{dt^{*2}} + \nu\omega_0 u_0\frac{du^*}{dt^*} + ku_0 u^* = 0. \tag{4.3}$$

Dividing throughout by the factor $m\omega_0^2 u_0$, we get

$$\frac{d^2u^*}{dt^{*2}} + \nu^*\frac{du^*}{dt^*} + u^* = 0 \tag{4.4}$$

where $\nu^* = \frac{\nu}{m\omega_0}$. The initial condition becomes

$$u^*(0) = 1; \frac{du^*}{dt^*}(0) = 0. \tag{4.5}$$

Thus, the solution to the present problem depends only on the single parameter ν^*, which represents the ratio of the damping force to the inertial force.

On the other hand, if we add a nonlinear function of u as a additional force term, the equation of motion becomes

$$m\frac{d^2u}{dt^2} + \nu\frac{du}{dt} + ku + k_1u^2 = 0 \tag{4.6}$$

where k and k_1 are constants. Introducing the same dimensionless quantities as in the preceding example, we get the equation of motion as

$$\frac{d^2u^*}{dt^{*2}} + \nu^*\frac{du^*}{dt^*} + u^* + \epsilon u^{*2} = 0 \tag{4.7}$$

where $\nu^* = \frac{\nu}{m\omega_0}$ and $\epsilon = \frac{k_1u_0}{k}$ are two dimensionless parameters. ν^* represents the ratio of the damping force to the inertial force or the linear restoring force and ϵ represents the ratio of the nonlinear and linear restoring force. Equation (4.7) is weakly nonlinear if u^* is small, i.e., k_1u_0/k is small. Even if k_1 is small compared with k, the nonlinearity will not be small if u_0 is large compared with k/k_1. Thus, ϵ is the parameter that characterizes the nonlinearity.

This is how the perturbation parameter ϵ takes a lead role in this technique. Now, we shall explain the perturbation technique. Let us consider a function $u(x, \epsilon)$ that satisfies the differential equation $L(u, x, \epsilon) = 0$ and the boundary condition $B(u, \epsilon) = 0$, where x is the independent variable and ϵ is a parameter. In general, these problems cannot be solved exactly. However, if we consider an $\epsilon(= \epsilon_0)$ (say) for which the above problem can be solved exactly, and let $u = u_0(x)$ be the solution of the problem for $\epsilon = \epsilon_0$, then, in general, we find the solution (for small ϵ) in the series power of ϵ as

$$u(x, \epsilon) = u_0(x) + \epsilon u_1(x) + \epsilon^2 u_2(x) + \cdots$$

where u_i are independent of ϵ and $u_0(x)$ is the solution of the problem for $\epsilon = \epsilon_0$. We first substitute this expansion into $L(u, x, \epsilon) = 0$ and $B(u, \epsilon) = 0$, and after that we collect the coefficients of each power of ϵ. This will help us in obtaining the result. Hence, in general, we can explain perturbation as follows: the full solution A can be expressed as a series in the small parameter (say ϵ), like the following

$$A = A_0 + \epsilon A_1 + \epsilon^2 A_2 + \cdots \tag{4.8}$$

where A_0 is the exact solution of the solvable part and $A_1, A_2, \ldots$ are the higher-order terms obtained by solving the perturbation problems in an iterative way. Naturally, as ϵ is considered small, so the higher-order terms of this series become successively smaller. Ultimately, the solution is obtained as a truncated series of the above series by keeping up certain order of A. The first approximate solution is

$$A \approx A_0 + \epsilon A_1. \tag{4.9}$$

So, the perturbation theory is considered in terms of the order to which the perturbation is carried out: first-order perturbation theory or second-order perturbation theory. If the perturbed states are degenerated, the theory is called singular perturbation theory. In the singular case, we must take some extra care and the theory is slightly more complicated (which is not our concern).

As an example, let us find the solution of the following differential equation by using perturbation technique:

$$\frac{d^2x}{dt^2} = -\frac{1}{(1+\epsilon x)^2}, \quad for \ 0 < t, \tag{4.10}$$

with initial condition

$$x(0) = 0, \quad \frac{dx(0)}{dt} = 1.$$

Considering the assumption for x as

$$x \approx x_0(t) + \epsilon^\alpha x_1(t) + \cdots \tag{4.11}$$

and substituting (4.11) into (4.10), we get

$$\frac{1}{(1+\epsilon x)^2} = 1 - 2\epsilon x + 3\epsilon^2 x^2 + \cdots$$

$$\approx 1 - 2\epsilon(x_0 + \epsilon^\alpha x_1 + \cdots + 3\epsilon^2(x_0 + \cdots)^2 + \cdots$$

$$= 1 - 2\epsilon x_0 + \cdots. \tag{4.12}$$

With this, the differential equation (4.10) becomes

$$x_0'' + \epsilon^\alpha x_1'' + \cdots = -1 + 2\epsilon x_0 + \cdots \tag{4.13}$$

and the initial conditions will be

$$x_0(0) + \epsilon^\alpha x_1(0) + \cdots = 0$$

$$x_0'(0) + \epsilon^\alpha x_1'(0) + \cdots = 0.$$

Now, we break the above equations into problems depending on the power of ϵ and get $O(1)$

$$\left.\begin{array}{l} x_0'' = -1 \\ x_0(0) = 0, \quad x_0'(0) = 1. \end{array}\right\} \tag{4.14}$$

The solution of this problem is $x_0 = t(1 - \frac{1}{2}t)$. With this the next highest term is left in (4.13) is $2\epsilon x_0$. The term available to balance with this is $\epsilon^\alpha x_1$, and from this we conclude $\alpha = 1$. This gives us the following problem $O(\epsilon)$:

$$\left.\begin{array}{l} x_1'' = 2x_0 \\ x_1(0) = 0, \quad x_1'(0) = 0. \end{array}\right\} \tag{4.15}$$

The solution of this problem is $x_1 = \frac{1}{12}t^3(4 - t)$.

Therefore, a two-term expansion of the solution is

$$x \approx t\left(1 - \frac{1}{2}t\right) + \frac{1}{12}\epsilon t^3(4 - t) + \cdots . \tag{4.16}$$

4.2 Reductive Perturbation Technique

The reductive perturbation technique (RPT) is a particular type of perturbation method that is different from the usual perturbation method discussed in the previous section. This method is considered as a method that reduces a set of nonlinear partial differential equations (PDEs) to a single solvable nonlinear evolution equation (NEE). Starting from fluid equations, the evolution equation is obtained in two steps or more. In the first step, the original coordinates x and t are transformed to new stretched coordinates ξ and τ (say) depending on the nature of the problem. Then, the perturbation parameter ϵ is introduced which has a connection with the wavenumber (and hence, with the frequency and the dispersion relation). In the second step, the same ϵ is used as a perturbation parameter where the dependent variables are expanded as a power series of ϵ in the neighbourhood of the equilibrium point. The perturbation of the parameters is considered at a near-equilibrium point not for finding the solution but for obtaining an evolution equation. It can be applied to more general systems that include dissipation/dispersion or both. It shows that for long waves, the set of equations can be reduced to Burgers' equation or the KdV equation, for a system with dissipation or dispersion, respectively. If we consider the propagation of a modulated wave of small amplitude, then the evolution equation would be a nonlinear Schrodinger equation (NLSE).

If the system is weakly dispersive, i.e., the wavenumber k is much less than $\epsilon^{1/2}$ ($k \ll \epsilon^{1/2}$), the hyperbolic approximation is justified, and the expansion and the stretching of RPT may be considered as

$$U = U^{(0)} + \epsilon U^{(1)} + \cdots \tag{4.17}$$

$$\xi = \epsilon^{1/2}(x - \lambda_0 t), \quad \tau = \epsilon^{3/2} t. \tag{4.18}$$

This will enable us to reduce a general dispersive system to the KdV equation, where $U, U^{(0)}$, and $U^{(1)}$ are the average velocity of the fluid, solution of the equilibrium point, and higher-order perturbation term, respectively. For example, we may consider

$$U_{,t} + AU_{,x} + K_1[K_2(K_3 U_{,x}),_x],_x = 0. \tag{4.19}$$

Similarly, in case of dissipative system, we get

$$\frac{\partial \phi^{(1)}}{\partial \tau} + \alpha \phi^{(1)} \frac{\partial \phi^{(1)}}{\partial \xi} + \nu \frac{\partial^3 \phi^{(1)}}{\partial \xi^3} = 0 \tag{4.20}$$

where $\phi^{(1)}$ may be considered as the first-order perturbation value of the potential. In 1968, Taniuti and Wei [2] first applied RPT to study the propagation of the long wave in both dispersive and dissipative systems in the framework of cold plasma. Su and Gardner [3] also obtained similar results independently. They considered the system of equation as

$$\frac{\partial U}{\partial t} + A \frac{\partial U}{\partial X} + \left\{ \sum_{\beta=1}^{s} \prod_{\alpha=1}^{p} \left(H_\alpha^\beta \frac{\partial}{\partial t} + K_\alpha^\beta \frac{\partial}{\partial x} \right) \right\} \cdot U = 0, \quad (p \geq 2) \tag{4.21}$$

where A, H_α^β, and K_α^β are $n \times n$ matrices and all of which are functions of U. So, in this method, a general transformation is introduced where the expansion of a stable solution U_0 in a small parameter is considered. It is assumed that at least one real and nondegenerate eigenvalue of A_0 (is denoted by λ_0) exists. This transformation is called Gardner–Morikawa transformation [4],

$$\left. \begin{array}{l} U = U_0 + \epsilon U_1 + \cdots \\ \xi = \epsilon^\alpha (x - \lambda_0 t) \\ \tau = \epsilon^{\alpha+1} t \\ \alpha = \dfrac{1}{(p-1)}. \end{array} \right\} \tag{4.22}$$

Using (4.22), one can easily obtain any nonlinear evolution equation like the KdV equation. One such equation is

$$\frac{\partial \phi^{(1)}}{\partial \tau} + \alpha \phi^{(1)} \frac{\partial \phi^{(1)}}{\partial \xi} + \mu \frac{\partial^p \phi^{(1)}}{\partial \xi^p} = 0. \tag{4.23}$$

It is a KdV equation with a higher-order dispersion.

4.3 Korteweg–de Vries (KdV) Equation

The theory of soliton is a very interesting discovery in physics. In 1895, Diederik Jonannes Korteweg and his Ph.D. scholar Gustav de Vries [5] derived a prototype equation of soliton theory known as Korteweg–De Varies (KdV) equation. This equation is derived from the basic equation of hydrodynamics. KdV equation is a nonlinear partial differential equation of two variables: the space and the time. Let us derive the KdV equation from a classical plasma model. We consider a collisionless unmagnetized electron–ion (e-i) plasma where ions are mobile and electrons obey Maxwell distribution.

Step 1: Basic fluid equations

The basic equations are given as follows:

Equation of continuity:

$$\frac{\partial N_i}{\partial T} + \frac{\partial N_i U_i}{\partial X} = 0 \tag{4.24}$$

Equation of motion:

$$\frac{\partial U_i}{\partial T} + U_i \frac{\partial U_i}{\partial X} = -\frac{e}{m_i} \frac{\partial \psi}{\partial X} \tag{4.25}$$

Poisson's equation:

$$\epsilon_0 \frac{\partial^2 \psi}{\partial X^2} = e(N_e - N_i) \tag{4.26}$$

where the electrons obey Maxwell distribution, i.e., $N_e = e n_0 e^{\frac{e\phi}{K_B T_e}}$. N_i, N_e, U_i, and m_i are the ion density, electron density, ion velocity, and ion mass, respectively. ψ is the electrostatic potential, K_B is the Boltzmann constant, T_e is the electron temperature, and e is the charge of the electrons.

Step 2: Normalization

To write Equations (4.24)–(4.26) in dimensionless form, we use the following dimensionless variables:

$$x = \frac{X}{\lambda_D}, \quad t = \omega_p T, \quad \phi = \frac{e\psi}{KT_e}, \quad n_i = \frac{N_i}{n_0}, \quad u_i = \frac{U_i}{C_s} \qquad (4.27)$$

where $\lambda_D = \sqrt{\epsilon_0 K_B T_e / n_0 e^2}$ is the Debye length, $C_s = \sqrt{K_B T_e / m_i}$ is the ion acoustic speed, $\omega_{pi} = \sqrt{n_0 e^2 / \epsilon_0 m_i}$ is the ion plasma frequency, and n_0 is the unperturbed density of ions and electrons. Hence, using (4.27) in (4.24)–(4.26), we obtain the set of normalized equations as

$$\frac{\partial n_i}{\partial t} + \frac{\partial (n_i u_i)}{\partial x} = 0 \qquad (4.28)$$

$$\frac{\partial u_i}{\partial t} + u_i \frac{\partial u_i}{\partial x} = -\frac{\partial \phi}{\partial x} \qquad (4.29)$$

$$\frac{\partial^2 \phi}{\partial x^2} = e^\phi - n_i. \qquad (4.30)$$

Step 3: Linearization

To linearize (4.28)–(4.30), we write the dependent variable as the sum of equilibrium and perturbed parts as $n_i = 1 + \bar{n}_i$, $u_i = \bar{u}_i$, and $\phi = \bar{\phi}$. Putting $n_i = 1 + \bar{n}_i$, where the values of parameters at equilibrium position are given by $n_1 = 1, u_1 = 0$, and $\phi_i = 0$ in Equation (4.28), we get

$$\frac{\partial}{\partial t}(1 + \bar{n}_i) + \frac{\partial}{\partial x}(\bar{u}_i + \bar{n}_i \bar{u}_i) = 0. \qquad (4.31)$$

Neglecting the nonlinear term $\frac{\partial (\bar{n}_i \bar{u}_i)}{\partial x}$ from (4.31), we get

$$\frac{\partial \bar{n}_i}{\partial \bar{t}} + \frac{\partial \bar{u}_i}{\partial \bar{x}} = 0 \qquad (4.32)$$

which is the linearized form of Equation (4.28).

Putting $u_i = \bar{u}_i$ and $\phi = \bar{\phi}$ in Equation (4.29), we get

$$\frac{\partial \bar{u}_i}{\partial t} + \bar{u}_i \frac{\partial \bar{u}_i}{\partial x} = -\frac{\partial \bar{\phi}}{\partial x}. \qquad (4.33)$$

Neglecting the nonlinear term of (4.33), we get

$$\frac{\partial \bar{u}_i}{\partial t} + \frac{\partial \bar{\phi}}{\partial \bar{x}} = 0. \qquad (4.34)$$

This is the linearized form of Equation (4.29).

Putting $n_i = 1 + \bar{n}_i$ and $\phi = \bar{\phi}$ in Equation (4.30) and neglecting $O(\bar{\phi}^2)$ term, we get

$$\frac{\partial^2 \bar{\phi}}{\partial x} = \bar{\phi} - \bar{n}_i. \tag{4.35}$$

Hence, Equations (4.32), (4.34), and (4.35) are the linearized form of Equations (4.28)–(4.30), respectively.

Step 4: Dispersion relation

To get dispersion relation for low-frequency wave, let us assume that the perturbation quantities are proportional to $e^{i(kx-\omega t)}$ and in the form of

$$\bar{n} = n_0 e^{i(kx-\omega t)}, \quad \bar{u} = u_0 e^{i(kx-\omega t)}, \quad \bar{\phi} = \phi_0 e^{i(kx-\omega t)}.$$

So,

$$\frac{\partial \bar{n}}{\partial t} = -in_0\omega e^{i(kx-\omega t)}, \quad \frac{\partial \bar{n}}{\partial x} = ikn_0 e^{i(kx-\omega t)}, \quad \frac{\partial \bar{u}}{\partial t} = -iu_0\omega e^{i(kx-\omega t)}$$

$$\frac{\partial \bar{u}}{\partial x} = iku_0 e^{i(kx-\omega t)}, \quad \frac{\partial \bar{\phi}}{\partial x} = ik\phi_0 e^{i(kx-\omega t)}, \quad \frac{\partial^2 \bar{\phi}}{\partial x^2} = (ik)^2 \phi_0 e^{i(kx-\omega t)}.$$

Putting these value in Equations (4.32), (4.34), and (4.35), we get

$$\left.\begin{array}{r} -i\omega n_0 + iku_0 = 0 \\ -i\omega u_0 + ik\phi_0 = 0 \\ n_0 - (k^2 + 1)\phi_0 = 0. \end{array}\right\} \tag{4.36}$$

Since system (4.36) is a system of linear homogeneous equation, so for existence of nontrivial solutions, we have

$$\begin{vmatrix} -i\omega & ik & 0 \\ 0 & -i\omega & ik \\ 1 & 0 & -(k^2+1) \end{vmatrix} = 0$$

$$\Rightarrow -i^2\omega^2(k^2+1) + i^2k^2 = 0$$

$$\Rightarrow \omega = \frac{k}{\sqrt{k^2+1}}. \tag{4.37}$$

This is the *dispersion relation*.

For small k (i.e., for weak dispersion), we can expand (4.37) as

$$\omega = k(1 + k^2)^{-\frac{1}{2}} = k - \frac{1}{2}k^3 + \cdot$$

The phase velocity

$$V_p = \frac{\omega}{k} = \frac{1}{\sqrt{(1 + k^2)}}. \tag{4.38}$$

So, $V_p \to 1$ as $k \to 0$ and $V_p \to 0$ as $k \to \infty$.

The group velocity $V_g = \frac{d\omega}{dk}$ is given by

$$V_g = \frac{1}{(1 + k^2)^{3/2}}. \tag{4.39}$$

In this case, we have $V_g < V_p$ for all $k > 0$.

If we consider the long-wave limit, i.e., the wavenumber $k \to 0$, then $V_p = \frac{\omega}{k}$ or $\omega = k$. It corresponds to a nondispersive acoustic wave with phase speed 1, i.e., in the original dimensional variable, the wave speed is equal to the ion acoustic speed C_s. Again, if the wavelength is much larger than the Debye length, i.e., $k\lambda_D \ll 1$, then the long wave dispersion will be very weak. In that case, the electrons and ions oscillate, but as a whole, they behave as a fluid. The inertia is given by the ions and, restoring force is given by the electrons.

At the next order in k, it is known as

$$\omega = k - \frac{1}{2}k^3 + O(k^5) \quad as \; k \to 0.$$

The $O(k^5)$ correction corresponds to weak KdV-type long wave dispersion.

In the short wave limit, the waves have constant frequency $\omega = 1$, corresponding in dimensional terms to the ion plasma frequency $\omega_{pi} = \frac{C_s}{\lambda_D}$. For such short waves, the ions oscillate in a fixed background of electrons.

Now, the phase of the waves can be written as

$$kx - \omega t = k(x - t) + \frac{1}{2}k^3 t.$$

Here, $k(x - t)$ and $k^3 t$ have same dynamic status (dimension) in the phase. Assuming k to be small order of $\epsilon^{1/2}$, ϵ being a small parameter measuring the weakness of the dispersion, $(x - t)$ is thus the traveling waveform and time t is the linear form.

Step 5: Perturbation

Accordingly, we consider new stretched coordinates ξ and τ such that

$$\xi = \epsilon^{1/2}(x - \lambda t), \quad \tau = \epsilon^{3/2}t \tag{4.40}$$

where ϵ is the strength of nonlinearity and λ is the Mach number (phase velocity of the wave). ϵ may be termed as the size of the perturbation. Let the variables be perturbed from the stable state in the following way (considering $n_i = 1$, $u_i = 0$, $\phi = 0$, and $n_e = e^\phi = e^0 = 1$ at equilibrium):

$$\left.\begin{aligned}
n_i &= 1 + \epsilon n_i^{(1)} + \epsilon^2 n_i^{(2)} + \epsilon^3 n_i^{(3)} + \cdots, \\
u_i &= 0 + \epsilon u_i^{(1)} + \epsilon^2 u_i^{(2)} + \epsilon^3 u_i^{(3)} + \cdots, \\
\phi &= 0 + \epsilon \phi^{(1)} + \epsilon^2 \phi^{(2)} + \epsilon^3 \phi^{(3)} + \cdots
\end{aligned}\right\} \tag{4.41}$$

where the numbers on the hat indicate the order of the perturbed quantities. $n_i^{(1)}$, $u_i^{(1)}$, and $\phi_i^{(1)}$ are the first-order perturbed quantities.

Step 6: Partial derivative in terms of stretched coordinates

(4.40) shows that x and t are function of ξ and τ. So, partial derivatives with respect to x and t can be transformed into partial derivative in terms of ξ and τ as

$$\frac{\partial}{\partial x} = \frac{\partial}{\partial \xi}\frac{\partial \xi}{\partial x} + \frac{\partial}{\partial \tau}\frac{\partial \tau}{\partial x}, \quad \Rightarrow \frac{\partial}{\partial x} = \epsilon^{\frac{1}{2}}\frac{\partial}{\partial \xi}$$

$$\frac{\partial}{\partial t} = \frac{\partial}{\partial \xi}\frac{\partial \xi}{\partial t} + \frac{\partial}{\partial \tau}\frac{\partial \tau}{\partial t}, \quad \Rightarrow \frac{\partial}{\partial t} = -\epsilon^{\frac{1}{2}}\frac{\partial}{\partial \xi} + \epsilon^{\frac{3}{2}}\frac{\partial}{\partial \tau}$$

$$\frac{\partial^2}{\partial x^2} = \frac{\partial}{\partial x}\left(\epsilon^{\frac{1}{2}}\frac{\partial}{\partial \xi}\right), \quad \Rightarrow \frac{\partial^2}{\partial x^2} = \epsilon\frac{\partial^2}{\partial \xi^2}.$$

We can express (4.28)–(4.30) in terms of ξ and τ as

$$\left.\begin{aligned}
\epsilon^{3/2}\frac{\partial n_i}{\partial \tau} - \epsilon^{1/2}\lambda\frac{\partial n_i}{\partial \xi} + \epsilon^{1/2}\frac{\partial(n_i u_i)}{\partial \xi} &= 0 \\
\epsilon^{3/2}\frac{\partial u_i}{\partial \tau} - \epsilon^{1/2}\lambda\frac{\partial u_i}{\partial \xi} + \epsilon^{1/2}u_i\frac{\partial u_i}{\partial x} + \epsilon^{1/2}\frac{\partial \phi}{\partial x} &= 0 \\
\epsilon\frac{\partial^2 \phi}{\partial \xi^2} - e^\phi + n_i &= 0.
\end{aligned}\right\} \tag{4.42}$$

Step 7: Phase velocity of the wave

Substituting Equations (4.40)–(4.41) in Equation (4.42) and collecting the lowest-order $O(\epsilon^{3/2})$ terms, we get

$$\left.\begin{array}{r}-\lambda\dfrac{\partial n_i^{(1)}}{\partial\xi}+\dfrac{\partial u_i^{(1)}}{\partial\xi}=0,\\[2mm]-\lambda\dfrac{\partial u_i^{(1)}}{\partial\xi}-\dfrac{\partial\phi^{(1)}}{\partial\xi}=0,\\[2mm]\phi^{(1)}-n_i^{(1)}=0.\end{array}\right\} \tag{4.43}$$

Integrating Equations (4.43), and all the variables tend to be zero as $\xi\to\infty$. We get

$$\left.\begin{array}{r}n_i^{(1)}=\dfrac{u_i^{(1)}}{\lambda},\\[2mm]u_i^{(1)}=\dfrac{\phi^{(1)}}{\lambda},\\[2mm]\phi^{(1)}=n_i^{(1)}.\end{array}\right\} \tag{4.44}$$

From Equation (4.44), we get the phase velocity as

$$\lambda^2=\pm 1. \tag{4.45}$$

Step 8: Nonlinear evolution equation

Substituting Equations (4.40)–(4.41) in Equation (4.42) and collecting order $O(\epsilon^{5/2})$, we get

$$\frac{\partial n_i^{(1)}}{\partial\tau}-\lambda\frac{\partial n_i^{(2)}}{\partial\xi}+\frac{\partial n_i^{(1)}u_i^{(1)}}{\partial\xi}+\frac{\partial u_i^{(2)}}{\partial\xi}=0, \tag{4.46}$$

$$\frac{\partial u_i^{(1)}}{\partial\tau}-\lambda\frac{\partial u_i^{(2)}}{\partial\xi}+u_i^{(1)}\frac{\partial u_i^{(1)}}{\partial\xi}=-\frac{\partial\phi^{(2)}}{\partial\xi^2}, \tag{4.47}$$

$$\frac{\partial\phi^{(1)}}{\partial\xi^2}-\phi^{(2)}-\frac{1}{2}(\phi^{(1)})^2+n_i^{(1)}=0. \tag{4.48}$$

Differentiating Equation (4.48) with respect to ξ and substituting for $\frac{\partial n_i^{(2)}}{\partial\xi}$ from Equation (4.46) and for $\frac{\partial u_i^{(2)}}{\partial\xi}$ from Equation (4.47), we finally obtain

$$\frac{\partial \phi^{(1)}}{\partial \tau} + \phi^{(1)} \frac{\partial \phi^{(1)}}{\partial \xi} + \frac{1}{2} \frac{\partial^3 \phi^{(1)}}{\partial \xi^3} = 0. \tag{4.49}$$

Equation (4.49) is known as the KdV equation. $\phi^{(1)} \frac{\partial \phi^{(1)}}{\partial \xi}$ is the nonlinear and $\frac{1}{2} \frac{\partial^3 \phi^{(1)}}{\partial \xi^3}$ is the dispersive term.

To obtain the steady-state solution of this KdV Equation (4.49), we introduce a transformation $\eta = \xi - u_0 \tau$, where u_0 is a constant velocity normalized by C_s and finally, we get the steady-state solution as

$$\phi^{(1)} = \phi_m sech^2 \left(\frac{\eta}{\Delta} \right) \tag{4.50}$$

where $\phi_m = 3u_0$ and $\Delta = \sqrt{\frac{2}{u_0}}$ are the amplitude and width of the solitary waves. It is clear that the height, width, and speed of the pulse are proportional to u_0, $\frac{1}{\sqrt{u_0}}$, and u_0, respectively. u_0 specifies the energy of the solitary waves. So, the larger the energy, the greater the speed, the larger the amplitude, and the narrower the width. Also, a finite number of solitons emerge with heights $\phi_{m1}, \phi_{m2}, \ldots$ and hence, each of the speed $u_1, u_2, \ldots$ travels to the right. These solitons interact with nonlinearly and preserve their soliton identity. As $t \to \infty$, the solitons are arranged in the order of increasing height with the tallest soliton in the extreme right. The solution of the KdV Equation (4.50) represents a single pulse as shown in Figure 4.1, having a peak at $\eta = 0$ and vanishing at $\eta \to \pm\infty$. It propagates along the positive direction of the ξ-axis with a constant velocity u_0 without any change of shape. Figure 4.1 also describes that as the wave speeds get larger and larger, the wavelength becomes smaller and smaller.

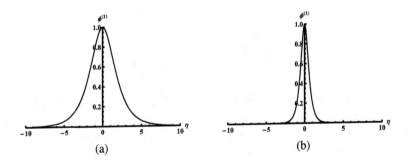

Fig. 4.1: (a) Plot of $\phi^{(1)}$ vs η for $u_0 = 1$ and (b) plot of $\phi^{(1)}$ vs. η for $u_0 = 10$.

4.4 Modified KdV (MKdV) Equation

For nonlinear waves in weakly dispersive media, there are two essential processes: the increase of steepness of the wave profile owing to nonlinear effects (as known from gas dynamics) and the dispersion of the profile. If the amplitude is not too large, the dispersion can compete with the nonlinearity. With the equilibrium of these two processes, the existing waves propagate with constant velocity without deformation of the profile. It would seem that with increasing amplitude, the nonlinear effects should prevail and lead to the formation of shock waves. If we take the nonlinear and dispersion terms in the equations only till the first nonvanishing approximation, we shall get the KdV equation. For smooth initial conditions, the Cauchy problem reduces to the soliton mode. As for the averaged solutions, they indeed behave like shock waves. There are many physical situations (if the coefficient of quadratic nonlinearity becomes zero) where the nonlinearity should be taken into account for up to cubic order. We then get the modified Korteweg–de Vries (MKdV) equation.

The MKdV equation has a significant role of soliton theory. It was used to construct an infinite number of conservation laws of the KdV equation that triggered the discovery of the Lax pair of the KdV equation and the breakthrough of the inverse scattering transformation. The MKdV equation is known to describe acoustic type waves in plasma.

To derive an MKdV equation in unmagnetized collisionless dusty plasma, we also consider a model consist of cold inertial ions, negatively stationary dusts, and q-nonextensive electrons. Accordingly, the one-dimensional normalized fluid equations are

$$\frac{\partial n_i}{\partial t} + \frac{\partial (n_i u_i)}{\partial x} = 0, \tag{4.51}$$

$$\frac{\partial u_i}{\partial t} + u_i \frac{\partial u_i}{\partial x} = -\frac{\partial \phi}{\partial x}, \tag{4.52}$$

$$\frac{\partial^2 \phi}{\partial x^2} = (1 - \mu)n_e - n_i + \mu \tag{4.53}$$

where $n_e = \left\{1 + (q-1)\phi\right\}^{\frac{q+1}{2(q-1)}}$. n_j ($j = i$, and e, for ion, and electron, respectively), u_i, and ϕ are the number density, ion fluid velocity, and electrostatic wave potential, respectively. Here, $\mu = \frac{Z_d n_{d0}}{n_0}$. n_0, Z_d, and n_{d0} are the unperturbed density of ions, the charge state of dust, and the unperturbed density of dust, respectively. μ is the density of the stationary dust. The normalization is represented by

$$n_i \to \frac{n_i}{n_0}, \quad u_i \to \frac{u_i}{C_s}, \quad \phi \to \frac{e\phi}{K_B T_e}, \quad x \to \frac{x}{\lambda_D}, \quad t \to \omega_{pi} t$$

where $C_s = \sqrt{\left(\frac{K_B T_e}{m_i}\right)}$, $\lambda_D = \left(\frac{T_e}{4\pi n_{e0} e^2}\right)^{\frac{1}{2}}$, and $\omega_{pi} = \left(\frac{4\pi n_{e0} e^2}{m_i}\right)^{\frac{1}{2}}$. C_s is the ion acoustic speed, λ_D is the Debye length, ω_{pi} is the ion plasma frequency, T_e is the electron temperature, K_B is the Boltzmann constant, e is the magnitude of electron charge, and m_i is the mass of the ion.

To obtain the KdV equation, we have used the same stretched coordinates as in Equation (4.40). The expansions of the dependent variables are also considered the same as in (4.41). Substituting the above expansions (4.41) along with stretching coordinates (4.40) into Equations (4.51)–(4.53) and equating the coefficients of the lowest order of ϵ, we obtain the phase velocity as

$$\lambda = \sqrt{\frac{2}{(q+1)(1-\mu)}}. \tag{4.54}$$

Taking the coefficients of next higher order of ϵ, and after some calculation, we obtain the KdV equation as

$$\frac{\partial \phi^{(1)}}{\partial \tau} + A\phi^{(1)} \frac{\partial \phi^{(1)}}{\partial \xi} + B \frac{\partial^3 \phi^{(1)}}{\partial \xi^3} = 0 \tag{4.55}$$

where $A = \left(\frac{3}{2\lambda} - \frac{b\lambda}{a}\right)$, $B = \frac{\lambda^3}{2}$, $a = \frac{q+1}{2}$, and $b = \frac{(q+1)(3-q)}{8}$.

The parameters q and μ may be chosen in such a way that $A = 0$. Then, for those values of q and μ, the nonlinear term vanishes, and Equation (4.55) is no longer a nonlinear equation. So, there are critical points where the quadratic nonlinearity vanishes. At the critical point, the stretching (4.40) is not valid, and a new stretching is necessary. Accordingly, we use the new stretched co-ordinate as

$$\xi = \epsilon(x - \lambda t), \quad \tau = \epsilon^3 t. \tag{4.56}$$

Now, substituting Equation (4.56) with Equations (4.41) into Equations (4.51)–(4.53) and equating the coefficients of the lowest order of ϵ (i.e., coefficients of ϵ^2 from Equations (4.51) and (4.52) and coefficients of ϵ from

Equation (4.53)), we obtain the following relations:

$$n_i^{(1)} = \frac{u_i^{(1)}}{\lambda}, \quad u_i^{(1)} = \frac{\phi^{(1)}}{\lambda}, \quad n_i^{(1)} = a(1-\mu)\phi^{(1)}. \tag{4.57}$$

Equating the coefficients of next higher order of ϵ (i.e., coefficients of ϵ^3 from Equations (4.51) and (4.52) and coefficients of ϵ^2 from Equation (4.53)), we obtain the following relations:

$$\left.\begin{array}{l} n_i^{(2)} = \dfrac{1}{\lambda}\left(u_i^{(2)} + n_i^{(1)}u_i^{(1)}\right) \\[2mm] u_i^{(2)} = \dfrac{1}{\lambda}\left\{\dfrac{1}{2}\left(u_i^{(1)}\right)^2 + \phi^{(2)}\right\} \\[2mm] n_i^{(2)} = (1-\mu)\left\{a\phi^{(2)} + b\left(\phi^{(1)}\right)^2\right\}. \end{array}\right\} \tag{4.58}$$

Equating the coefficients of next higher order of ϵ (i.e., coefficients of ϵ^4 from Equations (4.51) and (4.52) and coefficients of ϵ^3 from Equation (4.53)), we obtain the following relations:

$$\frac{\partial n_i^{(1)}}{\partial \tau} - \lambda\frac{\partial n_i^{(3)}}{\partial \xi} + \frac{\partial u_i^{(3)}}{\partial \xi} + \frac{\partial(n_i^{(1)}u_i^{(2)})}{\partial \xi} + \frac{\partial(n_i^{(2)}u_i^{(1)})}{\partial \xi} = 0 \tag{4.59}$$

$$\frac{\partial u_i^{(1)}}{\partial \tau} - \lambda\frac{\partial u_i^{(3)}}{\partial \xi} + \frac{\partial \phi^{(3)}}{\partial \xi} + \frac{\partial(u_i^{(1)}u_i^{(2)})}{\partial \xi} = 0 \tag{4.60}$$

$$\frac{\partial^2 \phi^{(1)}}{\partial \xi^2} = (1-\mu)(a\phi^{(3)} + 2b\phi^{(1)}\phi^{(2)} + c(\phi^{(1)})^3) - n_i^{(3)} \tag{4.61}$$

where $c = \frac{(1+q)(3-q)(5-3q)}{48}$.

From Equations (4.57), it is seen that the same phase velocity is obtained as (4.54).

Differentiating Equation (4.61) once with $\frac{\partial}{\partial \xi}$ and substituting the terms other than $\phi^{(1)}$ from Equations (4.57)–(4.60), we can obtain MKdV equation as

$$\frac{\partial \phi^{(1)}}{\partial \tau} + A_1(\phi^{(1)})^2\frac{\partial \phi^{(1)}}{\partial \xi} + B_1\frac{\partial^3 \phi^{(1)}}{\partial \xi^3} = 0 \tag{4.62}$$

where $A_1 = \frac{15}{4\lambda^3} - \frac{3\lambda^3 c(1-\mu)}{2}$ and $B_1 = \frac{\lambda^3}{2}$. This is similar to the KdV equation with a higher-order nonlinearity. The solitary wave solution of Equation (4.62) is

$$\phi^{(1)} = \phi_m \operatorname{sech}\left(\frac{\xi - u_0\tau}{\Delta}\right) \tag{4.63}$$

where $\phi_m \left(=\sqrt{\frac{6u_0}{A_1}}\right)$ and $\Delta \left(=\sqrt{\frac{B_1}{u_0}}\right)$ are the amplitude and the width of the solitary waves, respectively, and u_0 is the speed of the ion-acoustic solitary waves.

Figure 4.2 shows the plot of ϕ_m against q for different values of μ. It is seen from the figure that the amplitude of the solitary waves decreases with the increase of q. So, an increase in nonextensive electron distribution decreases the amplitude of the solitary wave. It is observed that as μ increases, the amplitude of the soliton increases. It is obvious from Figure 4.3 that as we increase μ, the width of the soliton increases.

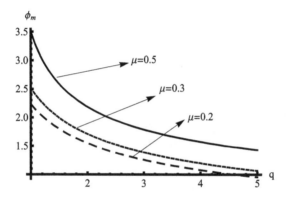

Fig. 4.2: Plot of ϕ_m vs. q for $\mu=$ 0.6, 0.3, and 0.2.

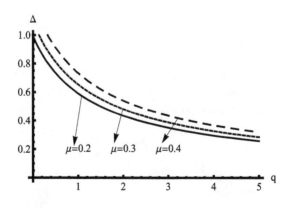

Fig. 4.3: Plot of Δ vs. q for $\mu=$ 0.4, 0.3, and 0.2.

4.5 Gardner's Equation

To obtain Gardner's equation, we consider a four components collision-free unmagnetized dusty plasma model consisting of electrons, ions, and both positive and negative dust grains. Electrons obey the superthermal distribution. Here, the charge neutrality condition is $n_{i0} + Z_{dp}n_{dp} = n_{e0} + Z_{dn}n_{dn}$, where n_{i0}, n_{e0}, n_{dp}, and n_{dn} are ion, electron, positively dust, and negatively dust number density at equilibrium, respectively. Z_{dp} and Z_{dn} represents the charge state of positive and negative dust. The basic normalization equations are as follows:

$$\frac{\partial n_i}{\partial t} + \frac{\partial}{\partial x}(n_i u_i) = 0 \tag{4.64}$$

$$\frac{\partial u_i}{\partial t} + u_i \frac{\partial u_i}{\partial x} = -\frac{\partial \phi}{\partial x} \tag{4.65}$$

$$\frac{\partial^2 \phi}{\partial x^2} = \rho \tag{4.66}$$

$$\rho = (1 - j\mu)n_e - n_i + j\mu \tag{4.67}$$

where $\mu = |Z_{dp}n_{dp} - Z_{dn}n_{dn}|/n_{io}$. Here, $j = 1$, -1 for positive, negative net dust charge. The electron distribution is represented by

$$n_e = \left(1 - \frac{\phi}{(\kappa - 1/2)}\right)^{-k-\frac{1}{2}}.$$

We have used the stretched coordinates (4.56) in Equations (4.64)–(4.66). The expansion of the dependent variables is also considered the same as (4.41), with an additional expression as

$$\rho = 0 + \sum_{p=1}^{\infty} \epsilon^p \rho^{(p)}. \tag{4.68}$$

Here, ρ is the net surface charge density. Now, expressing Equations (4.64)–(4.67) in terms of ξ and τ, substituting Equations (4.41) and (4.68) into the resulting equations, and collecting the lowest-order terms, we get

$$n_i^{(1)} = \frac{\phi^{(1)}}{\lambda^2}, \quad u_i^{(1)} = \frac{\phi^{(1)}}{\lambda}, \quad \frac{(1 - j\mu)(2\kappa + 1)}{(2\kappa - 1)}\phi^{(1)} = n_i^{(1)}. \tag{4.69}$$

Hence, from the condition for nontrivial first-order perturbed quantities, we get the phase velocity as

$$\lambda = \sqrt{\frac{(2\kappa - 1)}{(1 - j\mu)(2\kappa + 1)}}. \tag{4.70}$$

For the next order in ϵ, we get another set of equation that, after using (4.69)–(4.70), can be written as

$$
\left.
\begin{aligned}
n_i^{(2)} &= \frac{3(\phi^{(1)})^2}{2\lambda^4} + \frac{\phi^{(2)}}{\lambda^2}, \quad u_i^{(2)} = \frac{(\phi^{(1)})^2}{2\lambda^3} + \frac{\phi^{(2)}}{\lambda}, \\
\rho^{(2)} &= -\frac{1}{2}A(\phi^{(1)})^2 = 0, \quad A = \frac{3}{\lambda^4} - \frac{(1-j\mu)(2\kappa+1)(2\kappa+3)}{(2\kappa-1)^2}.
\end{aligned}
\right\} \quad (4.71)
$$

It is clear that $A = 0$ (since $\phi \neq 0$) and $A = 0$ when $\kappa = \kappa_c = \frac{3j\mu}{2(2-3j\mu)}$. It is obvious that (4.71) is satisfied for $\kappa = \kappa_c$ and $\kappa_c < 0$ when $j = -1$. In that case, solitary waves or double layers are not possible. So, for $|\kappa - \kappa_c| = \epsilon$ corresponding to $A = A_0$, one can write A_0 as

$$
A_0 \approx s\left(\frac{\partial A}{\partial \kappa}\right)_{\kappa=\kappa_c} |\kappa - \kappa_c| = sA_k\epsilon
$$

where $A_k = \frac{(1-j\mu)}{(2\kappa_c-1)^3}[24\kappa_c + 20 - 24(1-j\mu)(2\kappa_c+1)]$. Here, $s = 1$ for $\kappa > \kappa_c$ and $s = -1$ for $\kappa < \kappa_c$. So, for $\kappa \neq \kappa_c$, one can express $\rho^{(2)}$ as $\rho^{(2)} = -\frac{sA_k\epsilon\phi^2}{2}$, i.e, when $\kappa \neq \kappa_c \cdot \rho^{(2)}$ must be considered in the third-order Poisson's equation.

As the next higher order in ϵ, we get

$$
\frac{\partial n_i^{(1)}}{\partial \tau} - \lambda \frac{\partial n_i^{(3)}}{\partial \xi} + \frac{\partial u_i^{(3)}}{\partial \xi} + \frac{\partial}{\partial \xi}(n_i^{(1)}u_i^{(2)} + n_i^{(2)}u_i^{(1)}) = 0 , \quad (4.72)
$$

$$
\frac{\partial u_i^{(1)}}{\partial \tau} - \lambda \frac{\partial u_i^{(3)}}{\partial \xi} + \frac{\partial}{\partial \xi}(u_i^{(1)}u_i^{(2)}) = 0, \quad (4.73)
$$

$$
\frac{\partial^2 \phi}{\partial \xi^2} + \frac{1}{2}sA_k\phi^2 - (1-j\mu)\left[\frac{(2\kappa+1)}{(2\kappa-1)}\phi^{(3)} + \frac{(2\kappa+1)(2\kappa+3)}{(2\kappa-1)^2}\phi\phi^{(2)}\right.
$$

$$
\left. + \frac{(2\kappa+1)(2\kappa+3)(2\kappa+5)}{6(2\kappa-1)^3}\phi^3\right] + n_i^{(3)} = 0. \quad (4.74)
$$

Now, using (4.69)–(4.71) and (4.72)–(4.74), one finally obtains a nonlinear dynamical equation as follows:

$$
\frac{\partial \phi}{\partial \tau} + p\phi\frac{\partial \phi}{\partial \xi} + q\phi^2\frac{\partial \phi}{\partial \xi} + q_0\frac{\partial^3 \phi}{\partial \xi^3} = 0 \quad (4.75)
$$

where

$$
p = sA_kq_0, \quad q = p_0q_0,
$$

$$
p_0 = \frac{15}{2\lambda^6} - \frac{(1-j\mu)(2\kappa+1)(2\kappa+3)(2\kappa+5)}{2(2\kappa-1)^3}, \quad q_0 = \frac{\lambda^3}{2}.
$$

Equation (4.75) is called further modified KdV (FMKdV) equation or Gandner's equation.

To obtain the stationary solution of Gardner's equation, we have introduced a transformation $\zeta = \xi - u_0\tau$, where u_0 is the constant velocity. Using the conditions $\phi \to 0$, $\frac{d\phi}{d\zeta} \to 0$, $\frac{d^2\phi}{d\zeta^2} \to 0$ at $\zeta \to \pm\infty$, we finally get the stationary solitary wave solution of Gardner's equation as

$$\phi^{(1)} = \left[\frac{1}{\phi_{m2}} - \left(\frac{1}{\phi_{m2}} - \frac{1}{\phi_{m1}}\right)\cosh^2\left(\frac{\zeta}{\Delta}\right)\right]^{-1} \qquad (4.76)$$

where

$$u_0 = \frac{p}{3}\phi_{m1,2} + \frac{1}{6}\phi_{m1,2}^2, \quad \phi_{m1,2} = \phi_m\left[1 \mp \sqrt{1 + \frac{u_0}{V_0}}\right],$$

$$\phi_m = -\frac{p}{q}, \quad V_0 = \frac{p^2}{6q}$$

and the width Δ as

$$\Delta = \frac{2}{\sqrt{-\gamma\phi_{m1}\phi_{m2}}}, \quad \gamma = \frac{q}{6q_0}.$$

4.6 Gardner and Modified Gardner's (MG) Equation

For simple wave problems, like the nonlinear description of an ion-acoustic soliton in an electron–proton plasma, most of the compositional parameters are fixed or eliminated by proper normalization. It results in the ubiquitous KdV equation with quadratic nonlinearity. After the plasma model becomes more complicated, some critical choices for the compositional parameters which annul the coefficients of the nonlinear term in the KdV equation leading to an undesirable linear equation (the combination of stretching and expansion used) must then be adapted to account for nonlinear effects of higher degree. It is usually done for the stretching and results in the MKdV equation with cubic nonlinearity. An interesting question arises here that whether one can take this procedure to a higher level. What will happen if for complicated plasma models the coefficients of both the quadratic and the cubic nonlinearities can vanish simultaneously for a specific set of compositional parameters? For many models, such supercritical compositions will be impossible. However, there are situations where supercriticality is possible for the models with many restrictions. In mathematically inclined studies, it can be used as one of the higher-degree extensions of the KdV family of equations.

Let us consider a plasma model composed of cold ions and two temperature (cold and hot) q-nonextensive electrons. Propagation of ion acoustic waves is characterized by the normalized model equations as

$$\frac{\partial n_i}{\partial t} + \frac{\partial (n_i u_i)}{\partial x} = 0, \tag{4.77}$$

$$\frac{\partial u_i}{\partial t} + u_i \frac{\partial u_i}{\partial x} = -\frac{\partial \phi}{\partial x}, \tag{4.78}$$

$$\frac{\partial^2 \phi}{\partial x^2} = \mu n_c + (1 - \mu) n_h - n_i. \tag{4.79}$$

The normalized cold and hot electron densities are written as $n_c = (1 - (1 - q)\sigma_c \phi)^{\frac{(1+q)}{2(1-q)}}$ and $n_h = (1 - (1-q)\sigma_h \phi)^{\frac{(1+q)}{2(1-q)}}$, where $\sigma_c = \frac{T_{eff}}{T_c}$ and $\sigma_h = \frac{T_{eff}}{T_h}$ and q is the degree of efficiency of nonextensivity. Here, $\mu = \frac{n_{i0}}{n_0}$. Again, n_j ($j = i$, h, and e for ion, hot electron, and cold electron), u_i, and ϕ are the number density, ion velocity, and electrostatic potential, respectively. At equilibrium, we get $n_{c0} + n_{h0} = n_{i0}$.

We introduce the following dimensionless variables:

$$x = \frac{x}{\lambda_D}, \quad t = \omega_{pi} t, \quad \phi = \frac{e\psi}{K_B T_{eff}}, \quad n_i = \frac{n_i}{n_0}, \quad u_i = \frac{u_i}{C_s} \tag{4.80}$$

where $\lambda_D = \sqrt{T_h/(4\pi n_{i0} e^2)}$ is the Debye length, $C_s = \sqrt{T_{eff}/m}$ is the ion acoustic speed, $\omega_{pi} = \sqrt{m_i/4\pi n_{i0} e^2}$ is the ion plasma frequency, and n_0 is the unperturbed density of ions and electrons. T_c and T_h denote temperatures of cold and hot electrons, respectively. Also, $T_{eff} = \frac{T_c T_h}{\mu T_h + (1-\mu) T_c}$ stands for effective temperature and m is the ion mass.

We have derived the KdV equation using RPT with the same stretched coordinates as (4.40). We also expand the dependent variable, the same as (4.41). Using (4.41) in Equations (4.77)–(4.79), we get the relation $\frac{1}{\lambda^2} = \frac{(1+q)}{2}[\mu\sigma_c + (1-\mu)\sigma_h]$. After further calculations like the previous section, we get the KdV equation as follows:

$$\frac{\partial \phi^{(1)}}{\partial \tau} + A\phi^{(1)} \frac{\partial \phi^{(1)}}{\partial \xi} + B \frac{\partial^3 \phi^{(1)}}{\partial \xi^3} = 0 \tag{4.81}$$

where $A = \frac{3}{2\lambda} - A_1 \lambda^3$, $B = \frac{\lambda^3}{2}$, and $A_1 = \frac{1}{8}(1+q)(3-q)[\mu\sigma_c^2 + (1-\mu)\sigma_h^2]$.

At certain sets of critical values, the nonlinear coefficient is $A = 0$. This indicates the occurrence of singularity. In that case, using the new stretched coordinates $\xi = \epsilon(x - \lambda t)$ and $\tau = \epsilon^3 t$, we obtain the MKdV equation as

$$\frac{\partial \phi^{(1)}}{\partial \tau} + C(\phi^{(1)})^2 \frac{\partial \phi^{(1)}}{\partial \xi} + B \frac{\partial^3 \phi^{(1)}}{\partial \xi^3} = 0 \qquad (4.82)$$

where $C = \frac{15}{4\lambda^3} - \frac{3C_1\lambda^3}{2}$, and $C_1 = \frac{1}{48}(1+q)(3-q)(5-q)[\mu\sigma_c^3 + (1-\mu)\sigma_h^3]$. Also, there exists a set of critical values at which the nonlinear coefficient is $C = 0$. Furthermore, to deal with such a situation with the help of stretched coordinates $\xi = \epsilon^{3/2}(x - \lambda t)$ and $\tau = \epsilon^{9/2}t$, we find the FMKdV equation as follows:

$$\frac{\partial \phi^{(1)}}{\partial \tau} + D(\phi^{(1)})^3 \frac{\partial \phi^{(1)}}{\partial \xi} + B \frac{\partial^3 \phi^{(1)}}{\partial \xi^3} = 0 \qquad (4.83)$$

where $D = \frac{\lambda^3}{2}\left(\frac{35}{2\lambda^8} - 4D_1\right)$, and $D_1 = \frac{1}{384}(1+q)(3-q)(5-3q)(7-5q)[\mu\sigma_c^4 + (1-\mu)\sigma_h^4]$. To examine the small amplitude supernonlinear IASW feature, we further derive the modified Gardner's (MG) equation. To evolute the MG equation, we introduce new stretch coordinate $\xi = \epsilon^{3/2}(x - \lambda t)$ and $\tau = \epsilon^{9/2}t$. We then apply the stretched coordinate and Equation (4.41) in Equations (4.77)–(4.79). Similarly, we get the other nonlinear equations. We also obtain the following relations from coefficients of lowest order of ϵ:

$$n_3 = \frac{5(\phi^{(1)})^3}{2\lambda^6} + \frac{3\phi^{(1)}\phi^{(2)}}{\lambda^4} + \frac{\phi^{(3)}}{\lambda^2}, \quad u_3 = \frac{(\phi^{(1)})^3}{2\lambda^5} + \frac{\phi^{(1)}\phi^{(2)}}{\lambda^3} + \frac{\phi^{(3)}}{\lambda}. \qquad (4.84)$$

Comparing all coefficients with the next higher order of ϵ, we get

$$\frac{\partial n^{(4)}}{\partial \xi} = \frac{2}{\lambda^3}\frac{\partial \phi^{(1)}}{\partial \tau} + \frac{3}{\lambda^4}\frac{\partial}{\partial \xi}(\phi^{(1)}\phi^{(3)}) + \frac{35}{2\lambda^8}(\phi^{(1)})^3 \frac{\partial \phi^{(1)}}{\partial \xi}$$

$$+ \frac{15}{2\lambda^6}\frac{\partial}{\partial \xi}[(\phi^{(1)})^2\phi^{(3)}] + \frac{3}{2\lambda^4}\frac{\partial(\phi^{(2)})^2}{\partial \xi} + \frac{1}{2\lambda^2}\frac{\partial \phi^{(4)}}{\partial \xi} \qquad (4.85)$$

and

$$\frac{\partial^2 \phi^{(1)}}{\partial \xi} + \epsilon n^{(1)} + \epsilon^2 n^{(2)} + \epsilon^3 n^{(3)} + \epsilon^4 n^{(4)} - \epsilon\left(\frac{1+q}{2}\right)A_1\phi^{(1)}$$

$$- \epsilon^2\left(\frac{1+q}{2}\right)A_1\phi^{(2)} - \epsilon^3\left(\frac{1+q}{2}\right)A_1\phi^{(3)} - \epsilon^4\left(\frac{1+q}{2}\right)A_1\phi^{(4)}$$

$$- \epsilon^2\frac{1}{8}(1+q)(3-q)A_2(\phi^{(1)})^2 - \epsilon^3\frac{1}{8}(1+q)(3-q)A_22\phi^{(1)}\phi^{(2)}$$

$$-\epsilon^3 \frac{1}{48}(1+q)(3-q)(5-3q)A_3(\phi^{(1)})^3$$

$$-\epsilon^4 \frac{1}{8}(1+q)(3-q)A_2 2\phi^{(1)}\phi^{(3)}$$

$$-\epsilon^4 \frac{1}{48}(1+q)(3-q)(5-3q)3A_3(\phi^{(1)})^2\phi^{(2)}$$

$$-\epsilon^4 \frac{1}{348}(1+q)(3-q)(5-3q)(7-5q)A_4(\phi^{(1)})^4$$

$$-\epsilon^4 \frac{1}{8}(1+q)(3-q)A_2(\phi^{(2)})^2 = 0 \qquad (4.86)$$

where $A_l = \mu\sigma_c^l + (1-\mu)\sigma_h^l$, $l = 1,2,3,4$. After some calculations, we get the further modified KdV or supercritical KdV equation as follows:

$$\frac{\partial\phi^{(1)}}{\partial\tau} + a\phi^{(1)}\frac{\partial\phi^{(1)}}{\partial\xi} + b(\phi^{(1)})^2\frac{\partial\phi^{(1)}}{\partial\xi} + c(\phi^{(1)})^3\frac{\partial\phi^{(1)}}{\partial\xi} + B\frac{\partial^3\phi^{(1)}}{\partial\xi^3} = 0$$

$$(4.87)$$

where $a = \lambda^3 \left[\frac{12}{\lambda^4(1+q)(3-q)} - A_2\right]$, $b = \frac{3\lambda^3}{2}\left[\frac{120}{\lambda^6(1+q)(3-q)(5-3q)} - A_3\right]$, and $c = 2\lambda^3\left[\frac{35}{8\lambda^8} - \frac{1}{384}(1+q)(3-q)(5-3q)(7-5q)A_4\right]$. $A_2 = \frac{8}{(1+q)(3-q)}\frac{3}{2\lambda^4} - \epsilon^2 B_2$ and $A_3 = \frac{48}{(1+q)(3-q)(5-3q)}\frac{5}{2\lambda^6} - \epsilon^2 B_3$.

4.7 Damped Forced KdV (DFKdV) Equation

It is observed that the soliton solutions are damped in a dusty plasma due to dust–ion collision, and accordingly, a new equation is modeled through RPT. We consider an unmagnetized dusty plasma consisting of mobile ions and κ distributed electrons. Accordingly, the basic normalized fluid equations are

$$\frac{\partial n_i}{\partial t} + \frac{\partial(n_i u_i)}{\partial x} = 0, \qquad (4.88)$$

$$\frac{\partial u_i}{\partial t} + u_i\frac{\partial u_i}{\partial x} = -\frac{\partial\phi}{\partial x} - \nu_{id}u_i, \qquad (4.89)$$

$$\frac{\partial^2\phi}{\partial x^2} = (1-\mu)n_e - n + \mu \qquad (4.90)$$

where

$$n_e = \left(1 - \frac{\phi}{\kappa - 3/2}\right)^{-\kappa+1/2}.$$

Here, n_j ($j = i$ and e for ions and electrons), u_i, and ϕ are the number density, ion velocity, and the electrostatic potential, respectively. The normalization can be represented as

$$n_i \to \frac{n_i}{n_o}, \quad u_i \to \frac{u_i}{C_s}, \quad \phi \to \frac{e\phi}{K_B T_e}, \quad x \to \frac{x}{\lambda_D}, \quad t \to \omega_{pi} t$$

where n_0 is the unperturbed ion density, $C_s (= \sqrt{T_e/m_i})$ is the ion acoustic speed, $\omega_{pi} (= \sqrt{4\pi n_{e0} e^2/m_i})$ is the ion plasma frequency, $\lambda_D (= \sqrt{T_e/(4\pi n_{e0} e^2)})$ is the Debye length, T_e is the electron temperature, m_i is the ion mass, e is the electron charge, and K_B is the Boltzmann constant. Here, ν_{id} is the dust–ion collision frequency and $\mu = \frac{Z_d n_{d0}}{n_0}$.

We use the same stretched coordinates use in Equation (4.40) and the same expansion of the dependent variables considered in (4.41). We also consider

$$\nu_{id} \sim \epsilon^{3/2} \nu_{id0}. \tag{4.91}$$

Substituting (4.41) and (4.91) along with stretching coordinates into Equations (4.88)–(4.90) and equating the coefficients of the lowest order of ϵ, we obtain the phase velocity as

$$\lambda = \sqrt{\frac{(\kappa - 3/2)}{(\kappa - 1/2)(1 - \mu)}}. \tag{4.92}$$

Taking the coefficients of the next higher order of ϵ, we get the damped KDV equation as

$$\frac{\partial \phi^{(1)}}{\partial \tau} + A\phi^{(1)} \frac{\partial \phi^{(1)}}{\partial \xi} + B\frac{\partial^3 \phi^{(1)}}{\partial \xi^3} + C\phi^{(1)} = 0 \tag{4.93}$$

where $A = \left(\frac{3 - 2b(1-\mu)\lambda^4}{2\lambda}\right)$, $B = \frac{v^3}{2}$, $C = \frac{\nu_{id0}}{2}$, $a = \frac{\kappa - 1/2}{\kappa - 3/2}$, and $b = \frac{\kappa^2 - 1/4}{2(\kappa - 3/2)^2}$.

The behavior of nonlinear waves changes with the change of external periodic force [17, 18]. It shows that such a force can be produced by a flexible, high-speed waveform generator. Considering an external periodic force $f_0 cos(\omega\tau)$, the damped KdV Equation (4.93) takes the form

$$\frac{\partial \phi^{(1)}}{\partial \tau} + A\phi^{(1)} \frac{\partial \phi^{(1)}}{\partial \xi} + B\frac{\partial^3 \phi^{(1)}}{\partial \xi^3} + C\phi^{(1)} 1 = f_0 \cos(\omega\tau). \tag{4.94}$$

It is termed as damped and forced KdV (DFKdV) equation.

When $C = 0$ and $f_0 = 0$, then Equation (4.94) converts to KdV equation. The solitary wave solution of the KdV equation is written as

$$\phi_1 = \phi_m sech^2 \left(\frac{\xi - M\tau}{W} \right) \tag{4.95}$$

where $\phi_m = \frac{3M}{A}$ and $W = 2\sqrt{\frac{B}{M}}$, with M as the Mach number.

From the conservation properties of the KdV equation, the conserved quantity is

$$I = \int_{-\infty}^{\infty} \phi_1^2 \, d\xi. \tag{4.96}$$

Following the same procedure as in Chapter 3, Section 3.7.3, we finally get the approximate analytical solution of Equation (4.94) as

$$\phi_1 = \phi_m(\tau) sech^2 \left(\frac{\xi - M(\tau)\tau}{W(\tau)} \right) \tag{4.97}$$

where $\phi_m(\tau) = \frac{3M(\tau)}{A}$ and $W(\tau) = 2\sqrt{\frac{B}{M(\tau)}}$. $M(\tau)$ is given by the equation

$$M(\tau) = \left(M - \frac{8ACf_0}{16C^2 + 9\omega^2} \right) e^{-\frac{4}{3}C\tau} + \frac{6Af_0}{16C^2 + 9\omega^2} \left(\frac{4}{3}Ccos(\omega\tau) + \omega sin(\omega\tau) \right).$$

4.8 Damped Forced MKdV (DFMKdV) Equation

In the last case, we derived the DKdV equation due to the dust–ion collision. Damped and forced KdV equation appears if an additional force term appears on the right hand side of Poisson's equation. Similarly, one can also obtain the damped and forced MKdV equation in the plane. To derive the DFMKdV equation, let us consider an unmagnetized collisional dusty plasma, consisting of cold inertial ions, q-nonextensive electrons, and negative stationery charged dust. Accordingly, basic normalized fluid equations are

$$\frac{\partial n_i}{\partial t} + \frac{\partial (n_i u_i)}{\partial x} = 0, \tag{4.98}$$

$$\frac{\partial u_i}{\partial t} + u_i \frac{\partial u_i}{\partial x} = -\frac{\partial \phi}{\partial x} - \nu_{id} u, \tag{4.99}$$

$$\frac{\partial^2 \phi}{\partial x^2} = (1 - \mu) n_e - n_i + \mu + S(x, t) \tag{4.100}$$

where $n_e = n_{e0}\{1 + (q-1)\phi\}^{\frac{q+1}{2(q-1)}}$. Here, $\mu = \frac{Z_d n_{d0}}{n_0}$, ν_{id} is the dust–ion collisional frequency, and the term $S(x,t)$ [6, 7] is a charged density source that may be obtained from experimental conditions for a definite purpose. We have used the same normalization as in Section 4.7.

To obtain phase velocity and the nonlinear evolution equation, we introduced the same stretched coordinates as used in Equation (4.40). The expansions of the dependent variables are also considered the same as (4.41) and (4.91). We also consider

$$S \sim \epsilon^2 S_2. \tag{4.101}$$

Substituting expansions (4.41), (4.91), and (4.101) along with stretching coordinates (4.40) into Equations (4.98)–(4.100) and equating the coefficients of the lowest order of ϵ, the phase velocity is obtained the same as Equation (4.54).

Now, taking the coefficients of the next higher order of ϵ (i.e., coefficient of $\epsilon^{5/2}$ from Equations (4.98) and (4.99) and coefficient of ϵ^2 from Equation (4.100)), we obtain the DFKdV equation as

$$\frac{\partial \phi^{(1)}}{\partial \tau} + A\phi^{(1)}\frac{\partial \phi^{(1)}}{\partial \xi} + B\frac{\partial^3 \phi^{(1)}}{\partial \xi^3} + C\phi^{(1)} = B\frac{\partial S_2}{\partial \xi} \tag{4.102}$$

where $A = \left(\frac{3}{2\lambda} - \frac{b\lambda}{a}\right)$, $B = \frac{\lambda^3}{2}$, $C = \frac{\nu_{id0}}{2}$, $a = \frac{q+1}{2}$, and $b = \frac{(q+1)(3-q)}{8}$.

It is obvious that for some particular value of a, b, and λ, if $\frac{b\lambda}{a} = \frac{3}{2}$, then $A = 0$. So, at the critical point, the stretching (4.40) is not valid. In this situation, we have used stretched coordinate the same as (4.56) and expanded the dependent variables the same as (4.41). We also consider

$$\nu_{id} \sim \epsilon^3 \nu_{id0}, \quad S \sim \epsilon^3 S_2. \tag{4.103}$$

Now, substituting Equations (4.41), (4.56), and (4.103) into the basic equations (4.98)–(4.100) and equating the coefficients of the lowest order of ϵ (i.e., coefficients of ϵ^2 from Equations (4.98) and (4.99) and coefficients of ϵ from Equation (4.100)), we get

$$n_i^{(1)} = \frac{u_i^{(1)}}{\lambda}, \quad u_i^{(1)} = \frac{\phi^{(1)}}{\lambda}, \quad n_i^{(1)} = a(1-\mu)\phi^{(1)}. \tag{4.104}$$

Equating the coefficients of the next higher order of ϵ (i.e., coefficients of ϵ^3 from Equations (4.98) and (4.99) and coefficients of ϵ^2 from

Equation (4.100)), we obtain the following relations:

$$n_i^{(2)} = \frac{1}{\lambda}(u_i^{(2)} + n_i^{(1)}u_i^{(1)})$$

$$\frac{\partial u_i^{(2)}}{\partial \xi} = \frac{1}{\lambda}(u_i^{(1)}\frac{\partial u_i^{(1)}}{\partial \xi} + \frac{\partial \phi^{(2)}}{\partial \xi})$$

$$n_i^{(2)} = (1 - \mu)(a\phi^{(2)} + b(\phi^{(1)})^2).$$

$$(4.105)$$

Equating the coefficients of the next higher order of ϵ (i.e., coefficients of ϵ^4 from Equations (4.98) and (4.99) and coefficients of ϵ^3 from Equation (4.100)), we obtain the following relations:

$$\frac{\partial n_i^{(1)}}{\partial \tau} - \lambda \frac{\partial n_i^{(3)}}{\partial \xi} + \frac{\partial u_i^{(3)}}{\partial \xi} + \frac{\partial (n_i^{(1)}u_i^{(2)})}{\partial \xi} + \frac{\partial (n_i^{(2)}u_i^{(1)})}{\partial \xi} = 0$$

$$\frac{\partial u_i^{(1)}}{\partial \tau} - \lambda \frac{\partial u_i^{(3)}}{\partial \xi} + \frac{\partial \phi^{(3)}}{\partial \xi} + \frac{\partial (u_i^{(1)}u_i^{(2)})}{\partial \xi} + \nu_{id0}u_i^{(1)} = 0$$

$$\frac{\partial^2 \phi^{(1)}}{\partial \xi^2} - (1 - \mu)(a\phi^{(3)} + 2b\phi^{(1)}\phi^{(2)} + c(\phi^{(1)})^3) = n_i^{(3)} - S_2$$

$$(4.106)$$

where $c = \frac{(1+q)(3-q)(5-3q)}{48}$.

From Equation (4.104), one can obtain the phase velocity same as in (4.54) and from Equations (4.104)–(4.106), one can obtain the nonlinear evolution equation as

$$\frac{\partial \phi^{(1)}}{\partial \tau} + A_1(\phi^{(1)})^2 \frac{\partial \phi^{(1)}}{\partial \xi} + B_1 \frac{\partial^3 \phi^{(1)}}{\partial \xi^3} + C_1\phi^{(1)} = B_1 \frac{\partial S_2}{\partial \xi} \qquad (4.107)$$

where $A_1 = \frac{15}{4\lambda^3} - \frac{3\lambda^3 c(1-\mu)}{2}$, $B_1 = \frac{\lambda^3}{2}$, and $C_1 = \frac{\nu_{id0}}{2}$. It has been observed that the nature of nonlinear waves changes remarkably in the presence of external periodic force. It is important that the source term or forcing term may arise due to the presence of space debris in plasmas of a different kind. Several people have considered different types of forcing terms like Gaussian forcing term [6], hyperbolic forcing term [6] in the form of $sech^2(\xi, \tau)$ and $sech^4(\xi, \tau)$ functions, and trigonometric forcing term [8] in the form of $\sin(\xi, \tau)$ and $\cos(\xi, \tau)$ functions. Taking a clue from these works, we presume that S_2 is a linear function of ξ such as $S_2 = f_0\xi \cos(\omega\tau) + P$, where P is some constant, f_0 is the strength of the source, and ω is the frequency of the source, respectively. If we put the expression of S_2 in Equation (4.107), we get

$$\frac{\partial \phi^{(1)}}{\partial \tau} + A_1 (\phi^{(1)})^2 \frac{\partial \phi^{(1)}}{\partial \xi} + B_1 \frac{\partial^3 \phi^{(1)}}{\partial \xi^3} + C_1 \phi^{(1)} = B_1 f_0 \cos(\omega\tau). \quad (4.108)$$

Equation (4.108) is termed as damped forced modified KdV (DFMKdV) equation.

When $C_1 = 0$ and $f_0 = 0$, then Equation (4.108) converts to the MKdV Equation (4.62) with the solitary wave solution as (4.63).

Just like the previous section, we can find the approximate analytical solution of Equation (4.108) as

$$\phi^{(1)} = \phi_m(\tau) sech\left(\frac{\xi - M(\tau)\tau}{W(\tau)}\right) \quad (4.109)$$

where $M(\tau)$ is given by equation

$$M(\tau) = \left[\frac{\pi f_0 \sqrt{A_1/6}}{2} e^{-\nu_{id0}\tau}\left(\frac{\omega}{\omega^2 + 4C_1^2}\right)\left\{sin(\omega\tau) + \frac{2C_1}{\omega}cos(\omega\tau)\right\}\right.$$
$$\left. + \left\{\sqrt{M} - \pi f_0 B_1 \sqrt{A_1/24}\left(\frac{2C_1}{\omega^2 + 4C_1^2}\right)\right\}\right]^2.$$

The amplitude and width are as follows:

$$\phi_m(\tau) = \frac{1}{\sqrt{A}}\left(\sqrt{6}\left[\frac{\pi f_0 \sqrt{A_1/6}}{2} e^{-\nu_{id0}\tau}\left(\frac{\omega}{\omega^2 + 4C_1^2}\right)\left\{sin(\omega\tau)\right.\right.\right.$$
$$\left.\left.\left. + \frac{2C_1}{\omega}cos(\omega\tau)\right\} + \left\{\sqrt{M} - \pi f_0 B_1 \sqrt{A_1/24}\left(\frac{2C_1}{\omega^2 + 4C_1^2}\right)\right\}\right]\right)$$

$$W(\tau) = \frac{\sqrt{B_1}}{W_1 + W_2}$$

where

$$W_1 = \frac{\pi f_0 \sqrt{A_1/6}}{2} e^{-\nu_{id0}\tau}\left(\frac{\omega}{\omega^2 + 4C_1^2}\right)\left\{sin(\omega\tau) + \frac{2C_1}{\omega}cos(\omega\tau)\right\}$$
$$W_2 = \sqrt{M} - \pi f_0 B_1 \sqrt{A_1/24}\left(\frac{2C_1}{\omega^2 + 4C_1^2}\right).$$

The dependence of the amplitude of the DIA soliton of DFMKdV equation (4.108), which concerns the strength (f_0) of the external periodic force for different values of entropic index q, is shown in Figure 4.4. From Figure 4.4, it is seen that as we increase the entropic index q, with the strength (f_0) of the external periodic force, the amplitude of the solitary wave decreases.

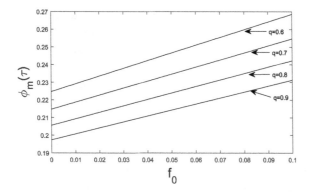

Fig. 4.4: Plot of $\phi_m(\tau)$ vs f_0 for several values of q.

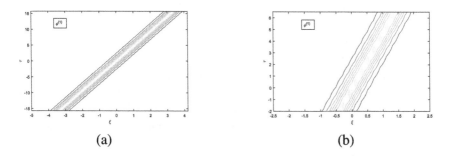

Fig. 4.5: (a) Contour plot of $\phi^{(1)}$ in the plane (ξ, τ) of Equation (4.108).

From Figures 4.5(a) and 4.5(b), it is seen that the outermost contour has the same value of $\phi^{(1)}$, and it increases with the value of the outermost contour towards the center of the solution space from both sides. It is how a solitary wave solution is represented. We can observe from the contours that the value of the maximum amplitude in Figure 4.5(a) is 0.2 and that of Figure 4.5(b) is 0.045.

4.9 Forced Schamel KdV (SKdV) Equation

Schamel [9] introduced a KdV type equation in plasmas, where the trapping of particles plays a vital role in the dynamics. Trapping of particles means that some plasma particles are confined to a finite region where they bounce back and forth, describing closed trajectories in phase space. The concept of trapping in plasmas occurs when there are momentum and energy exchanges between waves and resonant particles. The particles whose speed is near to the phase velocity of the waves are responsible for this. Electrons that have lesser kinetic energy are trapped in the nonlinear wave potential. It leads to the confinement of electrons by the wave potential to a region of the phase space where they oscillate. The amplitude, thickness, and speed of the solitary wave depend crucially upon the population of the trapped electrons.

When deriving the KdV equation for IAWs, the Boltzmann distribution for the electron density is usually considered. Hence, the isothermality and the electron inertia are neglected. It is obtained by assuming $f_e \propto exp\left\{-\left(\frac{1}{2}v^2 - \phi\right)\right\}$ (where the electron velocity is normalized by the electron thermal speed) and is motivated by the consideration that a thermal electron moves with a speed much higher than an ion acoustic wave. Thus, it would not be much affected by the wave as the isothermal behavior of the electrons needs to be reasonable.

The resonant particles interact strongly with the wave during its evolution and, therefore, cannot be treated on the same footing as the free ones. We remove the effects of external boundaries so that the collision-less behaviour is guaranteed. Laboratory experiments indicate that flat-topped electron distributions are typical. Two different distribution functions for the electrons (for the free and the trapped ones) must be used to generally describe the asymptotic, nearly stationary state.

To study the effects of nonisothermal electrons on the nonlinear ion-acoustic waves, vortex-like electron distribution function [9] is employed. The functions are as follows:

$$\left. \begin{aligned} f_{ef} &= \frac{1}{\sqrt{2\pi}} exp\left[\frac{(v^2 - 2\phi)}{2}\right], \quad |v| > \sqrt{2\phi}, \\ f_{et} &= \frac{1}{\sqrt{2\pi}} exp\left[-\frac{\beta(v^2 - 2\phi)}{2}\right], \quad |v| < \sqrt{2\phi}, \end{aligned} \right\} \qquad (4.110)$$

where the subscript ef (et) represents the free (trapped) electron contribution. Distribution functions that are written in Equation (4.110) are continuous in velocity space and satisfy the regularity requirements for an admissible Bernstein–Greene–Kruskal (BGK) solution. The velocity is normalized by the electron thermal velocity. It is a parameter that determines the number of trapped electrons, whose magnitude is defined by the ratio of free electron temperature (T_{ef}) and trapped electron temperature (T_{et}). Here, the velocity of the ion-acoustic wave is assumed less compared to the electron thermal velocity. Now, integrating the electron distribution function over the velocity space, the electron number density is obtained by

$$\left.\begin{array}{l} n_e = e^{\phi} erfc(\sqrt{\phi}) + \dfrac{e^{\beta\phi}}{\sqrt{|\beta|}} erf(\sqrt{\beta\phi}), \quad (\beta > 0) \\[4mm] n_e = e^{\phi} erfc(\sqrt{\phi}) + \dfrac{1}{\sqrt{\pi|\beta|}} W(\sqrt{-\beta\phi}), \quad (\beta < 0) \end{array}\right\} \quad (4.111)$$

where W is the Dawson integral and $erfc(\phi) = 1 - erf(\phi)$ is the complementary error function. Expending n_e for the small amplitude limit and keeping the terms up to ϕ^2, it is seen that n_e is same for both $\beta > 0$ and $\beta < 0$, and finally, we obtain

$$n_e = 1 + \phi - \frac{4}{3} b\phi^{3/2} + \frac{1}{2}\phi^2 \quad (4.112)$$

where $b = (1 - \beta)/\sqrt{\pi}$. Physically, b indicates the deviation from isothermality. If $b > 0$, then the contribution of the resonant electrons to the electron density is possible.

Now, we consider an *e-i* plasma model where the ions are mobile in the presence of superthermal trapped electrons. The external force is considered in the Poisson equation. Schamel [9] and Williams *et al.* [10] have considered electrons both superthermal and trapped. Both the superthermal and trapped electrons are defined in different energy regions. When the energy region lies between $-\sqrt{2\phi} < v < \sqrt{2\phi}$ (v is the velocity and ϕ is the electric potential), the electrons are considered trapped, and the corresponding κ distribution for the trapped electrons will be

$$f_{e,t}^k(v,\phi) = \frac{1}{\sqrt{2\pi}(\kappa - \frac{3}{2})^{1/2}} \frac{\Gamma(\kappa)}{\Gamma(\kappa - 1/2)}$$

$$\times \left[1 + \beta\left(\frac{v^2/2 - \phi}{\kappa - \frac{3}{2}}\right)\right]^{-\kappa} \quad for \; E_e \leq 0. \quad (4.113)$$

It is an extension of Schamel's distribution [11] for Maxwellian trapped electrons. If $\kappa \to \infty$ (4.113), it produces Schamel's equation [9]. Schamel considered the distribution which separates free electrons from trapped electrons. He also considered a trapped parameter β, which measures the inverse temperature of the trapped electrons. For superthermal free electrons, we have assumed the distribution as

$$f_{e,f}^\kappa(v,\phi) = \frac{1}{\sqrt{2\pi}(\kappa - \frac{3}{2})^{\frac{1}{2}}} \frac{\Gamma(\kappa)}{\Gamma(\kappa - \frac{1}{2})} \left(1 + \frac{\frac{v^2}{2} - \phi}{\kappa - \frac{3}{2}}\right)^{-\kappa}. \quad (4.114)$$

For simplicity, we assume $\kappa > 3/2$. So, the number density of electron $n_e(\phi)$ will be given by

$$n_e(\phi) = \int_{-\infty}^{-\sqrt{2\phi}} f_{e,f}^{\kappa}(v,\phi)dv + \int_{-\sqrt{2\phi}}^{\sqrt{2\phi}} f_{e,t}^{\kappa}(v,\phi)dv + \int_{\sqrt{2\phi}}^{+\infty} f_{e,f}^{\kappa}(v,\phi)dv$$

(4.115)

where $f_{e,f}^{\kappa}(v,\phi)$ is given by (4.114) and n_e is given by (4.115). After integrating with respect to velocity, we get

$$n_e(\phi) = (2\kappa - 3)^{\kappa-3/2}(2\kappa - 3 - 2\phi)^{-\kappa} \times \left[(2\kappa - 3)\sqrt{2\kappa - 3 - 2\phi} \right.$$

$$- \frac{4}{\Gamma[\kappa - 3/2]}\sqrt{2/\pi} \times \sqrt{\phi}\Gamma[\kappa]2^{F_1}\left[\frac{1}{2}, \kappa, \frac{3}{2}, \frac{2\phi}{3 - 2\kappa + 2\phi}\right] \Big] \Big]$$

$$+ \frac{2}{\Gamma[\kappa - 1/2]}\sqrt{2/\pi}(2\kappa - 3)^{\kappa-1/2}\sqrt{\phi} \times (2\kappa - 3 - 2\beta\phi)^{-\kappa}\Gamma[\kappa]$$

$$\times 2^{F_1}\left[\frac{1}{2}, \kappa, \frac{3}{2}, \frac{2\beta\phi}{3 - 2\kappa + 2\beta\phi}\right].$$

(4.116)

Expanding the hyper geometric function $F(a, b, c, x)$ as a power series expansion as $F(a, b, c, x) = 1 + \frac{ab}{c}x + \frac{a(a+1)b(b+1)}{c(c+1)}\frac{x^2}{2!} + \cdots$ and keeping term up to ϕ^2, the following function $n_e(\phi)$ is obtained:

$$n_e(\phi) \sim 1 + p\phi + q\phi^{3/2} + r\phi^2$$

(4.117)

where $p = \frac{2\kappa-1}{2\kappa-3}$, $q = \frac{8\sqrt{2/\pi}(\beta-1)\kappa\Gamma(\kappa)}{3(2\kappa-3)^{3/2}\Gamma(\kappa-1/2)}$, and $r = \frac{4\kappa^2-1}{2(2\kappa-3)^2}$.

Sen *et al.* [6] have studied nonlinear wave excitation by orbiting charged space debris objects. They considered the source term $S(x - v_d t)$ on the Poisson equation arising from the charged debris, moving at speed v_d. There is no work in that area where the externally applied force is solely dependent on τ.

Accordingly, the one-dimensional normalized fluid equations along with the source term are given by

$$\frac{\partial n_i}{\partial t} + \frac{\partial (n_i u_i)}{\partial x} = 0$$

(4.118)

$$\frac{\partial u_i}{\partial t} + u_i\frac{\partial u_i}{\partial x} = -\frac{\partial \phi}{\partial x}$$

(4.119)

$$\frac{\partial^2 \phi}{\partial x^2} = n_e - n_i + S(x,t)$$

$$\simeq (1 - n_i) + p\phi + q\phi^{3/2} + r\phi^2 + S(x,t). \quad (4.120)$$

Here, n_i, n_e, u_i, and ϕ represent the ion density, electron density, ion velocity, and electrostatic potential, respectively. The term $S(x,t)$ is a charge density source derived from experimental conditions for a definite objective. Here, the same normalization is used as in Section 4.7.

To obtain the phase velocity and the nonlinear evolution equation, the stretch coordinates are taken as

$$\xi = \epsilon^{1/4}(x - \lambda t), \quad \tau = \epsilon^{3/4} t \quad (4.121)$$

where ϵ is an infinitely small parameter. The dependent variables n_i, u_i, ϕ, and $S(x,t)$ can be expanded as

$$\left.\begin{aligned}
n_i &= 1 + \epsilon n_i^{(1)} + \epsilon^{3/2} n_i^{(2)} + \cdot \\
u_i &= 0 + \epsilon u_i^{(1)} + \epsilon^{3/2} u_i^{(2)} + \cdot \\
\phi &= 0 + \epsilon \phi^{(1)} + \epsilon^{3/2} \phi^{(2)} + \cdot \\
S(x,t) &\sim \epsilon^{3/2} S_2(x,t) + \cdot.
\end{aligned}\right\} \quad (4.122)$$

Substituting Equations (4.121)–(4.122) in the model Equations (4.118)–(4.120) and comparing the coefficients of different order of ϵ, one can obtain

$$\left.\begin{aligned}
&n_i^{(1)} = p\phi^{(1)} \\
&\frac{\partial^2 \phi^{(1)}}{\partial \xi^2} + n_i^{(2)} = p\phi^{(2)} + q(\phi^{(1)})^{3/2} + S_2(\xi, \tau) \\
&-\lambda \frac{\partial n_i^{(1)}}{\partial \xi} + \frac{\partial u_i^{(1)}}{\partial \xi} = 0, \lambda \frac{\partial u_i^{(1)}}{\partial \xi} - \frac{\partial \phi^{(1)}}{\partial \xi} = 0 \\
&-\lambda \frac{\partial n_i^{(2)}}{\partial \xi} + \frac{\partial u_i^{(2)}}{\partial \xi} + \frac{\partial n_i^{(1)}}{\partial \tau} = 0, -\lambda \frac{\partial u_i^{(2)}}{\partial \xi} + \frac{\partial u_i^{(1)}}{\partial \tau} + \frac{\partial \phi^{(2)}}{\partial \xi} = 0.
\end{aligned}\right\} \quad (4.123)$$

To obtain phase velocity, we eliminate the first-order perturbed quantities, and for the nontrivial values of the perturbed quantities, we have discussed the phase velocity of the wave as

$$\lambda^2 = \frac{1}{p}. \quad (4.124)$$

Now, considering the term of next order of ϵ and simply as above we get the nonlinear evolution equation as

$$\frac{\partial \phi^{(1)}}{\partial \tau} + A\sqrt{\phi^{(1)}}\frac{\partial \phi^{(1)}}{\partial \xi} + B\frac{\partial^3 \phi^{(1)}}{\partial \xi^3} = B\frac{\partial S_2}{\partial \xi} \qquad (4.125)$$

where $A = -\frac{3q}{4p^{3/2}}$ and $B = \frac{1}{2p^{3/2}}$.

We suppose $S_2 = \frac{f_0}{B}\xi \cos(\omega\tau)$, where f_0 and ω have respectively denoted the strength and frequency. Using this, we obtain from Equation (4.125)

$$\frac{\partial \phi^{(1)}}{\partial \tau} + A\sqrt{\phi^{(1)}}\frac{\partial \phi^{(1)}}{\partial \xi} + B\frac{\partial^3 \phi^{(1)}}{\partial \xi^3} = f_0 \cos(\omega\tau). \qquad (4.126)$$

It is known as forced KdV-like Schamel (SKdV) equation.

When $f_0 = 0$, Equation (4.126) represents KdV-like Schamel equation, and the solitary wave solution is of the form

$$\phi^{(1)} = \phi_m sech^4\left(\frac{\xi - U\tau}{W}\right) \qquad (4.127)$$

where $\phi_m = \left(\frac{15U}{8A}\right)^2$ and $W = \sqrt{\frac{16B}{U}}$ are the amplitude and width of the ion-acoustic solitary wave, respectively, and U is the speed of the ion-acoustic solitary wave.

When $f_0 \neq 0$, we consider the amplitude, width, and velocity of the solitary wave depending on τ, and the approximate solution of (4.126) is of the form

$$\phi^{(1)} = \phi_m(\tau)sech^4\left(\frac{\xi - U(\tau)\tau}{W(\tau)}\right) \qquad (4.128)$$

where amplitude $\phi_m(\tau) = \left(\frac{15U(\tau)}{8A}\right)^2$ and width $W(\tau) = \sqrt{\frac{16B}{U(\tau)}}$. Where $U(\tau)$ have to be determined from the equation

$$U(\tau) = \sqrt{\frac{64A^2}{135}\frac{f_0 \sin(\omega t)}{\omega} + k^2}.$$

So, the solution of (4.126) is of the form

$$\phi^{(1)} = \phi_m(\tau)sech^4\left(\frac{\xi - U(\tau)\tau}{W(\tau)}\right) \qquad (4.129)$$

where

$$\phi_m(\tau) = \frac{5f_0 sin(\omega\tau)}{3\omega} + \frac{225k^2}{64A^2}$$

$$W(\tau) = \left(\frac{16B}{\sqrt{\frac{64A^2 f_0 sin(\omega\tau)}{135\omega} + k^2}} \right)^{1/2}.$$

We can also examine the effects of the strength (f_0) of the external force by solitary wave solution of Equations (4.126), as shown in Figure 4.6. It is clear that as we increase f_0, the amplitude of the ion acoustic solitary wave increases.

Figure 4.7 reflects the variation of the amplitude of the ion acoustic solitary wave solution of Equation (4.126) for different values of ω. It is clear

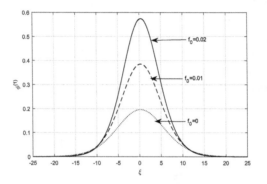

Fig. 4.6: Variation of the solitary wave solution of Equation (4.126) for $f_0 = 0$, 0.01, 0.02 with $k = 2.5$, $u_0 = 0.2$, $\beta = 0.5$, $\omega = 1$, $\tau = 1$.

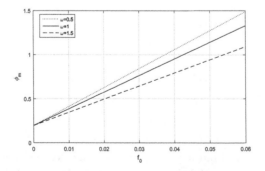

Fig. 4.7: Variation of the amplitude of the solitary wave solution of Equation (4.126) for $\omega = 0.5$, 1, 1.5 with other parameters the same as in Figure 4.6.

that the amplitude of the solitary wave increases as the force increases. At the same time, when the frequency of the external periodic forces increases, the rate of change of amplitude of the solitary wave decreases.

4.10 Burgers' Equation

In fluid mechanics, Burgers' equation is one of the most significant partial differential equations. The equation is named after Johannes Martinus Burgers (1895–1981). It is obtained due to the combination of a nonlinear wave motion with diffusion. The presence of the viscous term helps suppress the wave breaking and smooth out shock discontinuities. To derive Burgers' equation, we consider an unmagnetized, collisionless dusty plasma having q distributed electrons, Boltzmann distributed ions, and both positive and negative charged dust grains. Generally, negatively charged dust grains are considered in dusty plasmas as electrons move fast towards the dust and make it negatively charged. But, positively charge clouds of dust are also present in dusty plasmas. The principle of positively charged dust grains in space arises due to (i) photoemission in the presence of flux of ultraviolet photons, (ii) thermionic emission induced by radiative heating, and (iii) secondary emission of electrons from the surface of dust grains. Therefore, dust grains are both negatively and positively charged. They exist in different regions of space like comet tails, upper and lower mesosphere, Jupiter's magnetosphere, and planetary rings. The basic fluid equations are given as follows:

$$\frac{\partial N_1}{\partial T} + \frac{\partial (N_1 U_1)}{\partial X} = 0 \tag{4.130}$$

$$\frac{\partial U_1}{\partial T} + U_1 \frac{\partial U_1}{\partial X} = \frac{Z_1 e}{m_1} \frac{\partial \phi}{\partial X} + \eta_{11} \frac{\partial^2 U_1}{\partial X^2} \tag{4.131}$$

$$\frac{\partial N_2}{\partial T} + \frac{\partial (N_2 U_2)}{\partial X} = 0 \tag{4.132}$$

$$\frac{\partial U_2}{\partial T} + U_2 \frac{\partial U_2}{\partial X} = -\frac{Z_2 e}{m_2} \frac{\partial \phi}{\partial X} + \eta_{22} \frac{\partial^2 U_2}{\partial X^2} \tag{4.133}$$

$$N_e - N_i + Z_1 N_1 - Z_2 N_2 = 0 \tag{4.134}$$

where $N_e = N_{e0} \left[1 + (q-1) \frac{e\phi}{K_B T_e} \right]^{\frac{(1-q)}{2(q+1)}}$ and $N_i = N_{i0} e^{\left(-\frac{e\phi}{K_B T_i}\right)}$. Here, N_j ($j = 1$, 2, e, and i stand for negative dust particle, positive dust particle, electrons, and ions) is the number density, U_j is the fluid speed, $Z_1(Z_2)$ is the number of electrons (protons) residing on negative (positive) dust particles, m_j is the mass, e is the electronic charge, ϕ is the wave potential, $\eta_1(\eta_2)$ is the viscosity coefficient of negative (positive) dust fluid, T_j is the temperature, and K_B is the Boltzmann constant. In Equation (4.134), we have assumed the quasineutrality condition at equilibrium. Here, normalization is taken as follows:

$$n_1 \to N_1/n_{10}, n_2 \to N_2/n_{20}, u_1 \to U_1/c_1, u_2 \to U_2/c_1, \phi \to (e\phi)/(K_B T_i),$$

$$t \to T w_{pd}, x \to X/\lambda_D, \eta_1 \to \eta_{11} w_{pd}\lambda_D^2, \eta_2 \to \eta_{22} w_{pd}\lambda_D^2$$

where n_{j0} is the equilibrium value of n_j, $c_1 = \sqrt{Z_1 K_B T_i/m_1}$, $w_{pd} = \sqrt{4\pi Z_1^2 e^2 n_{10}/m_1}$, and $\lambda_D = \sqrt{(Z_1 K_B T_i)/(4\pi Z_1^2 e^2 n_{10})}$, and accordingly the basic normalized equations are expressed as

$$\frac{\partial n_1}{\partial t} + \frac{\partial(n_1 u_1)}{\partial x} = 0 \qquad (4.135)$$

$$\frac{\partial u_1}{\partial t} + u_1\frac{\partial u_1}{\partial x} = \frac{\partial \phi}{\partial x} + \eta_1\frac{\partial^2 u_1}{\partial x^2} \qquad (4.136)$$

$$\frac{\partial n_2}{\partial t} + \frac{\partial(n_2 u_2)}{\partial x} = 0 \qquad (4.137)$$

$$\frac{\partial u_2}{\partial t} + u_2\frac{\partial u_2}{\partial x} = -\alpha\beta\frac{\partial \phi}{\partial x} + \eta_2\frac{\partial^2 u_2}{\partial x^2} \qquad (4.138)$$

$$n_1 - \mu_i e^{-\phi} - (1 + \mu_e - \mu_i)n_2 = -\mu_e[1 + (q-1)\sigma\phi]^{\frac{q+1}{2(q-1)}} \qquad (4.139)$$

where $\alpha = Z_2/Z_1$, $\beta = m_1/m_2$, $\mu_e = N_{e0}/(Z_1 n_{10})$, $\mu_i = N_{i0}/(Z_1 n_{10})$, and $\sigma = T_i/T_e$. For RPT, we have used the same stretched coordinates used as in Equation (4.40). The expansions of the dependent variables are considered as

$$\left.\begin{array}{c} n_1 = 1 + \sum\limits_{k=1}^{\infty} \epsilon^k n_1^{(k)}, \; n_2 = 1 + \sum\limits_{k=1}^{\infty} \epsilon^k n_2^{(k)} \\[2mm] u_1 = 0 + \sum\limits_{k=1}^{\infty} \epsilon^k u_1^{(k)}, \; u_2 = 0 + \sum\limits_{k=1}^{\infty} \epsilon^k u_2^{(k)} \\[2mm] \phi = 0 + \sum\limits_{k=1}^{\infty} \epsilon^k \phi^{(k)}. \end{array}\right\} \qquad (4.140)$$

To obtain the phase velocity and nonlinear evolution equation, we substitute (4.140) and (4.40) into (4.135)–(4.139) and taking the coefficient of $\epsilon^{\frac{3}{2}}$

from (4.135)–(4.138) and ϵ from (4.139), we get

$$\left.\begin{array}{l} n_1^{(1)} = \dfrac{u_1^{(1)}}{\lambda}, \quad u_1^{(1)} = -\dfrac{\phi^{(1)}}{\lambda} \\[3mm] n_2^{(1)} = \dfrac{u_2^{(1)}}{\lambda}, \quad u_2^{(1)} = (\alpha\beta)\dfrac{\phi^{(1)}}{\lambda} \\[3mm] n_1^{(1)} = (1 + \mu_e - \mu_i)n_2^{(1)} - \mu_e\sigma\dfrac{(q+1)}{2}\phi^{(1)} - \mu_i\phi^{(1)}. \end{array}\right\} \quad (4.141)$$

Now, using the set of equations in (4.141), we get the phase velocity as

$$\lambda^2 = \frac{[1 + \alpha\beta(1 + \mu_e - \mu_i)]}{[\sigma\mu_e(q+1)/2 + \mu_i]}. \quad (4.142)$$

Substituting (4.140) into (4.135)–(4.139) and equating the coefficients of $O(\epsilon^{\frac{5}{2}})$ from (4.135)–(4.138) and $O(\epsilon^2)$ from (4.139), we obtain

$$\frac{\partial n_1^{(1)}}{\partial \tau} - \lambda\frac{\partial n_1^{(2)}}{\partial \xi} + \frac{\partial u_1^{(2)}}{\partial \xi} + \frac{\partial(n_1^{(1)}u_1^{(1)})}{\partial \xi} = 0 \quad (4.143)$$

$$\frac{\partial u_1^{(1)}}{\partial \tau} - \lambda\frac{\partial u_1^{(2)}}{\partial \xi} + u_1^{(1)}\frac{\partial u_1^{(1)}}{\partial \xi} = \frac{\partial\phi^{(2)}}{\partial \xi} + \eta_{10}\frac{\partial^2 u_1^{(1)}}{\partial \xi^2} \quad (4.144)$$

$$\frac{\partial n_2^{(1)}}{\partial \tau} - \lambda\frac{\partial n_2^{(2)}}{\partial \xi} + \frac{\partial u_2^{(2)}}{\partial \xi} + \frac{\partial(n_2^{(1)}u_2^{(1)})}{\partial \xi} = 0 \quad (4.145)$$

$$\frac{\partial u_2^{(1)}}{\partial \tau} - \lambda\frac{\partial u_2^{(2)}}{\partial \xi} + u_2^{(1)}\frac{\partial u_2^{(1)}}{\partial \xi} = -\alpha\beta\frac{\partial\phi^{(2)}}{\partial \xi} + \eta_{20}\frac{\partial^2 u_2^{(1)}}{\partial \xi^2} \quad (4.146)$$

$$n_1^{(2)} = (1 + \mu_e - \mu_i)n_2^{(2)} - \mu_e\sigma\frac{(q+1)}{2}\phi^{(2)}$$
$$- \mu_e\sigma^2\frac{(q+1)(3-q)}{8}(\phi^{(1)})^2 - \mu_i\phi^{(2)} + \frac{\mu_i}{2}(\phi^{(1)})^2. \quad (4.147)$$

Using Equations (4.141)–(4.142) and eliminating $n_1^{(2)}$, $n_2^{(2)}$, $u_1^{(2)}$, $u_2^{(2)}$, and $\phi^{(2)}$ from the above set of equations, we finally obtain

$$\frac{\partial\phi^{(1)}}{\partial \tau} + A\phi^{(1)}\frac{\partial\phi^{(1)}}{\partial \xi} - C\frac{\partial^2\phi^{(1)}}{\partial \xi^2} = 0. \quad (4.148)$$

(4.148) is known as Burgers' equation where the nonlinear coefficient A and the dissipation coefficient C are given by

$$A = \frac{12\alpha^2\beta^2(1 + \mu_e - \mu_i) - 12 + 4\mu_i\lambda^4 - \mu_e\sigma^2\lambda^4(q+1)(3-q)}{8\lambda[1 + \alpha\beta(1 + \mu_e - \mu_i)]} \quad \text{and}$$

$$C = \frac{\eta_{10} + \eta_{20}\alpha\beta(1 + \mu_e - \mu_i)}{2\{1 + \alpha\beta(1 + \mu_e - \mu_i)\}}.$$

To obtain the stationary solution of this Burgers' equation (4.148), we have introduced a transformation $\zeta = \xi - u_0\tau$. Now, applying the conditions $\phi^{(1)} \to 0$, $\frac{d\phi^{(1)}}{d\zeta} \to 0$ at $\zeta \to \infty$, the stationary solution is given by

$$\phi^{(1)} = \phi_m^{(1)}\left[1 - \tanh\left(\frac{\zeta}{\Delta}\right)\right] \tag{4.149}$$

where u_0 is a constant velocity normalized by C_s and the amplitude $\phi_m^{(1)}$ (normalized by $\frac{K_B T_i}{e}$) and width Δ (normalized by λ_D) of the shock waves are defined as

$$\phi_m^{(1)} = \frac{u_0}{A}, \quad \Delta = \frac{2C}{u_0}, \tag{4.150}$$

respectively. It is observed, from Equations (4.149)–(4.150), that the amplitude of the shock waves increases as u_0 increases, and the width of the shock waves decreases as u_0 increases. From Equation (4.149), it is clear that the shock potential profile is both positive and negative when $A > 0$ or $A < 0$.

To find the parametric regimes for which positive and negative shock wave (potential) profiles exist, we have numerically analyzed A and have obtained the $A = 0$ curve in the $\beta - q$ plane. Figure 4.8 shows that we can have positive shock wave (potential) profiles for the parameters, whose values lie above the curve $A = 0$, and a negative shock (potential) profile can be achieved for the parameters whose values lie below the curve $A = 0$. Obviously, for $A = 0$, the shock waves do not exist.

Figure 4.9(a) reflects the effects of the nonextensive parameter q on the propagation of dust acoustic shock structure. It is clear from Figure 4.9(a) that a small change in nonextensive parameters q exhibits different shock structures, and positive dust acoustic shock wave potential decreases as q increases. Also, from Figure 4.9(b), it is seen that the shock structures are different for different values of β. It is also seen that the amplitude of the positive dust acoustic shock wave potential decreases as β increases.

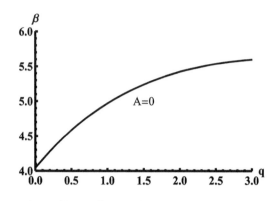

Fig. 4.8: Showing $A = 0$ (β vs. q) curve for $\alpha = 0.101$, $\sigma = 0.497$, $\mu_i = 0.5$, $\mu_e = 0.3$.

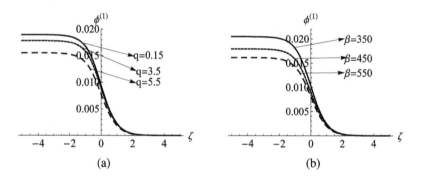

Fig. 4.9: (a) Variation of DA shock wave potential $\phi^{(1)}$ with spatial coordinates ζ for different values of q and (b) for different values of β.

4.11   Modified Burgers' Equation

Like the MKdV equation, the modified Burgers' equation is necessary if, for a particular set of parameters, the coefficient of the nonlinear term of the Burgers' equation vanishes. Here, we consider the propagation of an electrostatic perturbation in an unmagnetized, collisionless, dense plasma containing degenerate electron fluids (both nonrelativistic and ultra-relativistic) and inertial viscous ion fluids [12].

For understanding the different electrostatic nonlinear phenomena in astrophysical environments (where particle velocities are near the speed of light), relativistic effects should be taken into account. Many astrophysical compact objects such as white dwarfs and neutron stars have degenerate electron number densities. These are so high (in white dwarfs and neutron stars) that on the order of $10^{30} cm^{-3}$ and $10^{36} cm^{-3}$, or even more than their cores, it consists of strongly coupled nondegenerate ion lattices. These are immersed in degenerate electron fluids that follow the Fermi–Dirac distribution function. Chandrasekhar [13] developed a general expression for relativistic electron pressures in his classical papers. The electron fluid pressure can be satisfied by the following equation:

$$P_e = K_e n_e^\alpha = K_e n_e^\gamma.$$

The nonrelativistic limit can be written as

$$\alpha = \gamma = \frac{5}{3}, \quad K_e = \frac{3}{5}\left(\frac{\pi}{3}\right)^{1/3}\frac{\pi h^2}{m} \simeq \Lambda_c hc$$

where $\Lambda_c = \pi h/mc = 1.2 \times 10^{-10} cm$ and h is the plank constant divided by 2π, whereas in considering the ultra-relativistic case, it is

$$\alpha = \frac{5}{3}, \quad \gamma = \frac{4}{3}, \quad K_e = \frac{3}{4}\left(\frac{\pi}{9}\right)^{1/3} hc \simeq \frac{3}{4}hc.$$

The basic normalized fluid equations are

$$\frac{\partial n_i}{\partial t} + \frac{\partial(n_i u_i)}{\partial x} = 0 \tag{4.151}$$

$$\frac{\partial u_i}{\partial t} + u_i\frac{\partial u_i}{\partial x} = -\frac{\partial \phi}{\partial x} + \eta\frac{\partial^2 u_i}{\partial x^2} \tag{4.152}$$

$$n_e\frac{\partial \phi}{\partial t} = K\frac{\partial n_e^\gamma}{\partial x} \tag{4.153}$$

$$\frac{\partial^2 \phi}{\partial x^2} = -\rho \tag{4.154}$$

$$\rho = n_i - n_e. \tag{4.155}$$

n_j ($j = e$, and i, stands for electrons, and ions, respectively) is the number density, u_j is the fluid speed, m_j is the mass, ϕ is the wave potential, η is the viscosity coefficient, x is the space variable, and t is the time variable. At equilibrium, we have $n_{i0} = n_{e0}$ where the normalization is done as follows:

$$n_j \to n_j/n_{j0}, \quad u_i \to u_i/c_i, \quad \phi \to (e\phi)/(m_e c^2),$$

$$t \to t w_{pi}, \quad x \to x/\lambda_m, \quad \eta \to \frac{\eta}{w_{pi}\lambda_m^2 m_i n_{i0}}.$$

Here, n_{j0} is the equilibrium value of n_j, $c_i = \sqrt{m_e c^2/m_i}$, $w_{pi} = \sqrt{4\pi e^2 n_{i0}/m_i}$, and $\lambda_m = \sqrt{(m_e c^2)/(4\pi e^2 n_{e0})}$. c is the speed of light in vacuum, e is the magnitude of the charge of an electron, and $K = \frac{K_e n_{e0}^{\gamma-1}}{m_e c^2}$.

For perturbation analysis, let us consider new stretched coordinates ξ and τ such that

$$\xi = \epsilon^2(x - \lambda t), \quad \tau = \epsilon^4 t \tag{4.156}$$

where ϵ is a parameter measuring the weakness of the nonlinearity and λ is the phase speed of the waves. We can expand the variables n_j, u_i, and ψ in a power series of ϵ as

$$\left.\begin{array}{c} n_j = 1 + \displaystyle\sum_{k=1}^{\infty} \epsilon^k n_j^{(k)}, \quad u_i = 0 + \displaystyle\sum_{k=1}^{\infty} \epsilon^k u_1^{(k)} \\[3mm] \phi = 0 + \displaystyle\sum_{k=1}^{\infty} \epsilon^k \phi^{(k)}, \quad \rho = 0 + \displaystyle\sum_{k=1}^{\infty} \epsilon^k \rho^{(k)}. \end{array}\right\} \tag{4.157}$$

To obtain the phase velocity and nonlinear evolution equation, we substitute (4.156)–(4.157) into (4.151)–(4.155), and equating the lowest power of ϵ, we get

$$n_i^{(1)} = \frac{\phi^{(1)}}{\lambda^2}, \quad u_i^{(1)} = \frac{\phi^{(1)}}{\lambda}, \quad n_e^{(1)} = \frac{\phi^{(1)}}{\gamma K}. \tag{4.158}$$

We get from Equation (4.158)

$$\lambda = \sqrt{\gamma K}. \tag{4.159}$$

Equation (4.159) is the phase velocity. We substitute Equations (4.156)–(4.157) in Equations (4.151)–(4.155), equate the coefficient of ϵ^4 from Equations (4.151)–(4.154), and take the coefficient of ϵ^2 from Equation (4.155). We obtain a set of equations as follows:

$$\left.\begin{array}{c} n_i^{(2)} = \dfrac{\phi^{(2)}}{\lambda^2} + \dfrac{3(\phi^{(1)})^2}{2\lambda^4}, \quad u_i^{(2)} = \dfrac{\phi^{(2)}}{\lambda} + \dfrac{(\phi^{(1)})^2}{2\lambda^3} \\[3mm] n_e^{(2)} = \dfrac{\phi^{(2)}}{\lambda^2} - \dfrac{(\gamma-2)(\phi^{(1)})^2}{2\lambda^4}, \quad \rho^{(2)} = \dfrac{1}{2}\left[\dfrac{(\gamma-2)}{\lambda^4} + \dfrac{3}{\lambda^4}\right](\phi^{(1)})^2 = 0. \end{array}\right\} \tag{4.160}$$

For the next higher order in ϵ, we equate the coefficient of ϵ^5 from Equations (4.151)–(4.152) and ϵ^3 from Equation (4.155), thus we can derive the following sets of equations:

$$\frac{\partial n_i^{(1)}}{\partial \tau} - \lambda \frac{\partial n_i^{(3)}}{\partial \xi} + \frac{\partial u_i^{(3)}}{\partial \xi} + \frac{\partial}{\partial \xi}(n_i^{(1)} u_i^{(2)} + n_i^{(2)} u_i^{(1)}) = 0$$

$$\frac{\partial u_i^{(1)}}{\partial \tau} - \lambda \frac{\partial u_i^{(3)}}{\partial \xi} + \frac{\partial}{\partial \xi}(u_i^{(1)} u_i^{(2)}) + \frac{\partial \phi^{(3)}}{\partial \xi} - \eta \frac{\partial^2 u_i^{(1)}}{\partial \xi^2} = 0$$

$$\frac{\partial}{\partial \xi}\left[\phi^{(3)} - \lambda^2 \left\{ n_e^{(3)} + \frac{(\gamma - 2)(\phi^{(1)}\phi^{(2)})}{\lambda^4} - \frac{(\gamma - 2)(2\gamma - 3)(\phi^{(1)})^3}{6\lambda^6} \right\} \right] = 0$$

$$n_i^{(3)} - n_e^{(3)} = -\rho^{(3)}.$$

We finally obtain the modified Burgers' equation as

$$\frac{\partial \phi^{(1)}}{\partial \tau} + A(\phi^{(1)})^2 \frac{\partial \phi^{(1)}}{\partial \xi} = C \frac{\partial^2 \phi^{(1)}}{\partial \xi^2} \tag{4.161}$$

where $A = \frac{1}{4\lambda^3}[15 - (\gamma - 2)(2\gamma - 3)]$ and $C = \frac{\eta}{2}$.

The stationary shock solution of Equation (4.161) is written as

$$\phi^{(1)} = \left[\phi_m \left\{ 1 - \tanh\left(\frac{\zeta}{\Delta}\right) \right\} \right] \tag{4.162}$$

where the spacial coordinate is $\zeta = \xi - u_0 \tau$, the amplitude is $\phi_m = \frac{3u_0}{2A}$, and the width is $\Delta = \sqrt{\frac{C}{u_0}}$.

4.12 KdV Burgers' (KdVB) Equation

The propagation of IAWs in a collisionless plasma is described by the KdV equation. The KdV equation exhibits solitary wave solutions as well as cnoidal wave solutions without dissipation. On the other hand, ion acoustic shock waves arise in dissipative plasmas. We consider a dissipative mechanism to explain the existence of shock waves. One possible dissipative mechanism peculiar to plasmas is due to the kinematic viscosity. It is interesting and worthwhile to examine the effects of kinematic viscosity on the propagation of ion acoustic waves, where the dissipation plays a crucial role to form shock waves (than solitary waves) due to kinematic viscosity. KdVB equation is such an equation that can contain the dissipative and dispersion of the media simultaneously. The standard RPT is used to derive the KdVB equation for IAWs. To investigate the effects of kinematic viscosity on IAWs, we use the modified ion momentum equation, equation of continuity, and Poisson's equation. The basic fluid normalized equations are written as

$$\frac{\partial n_i}{\partial t} + \frac{\partial(n_i u_i)}{\partial x} = 0 \tag{4.163}$$

$$\frac{\partial u_i}{\partial t} + u_i \frac{\partial u_i}{\partial x} = -\frac{\partial \phi}{\partial x} + \eta_i \frac{\partial^2 u_i}{\partial x^2} \tag{4.164}$$

$$\frac{\partial^2 \phi}{\partial x^2} = \exp \phi - n_i \tag{4.165}$$

where $\eta_i = \frac{\mu_i \omega_{pi}}{C_s^2}$, and μ_i is the ion kinematic viscosity.

To obtain the KdVB equation, we have introduced the same stretched coordinates as in Equation (4.40). The expansions of the dependent variables are also considered the same as (4.41). Substituting expansions (4.41), along with the stretch coordinates (4.40) into Equations (4.163–4.165) and equating the coefficient of the lowest order of ϵ, we obtain the phase velocity as

$$\lambda^2 = \pm 1. \tag{4.166}$$

To obtain the nonlinear evolution equation, we substitute Equation (4.41) in Equations (4.163)–(4.165) and collect the next higher order of ϵ,

$$\frac{\partial n_i^{(1)}}{\partial \tau} - \lambda \frac{\partial n_i^{(2)}}{\partial \xi} + \frac{\partial n_i^{(1)} u_i^{(1)}}{\partial \xi} + \frac{\partial u_i^{(2)}}{\partial \xi} = 0, \tag{4.167}$$

$$\frac{\partial u_i^{(1)}}{\partial \tau} - \lambda \frac{\partial u_i^{(2)}}{\partial \xi} + u_i^{(1)} \frac{\partial u_i^{(1)}}{\partial \xi} + \frac{\partial \phi^{(2)}}{\partial \xi^2} = \eta_{i0} \frac{\partial^2 u_i^{(1)}}{\partial \xi^2}, \tag{4.168}$$

$$\frac{\partial \phi^{(1)}}{\partial \xi^2} - \phi^{(2)} - \frac{1}{2}(\phi^{(1)})^2 + n_i^{(1)} = 0. \tag{4.169}$$

Differentiating Equation (4.169) with respect to ξ and substituting $\frac{\partial n_i^{(2)}}{\partial \xi}$ from Equation (4.167) and for $\frac{\partial u_i^{(2)}}{\partial \xi}$ from Equation (4.168), we finally obtain

$$\frac{\partial \phi^{(1)}}{\partial \tau} + \frac{1}{\lambda} \phi^{(1)} \frac{\partial \phi^{(1)}}{\partial \xi} + \frac{\lambda}{2} \frac{\partial^3 \phi^{(1)}}{\partial \xi^3} - \frac{\eta_{i0}}{2} \frac{\partial^2 \phi^{(1)}}{\partial \xi^2} = 0. \tag{4.170}$$

Equation (4.170) is known as KdVB equation. The second, third, and fourth terms of Equation (4.170) respectively are nonlinear, dispersion, and dissipative. If the system is nondissipative, then we obtain the KdV equation (1.137). With the help of tanh method, we can also get the stationary

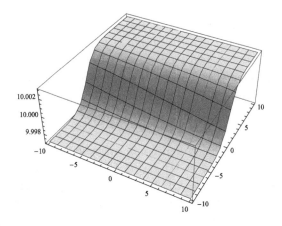

Fig. 4.10: The stationary shock structures (4.170) as a function of ξ and τ.

solution of Equation (4.170) as

$$\phi^{(1)}(\xi, \tau) = a_0 + a_1 \tanh\{\alpha(\xi - V\tau)\} + a_2 \tanh^2\{\alpha(\xi - V\tau)\} \quad (4.171)$$

where $a_0 = \frac{1}{A}(V + 12B\alpha^2)$, $a_1 = -\frac{6\eta_{i0}\alpha}{5A}$, $a_2 = -\frac{12B\alpha^2}{A}$, $\alpha = \pm\frac{\eta_{i0}}{20B}$, $A = \frac{1}{\lambda}$, and $B = \frac{\lambda}{2}$. Here, V is the shock wave velocity. The shock height is directly proportional to the square of η_{i0} and inversely to the product AB, whereas the shock width varies inversely with η_{i0} and directly with B.

Figure 4.10 represents the three-dimensional view of the stationary shock structures for different values of η_{i0}.

4.13 Damped KdVB Equation

To derive the damped KdVB equation, we consider an unmagnetized collisional dusty plasma model. It consists of cold inertial ions, stationary negative dust charge, and q-nonextensive electrons. Here, the damping is considered because of the dust–ion collision along with the usual kinetic viscosity. The basic normalized set of equations are

$$\frac{\partial n_i}{\partial t} + \frac{\partial(n_i u_i)}{\partial x} = 0 \quad (4.172)$$

$$\frac{\partial u_i}{\partial t} + u_i\frac{\partial u_i}{\partial x} = -\frac{\partial \phi}{\partial x} + \eta\frac{\partial^2 u_i}{\partial x^2} - \nu_{id}u_i \quad (4.173)$$

$$\frac{\partial^2 \phi}{\partial x^2} = (1 - \mu)n_e - n_i + \mu \quad (4.174)$$

where $n_e = \{1 + (q - 1)\phi\}^{\frac{q+1}{2(q-1)}}$. Here, we use the same normalization according as in Section 4.7. To obtain the Damped KdVB equation, we introduce the same stretched coordinates as in Equation (4.40). The expansions of the dependent variables are also considered the same as in Equation (4.41). We also consider

$$\eta = \epsilon^{1/2}\eta_0, \quad \nu_{id} \sim \epsilon^{3/2}\nu_{id0}. \tag{4.175}$$

To obtain the phase velocity and nonlinear evolution equation, we substitute the above expansions (4.41) and (4.175) along with stretched coordinates (4.40) into Equations (4.172)–(4.174) and equate the coefficients of the lowest order of ϵ. We thus get the phase velocity the same as in Equation (4.54). Taking the coefficients of next higher order of ϵ, we obtain the damped KdV Burgers' equation as

$$\frac{\partial \phi^{(1)}}{\partial \tau} + A\phi^{(1)}\frac{\partial \phi^{(1)}}{\partial \xi} + B\frac{\partial^3 \phi^{(1)}}{\partial \xi^3} + C\frac{\partial^2 \phi^{(1)}}{\partial \xi^2} + D\phi^{(1)} = 0 \tag{4.176}$$

where $A = \left(\frac{3}{2v} - v^3(1-\mu)b\right)$, $B = \frac{v^3}{2}$, $C = -\frac{\eta_{10}}{2}$, and $D = \frac{\nu_{id0}}{2}$ with $b = \frac{(q+1)(3-q)}{8}$. When $C = 0$ and $D = 0$, then Equation (4.176) converts to the KdV equation, and the solution of the KdV equation is

$$\phi_1 = \phi_m sech^2\left(\frac{\xi - M_0\tau}{W}\right) \tag{4.177}$$

where $\phi_m = \frac{3M_0}{A}$ and $W = 2\sqrt{\frac{B}{M_0}}$ are the amplitude and the width of the solitary waves, and M_0 is the Mach number. Like the previous section, similarly, we find the approximate solution of Equation (4.176) in the form of

$$\phi^{(1)} = \phi_m(\tau)sech^2\left(\frac{\xi - M(\tau)\tau}{W(\tau)}\right) \tag{4.178}$$

where the amplitude $\phi_m(\tau) = \frac{3M(\tau)}{A}$, width $W(\tau) = 2\sqrt{B/M(\tau)}$, and velocity $M(\tau)$ can be obtained by the relation $M(\tau) = \frac{PM_0}{M_0Q(1-e^{P\tau})+Pe^{P\tau}}$, where $P = \frac{4}{3}D$, $Q = \frac{4}{15}\frac{C}{B}$, and $M(0) = M_0$ as $\tau = 0$.

From Figure 4.11, it is clear that the solitary wave amplitude decreases monotonically if the viscosity coefficients η_{10} increase slowly. In Figure 4.12, the amplitude of the solitary wave is plotted concerning the collision frequency parameter ν_{id0}. It is obvious here that the amplitude of the solitary

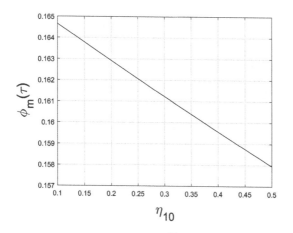

Fig. 4.11: Variation of the amplitude of the solitary wave from (4.176) with respect to η_{10} for $q = 0.6$, $\tau = 2$, $M = 0.1$, $\nu_{id0} = 0.01$, and $\mu = 0.5$.

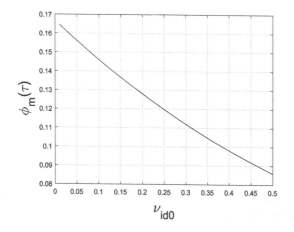

Fig. 4.12: Variation of the amplitude of the solitary wave from (4.176) with respect to ν_{id0} for $q = 0.6$, $\tau = 2$, $M = 0.1$, $\eta_{10} = 0.1$, and $\mu = 0.5$.

wave decreases as the dust–ion collision frequency parameter ν_{id0} increases gradually for positive nonzero values. Thus, the solitary wave solution does not exist for $\nu_{id0} = 0$. Figure 4.13 shows that the solitary wave width increases monotonically if the value of the viscosity coefficients η_{10} increases slowly.

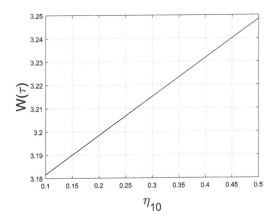

Fig. 4.13: Variation of width of the solitary wave from (4.176) with respect to η_{10} for $q = 0.6$, $\tau = 2$, $M_0 = 0.1$, $\nu_{id0} = 0.1$, and $\mu = 0.5$.

4.14 Kadomtsev–Petviashvili (KP) Equation

Soviet physicists Boris Kadomtsev (1928–1998) and Vladimir Petviashvili (1936–1993) [14] studied the evolution of the long IAWs of small amplitude propagating in plasma in their research work and derived an evolution equation named as KP equation. The KP equation can also be applied to model water waves of long wavelength with weakly nonlinear restoring forces and frequency dispersion. Here, we derive the KP equation for DIA waves in a three-component dusty plasma, subject to an external magnetic field. In this model, the plasma consists of negatively charged ions, massive dust grains, and q-nonextensive electrons. The dust dynamics are not taken into account, and the charges of dust grains are assumed to be constant. In the previous section of Chapter 2, we have already discussed the q-nonextensive distribution. The basic equations are written as

$$\frac{\partial n_i}{\partial t} + \vec{\nabla} \cdot (n_i \vec{u_i}) = 0, \tag{4.179}$$

$$\frac{\partial \vec{u_i}}{\partial t} + (\vec{u_i} \cdot \vec{\nabla})\vec{u_i} = -\frac{e\vec{\nabla}\phi}{m_i} + \frac{eB_0}{m_i c}\vec{u_i} \times e_z, \tag{4.180}$$

$$\vec{\nabla}^2 \phi = 4\pi e[n_e - n_i + z_d n_d] \tag{4.181}$$

where

$$n_e(\phi) = n_{e0}\left\{1 + (q-1)\frac{e\phi}{T_e}\right\}^{\frac{1}{q-1}+\frac{1}{2}}.$$

Here, n_j ($j = e, i$, and d stands for electron, ion, and dust particle respectively), $\vec{u}_i(u, v, w)$, and ϕ are the number densities, ion velocity, and the plasma potential, respectively. m_i, z_d, and e are the ion mass, the dust charge number, and the elementary charge, respectively.

Let us consider that the wave is propagating in the xz-plane. Accordingly, the normalized equations are

$$\frac{\partial n_i}{\partial t} + \frac{\partial(n_i u)}{\partial x} + \frac{\partial(n_i w)}{\partial z} = 0, \tag{4.182}$$

$$\frac{\partial u}{\partial t} + \left(u\frac{\partial}{\partial x} + w\frac{\partial}{\partial z} \right)u = -\frac{\partial \phi}{\partial x} + v, \tag{4.183}$$

$$\frac{\partial v}{\partial t} + \left(u\frac{\partial}{\partial x} + w\frac{\partial}{\partial z} \right)v = -u, \tag{4.184}$$

$$\frac{\partial w}{\partial t} + \left(u\frac{\partial}{\partial x} + w\frac{\partial}{\partial z} \right)w = -\frac{\partial \phi}{\partial z}, \tag{4.185}$$

$$\left(\frac{\partial^2}{\partial x^2} + \frac{\partial^2}{\partial z^2} \right)\phi + \beta\delta_1 n_i = \beta[(1 + (q-1)\phi)^{\frac{q+1}{2(q-1)}} + \delta_2] \tag{4.186}$$

where $\beta = r_g^2/\lambda_e^2$, $\delta_1 = n_{i0}/n_{e0}$, and $\delta_2 = n_d z_d/n_{e0}$. Here, $r_g = C_s/\Omega$ is the ion gyroradius and $\lambda_e = \sqrt{T_e/(4\pi n_{e0}e^2)}$ is the electron Debye length. The normalizations are taken as $\Omega t \to t$, $(C_s/\Omega)\nabla \to \nabla$, $u_i/C_s \to u_i$, $n_i/n_{i0} \to n_i$, $e\phi/T_e \to \phi$, where $C_s = \sqrt{T_e/m_i}$ is the ion acoustic velocity and $\Omega = (eB_0)/(m_i c)$ is the ion gyrofrequency. Also, n_{j0} ($j = i, e$) is the unperturbed density.

The stretch coordinates are taken as

$$\chi = \epsilon^2 x, \quad \xi = \epsilon(z - \lambda t), \quad \tau = \epsilon^3 t \tag{4.187}$$

where λ is the phase velocity of IAWs. The dependent variables are expanded as

$$\left.\begin{array}{l} n_i = 1 + \displaystyle\sum_{k=1}^{\infty} \epsilon^{2k} n_i^{(k)} + \cdots, \quad u = \displaystyle\sum_{k=1}^{\infty} \epsilon^{2k+1} u^{(k)} + \cdots \\[4mm] v = \displaystyle\sum_{k=1}^{\infty} \epsilon^{2k+1} v^{(k)} + \cdots, \quad w = \displaystyle\sum_{k=1}^{\infty} \epsilon^{2k+1} w^{(k)} + \cdots \\[4mm] \phi = \displaystyle\sum_{k=1}^{\infty} \epsilon^{2k} \phi^{(1)} + \cdots. \end{array}\right\} \tag{4.188}$$

To obtain the phase velocity and nonlinear evolution equation, we substitute the expansions given by Equations (4.187)–(4.188) into Equations (4.182)–(4.186) and equate the coefficients of lowest power of ϵ, thus we get the phase velocity as

$$\lambda^2 = \frac{2\delta_1}{1+q}. \tag{4.189}$$

Again, equating next higher-order terms of ϵ, we get

$$\left.\begin{array}{c} \dfrac{\partial n_i^{(1)}}{\partial \tau} - \lambda \dfrac{\partial n_i^{(2)}}{\partial \xi} + \dfrac{\partial u^{(1)}}{\partial \chi} + \dfrac{\partial w^{(2)}}{\partial \xi} + \dfrac{\partial(n_i^{(1)}w^{(1)})}{\partial \xi} = 0, \\[3mm] \dfrac{\partial w^{(1)}}{\partial \tau} - \lambda \dfrac{\partial w^{(2)}}{\partial \xi} + w^{(1)}\dfrac{\partial w^{(1)}}{\partial \xi} + \dfrac{\partial \phi^{(2)}}{\partial \xi} = 0, \\[3mm] \dfrac{\partial u^{(1)}}{\partial \tau} - \lambda \dfrac{\partial u^{(2)}}{\partial \xi} + w^{(1)}\dfrac{\partial u^{(1)}}{\partial \xi} + \dfrac{\partial \phi^{(2)}}{\partial \chi} = 0, \\[3mm] \dfrac{\partial^2 \phi^{(1)}}{\partial \xi^2} - \beta\left[\dfrac{q+1}{2}\phi^{(2)} + \dfrac{(q+1)(3-q)}{8}(\phi^{(1)})^2 - \delta_1 n_i^{(2)}\right] = 0. \end{array}\right\} \tag{4.190}$$

From relations (4.189)–(4.190), we obtain the KP equation as

$$\frac{\partial}{\partial \xi}\left[\frac{\partial \phi^{(1)}}{\partial \tau} + A\phi^{(1)}\frac{\partial \phi^{(1)}}{\partial \xi} + B\frac{\partial^3 \phi^{(1)}}{\partial \xi^3}\right] + C\frac{\partial^2 \phi^{(1)}}{\partial \chi^2} = 0 \tag{4.191}$$

where $A = -\frac{(3-q)\lambda^2-6}{4\lambda}$, $B = \frac{\lambda}{\beta(1+q)}$, and $C = \frac{\lambda}{2}$.
The tanh method is one of the famous methods to find a solution of the KP Equation (4.191). With the help of tanh method, we use the transformation $\zeta = \xi + \eta - u\tau$, where u is the speed of the nonlinear structure. Now applying the conditions $\phi^{(1)} \to 0$, $\frac{\partial \phi^{(1)}}{\partial \zeta} \to 0$, $\frac{\partial^2 \phi^{(1)}}{\partial \zeta^2} \to 0$, $\frac{\partial^3 \phi^{(1)}}{\partial \zeta^3} \to 0$ as $\zeta \to \infty$, we get the analytical solution of the KP Equation (4.191) as

$$\phi^{(1)}(\zeta) = \frac{12B}{A}\left[1 - \tanh^2\left\{\xi + \eta - (4B + C)\tau\right\}\right]. \tag{4.192}$$

The speed of the co-moving frame (say u) is related to the weak dispersive and diffraction coefficients such as $u = (4B + C)$, which has been obtained using the boundary conditions, i.e., $\zeta \to \infty$, $\phi^{(1)}(\zeta) \to 0$, and $\tanh^2(\zeta) \to 1$.

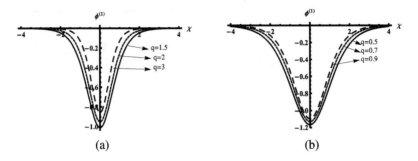

Fig. 4.14: (a) Variation of solitary wave potential $\phi^{(1)}$ with spatial coordinates χ for different values of $q > 1$ and (b) for different values of $q < 1$.

Also, the solution using the pseudo-potential approach is written as

$$\phi^{(1)}(\zeta) = \phi_m Sech^2\left(\frac{\xi + \eta - u\tau}{W}\right) \qquad (4.193)$$

where maximum amplitude $\phi_m = \frac{3(u-C)}{A}$ and width $W = \sqrt{4B/(u - C)}$ of the soliton has been defined. Here, it should be noted that both solutions have the same form with the same numerical results.

We illustrate the effect of the nonextensive parameter q by plotting $\phi^{(1)}$ versus χ as shown in Figure 4.14. It is also observed from Figure 4.14(a) that, as $q(> 1)$ increases, the amplitude and the width of the solitary waves decrease. Also, from Figure 4.14(b), it is seen that as the amplitude and the width of the solitary waves decrease accordingly, the value of $q(< 1)$ increases.

4.15 Modified KP (MKP) Equation

The KP equation is a two-dimensional analog of the KdV equation. We reconsider the derivation of the KP equation, which is modified to include the effects of rotation. The motivation for this work is that if the solution of the modified KP (MKP) equation is assumed to be locally confined, then they satisfy a certain constraint. It appears to restrict the class of allowed initial conditions considerably. Grimshaw [15] derived a MKP equation to describe long surface or initial waves in the presence of rotation. The MKP equation is the appropriate extension of the MKdV equation. The MKP equation provides a correct asymptotic description of the waves traveling to the right. In general, it cannot be assumed that the solutions are locally confined.

It is required to proceed with the MKP equation by considering the higher-order coefficients of ϵ. The same set of stretched coordinate Equation (4.187) are considered, but expansion (4.188) of the dependent variables are not valid. So, a set of new expansions of the dependent variables is taken into account

$$
\left.
\begin{aligned}
& n_i = 1 + \sum_{k=1}^{\infty} \epsilon^k n_i^{(k)} + \cdots , \quad u = 0 + \sum_{k=1}^{\infty} \epsilon^{k+1} u^{(k)} + \cdots \\[2mm]
& v = 0 + \sum_{k=1}^{\infty} \epsilon^{2k} v^{(k)} + \cdots , \quad w = 0 + \sum_{k=1}^{\infty} \epsilon^k w^{(k)} + \cdots \\[2mm]
& \phi = 0 + \sum_{k=1}^{\infty} \epsilon^k \phi^{(k)} + \cdots .
\end{aligned}
\right\} \quad (4.194)
$$

Substituting the above expansions (4.194), along with the same stretched coordinates (4.187) into Equations (4.179)–(4.186), and equating the coefficients of different powers of ϵ, one can obtain

$$
n_i^{(1)} = \frac{w^{(1)}}{\lambda}, \quad w^{(1)} = \frac{\phi^{(1)} 1}{\lambda}, \quad \phi^{(1)} = \frac{\delta_1 n_i^{(1)}}{a}, \quad \delta_1 = 1 + \delta_2 \quad (4.195)
$$

$$
n_i^{(2)} = \frac{n_i^{(1)} w^{(1)} + w^{(2)}}{\lambda}, \quad n_i^{(2)} = \frac{a\phi^{(2)} + b(\phi^{(1)})^2}{\delta_1}, \quad \frac{\partial u^{(1)}}{\partial \xi} = \frac{1}{\lambda}\frac{\partial \phi^{(1)}}{\partial X}
$$
$$
(4.196)
$$

$$
\left.
\begin{aligned}
& \frac{\partial n_i^{(1)}}{\partial \tau} - \lambda \frac{\partial n_i^{(3)}}{\partial \xi} + \frac{\partial u^{(1)}}{\partial \chi} + \frac{\partial}{\partial \xi}\left(n_i^{(1)} w^{(2)} + n_i^{(2)} w^{(1)}\right) = -\frac{\partial w^{(3)}}{\partial \xi}, \\[2mm]
& \frac{\partial w^{(1)}}{\partial \tau} - \lambda \frac{\partial w^{(3)}}{\partial \xi} + w^{(1)} \frac{\partial w^{(2)}}{\partial \xi} + w^{(2)} \frac{\partial w^{(1)}}{\partial \xi} + \frac{\partial \phi^{(3)}}{\partial \xi} = 0, \\[2mm]
& \frac{\partial^2 \phi^{(1)}}{\partial \xi^2} - \beta\{a\phi^{(3)} + 2b\phi^{(1)}\phi^{(2)} + k(\phi^{(1)})^3 - \delta_1 n_i^{(3)}\} = 0
\end{aligned}
\right\} \quad (4.197)
$$

where $a = \frac{(q+1)}{2}$, $b = \frac{1}{8}\{(q+1)(3-q)\}$, and $k = \frac{1}{48}\{(q+1)(3-q)(5-3q)\}$. From Equation (4.195), one can obtain the phase velocity as

$$
\lambda^2 = \frac{\delta_1}{a}. \quad (4.198)
$$

By eliminating $n_i^{(3)}, w^{(3)}$, and $\phi^{(3)}$ from Equation (4.197) with the help of Equations (4.195)–(4.196), one can obtain the MKP equation as

$$\frac{\partial}{\partial \xi}\left[\frac{\partial \phi^{(1)}}{\partial \tau} + A\frac{\partial(\phi^{(1)}\phi^{(2)})}{\partial \xi} - D(\phi^{(1)})^2\frac{\partial \phi^{(1)}}{\partial \xi} + B\frac{\partial^3 \phi^{(1)}}{\partial \xi^3}\right] + C\frac{\partial^2 \phi^{(1)}}{\partial \chi^2} = 0$$

(4.199)

where $A = -\frac{(3-q)V^2-6}{4V}$, $B = \frac{V}{\beta(1+q)}$, $C = \frac{V}{2}$, and $D = \frac{3V}{2a}\left(k - \frac{3b}{V^2} + \frac{2a}{V^4}\right)$.

There exists a set of critical values at which $A = 0$ and Equation (4.199) converts to the MKP equation as

$$\frac{\partial}{\partial \xi}\left[\frac{\partial \phi^{(1)}}{\partial \tau} - D(\phi^{(1)})^2\frac{\partial \phi^{(1)}}{\partial \xi} + B\frac{\partial^3 \phi^{(1)}}{\partial \xi^3}\right] + C\frac{\partial^2 \phi^{(1)}}{\partial \chi^2} = 0. \quad (4.200)$$

We assume the stationary wave solution of MKP Equation (4.200) as $\phi^{(1)} = \phi^{(1)}(\zeta)$ where $\zeta = k\xi + l\chi - u_0\tau$. Substituting this expression into the MKP Equation (4.200), we obtain

$$\phi^{(1)} = \phi_m Sech^2\left(\frac{\zeta}{\Delta}\right) \quad (4.201)$$

where the amplitude of the soliton is $\phi_m = 6(u_0 k - Cl^2/Dk^2)^{1/2}$ and the width of soliton is $\Delta = k^2\left[\frac{B}{(u_0 - cl^2)}\right]^{1/2}$.

4.16 Further MKP (FMKP) Equation

Let us consider a magnetoplasma consisting of ions and dust particles. Here, the ion obeys the nonextensive nonthermal distribution and the external magnetic field (M) acting analog the x-axis, i.e., $M = \hat{x}M_0$, where $\hat{x}$ is a unit vector along the x-axis. The basic normalized equations are

$$\frac{\partial n_d}{\partial t} + \vec{\nabla} \cdot (n_d\vec{u_d}) = 0, \quad (4.202)$$

$$\frac{\partial \vec{u_d}}{\partial t} + (\vec{u_d} \cdot \vec{\nabla})\vec{u_d} = \vec{\nabla}\phi - \vec{u_d} \times \hat{x}, \quad (4.203)$$

$$\vec{\nabla}^2\phi = \alpha_1(n_d - n_i) \quad (4.204)$$

where $\alpha_1 = r^2/\lambda_D^2$, $r = C_s/\Omega$, $\lambda_D = \sqrt{T_i/(4\pi e^2 n_0 z_{d0})}$, $C_s = \sqrt{T_i/m}$, and $\Omega = (eM_0)/m_d c$. r, λ_D, C_s, Ω, c, e, m_d, and z_d are the dust gyroradius,

Debye length, dust acoustic velocity, dust gyrofrequency, speed of the light, elementary charge, dust mass, and the number of the charge residing on the dust grains, respectively. The dust charge $q_d = -ez_d$. n_d and $\vec{u}_d(u, v, w)$ are the number density and velocity of the dust particles, respectively. The ions obey the nonextensive nonthermal distribution, i.e.,

$$n_i = n_{i0}\left(1 - M\left(\frac{e\phi}{T_i}\right) + N\left(\frac{e\phi}{T_i}\right)^2\right)\left\{1 - (q-1)\left(\frac{e\phi}{T_i}\right)\right\}^{\frac{1}{q-1}+\frac{1}{2}}$$

(4.205)

where $M = -\frac{16\alpha q}{(5q-3)(3q-1)+12\alpha}$ and $N = \frac{16\alpha q(2q-1)}{(5q-3)(3q-1)+12\alpha}$.

Here, the normalization is done as follows:

$$n_i \to \frac{n_i}{n_{i0}}, \quad n_d \to \frac{n_d}{n_0}, \quad u_d \to \frac{u_d}{C_s}, \quad \phi \to \frac{e\phi}{T_i}, \quad t \to t\Omega, \quad x \to \frac{x}{r}.$$

Let us consider that the wave is propagating in the xy-plane. Accordingly, the normalized equations are

$$\frac{\partial n_d}{\partial t} + \frac{\partial(n_d u)}{\partial x} + \frac{\partial(n_d v)}{\partial y} = 0,$$

(4.206)

$$\frac{\partial u}{\partial t} + \left(u\frac{\partial}{\partial x} + v\frac{\partial}{\partial y}\right)u = \frac{\partial\phi}{\partial x},$$

(4.207)

$$\frac{\partial v}{\partial t} + \left(u\frac{\partial}{\partial x} + v\frac{\partial}{\partial y}\right)v = \frac{\partial\phi}{\partial y} - w,$$

(4.208)

$$\frac{\partial w}{\partial t} + \left(u\frac{\partial}{\partial x} + v\frac{\partial}{\partial y}\right)w = v,$$

(4.209)

$$\left(\frac{\partial^2}{\partial x^2} + \frac{\partial}{\partial y^2}\right)\phi = \alpha_1\left[n_d - \left(1 - M\phi + N\phi^2\right)\left\{1 - (q-1)\phi\right\}^{\frac{1}{q-1}+\frac{1}{2}}\right].$$

(4.210)

To obtain the FMKP equation, we introduce the same stretched coordinates as in Equations (4.187). The expansions of the dependent variables are considered as follows:

$$
\left.
\begin{aligned}
n_d &= 1 + \sum_{k=1}^{\infty} \epsilon^k n_d^{(k)} + \cdots, \\
u &= 0 + \sum_{k=1}^{\infty} \epsilon^k u^{(k)} + \cdots, \\
v &= 0 + \sum_{k=1}^{\infty} \epsilon^{k+1} v^{(k)} + \cdots, \\
w &= 0 + \sum_{k=1}^{\infty} \epsilon^{2k} w^{(k)} + \cdots, \\
\phi &= 0 + \sum_{k=1}^{\infty} \epsilon^k \phi^{(k)} + \cdots, \\
\nu_{id} &\sim \epsilon^3 \nu_{id0}
\end{aligned}
\right\}
\tag{4.211}
$$

where ν_{ido} is the dust–ion collisional frequency. Substituting Equation (4.187) along with the stretched coordinates (4.211) into the system of Equations (4.206)–(4.210) and equating the coefficients of lowest order of ϵ, we get the phase velocity as

$$
\lambda^2 = \frac{2}{q + 1 + 2M}.
\tag{4.212}
$$

Equating the coefficient of different power of ϵ and eliminating $n_d^{(3)}$, $w^{(3)}$, and $\phi^{(3)}$, one can obtain the nonlinear equation

$$
\frac{\partial}{\partial \eta} \left[\frac{\partial \phi_1}{\partial \tau} - A \frac{\partial (\phi_1 \phi_2)}{\partial \eta} - D\phi_1^2 \frac{\partial \phi_1}{\partial \eta} + B \frac{\partial^3 \phi_1}{\partial \eta^3} \right] + C \frac{\partial^2 \phi_1}{\partial \chi^2} = 0
\tag{4.213}
$$

where $A = \frac{\lambda}{2P}[3P^2 - 2Q]$, $B = \frac{\lambda}{2P\alpha_1}$, $C = \frac{\lambda}{2}$, $P = \frac{q+1+2M}{2}$, $b = \frac{(q+1)(3-q)}{8}$, $Q = b + N + aM$, $a = \frac{q+1}{2}$, $D = \frac{3\lambda}{2P}(R + 2P^3 - 3PQ)$, and $R = K + bM + aN$. At certain sets of critical values, the nonlinear coefficients $A = 0$, and Equation (4.213) reduces to the following MKP equation:

$$
\frac{\partial}{\partial \eta} \left[\frac{\partial \phi_1}{\partial \tau} - D\phi_1^2 \frac{\partial \phi_1}{\partial \eta} + B \frac{\partial^3 \phi_1}{\partial \eta^3} \right] + C \frac{\partial^2 \phi_1}{\partial \chi^2} = 0.
\tag{4.214}
$$

If A is at the same order of ϵ, but not zero, we derive the FMKP equation using the same stretched coordinates and the expression as the MKP equation

$$\frac{\partial}{\partial \eta}\left[\frac{\partial \phi_1}{\partial \tau} - A\frac{\partial(\phi_1\phi_2)}{\partial \eta} - D\phi_1^2\frac{\partial \phi_1}{\partial \eta} + B\frac{\partial^3 \phi_1}{\partial \eta^3}\right] + C\frac{\partial^2 \phi_1}{\partial \chi^2} = 0. \quad (4.215)$$

4.17 KP Burgers' (KPB) Equation

In a nonlinear dissipative medium, shock-like structures arise due to the interaction of nonlinearity and dissipation. However, if a medium contains both dispersion and dissipation, then the propagation properties of a small amplitude disturbance can be adequately explained by the KP Burgers' (KPB) equation. While the viscosity, particle reflection, interparticle collisions, and Landau damping can lead to energy dissipation, the nonadiabaticity of the dust charge fluctuation provides an alternate physical mechanism causing the dissipation.

Now, we shall derive the KPB equation in a pair-ion plasma system. The pair-ion plasma is important in plasma physics because of the various astrophysical environment like the pulsar magnetosphere, active galactic nuclei, and neutron star. The energies are produced in intense, and in turn, they produce electron–positron with the help of pair producing and annihilation. The physics of the pair-ion plasma became interesting as it descended from its astrophysical heights to the terrestrial laboratory. The laboratory pair plasma generates a sufficiently dense pair-ion plasma, which consists of equal masses and positive and negative fullerene ions (C_{60}^+ and C_{60}^-). Generally, the pair plasma is different from the standard e-i plasma in which the different masses of species break the symmetry between the components. If the pair-ion plasma is produced under identical conditions, it must remain symmetric, for example, with regard to their thermal speed and temperature [16].

Let us consider a pair-ion plasma model, consisting of positive as well as negative ions and electrons. Here, both ions have equal mass ($m_+ = m_- = m$), and the electron obeys the kappa distribution. The basic equations are

$$\frac{\partial n_\alpha}{\partial t} + \vec{\nabla}\cdot(n_\alpha\vec{u_\alpha}) = 0 \qquad (4.216)$$

$$\frac{\partial \vec{u_\alpha}}{\partial t} + (\vec{u_\alpha}\cdot\vec{\nabla})\vec{u_\alpha} = \frac{q}{m}\vec{E} - \frac{1}{n_\alpha m}\vec{\nabla}p_\alpha + \mu\vec{\nabla}^2\vec{u_\alpha} \qquad (4.217)$$

where n_α ($\alpha = +, -$ stands for positive ion, negative ion), v_α, and p_α are the number density, fluid velocity, and the pressure, respectively. q and μ are the charges and the kinematic viscosity. The isothermal pressure for ions is written as

$$p_\alpha = n_\alpha T_\alpha. \tag{4.218}$$

Also, the Poisson equation is

$$\nabla^2 \phi = 4\pi e(\alpha n_-(1+\alpha)n_+ + n_e). \tag{4.219}$$

Here, $n_e = (1 - \phi/(k - 1/2))^{-(k+1/2)}$. T_α represents the temperature with $T_- \neq T_+$. The electric field is $\vec{E} = -\vec{\nabla}\phi$, and ϕ is the electrostatic wave potential. n_0 is the unperturbed number densities. The two-dimensional normalized basic equations are as follows:

$$\frac{\partial n_+}{\partial t} + \frac{\partial}{\partial x}(n_+ u_+) + \frac{\partial}{\partial y}(n_+ v_+) = 0 \tag{4.220}$$

$$\frac{\partial n_-}{\partial t} + \frac{\partial}{\partial x}(n_- u_-) + \frac{\partial}{\partial y}(n_- v_-) = 0 \tag{4.221}$$

$$\frac{\partial u_+}{\partial t} + u_+ \frac{\partial u_+}{\partial x} + v_+ \frac{\partial u_+}{\partial y} + \frac{\partial \phi}{\partial x} = -\frac{1}{n_+}\frac{\partial n_+}{\partial x} + \eta_+ \frac{\partial^2 u_+}{\partial x^2} \tag{4.222}$$

$$\frac{\partial v_+}{\partial t} + u_+ \frac{\partial v_+}{\partial x} + v_+ \frac{\partial v_+}{\partial y} + \frac{\partial \phi}{\partial y} = -\frac{1}{n_+}\frac{\partial n_+}{\partial y} + \eta_+ \frac{\partial^2 v_+}{\partial y^2} \tag{4.223}$$

$$\frac{\partial u_-}{\partial t} + u_- \frac{\partial u_-}{\partial x} + v_- \frac{\partial u_-}{\partial y} - \frac{\partial \phi}{\partial x} = -\frac{\beta}{n_-}\frac{\partial n_-}{\partial x} + \eta_- \frac{\partial^2 u_-}{\partial x^2} \tag{4.224}$$

$$\frac{\partial v_-}{\partial t} + u_- \frac{\partial v_-}{\partial x} + v_- \frac{\partial v_-}{\partial y} - \frac{\partial \phi}{\partial y} = -\frac{\beta}{n_-}\frac{\partial n_-}{\partial y} + \eta_- \frac{\partial^2 v_-}{\partial y^2} \tag{4.225}$$

$$\frac{\partial \phi}{\partial x^2} + \frac{\partial \phi}{\partial y^2} = \alpha n_- - (1 = \alpha)n_+ + n_e. \tag{4.226}$$

Here, u_α and v_α are the ion fluid velocity along the x-axis and the y-axis, respectively, and normalization is taken as

$$n_\alpha \to \frac{n_\alpha}{n_0}, \quad u_\alpha \to \frac{u_\alpha}{v_s}, \quad \phi \to \frac{e\phi}{T_+}, \quad x \to \frac{x}{\lambda_+}, \quad t \to \omega_p t.$$

Here, $\lambda_+ = \sqrt{T_+/(4\pi n_0 e^2)}$, $\omega_p = \sqrt{4\pi n_0 e^2/m}$, and $v_s = \sqrt{T_+/m}$. Also, $\beta = T_-/T_+$, $\eta_+ = \mu_+/(\lambda_+ v_s)$ and $\eta_- = \mu_-/(\lambda_- v_s)$. The viscosity coefficients of the fluids of the same mass are different since their temperatures are assumed to be different.

To obtain the KPB equation, we introduce the stretch co-ordinate as

$$\xi = \epsilon^{1/2}(x - \lambda t), \quad \chi = \epsilon y, \ \tau = \epsilon^{3/2} t. \tag{4.227}$$

Also, we expand the dependent variable as

$$\left.\begin{array}{l} n_\alpha = 1 + \epsilon n_\alpha^1 + \epsilon^2 n_\alpha^2 + \cdots, \ u_\alpha = 0 + \epsilon u_\alpha^1 + \epsilon^2 u_\alpha^2 + \cdots \\ v_\alpha = 0 + \epsilon^{3/2} v_\alpha^1 + \epsilon^{5/2} v_\alpha^2 + \cdots, \ \phi = 0 + \epsilon \phi^1 + \epsilon^2 \phi^2 + \cdots . \end{array}\right\} \tag{4.228}$$

Assuming the value of η to be small, i.e., $\eta_\pm = \epsilon^{1/2}\eta_{0\pm}$, where $\eta_{0\pm}$ is $o(1)$. Substituting Equations (4.227)–(4.228) into the normalized equation and collecting different powers of ϵ and equating the lowest order of ϵ, we get

$$\left.\begin{array}{l} n_+^1 = \dfrac{1}{\lambda^2 - 1}\phi^1, \ n_-^1 = \dfrac{-1}{\lambda^2 - \beta}\phi^1, \ u_+^1 = \dfrac{\lambda}{\lambda^2 - 1}\phi^1 \\[2mm] u_-^1 = \dfrac{-\lambda}{\lambda^2 - \beta}\phi^1, \ v_+^1 = \dfrac{\lambda}{\lambda^2 - 1}\phi^1, \ v_-^1 = \dfrac{-\lambda}{\lambda^2 - \beta}\phi^1. \end{array}\right\} \tag{4.229}$$

From these set of equations, we get the phase velocity of the wave as

$$\lambda = \sqrt{(1 + \beta)/2}. \tag{4.230}$$

Taking the next higher-order equation in ϵ, we get

$$\frac{\partial n_+^1}{\partial \tau} - \lambda \frac{\partial n_+^2}{\partial \xi} + \frac{\partial}{\partial \xi}(n_+^1 u_+^1) + \frac{\partial v_+^1}{\partial \chi} + \frac{\partial u_+^2}{\partial \xi} = 0 \tag{4.231}$$

$$\frac{\partial n_-^1}{\partial \tau} - \lambda \frac{\partial n_-^2}{\partial \xi} + \frac{\partial}{\partial \xi}(n_-^1 u_-^1) + \frac{\partial v_-^1}{\partial \chi} + \frac{\partial u_-^2}{\partial \xi} = 0 \tag{4.232}$$

$$\frac{\partial u_+^1}{\partial \tau} - \lambda \frac{\partial u_+^2}{\partial \xi} + u_+^1 \frac{\partial u_+^1}{\partial \xi} + \frac{\partial \phi^2}{\partial \xi} + \frac{\partial n_+^2}{\partial \xi} - n_+^1 \frac{\partial n_+^1}{\partial \xi} - \eta_{0+} \frac{\partial^2 u_+^1}{\partial \xi^2} = 0 \tag{4.233}$$

$$\frac{\partial u_-^1}{\partial \tau} - \lambda \frac{\partial u_-^2}{\partial \xi} + u_-^1 \frac{\partial u_-^1}{\partial \xi} - \frac{\partial \phi^2}{\partial \xi} + \beta \frac{\partial n_-^2}{\partial \xi} - \beta n_-^1 \frac{\partial n_-^1}{\partial \xi} - \eta_{0-} \frac{\partial^2 u_-^1}{\partial \xi^2} = 0 \tag{4.234}$$

$$\frac{\partial^2 \phi^1}{\partial \xi^2} = \alpha n_-^2 - (1 + \alpha)n_+^2 + \frac{k + 1/2}{k - 1/2}\phi^2 + \frac{(k + 3/2)(k + 1/2)}{2(k - 1/2)^2}(\phi^1)^2. \tag{4.235}$$

Then, eliminating n_α^2, u_α^2, and ϕ^2 from Equations (4.231)–(4.235) and using Equations (4.229)–(4.230), we obtain the KP Burgers' equation as

$$\frac{\partial}{\partial\xi}\left(\frac{\partial\phi^1}{\partial\tau} + A\phi^1\frac{\partial\phi^1}{\partial\xi} + B\frac{\partial^3\phi^1}{\partial\xi^3} - C\frac{\partial^2\phi^1}{\partial\xi^2}\right) + D\frac{\partial^2\phi^1}{\partial\chi^2} = 0 \quad (4.236)$$

where

$$A = \left[\frac{(1+\alpha)(3\lambda^2-1)}{(\lambda^2-1)^3} - \frac{\alpha(3\lambda^2-\beta)}{(\lambda^2-\beta)^3} - \frac{(k+3/2)(k+1/2)}{(k-1/2)^2}\right]B,$$

$$B = \frac{(\lambda^2-1)^2(\lambda^2-\beta)^2}{2\lambda[(1+\alpha)(\lambda^2-\beta)^2 + \alpha(\lambda^2-1)^2]},$$

$$C = \frac{(1+\alpha)\eta_{0+}(\lambda^2-\beta)^2 - (\lambda^2-1)^2\alpha\eta_{0-}}{2[(1+\alpha)(\lambda^2-\beta)^2 + \alpha(\lambda^2-1)^2]},$$

$$D = \frac{\lambda}{2}$$

where A and C are the coefficients of nonlinearity and dissipation, whereas B and D are the coefficients of the predominant and weak dispersion, respectively.

With the help of tanh method, we find the solution of Equation (4.236), where we use the transformation $\zeta = k(\xi + \chi - u_0\tau)$. Here, k is a dimensionless wave number and the solution is

$$\phi^1(\xi,\chi,\tau) = \frac{6C^2}{25AB}\left[1 - \tanh\left(\frac{C\xi}{10B}\right) + \chi - \left(\frac{6C^2}{25B} + D\right)\tau\right]$$

$$+ \frac{3C^2}{25AB}\left[Sech^2\left(\frac{C\xi}{10B}\right) + \chi - \left(\frac{6C^2}{25B} + D\right)\tau\right]. \quad (4.237)$$

The solution will exist only when $T_+ \neq T_-$. But when $T_+ = T_-$, the coefficients A, B, and C become undetermined, and the soliton structure can not be obtained.

4.18 Damped KP (DKP) Equation

In a two-dimensional system, the soliton was first modeled by Kadomstev and Petviashvili through a two-dimensional partial differential equation known as KP equation for a cold plasma system. It is a multidimensional extension of the well-known KdV equation. The investigations are done in the framework of the KP equation ignoring the collisional (dissipative) effects. These possesses the characteristics of an integrable system and were an extreme simplification of the real plasmas in nature. However, with the inclusion of the dissipative effects, the plasma remains no longer a Hamiltonian. The nonlinear localized structures in such types of non-Hamiltonian systems are known as dissipative solitons [17]. In addition to the interplay between nonlinearity and dispersion necessary for the formation of a solitary wave structure in an integrable system, a balance between gain and loss should exist to have a dissipative nonlinear localized structure. New features of dispersion and nonlinearity, in dissipative longitudinal solitons in a 2D system, have been pointed out in complex plasma [18]. It is, therefore, tempting to search for the role of dissipative effects due to plasma-neutral collisions on the propagation of ion solitary waves. Now, we investigate the dissipative solitons propagating in degenerate dense plasmas, inspired by the current interest in the dissipative solitons. This may link the dissipative solitons' paradigm to plasma dynamics.

To derive the DKP equation, we consider a collisional dusty plasma having negatively charged ions, massive dust grains, and isothermal electrons in presence of an external static magnetic field acting along z-axis. The dust dynamics are not considered, and dust charge is assumed to be constant. Let us also assume that the wave is propagating in the xz plane, and accordingly, the normalized basic equations are given by

$$\frac{\partial n}{\partial t} + \frac{\partial (nu)}{\partial x} + \frac{\partial (nw)}{\partial z} = 0, \tag{4.238}$$

$$\frac{\partial u}{\partial t} + u\frac{\partial u}{\partial x} + w\frac{\partial u}{\partial z} = -\frac{\partial \phi}{\partial x} + v, \tag{4.239}$$

$$\frac{\partial v}{\partial t} + u\frac{\partial v}{\partial x} + w\frac{\partial v}{\partial z} = -u, \tag{4.240}$$

$$\frac{\partial w}{\partial t} + u\frac{\partial w}{\partial x} + w\frac{\partial w}{\partial z} = -\frac{\partial \phi}{\partial z} - v_{id}w, \tag{4.241}$$

$$\frac{\partial^2 \phi}{\partial x^2} + \frac{\partial^2 \phi}{\partial z^2} = \delta_1 + \delta_2 n_e - n \tag{4.242}$$

where $n_e = e^{\sigma\phi}$. n_j ($j = e$, i, and d stands for electron, ion, and dust particle, respectively) and ϕ are the number density and the electrostatic potential. u, v, and w are velocity along the x, y, z axis, respectively. Here, $\sigma = T_e/T_i$. The charge neutrality condition is $n_{i0} = z_d n_{d0} + n_{e0}$. So, $\delta_1 + \delta_2 = 1$. $\delta_1 = \frac{n_{d0} z_d}{n_{i0}}$ and $\delta_2 = \frac{n_{e0}}{n_{i0}}$, where n_{j0} denotes unperturbed number densities. z_d denotes the dust charge number, and the dust charge is $q_d = -ez_d$, where e denotes the elementary charge.

Here, the normalization is done in the following way:

$$n_i \to \frac{n_i}{n_{i0}}, \quad u \to \frac{u}{C_i}, \quad v \to \frac{v}{C_i}, \quad w \to \frac{w}{C_i}, \quad \phi \to \frac{e\phi}{T_i}, \quad x \to \frac{x}{\lambda}, \quad t \to \omega t$$

where $C_i = \sqrt{T_i/m_i}$, $\lambda_D = \sqrt{T_i/(4\pi e^2 n_0)}$, ω_{pi}, ν_{id}, and m_i are the ion acoustic speed, Debye length, ion plasma frequency, dust–ion collisional frequency, and the ion mass, respectively.

To obtain phase velocity and the DKP equation, we introduce the same stretched coordinates as in Equation (4.187). The expansions of the dependent variables are considered the same as Equation (4.211). Substituting the above Equation (4.211) along with the same stretched coordinates (4.187) into Equations (4.238)–(4.242) and equating the coefficients of lowest powers of ϵ, we get

$$n_i^{(1)} = \frac{1}{\lambda} w^{(1)}, \quad w^{(1)} = \frac{1}{\lambda} \phi^{(1)}, \quad \phi^{(1)} = \frac{1}{\delta_2 \sigma} n_i^{(1)}, \quad \lambda \frac{\partial u^{(1)}}{\partial \xi} = \frac{\partial \phi^{(1)}}{\partial \chi}.$$

$$(4.243)$$

From relations (4.243), one can obtain the phase velocity as

$$\lambda^2 = \frac{1}{\delta_2 \sigma}. \tag{4.244}$$

Equating the coefficients of the next higher order of ϵ , we have

$$\frac{\partial n_i^{(1)}}{\partial \tau} + \frac{\partial u^{(1)}}{\partial \chi} + \frac{\partial n_i^{(1)} w^{(1)}}{\partial \xi} - \lambda \frac{\partial n_i^{(2)}}{\partial \xi} + \frac{\partial w^{(2)}}{\partial \xi} = 0, \tag{4.245}$$

$$\frac{\partial u^{(1)}}{\partial \tau} - \lambda \frac{\partial u_i^{(2)}}{\partial \xi} + w^{(1)} \frac{\partial u^{(1)}}{\partial \xi} + \frac{\partial \phi^{(2)}}{\partial \chi} = 0, \tag{4.246}$$

$$\frac{\partial w^{(1)}}{\partial \tau} - \lambda \frac{\partial w^{(2)}}{\partial \xi} + w^{(1)} \frac{\partial w^{(1)}}{\partial \xi} = -\frac{\partial \phi^{(2)}}{\partial \xi} - \nu_{id0} w^{(1)}, \tag{4.247}$$

$$\frac{\partial^2 \phi^{(1)}}{\partial \xi^2} = \delta_2 \left(\sigma \phi^{(2)} + \frac{\sigma^2 (\phi^{(1)})^2}{2} \right) - n_i^{(2)}. \tag{4.248}$$

From Equations (4.245)–(4.248), we get DKP equation as

$$\frac{\partial}{\partial \xi} \left[\frac{\partial \phi^{(1)}}{\partial \tau} + A \phi^{(1)} \frac{\partial \phi^{(1)}}{\partial \xi} + B \frac{\partial^3 \phi^{(1)}}{\partial \xi^3} + C \phi^{(1)} \right] + D \frac{\partial^2 \phi^{(1)}}{\partial \chi^2} = 0 \tag{4.249}$$

where $A = \frac{\lambda^3}{2}$, $B = \frac{3 - \sigma \lambda^2}{2\lambda}$, $C = \frac{\nu e_{id0}}{\lambda^3}$, and $D = \frac{\lambda}{2}$.

4.19   Zakharov–Kuznetsov (ZK) Equation

In 1974, Zakharov and Kuznetsov derived a nonlinear equation named the ZK equation as a nonlinear evolution equation to study IAWs in a strongly magnetized plasma in the z dimension. The dynamics of IASWs are the silent character in the nonlinear phenomena of modern plasma physics. Nonlinear differential equations, such as the KdV equation and the MKdV equation, describe the different properties of nonlinear plasma waves in one dimension. The Zakharov–Kuznetsov (ZK) equation, and KP equation, describe the different properties of nonlinear plasma waves in more than one dimension. Zakharov and Kuznetsov [19] derived and used to study three-dimensional acoustic ion waves in magnetized plasma. This equation regulates the nature of weakly nonlinear waves in a plasma that consists of cold ions and hot superthermal electrons in a magnetic field.

To derive the ZK equation, we consider a plasma model consisting of cold ions, superthermal distributed electrons in the presence of dust particles. Also, the external static magnetic field $\vec{B} = \hat{y}\vec{B}_0$ along the y-axis. Accordingly, the normalized equations are as follows:

$$\frac{\partial n_i}{\partial t} + \frac{\partial(n_i u)}{\partial x} + \frac{\partial(n_i v)}{\partial y} + \frac{\partial(n w)}{\partial z} = 0, \qquad (4.250)$$

$$\frac{\partial u}{\partial t} + \left(u\frac{\partial}{\partial x} + v\frac{\partial}{\partial y} + w\frac{\partial}{\partial z}\right)u = -\frac{\partial \phi}{\partial x} - \frac{\Omega_i}{\omega_{pi}}w, \qquad (4.251)$$

$$\frac{\partial v}{\partial t} + \left(u\frac{\partial}{\partial x} + v\frac{\partial}{\partial y} + w\frac{\partial}{\partial z}\right)v = -\frac{\partial \phi}{\partial y}, \qquad (4.252)$$

$$\frac{\partial w}{\partial t} + \left(u\frac{\partial}{\partial x} + v\frac{\partial}{\partial y} + w\frac{\partial}{\partial z}\right)w = -\frac{\partial \phi}{\partial z} + \frac{\Omega_i}{\omega_{pi}}u, \qquad (4.253)$$

$$\frac{\partial^2 \phi}{\partial x^2} + \frac{\partial^2 \phi}{\partial y^2} + \frac{\partial^2 \phi}{\partial z^2} = n_e - n_i \qquad (4.254)$$

where

$$n_e = \left(1 - \frac{\phi}{k - 1/2}\right)^{-(k+1/2)}.$$

Here, n, n_e, $u_i(= u, v, w)$, T_e, m_i, e, ϕ, Ω_i, ω_{pi}, νid, and λ_D are the ion number density, electron number density, ion velocity, electron temperature, ion mass, electron charge, electrostatic potential, ion cyclotron frequency, ion plasma frequency, dust–ion collision frequency, and Debye length, respectively.

The normalization is done in the following way:

$$n_i \to \frac{n_i}{n_0}, \quad n_e \to \frac{n_e}{n_{e0}}, \quad u_i \to \frac{u_i}{C_s}, \quad \phi \to \frac{e\phi}{T_e}, \quad x \to \frac{x}{\lambda_D}, \quad t \to \omega_{pi}t.$$

Here, $\delta_1 = \frac{n_{d0}}{n_{i0}}$ and $\delta_2 = \frac{n_{e0}}{n_{i0}}$ with the condition $\delta_1 + \delta_2 = 1$. $\lambda_D = \left(\frac{T_e}{4\pi n_{e0}e^2}\right)^{1/2}$, $\omega_{pi}^{-1} = \left(\frac{m_i}{4\pi n_{e0}e^2}\right)^{1/2}$, and $C_s = \sqrt{\frac{T_e}{m_i}}$.

To obtain the ZK equation, we introduce new stretched coordinates as

$$\xi = \epsilon^{1/2}x, \quad \zeta = \epsilon^{1/2}(x - \lambda t), \quad \eta = \epsilon^{1/2}y, \quad \tau = \epsilon^{3/2}t. \quad (4.255)$$

λ is the phase velocity of waves. The dependent variables are expanded in the following way:

$$\left.\begin{aligned}
n_i &= 1 + \epsilon n_i^{(1)} + \epsilon^2 n_i^{(2)} + \cdots \\
u &= 0 + \epsilon^{3/2}u^{(1)} + \epsilon^2 u^{(2)} + \cdots \\
v &= 0 + \epsilon v^{(1)} + \epsilon^2 v^{(2)} + \cdots \\
w &= 0 + \epsilon^{3/2}w^{(1)} + \epsilon^2 w^{(2)} + \cdots \\
\phi &= 0 + \epsilon \phi^{(1)} + \epsilon^2 \phi^{(2)} + \cdots .
\end{aligned}\right\} \quad (4.256)$$

To obtain the phase velocity and the ZK equation, we substitute the above expansions along with stretching coordinates (4.255) into Equations (4.250)–(4.254), and equating the coefficient of ϵ, we get

$$\left.\begin{aligned}
n_i^{(1)} &= \frac{v^{(1)}}{\lambda}, \quad w^{(1)} = -\frac{\omega_{pi}}{\Omega_i}\frac{\partial\phi^{(1)}}{\partial\xi}, \quad v^{(1)} = \frac{\phi^{(1)}}{\lambda}, \\
u^{(1)} &= \frac{\omega_{pi}}{\Omega_i}\frac{\partial\phi^{(1)}}{\partial\eta}, \quad w^{(2)} = \lambda\frac{\omega_{pi}}{\Omega_i}\frac{\partial u^{(1)}}{\partial\zeta}, \\
u^{(2)} &= -\lambda\frac{\omega_{pi}}{\Omega_i}\frac{\partial w^{(1)}}{\partial\zeta}, \quad \phi^{(1)} = n_i^{(1)}\frac{k - 1/2}{k + 1/2}.
\end{aligned}\right\} \quad (4.257)$$

Equating the coefficient of the next higher order of ϵ, we have

$$\left.\begin{aligned}
\frac{\partial n_i^{(1)}}{\partial\tau} - \lambda\frac{\partial n_i^{(2)}}{\partial\zeta} + \frac{\partial u^{(2)}}{\partial\xi} + \frac{\partial}{\partial\zeta}(n_i^{(1)}v^{(1)}) + \frac{\partial v^{(2)}}{\partial\zeta} + \frac{\partial w^{(2)}}{\partial\eta} &= 0 \\
\frac{\partial v^{(1)}}{\partial\tau} - \lambda\frac{\partial v^{(2)}}{\partial\zeta} + v^{(1)}\frac{\partial v^{(1)}}{\partial\zeta} + \frac{\partial\phi^{(2)}}{\partial\zeta} &= 0 \\
\frac{\partial^2\phi^{(1)}}{\partial\xi^2} + \frac{\partial^2\phi^{(1)}}{\partial\zeta^2} + \frac{\partial^2\phi^{(1)}}{\partial\eta^2} - A_1\phi^{(2)} - A_2\phi^{(1)^2} + n_i^{(2)} &= 0
\end{aligned}\right\} \quad (4.258)$$

where $A_1 = \frac{(k+1/2)}{(k-1/2)}$ and $A_2 = \frac{(k+1/2)}{2(k-1/2)}$.

From (4.257), one can obtain the phase velocity

$$1 - \lambda^2 A_1 = 0. \tag{4.259}$$

Expressing all the perturbed quantities in terms of $\phi^{(1)}$ from Equations (4.257)–(4.258), the ZK equation is obtained by

$$\frac{\partial \phi^{(1)}}{\partial \tau} + A\phi^{(1)} \frac{\partial \phi^{(1)}}{\partial \zeta} + B\frac{\partial^3 \phi^{(1)}}{\partial \zeta^3} + C\frac{\partial}{\partial \zeta}\left(\frac{\partial^2 \phi^{(1)}}{\partial \xi^2} + \frac{\partial^2 \phi^{(1)}}{\partial \eta^2}\right) = 0 \tag{4.260}$$

where

$$A = \frac{\lambda}{2A_1}\left(\frac{3A_1}{\lambda^2} - 2A_2\right), \quad B = \frac{\lambda}{2A_1}, \quad \text{and} \quad C = \frac{\lambda}{2A_1}\left(1 + A_1\lambda^2 \frac{\omega_{pi}^2}{\Omega_i^2}\right).$$

The ZK Equation (4.260) admits higher-dimensional solutions, such as plane solitons, 2-D cylindrical solitons, and 3-D spherical solitons. For the sake of simplicity, we here consider the plane solitary wave solutions $\phi = \phi(\chi)$ of the ZK equation, where χ is the coordinate

$$\chi = \zeta \cos \alpha + \xi \sin \alpha - u_0 \tau. \tag{4.261}$$

Here, α is the angle between the direction of propagation and the magnetic field B_0 and u is the soliton speed in the $(\xi - \eta - \zeta)$ frame. Without loss of generality, we assume that the wave propagates in the $(\xi - \zeta)$ plane because of cylindrical symmetry around the ζ-axis. Using transformation (4.261) and assuming that $\phi^{(1)}$ together with its χ-derivatives vanish at $\chi \to \infty$, the ZK Equation (4.260) yields the following solution:

$$\phi^{(1)} = \frac{3u}{A\cos\alpha} Sech^2\left[\left(\frac{1}{4}\frac{u/\cos\alpha}{B\cos^2\alpha + C\sin^2\alpha}\right)^{1/2} \chi\right] \tag{4.262}$$

where $\phi_m = \frac{3u}{A\cos\alpha}$ is the amplitude and $W = \left(\frac{1}{4}\frac{u/\cos\alpha}{B\cos^2\alpha + C\sin^2\alpha}\right)^{1/2}$ is the inverse of the width of the solitary waves.

The effects of k on the solitons are illustrated by plotting $\phi^{(1)}$ versus χ as shown in Figure 4.15. It is also observed from Figure 4.15 that k is directly proportional to the amplitude and the width of the solitary waves.

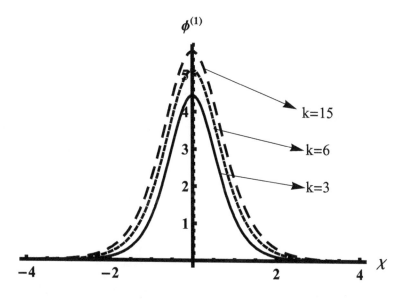

Fig. 4.15: Solitary wave solution of Equation (4.260) for different values of κ.

4.20 ZK Burgers' (ZKB) Equation

Like the KdVB equation or KPB equation, ZK Burgers' (ZKB) equation is also derived to study the two-dimensional solitons and shocks in a single equation in the presence of the magnetic field. To derive the ZKB equation, we consider a homogeneous, collisionless magnetoplasma consisting of ions and q-nonextensive distributed electrons. The viscosity is also considered. The plasma is confined in an external magnetic field $B_0 = \hat{x}B_0$, where $\hat{x}$ is the unit vector along the x-direction and B_0 is the external static magnetic field. Accordingly, the basic normalized equations are as follows:

$$\frac{\partial n_i}{\partial t} + \vec{\nabla} \cdot (n_i \vec{u}_i) = 0, \tag{4.263}$$

$$\frac{\partial \vec{u}_i}{\partial t} + (\vec{u}_i \cdot \vec{\nabla})\vec{u}_i = -\vec{\nabla}\phi + \Omega(\vec{u}_i \times \hat{\vec{x}}) + \mu\vec{\nabla}^2 \vec{u}_i, \tag{4.264}$$

$$\vec{\nabla}^2 \phi = n_e - (1+\alpha)n_i + \alpha \tag{4.265}$$

where n_j ($j = i$ and e stand for ions and electrons), u, v, and w are number density, the ion fluid speed in x, y, and z directions, respectively. Here, the normalization is done in the following way:

$$n_i \rightarrow \frac{n_i}{n_{e0}}, \quad u_i \rightarrow \frac{u_i}{C_s}, \quad \phi \rightarrow \frac{e\phi}{T_e}, \quad x \rightarrow \frac{x}{\lambda_D}, \quad t \rightarrow \omega_{pi}t$$

where n_{e0} is the electron unperturbed equilibrium plasma density and $\alpha = z_d n_{d0}/n_{e0}$. $C_s = \sqrt{K_B T_e/m_i}$ and K_B are the ion acoustic velocity and Boltzmann constant, respectively. $\omega_{pi}^{-1} = \sqrt{m_i/(4\pi e^2 n_{e0})}$ is the ion plasma frequency, and $\lambda_D = \sqrt{K_B T_e/(4\pi e^2 n_{e0})}$ is the Debye length. Ω is the ion cyclotron frequency, c is the velocity of light, and μ is the kinematic viscosity.

To obtain the ZK Burgers' equation, we introduce the stretched coordinate as

$$\xi = \epsilon^{1/2}(x - \lambda t), \eta = \epsilon^{1/2}y, \quad \zeta = \epsilon^{1/2}z, \quad \tau = \epsilon^{3/2}t, \quad \mu = \epsilon^{1/2}\mu_0$$

$$(4.266)$$

where μ is scaled in such a way that μ_0 becomes the effective viscosity. The viscosity is incorporated in nonlinear equations like KdVB, KPB, and ZKB, assumed to be the order of $\epsilon^{1/2}$ suggested in Equation (4.266) in the perturbation scheme. Let us expand the dependent variables as

$$\left.\begin{array}{l} n_i = 1 + \epsilon n_i^{(1)} + \epsilon^2 n_i^{(2)} + \cdots , \\[4pt] u = \epsilon u^{(1)} + \epsilon^2 u^{(2)} + \cdots , \\[4pt] v = \epsilon^{3/2}v^{(1)} + \epsilon^2 v^{(2)} + \cdots , \\[4pt] w = \epsilon^{3/2}w^{(1)} + \epsilon^2 w^{(2)} + \cdots , \\[4pt] \phi = \epsilon\phi^{(1)} + \epsilon^2\phi^{(2)} + \cdots . \end{array}\right\} \qquad (4.267)$$

By substituting Equations (4.266) and (4.267) into Equations (4.263) − (4.265) and equating the lowest power of ϵ, one gets

$$n_i^{(1)} = \frac{1}{\lambda}u^{(1)}, \quad u^{(1)} = \frac{1}{\lambda}\phi^{(1)}, \quad v^{(1)} = -\frac{1}{\Omega}\frac{\partial\phi^{(1)}}{\partial\zeta}. \qquad (4.268)$$

From Equations (4.268), we get the phase velocity as

$$\lambda = \sqrt{2(1+\alpha)/(q+1)}. \qquad (4.269)$$

The next order of ϵ is

$$\left.\begin{array}{l} w^{(1)} = \frac{1}{\Omega}\frac{\partial\phi^{(1)}}{\partial\eta}, \quad \frac{\partial v^{(1)}}{\partial\xi} = -\frac{\Omega}{\lambda}w^{(2)}, \quad \frac{\partial w^{(1)}}{\partial\xi} = \frac{\Omega}{\lambda}v^{(2)}, \\[10pt] \frac{\partial^2\phi^{(1)}}{\partial\xi^2} + \frac{\partial^2\phi^{(1)}}{\partial\eta^2} + \frac{\partial^2 w^{(1)}}{\partial\zeta^2} - \beta_1\phi^{(2)} = \beta_2(\phi^{(1)})^2 - (1+\alpha)n_i^{(2)} \end{array}\right\} \qquad (4.270)$$

where $\beta_1 = (q+1)/2$ and $\beta_2 = (q+1)(3-q)/8$. Considering the next higher order of ϵ, we get

$$
\left.
\begin{aligned}
&\frac{\partial n_i^{(1)}}{\partial \tau} - \lambda \frac{\partial n_i^{(2)}}{\partial \xi} + \frac{\partial}{\partial \xi}(n_i^{(1)} u^{(1)}) + \frac{\partial u^{(2)}}{\partial \xi} + \frac{\partial v^{(2)}}{\partial \eta} + \frac{\partial w^{(2)}}{\partial \zeta} = 0, \\
&\frac{\partial u^{(1)}}{\partial \tau} - \lambda \frac{\partial u^{(2)}}{\partial \xi} + u^{(1)} \frac{\partial u^{(1)}}{\partial \xi} + \frac{\partial \phi^{(2)}}{\partial \xi} \\
&\quad - \mu_0 \left(\frac{\partial^2 u^{(1)}}{\partial \xi^2} - \frac{\partial^2 u^{(1)}}{\partial \eta^2} - \frac{\partial^2 u^{(1)}}{\partial \zeta^2} \right) = 0.
\end{aligned}
\right\} \quad (4.271)
$$

Now, we eliminate $u^{(2)}$ and $n_i^{(2)}$ from Equation (4.271) by using Equation (4.270). After simplification and eliminating the second order of ϕ, we finally obtain the ZKB equation as

$$
\frac{\partial \phi^{(1)}}{\partial \tau} + A\phi^{(1)} \frac{\partial \phi^{(1)}}{\partial \xi} + B \frac{\partial^3 \phi^{(1)}}{\partial \xi^3} + C \frac{\partial}{\partial \xi} \left(\frac{\partial^2 \phi^{(1)}}{\partial \eta^2} + \frac{\partial^2 \phi^{(1)}}{\partial \zeta^2} \right)
$$
$$
- D \left(\frac{\partial^2 \phi^{(1)}}{\partial \xi^2} + \frac{\partial^2 \phi^{(1)}}{\partial \eta^2} + \frac{\partial^2 \phi^{(1)}}{\partial \zeta^2} \right) = 0 \quad (4.272)
$$

where

$$
A = \frac{v_0^3}{2} \left(\frac{3}{v_0^4} - \frac{2\beta_2}{1+\alpha} \right), \quad B = \frac{v_0^3}{2(1+\alpha)},
$$
$$
C = \frac{v_0^3}{2} \left(\frac{1}{1+\alpha} + \frac{1}{\Omega^2} \right), \quad \text{and} \quad D = \frac{\mu_0}{2}.
$$

4.21 Damped ZK (DZK) Equation

Like DKdV and DKP equations, now we shall derive the damped ZK (DZK) equation. For this, let us consider a plasma model consisting of cold ions, superthermal electrons in the presence of dust particles, and the external static magnetic field $B = \hat{y}B_0$ along the y-axis. The normalized continuity, momentum, and Poisson equations are as follows:

$$
\frac{\partial n_i}{\partial t} + \frac{\partial(n_i u)}{\partial x} + \frac{\partial(n_i v)}{\partial y} + \frac{\partial(n_i w)}{\partial z} = 0, \quad (4.273)
$$

$$
\frac{\partial u}{\partial t} + \left(u\frac{\partial}{\partial x} + v\frac{\partial}{\partial y} + w\frac{\partial}{\partial z} \right) u = -\frac{\partial \phi}{\partial x} - \frac{\Omega_i}{\omega_{pi}} w, \quad (4.274)
$$

$$
\frac{\partial v}{\partial t} + \left(u\frac{\partial}{\partial x} + v\frac{\partial}{\partial y} + w\frac{\partial}{\partial z} \right) v = -\frac{\partial \phi}{\partial y} - \nu_{id} v, \quad (4.275)
$$

$$\frac{\partial w}{\partial t} + \left(u\frac{\partial}{\partial x} + v\frac{\partial}{\partial y} + w\frac{\partial}{\partial z} \right)w = -\frac{\partial \phi}{\partial z} + \frac{\Omega_i}{\omega_{pi}}u, \qquad (4.276)$$

$$\frac{\partial^2 \phi}{\partial x^2} + \frac{\partial^2 \phi}{\partial y^2} + \frac{\partial^2 \phi}{\partial z^2} = \delta_1 + \delta_2 n_e - n_i. \qquad (4.277)$$

The normalized electron density is written as

$$n_e = \left(1 - \frac{\phi}{k - 1/2} \right)^{-(k+1/2)}$$

where n_i, n_e, $u_i (= u, v, w)$, ϕ, and ν_{id} are the ion number density, electron number density, ion velocity, electrostatic potential, and dust–ion collision frequency, respectively. Here, we use the same normalization like in Section 4.19.

To obtain the DZK equation, we introduce the same stretched coordinates as in Equation (4.255). The expressions of the dependent variables are considered the same as Equations (4.256) with

$$\nu_{id} \sim \epsilon^{3/2}\nu_{id0}. \qquad (4.278)$$

Substituting the above expansions along with stretching coordinates into Equations (4.273)–(4.277) and equating the coefficient of ϵ, we get

$$\phi^{(1)} = \frac{n_i^{(1)}}{\delta_1 A_1} \qquad (4.279)$$

where $A_1 = \frac{k+1/2}{k-1/2}$. Equating the coefficient of $\epsilon^{3/2}$, we get

$$n_i^{(1)} = \frac{v^{(1)}}{\lambda}, \quad w^{(1)} = -\frac{\omega_{pi}}{\Omega_i}\frac{\partial \phi^{(1)}}{\partial \xi}, \quad v^{(1)} = \frac{\phi^{(1)}}{\lambda}, \quad u^{(1)} = \frac{\omega_{pi}}{\Omega_i}\frac{\partial \phi^{(1)}}{\partial \eta}. \qquad (4.280)$$

Considering the coefficient of ϵ^2, we obtain

$$\left.\begin{array}{l} w^{(2)} = \lambda\dfrac{\omega_{pi}}{\Omega_i}\dfrac{\partial u^{(1)}}{\partial \zeta}, \quad u^{(2)} = -\lambda\dfrac{\omega_{pi}}{\Omega_i}\dfrac{\partial w^{(1)}}{\partial \zeta}, \\[2mm] \dfrac{\partial^2 \phi^{(1)}}{\partial \xi^2} + \dfrac{\partial^2 \phi^{(1)}}{\partial \zeta^2} + \dfrac{\partial^2 \phi^{(1)}}{\partial \eta^2} = \delta_1(A_1\phi^{(2)} + A_2\phi^{(1)^2}) - n_i^{(2)}. \end{array}\right\} \qquad (4.281)$$

Comparing the coefficients of $\epsilon^{5/2}$, we obtain

$$\left.\begin{array}{l} \dfrac{\partial n_i^{(1)}}{\partial \tau} - \lambda\dfrac{\partial n_i^{(2)}}{\partial \zeta} + \dfrac{\partial u^{(2)}}{\partial \xi} + \dfrac{\partial}{\partial \zeta}(n_i^{(1)}v^{(1)}) + \dfrac{\partial v^{(2)}}{\partial \zeta} + \dfrac{\partial w^{(2)}}{\partial \eta} = 0 \\[2mm] \dfrac{\partial v^{(1)}}{\partial \tau} - \lambda\dfrac{\partial v^{(2)}}{\partial \zeta} + v^{(1)}\dfrac{\partial v^{(1)}}{\partial \zeta} + \dfrac{\partial \phi^{(2)}}{\partial \zeta} - \nu_{id0}v^{(1)} = 0 \end{array}\right\} \qquad (4.282)$$

where $A_2 = \frac{(k+1/2)(k+3/2)}{2(k-1/2)^2}$. Using relationships (4.280), we get

$$1 - \lambda^2 A_1 \delta_2 = 0. \tag{4.283}$$

Expressing all the perturbed quantities in terms of $\phi^{(1)}$ from Equation (4.281), the damped ZK equation is obtained by

$$\frac{\partial \phi^{(1)}}{\partial \tau} + A\phi^{(1)} \frac{\partial \phi^{(1)}}{\partial \xi} + B\frac{\partial^3 \phi^{(1)}}{\partial \zeta^3} + D\phi^{(1)}$$

$$+ C\frac{\partial}{\partial \zeta}\left(\frac{\partial^2 \phi^{(1)}}{\partial \xi^2} + \frac{\partial^2 \phi^{(1)}}{\partial \eta^2}\right) = 0 \tag{4.284}$$

where

$$A = \frac{\lambda}{2A_1}\left(\frac{3A_1}{\lambda^2} - 2A_2\right),$$

$$B = \frac{\lambda}{2\delta_2 A_1},$$

$$C = \frac{\lambda}{2\delta_2 A_1}\left(1 + \delta_2 A_1 \lambda^2 \frac{\omega_{pi}^2}{\Omega_i^2}\right),$$

$$D = \frac{\nu_{id0}}{2}.$$

References

[1] A. H. Nayfeh, *Introduction to Perturbation Techniques*. Wiley-vch (2004).

[2] T. Taniuti and C. C. Wei, *J. Phys. Soc. Jpn.* 24, 941 (1968).

[3] C. H. Su and C. S. Gardner, *J. Math. Phys.* 10, 536 (1969).

[4] C. S. Gordner and G. K. Morikawa, Coutant Institute of Mathematical Sciences Report No. NY09082, 1960 (unpublished); *Comm. Pure Appl. Math.* 18, 35 (1965).

[5] D. J. Korteweg and G. deVries, *Phil. Mag.* 39, 422 (1985).

[6] A. Sen, S. Tiwary, S. Mishra, and P. Kaw, *Adv. Space Res.* 56(3), 429 (2015).

[7] S. Chowdhury, L. K. Mandi, and P. Chatterjee, *Phys. Plasmas* 25, 042112 (2018).

[8] V. S. Aslanov and V. V. Yudintsev, *Adv. Space Res.* 55, 660 (2015).

[9] H. Schamel, *Plasma Phys.* 14, 905 (1972).

[10] G. Williams, F. Verheest, M. A. Hellberg, M. G. M. Anowar, and I. Kourakis, *Phys. Plasmas* 21, 092103 (2014).

[11] H. Schamel, *J. Plasma Phys.*, 9, 377 (1973).

[12] M. A. Hossen, M. R. Hossen, and A. A. Mamun, *J. Korean Phys. Soc.* 65, 1883 (2014).

[13] S. Chandrasekhar, *Phi. Mag.* 11, 592 (1931).

[14] B. B. Kadomtsev and V. I. Petviashvili, *Soviet Phys. Dokl.* 15, 539 (1970).

[15] R. Grimshaw, *Stud. Appl. Math.* 73, 1 (1985).

[16] W. Oohara and R. Hatakeyama, *Phys. Rev. Lett.* 91, 205005 (2003).

[17] V. I. Karpman and E. M. Maslov, *Sov. Phys. JETP* 46, 281 (1977).

[18] D. Samsonov, A. V. Ivlev, R. A. Quinn, G. Morfill, and S. Zhdanov, *Phys. Rev. Lett.* 88, 095004 (2002).

[19] V. E. Zakharov and E. A. Kuznetsov, *Sov. Phys. JETP* 39, 285 (1974).

Chapter 5

Dressed Soliton and Envelope Soliton

5.1 Dressed Soliton

KdV, KP, and ZK type equations help us to describe solitary wave propagation in plasmas. Taylor and Ikezi [1] first showed that for ion acoustic solitary waves, the experimental observation data do not match with the soliton solution of KdV, KP, ZK, or similar equations. To get an accurate result, the theory needs to be improved so that the amplitude, width, and velocity of the solitary waves will be more accurate with the physical situation. Accordingly, a modification or correction of the amplitude, width, and velocity is necessary. One such modification is the inclusion of the higher-order perturbation correction of the KdV, KP, and ZK types of equations, and accordingly, the improvement of Mach number, amplitude, and width should be done properly. The solution of these equations with higher-order correction (source term) will surely give a better result. This improved solution is named Dressed Solution. In this chapter, we are going to derive the NLEEs with source term and to obtain higher-order correction of amplitude, width, and velocity for KdV or KdV type soliton in classical plasma, dusty plasma, and quantum plasma and higher-order correction of the same in the frame of the ZK equation.

5.2 Dressed Soliton in a Classical Plasma

To obtain the dressed soliton (higher-order correction to KdV equation) in a classical plasma model, we derive the KdV equation from the plasma model. Here, we consider a collisionless unmagnetized electron–ion plasma, where ions are mobile and electrons obey the Maxwell distribution.

Step 1: Basic normalized equation

The normalized fluid equations are written as

$$\frac{\partial n_i}{\partial t} + \frac{\partial(n_i u_i)}{\partial x} = 0 \tag{5.1}$$

$$\frac{\partial u_i}{\partial t} + u_i \frac{\partial u_i}{\partial x} = -\frac{\partial \phi}{\partial x} \tag{5.2}$$

$$\frac{\partial^2 \phi}{\partial x^2} = e^\phi - n_i \tag{5.3}$$

where n_i, u_i, and ϕ are the ion density, ion velocity, and electrostatic potential, respectively. Here, we apply the same normalization procedure as in Section 4.7.

Step 2: KdV equation evolution

To obtain the KdV equation, we introduce the same stretched coordinates as used in (4.40). Expansions of the dependent variables are also considered the same as in (4.41). Substituting (4.40) and (4.41) in (5.1)–(5.3), and equating the first order of ϵ, we get

$$n_i^{(1)} = u_i^{(1)} = \phi^{(1)} \quad \text{and} \quad \lambda = 1. \tag{5.4}$$

Taking the coefficient of the next higher-order of ϵ, we obtain the KdV equation as

$$\frac{\partial \phi^{(1)}}{\partial \tau} + \phi^{(1)} \frac{\partial \phi^{(1)}}{\partial \xi} + \frac{1}{2} \frac{\partial^3 \phi^{(1)}}{\partial \xi^3} = 0. \tag{5.5}$$

Step 3: Higher-order approximation

As stated earlier, the KdV soliton does not always match with observed data, and to overcome this discrepancy, a higher-order correction of the KdV equation has been prescribed here. So, we include the higher-order perturbation corrections to the KdV solitons. It has resulted in a better agreement with the experimental observations. When the higher-order perturbation corrections are included in the KdV soliton, then the improved soliton is the dressed soliton. However, from perturbation theory, it is known that the higher-order correction is to be considered only if the amplitude of the higher-order correction is much less than the amplitude of the original KdV soliton. If the amplitude of the higher-order correction is greater or equal to the amplitude of the KdV soliton, then the solution obtained is not physical and is to be ignored.

The KdV equation contains the lowest-order relation between the non-linearity and dispersion. To get a better result, we include the second-order perturbation term $\phi^{(2)}$, $n_i^{(2)}$, $u_i^{(2)}$ in (4.41). This will provide us a more accurate relationship between amplitude, width, and velocity of the wave. Now, we shall investigate the higher-order nonlinear and dispersion effect. So, we take the next order of ϵ and obtain second-order quantities $n_i^{(2)}$ and $u_i^{(2)}$, and it is expressed as

$$n_i^{(2)} = \phi^{(2)} + \frac{1}{2}\left(\phi^{(1)}\right)^2 - \frac{\partial^2 \phi^{(1)}}{\partial \xi^2}, \quad u_i^{(2)} = \phi^{(2)} - \frac{1}{2}\frac{\partial^2 \phi^{(1)}}{\partial \xi^2}. \tag{5.6}$$

The behavior of the second-order potential $\phi^{(2)}$ is determined from the linear inhomogeneous differential equation of $\phi^{(2)}$, whose source term is given as a function of $\phi^{(1)}$. Thus, we determine the nonsecular solution of $\phi^{(2)}$ from

$$\frac{\partial \phi^{(2)}}{\partial \tau} + \frac{\partial\left(\phi^{(1)}\phi^{(2)}\right)}{\partial \xi} + \frac{1}{2}\frac{\partial^3 \phi^{(2)}}{\partial \xi^3} = S\left(\phi^{(1)}\right) \tag{5.7}$$

where $S\left(\phi^{(1)}\right) = M\phi^{(1)}\frac{\partial^3 \phi^{(1)}}{\partial \xi^3} + N\frac{\partial^5 \phi^{(1)}}{\partial \xi^5} + P\frac{\partial}{\partial \xi}\left(\frac{\partial \phi^{(1)}}{\partial \xi}\right)^2; M = \frac{1}{2}, \ N = -\frac{3}{8}, \ P = -\frac{5}{8}.$

Step 4: Renormalization

Ichikawa and his collaborators [2–4] first prescribed the corrections to the KdV soliton in the next higher order of approximation in the RPT. However, their results included the secular terms, and hence, the theory of higher-order approximation in the RPT was not established.

For the general weakly dispersive system, the higher-order approximations come from the linearized KdV equation. It includes a source term inhomogeneous in nature. The reason is that the secular terms appear due to self-resonance, which in turn comes from nonlinear oscillation. Furthermore, the secular terms, resulting from the soliton part, are eliminated by adding them to the KdV equation. The derivatives of the higher-order conserved densities are expressed in terms of the conserved quantities also. The resultant equation is known as the generalized KdV equation. It is seen from the higher-order derivatives of conserved densities of the KdV equation that the overall solutions are solutions of the linearized KdV equation along with the secular solutions for the special initial data. The renormalization technique is a technique that is used to eliminate the secular terms that appeared in the one-soliton solution developed by Kodama and Taniuti [5]. Then, the nonsecular solutions are obtained in all order, as a particular solution to the higher-order equations. As a result, the solution to the original system becomes the KdV soliton with velocity shift plus nonlinear corrections, which are bounded all time. It is called the dress of the KdV soliton (dressed soliton) after Ichikawa [2].

To get a nonsecular solution for $\phi^{(2)}$, the method of renormalization is used. Accordingly, Equation (5.5) is modified as

$$\frac{\partial \widetilde{\phi}^{(1)}}{\partial \tau} + \widetilde{\phi}^{(1)} \frac{\partial \widetilde{\phi}^{(1)}}{\partial \xi} + \frac{1}{2} \frac{\partial^3 \widetilde{\phi}^{(1)}}{\partial \xi^3} + \delta\Lambda \frac{\partial \widetilde{\phi}^{(1)}}{\partial \xi} = 0. \tag{5.8}$$

The inhomogeneous Equation (5.7) for $\phi^{(2)}$ becomes

$$\frac{\partial \widetilde{\phi}^{(2)}}{\partial \tau} + \frac{\partial (\widetilde{\phi}^{(1)} \widetilde{\phi}^{(2)})}{\partial \xi} + \frac{1}{2} \frac{\partial^3 \widetilde{\phi}^{(2)}}{\partial \xi^3} + \delta\Lambda \frac{\partial \widetilde{\phi}^{(2)}}{\partial \xi} = S(\widetilde{\phi}^{(1)}) + \delta\Lambda \frac{\partial \widetilde{\phi}^{(1)}}{\partial \xi}. \tag{5.9}$$

The parameter $\delta\Lambda$ in Equations (5.8) and (5.9) is introduced in such a way that the secular (resonant) term in $S(\widetilde{\phi}^{(1)})$ is canceled by the term $\delta\Lambda \left(\frac{\partial \widetilde{\phi}^{(1)}}{\partial \xi} \right)$ in Equation (5.9).

Step 5: Second-order inhomogeneous differential equation evolution

Now, we introduce a new stationary frame variable η as

$$\eta = \xi - (\Lambda + \delta\Lambda)\tau \tag{5.10}$$

where $(\Lambda + \delta\Lambda) = X - 1$, and X is the Mach number. Hence, Equation (5.8) can be transformed into

$$-\Lambda \frac{d\widetilde{\phi}^{(1)}}{d\eta} + \widetilde{\phi}^{(1)} \frac{d\widetilde{\phi}^{(1)}}{d\eta} + \frac{1}{2} \frac{d^3 \widetilde{\phi}^{(1)}}{d\eta^3} = 0. \tag{5.11}$$

Integrating Equation (5.11), the boundary conditions $\phi^{(1)}$ and its derivatives vanish as $\eta \to \pm\infty$. We obtain the stationary renormalized solitary wave solution of Equation (5.8) (up to 1st order in Λ) as

$$\widetilde{\phi}^{(1)} = \phi_0 \, sech^2(\widetilde{D}\eta) \tag{5.12}$$

where $\phi_0 = 3\Lambda$, $\widetilde{D} = D = \left(\frac{\Lambda}{2}\right)^{1/2}$. Using Equations (5.10) and (5.12) in Equation (5.9), we obtain

$$-\Lambda\frac{d\widetilde{\phi}^{(2)}}{d\eta} + \phi_0\frac{d(sech^2(\widetilde{D}\eta)\widetilde{\phi}^{(2)})}{d\eta} + \frac{1}{2}\frac{d^3\widetilde{\phi}^{(2)}}{d\eta^3}$$

$$= -2\widetilde{D}\delta\Lambda\phi_0 sech^2(\widetilde{D}\eta)\tanh(\widetilde{D}\eta) + A_1 sech^2(\widetilde{D}\eta)\tanh(\widetilde{D}\eta)$$

$$+ A_2 sech^4(\widetilde{D}\eta)\tanh(\widetilde{D}\eta) + A_3 sech^6(\widetilde{D}\eta)\tanh(\widetilde{D}\eta) \qquad (5.13)$$

where $A_1 = -32ND^5\phi_0$, $A_2 = 480ND^5\phi_0 - 8MD^3\phi_0^2 - 16D^3P\phi_0^2$, $A_3 = -720N\phi_0 D^5 + 24M\phi_0^2 D^3 + 24PD^3\phi_0^2$.

Integrating Equation (5.13) with respect to η, the boundary conditions $\widetilde{\phi}^{(2)}$ and its derivatives vanish as $\eta \to \pm\infty$, and we obtain a second-order inhomogeneous differential equation for $\phi^{(2)}$.

$$-\Lambda\widetilde{\phi}^{(2)} + \phi_0\ sech^2(\widetilde{D}\eta)\widetilde{\phi}^{(2)} + \frac{1}{2}\frac{d^2\widetilde{\phi}^{(2)}}{d\eta^2} = \delta\Lambda\phi_0\ sech^2(\widetilde{D}\eta)$$

$$+ A_{11} sech^2(\widetilde{D}\eta) + A_{12} sech^4(\widetilde{D}\eta) + A_{13} sech^6(\widetilde{D}\eta) \qquad (5.14)$$

where $A_{11} = -\frac{A_1}{2D} = 4N\Lambda^2\phi_0$, $A_{12} = -\frac{A_2}{4D} = -90N\Lambda^3 + 9\Lambda^3(M + 2P)$, $A_{13} = -\frac{A_3}{6D} = 90N\Lambda^3 - 18(M + P)\Lambda^3$.

To cancel the secular term, we choose $A_{11} + \delta\Lambda\phi_0 = 0$ which gives

$$\delta\Lambda = -4N\Lambda^2. \qquad (5.15)$$

Hence, using Equation (5.15), and putting $\phi_0 = 3\Lambda$, Equation (5.14) becomes

$$\frac{1}{2}\frac{d^2\widetilde{\phi}^{(2)}}{d\eta^2} + \Lambda(3\ sech^2(\widetilde{D}\eta) - 1)\widetilde{\phi}^{(2)} = A_{12} sech^4(\widetilde{D}\eta) + A_{13} sech^6(\widetilde{D}\eta)$$

$$(5.16)$$

where the secular term is removed. Equation (5.16) is a second-order inhomogeneous differential equation with a solution that can be written as

$$\widetilde{\phi}^{(2)} = \widetilde{\phi}_{\text{comp}} + \widetilde{\phi}_p \qquad (5.17)$$

where $\widetilde{\phi}_{\text{comp}}$ is the complementary function and $\widetilde{\phi}_p$ is the particular solution.

Step 6: Particular solution evolution

A particular solution to the inhomogeneous equation only plays the role of the higher-order correction. Most authors' [6–8] remedy to an obtained particular solution of Equation (5.16), using the method of variation in parameter, will be lengthy. Chatterjee and collaborates [9, 10] developed a simpler series solution method similar to the tanh method. To obtain the particular solution to Equation (5.16), here the series considered as power series of $sech^2$ terms unlike in the tanh method is the series considered as power series of $tanh$ term. This technique is based on a truncated power series solution of the second-order evolution and the solution can easily be obtained as a power series of $sech^2$ terms.

Let $\widetilde{\phi}_p$ be defined as

$$\widetilde{\phi}_p = \sum_{i=1}^{K} a_i sech^{2i}(\widetilde{D}\eta) = a_1 sech^2(\widetilde{D}\eta) + a_2 sech^4(\widetilde{D}\eta) + \cdots \qquad (5.18)$$

and be a particular solution of Equation (5.16). The unknown K will be determined after equating the highest power of $sech\xi$ that arises in the left- and right-hand sides of Equation (5.16) after the substitution. The highest power term that arises on the left-hand side is $sech^{2K+2}(\widetilde{D}\eta)$ and on the right-hand side is $sech^6(\widetilde{D}\eta)$. Hence, the value of K will be 2. The appropriate series that is required to solve Equation (5.16) is then written as

$$\widetilde{\phi}_p = a_1 sech^2(\widetilde{D}\eta) + a_2 sech^4(\widetilde{D}\eta) \qquad (5.19)$$

where a_1 and a_2 are to be calculated by equating the coefficients of the different powers of $sech\xi$ (namely, $sech^2\xi$, $sech^4\xi$, and $sech^6\xi$), and after substituting Equation (5.19) in Equation (5.16), we get

$$\left(\frac{3}{2}a_1 + 3a_2\right)\Lambda sech^4(\widetilde{D}\eta) - 2a_2\Lambda sech^6(\widetilde{D}\eta)$$

$$= A_{12}sech^4(\widetilde{D}\eta) + A_{13}sech^6(\widetilde{D}\eta). \qquad (5.20)$$

Equating the coefficients of $sech^4(\widetilde{D}\eta)$ and $sech^6(\widetilde{D}\eta)$ of the above equation, we obtain $a_1 = \left(\frac{2}{3\Lambda}A_{12} + A_{13}/\Lambda\right) = 30N\Lambda^2 - 6(2M + P)\Lambda^2$, $a_2 = -\frac{A_{13}}{2\Lambda} = -45N\Lambda^2 + 9(M + P)\Lambda^2$.

Thus, the series is truncated at $k = 2$. Hence, the particular solution ϕ_p can be expressed as

$$\widetilde{\phi}_p = \left(30N\Lambda^2 - 6(2M + P)\Lambda^2\right)sech^2(\widetilde{D}\eta)$$

$$+ \left(-45N\Lambda^2 + 9(M + P)\Lambda^2\right)sech^4(\widetilde{D}\eta). \tag{5.21}$$

Step 7: To obtain complementary solution

The complementary solution ψ_{comp} of Equation (5.16) is given by

$$\widetilde{\psi}_{\text{comp}} = C_1 P_3^2(z) + C_2 Q_3^2(z) \tag{5.22}$$

where $P_3^2(z)$ and $Q_3^2(z)$ are the associated Legendre functions defined as

$$P_3^2(z) = 15z(1 - z^2) \tag{5.23}$$

$$Q_3^2(z) = \frac{15}{2}z(1 - z^2)ln\frac{1 + z}{1 - z} + \frac{2}{1 - z^2} + 5 - 15(1 - z^2) \tag{5.24}$$

where $z = tanh(\widetilde{D}\eta)$ [6–8]. The coefficients C_1 and C_2 can be determined using the boundary conditions. The first term in the complementary function is secular which can be eliminated by renormalizing the amplitude. Also, $\widetilde{\phi}^2(\eta) \to 0$ as $\eta \to \infty$, so, $C_2 = 0$. One can notice that the complementary part does not affect the stationary solution.

Step 8: Dressed soliton evolution

Using Equations (5.12) and (5.18), the stationary one soliton solution up to second-order in Λ, for ion acoustic waves in the classical plasma, is written as

$$\widetilde{\phi} = \widetilde{\phi}^{(1)} + \widetilde{\phi}^{(2)} = \widetilde{\phi}_0 \, sech^2(\widetilde{D}\eta) + a_1 sech^2(\widetilde{D}\eta) + a_2 sech^4(\widetilde{D}\eta). \tag{5.25}$$

The amplitude of the KdV soliton that includes the second-order contribution $\widetilde{\phi}_0$, the amplitude of the dressed soliton that includes the second-order contribution $\widetilde{\phi_0}^*$, and the width $\widetilde{W}$ of the dressed soliton are as follows:

$$\widetilde{\phi}_0 = 3(\Lambda + \delta\Lambda) = 3(\Lambda - 4N\Lambda^2),$$

$$\widetilde{\phi}_0^* = 3(\Lambda + \delta\Lambda) + a_1 + a_2 = 3(\Lambda - 4N\Lambda^2 + a_1 + a_2,$$

$$\widetilde{W} = \widetilde{D}^{-1} = \left(\frac{2}{\Lambda - 4N\Lambda^2}\right)^{1/2}.$$

Equation (5.5) is the standard *sech*^{2} type KdV soliton, whose amplitude $\phi_0 = 3\Lambda$ and width $W = \sqrt{2/\Lambda}$.

5.3 Dressed Soliton in a Dusty Plasma

To derive dressed soliton in dusty plasma, we consider a four-component dusty plasma model consisting of Boltzmann distributed electrons, non-thermal ions, and negatively and positively charged dust grains. The basic normalized equations are

$$\frac{\partial n_1}{\partial t} + \frac{\partial}{\partial x}(n_1 u_1) = 0 \tag{5.26}$$

$$\frac{\partial u_1}{\partial t} + u_1 \frac{\partial u_1}{\partial x} = \frac{\partial \phi}{\partial x} \tag{5.27}$$

$$\frac{\partial n_2}{\partial t} + \frac{\partial}{\partial x}(n_2 u_2) = 0 \tag{5.28}$$

$$\frac{\partial u_2}{\partial t} + u_2 \frac{\partial u_2}{\partial x} = -\alpha\beta\frac{\partial \phi}{\partial x} \tag{5.29}$$

$$\frac{\partial^2 \phi}{\partial x^2} = n_1 - (1 - \mu_i + \mu_e)n_2$$

$$+ \mu_e e^{\sigma\phi} - \mu_i(1 + \beta_1\phi + \beta_1\phi^2)e^{-\phi} \tag{5.30}$$

where n_j ($j = 1, 2$ stands for negatively charged and positively charged grains, respectively) is the number density, u_j is the charged dust fluid speed, and ϕ is the electric potential. Here, $\alpha = \frac{Z_2}{Z_1}$, $\beta = \frac{m_1}{m_2}$, $\mu_e = \frac{n_{e0}}{Z_1 n_{10}}$, $\mu_i = \frac{n_{i0}}{Z_1 n_{10}}$, $\sigma = \frac{T_i}{T_e}$, $\beta_1 = \frac{4\alpha_1}{1+3\alpha_1}$. α_1 is the ion nonthermal parameter that determines the number of fast (energetic) ions, and m_j are masses of dust particles. T_i, T_e, k_B, and e are ion temperature, electron temperatures, the Boltzmann constant, and electron charge, respectively. n_{j0}, n_{e0}, and n_{i0} are the equilibrium number density of dust particle, electron, and ions (with Z_1 and Z_2 being the number of electrons and protons residing on a negative and positive dust particle). Here, we use the same normalization as in Section 4.10.

Now, we derive the KdV equation from Equations (5.26)–(5.30) by employing the RPT, where the stretched coordinates are taken the same as (4.40) and the dependent variables are expanded the same as (4.140). Using Equation (4.140) in Equations (5.26)–(5.30), and equating terms of the first-order in ϵ, we get the phase velocity λ as

$$\lambda^2 = \frac{1 + \alpha\beta(1 + \mu_e - \mu_i)}{\sigma\mu_e + \mu_i - \mu_i\beta_1}. \tag{5.31}$$

Similarly, equating terms of the next higher-order of ϵ, we obtain the KdV equation as

$$\frac{\partial\phi^{(1)}}{\partial\tau} + A\phi^{(1)}\frac{\partial\phi^{(1)}}{\partial\xi} + B\frac{\partial^3\phi^{(1)}}{\partial\xi^3} = 0 \tag{5.32}$$

where $A = \frac{1}{2\lambda[1+\alpha\beta(1+\mu_e-\mu_i)]}\left[3\alpha^2\beta^2(1 + \mu_e - \mu_i) - 3 - \lambda^4(\mu_e\sigma^2 - \mu_i)\right]$, $B = \frac{\lambda^3}{2[1+\alpha\beta(1+\mu_e-\mu_i)]}$.

Next, we determine the higher-order nonlinear and dispersion effects of the KdV equation. We start by equating the next higher-order terms in ϵ, and after some standard algebra, we obtain the differential equation for the higher-order correction $\phi^{(2)}$ as

$$\frac{\partial\phi^{(2)}}{\partial\tau} + A\frac{\partial(\phi^{(1)}\phi^{(2)})}{\partial\xi} + B\frac{\partial^3\phi^{(2)}}{\partial\xi^3} = S(\phi^{(1)}) \tag{5.33}$$

where

$$S(\phi^{(1)}) = L(\phi^{(1)})^2\frac{\partial\phi^{(1)}}{\partial\xi} + M\phi^{(1)}\frac{\partial^3\phi^{(1)}}{\partial\xi^3} + N\frac{\partial^5\phi^{(1)}}{\partial\xi^5} + P\frac{\partial\left(\frac{\partial\phi^{(1)}}{\partial\xi}\right)^2}{\partial\xi},$$

$$L = \frac{1}{4\lambda^3[1 + \alpha\beta(1 + \mu_e - \mu_i)]}(L_1 + L_2 + L_3),$$

$$L_1 = (-6A^2\lambda^2 - 14A\lambda - 15),$$

$$L_2 = -(1 - \mu_i + \mu_e)(6A^2\alpha\beta\lambda^2 - 20A\alpha^2\beta^2\lambda + 15\alpha^3\beta^3),$$

$$L_3 = 2\lambda^6\left(\frac{\mu_e\delta^3}{2} + 3\frac{\mu_i\beta_1}{2} + \frac{\mu_i}{2}\right),$$

$$M = \frac{(-12AB\lambda^2 - 16B) - (1 - \mu_i + \mu_e)(6AB\alpha\beta - 8B\alpha^2\beta^2}{2[1 + \alpha\beta(1 - \mu_i + \mu_e)]4\lambda^2},$$

$$N = \frac{-3B^2}{2\lambda},$$

$$P = \frac{(-9AB\lambda - 4B) - (1 - \mu_i + \mu_e)(9AB\alpha\beta\lambda - 4B\alpha^2\beta^2)}{4\lambda^2[1 + \alpha\beta(1 + \mu_e - \mu_i)]}.$$

Equation (5.33) is the linear inhomogeneous differential equation in $\phi^{(2)}$, whose source term is given as a function of $\phi^{(1)}$, and the expression of $\phi^{(1)}$ is known from Equation (5.32). Equation (5.33) describes the effect of higher-order nonlinearity and dispersion, and to get the dressed soliton, this needs to be solved.

To get a nonsecular solution for $\phi^{(2)}$, we use the method of renormalization, developed by Kodama and Taniuti [5]. Accordingly, equations (5.32) and (5.33) are modified. Introducing the new stationary frame $\eta = \xi - (\Lambda + \delta\Lambda)\tau$ and proceeding the same way as before, we get

$$-\Lambda\frac{d\widetilde{\phi}^{(1)}}{d\eta} + A\widetilde{\phi}^{(1)}\frac{d\widetilde{\phi}^{(1)}}{d\eta} + B\frac{d^3\widetilde{\phi}^{(1)}}{d\eta^3} = 0. \tag{5.34}$$

Integrating Equation (5.34) under the boundary conditions $\phi^{(1)}$ and its derivatives vanish as $\eta \to \pm\infty$, we obtain the stationary renormalized solitary wave solution as

$$\widetilde{\phi}^{(1)} = \phi_0 \ sech^2(\widetilde{D}\eta) \tag{5.35}$$

where $\phi_0 = \frac{3\Lambda}{A}$ and $\widetilde{D} = D = \sqrt{\frac{\Lambda}{4B}}$. Similarly, proceeding the same way as before, we obtain a second-order inhomogeneous differential equation for $\phi^{(2)}$.

$$B\frac{d^2\widetilde{\phi}^{(2)}}{d\eta^2} + \Lambda(3 \ sech^2(\widetilde{D}\eta) - 1)\widetilde{\phi}^{(2)} = A_{12}sech^4(\widetilde{D}\eta) + A_{13}sech^6(\widetilde{D}\eta) \tag{5.36}$$

where $A_{12} = -\frac{45N\Lambda^3}{2AB^2} + \frac{9\Lambda^3(M+2P)}{2A^2B}$, $A_{13} = \frac{45N\Lambda^3}{2AB^2} - \frac{9(M+P)\Lambda^3}{A^2B} + \frac{9L\Lambda^3}{A^3}$ and $\delta\Lambda$ is given by $\delta\Lambda = -\frac{N\Lambda^2}{B^2}$.

Equation (5.36) is a second-order inhomogeneous differential equation with a solution that can be written as

$$\widetilde{\phi}^{(2)} = \widetilde{\phi}_{comp} + \widetilde{\phi}_p \tag{5.37}$$

where $\widetilde{\phi}_{comp}$ is the complementary function and $\widetilde{\phi}_p$ is the particular solution. Similarly, the series solution method is used to obtain the particular solution of Equation (5.36) as

$$
\widetilde{\phi}_p = \left(\frac{15N\Lambda^2}{2AB^2} - \frac{3(2M+P)\Lambda^2}{A^2B} + \frac{9L\Lambda^2}{A^3} \right) sech^2(\widetilde{D}\eta)
$$

$$
+ \left(-\frac{45N\lambda^2}{4AB^2} + \frac{9(M+P)\Lambda^2}{2A^2B} - \frac{9L\Lambda^2}{2A^3} \right) sech^4(\widetilde{D}\eta). \quad (5.38)
$$

The complementary solution ψ_{comp} of Equation (5.36) is given by

$$
\widetilde{\psi}_{\mathrm{comp}} = C_1 P_3^2(z) + C_2 Q_3^2(z), \quad (5.39)
$$

where $P_3^2(z)$ and $Q_3^2(z)$ are the associated Legendre functions. These are defined as

$$
P_3^2(z) = 15z(1 - z^2) \quad (5.40)
$$

$$
Q_3^2(z) = \frac{15}{2}z(1 - z^2)ln\frac{1+z}{1-z} + \frac{2}{1-z^2} + 5 - 15(1 - z^2), \quad (5.41)
$$

where $z = tanh(\widetilde{D}\eta)$. The coefficients C_1 and C_2 can be determined using the boundary conditions. The first term in the complementary function is secular which can be eliminated by renormalizing the amplitude. Also, $\widetilde{\phi}^2(\eta) \to 0$ as $\eta \to \infty$, so, $C_2 = 0$. One can notice that the complementary part has no effect on the stationary solution. Using Equations (5.35)–(5.37), the stationary one soliton solution up to the second-order in Λ for DAWs in the four component dusty plasma is written as

$$
\widetilde{\phi} = \widetilde{\phi}^{(1)} + \widetilde{\phi}^{(2)} = \widetilde{\phi}_0 \, sech^2(\widetilde{D}\eta) + a_1 sech^2(\widetilde{D}\eta) + a_2 sech^4(\widetilde{D}\eta). \quad (5.42)
$$

The amplitude of the KdV soliton that includes the second-order contribution $\widetilde{\phi}_0$, the amplitude of the dressed soliton that includes the second-order contribution $\widetilde{\phi}_0^{\,*}$, and the width $\widetilde{W}$ of the dressed soliton are as follows:

$$
\widetilde{\phi}_0 = \frac{3(\Lambda + \delta\Lambda)}{A} = \frac{3\left(\Lambda - \frac{N\Lambda^2}{B^2}\right)}{A},
$$

$$
\widetilde{\phi}_0^{\,*} = \frac{3(\Lambda + \delta\Lambda)}{A} + a_1 + a_2 = \frac{3\left(\Lambda - \frac{N\Lambda^2}{B^2}\right)}{A} + a_1 + a_2,
$$

$$
\widetilde{W} = \widetilde{D}^{-1} = \left(\frac{4B}{\Lambda - \frac{N\Lambda^2}{B^2}} \right)^{1/2}.
$$

Equation (5.35) is the standard $sech^2$ type KdV soliton, whose amplitude $\psi_0 = \frac{3\lambda}{A}$ and width $W = \left(\frac{4B}{\Lambda}\right)^{1/2}$.

We illustrate the effects of higher-order nonlinear terms, by plotting the KdV soliton $\widetilde{\phi}_{(1)}$ (dotted line), the higher-order correction $\widetilde{\phi}_{(2)}$ (dashed line), and the dressed soliton $\widetilde{\phi}$ (solid line) vs η as shown in Figure 5.1(a). It is seen that the amplitude of the dressed soliton $\widetilde{\phi}$ is larger than the amplitude of the KdV soliton $\widetilde{\phi}^{(1)}$. However, from the perturbation theory, it is known that the higher-order correction is to be considered only if $\frac{|\widetilde{\phi}_0|}{|\widetilde{\phi}_{20}|} \ll 1$, i.e., $|a_1 + a_2| < |\widetilde{\phi}_0|$. If $|a_1 + a_2| \geq |\widetilde{\phi}_0|$, then the solution obtained is not physical. The shapes of the dressed soliton and KdV soliton are shown in Figure 5.1(b) for the same set of parameters as above, but the value of $\beta_1 = 0.75$. From the above discussions, it is clear that the shape of the dressed soliton may exist, but the solution is not physical.

Figure 5.2 is drawn to show this situation. In this figure, the amplitudes of the KdV soliton $\widetilde{\phi}_0$ (dotted line), the second-order correction $\widetilde{\phi}_{20}$ (dashed line), and dressed soliton (solid line) are plotted against β_1.

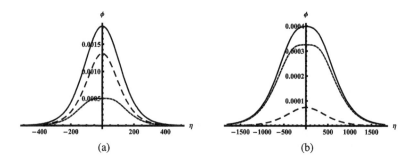

Fig. 5.1: The KdV soliton (dotted line), second-order correction (dashed line), and dressed soliton (solid line) are plotted (a) with $\beta_1 = 0.11$ and (b) with $\beta_1 = .75$.

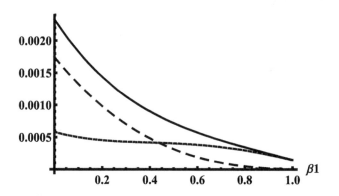

Fig. 5.2: The amplitude of the KdV soliton (dotted line), second-order correction (dashed line), and dressed soliton (solid line) are plotted against β_1.

It is seen that if $\beta_1 \geq 0.44$, the amplitude of the higher-order correction exceeds the amplitude of the first-order KdV soliton. So, the dressed soliton solution is invalid for $\beta_1 \geq 0.44$.

5.4 Dressed Soliton in Quantum Plasma

To derive the dressed soliton in quantum plasma, we consider an unmagnetized collision-free quantum pair-ion plasma model, having electrons, positive and negative ions, and immobile negatively charged dust grains. The basic normalized equations are

$$0 = \frac{\partial \phi}{\partial x} - 2n_e \frac{\partial n_e}{\partial x} + \frac{H^2}{2\mu} \frac{\partial}{\partial x} \left(\frac{\partial^2 \sqrt{n_e}/\partial x^2}{\sqrt{n_e}} \right), \quad (5.43)$$

$$\frac{\partial n_+}{\partial t} + \frac{\partial}{\partial x}(n_+ u_+) = 0, \quad (5.44)$$

$$\frac{\partial u_+}{\partial t} + u_+ \frac{\partial u_+}{\partial x} = -m \frac{\partial \phi}{\partial x}, \quad (5.45)$$

$$\frac{\partial n_-}{\partial t} + \frac{\partial}{\partial x}(n_- u_-) = 0, \quad (5.46)$$

$$\frac{\partial u_-}{\partial t} + u_- \frac{\partial u_-}{\partial x} = \frac{\partial \phi}{\partial x}, \quad (5.47)$$

$$\frac{\partial^2 \phi}{\partial x^2} = \mu n_e - \beta n_+ + n_- + \delta \quad (5.48)$$

where n_j, u_j, and m_j ($j = e$, d, $+$, and $-$ stands for electrons, dust grains, positive ions, and negative ions, respectively) are the number density, velocity, and mass, respectively. $\mu = n_{e0}/Z_- n_{-0}$ and $\beta = Z_+ n_{+0}/Z_- n_{-0}$ are connected through the charge neutrality condition $\mu = \beta - 1 - \delta$ with $\delta = Z_{d0} n_{d0}/Z_- n_{-0}$, $m = Z_+ m_-/Z_- m_+$. n_{j0} is the equilibrium number density. $\hbar$ is the scaled Planck's constant divided by 2π, ϕ is the electrostatic wave potential, and p_e is the electron pressure. The equilibrium charge neutrality condition is $n_{e0} + Z_- n_{-0} + Z_{d0} n_{d0} = Z_+ n_{+0}$, where $Z_\pm$ and Z_{d0} are the charge states for positive (negative) ions and dusts. We assume that the ions are cold, and the electrons obey the pressure law

$$p_e = \frac{m_e v_{Fe}^2}{3 n_{e0}^2} n_e^3$$

where $v_{Fe} = \sqrt{2K_B T_{Fe}/m_e}$ is the electron Fermi thermal speed, T_{Fe} is the particle Fermi temperature given by $K_B T_{Fe} = \hbar^2 (3\pi^2)^{2/3} n_{e0}^{2/3}/2m_e$, and

K_B is the Boltzmann constant. Here, the normalizations are taken as

$$x \to \omega_{p-} x/c_s, \quad t \to \omega_{p-} t, \quad n_\alpha \to n_\alpha/n_{\alpha 0},$$

$$u_\alpha \to u_\alpha/c_s, \quad \phi \to e\phi/(k_B T_{Fe}),$$

$\omega_{pj} = \sqrt{n_{j0}e^2/\epsilon_0 m_j}$ is the j-particle plasma frequency, and $c_s = \sqrt{K_B T_{Fe}/m_-}$ is the quantum ion-acoustic speed. In the following set of normalized equations, we introduce the nondimensional quantum parameter $H = \hbar\omega_{pe}/(K_B T_{Fe})$ (the ratio between the electron plasma energy and the electron Fermi energy) proportional to quantum diffraction.

Integrating Equation (5.43) with the boundary conditions $n_e \to 1$, $\partial n_e/\partial x \to 1$ and $\phi \to 0$ at $\pm\infty$, we have

$$\phi = -1 + n_e^2 - \frac{H^2}{2\mu} \frac{\partial^2 \sqrt{n_e}/\partial x^2}{\sqrt{n_e}}. \tag{5.49}$$

We consider stretched coordinate the same as Equation (4.40). The dependent variables are expanded as

$$n_\alpha = 1 + \sum_j^\infty \epsilon^j n_\alpha^{(j)} + \cdots, \quad u_\alpha = \sum_j^\infty \epsilon^j u_\alpha^{(j)} + \cdots, \quad \phi = \sum_j^\infty \epsilon^j \phi^{(j)} + \cdots \tag{5.50}$$

where $\alpha = e, +, -$, and ϵ is a small nonzero parameter proportional to the amplitude of the perturbation. Upon substituting expressions (5.50) into Equations (5.44)–(5.49) and collecting the terms in different powers of ϵ from the lowest-order of ϵ, we obtain the dispersion law as

$$\lambda = \pm\sqrt{\frac{2(1 + m\beta)}{\mu}}. \tag{5.51}$$

Comparing the next higher-order of ϵ and eliminating the second-order perturbed quantities from a set of equations, we obtain the KdV equation for DIAWs as

$$\frac{\partial \phi^{(1)}}{\partial \tau} + A\phi^{(1)} \frac{\partial \phi^{(1)}}{\partial \xi} + B\frac{\partial^3 \phi^{(1)}}{\partial \xi^3} = 0 \tag{5.52}$$

where the nonlinear coefficient A and the dispersion coefficient B are written as

$$A = \sqrt{\frac{1 + m\beta}{8\mu}} - \frac{3\sqrt{\mu}(1 - m^2\beta)}{\sqrt{8(1 + m\beta)^3}}, \quad B = \sqrt{\frac{1 + m\beta}{128\mu^3}}(16 - H^2).$$

Next, we determine the higher-order nonlinear and dispersion correction of the KdV equation. Equating the next higher-order terms in ϵ and after some standard algebra, we obtain the differential equation for the higher-order correction $\phi^{(2)}$ as

$$\frac{\partial \phi^{(2)}}{\partial \tau} + A\frac{\partial\left(\phi^{(1)}\phi^{(2)}\right)}{\partial \xi} + B\frac{\partial^3 \phi^{(2)}}{\partial \xi^3}$$

$$= L\left(\phi^{(1)}\right)^2\frac{\partial \phi^{(1)}}{\partial \xi} + M\phi^{(1)}\frac{\partial^3 \phi^{(1)}}{\partial \xi^3} + N\frac{\partial^5 \phi^{(1)}}{\partial \xi^5} + P\frac{\partial}{\partial \xi}\left(\frac{\partial \phi^{(1)}}{\partial \xi}\right)^2 \quad (5.53)$$

where

$$L = \frac{3\left(v_0^2 - A^2\right)}{16v_0} + \frac{4A\left(m^2\beta - 1\right)}{v_0^4\mu} - \frac{3\left(5m^2\beta - Av_0m^2\beta - 2Av_0 - 3\right)}{2v_0^5\mu}$$

$$M = \frac{1}{\mu}\left[-\frac{3H^2v_0}{32} + \frac{B}{v_0^4}\left(4 - 4m^2\beta + Am\beta v_0 + Av_0\right) - \frac{3}{2}\frac{AB\mu}{v_0}\right]$$

$$P = \frac{1}{\mu}\left[-\frac{3H^2v_0}{32} - \frac{9AB\mu}{4v_0} + \frac{2B}{v_0^4}\left(m^2\beta - 1\right)\right]$$

$$N = \frac{H^4v_0}{128\mu^2} - \frac{3B^2}{2v_0}.$$

Equation (5.53) is a linear inhomogeneous differential equation in $\phi^{(2)}$, whose source term is given as a function of $\phi^{(1)}$, and we determine the nonsecular solution for $\phi^{(2)}$.

Using the method of renormalization, to obtain a nonsecular solution for $\phi^{(2)}$, Equations (5.52) and (5.53) are modified as

$$\frac{\partial \widetilde{\phi}^{(1)}}{\partial \tau} + A\widetilde{\phi}^{(1)}\frac{\partial \widetilde{\phi}^{(1)}}{\partial \xi} + B\frac{\partial^3 \widetilde{\phi}^{(1)}}{\partial \xi^3} + \delta\Lambda\frac{\partial \widetilde{\phi}^{(1)}}{\partial \xi} = 0 \quad (5.54)$$

$$\frac{\partial \widetilde{\phi}^{(2)}}{\partial \tau} + A\frac{\partial\left(\widetilde{\phi}^{(1)}\widetilde{\phi}^{(2)}\right)}{\partial \xi} + B\frac{\partial^3 \widetilde{\phi}^{(2)}}{\partial \xi^3} + \delta\lambda\frac{\partial \widetilde{\phi}^{(2)}}{\partial \xi} = S\left(\widetilde{\phi}^{(1)}\right) + \delta\Lambda\frac{\partial \widetilde{\phi}^{(1)}}{\partial \xi}. \quad (5.55)$$

The parameter $\delta\Lambda$ in Equations (5.54) and (5.55) is introduced in the same way as it was introduced in the previous problems. Introducing a new stationary frame variable $\eta = \xi - (\Lambda + \delta\Lambda)\tau$, where $(\Lambda + \delta\Lambda) = X - 1$, and X is the Mach number. The stationary renormalized solitary wave solution of

Equation (5.54) up to the first order in Λ is obtained as

$$\widetilde{\phi}^{(1)} = \phi_0 \, sech^2(\widetilde{D}\eta) \tag{5.56}$$

where $\phi_0 = \frac{3\lambda}{A}$ and $\widetilde{D} = D = \sqrt{\frac{\lambda}{4B}}$. Similarly, proceeding in the same way as before, we obtain a second-order inhomogeneous differential equation for $\widetilde{\phi}^{(2)}$ as

$$B\frac{d^2\widetilde{\phi}^{(2)}}{d\eta^2} + \lambda(3 \, sech^2(\widetilde{D}\eta) - 1)\widetilde{\phi}^{(2)} = A_2 sech^4\widetilde{D}\eta + A_3 sech^6\widetilde{D}\eta \tag{5.57}$$

where $A_2 = -\frac{45N\lambda^2}{2AB^2} + \frac{9\lambda^3(M+2P)}{2A^2}B$, $A_3 = -\frac{45N\lambda^2}{2AB^2} + \frac{9M\lambda^2}{A^2B} + \frac{27P\lambda^3}{2A^3} - \frac{9L\lambda^3}{A^3}$, and $\delta\lambda$ is given by

$$\delta\lambda = -\frac{N\lambda^2}{B^2}. \tag{5.58}$$

Equation (5.57) is a second-order inhomogeneous differential equation whose solution can be written as

$$\widetilde{\phi}^{(2)} = \widetilde{\phi}_{\text{comp}} + \widetilde{\phi}_p \tag{5.59}$$

where $\widetilde{\phi}_{\text{comp}}$ is the complementary function and $\widetilde{\phi}_p$ is the particular solution. It can be shown easily that the complementary function $\widetilde{\phi}_{\text{comp}}$ has no role in the second-order correction $\widetilde{\phi}_2$, while the particular integral does. A series solution method developed by Chatterjee *et al.* [9] is adopted to determine $\widetilde{\phi}_p$, where $\widetilde{\phi}_p$ is defined as a truncated power series. The particular solution $\widetilde{\phi}_p$ can be obtained in a similar way as Step 6 in Section 5.2. So, the particular solution of Equation (5.57) is

$$\widetilde{\phi}_p = a_1 sech^2(\widetilde{D}\eta) + a_2 sech^4(\widetilde{D}\eta) \tag{5.60}$$

where $a_1 = \frac{15N\lambda^2}{2AB^2} - \frac{3(2M+P)\lambda^2}{A^2B} - \frac{9L\lambda^2}{A^3}$ and $a_2 = -\frac{45N\lambda^2}{4AB^2} + \frac{9(M+P)\lambda^2}{2A^2B} - \frac{9L\lambda^2}{2A^3}$. Using Equations (5.56), (5.59), and (5.60), the stationary one soliton solution up to the second order in Λ for pair-ion quantum plasma is written as

$$\widetilde{\phi} = \widetilde{\phi}^{(1)} + \widetilde{\phi}^{(2)} = \widetilde{\phi}_0 \, sech^2(\widetilde{D}\eta) + a_1 sech^2(\widetilde{D}\eta) + a_2 sech^4(\widetilde{D}\eta). \tag{5.61}$$

The amplitude of the KdV soliton that includes the second-order contribution $\widetilde{\phi}_0$, the amplitude of the dressed soliton that includes the second-order contribution $\widetilde{\phi}_0^{\,*}$, and the width $\widetilde{W}$ of the dressed soliton are then expressed as

$$\widetilde{\phi}_0 = \frac{3(\lambda + \delta\lambda)}{A}, \quad \widetilde{\phi}_0^{\,*} = \frac{3(\lambda + \delta\lambda)}{A} + a_1 + a_2, \quad \widetilde{W} = \left(\frac{4B}{\lambda + \delta\lambda}\right)^{1/2}.$$

Equation (5.56) gives the renormalized KdV soliton, whose amplitude and width are ϕ_0 and D. For a higher-order correction to the KdV soliton, the speed is $\lambda + \delta\lambda$, and amplitude and width are $\widetilde{\phi}_0^{\,*}$ and $\widetilde{W}$, respectively. The quantum correction to the pair-ion plasma system is also considered. The effects of higher-order nonlinear terms on solitons are illustrated by plotting the KdV soliton $\widetilde{\phi}^{(1)}$ (dotted line), the second-order correction $\widetilde{\phi}^{(2)}$ (dashed line), and the dressed soliton $\widetilde{\phi}$ (solid line) vs. η for $H = 1$ as shown in Figure 5.3. The amplitude of the dressed soliton $\widetilde{\phi}$ is found to be larger than the amplitude of the KdV soliton $\widetilde{\phi}^{(1)}$. Here, we recall the fact from the perturbation theory that one can only consider the higher-order correction if $\frac{|\widetilde{\phi}_0|}{|a_1 + a_2|} \ll 1$, i.e., $|a_1 + a_2| < |\widetilde{\phi}_0|$. On the contrary, a nonphysical solution is obtained if $|a_1 + a_2| \geq |\widetilde{\phi}_0|$. The shapes of the dressed soliton (solid line), second-order correction (dashed line), and the KdV soliton (dotted line) are shown in Figure 5.4 for $H = 2.8$. The amplitude of the dressed soliton is same as the KdV soliton, but the width is greater. Figure 5.5 shows the same plot as Figure (5.4) with the same parameters except $H = 3.55$. One can easily justify that this dressed soliton is not physical, as the amplitude of the second-order correction has exceeded that of the KdV soliton.

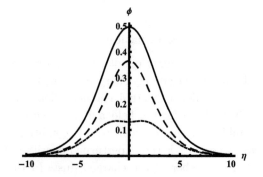

Fig. 5.3: KdV soliton $\widetilde{\phi}^{(1)}$ (dotted line), higher-order correction $\widetilde{\phi}^{(2)}$ (dashed line), and dressed soliton $\widetilde{\phi}$ (solid line) are plotted against η for $H = 1$.

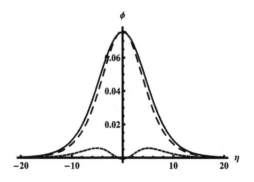

Fig. 5.4: KdV soliton $\widetilde{\phi}^{(1)}$ (dotted line), higher-order correction $\widetilde{\phi}^{(2)}$ (dashed line), and dressed soliton $\widetilde{\phi}$ (solid line) are plotted against η for $H = 2.8$.

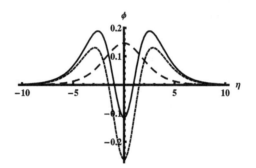

Fig. 5.5: KdV soliton $\widetilde{\phi}^{(1)}$ (dotted line), higher-order correction $\widetilde{\phi}^{(2)}$ (dashed line), and dressed soliton $\widetilde{\phi}$ (solid line) are plotted against η for $H = 3.55$.

5.5 Dressed Soliton of ZK Equation

We consider a three species dense quantum plasma composed of inertialess electrons and ions and negatively charged mobile heavy dust particles. The plasma is in the uniform external magnetic field $\vec{B}_0 = B_0 \hat{x}$, where B_0 is the strength of the magnetic field and $\hat{x}$ is the unit vector in the x-direction. At equilibrium, the charge neutrality condition applies, namely, $n_{i0} = n_{e0} + Z_d n_{d0}$, where n_{j0} is the unperturbed density of the jth species and Z_d is the charge number of the charged dust. In the low-frequency limit $\omega \ll \Omega_{cd}$, where ω is the wave frequency, $\Omega_{cd} = eB_0/m_d c$ is the dust cyclotron frequency, e is the electronic charge, m_d is dust particle mass, and c is the speed of the light in vacuum. The normalized basic set of equations in two dimensions (xy-plane) in such a quantum plasma system are as follows:

$$\nabla^2\phi = \alpha(\mu_e n_e + n_d - \mu_i n_i) \tag{5.62}$$

$$\frac{\partial u_{dx}}{\partial t} + \left(u_{dx}\frac{\partial}{\partial x} + u_{dy}\frac{\partial}{\partial y}\right)u_{dx} = \frac{\partial\phi}{\partial x} \tag{5.63}$$

$$\frac{\partial u_{dy}}{\partial t} + \left(u_{dx}\frac{\partial}{\partial x} + u_{dy}\frac{\partial}{\partial y}\right)u_{dy} = \frac{\partial\phi}{\partial y} - u_{dz} \tag{5.64}$$

$$\frac{\partial u_{dz}}{\partial t} + \left(u_{dx}\frac{\partial}{\partial x} + u_{dy}\frac{\partial}{\partial y}\right)u_{dz} = u_{dy} \tag{5.65}$$

$$\frac{\partial n_d}{\partial t} + \frac{\partial(n_d u_{dx})}{\partial x} + \frac{\partial(n_d u_{dy})}{\partial y} = 0 \tag{5.66}$$

$$\phi - \sigma\frac{n_e^2}{2} + \frac{H_e^2}{2\sqrt{n_e}}\nabla^2\sqrt{n_e} + \frac{\sigma}{2} = 0 \tag{5.67}$$

$$-\phi - \frac{n_i^2}{2} + \frac{H_i^2}{2\sqrt{n_i}}\nabla^2\sqrt{n_i} + \frac{1}{2} = 0. \tag{5.68}$$

Here, $\nabla = \hat{x}\frac{\partial}{\partial x} + \hat{y}\frac{\partial}{\partial y}$ ($\hat{y}$ is the unit vector in the y-direction). Furthermore, n_j, u_d, and ϕ are the number density of the jth species, dust fluid velocity, and electrostatic potential, respectively. $H_j = \sqrt{\frac{Z_d}{m_j m_d}}\left(\frac{\hbar\Omega_{cd}}{c_{sd}^2}\right)$ is the quantum diffraction for the jth species (electron and ion), where m_j and C_{sd} are the mass of the jth species and dust-acoustic speed, respectively. $\alpha = \frac{\omega_{pd}^2}{\Omega_{cd}^2}$, $\sigma = \frac{T_{Fe}}{T_{Fi}}$, $\omega_{pd} = \sqrt{\frac{4\pi Z_d^2 e^2 n_{d0}}{m_d}}$, $T_{Fe,i} = \frac{\hbar^2}{2m_{e,i}K_B}(3\pi^2 n_{e,i0})^{2/3}$, $\mu_j = \frac{n_{j0}}{Z_d n_{d0}}$ ($j = e, i$). The diffraction effects for the dust are ignored since $m_d \gg m_{e,i}$. To obtain Equations (5.67) and (5.68) from the electron and ion momentum equations along the magnetic field, we use the boundary conditions $n_e = 1$, $n_i = 1$, and $\phi = 0$ at infinity. Now, we use the normalization as follows:

$$n_j \to \frac{n_j}{n_{j0}}, \quad u_d \to \frac{u_d}{C_{sd}}, \quad \phi \to \frac{e\phi}{2K_B T_{Fi}}, \quad t \to \Omega_{cd}t. \tag{5.69}$$

Space is normalized by $\frac{\omega_{cd}}{C_{sd}}$, where $c_{sd} = \sqrt{\frac{2Z_d K_B T_{Fi}}{m_d}}$. We assume that the inertia-less electrons and ions obey the pressure law $p_{e,i} = \frac{1}{3}\frac{m_{e,i}V_{Fe,i}^2}{n_{e,i0}^2}n_{e,i}^3$ with $V_{Fe,i} = \sqrt{\frac{2K_B T_{Fe,i}}{m_{e,i}}}$ being the electron and ion Fermi velocity.

Now, to derive the ZK equation for the considered magnetized quantum plasma, the independent variables are stretched as $\xi = \epsilon^{1/2}(l_x x - \lambda t)$,

$\eta = \epsilon^{1/2} l_y y$, $\tau = \epsilon^{3/2} t$ with $l_x^2 + l_y^2 = 1$, and the dependent variables are expanded as

$$
\left.
\begin{aligned}
u_{dx} &= \epsilon u_{dx}^{(1)} + \epsilon^2 u_{dx}^{(2)} + \cdots \\
u_{dy} &= \epsilon^2 u_{dy}^{(1)} + \epsilon^3 u_{dy}^{(2)} + \cdots \\
u_{dz} &= \epsilon^{3/2} u_{dz}^{(1)} + \epsilon^{5/2} u_{dz}^{(2)} + \cdots \\
n_j &= 1 + \epsilon n_j^{(1)} + \epsilon^2 n_j^{(2)} + \cdots \\
\phi &= \epsilon \phi^{(1)} + \epsilon^2 \phi^{(2)} + \cdots
\end{aligned}
\right\}
\tag{5.70}
$$

where $j = e,\, i,\, d$, and ϵ is a small nonzero parameter proportional to the amplitude of the perturbation. Now, substituting the expression from Equation (5.70) into Equations (5.62)–(5.68) and collecting the coefficients of ϵ in the lowest order, we obtain the *dispersion relation* as

$$
\lambda = l_x \left(\frac{\sigma}{\mu_e + \sigma \mu_i} \right)^{1/2}.
\tag{5.71}
$$

In the higher order of ϵ, eliminating the second-order perturbed quantities, we obtain the ZK equation for the magnetized quantum dust acoustic waves

$$
\frac{\partial \phi^{(1)}}{\partial \tau} + A \phi^{(1)} \frac{\partial \phi^{(1)}}{\partial \xi} + B \frac{\partial^3 \phi^{(1)}}{\partial \xi^3} + C \frac{\partial^3 \phi^{(1)}}{\partial \xi \partial \eta^2} = 0
\tag{5.72}
$$

where $A = \frac{\lambda^3}{2 l_x^2} \left(\frac{\mu_e}{\sigma^2} - \mu_i - \frac{3 l_x^4}{\lambda^4} \right)$, $B = \frac{\lambda^3}{2\alpha} \left(1 - \frac{\alpha \mu_e H_e^2}{4\sigma^2} - \frac{\alpha \mu_i H_i^2}{4} \right)$, and $C = \frac{\lambda^3 l_y^2}{2\alpha l_x^2} \left[1 + \alpha \left(1 - \frac{\mu_e H_e^2}{4\sigma^2} - \frac{\mu_i H_i^2}{4} \right) \right]$.

Next, we determine the higher-order correction to the nonlinear and dispersion effect of the ZK equation. We start by equating the next higher-order terms in ϵ, and after some standard algebra, we obtain the differential equation for the higher-order correction $\phi^{(2)}$ as

$$
\frac{\partial \phi^{(2)}}{\partial \tau} + A \frac{\partial}{\partial \xi} \left(\phi^{(1)} \phi^{(2)} \right) + B \frac{\partial^3 \phi^{(2)}}{\partial \xi^3} + C \frac{\partial^3 \phi^{(2)}}{\partial \xi \partial \eta^2} = S^{(2)} \left(\phi^{(1)} \right)
\tag{5.73}
$$

with

$$
\begin{aligned}
S^{(2)} \left(\phi^{(1)} \right) = {}& L \left(\phi^{(1)} \right)^2 \frac{\partial \phi^{(1)}}{\partial \xi} + M \phi^{(1)} \frac{\partial^3 \phi^{(1)}}{\partial \xi^3} + N \frac{\partial^5 \phi^{(1)}}{\partial \xi^5} \\
& + P \frac{\partial \phi^{(1)}}{\partial \xi} \frac{\partial^2 \phi^{(1)}}{\partial \xi^2} + Q \frac{\partial^5 \phi^{(1)}}{\partial \xi^3 \partial \eta^2} + R \frac{\partial^5 \phi^{(1)}}{\partial \xi \partial \eta^4} + S \frac{\partial \phi^{(1)}}{\partial \xi} \frac{\partial^2 \phi^{(1)}}{\partial \eta^2} \\
& + T \frac{\partial \phi^{(1)}}{\partial \eta} \frac{\partial^2 \phi^{(1)}}{\partial \xi \partial \eta}
\end{aligned}
$$

where

$$L = \frac{\lambda^3}{2\alpha l_x^2}\left[\frac{3\alpha\mu_e}{2\sigma^3} + \frac{3\alpha\mu_i}{2} - \alpha\left(A - \frac{3l_x}{2\lambda}\right)\left(\frac{\mu_e - \mu_i\sigma^2}{\lambda\sigma^2}\right)\right.$$
$$\left. - \frac{\alpha A^2 l_x^2}{\lambda^3} - \frac{3\alpha A l_x^4}{\lambda^5} - \frac{9\alpha l_x^6}{2\lambda^6} - \frac{3\alpha A^2 l_x^5}{2\lambda^5}\right],$$

$$M = \frac{\lambda^3}{2\alpha l_x^2}\left[\frac{-3\alpha\mu_e l_x^2 H_e^2}{4\sigma^3} + \frac{3\alpha\mu_i l_x^2 H_i^2}{4} - \frac{l_x^2\gamma}{4\lambda}\left(\frac{A\alpha}{\sigma^2} - \frac{l_x}{\lambda}\right)\right.$$
$$\left. - \frac{B\alpha(\mu_e - \mu_i\sigma^2)}{\lambda\sigma^2} - \frac{2AB\alpha l_x^2}{\lambda^4} - \frac{2Bl_x^4}{\lambda^5} - \frac{3l_x^4}{\lambda^5}\right],$$

$$N = \frac{\lambda^3}{2\alpha l_x^2}\left[\frac{\alpha\mu_e l_x^4 H_e^4}{16\sigma^3} + \frac{\alpha\mu_i l_x^4 H_i^4}{16} - \frac{\alpha B\gamma l_x^2}{4\lambda\sigma^2} - \frac{\alpha B^2 l_x^2}{\lambda^4}\right],$$

$$P = \frac{\lambda^3}{2\alpha l_x^2}\left[\frac{-9\alpha\mu_e l_x^2 H_e^2}{8\sigma^3} + \frac{3\alpha\mu_i l_x^2 H_i^2}{2} - \frac{l_x^2\gamma\alpha(3A + l_x^2)}{4\lambda\sigma^2}\right.$$
$$\left. - \frac{3AB\alpha l_x^2}{\lambda^4} - \frac{l_x^3\alpha B}{\lambda^4} - \frac{l_x^4\alpha B}{\lambda^4\sigma}\right],$$

$$Q = \frac{\lambda^3}{2\alpha l_x^2}\left[\frac{\alpha\mu_e l_x^2 l_y^2 H_e^4}{8\sigma^3} + \frac{\alpha\mu_i l_x^2 l_y^2 H_i^4}{8} - \frac{\gamma\alpha(Cl_x + Bl_y^2)}{4\lambda\sigma^2}\right.$$
$$\left. - \frac{B\alpha l_y^2}{\lambda} - \frac{2BC\alpha l_x^2}{\lambda^4} + \alpha\lambda^2 l_y^2\right],$$

$$R = \frac{\lambda^3}{2\alpha l_x^2}\left[\frac{\alpha\mu_e l_y^4 H_e^4}{16\sigma^3} - \frac{\alpha l_x^2 C^2}{\lambda^4} - \frac{C\gamma\alpha l_y^2}{4\lambda\sigma^2} - \frac{C\alpha l_y^2}{\lambda} + \frac{\alpha\mu_i l_x l_y^4 H_i^4}{16}\right],$$

$$S = \frac{\lambda^3}{2\alpha l_x^2}\left[\frac{-3\alpha\mu_e l_y^2 H_e^2}{4\sigma^3} + \frac{3\alpha\mu_e l_y^2 H_i^2}{4} - \frac{\alpha\gamma l_y^2\left(A + \frac{l_x^2}{\lambda}\right)}{4\lambda\sigma^2}\right.$$
$$\left. - \frac{C\alpha}{l_x}{}^4\lambda^5 - \frac{AC\alpha l_x^2}{\lambda^4} - \frac{\alpha l_x^4}{\lambda^5} - \frac{Al_y^2}{\lambda}\right],$$

$$T = \frac{\lambda^3}{2\alpha l_x^2}\left[\frac{-3\alpha\mu_e l_y^2 H_e^2}{4\sigma^3} + \frac{3\alpha\mu_i l_y^2 H_i^2}{4} - \frac{A\alpha l_y^2\gamma}{2\lambda\sigma^2}\right.$$
$$\left. - \frac{2AC\alpha l_x^2}{\lambda^4} + \frac{\alpha l_x^2 l_y^2}{\lambda^2} - \frac{2A\alpha l_y^2}{\lambda}\right],$$

$$\gamma = \left(2\sigma^2 - \mu_e H_e^2 - \mu_i\sigma^2 H_i^2\right).$$

Thus, Equation (5.72) is obtained from the basic set of equations which is a ZK equation for the first-order perturbed potential $\phi^{(1)}$, whereas Equation (5.73) is a ZK-type equation with an inhomogeneous term (source term on the right-hand side of Equation (5.73)) for the second-order perturbed potential $\phi^{(2)}$.

Now, we use the method of renormalization [5]. Accordingly, Equations (5.72) and (5.73) become

$$\frac{\partial \bar{\phi}^{(1)}}{\partial \tau} + A\bar{\phi}^{(1)} \frac{\partial}{\partial \xi}\left(\bar{\phi}^{(1)}\right) + B\frac{\partial^3 \bar{\phi}^{(1)}}{\partial \xi^3} + C\frac{\partial^3 \bar{\phi}^{(1)}}{\partial \xi \partial \eta^2} + \frac{\delta\theta}{l_x}\frac{\partial \bar{\phi}^{(1)}}{\partial \xi} = 0 \quad (5.74)$$

$$\frac{\partial \bar{\phi}^{(2)}}{\partial \tau} + A\frac{\partial}{\partial \xi}\left(\bar{\phi}^{(1)}\bar{\phi}^{(2)}\right) + B\frac{\partial^3 \bar{\phi}^{(2)}}{\partial \xi^3} + C\frac{\partial^3 \bar{\phi}^{(2)}}{\partial \xi \partial \eta^2} + \frac{\delta\theta}{l_x}\frac{\partial \bar{\phi}^{(2)}}{\partial \xi}$$

$$= S^2\left(\bar{\phi}^{(1)}\right) + \frac{\delta\theta}{l_x}\frac{\partial \bar{\phi}^{(1)}}{\partial \xi}. \quad (5.75)$$

Here, $\bar{\phi}^{(1)}$ and $\bar{\phi}^{(2)}$ are the renormalized potentials. The parameter $\delta\theta$ is expanded only on the right-hand side of the added equation in the renormalization method as $\delta\theta = \varepsilon\theta_1 + \varepsilon^2\theta_2 + \cdots$, since θ_n, $n = 1, 2, 3, \ldots$, are chosen to cancel the resonant term in $S^{(2)}(\phi_1)$. Let us introduce a new variable ζ as

$$\zeta = l_x\xi + l_y\eta - (\theta + \delta\theta)\tau \quad (5.76)$$

where the parameter θ is related to the Mach number (M) by $\theta + \delta\theta = M - 1 = \Delta M$. Under this transformation, Equations (5.74) and (5.75), respectively, become

$$\chi\frac{d^3 \bar{\phi}^{(1)}}{d\zeta^3} + \left(A\bar{\phi}^{(1)} - \frac{\theta}{l_x}\right)\frac{d\bar{\phi}^{(1)}}{d\zeta} = 0 \quad (5.77)$$

$$\chi\frac{d^3 \bar{\phi}^{(2)}}{d\zeta^3} + A\frac{d}{d\zeta}\left(\bar{\phi}^{(1)}\bar{\phi}^{(2)}\right) - \frac{\theta}{l_x}\frac{d\bar{\phi}^{(2)}}{d\zeta} = \frac{1}{l_x}\left[S^{(2)}\left(\bar{\phi}^{(1)}\right) + \delta\theta\frac{d\bar{\phi}^{(1)}}{d\zeta}\right]. \quad (5.78)$$

Now, the first integral of the ordinary differential Equation (5.77) with the boundary conditions $\bar{\phi}^{(1)} = \frac{d\bar{\phi}^{(1)}}{d\zeta} = \frac{d^2 \bar{\phi}^{(1)}}{d\zeta^2} = 0$ as $|\zeta| \to \infty$ gives

$$\chi\frac{d^2 \bar{\phi}^{(1)}}{d\zeta^2} + \left(\frac{A}{2}\bar{\phi}^{(1)} - \frac{\theta}{l_x}\right)\bar{\phi}^{(1)} = 0. \quad (5.79)$$

Here, $\chi = (B-C)l_x + C$. One soliton solution of Equation (5.79) is written as

$$\phi^{(1)}(\zeta) = \phi_0 sech^2\left(\frac{\zeta}{w}\right) \tag{5.80}$$

where the width w and the amplitude ϕ_0 of the solitary wave are given by $w = 2\sqrt{\frac{l_x \chi}{\theta}}$ and $\phi_0 = \frac{3\theta}{Al_x}$. Using Equation (5.80) in Equation (5.78), we have

$$\chi \frac{d^3 \bar{\phi}^{(2)}}{d\zeta^3} + A\phi_0 \frac{d}{d\zeta}\left\{\bar{\phi}^{(2)} sech^2\left(\frac{\zeta}{w}\right)\right\} - \frac{\theta}{l_x}\frac{d\bar{\phi}^{(2)}}{d\zeta}$$
$$= \left(A_1 - \frac{2\phi_0 \delta\theta}{wl_x}\right) sech^2\left(\frac{\zeta}{w}\right) \tanh\left(\frac{\zeta}{w}\right) + A_2 sech^4\left(\frac{\zeta}{w}\right) \tanh\left(\frac{\zeta}{w}\right)$$
$$+ A_3 sech^6\left(\frac{\zeta}{w}\right) \tanh\left(\frac{\zeta}{w}\right) \tag{5.81}$$

where $A_1 = -\frac{32\phi_0}{w^3}\{(N-Q+R)l_x^4 + (Q-2R)l_x^2 + R\}$, $A_2 = -\frac{8\phi_0^2}{w^3}\{(M+P-S-T)l_x^2 + (S+T)\} + \frac{480\phi_0}{w^5}\{(N-Q+R)l_x^4 + (Q-2R)l_x^2 + R\}$, $A_3 = -\frac{2L\phi_0^3}{w} + \frac{12\phi_0^2}{w^3}\{(2M+P-S-T)l_x^2 + (S+T)\} - \frac{720\phi_0}{w^5}\{(N-Q+R)l_x^4 + (Q-2R)l_x^2 + R\}$.

Integrating Equation (5.81) with the boundary conditions $\bar{\phi}^{(2)} = \frac{d\bar{\phi}^{(2)}}{d\zeta} = \frac{d^2\bar{\phi}^{(2)}}{d\zeta^2} = 0$ as $|\zeta| \to \infty$ gives a second-order inhomogeneous ordinary differential equation in $\bar{\phi}^{(2)}$ as

$$\chi \frac{d^2 \bar{\phi}^{(2)}}{d\zeta^2} + A\phi_0 \bar{\phi}^{(2)} sech^2\left(\frac{\zeta}{w}\right) - \frac{\theta}{l_x}\bar{\phi}^{(2)}$$
$$= \left(\frac{\phi_0 \delta\theta}{l_x} - \frac{A_1 w}{2}\right) sech^2\left(\frac{\zeta}{w}\right) - \frac{wA_2}{4} sech^4\left(\frac{\zeta}{w}\right) - \frac{wA_3}{6} sech^6\left(\frac{\zeta}{w}\right). \tag{5.82}$$

To cancel the secular term, we consider

$$\delta\theta = \frac{wA_1 l_x}{2\phi_0} \tag{5.83}$$

Hence, using Equation (5.83) and putting $\phi_0 = \frac{3\theta}{Al_x}$, Equation (5.82) gives

$$\chi \frac{d^2 \bar{\phi}^{(2)}}{d\zeta^2} + \left(3 sech^2\left(\frac{\zeta}{w}\right) - 1\right)\frac{\theta}{l_x}\bar{\phi}^{(2)}$$
$$= -\frac{wA_2}{4} sech^4\left(\frac{\zeta}{w}\right) - \frac{wA_3}{6} sech^6\left(\frac{\zeta}{w}\right). \tag{5.84}$$

The complete solution of the second-order inhomogeneous differential Equation (5.84) can be written as

$$\bar{\phi}^{(2)} = \bar{\phi}_{\text{comp}} + \bar{\phi}_p \tag{5.85}$$

where $\bar{\phi}_{\text{comp}}$ and $\bar{\phi}_p$ are the complementary function and the particular solution of Equation (5.84). It can be shown easily that the complementary function $\bar{\phi}_{\text{comp}}$ has no role in the second-order correction $\bar{\phi}^{(2)}$, while the particular integral does play a role. The particular solution $\bar{\phi}_p$ can be obtained in a similar way as Step 6 in Section 5.2. So, the particular solution of Equation (5.84) is

$$\bar{\phi}_p = a_1 sech^2\left(\frac{\varsigma}{w}\right) + a_2 sech^4\left(\frac{\varsigma}{w}\right) \tag{5.86}$$

where $a_1 = \frac{w^3}{24\chi}(A_3 - A_2)$ and $a_2 = -\frac{w^3 A_3}{48\chi}$. Thus, Equations (5.80), (5.85), and (5.86) together give the stationary one soliton solution for the considered magnetized quantum plasma. This can be expressed as

$$\bar{\phi} = \bar{\phi}^{(1)} + \bar{\phi}^{(2)} = \bar{\phi}_0 sech^2\left(\frac{\varsigma}{w}\right) + a_1 sech^2\left(\frac{\varsigma}{w}\right) + a_2 sech^4\left(\frac{\varsigma}{w}\right). \tag{5.87}$$

The amplitude of the ZK soliton $\bar{\phi}_0$ (that includes the second-order contribution), the amplitude of the dressed soliton $\bar{\phi}_0^*$ (that includes the second-order contribution), and the width $\bar{w}$ of the dressed soliton are as follows ($\delta\theta$ is given in Equation (5.83)):

$$\bar{\phi}_0 = \frac{3(\theta + \delta\theta)}{Al_x}, \quad \bar{w} = 2\sqrt{\frac{l_x\chi}{\theta + \delta\theta}}, \quad \bar{\phi}_0^* = \bar{\phi}_0 + a_1 + a_2. \tag{5.88}$$

5.6 Envelope Soliton

In a dispersive system, when the leading-order nonlinear and dispersive effects are considered, then the envelope of a small amplitude narrow wave pulse may arise and satisfies the nonlinear Schrodinger equation. This equation admits envelope soliton solution under certain conditions. So, a group of waves with an envelope propagating without changing the form is known as envelope soliton. Envelope soliton survives when higher-order effects are considered. Envelope solitons are of two types: bright envelope soliton and dark envelope soliton. The ion acoustic dark or bright envelope solitons are formed for modulation of both stable or unstable waves in the plasma region.

5.7 Nonlinear Schrodinger Equation (NLSE)

Now, we will derive the NLSE from a classical plasma model. Here, we consider a collisionless unmagnetized *e-i* plasma, where ions are mobile and electrons obey the Maxwell distribution. The normalized set of equations are

$$\frac{\partial n}{\partial t} + \frac{\partial (nu)}{\partial x} = 0 \tag{5.89}$$

$$\frac{\partial u}{\partial t} + u\frac{\partial u}{\partial x} = -\frac{\partial \phi}{\partial x} \tag{5.90}$$

$$\frac{\partial^2 \phi}{\partial x^2} = e^\phi - n. \tag{5.91}$$

The normalization is similar to Section 4.3. To obtain the envelope soliton in the framework of NLSE, we employ a multiple scale perturbation. Taking

$$A = A^{(0)} + \sum_{n=1}^{\infty} \epsilon^n A^{(n)} \tag{5.92}$$

where A is any dependent variable (ϕ, n, u) and

$$A^{(n)} = \sum_{l=-\infty}^{\infty} A_l^{(n)}(X_m, T_m)e^{il(kx-wt)}, \quad m \geq 1. \tag{5.93}$$

Here, $T_m = \epsilon^m t$, $X_m = \epsilon^m x$. So, $\frac{\partial}{\partial x} = \epsilon^m \frac{\partial}{\partial X_m}$, $\frac{\partial}{\partial t} = \epsilon^m \frac{\partial}{\partial T_m}$. Now,

$$\frac{\partial}{\partial x}A = \frac{\partial}{\partial x}\left[A^{(0)} + \sum_{n=1}^{\infty} \epsilon^n A^{(n)}\right]$$

$$= \sum_{n=1}^{\infty} \epsilon^n \sum_{l=-\infty}^{\infty} e^{il(kx-wt)}\left(ilk + \sum_{m=1}^{\infty} \epsilon^m \frac{\partial}{\partial X_m}\right)A_l^{(n)}$$

Since this is true for all n and l, so we get

$$\frac{\partial}{\partial x} = ilk + \sum_{m=1}^{\infty} \epsilon^m \frac{\partial}{\partial X_m}$$

$$\frac{\partial^2}{\partial x^2} = -l^2 k^2 + 2ilk \sum_{m=1}^{\infty} \epsilon^m \frac{\partial}{\partial X_m} + \sum_{m,m'=1}^{\infty} \epsilon^{m+m'} \frac{\partial^2}{\partial X_m \partial X_{m'}}.$$

Similarly, we get

$$\frac{\partial}{\partial t} = -ilw + \sum_{m=1}^{\infty} \epsilon^m \frac{\partial}{\partial T_m}.$$

Accordingly, the variables are perturbed from the stable state in the following way (considering $n = 1, u = 0, \phi = 0$ at stable state equilibrium):

$$n = 1 + \sum_{n=1}^{\infty} \epsilon^n \sum_{l=-\infty}^{\infty} n_l^n e^{il(kx-wt)}$$

$$v = \sum_{n'=1}^{\infty} \epsilon^{n'} \sum_{l'=-\infty}^{\infty} v_{l'}^{n'} e^{il'(kx-wt)}$$

$$nv = \sum_{n'=1}^{\infty} \epsilon^{n'} \sum_{l'=-\infty}^{\infty} v_{l'}^{n'} e^{il'(kx-wt)} + \sum_{n,n'=1}^{\infty} \epsilon^{n+n'} \sum_{l,l'=-\infty}^{\infty} n_l^n v_{l'}^{n'} e^{i(l+l')(kx-wt)}.$$

Now,

$$\frac{\partial n}{\partial t} = \left(-ilw + \sum_{m=1}^{\infty} \epsilon^m \frac{\partial}{\partial T_m} \right) \left(-ilw \sum_{n=1}^{\infty} \epsilon^n \sum_{l=-\infty}^{\infty} n_l^n e^{il(kx-wt)} \right)$$

$$= -ilw - ilw \sum_{n=1}^{\infty} \epsilon^n \sum_{l=-\infty}^{\infty} n_l^n e^{il(kx-wt)}$$

$$+ \sum_{p=m+1}^{\infty} \sum_{m=1}^{\infty} \epsilon^p \sum_{l=-\infty}^{\infty} \frac{\partial n_l^{p-m}}{\partial T_m} e^{il(kx-wt)} \tag{5.94}$$

$$\frac{\partial}{\partial x}(nv) = \left(ilk + \sum_{m=1}^{\infty} \epsilon^m \frac{\partial}{\partial X_m} \right) \left[\sum_{n'=1}^{\infty} \epsilon^{n'} \sum_{l'=-\infty}^{\infty} v_{l'}^{n'} e^{il'(kx-wt)} \right.$$

$$\left. + \sum_{n,n'=1}^{\infty} \epsilon^{n+n'} \sum_{l,l'=-\infty}^{\infty} n_l^n v_{l'}^{n'} e^{i(l+l')(kx-wt)} \right]$$

$$= ilk \sum_{n'=1}^{\infty} \epsilon^{n'} \sum_{l'=-\infty}^{\infty} v_{l'}^{n'} e^{il'(kx-wt)}$$

$$+ ilk \sum_{q=n'+1}^{\infty} \sum_{n'=1}^{\infty} \epsilon^q \sum_{l,l'=-\infty}^{\infty} \left(n_l^{q-n'} v_{l'}^{n'} \right) e^{i(l+l')} e^{(kx-wt)}$$

$$+ \sum_{r=m+1}^{\infty} \sum_{m=1}^{\infty} \epsilon^r \sum_{l'=-\infty}^{\infty} \frac{\partial v_{l'}^{r-m}}{\partial X_m} e^{il'(kx-wt)}$$

$$+ \sum_{s=m+n'+1}^{\infty} \sum_{m=1}^{\infty} \sum_{n'=1}^{\infty} \epsilon^s \sum_{l=-\infty}^{\infty} \sum_{l'=-\infty}^{\infty}$$

$$\times \frac{\partial}{\partial X_m} \left(n_l^{s-m-n'} v_{l'}^{n'} \right) e^{i(l+l')} e^{(kx-wt)}.$$

So,

$$\frac{\partial}{\partial x}(nv) = ilk \sum_{n'=1}^{\infty} \epsilon^{n'} \sum_{l'=-\infty}^{\infty} v_{l'}^{n'} e^{il'(kx-wt)}$$

$$+ ilk \sum_{q=n'+1}^{\infty} \sum_{n'=1}^{\infty} \epsilon^q \sum_{l,l'=-\infty}^{\infty} \left(n_l^{q-n'} v_{l'}^{n'} \right) e^{i(l+l')} e^{(kx-wt)}$$

$$+ \sum_{r=m+1}^{\infty} \sum_{m=1}^{\infty} \epsilon^r \sum_{l'=-\infty}^{\infty} \frac{\partial v_{l'}^{r-m}}{\partial X_m} e^{il'(kx-wt)}$$

$$+ \sum_{s=m+n'+1}^{\infty} \sum_{m=1}^{\infty} \sum_{n'=1}^{\infty} \epsilon^s \sum_{l=-\infty}^{\infty} \sum_{l'=-\infty}^{\infty}$$

$$\times \frac{\partial}{\partial X_m} \left(n_l^{s-m-n'} v_{l'}^{n'} \right) e^{i(l+l')} e^{(kx-wt)}. \tag{5.95}$$

Putting the value of (5.94) and (5.95) in (5.89), and equating the coefficients of ϵ^n, we get

$$-ilw \sum_{l=-\infty}^{\infty} n_l^n e^{il(kx-wt)} + \sum_{m=1}^{\infty} \sum_{l=-\infty}^{\infty} \frac{\partial n_l^{(n-m)}}{\partial T_m} e^{il(kx-wt)}$$

$$+ ilk \sum_{l=-\infty}^{\infty} v_l^n e^{il(kx-wt)} + ilk \sum_{n'=1}^{\infty} \sum_{l=-\infty}^{\infty} \sum_{l'=-\infty}^{\infty} \left(n_{l-l'}^{n-n'} v_{l'}^{n'} \right) e^{il(kx-wt)}$$

$$+ \sum_{m=1}^{\infty} \sum_{l=-\infty}^{\infty} \frac{\partial v_l^{(n-m)}}{\partial X_m} e^{il(kx-wt)}$$

$$+ \sum_{m=1}^{\infty} \sum_{n'=1}^{\infty} \sum_{l=-\infty}^{\infty} \sum_{l'=-\infty}^{\infty} \frac{\partial}{\partial X_m} \left(n_{l-l'}^{(n-m-n')} v_{l'}^{(n')} \right) e^{il(kx-wt)} = 0.$$

Since this is true for all l and $e^{il(kx-wt)} \neq 0$, so, we get

$$-ilwn_l^n + \sum_{m=1}^{\infty} \frac{\partial n_l^{(n-m)}}{\partial T_m} + ilkv_l^n + ilk \sum_{n'=1}^{\infty} \sum_{l'=-\infty}^{\infty} \left(n_{l-l'}^{n-n'} v_{l'}^{n'}\right)$$

$$+ \sum_{m=1}^{\infty} \frac{\partial v_l^{(n-m)}}{\partial X_m} + \sum_{n'=1}^{\infty} \sum_{l'=-\infty}^{\infty} \sum_{m=1}^{\infty} \frac{\partial}{\partial X_m} \left(n_{l-l'}^{(n-m-n')} v_{l'}^{(n')}\right) = 0. \quad (5.96)$$

Also,

$$\frac{\partial v}{\partial t} = \left(-ilw + \sum_{m=1}^{\infty} \epsilon^m \frac{\partial}{\partial T_m}\right)\left(\sum_{n=1}^{\infty} \epsilon^n \sum_{l=-\infty}^{\infty} v_l^n e^{il(kx-wt)}\right)$$

$$= -ilw \sum_{n=1}^{\infty} \epsilon^n \sum_{l=-\infty}^{\infty} v_l^n e^{il(kx-wt)}$$

$$+ \sum_{p=m+1}^{\infty} \sum_{m=1}^{\infty} \epsilon^p \sum_{l=-\infty}^{\infty} \frac{\partial}{\partial T_m} v_l^{(p-m)} e^{il(kx-wt)}. \quad (5.97)$$

Now,

$$v\frac{\partial v}{\partial x} = \left[\sum_{n=1}^{\infty} \epsilon^n \sum_{l=-\infty}^{\infty} v_l^n e^{il(kx-wt)}\right]\left[\left(il'k + \sum_{m=1}^{\infty} \epsilon^m \frac{\partial}{\partial X_m}\right)\right.$$

$$\left. \times \left(\sum_{n'=1}^{\infty} \epsilon^{n'} \sum_{l'=-\infty}^{\infty} v_{l'}^{n'} e^{il'(kx-wt)}\right)\right]$$

$$= \sum_{p=n'+1}^{\infty} \sum_{n'=1}^{\infty} \epsilon^p \sum_{l=-\infty}^{\infty} \sum_{l'=-\infty}^{\infty} il'k v_l^{p-n'} v_{l'}^{n'} e^{i(l+l')(kx-wt)}$$

$$+ \sum_{q=n'+m+1}^{\infty} \sum_{n'=1}^{\infty} \sum_{m=1}^{\infty} \epsilon^p \sum_{l=-\infty}^{\infty} \sum_{l'=-\infty}^{\infty} v_l^{q-n'-m} \frac{\partial v_{l'}^{n'}}{\partial X_m} e^{i(l+l')(kx-wt)}. \quad (5.98)$$

Again,

$$\frac{\partial \phi}{\partial x} = \left(ilk + \sum_{m=1}^{\infty} \epsilon^m \frac{\partial}{\partial X_m}\right)\left(\sum_{n=1}^{\infty} \epsilon^n \sum_{l=-\infty}^{\infty} \phi_l^n e^{il(kx-wt)}\right)$$

$$= ilk \sum_{n=1}^{\infty} \epsilon^n \sum_{l=-\infty}^{\infty} \phi_l^n e^{il(kx-wt)} + \sum_{p=m+1}^{\infty} \sum_{m=1}^{\infty} \epsilon^p \sum_{l=-\infty}^{\infty} \frac{\partial \phi_l^{p-m}}{\partial X_m} e^{il(kx-wt)}. \quad (5.99)$$

Putting the values of (5.97), (5.98), and (5.99) in (5.90) and isolating the order ϵ^n, we get

$$
-ilw \sum_{l=-\infty}^{\infty} v_l^n e^{il(kx-wt)} + \sum_{m=1}^{\infty} \sum_{l=-\infty}^{\infty} \frac{\partial v_l^{n-m}}{\partial T_m} e^{il(kx-wt)} + \sum_{n'=1}^{\infty} \sum_{l=-\infty}^{\infty} \sum_{l'=-\infty}^{\infty}
$$

$$
\times \, il'k v_{l-l'}^{n-n'} v_{l'}^{n'} e^{il(kx-wt)} + \sum_{n'=1}^{\infty} \sum_{m=1}^{\infty} \sum_{l=-\infty}^{\infty} \sum_{l'=-\infty}^{\infty} v_{l-l'}^{n-n'-m} \frac{\partial v_{l'}^{n'}}{\partial X_m} e^{il(kx-wt)}
$$

$$
+ ilk \sum_{l=-\infty}^{\infty} \phi_l^n e^{il(kx-wt)} + \sum_{m=1}^{\infty} \sum_{l=-\infty}^{\infty} \frac{\partial \phi_l^{n-m}}{\partial X_m} e^{il(kx-wt)} = 0. \tag{5.100}
$$

Since this is true for all l and $e^{il(kx-wt)} \neq 0$, we get

$$
-ilwv_l^n + \sum_{m=1}^{\infty} \frac{\partial v_l^{(n-m)}}{\partial T_m} + ilk\phi_l^n + \sum_{m=1}^{\infty} \frac{\partial \phi_l^{(n-m)}}{\partial X_m} + \sum_{n'=1}^{\infty} \sum_{l'=-\infty}^{\infty} il'k v_{l-l'}^{n-n'} v_{l'}^{n'}
$$

$$
+ \sum_{n'=1}^{\infty} \sum_{m=1}^{\infty} \sum_{l'=-\infty}^{\infty} v_{l-l'}^{n-n'-m} \frac{\partial v_{l'}^{(n')}}{\partial X_m} = 0. \tag{5.101}
$$

Again,

$$
\frac{\partial^2 \phi}{\partial x^2} = \left[-l^2 k^2 + 2ilk \sum_{m=1}^{\infty} \epsilon^m \frac{\partial}{\partial X_m} + \sum_{m=1}^{\infty} \sum_{m'=1}^{\infty} \epsilon^{m+m'} \frac{\partial^2}{\partial X_m \partial X_{m'}} \right]
$$

$$
\times \left[\sum_{n=1}^{\infty} \epsilon^n \sum_{l=-\infty}^{\infty} \phi_l^n e^{il(kx-wt)} \right] = -l^2 k^2 \sum_{n=1}^{\infty} \epsilon^n \sum_{l=-\infty}^{\infty} \phi_l^n e^{il(kx-wt)}
$$

$$
+ 2ilk \sum_{p=m+1}^{\infty} \sum_{m=1}^{\infty} \epsilon^p \sum_{l=-\infty}^{\infty} \frac{\partial \phi_l^{p-m}}{\partial X_m} e^{il(kx-wt)}
$$

$$
\times \sum_{q=m+m'+1}^{\infty} \sum_{m=1}^{\infty} \sum_{m'=1}^{\infty} \epsilon^q \sum_{l=-\infty}^{\infty} \frac{\partial^2 \phi_l^{q-m-m'}}{\partial X_m \partial X_{m'}} e^{il(kx-wt)} \tag{5.102}
$$

as

$$
n = 1 + \sum_{n=1}^{\infty} \epsilon^n \sum_{l=-\infty}^{\infty} n_l^n e^{il(kx-wt)}. \tag{5.103}
$$

Now,

$$e^{\phi} = 1 + \phi + \frac{\phi^2}{2} + \frac{\phi^3}{6} + \cdots$$

$$= 1 + \sum_{n=1}^{\infty} \epsilon^n \sum_{l=-\infty}^{\infty} \phi_l^n \, e^{il(kx-wt)} + \frac{1}{2} \sum_{n=1}^{\infty} \sum_{n'=1}^{\infty} \epsilon^{n+n'}$$

$$\times \sum_{l=-\infty}^{\infty} \sum_{l'=-\infty}^{\infty} \phi_l^n \phi_{l'}^{n'} \, e^{i(l+l')} \, e^{kx-wt} + \frac{1}{6} \sum_{n=1}^{\infty} \sum_{n'=1}^{\infty} \sum_{n''=1}^{\infty} \epsilon^{n+n'+n''}$$

$$\times \sum_{l=-\infty}^{\infty} \sum_{l'=-\infty}^{\infty} \sum_{l''=-\infty}^{\infty} \phi_l^n \phi_{l'}^{n'} \phi_{l''}^{n''} \, e^{i(l+l'+l'')} \, e^{kx-wt} + \cdots$$

$$= 1 + \sum_{n=1}^{\infty} \epsilon^n \sum_{l=-\infty}^{\infty} \phi_l^n e^{il(kx-wt)} + \frac{1}{2} \sum_{p=n'+1}^{\infty} \sum_{n'=1}^{\infty} \epsilon^p \sum_{l=-\infty}^{\infty} \sum_{l'=-\infty}^{\infty} \phi_l^{p-n'} \phi_{l'}^{n'}$$

$$\times e^{i(l+l')} e^{kx-wt} + \frac{1}{6} \sum_{q=n'+n''+1}^{\infty} \sum_{n'=1}^{\infty} \sum_{n''=1}^{\infty} \epsilon^q$$

$$\times \sum_{l=-\infty}^{\infty} \sum_{l'=-\infty}^{\infty} \sum_{l''=-\infty}^{\infty} \phi_l^{q-n'-n''} \phi_{l'}^{n'} \phi_{l''}^{n''} \, e^{i(l+l'+l'')} e^{kx-wt} + \cdots$$

$$(5.104)$$

Now, putting the values of (5.102)–(5.104) in (5.91) and isolating the ϵ^n order equation, we get

$$-l^2 k^2 \sum_{l=-\infty}^{\infty} \phi_l^n e^{il(kx-wt)} + 2ilk \sum_{m=1}^{\infty} \sum_{l=-\infty}^{\infty} \frac{\partial \phi_l^{n-m}}{\partial X_m} e^{il(kx-wt)}$$

$$+ \sum_{m=1}^{\infty} \sum_{m'=1}^{\infty} \sum_{l=-\infty}^{\infty} \frac{\partial^2 \phi_l^{n-m-m'}}{\partial X_m \partial X_{m'}} e^{il(kx-wt)} + \sum_{l=-\infty}^{\infty} n_l^n e^{il(kx-wt)}$$

$$- \sum_{l=-\infty}^{\infty} \phi_l^n e^{il(kx-wt)} - \frac{1}{2} \sum_{n'=1}^{\infty} \sum_{l=-\infty}^{\infty} \sum_{l'=-\infty}^{\infty} \phi_{l-l'}^{n-n'} \phi_{l'}^{n'} e^{il(kx-wt)}$$

$$- \frac{1}{6} \sum_{n'=1}^{\infty} \sum_{n''=1}^{\infty} \sum_{l=-\infty}^{\infty} \sum_{l'=-\infty}^{\infty} \sum_{l''=-\infty}^{\infty} \phi_{l-l'-l''}^{n-n'-n''} \phi_{l'}^{n'} \phi_{l''}^{n''} e^{il(kx-wt)} - \cdots$$

$$(5.105)$$

Since this is true for all l and $e^{il(kx-wt)} \neq 0$, we get

$$-l^2 k^2 \phi_l^n + 2ilk \sum_{m=1}^{\infty} \frac{\partial \phi_l^{n-m}}{\partial X_m} + \sum_{m=1}^{\infty} \sum_{m'=1}^{\infty} \frac{\partial^2 \phi_l^{n-m-m'}}{\partial X_m \partial X_{m'}} + n_l^n - \phi_l^n$$

$$-\frac{1}{2} \sum_{n'=1}^{\infty} \sum_{l'=-\infty}^{\infty} \phi_{l-l'}^{n-n'} \phi_{l'}^{n'} - \frac{1}{6} \sum_{n'=1}^{\infty} \sum_{n''=1}^{\infty} \sum_{l'=-\infty}^{\infty} \sum_{l''=-\infty}^{\infty} \phi_{l-l'-l''}^{n-n'-n''} \phi_{l'}^{n'} \phi_{l''}^{n''}$$

$$- \cdots = 0. \tag{5.106}$$

1. Linear Part

A. Harmonic modes with $n = 1$, $l = 1$: Linear dispersion law

From Equations (5.96), (5.101), and (5.106) and equating the coefficients of ϵ for $n = 1, l = 1$, we get

$$\left. \begin{array}{l} n_1^1 = \dfrac{k}{w} v_1^1 \\[2ex] v_1^1 = \dfrac{k}{w} \phi_1^1 \\[2ex] n_1^1 = (1 + k^2)\phi_1^1 \end{array} \right\}. \tag{5.107}$$

From Equation (5.107), we obtain *the dispersion law*:

$$w^2 = \frac{k^2}{1+k^2}. \tag{5.108}$$

2. Nonlinear Part

B. Modes with $n = 2$, $l = 1$: Group Velocity

For $n = 2$ and $l = 1$, we have from Equations (5.96), (5.101), and (5.106)

$$-iwn_1^2 + ikv_1^2 + \frac{\partial n_1^1}{\partial T_1} + \frac{\partial v_1^1}{\partial X_1} = 0 \tag{5.109}$$

$$v_1^2 = \frac{k}{w}\phi_1^2 - i\frac{k}{w^2}\frac{\partial \phi_1^1}{\partial T_1} - \frac{i}{w}\frac{\partial \phi_1^1}{\partial X_1} \tag{5.110}$$

$$n_1^2 = (1 + k^2)\phi_1^2 - 2ik\frac{\partial \phi_1^1}{\partial X_1}. \tag{5.111}$$

Putting the values of $n_1^1, v_1^1, n_1^2,$ and v_1^2 in (5.109), we get

$$\frac{\partial \phi_1^1}{\partial T_1} + v_g \frac{\partial \phi_1^1}{\partial X_1} = 0 \tag{5.112}$$

where the *group velocity* is defined as $v_g = \frac{w^3}{k^3}$. Using (5.112), we get from (5.110)

$$v_1^2 = \frac{k}{w}\phi_1^2 - iw\frac{\partial \phi_1^1}{\partial X_1}. \tag{5.113}$$

C. Second Harmonic Modes with $n = l = 2$

For the second-order quantities with $n = l = 2$, we obtain from equation (5.106)

$$-(1 + 4k^2)\phi_2^2 + n_2^2 - \frac{1}{2}\left(\phi_1^1\right)^2 = 0. \tag{5.114}$$

From (5.101) and (5.96),

$$v_2^2 = \frac{k}{w}\phi_2^2 + \frac{k^3}{2w^3}\left(\phi_1^1\right)^2, \tag{5.115}$$

$$n_2^2 = \left(1 + k^2\right)\phi_2^2 + \frac{3}{2}\left(1 + k^2\right)^2\left(\phi_1^1\right)^2. \tag{5.116}$$

Putting n_2^2 in (5.114), we get

$$\phi_2^2 = \frac{2 + 6k^2 + 3k^4}{6k^2}\left(\phi_1^1\right)^2. \tag{5.117}$$

From (5.116), we get using (5.117)

$$n_2^2 = \frac{2 + 15k^2 + 12k^4}{6w^2}\left(\phi_1^1\right)^2. \tag{5.118}$$

Using (5.117), we get from (5.115)

$$v_2^2 = \frac{2 + 9k^2 + 6k^4}{6kw}\left(\phi_1^1\right)^2. \tag{5.119}$$

D. Zeroth Harmonic Modes with $n = 2, l = 0$ and $n = 3, l = 0$

Considering the terms corresponding to $n = 3$ and $l = 0$, we get from (5.96)

$$\frac{\partial n_0^2}{\partial T_1} = -\frac{\partial v_0^2}{\partial X_1} - 2\frac{k}{w}(1 + k^2)\frac{\partial}{\partial X_1}(|\phi_1^1|)^2 \tag{5.120}$$

and for $n = 2$ and $l = 0$, we get from (5.106)

$$\phi_0^2 = n_0^2 - |\phi_1^1|^2. \tag{5.121}$$

Also, for $n = 3$ and $l = 0$, we get from (5.101)

$$\frac{\partial v_0^2}{\partial T_1} + \frac{\partial \phi_0^2}{\partial X_1} + \frac{k^2}{w^2}\frac{\partial}{\partial X_1}(|\phi_1^1|)^2 = 0. \tag{5.122}$$

Now,

$$\phi_0^2 = n_0^2 - |\phi_1^1|^2$$

$$\frac{\partial}{\partial T_1}n_0^2 = \frac{\partial}{\partial T_1}\phi_0^2 + \frac{\partial}{\partial T_1}(|\phi_1^1|^2)$$

$$\frac{\partial}{\partial T_1}n_0^2 = \frac{\partial}{\partial T_1}\phi_0^2 - v_g\frac{\partial}{\partial X_1}(|\phi_1^1|^2). \tag{5.123}$$

As $\frac{\partial}{\partial T_1} + v_g\frac{\partial}{\partial X_1} = 0$, from Equation (5.120), we get

$$\frac{\partial n_0^2}{\partial T_1} = -\frac{\partial v_0^2}{\partial X_1} - 2\frac{k}{w}(1 + k^2)\frac{\partial}{\partial X_1}(|\phi_1^1|)^2$$

$$\frac{\partial n_0^2}{\partial T_1} = -\frac{\partial}{\partial X_1}\left(v_0^2 + \frac{2}{v_g}|\phi_1^1|^2\right)$$

$$\left(1 - v_g^2\right)\frac{\partial \phi_0^2}{\partial X_1} = -(3 + k^2 - v_g^2)\frac{\partial}{\partial X_1}(|\phi_1^1|^2) = 0.$$

Integrating, we get

$$\phi_0^2 = -\frac{3 + k^2 - v_g^2}{1 - v_g^2}|\phi_1^1|^2. \tag{5.124}$$

Using relation (5.124), we get from (5.121)

$$n_0^2 = -\left(\frac{2 + k^2}{1 - v_g^2}\right)|\phi_1^1|^2. \tag{5.125}$$

From (5.122), we get

$$\frac{\partial v_0^2}{\partial T_1} + \frac{\partial \phi_0^2}{\partial X_1} + \frac{k^2}{w^2}\frac{\partial}{\partial X_1}\left(|\phi_1^1|\right)^2 = 0$$

$$-v_g\frac{\partial v_0^2}{\partial X_1} - \left(\frac{3+k^2-v_g^2}{1-v_g^2}\right)\frac{\partial}{\partial X_1}(|\phi_1^1|)^2 + (1+k^2)\frac{\partial}{\partial X_1}\left(|\phi_1^1|\right)^2 = 0.$$

Integrating, we get

$$v_0^2 = -\frac{\left(2+k^2v_g^2\right)}{\left(1-v_g^2\right)v_g}\left(|\phi_1^1|\right)^2. \tag{5.126}$$

E. Harmonic Modes with $n = 3, l = 1$: The NLS equation

Now, for $n = 3$ and $l = 1$, we get from (5.106)

$$-(1+k^2)\phi_1^3 + n_1^3 + 2ik\frac{\partial \phi_1^1}{\partial X_2} + \frac{\partial^2 \phi_1^1}{\partial X_1^2} - \left(\phi_1^1\phi_0^2 + \phi_{-1}^1\phi_2^2\right) - \frac{1}{2}(|\phi_1^1|)^2\phi_1^1 = 0$$

$$-(1+k^2)\phi_1^3 + n_1^3 + 2ik\frac{\partial \phi_1^1}{\partial X_2} + \frac{\partial^2 \phi_1^1}{\partial X_1^2} - \left[-C_3^{(20)} + C_3^{(22)} + \frac{1}{2}\right](|\phi_1^1|)^2\phi_1^1 = 0. \tag{5.127}$$

From (5.96),

$$-iwn_1^3 + ikv_1^3 + \frac{\partial n_1^2}{\partial T_1} + \frac{\partial n_1^1}{\partial T_2} + \frac{\partial v_1^2}{\partial X_1} + \frac{\partial v_1^1}{\partial X_2}$$

$$+ ik\left[n_0^2v_1^1 + n_1^1v_0^2 + n_{-1}^1v_2^2 + n_2^2v_{-1}^1\right] = 0$$

$$-iwn_1^3 + ikv_1^3 - 2ikv_g\frac{\partial^2 \phi_1^1}{\partial X_1^2} + \left(1+k^2\right)\frac{\partial \phi_1^1}{\partial T_2} - iw\frac{\partial^2 \phi_1^1}{\partial X_1^2} + \frac{k}{w}\frac{\partial \phi_1^1}{\partial X_2}$$

$$+ ik\left[-C_1^{(20)}\frac{k}{w} - C_2^{(20)}\left(1+k^2\right) + (1+k^2)C_2^{(22)} + \frac{k}{w}C_1^{(22)}\right](|\phi_1^1|)^2\phi_1^1 = 0. \tag{5.128}$$

From (5.101),

$$-iwv_1^3 + ik\phi_1^3 + \frac{\partial v_1^2}{\partial T_1} + \frac{\partial v_1^1}{\partial T_2} + \frac{\partial \phi_1^1}{\partial X_2} + ik\left[v_0^2v_1^1 + 2v_{-1}^1v_2^2 - v_2^2v_{-1}^1\right] = 0$$

$$-iwv_1^3 + ik\phi_1^3 + iwv_g\frac{\partial^2 \phi_1^1}{\partial X_1^2} + \frac{k}{w}\frac{\partial \phi_1^1}{\partial T_2} + \frac{\partial \phi_1^1}{\partial X_2}$$

$$+ ik\left[-\frac{k}{w}C_2^{(20)} + \frac{k}{w}C_2^{(22)}\right](|\phi_1^1|)^2\phi_1^1 = 0. \tag{5.129}$$

Putting v_1^3 in (5.128), we get

$$
\begin{aligned}
n_1^3 = {}& -i\frac{k}{w^2}\left[ik\phi_1^3 + iwv_g\frac{\partial^2\phi_1^1}{\partial X_1^2} + \frac{k}{w}\frac{\partial\phi_1^1}{\partial T_2} + \frac{\partial\phi_1^1}{\partial X_2}\right.\\
&+ ik\left(-\frac{k}{w}C_2^{(20)} + \frac{k}{w}C_2^{(22)}\right)(|\phi_1^1|)^2\phi_1^1 \Bigg] + \frac{2k}{w}v_g\frac{\partial^2\phi_1^1}{\partial X_1^2}\\
&+ \frac{(1+k^2)}{iw}\frac{\partial\phi_1^1}{\partial T_2} - \frac{\partial^2\phi_1^1}{\partial X_1^2} - i\frac{k}{w^2}\frac{\partial\phi_1^1}{\partial X_2} + \frac{k}{w}\left[-C_1^{(20)}\frac{k}{w} - C_2^{(20)}(1+k^2)\right.\\
&+ (1+k^2)C_2^{(22)} + \frac{k}{w}C_1^{(22)}\bigg](|\phi_1^1|)^2\phi_1^1.
\end{aligned}
\tag{5.130}
$$

Putting n_1^3 in (5.127), we get

$$
i\left(\frac{\partial\phi_1^1}{\partial T_2} + v_g\frac{\partial\phi_1^1}{\partial X_2}\right) + P\frac{\partial^2\phi_1^1}{\partial X_1^2} + Q(|\phi_1^1|)^2\phi_1^1 = 0
\tag{5.131}
$$

where

$$
P = -\frac{3}{2}\frac{w^5}{k^4}, \quad Q = \frac{w^3}{2k^2}\left(\frac{1}{2} + C_3^{22} - C_3^{20}\right) + k(C_2^{20} - C_2^{22}) + \frac{w}{2}(C_1^{20} - C_1^{22}).
$$

This equation is called cubic *nonlinear Schrodinger equation*.

Now, applying the traveling wave transformation $\xi = x - v_gt$, $\tau = t$, one finds the standard form of the NLS equation as

$$
i\frac{\partial\psi}{\partial\tau} + P\frac{\partial^2\psi}{\partial\xi^2} + Q|\psi|^2\psi = 0
\tag{5.132}
$$

where ψ denotes the electric potential correction ϕ_1^1. The group velocity dispersion coefficient $P\left(= \frac{1}{2}\frac{d^2\omega}{dk^2}\right)$ is a real-valued parameter, and Q is the cubic nonlinear (local) coefficient. The coefficient P is proportional to the group dispersion $\frac{dv_g}{dK}$, and the coefficients Q is proportional to the nonlinear frequency shift.

If the amplitude of the plasma wave is not small, nonlinearities give rise to a modulation of the wave amplitude. When the amplitude varies slowly throughout oscillation, the equation describing the evolution of the wave amplitude (in certain cases) becomes the nonlinear Schrodinger equation.

In plasma, it is found that under certain conditions, conversion of an initially uniform wave train into a spatially modulated wave proves to be energetically favorable. This effect is known as *modulationally instability*. The plane wave solutions of Equation (5.132) are modulationally unstable if $PQ > 0$. Let us rewrite Equation (5.132) as

$$i\frac{\partial \psi}{\partial \tau'} = -\frac{\partial^2 \psi}{\partial \xi^2} - \frac{Q}{P}|\psi|^2\psi \tag{5.133}$$

where $\tau' = P\tau$. The Schrodinger equation for quasiparticles, the wave function of which is given by ψ, is trapped by a self-generated nonlinear potential $V = -\frac{Q}{P}|\psi|^2$. For $PQ > 0$, this potential will have an attractive sign. If somehow the quasiparticle density $|\psi|^2$ increases, the depth of this potential increases; more particles are attracted, leading to a further increase in the potential depth. In this respect, the instability may be the result of a consequence of the self-trapping of the quasiparticles.

For electron plasma waves, the modulational instability can be easily understood in terms of the pondermotive force. When an electromagnetic wave of vary high intensity interacts with plasma particles in a plasma nonlinear processes, the force due to radiation pressure is coupled to the plasma particles and is called the pondermotive force. Suppose we have a plasma wave with a ripple on the envelope. The gradient in wave intensity causes a pondermotive force, which pushes plasma out of the region with maximum intensity towards the region with minimum intensity.

It causes a ripple, in a density depression in the region of maximum intensity. The dispersion relation is

$$\omega^2 = \omega_{pe}^2 + \frac{3}{2}k^2 V_{Th}^2. \tag{5.134}$$

It indicates that waves of large k can exist only in a region of small ω_{pe} or low density. Thus, the density of the region's depression can trap plasma waves leading to further enhancement of local field and hence, the instability.

During the nonlinear evolution of the wave, when the nonlinear effects are balanced by the dispersion effect, a stable nonlinear wave structure is formed, called the envelope soliton. When both P and Q are positive, Equation (5.132) has a solitary wave solution.

Let us consider

$$\psi = f(\xi)exp.iA\tau \tag{5.135}$$

where $f(\xi)$ is real and A is an arbitrary constant. Substituting (5.135) in (5.132), we find that f satisfies the equation

$$-Af + P\frac{d^2 f}{d\xi^2} + Qf^3 = 0$$

$$\Rightarrow P\frac{d^2 f}{d\xi^2} = Af - Qf^3. \tag{5.136}$$

Multiplying both sides by $2\frac{df}{d\xi}$ and integrating, we get

$$P\left(\frac{df}{d\xi}\right)^2 = Af^2 - \frac{1}{2}Qf^4 + C \tag{5.137}$$

where C is a constant. Assuming that f and its derivatives vanish at $\xi \to \pm\infty$, we find that $C = 0$.

Therefore, Equation (5.137) can be rewritten as

$$\frac{df}{f\sqrt{1 - \frac{Q}{2A}f^2}} = \pm\sqrt{\frac{A}{P}}d\xi. \tag{5.138}$$

Substituting $f = \sqrt{\frac{2A}{Q}}sech\theta$ in Equation (5.138) and integrating, we get

$$\theta = \mp\sqrt{\frac{A}{P}}d\xi + C_1 \tag{5.139}$$

where C_1 is a constant. Therefore,

$$f = \sqrt{\frac{2A}{Q}}sech\left(\sqrt{\frac{A}{P}}\xi \mp C_1\right). \tag{5.140}$$

If we take the origin of the coordinate for ξ in such a way that f attains maximum at $\xi = 0$, then $C_1 = 0$. Therefore,

$$f = \sqrt{\frac{2A}{Q}}sech\left(\sqrt{\frac{A}{P}}\xi\right). \tag{5.141}$$

Hence, the solitary wave solution of the nonlinear Schrodinger Equation (5.132) becomes

$$\psi = \sqrt{\frac{2A}{Q}}sech\left(\sqrt{\frac{A}{P}}\xi\right)e^{iA\tau}. \tag{5.142}$$

Suppose the wave field is described by

$$E = Re\,\psi\,e^{i(kx-\omega t)} \tag{5.143}$$

then using (5.142) we can write

$$E = \sqrt{\frac{2A}{Q}}sech\left(\sqrt{\frac{A}{P}}\epsilon(x - v_g t)\right)\cos(kx - \omega t + A\epsilon^2 t). \tag{5.144}$$

Setting $\epsilon = 1$ and $\sqrt{\frac{2A}{Q}} = a$, we get

$$E = a\ sech\left(a\sqrt{\frac{Q}{2P}}(x - v_g t)\right) \cos\left[kx - \left(\omega - \frac{a^2 Q}{2}\right)t\right]. \quad (5.145)$$

Thus, there is a nonlinear frequency shift of the wave, and this frequency shift is equal to $\frac{a^2 Q}{2}$, where a is the amplitude of the solitary wave. Solution (5.146) shows that the amplitude of the wave moves with the group velocity v_g. At $t = 0$, the wave profile is written as

$$E = a\ sech\left(a\sqrt{\frac{Q}{2P}}x\right) \cos kx. \quad (5.146)$$

The wave profile resembles a simple soliton but oscillating between positive and negative values, and it is known as envelope soliton.

References

[1] H. Ikezi and R. J. Taylor, *Phys. Rev. Lett.* 22, 923 (1969).

[2] Y. H. Ichikawa, T. Mitsuhashi, and K. Konno, *J. Phys. Soc. Jpn.* 41, 1382 (1976).

[3] T. Aoyama and Y. H. Ichikawa, *J. Phys. Soc. Jpn.* 42, 313 (1977).

[4] Y. H. Ichikawa, T. Mitsuhashi, and K. Konno, *J. Phys. Soc. Jpn.* 43, 675 (1977).

[5] Y. Kodama and T. Taniuti, *J. Phys. Soc. Jpn.* 45, 298 (1978); 45, 1765 (1978).

[6] R. S. Tiwari and M. K. Misra, *Phys. Plasmas* 13, 062112 (2006).

[7] T. S. Gill, P. Bala, and H. Kaur, *Phys. Plasmas* 15, 122309 (2008).

[8] A. Esfandyari-Kalejahi, I. Kourakis, and P. K. Shukla, *Phys. Plasmas* 15, 022303 (2008).

[9] P. Chatterjee, G. Mandal, K. Roy, S. V. Muniandy, S. L. Yap, and C. S. Wong, *Phys. Plasmas* 16, 072102 (2009).

[10] K. Roy and P. Chatterjee, *Indian J. Phys.* 85, 1653 (2011).

Chapter 6

Evolution Equations
in Nonplanar Geometry

6.1 Introduction

The applications of solitons or shocks in different areas of plasmas are well known. In the past few decades, the propagation of IASWs, DASWs, DIASWs, etc., has been studied experimentally in the framework of KdV equation, Burgers' equation, KP equation, ZK equation, or some modified form of these equations. These have been explained clearly in Chapter 4. But, these studies are limited to unbounded planar geometry and are neither realistic in laboratory plasma nor space plasma. In reality, nonplanar geometry changes the shape of the waves. In nature, distorted waves are observed in the laboratory and space and are certainly not bounded in one or two-dimensional planar geometry. Frenz *et al.* [1] have observed the features in the auroral region, especially at the higher polar altitudes. Maxon and Viecelli [2, 3] initiated this problem theoretically and observed the propagation of radially ingoing acoustic type waves in cylindrical geometry and spherical geometry. It is seen that as the amplitude grows, the width decreases, and the propagation speed increases, while the soliton travels inward, which is different than the usual KdV soliton. However, the square root of the peak amplitude multiplies by the width and remains constant for a long span. They have also seen that the cylindrical soliton travels slower than the spherical soliton but faster than the soliton of the same amplitude of planar geometry.

6.2 Basic Equations of Motion in Nonplanar Geometry

The basic system of equations in a plasma model is mainly governed by the equation of continuity, the equation of motion, and the Poisson equation. For a classical electron-ion plasma, where ions are mobile in the background of electrons, may be modeled as

$$\frac{\partial n_i}{\partial t} + \vec{\nabla} \cdot (n_i \cdot \vec{u}) = 0, \tag{6.1}$$

$$\frac{\partial \vec{u}}{\partial t} + (\vec{u} \cdot \vec{\nabla})\vec{u} = -(\vec{\nabla}\phi) + \Omega(\vec{u} \times \hat{\vec{x}}) + \mu\vec{\nabla}^2\vec{u}, \tag{6.2}$$

$$\vec{\nabla}^2\phi = n_i - n_e \tag{6.3}$$

where n_i and n_e are the ion and electron number density, respectively. u_i, v_i, and w_i are the ion fluid speed in x, y, and z directions. Equations (6.1)–(6.3) refer to the equation of continuity, the equation of motion, and the Poisson equation, respectively.

To study nonlinear waves in nonplanar geometry, let us first express the equation of continuity in cylindrical and spherical geometry.

(a) **Continuity equation in cylindrical geometry:** The continuity equation arises from the fundamental physical principle of the conservation of mass. To derive this equation, we choose a convenient control volume inside the fluid and assume that all the fluid particles flowing inside the control volume must flow out. In planer geometry, the cubic control volume is taken into consideration where the sides of the cube are parallel to the coordinate axes. For cylindrical coordinate, a point P is represented by the triple (r, θ, z), where r and θ are the polar coordinates of the projection of P onto the xy-plane and z has the same meaning as in cartesian coordinate.

We choose the control volume $dV = rd\theta drdz$. As the mass conservation inside the control volume is zero, so

the rate of flow in = Rate of flow out + Accumulation,
i.e., Rate of flow out – Rate of flow in + Accumulation = 0.

If we assume the velocity field $\vec{u} = ue_r + ve_\theta + we_z$ and write the velocity component r, θ, z direction as u, v, w in place of u_r, u_θ, u_z, respectively. The mass of the fluid in the control volume is $M = \rho dV$, and the rate of change of mass or accumulation in the control volume is $\frac{\partial \rho}{\partial t}rdrd\theta dz$.

For the net flow through the control volume, let us deal with one face at a time. First, we consider the r faces. The net inflow is $\dot{m}_{r,in} = \rho urd\theta dz$, while the outflow in the r direction is $\dot{m}_{r,out} = (\rho u + \frac{\partial \rho u}{\partial r})(r + dr)d\theta dz$. So, the net flow in the r direction is $\dot{m}_{r,out} - \dot{m}_{r,in} = \rho u dr d\theta dz + \frac{\partial \rho u}{\partial r}r dr d\theta dz + \frac{\partial \rho u}{\partial r}r dr^2 d\theta dz = \frac{1}{r}\rho u dV + \frac{\partial(\rho u)}{\partial r} + O(dr^2)$.

We shall now complete the net flow in the θ direction. Here, the areas of the inflow and outflow faces are the same. The net flow in the θ direction is

$$\dot{m}_{\theta,net} = \frac{1}{r}\frac{\partial \rho V}{\partial r}dV.$$

We now turn our attention to the z-direction. The face area of a sector of angle $d\theta$ is

$$A_z = \frac{1}{2}(r + dr)^2 d\theta - \frac{1}{2}r^2 d\theta = rdrd\theta + \frac{1}{2}dr^2 d\theta = rdrd\theta + O(dr^2 d\theta).$$

The inflow at the lower z face is $\dot{m}(z,in) = \rho w A_z = \rho w r dr d\theta$, and the outflow at the upper z face is $\dot{m}_{r,out} = (\rho w + \frac{\partial \rho w}{\partial z}dz)$. $A_z = \rho w r dr d\theta + \frac{\partial \rho w}{\partial z}r dr d\theta dz$.

Hence, the net flow in the z direction is $\dot{m}_{z,out} - \dot{m}_{z,in} = \frac{\partial \rho w}{\partial z}r dr d\theta dz$.

Putting things together, we obtain the continuity equation as

$$\frac{\partial \rho}{\partial t}dV + \frac{1}{r}\rho u dV + \frac{\partial(\rho u)}{\partial r}dV + \frac{\partial(\rho v)}{\partial \theta}dV + \frac{\partial(\rho w)}{\partial z}dV = 0.$$

Conventionally, we take n as the plasma number density. So, by replacing fluid density ρ by n and dividing both the sides by dV, we get the continuity equation for plasma model in cylindrical coordinate system as

$$\frac{\partial n}{\partial t} + \frac{1}{r}\frac{\partial}{\partial r}(rnu_r) + \frac{1}{r}\frac{\partial}{\partial \theta}(nu_\theta) + \frac{\partial}{\partial z}(nu_z) = 0, \qquad (6.4)$$

where the component of the velocity vector is written as $\vec{u} = (u_r, u_\theta, u_z)$.

(b) Continuity equation in spherical geometry: Here, we start with a spherical control volume $dV = r^2 \sin\theta dr d\theta d\phi$, where r, θ, and ϕ stand for the radius, polar, and azimuthal angles, respectively. The azimuthal angle is also referred to as the zenith or colatitude angle, and the differential mass is $dM = \rho r^2 \sin\theta dr d\theta d\phi$. Let the velocity field be $\vec{u} = ue_r + ve_\theta + we_\phi$.

Like the previous case, mass conservation is represented by accumulation, net flow, and source terms in a control volume. The accumulation term is the rate of time of the change of mass. We, therefore, have $\frac{\partial \rho}{\partial t}r^2 \sin\theta dr d\theta d\phi$. The net flow through the control volume can be separated into that corresponding to each direction.

For radial flow: We start with the radial direction. So, we have $\dot{m}_{in} = \rho u A_{in}$. The inflow area A_{in} is a trapezoid, whose area is given by $A_{in} = \frac{1}{2}[r\sin\theta d\phi + r\sin(\theta + d\theta)d\phi]rd\theta$. The midsegment is considered as the average of the bases. Expanding $\sin(\theta + d\theta) = \sin\theta\cos d\theta + \cos\theta\sin d\theta = \sin\theta + \cos\theta d\theta$ and substituting into A_{in}, we have $A_{in} = r^2\sin\theta d\theta d\phi + \frac{1}{2}r^2\cos\theta d\theta^2 d\phi = r^2\sin\theta d\theta d\phi$, where high-order terms have been dropped. The outflow in the radial direction is $\dot{m}_{out} = \left(\rho u + \frac{\partial\rho u}{\partial r}dr\right)A_{out}$, but $A_{out} = \frac{1}{2}[r\sin\theta d\phi + (r + dr)\sin(\theta + d\theta)d\phi]$. By only keeping the lowest order (second- and third-order terms in the resulting expression), we have $A_{out} = r^2\sin\theta d\theta d\phi + 2\sin\theta dr d\theta d\phi$.

In A_{out}, we kept both second-order and third-order terms. The reason is that this term will be multiplied by 'dr' and, therefore, the overall order will be three. In principle, one must carry all those terms until the final substitution is made, and only then one can compare the terms and keep those with the lowest order. Hence, the net flow in the radial direction is given by $\dot{m}_{out} - \dot{m}_{in} = 2\rho u r\sin\theta dr d\theta d\phi + \frac{\partial\rho u}{\partial r}r^2\sin\theta dr d\theta d\phi$.

For polar flow (θ): The inflow in the polar direction is $\dot{m}_{in} = \rho v A_{in}$, where $A_{in} = r\sin\theta dr d\phi$. The outflow in the θ direction is $\dot{m}_{out} = (\rho v + \frac{\partial\rho v}{\partial\theta}d\theta)A_{out}$, where $A_{out} = \frac{1}{2}[r\sin(\theta + d\theta)d\phi + (r + dr)\sin(\theta + d\theta)d\phi]dr$. Expanding and keeping both second- and third-order terms, we get $A_{out} = r\cos\theta dr d\theta d\phi + r\sin\theta dt d\phi$. Finally, the net flow obtained in the polar direction is $\dot{m}_{out} - \dot{m}_{in} = \rho v r\cos\theta dr d\theta d\phi + \frac{\partial\rho v}{d\theta}r\sin\theta dr d\theta d\phi$.

For azimuthal flow (ϕ): The inflow in the azimuthal direction is given by $\dot{m}_{in} = \rho w A_{in}$, with $A_{in} = r dr d\theta$, while the outflow is $\dot{m}_{out} = (\rho w + \frac{\partial\rho w}{\partial\phi}d\phi)A_{out}$, and $A_{out} = r dr d\theta$. At the outset, the net flow in the azimuthal direction is $\dot{m}_{out} - \dot{m}_{in} = \frac{\partial\rho w}{\partial\phi}r dr d\theta d\phi$. Now, by collecting all mass fluxes we have $\frac{\partial\rho}{\partial t}dV + 2\rho u\frac{dV}{r} + \frac{\partial\rho u}{\partial r}dV + \rho v\cos\theta\frac{dV}{r\sin\theta} + \frac{\partial\rho v}{\partial\theta}\frac{dV}{r} + \frac{\partial\rho w}{\partial\phi}\frac{dV}{r\sin\theta} = 0$.

Dividing by dV and combining terms and replacing fluid density ρ by plasma density n as convention, the above equation reduces to

$$\frac{\partial n}{\partial t} + \frac{1}{r^2}\frac{\partial}{\partial r}(r^2 n u_r) + \frac{1}{r\sin\theta}\frac{\partial}{\partial\theta}(n u_\theta\sin\theta) + \frac{1}{r\sin\theta}\frac{\partial}{\partial\phi}(n u_\phi) = 0, \quad (6.5)$$

which is the continuity equation in spherical coordinates.

(ii) Equation of motion: The Navier–Stokes equation for incompressible fluid motion gives

$$n\left(\frac{\partial\vec{u}}{\partial t} + \vec{u}.\vec{\nabla}\vec{u}\right) = -\vec{\nabla}P + \mu\vec{\nabla}^2\vec{u} + \vec{F} \qquad (6.6)$$

where left-hand side represents inertia per volume. The first term is for unsteady acceleration, and the second term is for convective acceleration. The first two terms of the right-hand side represents the divergence of stress. The first term is for pressure gradient, the second term is for viscosity, and the third term is for other body forces.

In cylindrical coordinates, the Navier–Stokes equation along r direction is written as

$$n\left(\frac{\partial u_r}{\partial t} + u_r\frac{\partial u_r}{\partial r} + \frac{u_\theta}{r}\frac{\partial u_r}{\partial \theta} + u_z\frac{\partial u_r}{\partial z} - \frac{u_\theta^2}{r}\right)$$

$$= -\frac{\partial P}{\partial r} + \mu\left[\frac{\partial}{\partial r}\left(\frac{1}{r}\frac{\partial}{\partial r}(ru_r)\right) + \frac{1}{r^2}\frac{\partial^2 u_r}{\partial\theta^2} + \frac{\partial^2 u_r}{\partial z^2} - \frac{2}{r^2}\frac{\partial u_\theta}{\partial\theta}\right] + F_r,$$

(6.7)

along θ direction is expressed as

$$n\left(\frac{\partial u_\theta}{\partial t} + u_r\frac{\partial u_\theta}{\partial r} + \frac{u_\theta}{r}\frac{\partial u_\theta}{\partial \theta} + \frac{u_r u_\theta}{r} + u_z\frac{\partial u_\theta}{\partial z}\right)$$

$$= -\frac{1}{r}\frac{\partial P}{\partial \theta} + \mu\left[\frac{\partial}{\partial r}\left(\frac{1}{r}\frac{\partial}{\partial r}(ru_\theta)\right) + \frac{1}{r^2}\frac{\partial^2 u_\theta}{\partial\theta^2} + \frac{\partial^2 u_\theta}{\partial z^2} + \frac{2}{r^2}\frac{\partial u_r}{\partial\theta}\right] + F_\theta,$$

(6.8)

and along z direction is expressed as

$$n\left(\frac{\partial u_z}{\partial t} + u_r\frac{\partial u_z}{\partial r} + \frac{u_\theta}{r}\frac{\partial u_z}{\partial \theta} + u_z\frac{\partial u_z}{\partial z}\right)$$

$$= -\frac{\partial P}{\partial z} + \mu\left[\frac{1}{r}\left(\frac{\partial}{\partial r}\left(r\frac{\partial u_z}{\partial r}\right)\right) + \frac{1}{r^2}\frac{\partial^2 u_z}{\partial\theta^2} + \frac{\partial^2 u_z}{\partial z^2}\right] + F_z. \quad (6.9)$$

In spherical coordinates, the Navier–Stokes equation along r direction is written as

$$n\left(\frac{\partial u_r}{\partial t} + u_r\frac{\partial u_r}{\partial r} + \frac{u_\theta}{r}\frac{\partial u_r}{\partial \theta} + \frac{u_\phi}{r\sin\theta}\frac{\partial u_r}{\partial \phi} - \frac{u_\theta^2}{r} - \frac{u_\phi^2}{r}\right)$$

$$= -\frac{\partial P}{\partial r} + \mu\left[\frac{1}{r^2}\frac{\partial}{\partial r}\left(r^2\frac{\partial u_r}{\partial r}\right) + \frac{1}{r^2\sin\theta}\frac{\partial}{\partial \theta}\left(\sin\theta\frac{\partial u_r}{\partial \theta}\right) + \frac{1}{r^2\sin\theta}\frac{\partial^2 u_r}{\partial\phi^2}\right.$$

$$\left. + \frac{1}{r^2\sin^2\theta}\frac{\partial^2 u_r}{\partial\phi^2}\right] + \mu\left[-\frac{2u_r}{r^2} - \frac{2}{r^2}\frac{\partial u_\theta}{\partial\theta} - \frac{2u_\theta}{r^2}\cot\theta - \frac{2}{r^2\sin\theta}\frac{\partial u_\phi}{\partial\phi}\right] + F_r,$$

(6.10)

along θ direction is expressed as

$$n\left(\frac{\partial u_\theta}{\partial t} + u_r \frac{\partial u_\theta}{\partial r} + \frac{u_\theta}{r}\frac{\partial u_\theta}{\partial \theta} + \frac{u_\phi}{r\sin\theta}\frac{\partial u_\theta}{\partial \phi} + \frac{u_r u_\theta}{r} - \frac{u_\phi^2 \cot\theta}{r}\right)$$

$$= -\frac{1}{r}\frac{\partial P}{\partial \theta} + \mu\left[\frac{1}{r^2}\frac{\partial}{\partial r}\left(r^2\frac{\partial u_\theta}{\partial r}\right) + \frac{1}{r^2}\frac{\partial}{\partial \theta}\left(\frac{1}{\sin\theta}\frac{\partial}{\partial \theta}(u_\theta \sin\theta)\right)\right.$$

$$\left. + \frac{1}{r^2\sin\theta}\frac{\partial^2 u_\theta}{\partial \phi^2} + \frac{2}{r^2}\frac{\partial u_r}{\partial \theta} - \frac{2\cot\theta}{r^2\sin\theta}\frac{\partial u_\theta}{\partial \phi}\right] + F_\theta, \qquad (6.11)$$

and along ϕ direction is expressed as

$$n\left(\frac{\partial u_\phi}{\partial t} + u_r \frac{\partial u_\phi}{\partial r} + \frac{u_\theta}{r}\frac{\partial u_\phi}{\partial \theta} + \frac{u_\phi}{r\sin\theta}\frac{\partial u_\phi}{\partial \phi} + \frac{u_r u_\phi}{r} + \frac{u_\theta u_\phi \cot\theta}{r}\right)$$

$$= -\frac{1}{r\sin\theta}\frac{\partial P}{\partial \phi} + \mu\left[\frac{1}{r^2}\frac{\partial}{\partial r}\left(r^2\frac{\partial u_\phi}{\partial r}\right) + \frac{1}{r^2}\frac{\partial}{\partial \theta}\left(\frac{1}{\sin\theta}\frac{\partial}{\partial \theta}(u_\phi \sin\theta)\right)\right.$$

$$\left. + \frac{1}{r^2\sin\theta}\frac{\partial^2 u_\phi}{\partial \phi^2} + \frac{2}{r^2\sin\theta}\frac{\partial u_r}{\partial \phi} + \frac{2\cot\theta}{r^2\sin\theta}\frac{\partial u_\theta}{\partial \phi}\right] + F_\phi. \qquad (6.12)$$

The Navier–Stokes equation with no body force (i.e., $\vec{F} = 0$) is considered if $F_r = 0 = F_\theta = F_z = F_\phi$.

(iii) Poisson's equation: In the cylindrical coordinates, Poisson's equation is written as

$$\frac{1}{r}\frac{\partial}{\partial r}\left(r\frac{\partial \psi}{\partial r}\right) + \frac{1}{r^2}\frac{\partial^2 \psi}{\partial \theta^2} + \frac{\partial^2 \psi}{\partial z^2} = -4\pi n, \qquad (6.13)$$

while in the spherical coordinates, Poisson's equation is written as

$$\frac{1}{r^2}\frac{\partial}{\partial r}\left(r^2\frac{\partial \psi}{\partial r}\right) + \frac{1}{r^2\sin\theta}\frac{\partial}{\partial \theta}\left(\sin\theta\frac{\partial \psi}{\partial \theta}\right) + \frac{1}{r^2\sin^2\theta}\frac{\partial^2 \psi}{\partial \phi^2} = -4\pi n. \qquad (6.14)$$

6.3 Nonplanar KdV Equation in Classical Plasma

Now, we are going to derive the nonplanar KdV equation from a three component unmagnetized, collision-free plasma, consisting of warm ion fluid and superthermal distributed electrons and positrons in cylindrical or spherical geometry. The basic equations will be written as

$$\frac{\partial n_i}{\partial t} + \vec{\nabla} \cdot (n_i \vec{u}) = 0 \tag{6.15}$$

$$\frac{\partial \vec{u}}{\partial t} + (\vec{u} \cdot \vec{\nabla})\vec{u} = \frac{e}{m_i}\vec{E} - \frac{1}{n_i m_i}\vec{\nabla}p_i \tag{6.16}$$

where n_i, u, m_i, e, and E are the ion number density, ion fluid velocity, ion mass, the electron charge, and the electric field, respectively. p_i is the pressure of the adiabatically hot ions, given by the following thermodynamic equation of state

$$p_i = p_{i0}\left(\frac{n_i}{n_{i0}}\right)^\gamma. \tag{6.17}$$

At equilibrium, $p_{i0} = n_{i0}T_{i0}$, where n_{i0} is the unperturbed number density of ions, T_{i0} is the ion equilibrium temperature, and the adiabatic constant is defined as $\gamma = \frac{(N+2)}{N}$, where N represents the number of degrees of freedom of the ions. Here, $N = 1$.

Also, Poisson's equation is

$$\vec{\nabla} \cdot \vec{E} = 4\pi e(n_e - n_i - n_p) \tag{6.18}$$

where n_j ($j = e$, and p, stands for electron, and positron, respectively) and T_j are the number densities and temperature, respectively. The electric field $\vec{E} = -\vec{\nabla}\phi$ so that ϕ is the electrostatic wave potential. In equilibrium, $n_{e0} = n_{i0} + n_{p0}$, n_{j0} is the unperturbed number density.

We consider $\vec{u} = (u_r, 0, 0)$ (motion takes place along the direction of r only). For simplicity, we take $u_r = u_i$. Accordingly, the normalized equations are as follows:

$$\frac{\partial n_i}{\partial t} + \frac{1}{r^\nu}\frac{\partial}{\partial r}(r^\nu n_i u_i) = 0 \tag{6.19}$$

$$\frac{\partial u_i}{\partial t} + u_i\frac{\partial u_i}{\partial r} + 3\sigma_i n_i\frac{\partial n_i}{\partial r} = -\frac{\partial \phi}{\partial r} \tag{6.20}$$

$$\frac{1}{r^\nu}\frac{\partial}{\partial r}\left(r^\nu\frac{\partial \phi}{\partial r}\right) = n_e - n_p - n_i \tag{6.21}$$

where $n_e = \frac{1}{1-p}\left[1 - \frac{\phi}{\kappa}\right]^{-\kappa+\frac{1}{2}}$ and $n_p = \frac{p}{1-p}\left[1 + \sigma_p\frac{\phi}{\kappa}\right]^{-\kappa+\frac{1}{2}}$. $p = n_{p0}/n_{e0}$ and $\sigma_p = T_e/T_p$, $\sigma_i = T_{i0}/T_e$. κ is the real parameter measuring deviation from the Maxwellian equilibrium (recovered for κ infinite). $\nu = 0$ in the case of planar geometry, and $\nu = 1$, 2 in the case of cylindrical and spherical geometries, respectively.

The normalization is taken as

$$n_j \to \frac{n_j}{n_{j0}}, \quad u_i \to \frac{u_i}{C_s}, \quad r \to \frac{r}{\lambda_D}, \quad t \to \omega_{pi} t, \quad \phi \to \frac{e\phi}{K_B T_e}.$$

Here, $j = i, e, p$. $C_i = \sqrt{\frac{T_e}{m_i}}$, $\lambda_D = \sqrt{\frac{T_e}{4\pi n_{i0} e^2}}$, and $\omega_{pi} = \sqrt{\frac{4\pi n_{i0} e^2}{m_i}}$ are the ion-acoustic speed, the electron Debye length, and the ion plasma frequency, respectively.

Derivation of cylindrical/spherical KdV equation: To obtain the KdV equation in nonplanar geometry, we introduce the stretched coordinates as

$$\xi = \epsilon^{\frac{1}{2}}(r - \lambda t), \quad \tau = \epsilon^{\frac{3}{2}} t \tag{6.22}$$

where ϵ is a small expansion parameter and λ is a wave phase velocity normalized to C_s. The expansions of the dependent variables are also considered as

$$n_i = 1 + \sum_{k=1}^{\infty} \epsilon^k n_i^{(k)} + \cdots, \quad u_i = \sum_{k=1}^{\infty} \epsilon^k u_i^{(k)} + \cdots, \quad \phi = \sum_{k=1}^{\infty} \epsilon^k \phi^{(k)} + \cdots. \tag{6.23}$$

Substituting Equation (6.23) in Equations (6.19)–(6.21) and collecting different powers of ϵ, we obtain the following equations to the lowest order in ϵ:

$$n_i^{(1)} = \frac{u_i^{(1)}}{\lambda}, \quad u_i^{(1)} = \frac{\lambda}{\lambda^2 - 3\sigma_i} \phi^{(1)}. \tag{6.24}$$

From (6.24), we get the value of phase velocity as

$$\lambda = \sqrt{\frac{(1-p)\kappa + 3\sigma_i(\kappa - \frac{1}{2})(1 + p\sigma_p)}{(\kappa - \frac{1}{2})(1 + p\sigma_p)}}. \tag{6.25}$$

Taking the next higher order of ϵ, we get

$$\left.\begin{aligned}
&\frac{\partial n_i^{(1)}}{\partial \tau} - \lambda \frac{\partial n_i^{(2)}}{\partial \xi} + \frac{\partial u_i^{(2)}}{\partial \xi} + \frac{\partial}{\partial \xi}(n_i^{(1)} u_i^{(1)}) + \frac{\nu}{\lambda \tau} u_i^{(1)} = 0 \\
&\frac{\partial u_i^{(1)}}{\partial \tau} - \lambda \frac{\partial u_i^{(2)}}{\partial \xi} + 3\sigma_i \frac{\partial n_i^{(2)}}{\partial \xi} + u_i^{(1)} \frac{\partial u_i^{(1)}}{\partial \xi} + \frac{\partial \phi^{(2)}}{\partial \xi} = -3\sigma_i n_i^{(1)} \frac{\partial n_i^{(1)}}{\partial \xi} \\
&\frac{\partial^2 \phi^{(1)}}{\partial \xi^2} + n_i^{(2)} = \frac{(\kappa - \frac{1}{2})(1 + p\sigma_p)}{(1-p)\kappa} \phi^{(2)} + \frac{(\kappa - \frac{1}{2})(\kappa + \frac{1}{2})(1 - p\sigma_p^2)}{2(1-p)\kappa^2}(\phi^{(1)})^2.
\end{aligned}\right\} \tag{6.26}$$

Now, eliminating $n_i^{(2)}$, $u_i^{(2)}$, and $\phi^{(2)}$ from Equation (6.26) and using relations given in Equations (6.24)–(6.25), we obtain the nonplanar modified KdV equation as

$$\frac{\partial \phi^{(1)}}{\partial \tau} + \frac{\nu}{2\tau}\phi^{(1)} + A\phi^{(1)}\frac{\partial \phi^{(1)}}{\partial \xi} + B\frac{\partial^3 \phi^{(1)}}{\partial \xi^3} = 0 \qquad (6.27)$$

where $\frac{\nu}{2\tau}\phi^{(1)}$ is the additional term that has arisen due to the nonplanar geometry. Here, $A = \frac{1}{2\lambda}\left[3 + \frac{12\sigma_i(\kappa - \frac{1}{2})(1+p\sigma_p)}{(1-p)\kappa} - \frac{(1-p)(\kappa+\frac{1}{2})(1-p\sigma_p^2)}{(\kappa-\frac{1}{2})(1+p\sigma_p)^2}\right]$ and $B = \frac{1}{2\lambda}\frac{\kappa^2(1-p)^2}{(\kappa-\frac{1}{2})^2(1+p\sigma_p)^2}$. A and B are the coefficients of nonlinearity and dispersion, respectively. If we put $\nu = 0$ in Equation (6.27), we get the planar KdV equation. $\nu = 1$, 2 correspond to the KdV equations in the cylindrical and spherical geometries. The term $\frac{\nu}{2\tau}$ in the modified KdV equation appears due to a geometrical effect, and at longer time τ, the effect of this geometrical effect is reduced.

For planar geometry ($\nu = 0$), a stationary solution of Equation (6.27) has the following form:

$$\phi^{(1)} = \frac{3V}{A}Sech^2\left(\sqrt{\frac{V}{4B}}\left(\xi - V\tau\right)\right) \qquad (6.28)$$

where V is the constant velocity normalized by C_s. Now, we can solve Equation (6.27) numerically. The initial condition that we have used in our numerical results is the form of the stationary solution (6.28) at $\tau = -10$. In Figure 6.1, we have plotted the negative potential solitary structure for different values of the superthermal parameter κ and at different times ranging from $\tau = -3$ to $\tau = -10$ in cylindrical geometry. It is clear from the figure that both the amplitude and width of the negative potential electrostatic soliton decreases with a decrease of κ (i.e., an increase in superthermal). The pulse amplitude and width of the negative soliton become larger with an increase in the time duration. Figure 6.2(a) shows the formation of the positive potential wells for several values of κ and at different times in cylindrical geometry. As the superthermal parameter κ increases, the amplitude as well as width decreases. Moreover, the amplitude of the pulses increases when $|\tau|$ decreases. The numerical plots of solitons in spherical geometry, at different times, have been plotted for several values of κ in Figure 6.2(b). As the magnitude of $|\tau|$ increases, the solution looks like those for planar KdV solitons. This is because of the extra term $(\nu/2\tau)\phi^{(1)}$, and it becomes small for large values of $|\tau|$. As κ decreases (the superthermal character of

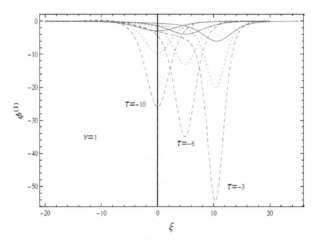

Fig. 6.1: Plot of $\phi^{(1)}$ against ξ for different values of ν for the solution of (6.27), where $\chi = -50$, $\sigma = 0.052$, $\alpha = 0.1$, $\kappa = 0.5$, $\gamma = 3$, $\tau = -5$, and $\eta_0 = 0.98$.

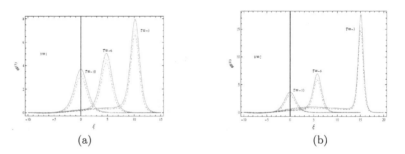

(a)   (b)

Fig. 6.2: The profiles of shock wave in (a) cylindrical geometry and (b) spherical geometry, where the other parameters are same as those in Figure 6.1.

the plasma increases), the potential pulse amplitude and width increase. Furthermore, it is observed that increasing the parameter κ leads to a decrease in the velocity of solitary waves, and the solitary peaks are well separated over time. However, the positive solitary pulses have the same qualitative behavior as the negative solitary waves.

6.4   Nonplanar KdV Equation in Quantum Plasma

The nonlinear dynamics of IASWs in a three-component unmagnetized, collisionless quantum plasma, consisting of inertialess electrons and positrons (the phase velocity of the wave is assumed to be much less than the Fermi velocities of electrons and positrons), inertial ions, are governed by the following normalized equations:

$$\frac{\partial n_i}{\partial t} + \frac{\nu}{r}(n_i u_i) + \frac{\partial(n_i u_i)}{\partial r} = 0, \tag{6.29}$$

$$\frac{\partial u_i}{\partial t} + u_i \frac{\partial u_i}{\partial r} = -\frac{\partial \phi}{\partial r}, \tag{6.30}$$

$$\frac{\partial \phi}{\partial r} - n_e \frac{\partial n_e}{\partial r} + \frac{H_e^2}{2} \frac{\partial}{\partial r}\left(\frac{\frac{\partial^2}{\partial r^2}\sqrt{n_e}}{\sqrt{n_e}}\right) = 0, \tag{6.31}$$

$$-\frac{\partial \phi}{\partial r} - \sigma n_p \frac{\partial n_p}{\partial r} + \frac{H_p^2}{2} \frac{\partial}{\partial r}\left(\frac{\frac{\partial^2}{\partial r^2}\sqrt{n_p}}{\sqrt{n_p}}\right) = 0, \tag{6.32}$$

$$\frac{\partial^2 \phi}{\partial r^2} = (1+p)n_e - p n_p - n_i. \tag{6.33}$$

Here, we consider that the Fermi temperature of electrons or positron is much larger than that of ions, i.e., $T_{Fj} \gg T_{Fi}$ ($j=e$, p). The electron/positron obeys the pressure law $P_j = m_j n_j^3 v_{Fj}^2 / 3 n_{j0}^2$, $v_{Fj} = (2K_B T_{Fj}/m_j)^{1/2}$ is the electron/positron Fermi thermal speed, and K_B is the Boltzmann constant. T_{Fj} ($j = i, e$, and p stands for ion, electron, and positron, respectively), m_j, and n_j are the Fermi temperature, the mass, and the number density, respectively. Also, n_{j0} is the unperturbed density. At equilibrium, $n_{e0} = n_{i0} + n_{p0}$. The electrons/positrons are considered to be degenerative owing to their small mass compared to the ions. Here, the normalizations are taken as

$$n_j \to \frac{n_j}{n_{j0}}, \quad u_i \to \frac{u_i}{c_{si}}, \quad t \to \omega_{pi} t, \quad r \to r \frac{c_{si}}{\omega_{pi}}, \quad \phi \to \frac{e\phi}{2K_B T_{Fe}}$$

where $c_{si} = \sqrt{2K_B T_{Fe}/m_i}$ and $\omega_{pi} = \sqrt{(n_{i0}e^2)/(m_i \epsilon_0)}$ are the quantum ion-acoustic speed and ion plasma frequency, respectively. Also, $H_j = \sqrt{\frac{\hbar^2 \omega_{pi}^2}{m_i m_j c_{si}^2}}$ is the quantum diffraction parameter, and $p = n_{p0}/n_{i0}$. Here, $\hbar$ is the Planck constant divided by 2π, e is the charge of electron, and ϵ_0 is the permeability of the free space. Finally, ν represents the geometry factor, $\nu = 0$ for the planar geometry, whereas $\nu = 1$ and 2 for the cylindrical and spherical geometry, respectively.

Integrating Equations (6.31) and (6.32) and using the boundary conditions $n_e = 1$, $n_p = 1$, and $\phi = 0$ at infinity, we obtain

$$n_e = \left(1 + 2\phi + H_e^2 \frac{\frac{\partial^2}{\partial r^2}(\sqrt{n_e})}{\sqrt{n_e}}\right)^{1/2}, \tag{6.34}$$

$$n_p = \left(1 - \frac{2\phi}{\sigma} + \frac{H_p^2}{\sigma} \frac{\frac{\partial^2}{\partial r^2}(\sqrt{n_p})}{\sqrt{n_p}}\right)^{1/2}. \tag{6.35}$$

To derive the KdV equation for a one-dimensional quantum ion acoustic solitary waves from Equations (6.29), (6.30), and (6.33)–(6.35), we have used the RPT, and the independent variables are stretched in the the the same way as in Equation (6.22). Let us expand the dependent variables as

$$\psi = \psi^{(0)} + \sum_{n=1}^{\infty} \epsilon^{n+1}\psi^{(n)} \tag{6.36}$$

where $\psi = (n_e, n_p, n_i, u_i, \phi)$ with $\psi^{(0)} = (1, 1, 1, 0, 0)$. Using the expressions in (6.22) and (6.36) into Equations (6.29), (6.30), and (6.33)–(6.35), at the lowest order of ϵ, we get the dispersion relation as

$$\lambda = \sqrt{\frac{\sigma}{p + (1+p)\sigma}}. \tag{6.37}$$

In the next higher order of ϵ, we eliminate the second-order perturbed quantities, and after doing some simple algebraic operations, we obtain the nonplanar KdV equation as

$$\frac{\partial \phi^{(1)}}{\partial \tau} + A\phi^{(1)}\frac{\partial \phi^{(1)}}{\partial \xi} + B\frac{\partial^3 \phi^{(1)}}{\partial \xi^3} + \frac{\nu}{2\tau}\phi^{(1)} = 0, \tag{6.38}$$

with $A = \frac{\lambda^3}{2}\left(\frac{3}{\lambda^4} + 1 + p - \frac{p}{\sigma^2}\right)$ and $B = \frac{\lambda^3}{2}\left(1 - (1+p)\frac{H_e^2}{4} - \frac{pH_p^2}{4\sigma^2}\right)$. A and B are the coefficients of nonlinearity and dispersion, respectively. If we put $\nu = 0$ in Equation (6.38), we get the planar KdV equation, $\nu = 1, 2$ corresponding to the KdV equation in cylindrical and spherical geometries. It is important to mention here that the quantum diffraction of electrons and positrons plays a vital role in the wave dispersion but not in the nonlinear properties of the waves.

6.5   Nonplanar Gardner's or Modified Gardner's Equation

To derive the Modified Gardner's (MG) equation in nonplanar geometry, we consider a four-component, collision-free, unmagnetized dusty plasma, consisting of inertial ions, q-nonextensive distributed electrons, and stationary positively as well as negatively charged dust. At equilibrium, $n_{i0} + Z_{dp}n_{dp} = n_{e0} + Z_{dn}n_{dn}$, where n_{i0}, n_{e0}, n_{dp}, and n_{dn} are ion, electron, positive dust, and negative dust number density at equilibrium, respectively. Z_{dp} and Z_{dn} represent the charge state of positive and negative dust, respectively. The dynamics of DIAWs in such plasma can be explained by a set of normalized equations as follows:

$$\frac{\partial n_i}{\partial t} + \frac{1}{r^\nu}\frac{\partial}{\partial r}(r^\nu n_i u_i) = 0 \tag{6.39}$$

$$\frac{\partial u_i}{\partial t} + u_i\frac{\partial u_i}{\partial r} = -\frac{\partial \phi}{\partial r} \tag{6.40}$$

$$\frac{1}{r^\nu}\frac{\partial}{\partial r}\left(r^\nu \frac{\partial \phi}{\partial r}\right) = \rho \tag{6.41}$$

$$\rho = (1 - j\mu)n_e - n_i + j\mu \tag{6.42}$$

where $n_e = [1 + (q-1)\phi]^{\frac{1+q}{2(q-1)}}$. Here, n_j ($j = i$, and e, stands for ion, and electron, respectively), u_i, and ϕ are the number density, ion fluid velocity, and electrostatic potential, respectively. The normalizations are taken as

$$n_i \to \frac{n_i}{n_{i0}}, \quad u_i \to \frac{u_i}{C_i}, \quad \phi \to \frac{e\phi}{K_B T_e}, \quad r \to \frac{r}{\lambda_D}, \quad t \to \omega_{pi}t, \quad \rho \to \frac{\rho}{n_{i0}}$$

where $C_i = \sqrt{T_e/m_i}$, $\lambda_D = \sqrt{T_e/(4\pi n_{i0}e^2)}$, and $\omega_{pi} = \sqrt{4\pi n_{i0}e^2/m_i}$ are the ion-acoustic speed, the ion Debye radius, and the ion plasma frequency, respectively. T_e, e, m_i, and ρ are the electron temperature, electron charge, ion mass, and the net surface charge density, respectively. Here, $\mu = |Z_{dp}n_{dp} - Z_{dn}n_{dn}|/n_{i0}$. Also, $j = 1$ for $Z_{dn}n_{dn} > Z_{dp}n_{dp}$ and $j = -1$ for $Z_{dn}n_{dn} < Z_{dp}n_{dp}$. $j = -1$ and 1 stand for the positive and negative net dust charge, respectively. Relation (6.42) is valid for stationary or static (positive and negative) dust. This is a correct approximation for the DIA waves, whose frequency (ω) is much larger than both the positive dust plasma frequency (ω_{pdp}), and negative dust plasma frequency (ω_{pdn}), i.e., $\omega \gg \omega_{pdp}, \omega_{pdn}$.

To study finite amplitude DIA, DLs in a dusty plasma by using (6.39)–(6.42) by RPT, we use the new stretched coordinates as $\xi = \epsilon(r - \lambda t)$, $\tau = \epsilon^3 t$, and expand all the dependent variables in power series of ϵ as

$$\psi = \psi^{(0)} + \sum_{k=1}^{\infty}\epsilon^k \psi^{(k)} + \cdots \tag{6.43}$$

where $\psi = (n_i, u_i, \phi, \rho)$ with $\psi^{(0)} = (1,0,0,0)$. Now, expressing (6.39)–(6.42) in terms of ξ and τ, substituting (6.43) into the resulting equations, and equating the lowest order in ϵ, we get

$$u_i^{(1)} = \frac{\phi^{(1)}}{\lambda}, \quad n_i^{(1)} = \frac{\phi^{(1)}}{\lambda^2}, \quad \rho^{(1)} = 0, \quad \lambda = \sqrt{\frac{2}{(1-j\mu)(q+1)}}. \quad (6.44)$$

Again, equating the next order in ϵ, we get

$$\left.\begin{array}{c} u_i^{(2)} = \dfrac{\phi^2}{2\lambda^3} + \dfrac{\phi^{(2)}}{\lambda}, \quad n_i^{(2)} = \dfrac{3\phi^2}{2\lambda^4} + \dfrac{\phi^{(2)}}{\lambda^2}, \quad \rho^{(1)} = 0 \\[2mm] \rho^{(2)} = -\dfrac{1}{2}A\phi^2 = 0, \quad A = \dfrac{3}{\lambda^4} - \dfrac{(1-j\mu)(q+1)(3-q)}{4}. \end{array}\right\} \quad (6.45)$$

It is clear that $A = 0$ (since $\phi \neq 0$) and $A = 0$ when $q = q_c = \frac{3\{1-(1-j\mu)\}}{1+3(1-j\mu)}$. It is obvious that (6.45) is satisfied when $q = q_c$. We have numerically shown how q_c varies with μ. The results are displayed in Figure 6.3, which, in fact, represents the parametric regimes that correspond to $A = 0, A > 0$, and $A < 0$. So, for $|q - q_c| = \epsilon$ corresponding to $A = A_0$, one can write A_0 as $A_0 \simeq s \left(\frac{\partial A}{\partial q}\right)_{q=q_c} |q - q_c| = sA_q\epsilon$, where $A_q = \frac{(1-j\mu)}{2}\{3(1-j\mu)(q+1) + (q-1)\}$. Here, $s = 1$ for $q > q_c$, and $s = -1$ for $q < q_c$. So, when $q \neq q_c$, one can express $\rho^{(2)}$ as $\rho^{(2)} \simeq -\frac{1}{2}s\epsilon A_q\phi^2$, i.e., when $q \neq q_c$, $\rho^{(2)}$, it must be considered in the third-order Poisson's equation.

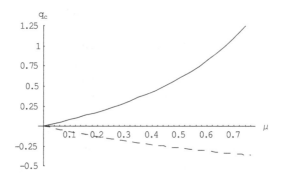

Fig. 6.3: Showing the variation of q_c [obtained from $A(q = q_c) = 0$] with μ for $j = 1$ and $j = -1$. The solid (dash) line represents this variation for $j = 1(-1)$.

To the next higher order in ϵ, we get

$$\left.\begin{array}{l} \dfrac{\partial n_i^{(1)}}{\partial \tau} - \lambda \dfrac{\partial n_i^{(3)}}{\partial \xi} + \dfrac{\partial u_i^{(3)}}{\partial \xi} + \dfrac{\partial}{\partial \xi}(n_i^{(1)} u_i^{(2)} + n_i^{(2)} u_i^{(1)}) + \dfrac{\nu}{\lambda \tau} u_i^{(1)} = 0 \\[3mm] \dfrac{\partial u_i^{(1)}}{\partial \tau} - \lambda \dfrac{\partial u_i^{(3)}}{\partial \xi} + \dfrac{\partial}{\partial \xi}(u_i^{(1)} u_i^{(2)}) + \dfrac{\partial \phi^{(3)}}{\partial \xi} = 0 \\[3mm] \dfrac{\partial^2 \phi}{\partial \xi^2} + \dfrac{1}{2} s A_q \phi^2 - (1 - j\mu) \left[\dfrac{(q+1)}{2} \phi^{(3)} \right. \\[3mm] \qquad + \dfrac{(q+1)(3-q)}{4} \phi \phi^{(2)} + \left. \dfrac{(q+1)(3-q)(5-3q)}{48} \phi^3 \right] + n_i^{(3)} = 0 \end{array}\right\}.$$

$$(6.46)$$

Now, using (6.44)–(6.46), finally, we obtain the MG equation as

$$\frac{\partial \phi}{\partial \tau} + \frac{\nu}{2\tau} \phi + m\phi \frac{\partial \phi}{\partial \zeta} + n\phi^2 \frac{\partial \phi}{\partial \zeta} + n_0 \frac{\partial^3 \phi}{\partial \zeta^3} = 0 \qquad (6.47)$$

where $m = sA_q n_0$, $n = m_0 n_0$, $m_0 = \dfrac{15}{2\lambda^6} - \dfrac{(1-j\mu)(q+1)(3-q)(5-3q)}{16}$, and $n_0 = \dfrac{\lambda^3}{2}$. For $\nu = 0$, Equation (6.47) converts to a standard Gardner's equation. We have derived the MG equation using RPT, which is valid beyond the KdV limit. We now turn to Equation (6.47) with the term $\dfrac{\nu}{2\tau} \phi$, which is due to the effect of nonplanar geometry. An exact analytical solution of Equation (6.47) is not possible. To study the effects of non-planar geometry on time-dependent DIAGSNs, we have solved Equation (6.47) numerically. We have used our numerical analysis taking the initial condition in the form of the stationary solution of Equation (6.47) without the term $\dfrac{\nu}{2\tau} \psi$. Our aim is now to numerically analyze the MG equation. However, for clear understanding, we first discuss the stationary solution of this standard Gardner's equation briefly (i.e., Equation (6.47) with $\nu = 0$).

To obtain the stationary solution of this Gardner's equation, we use the transformation $\zeta = \xi - u_0 \tau$, where u_0 is the constant speed. Now, we apply the conditions $\phi \to 0$, $\dfrac{d\phi}{d\xi} \to 0$, $\dfrac{d^2\phi}{d\xi^2} \to 0$ at $\xi \to \infty$. Thus, we get the stationary solution of the standard Gardner's equation as

$$\phi = \frac{\phi_m}{2} \left[1 + tanh\left(\frac{\xi}{\Delta}\right) \right] \qquad (6.48)$$

where $\phi_m = \dfrac{6su_0}{A_q n_0}$ and $\Delta = \sqrt{\dfrac{24}{-\phi_m^2 m_0}}$ are the amplitude and the width, respectively.

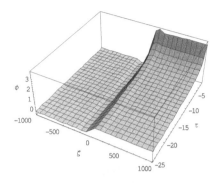

Fig. 6.4: Showing the effects of cylindrical geometry on DIA GSs for $j = 1$, $\mu = 0.509$, $s = 1$, and $q = 0.298$.

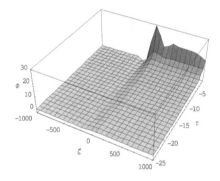

Fig. 6.5: Showing the effects of spherical geometry on DIA GSs for $j = 1$, $\mu = 0.509$, $s = 1$, and $q = 0.298$.

We have numerically solved Equation (6.47) and have studied the effects of cylindrical and spherical geometries on the time-dependent DIAGSNs. The results are depicted in Figures 6.4 and 6.5. Figure 6.4 explores how the effect of cylindrical geometry modifies DIA GSs for $j = 1$, while Figure 6.5 shows that the spherical geometry effect on the DIA for $j = 1$. It is displayed in Figures 6.4 and 6.5 that for a large value of $|\tau|$, i.e., at $\tau = -25$, the spherical and cylindrical SWs are similar to one-dimensional geometry. It can be concluded that for large $|\tau|$, $\frac{\nu}{2\tau}\psi$ is no longer dominant. But, when the value of $|\tau|$ decreases, the modified term $\frac{\nu}{2\tau}\psi$ becomes dominant, and cylindrical and spherical SW structures differ from the one-dimensional structure.

6.6 Nonplanar KP and KP Burgers' Equation

To derive the cylindrical/spherical KPB and the same type KP equation, we consider a plasma model having superthermal electrons, Boltzmann distributed positrons, and singly charged adiabatically hot positive ions. The phase velocity of IAWs is assumed to be much smaller than the electron and positron thermal velocities and larger than the ion thermal velocity $(v_{thi} \ll \omega/k \ll v_{the}, v_{thp})$. It should be noted that typically $T_e = T_p$. We, therefore, ignore the electron and positron inertia and write down the equation of motion for the ions. The basic system of equations in cylindrical and spherical geometry in such a plasma model is governed by

$$\frac{\partial n_i}{\partial t} + \vec{\nabla} \cdot (n_i \vec{v}_i) = 0, \tag{6.49}$$

$$\frac{\partial \vec{v}_i}{\partial t} + (\vec{v}_i \cdot \vec{\nabla})\vec{v}_i = \frac{e}{m_i}\vec{E} - \frac{1}{n_i m_i}\vec{\nabla}p_i + \mu\vec{\nabla}^2 \vec{v}_i \tag{6.50}$$

where n_i is the ion number density, v_i is the ion fluid velocity, m_i is the ion mass, e is the magnitude of the electron charge, E is the electric field, and μ is the kinematic viscosity, respectively. p_i is the pressure of the adiabatically hot ions and is represented by the following thermodynamic equation of state:

$$p_i = p_{i0}\left(\frac{n_i}{n_{i0}}\right)^{\gamma}. \tag{6.51}$$

Here, $p_{i0} = n_{i0}T_{i0}$ is the ion pressure at equilibrium, n_{i0} is the unperturbed ion density, T_{i0} is the ion equilibrium temperature, and the adiabatic constant is defined as $\gamma = \frac{(N+2)}{N}$, where N represents the number of degrees of freedom of the ions. Since the kinematic viscosity represents the diffusion in momentum, therefore, we include this contribution from ions and neglect the contribution of electrons and positrons. The electrons and positrons are assumed to obey the Kappa distribution and Boltzmann distribution, respectively, on the ion acoustic timescale and are expressed as $n_e = n_{e0}\left(1 - \frac{\phi}{\kappa - \frac{1}{2}}\right)^{-\kappa + \frac{1}{2}}$ and $n_p = n_{p0}exp\left(-\frac{e\phi}{T_p}\right)$. The parameter κ shapes predominantly the superthermal tail of the distribution, and the normalization has been provided for any value of the $\kappa > 1/2$. The system of equations is closed with the help of Poisson's equation,

$$\vec{\nabla} \cdot E = 4\pi e(n_i + n_p - n_e) \tag{6.52}$$

where n_p and n_e are the number densities, while T_p and T_e are temperatures of positrons and electrons, respectively. The electric field $E = -\nabla\phi$ so that ϕ represents the electrostatic wave potential. At equilibrium, $n_{i0} + n_{p0} = n_{e0}$, where n_{p0} and n_{e0} are the unperturbed positron and electron number densities, respectively.

The normalized form of continuity, momentum, and Poisson's equations in nonplanar cylindrical and spherical geometries are

$$\frac{\partial n_i}{\partial t} + \frac{1}{r^\nu}\frac{\partial(r^\nu n_i u_i)}{\partial r} + \frac{1}{r}\frac{\partial(n_i v_i)}{\partial \theta} + (\nu - 1)\frac{n_i v_i}{r}\cot\theta = 0, \tag{6.53}$$

$$\frac{\partial u_i}{\partial t} + u_i\frac{\partial u_i}{\partial r} + \frac{v_i}{r}\frac{\partial u_i}{\partial \theta} - \frac{v_i^2}{r} = -\frac{\partial\phi}{\partial r} - \frac{\sigma}{(1-\alpha)^{\gamma-1}}\gamma n_i^{\gamma-2}\frac{\partial n_i}{\partial r}$$

$$+ \eta\left[\nabla^2 u_i - \frac{\nu u_i}{r^2} - \frac{2}{r^2}\frac{\partial v_i}{\partial \theta} - \frac{2(\nu-1)v_i}{r^2}\cot\theta\right], \tag{6.54}$$

$$\frac{\partial v_i}{\partial t} + u_i\frac{\partial v_i}{\partial r} + \frac{v_i}{r}\frac{\partial v_i}{\partial \theta} + \frac{v_i u_i}{r} = -\frac{1}{r}\frac{\partial\phi}{\partial \theta} - \frac{\sigma}{r(1-\alpha)^{\gamma-1}}\gamma n_i^{\gamma-2}\frac{\partial n_i}{\partial \theta}$$

$$+ \eta\left[\nabla^2 v_i + \frac{2}{r^2}\frac{\partial u_i}{\partial \theta} - \frac{v_i}{r^2(sin^2\theta)^{\nu-1}}\right], \tag{6.55}$$

$$\frac{1}{r^\nu}\frac{\partial(r^\nu\frac{\partial\phi}{\partial r})}{\partial r} + \frac{1}{r^2}\frac{\partial^2\phi}{\partial\theta^2} + \frac{(\nu-1)}{r^2}\cot\theta\frac{\partial\phi}{\partial\theta} = \left(1 - \frac{\phi}{\kappa - \frac{1}{2}}\right)^{-\kappa+\frac{1}{2}}$$

$$- \alpha exp(-\phi) - n_i \tag{6.56}$$

where $\nu = 1, 2$ for cylindrical and spherical geometries, respectively. The expression for ∇^2 is different for cylindrical and spherical geometries and, therefore, caution needs to be exercised while opening it in the said geometries.

$$n_i \to \frac{n_i}{n_{e0}}, \quad v_i \to \frac{v_i}{C_s}, \quad \phi \to \frac{e\phi}{T_e}, \quad r \to \frac{r}{\lambda_{De}}, \quad t \to \frac{C_s}{\lambda_{De}}t. \tag{6.57}$$

$C_s = \sqrt{T_e/m_i}$, n_{e0}, and ϕ are the ion acoustic speed, electron equilibrium density, and the electrostatic wave potential, respectively. $\lambda_{De} = \sqrt{T_e/(4\pi n_{e0}e^2)}$ is the electron Debye length. Also, defined $\alpha = n_{p0}/n_{e0}$, $\sigma = T_{i0}/T_e$, and $\eta = \mu/(\lambda_{De}C_s)$.

To investigate the IASWs in unmagnetized *e-p-i* plasma, we stretch the independent variables as

$$\xi = \epsilon^{\frac{1}{2}}(r - \lambda t), \quad \chi = \epsilon^{-\frac{1}{2}}\theta, \quad \tau = \epsilon^{\frac{3}{2}}t \tag{6.58}$$

where λ is the wave phase velocity. Let us expand the perturbed quantities as

$$
\left.
\begin{aligned}
n_i &= (1 - \alpha) + \epsilon n_i^{(1)} + \epsilon^2 n_i^{(2)} + \epsilon^3 n_i^{(3)} + \cdots, \\
u_i &= \epsilon u_i^{(1)} + \epsilon^2 u_i^{(2)} + \epsilon^3 u_i^{(3)} + \cdots, \\
v_i &= \epsilon^{\frac{3}{2}} v_i^{(1)} + \epsilon^{\frac{5}{2}} v_i^{(2)} + \epsilon^{\frac{7}{2}} v_i^{(3)} + \cdots, \\
\phi &= \epsilon \phi^{(1)} + \epsilon^2 \phi^{(2)} + \epsilon^3 \phi^{(3)} + \cdots.
\end{aligned}
\right\}
\tag{6.59}
$$

The value of η is assumed to be small so that we may let $\eta = \epsilon^{\frac{1}{2}} \eta_0$, where η_0 is $O(1)$. Substituting Equations (6.58)–(6.59) in Equations (6.53)–(6.56) and collecting different powers of ϵ, we obtain the following equations to the lowest order in ϵ,

$$
n_i^{(1)} = \frac{(1 - \alpha)\phi^{(1)}}{\lambda^2 (1 - \frac{\gamma\sigma}{\lambda^2})}, \quad u_i^{(1)} = \frac{\phi^{(1)}}{\lambda(1 - \frac{\gamma\sigma}{\lambda^2})}.
\tag{6.60}
$$

From (6.60), we get

$$
\lambda = \sqrt{\frac{(1 - \alpha)(\kappa - \frac{1}{2}) + \gamma\sigma\{(\kappa + \frac{1}{2}) + \alpha(\kappa - \frac{1}{2})\}}{(\kappa + \frac{1}{2}) + \alpha(\kappa - \frac{1}{2})}}.
\tag{6.61}
$$

The next higher-order equations in ϵ are written as

$$
\frac{\partial n_i^{(1)}}{\partial \tau} - \lambda \frac{\partial n_i^{(2)}}{\partial \xi} + (1 - \alpha) \frac{\partial u_i^{(2)}}{\partial \xi} + \frac{\partial \left(n_i^{(1)} u_i^{(1)} \right)}{\partial \zeta}
$$

$$
+ \frac{(1 - \alpha)\nu}{\lambda\tau} u_i^{(1)} + \frac{(1 - \alpha)}{\lambda\tau} \frac{\partial v_i^{(1)}}{\partial \chi} + \frac{(1 - \alpha)}{\lambda\tau} \frac{(\nu - 1)}{\chi} v_i^{(1)} = 0,
\tag{6.62}
$$

$$
\frac{\partial u_i^{(1)}}{\partial \tau} - \lambda \frac{\partial u_i^{(2)}}{\partial \xi} + \frac{\gamma\sigma}{(1 - \alpha)} \frac{\partial n_i^{(2)}}{\partial \zeta} + u_i^{(1)} \frac{\partial u_i^{(1)}}{\partial \xi} + \frac{\partial \phi^{(2)}}{\partial \xi}
$$

$$
+ \frac{\gamma(\gamma - 2)\sigma}{(1 - \alpha)^2} n_i^{(1)} \frac{\partial n_i^{(1)}}{\partial \xi} - \eta_0 \frac{\partial^2 u_i^{(1)}}{\partial \xi^2} = 0,
\tag{6.63}
$$

$$
\frac{\partial v_i^{(1)}}{\partial \xi} - \frac{1}{\lambda^2 \tau} \left[1 + \frac{\gamma\sigma}{\lambda^2 (1 - \frac{\gamma\sigma}{\lambda^2})} \right] \frac{\partial \phi^{(1)}}{\partial \chi} = 0,
\tag{6.64}
$$

$$
n_i^{(2)} - \frac{(\kappa + \frac{1}{2})}{(\kappa - \frac{1}{2})} \phi^{(2)} - \frac{(\kappa + \frac{1}{2})(\kappa + \frac{3}{2})}{2(\kappa - \frac{1}{2})^2} (\phi^{(1)})^2
$$

$$
- \alpha\phi^{(2)} + \frac{\alpha}{2} (\phi^{(1)})^2 + \frac{\partial^2 \phi^{(1)}}{\partial \xi^2} = 0.
\tag{6.65}
$$

Now, eliminating $n_i^{(2)}$, $u_i^{(2)}$, and $\phi^{(2)}$ from Equations (6.62)–(6.65) and using relations given in Equations (6.60)–(6.61), we obtain KPB equation as

$$\frac{\partial}{\partial \xi}\left(\frac{\partial \phi^{(1)}}{\partial \tau} + A\phi^{(1)}\frac{\partial \phi^{(1)}}{\partial \xi} + B\frac{\partial^3 \phi^{(1)}}{\partial \xi^3} - C\frac{\partial^2 \phi^{(1)}}{\partial \xi^2} + \frac{\nu}{2\tau}\phi^{(1)}\right)$$
$$+ \frac{D}{\tau^2}\left(\frac{\partial^2 \phi^{(1)}}{\partial \chi^2} + \frac{\Xi(\nu-1)}{\chi}\frac{\partial \phi^{(1)}}{\partial \chi}\right) = 0 \qquad (6.66)$$

where $A = \frac{1}{2\lambda}\left[3 + \frac{\gamma\sigma(\gamma+1)\{(\kappa+\frac{1}{2})+\alpha(\kappa-\frac{1}{2})\}}{(1-\alpha)(\kappa-\frac{1}{2})} + \frac{(1-\alpha)\{\alpha(\kappa-\frac{1}{2})^2-(\kappa+\frac{1}{2})(\kappa+\frac{3}{2})\}}{\{(\kappa+\frac{1}{2})+\alpha(\kappa-\frac{1}{2})\}^2}\right]$,
$B = \frac{(1-\alpha)}{2\lambda}\frac{(\kappa-\frac{1}{2})^2}{\{(\kappa+\frac{1}{2})+\alpha(\kappa-\frac{1}{2})\}^2}$, $C = \frac{\eta_0}{2}$, and $D = \frac{1}{2\lambda}$. Here, $\Xi = 0, 1$ for planar and nonplanar geometries, respectively. A and C are the coefficients of nonlinearity and dissipation, respectively, whereas B and D are the coefficients of dispersion. If we put ν and Ξ equal to zero in Equation (6.66), we get the planar KPB equation with the only difference that the coefficient D would be $\frac{1}{2\lambda}$ in that case. The factor τ^2 comes due to the nonplanar effects. $\nu = 1, 2$ together with $\Xi = 1$ and corresponds to the KPB equations in the cylindrical and spherical geometries, respectively.

When $\eta_0 = 0$, i.e., the value of $C = 0$, then we find the KP equation in nonplanar geometry. Now putting $\eta_0 = 0$ in Equation (6.66), we get the KP equation as

$$\frac{\partial}{\partial \xi}\left(\frac{\partial \phi^{(1)}}{\partial \tau} + A\phi^{(1)}\frac{\partial \phi^{(1)}}{\partial \xi} + B\frac{\partial^3 \phi^{(1)}}{\partial \xi^3} + \frac{\nu}{2\tau}\phi^{(1)}\right)$$
$$+ \frac{D}{\tau^2}\left(\frac{\partial^2 \phi^{(1)}}{\partial \chi^2} + \frac{\Xi(\nu-1)}{\chi}\frac{\partial \phi^{(1)}}{\partial \chi}\right) = 0. \qquad (6.67)$$

The planar KPB equation is

$$\frac{\partial}{\partial \xi}\left(\frac{\partial \phi^{(1)}}{\partial \tau} + A\phi^{(1)}\frac{\partial \phi^{(1)}}{\partial \xi} + B\frac{\partial^3 \phi^{(1)}}{\partial \xi^3} - C\frac{\partial^2 \phi^{(1)}}{\partial \xi^2}\right) + D\frac{\partial^2 \phi^{(1)}}{\partial \chi^2} = 0. \qquad (6.68)$$

Using the transformation $\zeta = k(\xi + \chi - U\tau)$, where k is the dimensionless nonlinear wavenumber and U is the velocity of the nonlinear structure in the moving frame, the solution of the KPB Equation (6.68) is written as [?]

$$\phi^{(1)}(\xi, \chi, \tau) = \frac{6}{25}\frac{C^2}{AB}\left[1 - \tanh\frac{C}{10B}\left\{\xi + \chi - \left(\frac{6C^2}{25B} + D\right)\tau\right\}\right]$$
$$+ \frac{3}{25}\frac{C^2}{AB}\left[\text{sech}^2\frac{C}{10B}\left\{\xi + \chi - \left(\frac{6C^2}{25B} + D\right)\tau\right\}\right] \qquad (6.69)$$

where $k = C/10B$ and $U = \frac{6C^2}{25B} + D$.

We have numerically solved the nonplanar KPB Equation (6.68). The initial profile that we have used in our numerical analysis is (6.69). As Equation (6.69) is just a particular solution of Equation (6.68), it is necessary to plot numerical solutions of Equation (6.68) to clearly understand the behavior of the shock wave. The initial condition that we have used in our numerical results, in the form of the stationary solution (6.68) at $\tau = -20$. Figure 6.6 shows the cylindrical and spherical shock structures at different spectral indexes (κ). The shock height and width decrease as the value of the spectral index increases. Therefore, spectral index κ has a significant impact on the formation of shock structures. This result indicates that for small values of κ, the superthermal electrons in the tail of the distribution function increase, which plays a role to increase the height and width of the nonlinear structure. Figure 6.7 depicts the change in shock wave structure due to the variation of η_0. It is found that an increase in η_0 (meaning an increase in dissipation) considerably enhances the amplitude as well as the steepness of the shock front. By increasing the value of viscosity, i.e., dissipation in the system, the strength of shocks increases. It acquires more propagation speed in the case of spherical geometry.

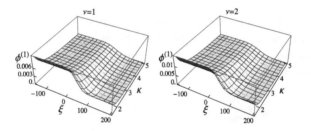

Fig. 6.6: Cylindrical and spherical shock structures evolved at $\tau = -10$ for several κ.

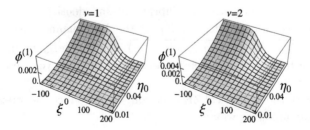

Fig. 6.7: Cylindrical and spherical shock structures evolved at $\tau = -10$ for several η_0.

6.7 Nonplanar ZK Equation

Now, we are going to investigate the characteristics of nonlinear wave structures in a homogeneous, collisionless magnetized plasma, comprising of nonextensive electrons and inertial ions in the framework of the cylindrical ZK equation. Here, the external magnetic field is $\vec{B}_0 = \hat{z}B_0$, where $\hat{z}$ is the unit vector along the z-direction and B_0 is the external static magnetic field. Accordingly, the basic system of normalized equations are as follows:

$$\frac{\partial n_i}{\partial t} + \frac{1}{r}\frac{\partial}{\partial r}(rn_iu_i) + \frac{1}{r}\frac{\partial}{\partial \theta}(n_iv_i) + \frac{\partial}{\partial z}(n_iw_i) = 0, \tag{6.70}$$

$$\frac{\partial u_i}{\partial t} + u_i\frac{\partial u_i}{\partial r} + \frac{v_i}{r}\frac{\partial u_i}{\partial \theta} + w_i\frac{\partial u_i}{\partial z} - \frac{v_i^2}{r} = -\frac{\partial \phi}{\partial r} + \Omega v_i, \tag{6.71}$$

$$\frac{\partial v_i}{\partial t} + u_i\frac{\partial v_i}{\partial r} + \frac{v_i}{r}\frac{\partial v_i}{\partial \theta} + w_i\frac{\partial v_i}{\partial z} - \frac{u_iv_i}{r} = -\frac{1}{r}\frac{\partial \phi}{\partial \theta} - \Omega u_i, \tag{6.72}$$

$$\frac{\partial w_i}{\partial t} + u_i\frac{\partial w_i}{\partial r} + \frac{v_i}{r}\frac{\partial w_i}{\partial \theta} + w_i\frac{\partial w_i}{\partial z} = -\frac{\partial \phi}{\partial z}, \tag{6.73}$$

$$\frac{1}{r}\frac{\partial}{\partial r}\left(r\frac{\partial \phi}{\partial r}\right) + \frac{1}{r^2}\frac{\partial^2 \phi}{\partial \theta^2} + \frac{\partial^2 \phi}{\partial z^2} = n_e - n_p - n_i \tag{6.74}$$

where $n_e = [1 + (q-1)\phi]^{\frac{1+q}{2(q-1)}}$ and n_j ($j = i, e$, and p stands for ion, electron, and positron, respectively) is the number density. Here, u_i, v_i, and w_i are the ion fluid speed in r, θ, and z directions, respectively. The normalizations are taken as

$$n_i \rightarrow \frac{n_i}{n_{i0}}, \quad u_i \rightarrow \frac{u_i}{v_s}, \quad v_i \rightarrow \frac{v_i}{v_s}, \quad w_i \rightarrow \frac{w_i}{v_s},$$

$$\phi \rightarrow \frac{e\phi}{K_BT_e}, \quad r \rightarrow \frac{r}{\lambda_D}, \quad t \rightarrow \omega_{i0}t$$

where n_{j0} is the unperturbed equilibrium plasma density, $v_s = \sqrt{K_BT_i/m_i}$ is the ion acoustic speed, and K_B is the Boltzmann constant. $\omega_{pi}^{-1} = \sqrt{m_i/(4\pi e^2n_{i0})}$, $\lambda_D = \sqrt{K_BT_e/(4\pi e^2n_{i0})}$, and $\Omega = (eB_0/m_ic)/\omega_{pi}$ are the ion plasma frequency, the Debye radius, and the ion cyclotron frequency, respectively.

To derive the cylindrical ZK equation, we introduce the stretch coordinates in the following way:

$$\xi = \epsilon^{1/2}(r - \lambda t), \quad \eta = \epsilon^{-1}\theta, \quad \zeta = \epsilon^{1/2}z, \quad \tau = \epsilon^{3/2}t. \tag{6.75}$$

Expanding the dependent variables as

$$\left.\begin{array}{l} n_i = 1 + \epsilon n_i^{(1)} + \epsilon^2 n_i^{(2)} + \cdots , \\ u_i = \epsilon u_i^{(1)} + \epsilon^2 u_i^{(2)} + \cdots , \\ v_i = \epsilon^{3/2} v_i^{(1)} + \epsilon^2 v_i^{(2)} + \cdots , \\ w_i = \epsilon^{3/2} w_i^{(1)} + \epsilon^2 w_i^{(2)} + \cdots , \\ \phi = \epsilon \phi^{(1)} + \epsilon^2 \phi^{(2)} + \cdots . \end{array}\right\} \tag{6.76}$$

Substituting Equations (6.75)–(6.76) into Equations (6.70)–(6.74) and equating the lowest power of ϵ, we get

$$n_i^{(1)} = \frac{1}{\lambda^2}\phi^{(1)}, u_i^{(1)} = \frac{1}{\lambda}\phi^{(1)}, v_i^{(1)} = -\frac{1}{\Omega}\frac{\partial \phi^{(1)}}{\partial \zeta}. \tag{6.77}$$

From (6.77), we get

$$\lambda = \sqrt{\frac{2(1-p)}{(q_e + 1)(q_p + 1)\sigma p}}. \tag{6.78}$$

To the next order of ϵ, one can get

$$\left.\begin{array}{l} w_i^{(1)} = \frac{1}{\lambda \Omega \tau}\frac{\partial \phi^{(1)}}{\partial \eta}, \frac{1}{\lambda \tau}\frac{\partial v_i^{(1)}}{\partial \eta} + \frac{\partial w_i^{(1)}}{\partial \zeta} = 0, \\[2mm] \frac{\partial v_i^{(1)}}{\partial \xi} = -\frac{\Omega}{\lambda}w_i^{(2)}, \frac{\partial w_i^{(1)}}{\partial \xi} = \frac{\Omega}{\lambda}v_i^{(2)}, \\[2mm] \frac{\partial^2 \phi^{(1)}}{\partial \xi^2} + \frac{1}{\lambda^2 \tau^2}\frac{\partial^2 \phi^{(1)}}{\partial \eta^2} + \frac{\partial^2 w_i^{(1)}}{\partial \zeta^2} = \beta_1 \phi^{(2)} + \beta_2 [\phi^{(1)}]^2 - n_i^{(2)} \end{array}\right\} \tag{6.79}$$

where $\beta_1 = \frac{1}{\lambda^2}$ and $\beta_2 = \frac{1}{4(1-p)}[(1 + q_e)(3 - q_e) - (1 + q_p)(3 - q_p)p\sigma^2]$.
    The next higher order of ϵ gives

$$\left.\begin{array}{l} \frac{\partial n_i^{(1)}}{\partial \tau} - \lambda \frac{\partial n_i^{(2)}}{\partial \xi} + \frac{\partial}{\partial \xi}(n_i^{(1)} u_i^{(1)}) = 0, \\[2mm] \frac{\partial u_i^{(2)}}{\partial \xi} + \frac{u_i^{(1)}}{\lambda \tau} + \frac{1}{\lambda \tau}\frac{\partial v_i^{(2)}}{\partial \eta} + \frac{\partial w_i^{(2)}}{\partial \zeta} = 0, \\[2mm] \frac{\partial u_i^{(1)}}{\partial \tau} - \lambda \frac{\partial u_i^{(2)}}{\partial \xi} + u_i^{(1)}\frac{\partial u_i^{(1)}}{\partial \xi} = -\frac{\partial \phi^{(2)}}{\partial \xi}. \end{array}\right\} \tag{6.80}$$

Eliminating the second-order derivatives of n_i, u_i, and ϕ from the Equations (6.79)–(6.81) with the help of Equation (6.77), we finally obtain the

ZK equation in cylindrical geometry as

$$\frac{\partial \phi^{(1)}}{\partial \tau} + \frac{\phi^{(1)}}{2\tau} + A\phi^{(1)}\frac{\partial \phi^{(1)}}{\partial \xi} + B\frac{\partial^3 \phi^{(1)}}{\partial \xi^3}$$

$$+ C\frac{\partial}{\partial \xi}\left(\frac{1}{v_0^2 \tau^2}\frac{\partial^2 \phi^{(1)}}{\partial \eta^2} + \frac{\partial^2 \phi^{(1)}}{\partial \zeta^2}\right) = 0 \tag{6.81}$$

where $A = \frac{1}{2v_0}[3 - 2\lambda^4 \beta_2]$, $B = \frac{\lambda^3}{2}$, and $C = \frac{\lambda^3}{2}\left(1 + \frac{1}{\Omega^2}\right)$. Equation (6.81) differs with the ZK equation (in planar geometry) in terms of $\frac{\phi^{(1)}}{2\tau}$ and $\frac{1}{v_0^2 \tau^2}$ $\left(\text{the coefficient of } \frac{\partial^2 \phi^{(1)}}{\partial \eta^2}\right)$. These mentioned terms occur in the equation due to the cylindrical geometry, which does not appear in planar geometry.

6.8 Nonplanar ZKB Equation

We consider a homogeneous, collisionless magnetoplasma, consisting of ions and q-nonextensive distributed electrons, by taking into account the viscosity. The plasma is confined to an external magnetic field $\vec{B}_0 = \hat{x}B_0$, where $\hat{x}$ is the unit vector along the x-direction and B_0 is the external static magnetic field. Accordingly, the basic normalized equations are

$$\frac{\partial n_i}{\partial t} + \vec{\nabla} \cdot (n_i \cdot \vec{u}) = 0, \tag{6.82}$$

$$\frac{\partial \vec{u}}{\partial t} + (\vec{u} \cdot \vec{\nabla})\vec{u} = -(\vec{\nabla}\phi) + \Omega(\vec{u} \times \hat{x}) + \mu\vec{\nabla}^2\vec{u}, \tag{6.83}$$

$$\vec{\nabla}^2\phi = n_e - (1 + \alpha)n_i + \alpha \tag{6.84}$$

where n_j ($j = i$ and e for ion and electron, respectively) is the number density and $\vec{u}(u_i, v_i, w_i)$ is the ion fluid speed. Here, the normalizations are taken as

$$n_i \to \frac{n_i}{n_{e0}}, \quad u \to \frac{u}{v_s}, \quad \phi \to \frac{e\phi}{K_B T_e}, \quad r \to \frac{r}{\lambda_D}, \quad t \to \omega_{pi}t \tag{6.85}$$

where n_{j0} is the unperturbed equilibrium plasma density and $\alpha = z_d n_{d0}/n_{e0}$. Here, $v_s = \sqrt{K_B T_e/m_i}$, K_B are the ion acoustic velocity and the Boltzmann constant, respectively. $\omega_{pi}^{-1} = \sqrt{m_i/(4\pi e^2 n_{e0})}$, $\lambda_D = \sqrt{K_B T_e/(4\pi e^2 n_{e0})}$, and $\Omega = (eB_0/m_i c)/\omega_{pi}$ are the ion plasma period, the Debye radius, and the ion cyclotron frequency, respectively. c is the velocity of light and μ is the kinematic viscosity.

To derive the ZK Burgers' equation, we use the stretched variables as

$$\xi = \epsilon^{1/2}(x - \lambda t), \quad \eta = \epsilon^{1/2}y, \quad \zeta = \epsilon^{1/2}z, \quad \tau = \epsilon^{3/2}t, \quad \mu = \epsilon^{1/2}\mu_0 \tag{6.86}$$

where μ is scaled in such a way that μ_0 becomes the effective viscosity. Expanding the dependent variables as

$$\left.\begin{aligned}
n_i &= 1 + \epsilon n_i^{(1)} + \epsilon^2 n_i^{(2)} + \cdots, \\
u_i &= \epsilon u_i^{(1)} + \epsilon^2 u_i^{(2)} + \cdots, \\
v_i &= \epsilon^{3/2} v_i^{(1)} + \epsilon^2 v_i^{(2)} + \cdots, \\
w_i &= \epsilon^{3/2} w_i^{(1)} + \epsilon^2 w_i^{(2)} + \cdots, \\
\phi &= \epsilon \phi^{(1)} + \epsilon^2 \phi^{(2)} + \cdots.
\end{aligned}\right\} \tag{6.87}$$

Substituting Equations (6.86)–(6.87) into Equations (6.82)–(6.86) and equating the lowest power of ϵ, we obtain

$$n_i^{(1)} = \frac{1}{\lambda} u_i^{(1)}, \quad u_i^{(1)} = \frac{1}{\lambda}\phi^{(1)}, \quad v_i^{(1)} = -\frac{1}{\Omega}\frac{\partial \phi^{(1)}}{\partial \zeta}, \quad \lambda = \sqrt{\frac{2(1+\alpha)}{q+1}}. \tag{6.88}$$

To the next order of ϵ, one gets

$$\left.\begin{aligned}
w_i^{(1)} &= \frac{1}{\Omega}\frac{\partial \phi^{(1)}}{\partial \eta}, \quad \frac{\partial v_i^{(1)}}{\partial \xi} = -\frac{\Omega}{\lambda} w_i^{(2)}, \quad \frac{\partial w_i^{(1)}}{\partial \xi} = \frac{\Omega}{\lambda} v_i^{(2)}, \\
\frac{\partial^2 \phi^{(1)}}{\partial \xi^2} &+ \frac{\partial^2 \phi^{(1)}}{\partial \eta^2} + \frac{\partial^2 w_i^{(1)}}{\partial \zeta^2} = \beta_1 \phi^{(2)} + \beta_2 (\phi^{(1)})^2 - (1+\alpha)n_i^{(2)}
\end{aligned}\right\} \tag{6.89}$$

where $\beta_1 = \frac{q+1}{2}$ and $\beta_2 = \frac{(q+1)(3-q)}{8}$.

The next higher order of ϵ gives

$$\left.\begin{aligned}
\frac{\partial n_i^{(1)}}{\partial \tau} &- \lambda \frac{\partial n_i^{(2)}}{\partial \xi} + \frac{\partial}{\partial \xi}(n_i^{(1)} u_i^{(1)}) + \frac{\partial u_i^{(2)}}{\partial \xi} + \frac{\partial v_i^{(2)}}{\partial \eta} + \frac{\partial w_i^{(2)}}{\partial \zeta} = 0, \\
\frac{\partial u_i^{(1)}}{\partial \tau} &- \lambda \frac{\partial u_i^{(2)}}{\partial \xi} + u_i^{(1)}\frac{\partial u_i^{(1)}}{\partial \xi} + \frac{\partial \phi^{(2)}}{\partial \xi} = \mu_0 \left(\frac{\partial^2 u_i^{(1)}}{\partial \xi^2} + \frac{\partial^2 u_i^{(1)}}{\partial \eta^2} + \frac{\partial^2 u_i^{(1)}}{\partial \zeta^2} \right).
\end{aligned}\right\} \tag{6.90}$$

Eliminating $u_i^{(2)}$ and $n_i^{(2)}$ from Equation (6.90) by using Equations (6.88)–(6.89), we get

$$(1+\alpha)\left(\frac{2}{\lambda^3}\frac{\partial \phi^{(1)}}{\partial \tau} + \frac{3}{\lambda^4}\phi^{(1)}\frac{\partial \phi^{(1)}}{\partial \xi} + \frac{1}{\lambda^2}\frac{\partial \phi^{(2)}}{\partial \xi}\right.$$
$$\left. + \frac{1}{\Omega^2}\frac{\partial}{\partial \xi}\left(\frac{\partial^2 \phi^{(1)}}{\partial \eta^2} + \frac{\partial^2 \phi^{(1)}}{\partial \zeta^2}\right)\right) + \frac{\partial}{\partial \xi}\left(\frac{\partial^2 \phi^{(1)}}{\partial \eta^2} + \frac{\partial^2 \phi^{(1)}}{\partial \zeta^2}\right) + \frac{\partial^3 \phi^{(1)}}{\partial \xi^3}$$
$$- \beta_1 \frac{\partial \phi^{(2)}}{\partial \xi} - 2\beta_2 \phi^{(1)}\frac{\partial \phi^{(1)}}{\partial \xi} - \frac{\mu_0}{\lambda^3}\left(\frac{\partial^2 \phi^{(1)}}{\partial \xi^2} + \frac{\partial^2 \phi^{(1)}}{\partial \eta^2} + \frac{\partial^2 \phi^{(1)}}{\partial \zeta^2}\right) = 0.$$

$$(6.91)$$

Thus, we finally obtain

$$\frac{\partial \phi^{(1)}}{\partial \tau} + A\phi^{(1)}\frac{\partial \phi^{(1)}}{\partial \xi} + B\frac{\partial^3 \phi^{(1)}}{\partial \xi^3} + C\frac{\partial}{\partial \xi}\left(\frac{\partial^2 \phi^{(1)}}{\partial \eta^2} + \frac{\partial^2 \phi^{(1)}}{\partial \zeta^2}\right)$$
$$- D\left(\frac{\partial^2 \phi^{(1)}}{\partial \xi^2} + \frac{\partial^2 \phi^{(1)}}{\partial \eta^2} + \frac{\partial^2 \phi^{(1)}}{\partial \zeta^2}\right) = 0,$$

$$(6.92)$$

which is the ZKB equation, where $A = \frac{\lambda^3}{2}\left(\frac{3}{\lambda^4} - \frac{2\beta_2}{1+\alpha}\right)$, $B = \frac{\lambda^3}{2(1+\alpha)}$, $C = \frac{\lambda^3}{2}\left(\frac{1}{1+\alpha} + \frac{1}{\Omega^2}\right)$, and $D = \frac{\mu_0}{2}$.

References

[1] J. R. Franz, P. M. Kintner, and J. S. Pickett, *Geophys. Res. Lett.* 25, 2041 (1998).

[2] S. Maxon and J. Viecelli, *Phys. Rev. Lett.* 32, 4 (1974a).

[3] S. Maxon and J. Viecelli, *Phys. Fluids* 17, 1614 (1974b).

Chapter 7

Collision of Solitons

7.1 Introduction

In theoretical studies of nonlinear science, propagation and collision of solitary waves occupy an important place. The interesting features of soliton collision are as follows: when two solitons collide, they interact, exchange energies and positions with each other, then separate, and finally regain their original waveforms. Solitons ensure their asymptotic preservation of form following an interaction. We can realize this by applying two consecutive voltage pulses in plasmas: the first pulse generates a small amplitude soliton and the second pulse produces a large amplitude one. Since the large amplitude soliton travels faster, it will overtake the smaller one. The larger pulse overtakes the smaller pulse, and the amplitude of the front pulse increases when the amplitude of the larger pulse decreases. Generally, two kinds of one-dimensional interaction occur. First, when two or more different amplitude solitons propagate in the same direction, they will overtake each other after some time. This phenomenon is called an overtaking collision. Second, when two solitons propagate in opposite directions, they interact for a relatively short time, emerge, and finally separate with phase shifts. This phenomenon is known as a head-on collision. Moreover, solitons may also interact obliquely while moving in a plane at an arbitrary angle to each other. This interaction occurs at some event altering the trajectories of colliding waves, and this kind of interaction is known as an oblique collision.

7.2 Head-on Collision

Following voltage pulse generation between two plasmas, two types of scenarios may be seen. As a consequence, the generation of the voltage pulse is made from the same end of the plasma and then the so-called overtaking collision is depicted. When a third independent discharge is put at the opposite end of the plasma, in which the waves are detected, then a soliton is excited at each end of the main plasma simultaneously. The solitons propagate towards each other and interact near the center of the plasma. It is a relatively new concept in plasma dynamics. Initially, they interact, exchange their energies and positions with one another, then separate off, and finally regain their original waveforms. Throughout the whole process of collision, the solitary waves are stable and preserve their identities. The main effect due to the collision is their phase shift. This property of solitary waves can only be preserved in a conservative system.

Let us take two independent moving solitary waves: $aS(\xi)$ and $bS(\eta)$. $S(x) = sech^2(\frac{x}{2})$ is a progressive wave of the permanent type that satisfies the KdV equation. The variables ξ and η denote the right and left going wave frame coordinates, respectively. The constants a and b specify the height of the waves. The experimental results show no observable nonlinear behavior upon interaction. The two peaks add up linearly when they overlap and penetrate each other. No deformation of the trajectories of the solitons is observed by H. Ikezi *et al.* [1]. T. Maxworthy [2] tested the higher-order effects in the head-on collision of two solitons, demonstrated by numerical computation. To illustrate this theoretically, let us take two solitons ϕ_α and ϕ_β in the plasma. They are asymptotically far apart in the initial state, then travel toward each other, and after a certain time, they interact, collide, and finally depart. Hence, we expect that the collision will be quasielastic, so it will only cause shifts of the post-collision trajectories (phase shift). To analyze the effects of a collision, we employ an extended version of the PLK method which is discussed in the following:

PLK method: Poincaré developed a method for finding the periodic solution of a system of the first-order equation. The equation is written as

$$\frac{dx_i}{dt} = X_i(x_1, x_2, \ldots \ldots x_i, \ldots \ldots x_n; \varepsilon) \quad (i = 1, 2, \ldots n)$$

where t is the time variable and ε is a small parameter representing the perturbation influence. The equation with $\varepsilon = 0$ corresponds to the unperturbed system, and a periodic solution with period $T^{(0)}$ can be easily obtained from it. The essence of Poincaré's method is that not only the variables $x_i = x_i^0 + \sum_{k=1}^{\infty} \varepsilon^k x_i^k + \cdots$ are expanded but also the period $T = T^0 + \sum_{k=1}^{\infty} \varepsilon^k T^k + \cdots$ is expanded. This method has many applications in the theory of nonlinear oscillation. Poincaré's method of perturbation is based on the concept of expansion of the exact solution in a power series of small parameter ε, where the zeroth-order solution being independent of ε, the first-order solution is proportional to ε, etc. Lighthill's method removes these difficulties. In this principle, the dependent variable u is expanded, and the independent variables x and y are also expanded in the power series of ε. By letting $u = u^0(\xi, \eta) + \sum_{k=1}^{\infty} \varepsilon^k u^k(\xi, \eta) + \cdots$, $x = \xi + \sum_{k=1}^{\infty} \varepsilon^k x^k(\xi, \eta) + \cdots$, and $y = \eta + \sum_{k=1}^{\infty} \varepsilon^k y^k(\xi, \eta) + \cdots$, where ξ and η take the place of the original independent variables x and y. $u^0(\xi, \eta)$ is simply the zeroth-order solution of the classical perturbation method with ξ and η replacing x and y. When we neglect the higher-order terms in u, the approximate solution is simply the zeroth-order perturbation solution with the stretched coordinates. Lighthill applied this method to solve the problems involving partial differential equations when the zeroth-order solution was obtained from a reduced linear equation of equal order. In many problems, a good zeroth-order approximation can be obtained only if a boundary layer solution is used. Kuo first recognized this necessity in his solution to the problem of the laminar incompressible boundary layer on a flat plate. It constitutes a further extension of Poincaré's original concept.

Extended PLK method: In PLK method, the dependent variables are expanded and the independent variables are also stretched. The extended PLK method in one-dimensional plasma evolves and the dependent variables are expanded as earlier. The independent variables are stretched in opposite directions (one in positive direction and another in negative direction). We consider $n_i = 1 + \sum_{k=1}^{\infty} \varepsilon^{k+1} n_k + \cdots$, $u_i = u_0 + \sum_{k=1}^{\infty} \varepsilon^{k+1} u_k \cdots$, and $\psi = \sum_{k=1}^{\infty} \varepsilon^{k+1} \psi_k + \cdots$.

The independent variables are expressed as

$$\xi = \varepsilon(x - c_1 t) + \varepsilon^2 P_0(\eta, \tau) + \varepsilon^3 P_1(\eta, \xi, \tau) + \cdots,$$

$$\eta = \varepsilon(x + c_2 t) + \varepsilon^2 Q_0(\xi, \tau) + \varepsilon^3 Q_1(\eta, \xi, \tau) + \cdots,$$

$$\tau = \varepsilon^3 t$$

where ξ and η denote the trajectories of two solitons traveling towards each other and c_1 and c_2 are the unknown phase velocities.

Perturbation solution for two solitary waves colliding head-on: Let us consider two solitary waves initially far apart, of small but finite amplitude and moving towards each other. The time evolution of their interaction and the final state after their collision will be our main concern.

We introduce the following co-ordinates transformations (wave frames) as

$$\xi_0 = \varepsilon^{\frac{1}{2}} k (x - C_R t), \quad \eta_0 = \varepsilon^{\frac{1}{2}} l (x + C_L t) \tag{7.1}$$

where $0 < \varepsilon < 1$, and ε is the dimensionless parameter representing the order of magnitude of the wave amplitude. The scaling of the horizontal wavelength following Ursell's relationship is taken as $\varepsilon^{\frac{1}{2}}$, leaving k and l as the wavenumbers of order unity for the right and left going waves, respectively. The right and left going wave speeds are C_R and C_L and are related to the amplitudes of the waves. Anticipating that difficulty (might show up in our perturbation method), we introduce the following transformations of wave-framed co-ordinates with phase functions as

$$\xi_0 = \xi - \varepsilon k \theta(\xi, \eta), \quad \eta_0 = \eta - \varepsilon l \phi(\xi, \eta) \tag{7.2}$$

where $\theta(\xi, \eta)$ and $\phi(\xi, \eta)$ are to be determined in the process of the perturbational solution. These functions, introduced to make asymptotic approximations, allow us to calculate phase changes due to collision. Using (7.1) and (7.2), we obtain the transformation between derivatives as

$$\left. \begin{aligned} \frac{\partial}{\partial t} + C_R \frac{\partial}{\partial x} &= \frac{\varepsilon^{\frac{1}{2}}}{D} (C_R + C_L) \left[l \frac{\partial}{\partial \eta} + \varepsilon k l \left(\frac{\partial \theta}{\partial \eta} \frac{\partial}{\partial \xi} - \frac{\partial \theta}{\partial \xi} \frac{\partial}{\partial \eta} \right) \right] \\ \frac{\partial}{\partial t} - C_L \frac{\partial}{\partial x} &= -\frac{\varepsilon^{\frac{1}{2}}}{D} (C_R + C_L) \left[k \frac{\partial}{\partial \xi} + \varepsilon k l \left(\frac{\partial \phi}{\partial \xi} \frac{\partial}{\partial \eta} - \frac{\partial \phi}{\partial \eta} \frac{\partial}{\partial \xi} \right) \right] \end{aligned} \right\} \tag{7.3}$$

where $D = \left(1 - \varepsilon k \frac{\partial \theta}{\partial \xi} \right) \left(1 - \varepsilon l \frac{\partial \phi}{\partial \eta} \right) - \varepsilon^2 k l \frac{\partial \theta}{\partial \eta} \frac{\partial \phi}{\partial \xi}$, $\theta(\xi, \eta) = \theta_0(\eta) + \varepsilon \theta_1(\xi, \eta) + \cdots$, $\phi(\xi, \eta) = \phi_0(\xi) + \varepsilon \phi_1(\xi, \eta) + \cdots$.

Phase shifts in head-on collisions: We know that the general solution of the standard wave equation $\frac{\partial^2 \phi}{\partial t^2} = c^2 \frac{\partial^2 \phi}{\partial x^2}$ is given by $\phi(x, t) = f(x - ct) + g(x + ct)$, where ϕ has some property associated with the wave and f and g are arbitrary functions. $f(x - ct)$ represents a progressive wave, moving in the positive direction of the x-axis with a constant speed c, while $g(x + ct)$ represents a progressive wave, moving in the negative direction of the x-axis with the same speed c. The arguments $x - ct$ and $x + ct$ are called the phase of f and g waves, respectively. Both of these are constants for space–time.

The phase shift is any change that occurs in the phase due to collision. In a head-on collision, the change of position occurs due to the interaction of two solitons. Let the trajectories of the two solitary waves be given by

$$\left. \begin{array}{l} \xi = \epsilon(x - ct) + \epsilon^2 P^{(0)}(\eta, \tau) + \epsilon^3 P^{(1)}(\xi, \eta, \tau) + \cdots \\ \eta = \epsilon(x + ct) + \epsilon^2 Q^{(0)}(\xi, \tau) + \epsilon^3 Q^{(1)}(\xi, \eta, \tau) + \cdots \end{array} \right\} \qquad (7.4)$$

where ξ and η denote the trajectories of two solitons traveling toward each other (i.e., to the right and left, respectively), both with the same phase velocity c. Then, clearly $P^{(0)}(\eta, \tau)$ and $Q^{(0)}(\xi, \tau)$ are the leading phase changes due to head-on collision. The corresponding phase shifts $\triangle P^{(0)}$ and $\triangle Q^{(0)}$ and the difference between the post-collision and past-collision leading phase changes are

$$\left. \begin{array}{l} \triangle P^{(0)} = P^{(0)}_{post\text{-}collision} - P^{(0)}_{past\text{-}collision} \\ \qquad = \epsilon(x - ct)|_{\xi=0, \eta=\infty} - \epsilon(x - ct)|_{\xi=0, \eta=-\infty} \\ \triangle Q^{(0)} = Q^{(0)}_{post\text{-}collision} - Q^{(0)}_{past\text{-}collision} \\ \qquad = \epsilon(x + ct)|_{\xi=\infty, \eta=0} - \epsilon(x + ct)|_{\xi=-\infty, \eta=0}. \end{array} \right\} \qquad (7.5)$$

7.2.1 *Head-on collision of solitary waves in planar geometry*

Now, we shall study the variation of phase shift and the trajectories of the two solitary waves after the collision. To obtain the phase shift and the trajectories, a couple of KdV equations have to be derived by employing the extended PLK method.

Derivation of KdV equations: Let us consider two-component plasma consisting of cold ions and nonextensive electrons. Let us analyze the head-on collision of IASWs in this model. Accordingly, the set of normalized equations are

$$\frac{\partial n_i}{\partial t} + \frac{\partial(n_i u_i)}{\partial x} = 0, \qquad (7.6)$$

$$\frac{\partial u_i}{\partial t} + u_i \frac{\partial u_i}{\partial x} = -\frac{\partial \phi}{\partial x}, \qquad (7.7)$$

$$\frac{\partial^2 \phi}{\partial^2 x} = n_e - n_i \qquad (7.8)$$

where $n_e = [1 + (q-1)\phi]^{\frac{1+q}{2(q-1)}}$. The normalization and notation are accordingly the same as in Section 4.4. Now, we assume that the two solitons α and β in the plasma, which are asymptotically far apart in the initial state,

travel towards each other. After some time, they interact, collide, and
then depart. Let the solitons have small amplitudes $\sim\varepsilon$, where ε is a small
parameter characterizing the strength of nonlinearity, and the interaction
between two solitons is weak. Hence, we expect that the collision will be
quasielastic, and so it will only cause shifts of the post-collision trajectories (phase shift). To analyze the effects of a collision, let us employ the
extended PLK method. According to this method, the dependent variables
are expanded as

$$n_i = 1 + \sum_{k=1}^{\infty} \varepsilon^{k+1} n_k, \quad u_i = 0 + \sum_{k=1}^{\infty} \varepsilon^{k+1} u_k, \quad \phi = 0 + \sum_{k=1}^{\infty} \varepsilon^{k+1} \phi_k. \quad (7.9)$$

The independent variables are written as

$$\left. \begin{array}{l} \xi = \varepsilon(x - \lambda t) + \varepsilon^2 P_0(\eta, \tau) + \varepsilon^3 P_1(\eta, \xi, \tau) + \cdots, \\[2mm] \eta = \varepsilon(x + \lambda t) + \varepsilon^2 Q_0(\xi, \tau) + \varepsilon^3 Q_1(\eta, \xi, \tau) + \cdots, \\[2mm] \tau = \varepsilon^3 t \end{array} \right\} \quad (7.10)$$

where ξ and η denote the trajectories of two solitons traveling towards each
other and λ is the unknown phase velocity of IASWs to be determined.
The variables of $P_0(\eta, \tau)$ and $Q_0(\xi, \tau)$ are also to be determined. Substituting Equations (7.9) and (7.10) into Equations (7.6)–(7.8) and equating
the quantities with equal power of ε, we obtain the coupled equations in
different orders of ε. For the leading order, we have

$$\left. \begin{array}{l} -\lambda \dfrac{\partial n_1}{\partial \xi} + \lambda \dfrac{\partial n_1}{\partial \eta} + \left(\dfrac{\partial u_1}{\partial \xi} + \dfrac{\partial u_1}{\partial \eta} \right) = 0, \\[4mm] -\lambda \dfrac{\partial u_1}{\partial \xi} + \lambda \dfrac{\partial u_1}{\partial \eta} + \left(\dfrac{\partial \phi_1}{\partial \xi} + \dfrac{\partial \phi_1}{\partial \eta} \right) = 0, \\[4mm] n_1 - \left(\dfrac{1+q}{2} \right) \phi_1 = 0. \end{array} \right\} \quad (7.11)$$

Solving Equation (7.11), we get

$$\phi_1 = \phi_\xi(\xi, \tau) + \phi_\eta(\eta, \tau), \quad (7.12)$$

$$n_1 = \left(\frac{1+q}{2} \right) [\phi_\xi(\xi, \tau) + \phi_\eta(\eta, \tau)], \quad (7.13)$$

$$u_1 = \frac{1}{\lambda} \phi_\xi(\xi, \tau) - \frac{1}{\lambda} \phi_\eta(\eta, \tau). \quad (7.14)$$

With the solvability condition [i.e., the condition required to obtain a uniquely defined n_1 and u_1 from Equations (7.13) and (7.14), when ϕ_1 is given by (7.12)], the phase velocities $\lambda = \left(\frac{2}{q+1}\right)^{1/2} + u_0$ and $\lambda = \left(\frac{2}{q+1}\right)^{1/2} - u_0$ are also obtained. Now, we shall determine the unknown function ϕ_ξ and ϕ_η in the next orders. Relations (7.12)–(7.14) imply that, at the leading order, we have two waves: one $\phi_\xi(\xi, \tau)$ that travels to the right and another $\phi_\eta(\eta, \tau)$ that travels to the left.

The next higher order leads to

$$\lambda_1 \frac{\partial^2 u_3}{\partial\xi\partial\eta} = -\frac{\partial}{\partial\xi}\left(\frac{\partial\phi_\xi}{\partial\tau} + A\phi_\xi\frac{\partial\phi_\xi}{\partial\xi} + B\frac{\partial^3\phi_\xi}{\partial\xi^3}\right) - \frac{\partial}{\partial\eta}\left(\frac{\partial\phi_\eta}{\partial\tau} - A\phi_\eta\frac{\partial\phi_\eta}{\partial\eta}\right.$$

$$\left. - B\frac{\partial^3\phi_\eta}{\partial\eta^3}\right) - \left(C\frac{\partial P0}{\partial\eta} - D\phi_\eta\right)\frac{\partial^2\phi_\xi}{\partial\xi^2} + \left(C\frac{\partial Q0}{\partial\xi} - D\phi_\xi\right)\frac{\partial^2\phi_\eta}{\partial\eta^2}$$

$$(7.15)$$

where $A = \frac{1}{2}\left[-(\lambda_1)^{3/2}\left\{1 - \left(\frac{q-1}{2}\right)^2\right\} + 3\left(\frac{1}{\lambda_1}\right)^{1/2}\right]$, $B = \frac{1}{2}(\lambda_1)^{3/2}$, $C = \frac{1}{2}(\lambda_1)^{1/2}$, $D = \frac{1}{2}\left[(\lambda_1)^{3/2}\left\{1 - \left(\frac{q-1}{2}\right)^2\right\} + (\lambda_1)^{1/2}\right]$, and $\lambda_1 = \left(\frac{2}{q+1}\right)$.

On integration of the above equation with respect to the variables ξ and η, one can get

$$\lambda_1 u_3 = -\int\left(\frac{\partial\phi_\xi}{\partial\tau} + A\phi_\xi\frac{\partial\phi_\xi}{\partial\xi} + B\frac{\partial^3\phi_\xi}{\partial\xi^3}\right)d\eta$$

$$-\int\left(\frac{\partial\phi_\eta}{\partial\tau} - A\phi_\eta\frac{\partial\phi_\eta}{\partial\eta} - B\frac{\partial^3\phi_\eta}{\partial\eta^3}\right)d\xi$$

$$-\int\int\left(C\frac{\partial P0}{\partial\eta} - D\phi_\eta\right)\frac{\partial^2\phi_\xi}{\partial\xi^2}\,d\xi d\eta$$

$$+\int\int\left(C\frac{\partial Q0}{\partial\xi} - D\phi_\xi\right)\frac{\partial^2\phi_\eta}{\partial\eta^2}\,d\xi d\eta. \qquad (7.16)$$

The integrand of the first integral on the right-hand side of Equation (7.16) will be proportional to η because the integrand is independent of η. The second term in the right-hand side of Equation (7.16) is dependent only on ξ and τ and, therefore, if the integrand is not identically equal to zero, then the integral will be proportional to η, which will give rise to secular terms. Hence, we must have the integrand to be identically zero. The same argument holds for the second integral. Hence, we obtain the following equations:

$$\frac{\partial \phi_\xi}{\partial \tau} + A\phi_\xi \frac{\partial \phi_\xi}{\partial \xi} + B\frac{\partial^3 \phi_\xi}{\partial \xi^3} = 0, \qquad (7.17)$$

$$\frac{\partial \phi_\eta}{\partial \tau} - A\phi_\eta \frac{\partial \phi_\eta}{\partial \eta} - B\frac{\partial^3 \phi_\eta}{\partial \eta^3} = 0. \qquad (7.18)$$

Equations (7.17) and (7.18) are the famous KdV equations. The solitary waves are traveling in opposite directions in the reference frames of ξ and η, respectively, and their expressions are

$$\phi_\xi = \phi_A sech^2\left[\left(\frac{A\phi_A}{12B}\right)^{1/2}\left(\xi - \frac{1}{3}A\phi_A\tau\right)\right], \qquad (7.19)$$

$$\phi_\eta = \phi_B sech^2\left[\left(\frac{A\phi_B}{12B}\right)^{1/2}\left(\eta + \frac{1}{3}A\phi_B\tau\right)\right] \qquad (7.20)$$

where ϕ_A and ϕ_B are the amplitudes of the two solitons in their initial positions. The soliton-like solutions are formed because of the balance between the nonlinearity and dispersion in nonlinear dispersive media. The soliton-like solutions are obtained from Equations (7.17) and (7.18). The coefficients A and B, appearing in the soliton solutions, are represented by Equations (7.17) and (7.18). These may create two possibilities: (i) $AB > 0$ and (ii) $AB < 0$.

Case (i): When $AB > 0$, Equations (7.19) and (7.20) give the compressive IASW solutions ($\phi_A > 0$ and $\phi_B > 0$).

Case (ii): When $AB < 0$, Equations (7.19) and (7.20) give the rarefactive IASW solutions ($\phi_A < 0$ and $\phi_B < 0$).

The third and fourth terms in Equation (7.16) are not secular in this order though they could be secular in the next order. Hence, we have

$$C\frac{\partial P_0}{\partial \eta} = D\phi_\eta, \quad C\frac{\partial Q_0}{\partial \xi} = D\phi_\xi. \qquad (7.21)$$

The leading phase changes due to the collision can be calculated by integral Equation (7.21) and are written as

$$P_0(\eta, \tau) = \frac{D}{C}\left(\frac{12B\phi_B}{A}\right)^{1/2}\left[\tanh\left(\frac{A\phi_B}{12B}\right)^{1/2}\left(\eta + \frac{1}{3}A\phi_B\tau\right) + 1\right], \qquad (7.22)$$

$$Q_0(\xi, \tau) = \frac{D}{C}\left(\frac{12B\phi_B}{A}\right)^{1/2}\left[\tanh\left(\frac{A\phi_B}{12B}\right)^{1/2}\left(\xi - \frac{1}{3}A\phi_A\tau\right) - 1\right].$$

$$(7.23)$$

Therefore, up to $O(\varepsilon^2)$, the trajectories of the two solitary waves for head-on interactions are

$$\xi = \varepsilon(x - \lambda t) + \varepsilon^2\frac{D}{C}\left(\frac{12B\phi_B}{A}\right)^{1/2}$$

$$\times\left[\tanh\left(\frac{A\phi_B}{12B}\right)^{1/2}\left(\eta + \frac{1}{3}A\phi_B\tau\right) + 1\right] + \cdots,\qquad(7.24)$$

$$\eta = \varepsilon(x + \lambda t) + \varepsilon^2\frac{D}{C}\left(\frac{12B\phi_B}{A}\right)^{1/2}$$

$$\times\left[\tanh\left(\frac{A\phi_B}{12B}\right)^{1/2}\left(\xi - \frac{1}{3}A\phi_A\tau\right) - 1\right] + \cdots.\qquad(7.25)$$

To obtain the phase shift after a head-on collision of the two solitons, let us assume that in the initial state $(t = -\infty)$ the solitons are asymptotically far from each other (first soliton is at $\xi = 0, \eta = -\infty$ and the second soliton is at $\eta = 0, \xi = +\infty$). After the collision $(t = +\infty)$, the first soliton is far to the right of the second soliton (soliton α is at $\xi = 0, \eta = +\infty$ and soliton β is at $\eta = 0, \xi = -\infty$). Using Equations (7.24) and (7.25), we obtain the corresponding phase shifts ΔP_0 and ΔQ_0 as follows from (7.5) and finally we get

$$\Delta P_0 = -2\varepsilon^2\frac{D}{C}\left(\frac{12B\phi_B}{A}\right)^{1/2}, \quad \Delta Q_0 = 2\varepsilon^2\frac{D}{C}\left(\frac{12B\phi_A}{A}\right)^{1/2}.\quad(7.26)$$

From (7.21), it is clear that the phase shift will be positive or negative depending on the coefficient D/C in Equation (7.21). It is also seen from Equation (7.26) that the magnitudes of the phase shifts are directly related to the physical parameters ε, ϕ_A, and ϕ_B. Since the first soliton is traveling to the right and the second soliton is traveling to the left, it is seen from Equation (7.26) that due to the collision, each soliton has a negative phase shift in its traveling direction. The negative phase shift means that the solitons reduce their velocities during the interaction stage. It is clear from Figure 7.1 that for several values of τ, the time evolution of the head-on collision solitary wave solution ϕ_ξ will be shifted towards the right with the

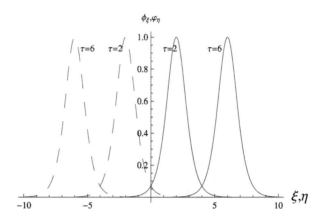

Fig. 7.1: Plot of ϕ_ξ (solid line) and ϕ_η (dashed line) against ξ and η, respectively, for several values of τ.

progress of time. But whereas the solution ϕ_η will be shifted towards the left with the progress of time.

7.2.2 Head-on collision of solitons in a Magnetized Quantum Plasma

We have studied the linear and nonlinear wave propagation in classical e-p-i plasmas using a variety of plasma models. The subfield quantum plasma of plasma physics is also enriched with various investigations on e-p-i plasma. Chatterjee *et al.* [3] have investigated the nonlinear propagation of quantum ion acoustic waves in dense quantum plasma containing electrons, positrons, and positive ions. When an e-p-i plasma is cooled under extremely low temperatures, the de Broglie wavelength of the charge carriers becomes comparable to the dimension of the system. In such a situation, ultra-cold e-p-i plasma behaves like a Fermi gas, and quantum mechanical effects are expected to play a vital role in the behavior of charged particles. All the works we have discussed earlier on head-on collision intend to find the KdV solitons with their phase shifts and the effects of different parameters on it, avoiding the detailed discussion on the critical composition. However, after the works of Verheest *et al.* [4, 5], there has been a surge of interest in the mKdV solitons for the critical composition, where the cubic nonlinearity, rather than the quadratic nonlinearity of the KdV equations, will appear in the evolution equations.

Let us consider a three species dense quantum plasma composed of electrons, positrons, and singly charged positive ions. The plasma is considered to be in the uniform external magnetic field $\vec{B}_0 = B_0 \hat{z}$, where B_0 is the strength of the magnetic field and $\hat{z}$ is the unit vector in the z-direction. At equilibrium, the charge neutrality condition is $n_{e0} = n_{i0} + n_{p0}$, where n_{j0} ($j = e$, p, and i stand for electrons, positrons, and ions, respectively) is the unperturbed number density. We assume that the Fermi temperature of electrons or positron is much larger than that of ions (i.e., $T_{Fe,p} \gg T_{Fi}$). The electron/positron obeys the pressure law $P_{e,p} = mn_{e,p}^3 V_{Fe,p}^2 / 3n_{e,p0}^2$, where $V_{Fe,p} = (2K_B T_{Fe,p}/m)^{1/2}$ is the electron/positron Fermi thermal speed, K_B is the Boltzmann constant, $T_{Fe,p}(T_{Fi})$ is the electron/positron (ion) Fermi temperature, m is the mass of electron and positron, and the number density of electron/positron is $n_{e,p}$ with the equilibrium value $n_{e,p0}$. The basic normalized equations are

$$\frac{\partial n_i}{\partial t} + \vec{\nabla} \cdot (n_i \vec{u}_i) = 0 \tag{7.27}$$

$$\frac{\partial \vec{u}_i}{\partial t} + \vec{u}_i \cdot \vec{\nabla} \vec{u}_i = -\vec{\nabla}\phi + \vec{u}_i \times \vec{z} \tag{7.28}$$

$$\Omega \vec{\nabla}^2 \phi = n_e - n_p - n_i \tag{7.29}$$

where $n_e = \mu_e \left(1 + 2\phi + H_e^2 \frac{\nabla^2 \sqrt{n_e}}{\sqrt{n_e}}\right)^{1/2}$ and $n_p = \mu_p \left(1 - 2\sigma\phi + \sigma H_e^2 \frac{\nabla^2 \sqrt{n_p}}{\sqrt{n_p}}\right)^{1/2}$. u_i, m_i, and ϕ are the ion fluid velocity, the ion mass, and the electrostatic potential, respectively. $\sigma = T_{Fe}/T_{Fp}$ is the electron to positron Fermi temperature ratio, and $H_e = eB_0\hbar/2c\sqrt{m_i m K_B T_{Fe}}$ is the quantum diffraction parameter. Here, the normalizations are taken as

$$n_j \to \frac{n_j}{n_{i0}}, \quad u_i \to \frac{u_i}{C_s}, \quad \phi \to \frac{e\phi}{2K_B T_{Fe}}, \quad \nabla \to \frac{\nabla C_s}{\omega_{ci}}, \quad t \to t\omega_{ci}$$

where $\omega_{ci} = eB_0/m_i c$ and $\omega_{pi} = \sqrt{4\pi e^2 n_{i0}/m_i}$ are the ion gyrofrequency and the ion plasma frequency. Also, $\Omega = \omega_{ci}^2/\omega_{pi}^2$ and $C_s = \sqrt{2K_B T_{Fe}/m_i}$, where $\hbar$ is the Planck constant divided by 2π and c is the speed of light in vacuum.

As usual, two solitary waves S_1 and S_2 are considered. To analyze the effect of collision, we employ the extended PLK method, and hence, the dependent variables are expanded in different powers of ϵ in

$$\psi = \psi_0 + \sum_{n=1}^{\infty} \epsilon^n \psi^{(n)} \tag{7.30}$$

where $\psi = (n_e, n_i, n_p, u_{ix}, u_{iy}, u_{iz}, \phi)$ with $\psi_0 = (\mu_e, 1, \mu_p, 0, 0, 0, 0)$. The stretched independent variables are expanded as

$$\left.\begin{array}{l} \xi = \epsilon(l_x x + l_y y + l_z z - \lambda t) + \epsilon^2 P(\xi, \eta, \tau) + \cdots , \\[2mm] \eta = \epsilon(l_x x + l_y y + l_z z + \lambda t) + \epsilon^2 Q(\xi, \eta, \tau) + \cdots , \\[2mm] \tau = \epsilon^3 t \end{array}\right\} \tag{7.31}$$

where ξ and η denote the trajectories of the two solitary waves during a head-on collision in the direction having direction cosine (l_x, l_y, l_z), with equal but opposite directional velocities. The variables P, Q, etc., will be determined later.

Using the extended PLK method, and after some calculation, we get [the same as the previous section] the coupled KdV equation as

$$\frac{\partial \phi_\xi^{(2)}}{\partial \tau} + A \phi_\xi^{(2)} \frac{\partial \phi_\xi^{(2)}}{\partial \xi} + B \frac{\partial^3 \phi_\xi^{(2)}}{\partial \xi^3}^{\,3} = 0 \tag{7.32}$$

$$\frac{\partial \phi_\eta^{(2)}}{\partial \tau} - A \phi_\eta^{(2)} \frac{\partial \phi_\eta^{(2)}}{\partial \eta} - B \frac{\partial^3 \phi_\eta^{(2)}}{\partial \eta^3} = 0 \tag{7.33}$$

where $A = \frac{\lambda^3}{2l_z^2}\left(\mu_e - \sigma^2 \mu_p + \frac{3l_z^4}{\lambda^4}\right)$ and $B = \frac{\lambda^3}{2l_z^2}\left[1 + \Omega - l_z^2 - \frac{H_e^2}{4\mu_e \mu_p}(\mu_p + \sigma^2 \mu_e)\right]$.

Also, we get

$$\frac{\partial P}{\partial \eta} - \frac{l_z^2}{4\lambda^2}\phi_\eta^{(2)} = 0, \qquad \frac{\partial Q}{\partial \xi} - \frac{l_z^2}{4\lambda^2}\phi_\xi^{(2)} = 0. \tag{7.34}$$

Equation (7.32) is a KdV equation. This wave is traveling in the ξ direction. Equation (7.33) is another KdV equation. This wave is propagating in the η direction, which is opposite to ξ. Their one soliton solutions are given as follows:

$$\phi_\xi^{(2)} = \phi_A \sec h^2\left[\left(\frac{A\phi_A}{12B}\right)^{1/2}\left(\xi - \frac{1}{3}A\phi_A \tau\right)\right] \tag{7.35}$$

$$\phi_\eta^{(2)} = \phi_B \sec h^2\left[\left(\frac{A\phi_B}{12B}\right)^{1/2}\left(\eta + \frac{1}{3}A\phi_B \tau\right)\right] \tag{7.36}$$

where ϕ_A and ϕ_B are the amplitudes of the two solitary waves in their initial positions. The leading phase changes $P(\eta, \tau)$ and $Q(\xi, \tau)$ are due to the head-on collision and are calculated from Equation (7.34).

To obtain the phase shifts after the head-on collision of the two solitary waves, we assume that the waves S_1 and S_2 are asymptotically far from each other at the initial time $\tau = -\infty$, S_1 is at $\xi = 0$, $\eta = -\infty$ and S_2 is at $\xi = \infty$, $\eta = 0$. After the collision, at time $\tau = +\infty$, S_1 is far to the right of S_2, i.e., S_1 is at $\xi = 0$, $\eta = \infty$ and S_2 is at $\xi = -\infty$, $\eta = 0$. We obtain the corresponding phase shifts

$$\triangle P = -\epsilon^2 \frac{l_z^2}{\lambda^2} \left(\frac{3B\phi_B}{A} \right)^{\frac{1}{2}}, \quad \triangle Q = \epsilon^2 \frac{l_z^2}{\lambda^2} \left(\frac{3B\phi_A}{A} \right)^{\frac{1}{2}}. \tag{7.37}$$

Derivation of phase shifts at critical compositions: At the critical composition when $A = 0$, the quadratic nonlinearity in the KdV Equations (7.32) and (7.33) will disappear, and the cubic nonlinearity will appear. Then, we consider $\phi^{(2)} - \phi_\xi^{(2)} - \phi_\eta^{(2)} \neq 0$. We can cancel [4] the solutions of the linear operator without loss of generality. Hence, $\phi_\xi^{(2)} = \phi_\eta^{(2)} = 0$ and according to the same procedure, we get the mKdV equations as

$$\frac{\partial \phi_\xi^{(1)}}{\partial \tau} + A_1 (\phi_\xi^{(1)})^2 \frac{\partial \phi_\xi^{(1)}}{\partial \xi} + B \frac{\partial^3 \phi_\xi^{(1)}}{\partial \xi^3} = 0 \tag{7.38}$$

$$\frac{\partial \phi_\eta^{(1)}}{\partial \tau} + A_1 (\phi_\eta^{(1)})^2 \frac{\partial \phi_\eta^{(1)}}{\partial \eta} + B \frac{\partial^3 \phi_\eta^{(1)}}{\partial \eta^3} = 0 \tag{7.39}$$

where $A_1 = \frac{\lambda^3}{2l_z^2} \left[\frac{15 l_z^6}{2\lambda^6} - \frac{3(\mu_e + \sigma^3 \mu_p)}{2} \right]$ and $B = \frac{\lambda^3}{2l_z^2} \left[1 + \Omega - l_z^2 - \frac{H_e^2}{4\mu_e \mu_p} (\mu_p + \sigma^2 \mu_e) \right]$.

Also, we get

$$\frac{\partial P}{\partial \eta} - C(\phi_\eta^{(1)})^2 = 0, \quad \frac{\partial Q}{\partial \xi} - C(\phi_\xi^{(1)})^2 = 0 \tag{7.40}$$

where $C = \frac{\lambda^2}{8l_z^2} \left[\mu_e + \sigma^2 \mu_p - \frac{l_z^6}{\lambda^6} \right]$.

Now the mKdV Equations (7.38) and (7.39) will keep the same form, whatever may be the sign of $\phi_\xi^{(1)}$ or $\phi_\eta^{(1)}$. The one soliton solutions of Equations (7.38) and (7.39) are

$$\phi_\xi^{(1)} = \pm \phi_a \sec h \left[\left(\frac{A_1}{6B} \right)^{1/2} \phi_a \left(\xi - \frac{A_1 \phi_a^2}{6} \tau \right) \right] \tag{7.41}$$

$$\phi_\eta^{(1)} = \pm \phi_b \sec h \left[\left(\frac{A_1}{6B} \right)^{1/2} \phi_b \left(\eta - \frac{A_1 \phi_b^2}{6} \tau \right) \right]. \tag{7.42}$$

Now, proceeding as in the case of KdV solitons, we obtain the corresponding colliding phase shifts as

$$\triangle P = -2\epsilon^2 C \phi_b \left(\frac{6B}{A_1} \right)^{1/2}, \quad \triangle Q = 2\epsilon^2 C \phi_a \left(\frac{6B}{A_1} \right)^{1/2}. \quad (7.43)$$

Since, the balance between the nonlinear and the dispersion terms in Equations (7.32), (7.33), (7.38), and (7.39) creates the KdV and the mKdV soliton-like solutions, respectively. So, the coefficients A, B, and A_1, (with the restriction $\mu_e - \sigma^2 \mu_p + \frac{3l_z^4}{\lambda^4} = 0$) are responsible for such situations. Here, two possibilities are created: (i) If $AB > 0$ (i.e., both ϕ_A and ϕ_B are positive), the solutions of Equations (7.35) and (7.36) are the compressive IASWS solutions (CIASWs). (ii) If $AB < 0$ (both ϕ_A and ϕ_B are negative), the solutions of Equations (7.35) and (7.36) are rarefactive IASWs (RIASWs). But the mKdV solitons are compressive as well as rarefactive if $A_1 B > 0$ for positive, as well as negative polarities. To illustrate the statements (i) and (ii), we draw Figure 7.2, where we plot the regions of CIASWS and RIASW solutions in the generic case in the H_e-Ω plane with $\mu_p = 1$, $\sigma = 1.585$, and $l_z = 0.9$. We plot the region of CIASWs and RIASWs for critical case and also the region where the mKdV soliton does not exist in the H_e-Ω plane (see Figure 7.3) for $l_z = 0.89$ and $\mu_p = 0.249$. Thus, there

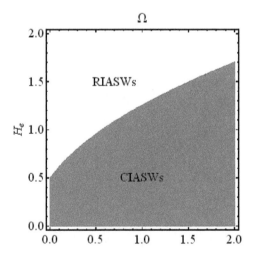

Fig. 7.2: The regions for CIASWs and RIASWs in $\Omega - H_e$ plane for $\sigma = 1.585$, $l_z = 0.9$, and $\mu_p = 1$ in the generic case.

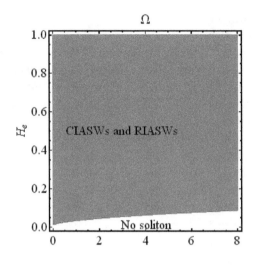

Fig. 7.3: The region in the $\Omega - H_e$ plane for $l_z = 0.89$ and $\mu_p = 0.249$, where the two types of MKdV solitons exist.

is no limitation for the existence of KdV solitons on the parameters, but limitations are there for the mKdV solitons.

7.2.3 *Head-on collision of magneto-acoustic solitons in spin-1/2 fermionic quantum plasma*

In dense plasmas, degenerate electrons follow the Fermi–Dirac pressure law, and the quantum force is connected with the Bohm–de Broglie potential, and as a product of which the waves disperse at nanoscales. Not only that, the effects of the electron spin appear themselves in terms of a magnetic dipole force and spin precession. It can be obtained by transforming the Pauli equation to fluid-like variables. Hence, the dynamics of electrons in Fermi's degenerate plasmas will be intervened not only by the Lorentz force but also by the effects of quantum statistical pressure, the Bohm force, and the intrinsic spin of electrons.

Marklund and Brodin [6] introduced the dynamics of spin-1/2 quantum plasma in the nonrelativistic magnetoplasma. They [7] showed that the spin properties of the electrons and positrons might lead to interesting collective effects in quantum magnetoplasma by the equation of Schrodinger Pauli. Marklund, Eliasson, and Shukla [8] also showed the existence of magneto solitons in fermionic quantum plasma. They found that if one neglects the magnetic diffusivity, the magnetic field satisfies an equation identical to the continuity equation. Hence, one can take the magnetic field linearly proportional to the density of plasma fluid by applying a simplification of the governing equations. Later, Misra and Ghosh [9] obtained the spin magnetosonic shock-like waves in quantum plasma considering the magnetic diffusivity. Linear and nonlinear compressional magnetosonic waves in magnetized degenerate spin-1/2 Fermi plasmas are investigated [10]. Relativistic corrections to the Pauli Hamiltonian in the context of a scalar kinetic theory for spin-1/2 quantum plasmas have also been established by Asenjo *et al.* [11].

Here, we are going to study the head-on collision of magnetosonic solitons in a fermionic quantum plasma, taking into account spin effects. The total mass density, the center-of-mass fluid flow velocity, and the current density are defined respectively as $\rho = (m_e n_e + m_i n_i)$, $\vec{V} = (m_e n_e v_e + m_i n_i v_i)/\rho$, and $j = (-e n_e v_e + e n_i v_i)$. m_k, n_k, v_k, and e ($k = e$, and i, stands for electron, and ion, respectively) are the mass, the number density, the fluid velocity, and the electron charge, respectively. Assuming the quasineutrality condition ($n_e = n_i$) and taking the magnetic field along the z-axis so that $\vec{B} = B(x,t)\hat{z}$ and taking the velocity $\vec{V} = V(x,t)\hat{x}$ and the density as $\rho(x,t)$, we get the following system of normalized basic equations:

$$\frac{\partial b}{\partial t} + \frac{\partial (bv)}{\partial x} = 0 \tag{7.44}$$

$$\frac{\partial v}{\partial t} + v\frac{\partial v}{\partial x} = -\frac{\partial b}{\partial x} - c_s^2 \frac{\partial (\ln b)}{\partial x} + \frac{2\omega_{pe}^2}{\omega_c |\omega_{ce}|}\frac{\partial}{\partial x}\left(\frac{1}{\sqrt{b}}\frac{\partial^2 \sqrt{b}}{\partial x^2}\right)$$
$$+ v_B^2 \frac{\partial}{\partial x}[ln(\cosh(z_e b)) + z_e b(\tanh(z_e b))] \tag{7.45}$$

where $\rho = \rho_0 b$, $b = B/B_0$, $c_s = C_s/C_A$, and $v = V/C_A$. Also, $C_A = \sqrt{B_0^2/(\mu_0 \rho_0)}$ is the Alfven speed, $C_s = \sqrt{K_B(T_e + T_i)/m_i}$ is the sound speed, $\omega_{pk} = \sqrt{(n_{k0}e^2)/(\epsilon_0 m_i)}$ is the plasma frequency, $\omega_c = 2m_e c^2/h$ is the Compton frequency, $z_e = (\mu_B B_0)/(K_B T_e)$ is the temperature-normalized Zeeman energy, and $v_B^2 = (\mu_B B_0)/(\varepsilon m_i C_A^2)$, where μ_0 is the permeability of the vacuum, B_0 is the magnetic field strength, ρ_0 is the total mass density of the charged plasma particles, T_i and T_e are ion and electron temperatures, K_B is the Boltzmann constant, and μ_B is the magnitude of Bohr magneton. The normalized variables are taken as $t \to \omega_{ci}t$ and $x \to (\omega_{ci}x)/C_A$. In deriving Equations (7.44) and (7.45), the magnetic resistivity is neglected.

Now, we assume that the two solitons α and β are asymptotically far apart in the initial state and travel towards each other. To analyze the effects of a collision, we employ an extended PLK method. According to this method, the dependent variables are expanded as

$$b = 1 + \epsilon b_1 + \epsilon^{3/2} b_2 + \epsilon^2 b_3 + \cdots \left.\vphantom{\begin{matrix}a\\a\end{matrix}}\right\} $$
$$v = \epsilon v_1 + \epsilon^{3/2} v_2 + \epsilon^2 v_3 + \cdots \tag{7.46}$$

and the independent variables are given by

$$\xi = \epsilon^{1/2}(x - \lambda t) + \epsilon^{3/2} P_0(\eta, \tau) + \epsilon^{5/2} P_1(\xi, \eta, \tau) + \cdots \left.\vphantom{\begin{matrix}a\\a\\a\end{matrix}}\right\}$$
$$\eta = \epsilon^{1/2}(x + \lambda t) + \epsilon^{3/2} Q_0(\xi, \tau) + \epsilon^{5/2} Q_1(\xi, \eta, \tau) + \cdots \tag{7.47}$$
$$\tau = \varepsilon^3 t.$$

Here, ξ and η denote the trajectories of two solitons traveling towards each other and λ is the unknown phase speed normalized by C_A. $P_0(\eta, \tau)$ and $Q_0(\xi, \tau)$ are also needed to be determined.

Using extended PLK method, and after some calculations, we get

$$\frac{\partial b_{11}}{\partial \tau} + A_1 b_{11} \frac{\partial b_{11}}{\partial \xi} + B_1 \frac{\partial^3 b_{11}}{\partial \xi^3} = 0 \tag{7.48}$$

$$\frac{\partial b_{12}}{\partial \tau} - A_1 b_{12} \frac{\partial b_{12}}{\partial \eta} - B_1 \frac{\partial^3 b_{12}}{\partial \eta^3} = 0 \tag{7.49}$$

where $A_1 = \frac{3\lambda^2 - c_s^2 - z_e^2 v_B^2 \sec h^2 z_e (3 - 2z_e \tanh z_e)}{2\lambda}$, $B_1 = -\frac{\omega_{pe}^2}{2|\omega_{ce}|\lambda\omega_c}$, and $\lambda = \sqrt{1 + c_s^2 - z_e v_B^2 (2 \tanh z_e + z_e \sec h^2 z_e)}$.

Also, we get

$$C_1 \frac{\partial P_0}{\partial \eta} = D_1 b_{12}, \quad C_1 \frac{\partial Q_0}{\partial \xi} = D_1 b_{11} \tag{7.50}$$

where $C_1 = 2\lambda$ and $D_1 = \frac{\lambda^2 + c_s^2 + z_e^2 v_B^2 \sec h^2 z_e (3 - 2z_e \tanh z_e)}{2\lambda}$.

Equations (7.48) and (7.49) are the two side of traveling wave KdV equations in the reference frames of ξ and η, respectively. Their special solutions are

$$b_{11} = b_A \sec h^2 \left[\left(\frac{A_1 b_A}{12 B_1} \right)^{1/2} \left(\xi - \frac{1}{3} A_1 b_A \tau \right) \right] \tag{7.51}$$

$$b_{12} = b_B \sec h^2 \left[\left(\frac{A_1 b_B}{12 B_1} \right)^{1/2} \left(\eta + \frac{1}{3} A_1 b_B \tau \right) \right] \tag{7.52}$$

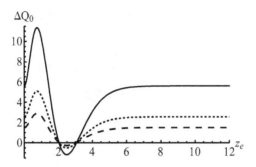

Fig. 7.4: Graphs of the variation of phase shift $\triangle Q_0$ against the Zeeman energy z_e for phase velocities $v_p = 0.0098$ (solid line), 0.0152 (dotted line), and 0.0198 (dashed line).

where b_A and b_B are the amplitudes of the two solitons in their initial positions. We obtain the corresponding phase shifts as

$$\triangle P_0 = -2\epsilon^2 \frac{D_1}{C_1} \left(\frac{12B_1 b_B}{A_1} \right)^{1/2}, \quad \triangle Q_0 = 2\epsilon^2 \frac{D_1}{C_1} \left(\frac{12B_1 b_A}{A_1} \right)^{1/2}. \quad (7.53)$$

To draw Figure 7.4, we consider $\epsilon = 0.1$, $B_A = 0.1$, $\omega_{pe}^2/(\omega_c|\omega_{ce}|) = 1$, and $v_B = 0.2$. Figure 7.4 represents the variations of the phase shift $\triangle Q_0$ with the Zeeman energy (z_e) for different values of v_p, when $c_s = 0.1$. The phase shift $\triangle Q_0$ is (i) positive and increasing when $0 < z_e < 0.8$ and $3 < z_e < 7$, (ii) positive and decreasing when $0.8 < z_e < 2$, (iii) negative and decreasing when $2 < z_e < 2.5$, (iv) negative and increasing for $2.5 < z_e < 3$, and (v) positive and constant for $z_e > 7$. Thus, the phase shift is positive and negative for different domains for the Zeeman energy. With a particular value of z_e, the magnitude of the phase shifts increases as the speed of the wave decreases. Qualitatively, one can say that the phase shifts become flat when the Zeeman energy is large. We consider the case where the Zeeman energy $z_e \geq 1$ so that the spin contribution to the soliton dynamics is enhanced, and the Zeeman energy plays a crucial role in the phase shifts.

The KdV-type soliton-like solutions are formed due to the balance between the nonlinearity and dispersion in nonlinear dispersive media. So, the condition for the existence of soliton-like solutions is $A_1 \neq 0$ and $B_1 \neq 0$. Since, the soliton α is traveling from the left and β is traveling from the right, Equation (7.53) imply that each soliton has a positive or a negative phase shift, depending upon the sign of the coefficient D. Moreover, from Equation (7.53), it is clear that both $B_1 b_B/A_1$ and $B_1 b_A/A_1$ must be positive, if both $\triangle P_0$ and $\triangle Q_0$ are real. It follows logically that b_B and b_A

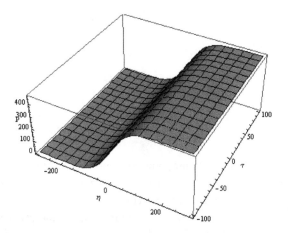

Fig. 7.5: The leading phase changes $P(\eta, \tau)$ due to head-on collision against η and τ for the parametric values as in Figure 7.4 and for $z_e = 0.498$.

must have the same sign. Hence, both the solitons will be either hump types or dip types. Thus, the positive or negative phase shift does not depend on the type of mode (i.e., ion-acoustic, dust-ion-acoustic, dust-acoustic, magneto-acoustic, and electrostatic waves).

In Figure 7.5, we consider the three-dimensional plot of the leading phase changes due to head-on collision against the space–time variables for the parametric values as in Figure 7.4 and three different values of Zeeman energy. It is clear from these three figures that the leading phase changes due to the head-on collision that is initially positive, and after a certain value of Zeeman energy, it is negative. Finally, it remains positive after a certain value of Zeeman energy although the other plasma parameters are the same.

7.2.4 *Interaction of DIASWs in nonplanar geometry*

In this section, we will consider the nonlinear propagation of finite-amplitude DIA waves in a four-component collisionless, unmagnetized, dusty plasma consisting of q-nonextensive distributed electrons, stationary positive and negative dust charge, and inertial ions in a nonplanar geometry. At equilibrium, we have $n_{i0}+Z_{dp}n_{dp}=n_{e0}+Z_{dn}n_{dn}$, where n_{i0}, n_{e0}, n_{dp}, and n_{dn} are, respectively, ion, electron, positive dust, and negative dust number density at equilibrium, and $Z_{dp}(Z_{dn})$ represents the charge state of positive (negative) dust. The dynamics of DIAWs in such plasma can be described by the following set of normalized equations:

$$\frac{\partial n_i}{\partial t} + \frac{1}{r^\nu}\frac{\partial}{\partial r}(r^\nu n_i u_i) = 0 \tag{7.54}$$

$$\frac{\partial u_i}{\partial t} + u_i \frac{\partial u_i}{\partial r} = -\frac{\partial \phi}{\partial r} \tag{7.55}$$

$$\frac{1}{r^\nu}\frac{\partial}{\partial r}\left(r^\nu \frac{\partial \phi}{\partial r}\right) = (1 - j\mu)n_e - n_i + j\mu \tag{7.56}$$

where $\nu = 0$ in case of 1D planar geometry and $\nu = 1, 2$ in case of nonplanar (cylindrical or spherical) geometries, respectively. All the notations and normalizations are the same as in Section 6.5.

Suppose that two solitary waves in nonplanar geometry, R and L, have been excited in the system. The solitary wave $R(L)$ is traveling outward (inward) from (to) the initial point of the coordinate system. The initial position (at time $t = 0$) of the solitary wave $R(L)$ is at $r = r_R$ ($r = r_L$), $r_L \gg r_R$. Since $0 < r < \infty$, this consideration is different from cartesian solitons, where $-\infty < x < \infty$ in one dimension. For the head-on collision between two Cartesian solitons, one can consider one soliton is at $x \approx -\infty$ and the other one at $x \approx \infty$ (at the initial time $t = 0$). After some time, they interact, following a collision, and then depart from each other. To investigate the head-on collision between the two solitary waves in a nonplanar geometry, we extend the PLK method to the nonplanar geometry. We anticipate that the collision will result in phase shifts in their postcollision trajectories. Thus, we introduce the following transformations:

$$\left.\begin{array}{l} \xi = \varepsilon(r - ct - r_R) + \varepsilon^2 A_1(\eta, L) + \varepsilon^3 A_2(\eta, \xi, L) + \cdots, \\ \eta = \varepsilon(r + ct - r_L) + \varepsilon^2 B_1(\xi, L) + \varepsilon^3 B_2(\eta, \xi, L) + \cdots, \\ L = \varepsilon^3 r \end{array}\right\} \tag{7.57}$$

where ξ and η denote the trajectories of two solitons traveling towards each other and c is the unknown phase velocity of DIASWs. The variables of $A_1(\eta, L)$ and $B_1(\xi, L)$ are also to be determined. Introducing the asymptotic expansion

$$n_i = 1 + \sum_{k=1}^{\infty} \varepsilon^{k+1} n_k + \cdots, \quad u_i = u_0 + \sum_{k=1}^{\infty} \varepsilon^{K+1} u_k + \cdots,$$

$$\phi = \sum_{k=1}^{\infty} \varepsilon^{K+1} \phi_k + \cdots \tag{7.58}$$

where u_0 is the drift fluid velocity. Proceeding the same way as the previous problem, we have

$$\frac{\partial \phi_\xi}{\partial L} + A\phi_A \frac{\partial \phi_\xi}{\partial \xi} + B\frac{\partial^3 \phi_\xi}{\partial \xi^3} + \frac{\nu}{2L}\phi_\xi = 0, \tag{7.59}$$

$$\frac{\partial \phi_\eta}{\partial L} + A\phi_\eta \frac{\partial \phi_\eta}{\partial \eta} + B\frac{\partial^3 \phi_\eta}{\partial \eta^3} + \frac{\nu}{2L}\phi_\eta = 0 \tag{7.60}$$

where $A = \frac{3}{4}(q+1)(1-j\mu) - \frac{1}{4}(3-q)$ and $B = \frac{1}{(q+1)(1-j\mu)}$.
    Also, we get

$$2\frac{\partial A_1}{\partial \eta} = D\phi_\eta, \quad 2\frac{\partial B_1}{\partial \xi} = D\phi_\xi \tag{7.61}$$

where $D = \frac{1}{4}(q+1)(1-j\mu) + \frac{1}{4}(3-q)$. Equations (7.59) and (7.60) are the two side traveling wave KdV equations in the reference frames of ξ and η, respectively. Their special solutions are

$$\phi_\xi = U_A\Theta_A^{2\nu/3}\sec h^2\left[\Gamma_A^{1/2}\Theta_A^{\nu/3}\left(\xi - \frac{1}{3}AU_A\Theta_A^{2\nu/3}L\right)\right], \tag{7.62}$$

$$\phi_\eta = U_B\Theta_B^{2\nu/3}\sec h^2\left[\Gamma_B^{1/2}\Theta_B^{\nu/3}\left(\eta - \frac{1}{3}AU_B\Theta_B^{2\nu/3}L\right)\right] \tag{7.63}$$

where U_A and U_B are the amplitude of two DIASWs R, and L, respectively. Here, $\Theta_A = L_A/L$, $\Theta_B = L_B/L$, $\Gamma_A = AU_A/12B$, and $\Gamma_B = AU_B/12B$ with $L_A = \varepsilon^3 r_R$ and $L_B = \varepsilon^3 r_L$. It is noted that the amplitude decreases drastically as $L(r)$ increases in cylindrical and spherical geometries. In Equations (7.59) and (7.60), A and B are the coefficients of nonlinearity and dispersion, respectively. If we set $\nu = 0$, Equations (7.59) and (7.60) will become the planar KdV equations. $\nu = 1$ and $\nu = 2$ correspond to the cylindrical and spherical KdV equations, respectively. We obtain the corresponding phase shifts ΔP_0 and ΔQ_0 if the initial separation between the two solitons is large enough, i.e., $r_L \gg r_R$, and the observation time is much larger than the collision time, i.e., $t \gg t_c = (r_L - r_R)/2$, as

$$\Delta P_0 = -\varepsilon^2 D\left(\frac{12BU_B}{A}\right)^{1/2}\left(\frac{r_L}{r}\right)^{\nu/3}, \Delta Q_0 = \varepsilon^2 D\left(\frac{12BU_A}{A}\right)^{1/2}\left(\frac{r_L}{r}\right)^{\nu/3}. \tag{7.64}$$

For cylindrical case, Equations (7.59) and (7.60) are the outward (R) and inward (L) traveling wave KdV equations, respectively. Now, we want to show how the interaction takes place. At the initial position, these two solitary waves R and L are at $r = r_R = 57.5$ and $r = r_L = 137.5$, respectively, at time $t = 0$. With the progress of time, as seen in Figures 7.6, the outward solitary waves R and inward solitary waves L come closer and closer, and ultimately they collide. After colliding with each other, they interchange their position, and, finally, they depart from each other so that the soliton R has the radius $r = r_L = 137.5$ and soliton L has the radius $r = r_R = 57.5$, as depicted in Figure 7.6.

For fixed physical parameters and initial soliton position, the phase shifts are proportional to $r^{-\nu/3}$. So, the collision-induced phase shifts in cylindrical/spherical geometry decrease with r according to $r^{-\nu/3}$.

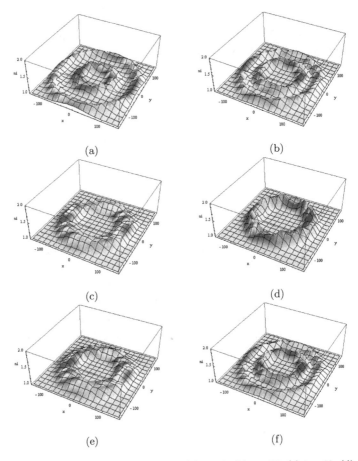

Fig. 7.6: Graphs of cylindrical collision for (a) $t = 0$, (b) $t = 30$, (c) $t = 60$, (d) $t = 90$, (e) $t = 120$, and (f) $t = 150$.

When the physical parameters and solitons' positions are the same, the phase shifts in spherical and cylindrical geometry are different. But, when $\nu = 0$, the phase shifts represented by Equation (7.64) reduce to the planar case.

We have plotted all the figures by taking the negative dust charge (i.e., $j = 1$) and have discussed accordingly. If we consider the positive dust charge (i.e., $j = -1$), we will obtain some interesting behavior of the phase shift.

7.3 Oblique Collision

Now, we are going to explain the oblique collision of soliton. The oblique collisions between solitary waves are interesting nonlinear phenomena in plasmas. When two solitary waves approach closely, they interact, exchange their energies and positions with each other, and then separate off, regaining their original waveforms. During the collision, the solitary waves are remarkably stable entities, preserving their identities through collisions. The unique effect due to the collisions is their phase shift and the trajectories.

Let us consider two small but finite amplitude solitary excitations, which propagate obliquely in the XY plane at an arbitrary angle with different velocities. Their interaction occurs at some event altering the trajectories of colliding waves, and then phase shifts appear. Realization of an acceptable physical profile of elastic interaction between waves through asymptotic expansion of plasma variables is possible. It is done with appropriate coordinates using stretching. The stretching process admits successful separation of variables to the desired nonlinear evolution and interaction profile by eliminating the secular terms with the help of an extended PLK method. The stretching coordinates are taken as

$$\left.\begin{array}{l} \xi = \varepsilon(k_1 x + l_1 y - c_1 t) + \varepsilon^2 P_0(\eta, \tau) + \cdots \\ \eta = \varepsilon(k_2 x + l_2 y - c_2 t) + \varepsilon^2 Q_0(\xi, \tau) + \cdots \\ \tau = \varepsilon^3 t \end{array}\right\} \tag{7.65}$$

where the functions P_j and Q_j ($j = 0, 1, 2, \ldots$) give the phase description of the interacting solitary waves in space–time evolution. These types of stretched coordinates were used in fluid dynamics also. Furthermore, we assume that before the collision takes place, the waves initially travel at directions given by $\mathbf{r}_1 = (k_1, l_1)$ and $\mathbf{r}_2 = (k_2, l_2)$. Therefore, they collide through an angle θ defined by $\cos\theta = \mu/(\lambda_1 \lambda_2)$, where $\mu = (k_1 k_2 + l_1 l_2)$,

$\lambda_1 = \sqrt{(k_1^2 + l_1^2)}$, and $\lambda_2 = \sqrt{(k_2^2 + l_2^2)}$. Here, λ_1 and λ_2 represent the normalized wavenumbers. If a wave that is slowly varying in a reference frame moving with the basic waves speed at an angle θ with respect to the x-axis may be described by $\phi = F(\xi, \tau)$, where $\xi = \mathbf{n} \cdot \mathbf{x} - \lambda t$, $\mathbf{n} = (\cos\theta, \sin\theta)$, $\tau = \alpha t$, and F satisfies the KdV-like equation $2\alpha F_\tau + \frac{3}{2}\alpha F_\xi^2 + \frac{1}{2}\beta F_{\xi\xi\xi} + O(\alpha^2) = 0$ in the first approximation. We proceed on the hypothesis that the interaction between two such waves may be described by $\phi(\xi_1, \xi_2, \tau) = F_1(\xi_1, \tau) + F_2(\xi_2, \tau) + \alpha F_{12}(\xi_1, \xi_2, \tau)$, where $\xi_n (n = 1, 2)$ is given by the above equation.

The general problem is characterized by three parameters, which comprise the amplitudes of the two basic waves and the relative inclination of their normals. Let c_n be the wave speed of the nth wave $(n = 1, 2)$ and 2θ the angle between the wave normals n_1 and n_2, then α, $\varepsilon(c_2 - c_1)/(c_2 + c_1)$, and $k = \sin^2\theta$ are suitable measures of mean strength, relative strength, and obliquity, respectively. It follows from the perturbation equations that interaction is weak if $k \gg \alpha$ or strong if $k = 0(\alpha)$ as $\alpha \to 0$ (the adjective strong is used here in the sense of scattering theory, but it should be emphasized that the actual nonlinearity remains weak in the sense that the perturbation equations are valid). It also follows from the perturbation equations that $\varepsilon = \frac{1}{4}(\alpha_2 - \alpha_1) + O(\alpha^2)$, where $\alpha_{1,2}d$ (d = quiescent depth) are the maximum amplitudes of the incoming waves. The more general case of solitary interaction involves two dimensions for the collision angle θ, which can be an arbitrary angle in the range $0 \leq \theta \leq \pi$, where the one-dimensional collisions are only special cases.

7.3.1 *Oblique collision of DIASWs in quantum plasmas*

In a three-dimensional system, the angle θ between two wave propagation directions of the two solitary waves lies between $0 < \theta < \pi$. The head-on collision and the overtaking collisions are only two special cases for $\theta = \pi$ and $\theta = 0$, respectively. In general, for the oblique interaction between two solitary waves in 3D, we must search for the evolution of the solitary waves propagating in two different directions. Hence, we need to employ a suitable asymptotic expansion to solve the original problem. However, when the included angle between the directions of propagation of impinging solitary waves is less than 120°, the effect of oblique interaction is stronger than that of the head-on one, but when the angle concerned is greater than 120°, the former is slightly weaker than the latter. The reality cannot be ignored that the one-dimensional geometry may not be a realistic situation in a laboratory device and space. However, the oblique collision of solitary waves in a two-dimensional geometry is more realistic in a magnetized dusty electronegative plasma, especially of the D and F regions of the Earth's ionosphere.

Now, we are going to investigate the oblique collision of two DIAWs in three-species quantum plasma. Like the previous problems, the extended PLK method is adopted to obtain a two-sided KdV equation, and Hirota's method is employed to investigate the two soliton solutions.

Quantum effects play a major role in collective nonlinear wave interactions in dense plasmas. The importance of quantum effects has also been recognized in the context of collective interactions in semiconductors [12]. There has been a growing interest in investigating new aspects of dense quantum plasmas by developing the quantum hydrodynamic (QHD) [13] and quantum kinetic equations [14] by incorporating the quantum force associated with the Bohm potential [15]. The Winger–Poisson (W-P) model [16] has been used to derive a set of QHD equations for a dense electron plasma. The QHD equations are composed of electron continuity, nonrelativistic electron momentum, and Poisson equations. The quantum nature appears in the electron momentum equations through the quantum statistical pressure, which requires the knowledge of the Winger distribution for a quantum mixture of electron wave functions, each characterized by the occupation probability. The quantum part of the electron pressure is represented as a quantum force $-\nabla \phi_B$, where $\nabla \phi_B = -(\hbar^2/2m_e\sqrt{n_e})\nabla^2 \sqrt{n_e}$, $\hbar$ is the Planck constant divided by 2π, m_e is the electron mass, and n_e is the electron number density. In dense plasmas, quantum mechanical effects are important, since the de Broglie length of the charge carriers is comparable to the interparticle spacing. Let us study the two-dimensional obliquely propagating DIAWs in a three-species quantum dusty plasmas, whose constituents are dust particles, inertial ions with a background stationary dust of constant charge while the electrons are inertialess. DIAW in such a quantum plasma system is described by the normalized 2D basic equations as follows:

$$\frac{\partial n_i}{\partial t} + \frac{\partial}{\partial x}(n_i u) + \frac{\partial}{\partial y}(n_i v) = 0 \tag{7.66}$$

$$\frac{\partial u}{\partial t} + u\frac{\partial u}{\partial x} + v\frac{\partial u}{\partial y} + \frac{\partial \phi}{\partial x} = 0 \tag{7.67}$$

$$\frac{\partial v}{\partial t} + u\frac{\partial v}{\partial x} + v\frac{\partial v}{\partial y} + \frac{\partial \phi}{\partial x} = 0 \tag{7.68}$$

$$\frac{\partial^2 \phi}{\partial x^2} + \frac{\partial^2 \phi}{\partial y^2} = \beta n_e - \alpha N_{d0} - n_i \tag{7.69}$$

$$\phi - n_e + 1 + \frac{H_e^2}{2\sqrt{n_e}} \nabla^2 \sqrt{n_e} = 0 \tag{7.70}$$

where n_j ($j = i$, and e, stands for ion, and electron, respectively) and ϕ are the number density and the electrostatic potential, respectively. u and v are the velocities of ions in the x and y directions, respectively.

Normalization

$$n_i \to \frac{n_i}{n_o}, \quad n_e \to \frac{n_e}{n_{eo}}, \quad \phi \to \frac{eL}{K_B T_e}, \quad x \to \frac{x}{L}, \quad t \to \omega_0 t, \quad u \to \frac{u}{L\omega_0},$$

$$v \to \frac{v}{L\omega_0}$$

where $L = \sqrt{(K_B T_e)/(4\Pi Z e^2 n_0)}$ and $\omega_0 = \sqrt{(4\Pi Z^2 e^2 n_0)/(m_i)}$. e, K_B, and T_e are the electron charge, the Boltzmann constant, and the Fermi temperature, respectively. $\alpha = \pm 1$ for positive/negative dust particles, $\beta = 1 + \alpha N_{d0}$, where $\beta = \frac{n_{i0}}{n_{e0}}$ is the density ratio parameter with $N_{d0} = \frac{z_{d0} n_{d0}}{n_{i0}}$, and H_e is the quantum diffraction parameter. The terms proportional to m_e/m_i have been disregarded in Equation (7.70) in the limit $m_e/m_i \ll 1$.

Now, let us consider two small but finite-amplitude wave-like perturbations that propagate obliquely at some angle θ in the XY plane with different velocities. They approach and interact after some time. Due to this interaction, they depart from each other, leaving a collision signature on waves which is nothing but a phase shift in the trajectories. Here, we use asymptotic expansions of plasma variables around the thermodynamics equilibrium state in a stretched coordinate that includes the phase variables. Here, the PLK method is used, and the following new oblique coordinates are (7.65). The directions of initial wave velocities are given by vectors $\vec{r}_1 = (l'_1, l_1)$ and $\vec{r}_2 = (l'_2, l_2)$, and the collision that acts through an angle θ is defined by $\cos\theta = \frac{\mu}{\lambda_1 \lambda_2}$, where $\mu = (l'_1 l'_2 + l_1 l_2)$, $\lambda_1 = (l'^2_1 + l^2_1)^{1/2}$, and $\lambda_2 = (l'^2_2 + l^2_2)^{1/2}$. λ_1 and λ_2 represent the normalized wavenumbers. Here, we must know that $\theta \neq 0$, i.e., $\cos\theta \neq 1$, otherwise the perturbation method used would not be valid. We take the asymptotic expansion of plasma variables away from thermodynamic equilibrium in the following way:

$$n_j = 1 + \sum_{k=1}^{\infty} \epsilon^{2k} n_j^{(k)} + \cdots, \quad u = \sum_{k=1}^{\infty} \epsilon^{2k} u_1 + \cdots, \quad v = \sum_{k=1}^{\infty} \epsilon^{2k} v_1 + \cdots,$$

$$\phi = \sum_{k=1}^{\infty} \epsilon^{2k} \phi^{(k)} + \cdots.$$

Proceeding the same way as the previous problem, we have

$$\frac{\partial \phi_\xi^{(1)}}{\partial \tau} + A \phi_\xi^{(1)} \frac{\partial \phi_\xi^{(1)}}{\partial \xi} + B \frac{\partial^3 \phi_\xi^{(1)}}{\partial \xi^3} = 0 \tag{7.71}$$

$$\frac{\partial \phi_\eta^{(1)}}{\partial \tau} + A_1 \phi_\eta^{(1)} \frac{\partial \phi_\eta^{(1)}}{\partial \eta} + B_1 \frac{\partial^3 \phi_\eta^{(1)}}{\partial \eta^3} = 0 \tag{7.72}$$

where $A = \frac{3}{2}\beta c_1$, $B = \frac{c_1^3}{2}\left(1 - \frac{\beta H_e^2}{4}\right)$, $A_1 = \frac{3}{2}\beta c_2$, and $B_1 = \frac{c_2^3}{2}\left(1 - \frac{\beta H_e^2}{4}\right)$. Also $(l_1' l_2' + l_1 l_2) = \beta c_1 c_2 \cos \theta$. Thus, we obtain

$$\frac{\partial P^{(0)}}{\partial \eta} = C \phi_\eta^{(1)}, \quad \frac{\partial Q^{(0)}}{\partial \xi} = D \phi_\xi^{(1)} \tag{7.73}$$

where $C = \frac{\beta c_1 (1 + 2 \cos \theta)}{c_2 (3 - 2 \cos \theta)}$ and $D = \frac{\beta c_2 (1 + 2 \cos \theta)}{c_1 (3 - 2 \cos \theta)}$.

Equations (7.71) and (7.72) are two KdV equations. These waves are traveling in the ξ direction and η direction, respectively. To obtain a multi-soliton solution of the KdV equation, let us employ Hirota's direct method to (7.71) and (7.72). Accordingly,

$$\phi_\xi^{(1)} = \frac{12B}{A} \frac{\partial^2}{\partial \xi^2} (\log f) \tag{7.74}$$

where $f = 1 + e^{\theta_1}$ and $\theta_1 = kB^{-1/3}\xi - k^3 \tau + \delta$. Using (7.74) in Equation (7.73), we get

$$Q^{(0)}(\xi, \tau) = \frac{12BD}{AC} \frac{\partial}{\partial \xi} (\log f) = \frac{12B^{2/3}D}{AC} \frac{ke^{\theta_1}}{1 + e^{\theta_1}}. \tag{7.75}$$

Therefore, the corresponding phase shift is

$$\triangle Q^{(0)} = \epsilon(l_2' x + l_2 y - c_2 t)|_{\xi = -\infty, \eta = 0} - \epsilon(l_1' x + l_1 y - c_1 t)|_{\xi = \infty, \eta = 0}$$

$$= \epsilon^2 Q^{(0)}(\infty, \tau) - \epsilon^2 Q^{(0)}(-\infty, \tau) = \frac{12\epsilon^2 DB^{2/3}}{AC} k. \tag{7.76}$$

Similarly, the other phase shift is

$$\triangle P^{(0)} = -\frac{12\epsilon^2 DB^{2/3}}{AC}k. \tag{7.77}$$

Phase shifts in Equations (7.76) and (7.77) are similar to the investigations of different plasma models, but the approaches are different.

Two soliton: Each of the KdV equations given by (7.71) and (7.72) has many soliton solutions. We consider here two-soliton solutions of each of the KdV equations. The two solitons for a particular KdV equation move in the same directions. The fast-moving soliton eventually overtakes the slower one. The two soliton solutions of (7.71) and (7.72) are propagated from the opposite directions. Initially, they are far from each other, but after some time, they come together, and the head-on collision will take place, and the solitons will finally depart. Using Hirota's method, the two-soliton solution of the KdV equation (7.71) is given by

$$\phi_\xi^{(1)} = \frac{12B}{A}\frac{\partial^2}{\partial\xi^2}(\log g) \tag{7.78}$$

where $g = 1 + e^{\theta_1} + e^{\theta_2} + a_{12}e^{\theta_1+\theta_2}$, $\theta_i = k_i B^{-1/3}\xi - k_i^3\tau + \delta_i$ $(i = 1, 2)$, and $a_{12} = (k_1 - k_2)^2/(k_1 + k_2)^2$. Using (7.78) in Equation (7.73), we obtain the corresponding phase shifts as

$$\triangle Q^{(0)} = \frac{12\epsilon^2 DB^{2/3}}{AC}(k_1 + k_2), \quad \triangle P^{(0)} = -\frac{12\epsilon^2 DB^{2/3}}{AC}(k_1 + k_2). \tag{7.79}$$

Three soliton: The three-soliton solution of (7.71) has the form

$$\phi_\xi^{(1)} = \frac{12B}{A}\frac{\partial^2}{\partial\xi^2}(\log h) \tag{7.80}$$

where $h = 1 + e^{\theta_1} + e^{\theta_2} + e^{\theta_3} + a_{12}^2 e^{\theta_1+\theta_2} + a_{13}^2 e^{\theta_3+\theta_1} + a_{23}^2 e^{\theta_2+\theta_3} + a^2 e^{\theta_1+\theta_2+\theta_3}$, $\theta_i = k_i B^{-1/3}\xi - k_i^3\tau + \delta_i$ $(i = 1, 2, 3)$ and $a_{lm}^2 = \left(\frac{k_l - k_m}{k_l + k_m}\right)^2$; $l, m = 1, 2, 3, l < m$. $a^2 = \prod_{l,m=1,l<m}^3 a_{lm}^2$. δ_i is the initial phase of the ith soliton in a three-soliton, and the corresponding phase shifts are given by

$$\triangle P^{(0)} = -\frac{12\epsilon^2 DB^{2/3}}{AC}(k_1 + k_2 + k_3),$$
$$\triangle Q^{(0)} = \frac{12\epsilon^2 DB^{2/3}}{AC}(k_1 + k_2 + k_3). \tag{7.81}$$

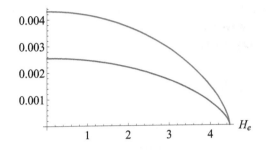

Fig. 7.7: Variation of phase shift $\triangle Q^{(0)}$ against the parameter H_e.

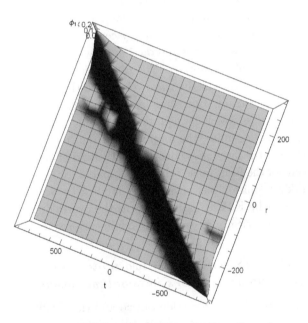

Fig. 7.8: Propagation of two solitons in three dimensions.

Figure 7.7 shows how the phase shifts are affected by the quantum diffraction parameter H_e. We consider $\epsilon = 0.01, k_1 = 0.1, k_2 = 0.2, l_1 = 0.5$, and $l_2 = 0.3$. It is seen that $Q^{(0)}$ is decreasing rapidly as H_e is increasing.

Figure 7.8 shows that two propagated dust ion-acoustic solitons approach each other, collide, and asymptotically separate away. We observe that during oblique collision, one practically motionless composite structure is formed for some time interval. In other words, it is shown that when two ion-acoustic solitary waves of the same amplitude interact obliquely, a new nonlinear wave is formed during their interaction which moves ahead of the colliding solitary waves; both its amplitude and width are larger than those of colliding solitary waves.

7.4 Overtaking Collision

We get this type of collision by applying two consecutive voltage pulses between the two plasmas, with amplitudes such that the first pulse generates a small-amplitude soliton and the second pulse produces a large-amplitude one. Since the larger-amplitude soliton propagates faster, it will overtake the smaller one. The interaction is depicted in the wave frame so that the small pulse is initially stationary. H. Ikezi *et al.* [1] observed that the time difference between each adjacent two waves is $10\mu sec$. Due to the velocity of the waves, the interaction shown takes place over 15 cm, resulting in considerable damping. The difference of velocity between the two pulses is much less than the wave velocity so that not much motion is evident in the wave train. But some features of the nonlinear interaction, described by the loss-free KdV equation, are evident. As the larger pulse overtakes the smaller pulse, the amplitude of the front pulse increases as the amplitude of the large pulse decreases. H. Ikezi *et al.* [1] also observed the amplitude of the front pulse is larger compared to the pulse in the back. This overtaking collision has been widely studied by Scott *et al.* [17] and Whitham [18]. The KdV equation governs the overtaking collision and is characterized analytically as essentially nonlinear or strong.

7.4.1 *Overtaking interaction of two solitons and three solitons of EAWs in quantum plasma*

To study the overtaking interaction of two and three solitons, we consider an unmagnetized and collisionless quantum plasma consisting of ions and both hot and cold electrons. Also, we consider the dynamics of cold electrons in the background of hot electrons and ions. The phase speed of EAWs lies in between v_{Fc} and v_{Fh}, i.e., $v_{Fc} \ll \omega \ll v_{Fh}$, where v_{Fc} and v_{Fh} are Fermi velocities of cold and hot electrons, respectively. The basic normalized equations are

$$\frac{\partial n}{\partial t} + \frac{\partial (nu)}{\partial x} = 0, \tag{7.82}$$

$$\frac{\partial u}{\partial t} + u\frac{\partial u}{\partial x} = \alpha\frac{\partial \phi}{\partial x}, \tag{7.83}$$

$$\frac{\partial \phi}{\partial x} - n_h \frac{\partial n_h}{\partial x} + \frac{H^2}{2} \frac{\partial}{\partial x} \left[\frac{\partial^2 \sqrt{n_h}/\partial x}{\sqrt{n_h}} \right] = 0, \tag{7.84}$$

$$\frac{\partial^2 \phi}{\partial x^2} = n_h + \frac{1}{\alpha} n - \left(1 + \frac{1}{\alpha} \right). \tag{7.85}$$

Integrating Equation (7.84) once with the boundary condition $n_h \to 1$ and $\phi \to 0$ at $\pm\infty$, we have

$$\phi = -\frac{1}{2} + \frac{n_h^2}{2} - \frac{H^2}{2\sqrt{n_h}} \frac{\partial^2 \sqrt{n_h}}{\partial x^2} \tag{7.86}$$

where n, n_h, u, and m_e are the cold electron number density, the hot electron number density, the cold electron velocity, and the electron mass, respectively. ϕ is the electrostatic wave potential, H is the nondimensional quantum parameter due to hot electron determined by $H = \hbar\omega_{ph}/2K_B T_{Fh}$, $\omega_{ph} = \sqrt{4\pi n_{h0}e^2/m_e}$ is the hot electron plasma frequency, and $\hbar$ is the Planck constant. In an unperturbed state, neutrality condition gives $n_0 + n_{h0} = n_{i0}$.

Normalization

$$n \to \frac{n}{n_0}, \quad n_h \to \frac{n_h}{n_{h0}}, \quad u \to \frac{\alpha_e u}{\sqrt{2K_B T_{Fh}}}, \quad \phi \to \frac{e\phi}{2K_B T_{Fh}},$$

$$x \to \frac{x}{\lambda_{Fh}}, \quad t \to \omega_{pc} t \tag{7.87}$$

where $\alpha = n_{h0}/n_0 (> 1)$, $\lambda_{Fh} = \sqrt{2k_B T_{Fh}/4\pi n_{h0}e^2}$, $\omega_{pc}^{-1} = \sqrt{m_e/4\pi n_0 e^2}$, T_{Fh} is the Fermi temperature of hot electron, K_B is the Boltzmann constant, and e is the electron charge. The Fermi temperature of hot electrons is given by the relation $m_e v_{Fh}^2/2 = k_B T_{Fh}$.

Now, we derive the KdV equation from Equations (7.82)–(7.86) employing the RPT. The independent variables are stretched as $\xi = \epsilon(x - \lambda t)$ and $\tau = \epsilon^3 t$ and the dependent variables are expanded as

$$n = 1 + \sum_{k=1}^{\infty} \epsilon^k n^{(k)} + \cdots, \quad u = \sum_{k=1}^{\infty} \epsilon^k u^{(k)} + \cdots,$$

$$n_h = 1 + \sum_{k=1}^{\infty} \epsilon^k n_h^{(k)} + \cdots, \quad \phi = \sum_{k=1}^{\infty} \epsilon^k \phi^{(k)} + \cdots \tag{7.88}$$

where ϵ is a small nonzero parameter proportional to the amplitude of the perturbation. Now, substituting (7.88) into (7.82)–(7.86) and taking the terms in different power of ϵ, we obtain in the lowest order of ϵ the dispersion relation as $\lambda^2 = 1$.

In the next higher order of ϵ, we eliminate the second-order perturbed quantities from a set of equations to obtain the required KdV equation. Since this is a standard procedure, we skip the details and write the KdV equation

$$\frac{\partial \phi^{(1)}}{\partial \tau} - A\phi^{(1)} \frac{\partial \phi^{(1)}}{\partial \xi} + B \frac{\partial^3 \phi^{(1)}}{\partial \xi^3} = 0 \tag{7.89}$$

where $A = \frac{\lambda}{2}(3\alpha - 1)$ and $B = \frac{\lambda}{2}\left(1 - \frac{H^2}{4}\right)$. The amplitude and width of a single soliton are respectively $\phi_m = -\frac{3M}{A}$ and $W = \sqrt{\frac{4B}{M}}$, where M is the normalized constant speed of the wave frame. We get the two solitons' solution of the KdV equation (7.89) as

$$\phi^{(1)} = -12\frac{B^{1/3}}{A}$$
$$\times \frac{k_1^2 e^{\theta_1} + k_2^2 e^{\theta_2} + a_{12}e^{\theta_1+\theta_2}(k_2^2 e^{\theta_1} + k_1^2 e^{\theta_2}) + 2(k_1 - k_2)^2 e^{\theta_1+\theta_2}}{(1 + e^{\theta_1} + e^{\theta_2} + a_{12}e^{\theta_1+\theta_2})^2}$$
$$\tag{7.90}$$

with $\theta_i = \frac{k_i}{B^{1/3}}\xi - k_i^3\tau + \alpha_i$ and $a_{12} = (k_1 - k_2)^2/(k_1 + k_2)^2$. a_{12} determines the phase shifts of the respective solitons after overtaking takes place.

When $\tau \gg 1$, the solution of Equation (7.89) asymptotically transforms into a superposition of two single soliton solutions

$$\phi^{(1)} \approx -\frac{3B^{1/3}}{A}\left[\frac{k_1^2}{2}\operatorname{sech}^2\left\{\frac{k_1}{2B^{1/3}}\left(\xi - B^{1/3}k_1^2\tau - \Delta_1\right)\right\}\right.$$
$$\left. + \frac{k_2^2}{2}\operatorname{sech}^2\left\{\frac{k_2}{2B^{1/3}}\left(\xi - B^{1/3}k_2^2\tau - \Delta_2\right)\right\}\right] \tag{7.91}$$

where $\Delta_i = \pm\frac{2B^{1/3}}{K_i}ln|\sqrt{a_{12}}|$ $(i = 1, 2)$. It is to be noted that the phase shifts Δ_1 and Δ_2 are of the same sign, and both of them are proportional to $B^{1/3}$ and amplitude. It is to be noted that B depends on H. The phase shifts will also depend on the parameter H.

Here, the coefficient A is independent of H, but the coefficient B depends on H. The dispersion coefficient B vanishes at $H = 2$. This critical value of H destroys the KdV equation (Equation (7.89)), and no soliton can occur in this case. No soliton solution is possible for $H > 2$. However, we find that the $H < 2$ formation of soliton structure is possible.

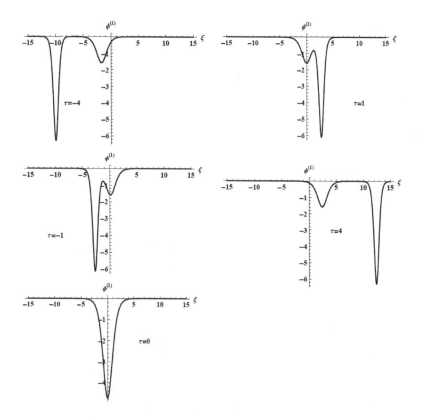

Fig. 7.9: Variation of the two soliton profiles $\phi^{(1)}$ (Equation (7.90)) for different values of τ with $H = 1.5$, $\alpha = 1.1$.

In Figure 7.9, the time evaluation of the interaction of two soliton solution $\phi^{(1)}$ vs ξ is plotted for the several values of τ. At $\tau = -4$, the larger amplitude soliton is behind the smaller amplitude solitary wave. When $\tau = -1$, two solitons merge and become one soliton at $\tau = 0$. But at $\tau = 1$, they separate from each other, and then finally, each appears as a separate soliton acquiring their respective unchanged speed and shape. It can be seen from the exact two soliton solutions and asymptotical solution that the amplitude of the merged soliton is greater than the amplitude of the shorter soliton but less than the amplitude of the taller soliton.

Three soliton solution: To construct three soliton solution, we use the Hirota perturbation and finally, we get the three solitons solution of the

KdV equation (7.89) as

$$\phi^{(1)} = -12\frac{B^{1/3}}{A}\frac{L_1}{M_1} \tag{7.92}$$

where

$$
\begin{aligned}
L_1 =\ & e^{\theta_1+\theta_2}\left[2(k_1-k_2)^2 + 2(k_1-k_2)^2 a_{13}a_{23}e^{2\theta_3} + a_{12}k_1^2 e^{\theta_2} + a_{12}k_2^2 e^{\theta_1}\right] \\
& + e^{\theta_1+\theta_3}\left[2(k_1-k_3)^2 + 2(k_1-k_3)^2 a_{12}a_{23}e^{2\theta_2} + a_{13}k_1^2 e^{\theta_3} + a_{13}k_3^2 e^{\theta_1}\right] \\
& + e^{\theta_2+\theta_3}\left[2(k_2-k_3)^2 + 2(k_2-k_3)^2 a_{12}a_{13}e^{2\theta_1} + a_{23}k_2^2 e^{\theta_3} + a_{23}k_3^2 e^{\theta_2}\right] \\
& + k_1^2 e^{\theta_1} + k_2^2 e^{\theta_2} + k_3^2 e^{\theta_3} + B_1 e^{\theta_1+\theta_2+\theta_3} \\
& \times \left[a_{12}k_3^2 e^{\theta_1+\theta_2} + a_{13}k_2^2 e^{\theta_1+\theta_3} + a_{23}k_1^2 e^{\theta_2+\theta_3}\right] \\
& + e^{\theta_1+\theta_2+\theta_3}\left[a_{12}(k_1^2 + k_2^2 + k_3^2 + 2k_1k_2 - 2k_1k_3 - 2k_2k_3)\right. \\
& + a_{13}(k_1^2 + k_2^2 + k_3^2 + 2k_1k_3 - 2k_1k_2 - 2k_2k_3) \\
& + a_{23}(k_1^2 + k_2^2 + k_3^2 + 2k_2k_3 - 2k_1k_2 - 2k_1k_3) \\
& \left. + B_1(k_1^2 + k_2^2 + k_3^2 + 2k_1k_2 + 2k_1k_3 + 2k_2k_3)\right] \\
M_1 =\ & \left[1 + e^{\theta_1} + e^{\theta_2} + e^{\theta_3} + a_{12}e^{\theta_1+\theta_2} + a_{13}e^{\theta_1+\theta_3}\right. \\
& \left. + a_{23}e^{\theta_2+\theta_3} + B_1 e^{\theta_1+\theta_2+\theta_3}\right]^2 \\
B_1 =\ & a_{12}a_{13}a_{23}, \quad \theta_i = \frac{k_i}{B^{1/3}}\xi - k_i^3\tau + \alpha_i, \quad i = 1,2,3.
\end{aligned}
$$

For $\tau \gg 1$, the above solution is asymptotically transformed into a superposition of three single-soliton solutions as

$$\phi^{(1)} \approx -\sum_i^3 A_i \operatorname{sech}^2\left[\frac{k_i}{2B^{1/3}}\left(\xi - k_i^2 B^{1/3}\tau - \Delta_i'\right)\right] \tag{7.93}$$

where $A_i = 3B^{1/3}k_i^2/2A$ $(i = 1,2,3)$ is the amplitudes, and $\Delta_1' = \pm\frac{2B^{1/3}}{k_1}ln|\frac{B_1}{a_{23}}|$, $\Delta_2' = \pm\frac{2B^{1/3}}{k_2}ln|\frac{B_1}{a_{13}}|$, and $\Delta_3' = \pm\frac{2B^{1/3}}{k_3}ln|\frac{B_1}{a_{12}}|$ are the phase shifts of the solitons.

In Figure 7.10, the time evaluation of the interaction of three-soliton solution $\phi^{(1)}$ vs ξ is plotted for the several values of τ. At $\tau = -8$, the larger amplitude soliton is behind the smaller amplitude solitary wave. When $\tau = -4$, two solitons merge and become one soliton at $\tau = 0$. But at $\tau = 1$, they separate from each other, and then finally, each appears as a separate soliton acquiring their original speed and shape.

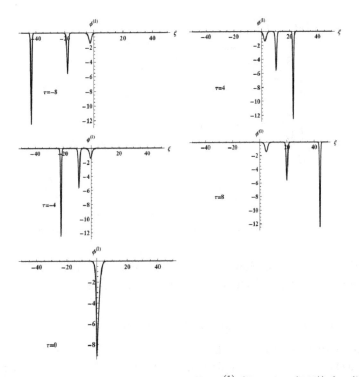

Fig. 7.10: Variation of the three soliton profiles $\phi^{(1)}$ (Equation (7.92)) for different values of τ.

Figure 7.11 shows the variation of phase shift for respective solitons against H when the values of the other parameters are kept fixed. The phase shifts decrease with the increase in H, and the value of B decreases with the increase in H.

Here, we have investigated the nature of the nonlinear propagation of two and three-electron acoustic soliton solutions in an unmagnetized quantum plasma consisting of ions and both cold and hot electrons. The KdV equation is derived by using RPT. Standard KdV equation is obtained by suitable transformation. Using Hirota's direct method, we have obtained a two-soliton solution of the KdV equation. The propagation of the two solitons and the three solitons has been discussed. We have observed that the larger soliton moves faster, approaches the smaller ones, and after overtaking collision, both resume their original shape and speed. Although head-on collision and overtaking collision are different phenomena, they are qualitatively consistent with each other. In two solitons' solutions, $k_i\Delta_i$ $(i = 1, 2)$

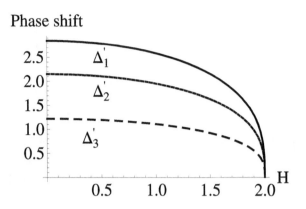

Fig. 7.11: Variation of the phase shift for three solitons against the parameter H.

have the same values. However, in the three soliton case, $k_i \Delta_i$ is not the same for $(i = 1, 2, 3)$. Each of them is different from the others.

7.5 Soliton Interaction and Soliton Turbulence

In weakly dispersive media, the soliton is an essential part of the nonlinear wavefield. Their deterministic dynamics in the framework of the KdV equation is thoroughly researched [19–21]. Several authors have also studied soliton and multisoliton solutions of the KdV and KdV-like equations and their mutual interactions [22–26]. When a huge number of interacting waves propagate in different directions with different velocities, their interactions lead to a fast change in the wave pattern. The characteristics of the wavefield are thus described within the framework of statistical theory. Such theory is termed the theory of wave turbulence [27, 28]. Zakharov [29, 30] has discussed the characteristics of wave turbulence in an integrable system. The soliton turbulence is specified by the kinetic equations describing the parameters of the associated scattering problem and is a specific part of wave turbulence. In 1971, Zakharov [29] first described the fundamental role of pairwise soliton collisions within the framework of the KdV equation. Later, the fact was confirmed in Refs. [31–33]. The soliton turbulence in the integrable system is slightly degenerative because of the conservation of solitons in the interacting process. In the turbulence theory, the wavefield distribution and the moments (mean, variance, skewness, and kurtosis) of the random wavefield are obtained from the measurements [34–37]. Pelinovsky *et al.* [38, 39] studied the two soliton interactions as an elementary act of soliton turbulence in the framework of the KdV and modified KdV equation. They have shown that the nonlinear interaction of two solitons leads to a decrease in third and fourth-order moments of the wavefield, whereas the first and second moments remain constant. Some works have been reported on soliton turbulence [40–44]. Shurgalina [45, 46] has studied different features of soliton turbulence in the framework of Gardner's equation with negative and positive cubic nonlinearities.

Let us consider an unmagnetized dusty plasma consisting of cold inertial ions, stationary negative dust charge, and inertialess κ distributed electrons. The normalized basic equations governing the DIA waves are given by

$$\frac{\partial n}{\partial t} + \frac{\partial(nu)}{\partial x} = 0, \tag{7.94}$$

$$\frac{\partial u}{\partial t} + u\frac{\partial u}{\partial x} = -\frac{\partial \phi}{\partial x}, \tag{7.95}$$

$$\frac{\partial^2 \phi}{\partial x^2} = (1-\mu)\left(1 - \frac{\phi}{\kappa - 3/2}\right)^{-\kappa + 1/2} - n + \mu \tag{7.96}$$

where n is the ion number density normalized to n_0, n_e is the number density of the electrons, u is the ion velocity normalized to ion fluid speed, $C_s = \sqrt{K_B T_e/m_i}$, m_i is the mass of ion, T_e is the temperature of electron, and K_B is the Boltzmann constant. The electrostatic wave potential ϕ is normalized to $K_B T_e/e$. Space and time variables are normalized to electron Debye radius $\lambda_D = \sqrt{K_B T_e/4\pi n_{e0}e^2}$ and the inverse of cold electron plasma frequency $\omega_{pi}^{-1} = \sqrt{m_i/4\pi n_{e0}e^2}$, respectively. Here, $\mu = \frac{Z_d n_{d0}}{n_0}$, with n_{d0} being the number density of dusts and Z_d being the dust charge number.

To derive the KdV equation, RPT is applied. According to RPT, the independent variables are stretched as

$$\xi = \epsilon^{1/2}(x - vt), \quad \tau = \epsilon^{3/2}t. \tag{7.97}$$

The dependent variables are expanded as

$$n = 1 + \sum_{k=1}^{\infty} \epsilon^k n_k + \cdots, \quad u = \sum_{k=1}^{\infty} \epsilon^k u_1 + \cdots,$$

$$\phi = \sum_{k=1}^{\infty} \epsilon^k \phi_k + \cdots. \tag{7.98}$$

Using Equations (7.97) and (7.98) in Equations (7.94)–(7.96) and comparing coefficients of lowest powers of ϵ, we obtain the linear propagation speed in a low-frequency limit as

$$v^2 = \frac{1}{a(1-\mu)}, \tag{7.99}$$

with $a = \frac{\kappa-1/2}{\kappa-3/2}$.

Taking the coefficients of the next higher order of ϵ, we obtain the following KdV equation:

$$\frac{\partial \phi_1}{\partial \tau} + A\phi_1 \frac{\partial \phi_1}{\partial \xi} + B\frac{\partial^3 \phi_1}{\partial \xi^3} = 0 \tag{7.100}$$

where $A = \left(\frac{3-2b(1-\mu)v^4}{2v}\right)$, $B = \frac{v^3}{2}$, and $b = \frac{(\kappa-1/2)(\kappa+1/2)}{2(\kappa-3/2)^2}$.

The coefficient A of the nonlinear term $\phi_1 \frac{\partial \phi_1}{\partial \xi}$ of the KdV Equation (7.100) becomes zero for $\kappa = \frac{(4-3\mu)}{2(2-3\mu)}$. So, assuming $\kappa \neq \frac{(4-3\mu)}{2(2-3\mu)}$ ($\mu < 1$) and making the transformations $\xi = B^{1/3}\,\bar{\xi}$, $\phi_1 = 6A^{-1}B^{1/3}\,\bar{\phi}_1$, and $\tau = \bar{\tau}$ to the KdV Equation (7.100), we obtain the following standard KdV equation:

$$\frac{\partial \bar{\phi}_1}{\partial \bar{\tau}} + 6\bar{\phi}_1 \frac{\partial \bar{\phi}_1}{\partial \bar{\xi}} + \frac{\partial^3 \bar{\phi}_1}{\partial \bar{\xi}^3} = 0. \tag{7.101}$$

Using Hirota's bilinear method, the two-soliton solution of Equation (7.101) is obtained [47] as

$$\bar{\phi}_1 = 2\frac{\partial^2}{\partial \bar{\xi}^2}(\ln f) \tag{7.102}$$

where $f(\xi, \tau) = 1 + e^{\bar{\theta}_1} + e^{\bar{\theta}_2} + A_{12}^2 e^{\bar{\theta}_1+\bar{\theta}_2}$, $A_{12} = \frac{\eta_1-\eta_2}{\eta_1+\eta_2}$, and $\bar{\theta}_i = -2(\eta_i\bar{\xi} - 4\eta_i^3\bar{\tau} - \alpha_i)$ for $i = 1, 2$. Here, α_i are the initial phase of the solitons. Thus, the two-soliton solution of the KdV Equation (7.100) is

$$\phi_1 = \frac{12B}{A}\frac{\partial^2}{\partial \xi^2}(\ln f) \tag{7.103}$$

where $f(\xi, \tau) = 1 + e^{\theta_1} + e^{\theta_2} + A_{12}^2 e^{\theta_1+\theta_2}$, and $\theta_i = -2\left(\frac{\eta_i}{B^{1/3}}\xi - 4\eta_i^3\tau - \alpha_i\right)$ for $i = 1, 2$.

From Equation (7.103), we have

$$\phi_1 = \frac{12B^{1/3}}{A}\frac{N}{D} \qquad (7.104)$$

where $D = (1 + e^{\theta_1} + e^{\theta_2} + A_{12}^2 e^{\theta_1+\theta_2})^2$ and $N = \eta_1^2 e^{\theta_1} + \eta_2^2 e^{\theta_2} + A_{12}^2 (\eta_2^2 e^{\theta_1} + \eta_1^2 e^{\theta_2})e^{\theta_1+\theta_2} + 2(\eta_1 - \eta_2)^2 e^{\theta_1+\theta_2}$. From Equation (7.104), we have

$$\begin{aligned}
\phi_1 &= \frac{12B^{1/3}}{A} \\
&\quad \times \frac{\eta_1^2 e^{\theta_1} + \eta_2^2 e^{\theta_2} + A_{12}^2(\eta_2^2 e^{\theta_1} + \eta_1^2 e^{\theta_2})e^{\theta_1+\theta_2} + 2(\eta_1 - \eta_2)^2 e^{\theta_1+\theta_2}}{(1 + e^{\theta_1} + e^{\theta_2} + A_{12}^2 e^{\theta_1+\theta_2})^2}, \\
&= \frac{12B^{1/3}}{A} \\
&\quad \times \frac{\eta_1^2 e^{-\theta_1-2\theta_2} + \eta_2^2 e^{-2\theta_1-\theta_2} + A_{12}^2(\eta_1^2 e^{-\theta_1} + \eta_2^2 e^{-\theta_2}) + 2(\eta_1 - \eta_2)^2 e^{-\theta_1-\theta_2}}{(e^{-\theta_1-\theta_2} + e^{-\theta_1} + e^{-\theta_2} + A_{12}^2)^2}.
\end{aligned}$$

$$(7.105)$$

Assuming $\tau \gg 1$, Equation (7.105) is asymptotically (up to exponentially small terms) approximated as

$$\begin{aligned}
\phi_1 &\approx \frac{12B^{1/3}}{A}\left(\frac{\eta_1^2 A_{12}^2 e^{-\theta_1}}{(e^{-\theta_1} + A_{12}^2)^2} + \frac{\eta_2^2 A_{12}^2 e^{-\theta_2}}{(e^{-\theta_2} + A_{12}^2)^2} \right) \\
&= \frac{48A^2 B^{1/3}}{A}\left(\frac{\eta_1^2}{(A_{12}e^{\theta_1/2} + \frac{e^{-\theta_1/2}}{A_{12}})^2} + \frac{\eta_2^2}{(A_{12}e^{\theta_2/2} + \frac{e^{-\theta_2/2}}{A_{12}})^2} \right) \\
\phi_1 &\approx \frac{12B^{1/3}}{A}\left(\eta_1^2 \operatorname{sech}^2(\theta_1/2 + \ln A_{12}) + \eta_2^2 \operatorname{sech}^2(\theta_2/2 + \ln A_{12}) \right).
\end{aligned}$$

$$(7.106)$$

Therefore, for $\tau \gg 1$, the two-soliton solution (7.103) of the KdV Equation (7.100) is asymptotically transformed into a superposition of two single solitons [26]

$$\phi_1 = \sum_{i=1}^{2} A_i \operatorname{sech}^2\left[\frac{\eta_i}{B^{1/3}}\left(\xi - 4\eta_i^2 B^{1/3}\tau - \frac{B^{1/3}}{\eta_i}\alpha_i - \Delta_i \right) \right] \qquad (7.107)$$

where the amplitudes of the solitons are given by

$$A_i = \frac{12B^{1/3}\eta_i^2}{A}, \quad i = 1, 2,$$

and the phase shifts (Δ_i, $i = 1, 2$) of the solitons due to interaction are given by

$$\Delta_1 = \frac{B^{1/3}}{\eta_1} \ln(A_{12}), \quad \Delta_2 = \frac{B^{1/3}}{\eta_2} \ln(A_{12}).$$

7.6 Statistical Characteristics of the Wavefield

In this section, we will discuss the propagation and mutual interaction of the two solitons of the KdV Equation (7.100). Due to the complete integrability of the KdV Equation (7.100), the interaction of solitons is elastic. After the interaction, they regain the properties of soliton [29, 31–33, 47]. Two solitons with different amplitudes propagate in time since the speed of the solitons is proportional to their amplitudes, and the nonlinear interaction of the two solitons takes place at a certain time and space. Choosing $\alpha_1 = -\frac{\eta_1}{2B^{1/3}}\Delta_1$, $\alpha_2 = -\frac{\eta_2}{2B^{1/3}}\Delta_2$. The interaction of the soliton elements occurs at the origin, i.e., at the point $\xi = 0, \tau = 0$ [48]. For the above choice of α_1 and α_2 and assuming $\eta_1 > \eta_2$, the amplitude of the resulting peak is obtained as

$$\phi_1^* = \frac{12B^{1/3}}{A}(\eta_1^2 - \eta_2^2). \tag{7.108}$$

The pulse shape at the soliton interaction is instantly determined by the following equation:

$$\frac{\partial^2 \phi_1}{\partial \xi^2}(0,0) = -\frac{24}{AB^{1/3}}\left(\eta_1^4 - 4\eta_1^2\eta_2^2 + 3\eta_2^4\right). \tag{7.109}$$

Equation (7.109) indicates the concavity of wave profile at the strongest interaction point. The negative value of Equation (7.109) indicates that the wave profile is concave downwards. Therefore, the wave profile may maintain a single peak status at the strongest interaction point. The positive value of Equation (7.109) implies that the wave profile is concave upwards, and it will maintain two peak statuses at $\xi = 0, \tau = 0$. Equation (7.109) is positive or negative according to whether $(1 - R)(1 - 3R)$ is negative or positive, where $R = \frac{\eta_2^2}{\eta_1^2}$ and $\eta_1 > \eta_2$. Equation (7.109) is negative for $R < \frac{1}{3}$ and is positive for $\frac{1}{3} < R < 1$.

Figure 7.12 shows the interaction process of two solitons of Equation (7.100) for $R = 0.3$, $\kappa = 2$, $\mu = 0.1$, and $\eta_1 = 0.4$. When $R < \frac{1}{3}$, the larger soliton grabs the smaller soliton and merge as a single soliton at $\xi = 0, \tau = 0$ and overtakes the smaller soliton.

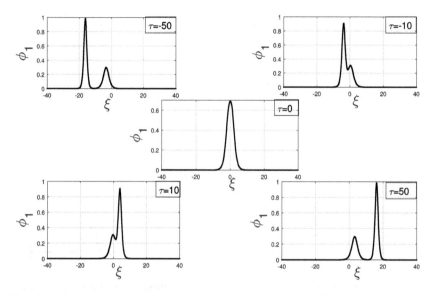

Fig. 7.12: Interaction process of two solitons of Equation (7.100) for $\kappa = 2$, $\mu = 0.1$, $\eta_1 = 0.4$, and $R = 0.3$.

Figure 7.13 presents the interaction process of two solitons for $R = 0.5$, $\kappa = 2, \mu = 0.1$, and $\eta_1 = 0.4$. When $\frac{1}{3} < R < 1$, the bigger and smaller solitons exchange their energy. In this case, the solitons never merge into a single soliton.

The interaction of a large number of propagating waves in conservative systems results in changing the wave patterns fast. In such a scenario, the statistical theory is suitable for describing the wavefield. Such a theory is called weak wave turbulence. Soliton turbulence is stronger than the ordinary, weak turbulent plasma description. The conservation laws are important aspects in the study of turbulence theory. For a scalar partial differential equation with two independent variables x and t, and a single dependent variable u, the conservation law can be written as

$$\frac{\partial T}{\partial t} + \frac{\partial X}{\partial x} = 0 \tag{7.110}$$

where T and X are conserved density and flux, respectively. Moreover, both are polynomials of the solution u and its derivatives with respect to the space variable x [49]. If both T and $\frac{\partial X}{\partial x}$ are integrable over the interval $(-\infty, \infty)$, then on the assumption that $X \longrightarrow 0$ as $|X| \longrightarrow \infty$,

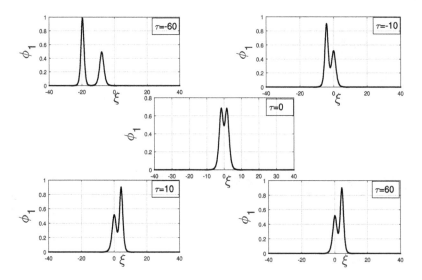

Fig. 7.13: Interaction process of two solitons of Equation (7.100) for $\kappa = 2$, $\mu = 0.1$, $\eta_1 = 0.4$, and $R = 0.5$.

Equation (7.110) can be integrated as

$$\frac{d}{dt}\left(\int_{-\infty}^{\infty} T dx\right) = 0,$$

$$\Rightarrow \int_{-\infty}^{\infty} T dx = constant. \tag{7.111}$$

Equation (7.111) is invariant with time and is termed as the invariant of motion or constant of motion [50, 51]. The KdV equation forms a completely integrable Hamiltonian system. Hence, it possesses an infinite number of conserved quantities [19–21]. The first four conservation laws of the KdV Equation (7.100) are

$$I_1 = \int_{-\infty}^{\infty} \phi_1(\xi, \tau) d\xi, \tag{7.112}$$

$$I_2 = \int_{-\infty}^{\infty} \phi_1^2(\xi, \tau) d\xi, \tag{7.113}$$

$$I_3 = \int_{-\infty}^{\infty} \left[\phi_1^3(\xi, \tau) - \frac{3B}{A}\left(\frac{\partial \phi_1}{\partial \xi}\right)^2\right] d\xi, \tag{7.114}$$

$$I_4 = \int_{-\infty}^{\infty} \left[\phi_1^4(\xi,\tau) - \frac{12B}{A}\phi_1 \left(\frac{\partial\phi_1}{\partial\xi} \right)^2 + \frac{36B^2}{5A^2} \left(\frac{\partial^2\phi_1}{\partial\xi^2} \right)^2 \right] d\xi. \quad (7.115)$$

The first three integrals (7.112)–(7.114) correspond to the conservation of mass, momentum, and energy, respectively. These integrals are preserved in the process of the wavefield evolution, and using the noninteracting solitons (7.107), the analytical calculations of $I_1, I_2, I_3,$ and I_4 are presented as follows:

$$I_1 = \frac{4\sqrt{3B}}{\sqrt{A}} (A_1^{1/2} + A_2^{1/2}), \quad (7.116)$$

$$I_2 = \frac{8\sqrt{3B}}{3\sqrt{A}} (A_1^{3/2} + A_2^{3/2}), \quad (7.117)$$

$$I_3 = \frac{8\sqrt{3B}}{5\sqrt{A}} (A_1^{5/2} + A_2^{5/2}), \quad (7.118)$$

$$I_4 = \frac{32\sqrt{3B}}{35\sqrt{A}} (A_1^{7/2} + A_2^{7/2}). \quad (7.119)$$

From Equations (7.116)–(7.119), it is observed that values of the integrals $I_1, I_2, I_3,$ and I_4 increase as amplitudes of the interacting solitons increase.

The dynamics of multisoliton is affected significantly by mutual interactions of the solitons [29, 30]. To understand the effects of two soliton interactions on the statistical moments of the random wavefield, we consider the following integrals:

$$\mu_n = \int_{-\infty}^{\infty} \phi_1^n d\xi, \quad n = 1, 2, 3, \ldots. \quad (7.120)$$

The integrals (7.120) are related to the statistical moments of the wavefield. The first integral moment (μ_1) and the second integral moment (μ_2) represent the mean and variance of the random wavefield, respectively. The first and second integral moments μ_1 and μ_2 are similar to Kruskal's integral I_1 and I_2. Hence, they are conserved for the two-soliton solution (7.103) which agrees with (7.116) and (7.117) (see Figure 7.14). Thus, the nonlinear interactions of the two solitons do not affect the mean and the variance of the wavefield. The third and fourth integral moments are defined by

$$M_3(\tau) = \frac{\mu_3}{\mu_2^{3/2}}, \quad (7.121)$$

$$M_4(\tau) = \frac{\mu_4}{\mu_2^2}. \quad (7.122)$$

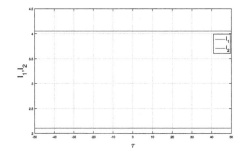

Fig. 7.14: The time dependence of the integrals I_1 and I_2 in the two soliton interaction with $\kappa = 2$, $\mu = 0.1$, $R = 0.5$, and $\eta_1 = 0.4$.

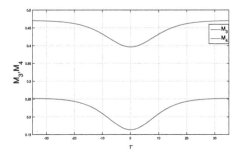

Fig. 7.15: The time dependence of skewness $(M_3(\tau))$ and kurtosis $(M_4(\tau))$ in the two-soliton interaction for $\kappa = 2$, $\mu = 0.1$, $R = 0.5$, and $\eta_1 = 0.4$.

The third and fourth moments $M_3(\tau)$ and $M_4(\tau)$ characterize the skewness and kurtosis (the word 'kurtosis' refers to the normalized fourth moment and not its difference from the Gaussian value 3-'excess kurtosis') of the random wavefield. The statistical measure of the vertical asymmetry of the wavefield is given by the skewness $(M_3(\tau))$ and the kurtosis that provides information on the probability of occurrence of extreme waves [52]. The structures of μ_3 and μ_4 are different from Kruskal's integrals I_3 and I_4. Therefore, the skewness $(M_3(\tau))$ and kurtosis $(M_4(\tau))$ will not be conserved in the dominant interaction region. Figure 7.15 represents the numerical evolution of $M_3(\tau)$ and $M_4(\tau)$ for the two-soliton solution (7.103) with $\kappa = 2, \mu = 0.1, R = 0.5$, and $\eta_1 = 0.4$. In Figure 7.15, the skewness and kurtosis decrease in the dominant interaction region of the random wavefield. If the solitons do not interact with each other, then the skewness (M_3^0) and kurtosis (M_4^0) can be calculated using the noninteracting solitons (7.107)

$$M_3^0 = \frac{\sqrt{6}A^{1/4}}{5(3B)^{1/4}} \frac{(A_1^{5/2} + A_2^{5/2})}{(A_1^{3/2} + A_2^{3/2})^{3/2}}, \qquad (7.123)$$

$$M_4^0 = \frac{3\sqrt{3A}}{35\sqrt{B}} \frac{(A_1^{7/2} + A_2^{7/2})}{(A_1^{3/2} + A_2^{3/2})^2}. \qquad (7.124)$$

Also, from Figure 7.15, it is observed that the skewness $(M_3(\tau))$ is calculated using (7.103). It varies about 7.25% from M_3^0 that is calculated using the noninteracting solitons (7.107). Hence, the kurtosis $(M_4(\tau))$ deviates about 8.03% from M_4^0 due to two soliton interactions. Here, the skewness and kurtosis are always positive as all the two solitons are positive.

7.7 Plasma Parameters on Soliton Turbulence

The soliton amplitude increases as the parameters κ and μ increase, as observed earlier. To show the effects of plasma parameters κ and μ on soliton turbulence, the maximum deviation $M_i^* = M_i^{\max} - M_i^{\min}(i = 3, 4)$ and the relative deviation $M_i^{**} = \frac{M_i^{\max} - M_i^{\min}}{M_i^{\max}}(i = 3, 4)$ in third and fourth moments as a function of κ and μ have been calculated (Figures 7.16–7.19). From Figure 7.16, it is observed that the increase in the value of κ decreases the maximum deviation in the third and fourth moments. Also, the maximum deviation in third and fourth moments due to the interaction of solitons decreases as the parameter μ increases (Figure 7.17). Therefore, the spectral index κ and the parameter μ (unperturbed dust to ion ratio) have a strong influence on the soliton turbulence for the DIA waves for dusty plasma systems.

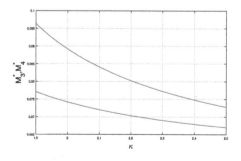

Fig. 7.16: Plot of maximum deviation of the third and fourth moments due to interaction as a function of κ with $\mu = 0.1$, $R = 0.5$, and $\eta_1 = 0.4$.

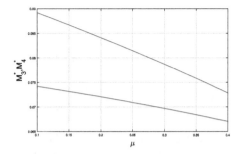

Fig. 7.17: Plot of maximum deviation of the third and fourth moments due to interaction as a function of μ with $\kappa = 2$, $R = 0.5$, and $\eta_1 = 0.4$.

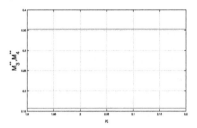

Fig. 7.18: Relative deviation in third and fourth moments due to interaction as a function of κ with $\mu = 0.1$, $R = 0.5$, and $\eta_1 = 0.4$.

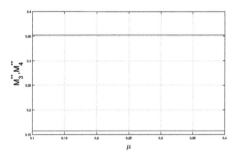

Fig. 7.19: Relative deviation in third and fourth moments due to interaction as a function of μ with $\kappa = 2$, $R = 0.5$, and $\eta_1 = 0.4$.

References

[1] H. Ikezi, R. Taylor, and D. Baker, *Phys. Rev. Lett.* 25, 11 (1970).

[2] T. Maxworthy, *J. Fluid Mech.* 76, 177 (1976).

[3] P. Chatterjee, K. Roy, G. Mandal, S. V. Muniandy, and S. L. Yap, *Phys. Plasmas* 16, 122112 (2009).

[4] F. Verheest, M. A. Hellberg, and W. A. Hereman, *Phys. Rev. E* 86, 036402 (2012).

[5] F. Verheest, M. A. Hellberg, and W. A. Hereman, *Phys. Plasmas* 19, 092302 (2012).

[6] M. Marklund and G. Brodin, *Phys. Rev. Lett.* 98, 025001 (2007).

[7] G. Brodin and M. Marklund, *New J. Phys.* 9, 277 (2007).

[8] M. Marklund, B. Eliasson, and P. K. Shukla, *Phys. Rev. E* 76, 067401 (2007).

[9] A. P. Misra and N. K. Ghosh, *Phys. Lett. A* 372, 6412 (2008).

[10] A. Mushtaq and S. V. Vladimirov, *Eur. Phys. J. D.* 64, 419 (2011).

[11] F. A. Asenjo, J. Zamanian, N. Marklund, G. Brodin, and P. Johansson, *New J. Phys.* 14, 073042 (2012).

[12] M. Bonitz, *Phys. Rev. E* 49, 5535 (1994).

[13] G. Manfredi and F. Hass, *Phys. Rev. B* 64, 075316 (2001).

[14] D. Kremp, T. Bornath, M. Bonitz, and M. Schlanges, *Phys. Rev. E* 60, 4725 (1999).

[15] C. L. Gardener and C. Ringhofer, *Phys. Rev. E* 53, 157 (1996).

[16] E. P. Winger, *Phys. Rev.* 40, 749 (1932).

[17] A. C. Scott, F. Y. F. Chu, and D. W. McLaughlin, *Proc. IEEE.* 61, 1443 (1973).

[18] G. B. Whitham, *Linear and Nonlinear Waves.* Wiley (1974).

[19] S. P. Novikov, S. V. Manakov, L. P. Pitaevskii, and V. E. Zakharov, *The Theory of Solitons: The Inverse Scattering Method.* New York: Consultants (1984).

[20] A. C. Newell, *Solitons in Mathematics and Physics.* Philadelphia: SIAM (1985).

[21] P. G. Drazin and R. S. Johnson, *Solitons: An Introduction.* Cambridge University Press (1993).

[22] B. Sahu and R. Roychoudhury, *Astrophys. Space Sci.* 345, 91–98 (2013).

[23] B. Sahu, *EPL* 101, 55002 (2013).

[24] A. Saha and P. Chatterjee, *Astrophys. Space Sci.* 353, 169–177 (2014).

[25] G. Mandal, K. Roy, A. Paul, A. Saha, and P. Chatterjee, *Z. Naturforsch.* 70, 703–711 (2015).

[26] K. Roy, S. K. Ghosh, and P. Chatterjee, *Pramana J. Phys.* 86, 873–883 (2016).

[27] V. E. Zakharov, V. S. L'vov, and G. Falkovich, *Kolmogorov Spectra of Turbulence.* Berlin: Springer (1992), p. 6.

[28] S. Nazarenko, Wave turbulence. *Lecture Notes in Physics*, p. 279. Berlin: Springer (2011) Vol. 26.

[29] V. E. Zakharov, *Sov. Phys. JETP* 33, 538 (1971).

[30] V. E. Zakharov, *Stud. Appl. Math.* 122, 219 (2009).

[31] G. A. El and A. M. Kamchatnov, *Phys. Rev. Lett.* 95, 204101 (2005).

[32] G. A. El, A. L. Krylov, S. A. Molchanov, and S. Venakides, *Physica D* 152–153, 653–664 (2001).

[33] G. A. El, A. M. Kamchatnov, M. V. Pavlov, and S. A. Zykov, *J. Nonlinear Sci.* 21, 151–191 (2011).

[34] K. Hasselmann, *J. Fluid Mech.* 12, 481 (1962).

[35] S. Dyachenko, A. C. Newell, and V. E. Zakharov, *Physica D* 57, 96 (1992).

[36] V. E. Zakharov and V. S. L'vov, *Radiophys. Quantum Electron.* 18, 1084 (1975).

[37] V. S. Lvov, Y. V. Lvov, A. C. Newell, and V. E. Zakharov, *Phys. Rev. E* 56, 390 (1997).

[38] E. N. Pelinovsky, E. G. Shurgalina, A. V. Sergeeva, T. G. Talipova, G. A. El, and R. H. J. Grimshaw, *Phys. Lett. A* 377, 272 (2013).

[39] E. N. Pelinovsky and E. G. Shurgalina, *Radiophys. Quan. Electr.* 57, 737 (2015).

[40] D. Dutykh and E. N. Pelinovsky, *Phys. Lett A* 378, 3102–3110 (2014).

[41] E. G. Shurgalina and E. N. Pelinovsky, *Phys. Lett. A* 380, 2049–2053 (2016).

[42] E. N. Pelinovsky and E. G. Shurgalina, "KDV soliton gas: Interactions and turbulence," in I. Aronson, N. Rulkov, A. Pikovsky, and L. Tsimring (eds.), *Challenges in Complexity: Advances in Dynamics, Patterns, Cognition.* Springer (2017), pp. 295–306.

[43] E. G. Shurgalina, E. N. Pelinovsky, and K. A. Gorshkov, *Moscow Univ. Phys. Bull.* 72, 441–448 (2017).

[44] A. V. Slunyaev and E. N. Pelinovsky, *Phys. Rev. Lett.* 117, 214501 (2016).

[45] E. G. Shurgalina, *Radiophys. Quan. Electr.* 60, 703–708 (2018).

[46] E. G. Shurgalina, *Fluid Dyn.* 53, 59–64 (2018).

[47] R. Hirota, *The Direct Method in the Soliton Theory.* Cambridge University Press (2004).

[48] T. P. Moloney and P. F. Hodnett, *Proc. R. Irish Acad. Sec. A Math. Phys. Sci.* 89A, 205–217 (1989).

[49] P. G. Drazin and R. S. Johnson, *Solitons: An Introduction.* Cambridge University Press (1996).

[50] F. Verheest and W. Hereman, *Phys. Scripta* 50, 611 (1994).

[51] U. Goktas and W. Hereman, *J. Symb. Comput.* 11, 1 (1999).

[52] N. Mori and P. A. E. M. Janssen, *J. Phys. Ocean* 36, 1471–1483 (2006).

Chapter 8

Sagdeev's Pseudopotential Approach

8.1 Nonperturbative Approach

Nonlinear waves are classified as small-amplitude waves and large-amplitude waves. The major problems of nonlinear waves in plasma physics are treated by the perturbation method. However, the perturbation method is applicable only to study small-amplitude waves. The reason is that for large-amplitude waves, the infinite series of perturbed quantities will not converge to the stable or equilibrium position. To study large-amplitude solitary waves, perturbation technique will not work, and accordingly, several nonperturbation techniques have been developed. For these techniques, the total nonlinearity of the system is taken into account and then the wave solutions are obtained from this consideration. One such method is Sagdeev's pseudopotential method. In 1966, famous scientist R. Z. Sagdeev [1] pioneered a technique that later came to be known as Sagdeev's pseudopotential approach or Sagdeev's energy integral method. This method is used to study large amplitude solitary waves and shock waves, large-amplitude double layers, speed and shape of the solitary waves, and similar features of the wave.

8.2 Sagdeev's Pseudopotential Approach

In 1966, R. Z. Sagdeev introduced an equation $\frac{d^2\phi}{d\xi^2} = -\frac{d\psi}{d\phi}$, where ϕ is the electric potential, the stretched co-ordinate $\xi = x - vt$, x is the position and t is the time, v is the velocity of the wave, and ψ is an unknown quantity. This equation is named after him. The analogy of this equation with that of the newton potential equation is shown in Figure 8.1. From Figure 8.1, it is seen that the unknown quantity $\psi(\phi)$ can be taken as the potential if one considers the potential ϕ as position and $\xi(= x - vt)$

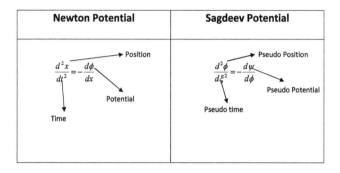

Fig. 8.1: Comparison between the Newton potential and Sagdeev potential.

as time, i.e., if ϕ behaves as pseudo particle and ξ as pseudo time, then ψ is the pseudopotential. This is the reason why $\psi(\phi)$ is called pseudopotential or Sagdeev's potential. Sagdeev's potential plays an important role to find the shape and size of the large-amplitude solitary waves in plasmas. Let us evaluate the pseudopotential as well as the large-amplitude solitary waves in a simple plasma model, given in the following:

Basic equations: Let us consider an unmagnetized, collisionless *e-i* plasma, where ions are mobile and electrons obey the Maxwell distribution. The basic equations in normalized forms are written as follows:

Equation of continuity:

$$\frac{\partial n_i}{\partial t} + \frac{\partial(n_i u_i)}{\partial x} = 0 \tag{8.1}$$

Equation of momentum balance:

$$\frac{\partial u_i}{\partial t} + u_i \frac{\partial u_i}{\partial x} = -\frac{\partial \phi}{\partial x} \tag{8.2}$$

and Poisson equation:

$$\frac{\partial^2 u_i}{\partial x^2} = n_e - n_i \tag{8.3}$$

where $n_e = e^\phi$.

Energy integral and the Sagdeev potential: Let us assume that the wave moves with the velocity of M. We consider the Galilean-type transformation (a traveling wave transformation), where the wave frame moves with the wave velocity M as

$$\xi = x - Mt. \tag{8.4}$$

By substitution $\frac{\partial}{\partial x} = \frac{d}{d\xi}$ and $\frac{\partial}{\partial t} = -M\frac{d}{d\xi}$, (8.1)–(8.3) reduce to

$$-M\frac{dn_i}{d\xi} + \frac{d(n_i u_i)}{d\xi} = 0 \tag{8.5}$$

$$-M\frac{du_i}{d\xi} + u_i\frac{du_i}{d\xi} = -\frac{d\phi}{d\xi} \tag{8.6}$$

$$\frac{d^2\phi}{d\xi^2} = e^\phi - n_i. \tag{8.7}$$

We assume that the equilibrium state is reached at both infinities ($\xi \to \pm\infty$). Accordingly, we integrate and apply the boundary condition $n_i = 1$, $u_i = 0$, and $\phi = 0$ at $\xi \pm \infty$. After integrating and using these initial conditions, from (8.5) and (8.6), one obtains

$$n_i = \frac{M}{M - u_i} \tag{8.8}$$

$$-Mu_i + \frac{u_i^2}{2} = -\phi. \tag{8.9}$$

After some simple algebra, we get

$$\frac{M - u_i}{M} = \left(1 - \frac{2\phi}{M^2}\right)^{1/2}. \tag{8.10}$$

Using Equations (8.8) and (8.10) in Equation (8.7), we get

$$\frac{\partial^2\phi}{\partial\xi^2} = e^\phi - \left(1 - \frac{2\phi}{M^2}\right)^{-1/2}. \tag{8.11}$$

Now, we introduce the pseudopotential ψ as

$$\frac{d^2\phi}{d\xi^2} = -\frac{d\psi}{d\phi}. \tag{8.12}$$

Integrating the above equation, we get

$$\psi = -\int \frac{d^2\phi}{d\xi^2}d\phi = -e^\phi - M(M^2 - 2\phi)^{\frac{1}{2}} + c_1.$$

Putting the condition as when $|\xi| \to \infty$, then $\psi \to 0$, $\phi \to 0$, we obtain $c_1 = 1 + M^2$. Therefore, ψ can be expressed as

$$\psi = 1 - e^\phi + M^2 \left[1 - \left(1 - \frac{2\phi}{M^2}\right)^{1/2}\right] = \psi_e + \psi_i \qquad (8.13)$$

where

$$\psi_e = 1 - e^\phi, \quad \psi_i = M^2 \left[1 - \left(1 - \frac{2\phi}{M^2}\right)^{1/2}\right].$$

Therefore,

$$\boxed{\psi(\phi) = 1 - e^\phi + M^2 \left[1 - \left(1 - \frac{2\phi}{M^2}\right)^{1/2}\right].} \qquad (8.14)$$

The expression in the box is called the "Sagdeev's pseudopotential", and ψ_i and ψ_e are the contributions of Sagdeev's potential for ions and electrons, respectively.

8.2.1 *Physical interpretation of Sagdeev's potential*

Let us compare Equation (8.12) with Newton's potential equation $\frac{d^2x}{dt^2} = -\frac{d\phi}{dx}$, where x is the position, t is the time, and ϕ is the potential. We can see that Equation (8.12) can be considered as a one-dimensional motion of a particle of unit mass, whose pseudo position is ϕ at pseudo time ξ with pseudo velocity $d\phi/d\xi$ in a pseudopotential well $\psi(\phi)$[2, 3]. If the potential ϕ is treated as pseudo position and ξ as pseudo time, then $\psi(\phi)$ can be treated as pseudopotential. If the first term in integral (8.12) is multiplied by $2d\phi/d\xi$ and integrated, it can be written as $(d\phi/d\xi)^2 + 2\psi(\phi) = $ constant. It can be considered as the kinetic energy of a particle with position coordinate ϕ. $\psi(\phi)$ can be considered as the potential energy at that instant. Since kinetic energy is always non-negative, $\psi(\phi)$ should be negative (i.e., $\psi(\phi) \leq 0$) for the entire motion and zero is the maximum value of $\psi(\phi)$. Again, from Equation (8.12), it is seen that $\frac{d^2\phi}{d\xi^2} + \psi'(\phi) = 0$, i.e., the force acting on the particle is $\psi'(\phi)$, where $\psi'(\phi) = \frac{d\psi}{d\phi}$. It can be shown that $\psi(0) = \psi'(0) = 0$. The particle is in equilibrium at $\phi = 0$ because both the velocity and the force acting on the particle at $\phi = 0$ are zero. Now, if $\phi = 0$ is an unstable equilibrium, the integral shows the motion of an oscillatory particle if $\psi(\phi_m) = 0$ for $\phi_m \neq 0$. If the particle is displaced slightly from the position of unstable equilibrium, it moves away from the position and continues its motion until its velocity reaches zero, at $\phi = \phi_m$.

The force acting on the particle at $\phi = \phi_m$ is $-\psi'(\phi_m)$. If $\phi_m < 0$, then the force acting on the particle at the point $\phi = \phi_m$ is directed towards the point $\phi = 0$ (if $-\psi'(\phi_m) > 0$, i.e., if $\psi'(\phi_m) < 0$). If $\phi_m > 0$, then the force acting on the particle at the point $\phi = \phi_m$ is directed towards the point $\phi = 0$ (if $-\psi'(\phi_m) < 0$, i.e. if $\psi'(\phi_m) > 0$). As for the positive potential side $\psi'(\phi_m) > 0$ and for the negative potential side $\psi'(\phi_m) < 0$, the particle reflects back again to $\phi = 0$ in both cases. Due to initial conditions assumed for $\psi(\phi)$, $\phi = 0$ is a double root. Due to the above observations, the conditions for the existence of soliton solutions are as follows:

Hence, the existence conditions for solitary waves can be written mathematically as

(i)

$$\psi(\phi) = 0 \quad \text{at } \phi = 0 \text{ and } \phi = \phi_m \tag{8.15}$$

(ii)

$$\left.\frac{d\psi(\phi)}{d\phi}\right|_{\phi=0} = 0 \quad \text{and} \quad \left.\frac{d\psi(\phi)}{d\phi}\right|_{\phi=\phi_m} \neq 0. \tag{8.16}$$

There is also an additional requirement that the double root at $\phi = 0$ corresponds to a local maximum at $\phi = 0$.

Hence, another condition is

(iii)

$$\left.\frac{d^2\psi(\phi)}{d\phi^2}\right|_{\phi=0} \leq 0 \tag{8.17}$$

(should it be < 0, otherwise $= 0$, will not give maximum, the $\frac{d^4\psi}{d\phi^4} < 0$, etc.)

(iv)

$$\psi(\phi) < 0 \quad \text{when } \phi \text{ lies between } 0 \text{ and } \phi_m. \tag{8.18}$$

If $\phi_m < \phi < 0$, rarefactive solitary waves exist, and if $0 < \phi < \phi_m$, compressive solitary waves exist. Here, ϕ_m is the amplitude of the solitary wave.

$\psi(\phi)|_{\phi=0} = \frac{d\psi}{d\phi}|_{\phi=0}$ are already satisfied by the equilibrium charge neutrality condition and by the boundary condition chosen for the integrating constant.

8.2.2 *Determination of the range of Mach number*

We have $\psi(\phi) = 1 - e^{\phi} + M^2 \left[1 - \left(1 - \frac{2\phi}{M^2}\right)^{1/2}\right] = \psi_e + \psi_i$. From Equation (8.13), it is clear that ψ_e is negative for $\phi > 0$. It is clear from Equation (8.14) that for $\phi > \frac{M^2}{2}$, then ψ_i becomes complex. But physically a complex ion number density is not allowed. If $0 < \phi \leq \frac{M^2}{2}$, then $0 < \psi \leq M^2$. So $\phi = \frac{M^2}{2}$, then ψ_i is maximum and is equal to M^2. The maximum value of ϕ is allowed as $\phi_m = \frac{M^2}{2}$. So, for that maximum value of $\phi_m = \frac{M^2}{2}$, we get solitary wave $\psi(\phi_m) = 0$, i.e.,

$$\psi(M^2/2) = 0$$

$$\text{or} \quad 1 - e^{M^2/2} + M^2 \left[1 - \left(1 - \frac{2}{M^2}\frac{M^2}{2}\right)^{1/2}\right] = 0$$

$$\Rightarrow 1 - \left[1 + \frac{M^2}{2} + \left(\frac{M^2}{2}\right)^2\frac{1}{2!} + \left(\frac{M^2}{2}\right)^3\frac{1}{3!} + M^2 = 0.\right.$$

So, neglecting higher-order terms, we get

$$1 - 1 - \frac{M^2}{2} - \frac{< M^4}{8} - \frac{M^6}{48} + M^2 = 0 \Rightarrow M^2(24 - 6M^2 - M^4) = 0.$$

This implies that either

$$M^2 = 0 \quad \text{or} \quad 24 - 6M^2 - M^4 = 0$$

$$\Rightarrow M = 0 \quad \text{or} \quad M^2 = \frac{-6 \pm \sqrt{132}}{2}.$$

Taking positive sign, we have $M^2 = -3 + \sqrt{33} \Rightarrow M = \sqrt{-3 + \sqrt{33}} \approx 1.66$.

Therefore, the range of Mach number for the existence of solitary waves is $0 < M < 1.66$.

8.2.3 *Shape of the solitary waves*

Multiplying both sides of Equation (8.12) by $2\frac{d\psi}{d\xi}$ and integrating with respect to ξ, we get

$$\left(\frac{d\phi}{d\xi}\right)^2 = -2\psi(\phi) + C.$$

Using the boundary conditions $|\xi| \to \infty$, $\psi \to 0$, and $\frac{d\phi}{d\xi} \to 0$, ultimately we get

$$\frac{d\phi}{d\xi} = \pm\sqrt{-2\psi}.$$

Integrating, we obtain

$$\pm\xi = \int_{\phi}^{\phi_0} \frac{1}{\sqrt{-2\psi(\phi)}} d\phi. \tag{8.19}$$

The shape of the soliton solution can be obtained from Equation (8.19). When ϕ_0 is the value of ϕ, where $\psi(\phi)$ crosses the ϕ axis from below, i.e., ϕ_0 is the amplitude of the soliton. From the above discussions, it is clear that soliton solution will exist if $\psi(\phi)$ is negative throughout the interval of integration, and $\psi(\phi)$ crosses ϕ axis from below at some value of ϕ (say ϕ_0). Thus, ϕ_0 is the amplitude of the wave.

8.2.4 *Physical interpretation of double layers*

The double layer is a nonlinear potential structure in a plasma consisting of two adjacent layers with opposite electric charges, in which the existing potentials' jump creates an electric field. Ions and electrons which enter the double layers are accelerated, decelerated, or reflected by the electric field. The double layer in plasma is the region of self-consistent potential drop, maintained by the appropriate distributions of accelerated and reflected particles. We classify double layers into two types: weak and strong double layers. It is based on the ratio of the potential drop in comparison with the plasma's equivalent thermal potential. A double layer is said to be strong if the potential drop across the layer is greater than the equivalent thermal potential of the plasma's component. It may be useful to note that the condition $\psi(0) = \psi(\phi_m) = 0$ is required to satisfy global charge neutrality and to balance the pressure on both sides of the double layers (known as Langmuir condition). Moreover, the boundary condition $\psi'(0) = \psi'(\phi_m) = 0$ must be fulfilled to ensure that the local charge is neutral and the electric field is zero at the boundaries. The conditions $\psi''(0) < 0$ and $\psi''(\phi_m) < 0$ are the generalized Bohm criteria. These have a simple physical interpretation of the net charges inside the double layers, and they must have the correct sign that is consistent with the electric field.

Existence conditions for double layers: For a double layer, one needs successive double roots. It is because, in the parlance of classical mechanics,

ϕ can transit from one value to another without coming back, with a rather sharp and shock, or kink-like transition between the two. Also, the double roots correspond to local maxima. The conditions on the Sagdeev potential now are

(i)

$$\psi(\phi) = \psi'(\phi) = 0 \quad \text{and} \quad \psi''(\phi) < 0 \quad \text{at } \phi = 0 \tag{8.20}$$

(ii)

$$\psi(\phi_m) = \psi'(\phi_m) = 0 \quad \text{and} \quad \psi''(\phi_m) < 0 \; (\phi_m \neq 0) \tag{8.21}$$

(iii)

$$\psi(\phi) \text{ is negative in the interval } (0, \phi_m). \tag{8.22}$$

If $\phi_m > 0$, then the double layer is called a compressive double layer, and if $\phi_m < 0$, then the double layer is called a rarefractive double layer, where ϕ_m is some extremum value of the potential and is called the amplitude of the double layers.

8.2.5 *Small amplitude approximation*

We shall now obtain the small amplitude approximation of $\psi(\phi)$. Expanding $\psi(\phi)$ about $\phi = 0$, we get

$$\psi(\phi) = A + A_0\phi + A_1\phi^2 + A_2\phi^3 + A_3\phi^4 + O(\phi^5) \tag{8.23}$$

where

$$A = \left(\psi(\phi) \right)_{\phi=0} = 0$$

$$A_0 = \left(\frac{d\psi(\phi)}{d\phi} \right)_{\phi=0} = 0$$

$$A_1 = \left(\frac{d^2\psi(\phi)}{d\phi^2} \right)_{\phi=0} = \frac{1 - M^2}{2}$$

$$A_2 = \left(\frac{d^3\psi(\phi)}{d\phi^3} \right)_{\phi=0} = \frac{3 - M^4}{6}$$

$$A_3 = \left(\frac{d^4\psi(\phi)}{d\phi^4} \right)_{\phi=0} = \frac{15 - M^6}{24M^6}.$$

Expanding up to ϕ^3: Using the boundary condition $\psi \to 0$ and $\frac{d\psi}{d\phi} \to 0$ as $\phi \to 0$, and if we consider up to ϕ^3 terms, we get

$$\psi(\phi) = A_1\phi^2 + A_2\phi^3.$$

It is evident that the pseudopotential is reflected back at $\phi = -\frac{3A_1}{A_2}$, which is the maximum potential ϕ_0 of the solitary waves. The small-amplitude results are valid if ϕ_0 is small, i.e., if A_2 is small. Hence, it is valid near the boundary $\left(\frac{\partial^2\psi}{\partial\phi^2}\right)_{\phi=0}$.

Therefore,

$$\frac{d\phi}{\sqrt{-2(A_1\phi^2 + A_2\phi^3)}} = d\xi.$$

Hence, the KdV-type soliton solution is written as

$$\phi = \phi_0 sech^2\left(\frac{\xi}{\delta}\right) \tag{8.24}$$

where $\psi_0 = -\frac{3A_1}{A_2}$ is the amplitude of the solitary wave and $\delta = \frac{2}{\sqrt{-A_1}}$ is the width of the solitary wave.

Expanding up to ϕ^4: If we consider up to ϕ^4 term, we get

$$\psi(\phi) = A_1\phi^2 + A_2\phi^3 + A_3\phi^4.$$

Therefore,

$$\frac{d\phi}{\sqrt{-2(A_1\phi^2 + A_2\phi^3 + A_3\phi^4)}} = d\xi.$$

Integrating, we get

$$\phi = \left[-\frac{A_2}{3A_1} - \sqrt{\frac{A_2^2}{9A_1^2} - \frac{A_3}{2A_1}} \cosh\left(\sqrt{A_1}\xi\right)\right]^{-1}. \tag{8.25}$$

Equation (8.25) is the modified KdV soliton solution provided $A_1 > 0$. Again, if $A_2^2 = \frac{9A_1A_3}{2}$, the above soliton solution would not exist. In that case, a shock wave solution is obtained from Equation (8.25), which is written as

$$\phi = -\frac{3A_1}{2A_2}[1 + \tanh\alpha(\xi + \xi_0)] \tag{8.26}$$

where ξ_0 is the integration constant and $\alpha = -\frac{A_2}{3\sqrt{2A_3}}$. Equation (8.25) is the small-amplitude cnoidal wave solution, and (8.26) is the small-amplitude shock wave solution.

8.3 Effect of Finite Ion Temperature

In Section 8.2, we have discussed the large-amplitude solitary waves in unmagnetized plasma neglecting the ion temperature. But there are real situations where the temperature of ions is considerable with the temperature of electrons. Incorporating that phenomena we may include the temperature ration $\sigma = \frac{T_i}{T_e}$, where T_e and T_i are electron and ion temperature, respectively. Also, considering the electron inertia along with the ion continuity equation (8.1) and Poisson equation (8.3), we use the modified ion momentum equation as

$$\frac{\partial u_i}{\partial t} + u_i \frac{\partial u_i}{\partial x} + \frac{\sigma}{n_i} \frac{\partial p_i}{\partial x} = -\frac{\partial \phi}{\partial x}. \tag{8.27}$$

Supplementing the energy equation by

$$\frac{\partial p_i}{\partial t} + u_i \frac{\partial p_i}{\partial x} + 3p_i \frac{\partial p_i}{\partial x} = 0. \tag{8.28}$$

The electron continuity equation

$$\frac{\partial n_e}{\partial t} + \frac{\partial (n_e u_e)}{\partial x} = 0. \tag{8.29}$$

The electron momentum equation

$$\frac{\partial u_e}{\partial t} + u_e \frac{\partial u_e}{\partial x} = \frac{1}{\mu} \left(\frac{\partial \phi}{\partial x} - \frac{1}{n_e} \frac{\partial n_e}{\partial x} \right). \tag{8.30}$$

Here, p_i is the ion pressure and $\mu = \frac{m_e}{M_i} = \frac{1}{1836}$. m_i and m_e are ion mass and electron mass, respectively. To obtain a solitary wave solution, we make all the dependent variables depend on a single independent variable $\xi = x - Mt$. Thus, Equations (8.1), (8.27)–(8.30) are written as

$$-M \frac{dn_i}{d\xi} + \frac{d(n_i u_i)}{d\xi} = 0 \tag{8.31}$$

$$-M \frac{du_i}{d\xi} + u_i \frac{du_i}{d\xi} + \frac{\sigma}{n_i} \frac{dp_i}{d\xi} = -\frac{d\phi}{d\xi} \tag{8.32}$$

$$-M \frac{dp_i}{d\xi} + u_i \frac{dp_i}{d\xi} + 3p_i \frac{du_i}{d\xi} = 0 \tag{8.33}$$

$$-M \frac{dn_e}{d\xi} + \frac{d(n_e u_e)}{d\xi} = 0 \tag{8.34}$$

$$-M\frac{du_e}{d\xi} + u_e\frac{du_e}{d\xi} = \frac{1}{\mu}\left(\frac{d\phi}{d\xi} - \frac{1}{n_e}\frac{du_e}{d\xi}\right) \tag{8.35}$$

$$\frac{d^2\phi}{d\xi^2} = n_e - n_i. \tag{8.36}$$

Integrating Equations (8.31)–(8.36) and using the boundary conditions for localized perturbations, namely $\phi \to 0, n_i \to 1,\ n_e \to 1,\ u_i \to 1, u_e \to 0$, and $p_i \to 1$ as $\xi \to \pm\infty$, we obtain from Equations (8.31) and (8.33)

$$n_i = \frac{M}{M - u_i} \tag{8.37}$$

$$p_i = n_i^3. \tag{8.38}$$

Replacing $\frac{1}{n}$ in (8.27) by $\left(1 - \frac{u_i}{M}\right)$, multiplying it by 2, and subtracting $\frac{\sigma}{M}$ times (8.28) from it, we get

$$-2M\frac{du_i}{d\xi} + 2u_i\frac{du_i}{d\xi} + 3\sigma\frac{dp_i}{d\xi} - \frac{3\sigma}{M}\frac{du_i p_i}{d\xi} = -2\frac{d\phi}{d\xi}. \tag{8.39}$$

Integrating Equation (8.39) and using the boundary conditions, we get

$$-2Mu_i + 2u_i^2 + 3\sigma p_i - 3\sigma - \frac{3\sigma u_i p_i}{M} = -2\phi. \tag{8.40}$$

Using Equations (8.37), (8.38), and (8.40), we get

$$n = \left[\frac{(M^2 + 3\sigma - 2\phi) - \left\{(M^2 + 3\sigma - 2\phi)^2 - 12\sigma M^2\right\}^{1/2}}{6\sigma}\right]^{1/2}. \tag{8.41}$$

Similarly, integrating Equations (8.34) and (8.35) and using the boundary condition, we get

$$n_e = \frac{M}{M - u_e} \tag{8.42}$$

$$\phi = \log\left[\frac{M}{M - u_e}\right] + \frac{1}{\mu}\left[(M - u_e)^2 - M^2\right]. \tag{8.43}$$

The pseudopotential ψ may be defined as

$$\frac{d\phi}{d\xi} = -\frac{d\psi}{d\phi} \tag{8.44}$$

where

$$\psi = \psi_i + \psi_e \tag{8.45}$$

$$\psi_i = -(3\sigma M^6)^{1/4} \left[\left(e^{\frac{\theta}{2}} - e^{\frac{\theta_0}{2}} \right) + \frac{1}{3} \left(e^{\frac{-3\theta}{2}} - e^{\frac{-3\theta_0}{2}} \right) \right],$$

$$\psi_e = 1 - \frac{M}{M - u_e} + \mu M u_e$$

$$\theta = \cosh^{-1} \left[\frac{M^2 + 3\sigma - 2\phi}{\sqrt{12\sigma M^2}} \right], \quad \theta_0 = \cosh^{-1} \left[\frac{M^2 + 3\sigma}{\sqrt{12\sigma M^2}} \right].$$

Soliton solution: The form of the pseudopotential ψ would determine whether a soliton like solution of Equation (8.45) will exist or not. From (8.17), we get $\left(-\frac{1}{1-\mu M^2} + \frac{1}{M^2-3\sigma} \right) < 0$. Also, from another condition $\psi(\phi_m) \geq 0$, when $\phi_m = \min(\phi_{m1}, \phi_{m2})$ and $\phi_{m1} = \frac{M^2-3\sigma}{2}$, $\phi_{m2} = \frac{1}{2}M^2$.

8.4 Large-amplitude DASWs

To study the effect of nonthermal ions on large-amplitude solitary waves, let us assume a four-component unmagnetized collisionless plasma consisting of negatively charged dust grains, electrons, and ions. The above nonthermal distribution for ion density has been discussed in Chapter 1. In this model, two types of dust grains are considered: smaller size positively and larger size negatively charged dust grains. Most of the researchers have considered the negatively charged dust only. The consideration of negatively charged dust is valid when the dust charging process by a collection of plasma particles (viz. electrons and ions) is much more important than other charging processes. But the dust grains can be positively charged by other charging processes also. The dust grains can be positively charged by three principal mechanisms. These are (i) photoemission in the presence of a flux of ultraviolet photons, (ii) thermionic emission induced by radiative heating, and (iii) secondary emission of electrons from the surface of the dust grains. Here, the electrons and ions obey the Boltzmann and nonthermal distribution, respectively. The basic normalized equations are

$$\frac{\partial n_1}{\partial t} + \frac{\partial}{\partial x}(n_1 u_1) = 0, \tag{8.46}$$

$$\frac{\partial u_1}{\partial t} + u_1 \frac{\partial u_1}{\partial x} = \frac{\partial \phi}{\partial x}, \tag{8.47}$$

$$\frac{\partial n_2}{\partial t} + \frac{\partial}{\partial x}(n_2 u_2) = 0, \tag{8.48}$$

$$\frac{\partial u_2}{\partial t} + u_2 \frac{\partial u_2}{\partial x} = -\alpha\beta\frac{\partial\phi}{\partial x}, \tag{8.49}$$

$$\frac{\partial^2\phi}{\partial x^2} = n_1 - (1 - \mu_i + \mu_e)n_2 + \mu_e e^{\sigma\phi}$$
$$- \mu_i(1 + \beta_1\phi + \beta_1\phi^2)e^{-\phi}. \tag{8.50}$$

Here, all the notations and normalization are the same as in Section 5.3.

Energy integral and the Sagdeev potential: By using the traveling wave transformation (8.4), Equations (8.46)–(8.50) are reduced to

$$-M\frac{dn_1}{d\xi} + \frac{d(n_1 u_1)}{d\xi} = 0, \tag{8.51}$$

$$-M\frac{du_1}{d\xi} + u_1\frac{du_1}{d\xi} = \frac{d\phi}{d\xi}, \tag{8.52}$$

$$-M\frac{dn_2}{d\xi} + \frac{d(n_2 u_2)}{d\xi} = 0, \tag{8.53}$$

$$-M\frac{du_2}{d\xi} + u_2\frac{du_2}{d\xi} = -\alpha\beta\frac{d\phi}{d\xi}, \tag{8.54}$$

$$\frac{d^2\phi}{d\xi^2} = n_1 - (1 - \mu_i + \mu_e)n_2 + \mu_e e^{\sigma\phi} - \mu_i(1 + \beta_1\phi + \beta_1\phi^2)e^{-\phi}. \tag{8.55}$$

Now, integrating with respect to ξ and using the boundary conditions ψ, u_1, $u_2 \to 0$, n_1, and $n_2 \to 1$ as $|\xi| \to \infty$.

From Equation (8.51)–(8.54), we get

$$n_1 = \frac{M}{M - u_1}, \quad n_2 = \frac{M}{M - u_2}, \quad \phi = -Mu_1 + \frac{u_1^2}{2}, \quad \alpha\beta\phi = Mu_2 - \frac{u_2^2}{2}. \tag{8.56}$$

Now, using (8.56) in (8.55) and introducing Sagdeev pseudopotential $\psi(\phi)$, we get Sagdeev's equation as

$$\frac{d^2\phi}{d\xi^2} = -\frac{d\psi(\phi)}{d\phi}. \tag{8.57}$$

Sagdeev's potential can be obtained by the similar procedure as discussed in the earlier section

$$\psi(\phi) = M^2 \left[1 - \left(1 + \frac{2\phi}{M^2} \right)^{\frac{1}{2}} \right] + \frac{M^2}{\alpha\beta}(1 - \mu_i + \mu_e)\left[1 - \left(1 - \frac{2\alpha\beta\phi}{M^2} \right)^{\frac{1}{2}} \right]$$

$$+ \frac{\mu_e}{\sigma}(1 - e^{\sigma\phi}) + \mu_i[1 + 3\beta_1 - (1 + 3\beta_1 + 3\beta_1\phi + \beta_1\phi^2)e^{-\phi}].$$

$$(8.58)$$

Lower bounds of Mach number for the existence of solitary waves:
Using soliton conditions (8.15)–(8.18), we can get an analytical condition to find a range of Mach number M for the existence of solitary waves. It can be easily checked that the condition $\psi(\phi) = 0$ and $\psi'(\phi) = 0$ at $\phi = 0$ are satisfied. The condition $\psi''(\phi) < 0$ at $\phi = 0$ gives rise to the condition $M > M_c$, where

$$M_c^2 = \frac{1 + \alpha\beta(1 - \mu_i + \mu_e)}{\mu_e\sigma + (1 - \beta_1)\mu_i}.$$

Small-amplitude approximation: To study the small-amplitude approximation of $\psi(\phi)$, let us expand $\psi(\phi)$ about $\phi = 0$. Using the boundary condition $\psi \to 0$ and $\frac{d\psi}{d\phi} \to 0$ as $\phi \to 0$ and keeping up to ϕ^3 terms, we get

$$\psi(\phi) = A_1 \frac{\phi^2}{2} + A_2 \frac{\phi^3}{6} \qquad (8.59)$$

where $A_1 = \frac{1}{M^2} + (1 - \mu_i + \mu_e)\frac{\alpha\beta}{M^2} - \sigma\mu_e + (\beta_1 - 1)\mu_i$ and $A_2 = -\frac{3}{M^4} + (1 - \mu_i + \mu_e)\frac{3\alpha^2\beta^2}{M^4} - \sigma^2\mu_e - (1 + 4\beta_1)\mu_i$.

Hence, the KdV-type soliton solution is

$$\psi = \psi_0 sech^2\left(\frac{\xi}{\delta}\right) \qquad (8.60)$$

where $\psi_0 = -\frac{3A_1}{A_2}$ is the amplitude of the solitary wave and $\delta = \frac{2}{\sqrt{-A_1}}$ is the width of the solitary wave. Neglecting the nonthermal effect of ions (i.e., putting $\beta_1 = 0$), (8.59) will become

$$\psi(\phi) = A_1 \frac{\phi^2}{2} + A_2 \frac{\phi^3}{6} \qquad (8.61)$$

where $A_1 = \frac{1}{M^2} + (1 - \mu_i + \mu_e)\frac{\alpha\beta}{M^2} - \sigma\mu_e - \mu_i$ and $A_2 = -\frac{3}{M^4} + (1 - \mu_i + \mu_e)\frac{3\alpha^2\beta^2}{M^4} - \sigma^2\mu_e - \mu_i$.

Comparison between small- and large-amplitude solitary waves:
Sayed and Mamun [4] studied this model for small-amplitude solitary waves using the RPT, and they obtained the KdV equation as

$$\frac{\partial\psi_1}{\partial\tau} + A\psi_1\frac{\partial\psi_1}{\partial\xi} + B\frac{\partial^3\psi_1}{\partial\xi^3} = 0 \tag{8.62}$$

where $A = \frac{1}{2V_0[(1-\mu_i+\mu_e)\alpha\beta]}[(1 - \mu_i + \mu_e)3\alpha^2\beta^2 - 3 - V_0^4(\mu_e\sigma^2 - \mu_i)]$ and $B = \frac{V_0^3}{2[1+(1+\mu_e-\mu_i)\alpha\beta]}$. V_0, the phase speed of the DAW, is given by

$$V_0^2 = \frac{1 + (1 + \mu_e - \mu_i)\alpha\beta}{\sigma\mu_e + \mu_i}. \tag{8.63}$$

To get the steady-state solution, they used the transformation $\xi = \eta - U_0\tau$ and the usual boundary conditions, where U_0 is the velocity of the frame of the transformed coordinate. Using the usual technique, one obtains

$$\frac{d^2\psi_1}{d\xi^2} = \frac{2}{B}\left(U_0\psi_1 - \frac{\psi_1^2}{2}\right) = -\frac{\partial V_1}{\partial\psi_1} \tag{8.64}$$

where

$$V_1(\psi_1) = -\frac{U_0}{B}\psi_1^2 + \frac{1}{3B}\psi_1^3. \tag{8.65}$$

Now, to compare the small-amplitude approximation of $\psi(\phi)$ of (8.61) with the values of $V_1(\psi_1)$ of (8.65) obtained by the RPT [4], we first replace M by $V_0 + U_0$, when U_0 is small. Then, keeping only first-order terms (in U_0), it can easily be verified that $\psi(\phi)$ in (8.61) reduces to $V_1(\psi_1)$ given in (8.65). Hence, $V_1(\psi_1)$ obtained by the RPT in Ref. [4] is nothing but a small-amplitude approximation of $\psi(\phi)$ of (8.61).

It is obvious from Equation (8.57) that $\psi(\phi)$ satisfies the existence conditions (8.15)–(8.17) for solitary waves. It can be shown that $\psi(\phi)$ crosses the ϕ axis for $\phi < 0$ for $1.60 \leq M \leq 1.88$. So, the rarefractive solitary waves exist. For $M = 1.88$, $\psi(\phi)$ crosses the ϕ axis at $\phi = -1.765$. Hence, $|\phi_m| = \psi_0 = 1.765$ is the amplitude of the rarefractive solitary waves. It is also seen that from Figure 8.2 that the amplitude of the solitary waves increases with the increase in the Mach number, i.e., phase velocity of the waves.

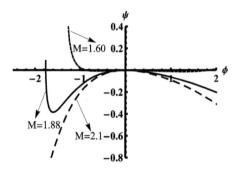

Fig. 8.2: Plot of $\psi(\phi)$ vs. ϕ for $M=$ 1.6, 1.88, and 2.1. The other parameters are $\alpha = 0.01, \beta = 40, \mu_i = 0.5, \mu_e = 0.2, \sigma = 0.5, \alpha_1 = 0.03$.

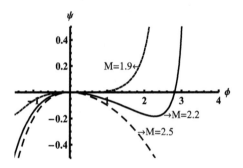

Fig. 8.3: Plot of $\psi(\phi)$ vs. ϕ for $M=$ 1.9, 2.2, and 2.5. The other parameters are $\alpha = 0.02, \beta = 40, \mu_i = 0.4, \mu_e = 0.3, \sigma = 0.6, \alpha_1 = 0.04$.

It is clear from Figure 8.3 that $\psi(\phi)$ crosses the ϕ axis for positive values of ψ for $1.9 \leq M \leq 2.2$. So, the compressive solitary waves exist. For $M = 2.2$, $\psi(\phi)$ crosses the ϕ axis at $\phi = 2.82$. Hence, $|\psi_m| = \psi_0 = 2.82$ is the amplitude of the compressive solitary waves. It is also seen from this figure that the amplitude of the solitary waves increases with the increase in velocity.

To see the effect of α_1 on the amplitude of rarefractive solitary waves, Figure 8.4 is drawn. Here, the amplitude of the solitary wave $|\psi_0|$ is plotted against α_1. It is seen that the amplitude of the rarefractive solitary waves increases very slowly with the increase in α_1. Hence, α_1 has a significant effect on the speed and shape of solitary waves in four-component plasmas.

Figure 8.5 shows that if the value of α_1 is between 0.0 and 0.2, the width of the solitary waves starts increasing. Again, when the value of $\alpha_1 > 0$, then the width of the solitary waves starts decreasing.

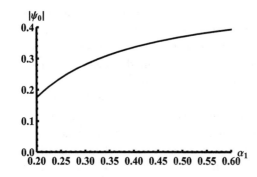

Fig. 8.4: Plot of $|\psi_0|$ against α_1 with the parameters of Figure 8.2.

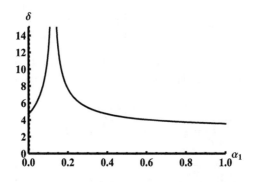

Fig. 8.5: Plot of δ vs. α_1 with parameters of Figure 8.2.

8.5 Large-amplitude Double Layers

In Chapter 1, we have discussed dusty plasma. Here, we consider a dusty plasma model consisting of massive, micron-sized, negatively charged inertial dust grains, high- and low-temperature isothermal ions, and nonthermal electrons having Tsallis distribution. The presence of energetic particles in a plasma can change the astrophysical plasma environment, and the distribution functions are considered highly nonthermal. In Chapter 1, we have already discussed the above q distribution. The nonextensive nonthermal velocity of electron distribution is physically meaningful because the distribution shoulders and high energy states are more prominent in the case of the extensive nonthermal electron. Accordingly, we have studied the effect of the nonthermal electron nonextensivity on DA double layers. However, expressions for electron number density are different for the values of $q > 1$

and $-1 < q < 1$. It is surprising that the previous analysis [5, 6], involving the pure Tsallis-type distribution (i.e., for $\alpha = 0$), uses the same electron number density distribution for both the regions. In this study, we have restricted the values of q in a limited range $0.6 < q < 1$ (arguments for selecting this range are discussed in Ref. [7]).

For simplicity, we assume the dust grains' charge $q_d = -z_d e$, where z_d is the number of charges residing on the dust grain. Charge neutrality at equilibrium requires $n_{ih0} + n_{ic0} = n_{e0} + z_d n_{d0}$, where n_{j0} is the equilibrium particle density and n_j ($j = d$, e, ih, and ic stands for the negative dust particle, electron, high-temperature isothermal ion, and low-temperature isothermal ion, respectively) is the density. The electrons are assumed to follow a nonextensive nonthermal velocity distribution function given by

$$f_e(v_x) = C_{q,\alpha}\left(1 + \alpha \frac{v_x^4}{v_{te}^4}\right)\left\{1 - (q-1)\frac{v_x^2}{2v_{te}^2}\right\}^{1/(q-1)} \tag{8.66}$$

where $v_{te} = (T_e/m_e)^{1/2}$, T_e, and m_e are the electron thermal velocity, the electron temperature, and the electron mass, respectively.

$$C_{q,\alpha} = \begin{cases} n_{e0}\sqrt{\dfrac{m_e}{2\pi T_e}}\,\dfrac{\Gamma(\frac{1}{1-q})(1-q)^{5/2}}{\Gamma(\frac{1}{1-q} - \frac{5}{2})[3\alpha + (\frac{1}{1-q} - \frac{3}{2})(\frac{1}{1-q} - \frac{5}{2})(1-q)^2]}, \\[4mm] \hspace{6cm} -1 < q < 1 \\[5mm] n_{e0}\sqrt{\dfrac{m_e}{2\pi T_e}}\,\dfrac{\Gamma(\frac{1}{q-1} + \frac{3}{2})(q-1)^{5/2}(\frac{1}{q-1} + \frac{3}{2})(\frac{1}{q-1} + \frac{5}{2})}{\Gamma(\frac{1}{q-1} + 1)[3\alpha + (q-1)^2(\frac{1}{q-1} + \frac{3}{2})(\frac{1}{q-1} + \frac{5}{2})]}, \\[4mm] \hspace{6cm} q > 1 \end{cases} \tag{8.67}$$

is the constant of normalization. Here, α, q, and Γ are the number of non-thermal electrons, the strength of nonextensivity, and the Gamma function, respectively. For $q > 1$, the distribution function (8.66) represents a thermal cut-off on the maximum value of the velocity of the electrons, given by

$$v_{max} = \sqrt{\frac{2T_e}{m_e(q-1)}}, \tag{8.68}$$

beyond which no probable states exist. For $q = 1$, the distribution [8] is obtained. High energy states are more probable than in the extensive case, when $q < 1$. Integrating Equation (8.66) overall velocity space, we get the electron density as

$$
n_e(\phi) = \begin{cases} \displaystyle\int_{-\infty}^{+\infty} f_e(v_x)dv_x & \text{for } -1 < q < 1, \\ \displaystyle\int_{-v_{max}}^{+v_{max}} f_e(v_x)dv_x & \text{for } q > 1 \end{cases}
$$

$$
= n_{e0}\left\{1 + (q-1)\frac{e\phi}{T_e}\right\}^{(q+1)/2(q-1)}\left\{1 + A\left(\frac{e\phi}{T_e}\right) + B\left(\frac{e\phi}{T_e}\right)^2\right\} \tag{8.69}
$$

where $A = -16q\alpha/(3 - 14q + 15q^2 + 12\alpha)$ and $B = 16(2q-1)q\alpha/(3 - 14q + 15q^2 + 12\alpha)$. In the extensive limiting case ($q \to 1$), density (8.69) reduces to the nonthermal electron density,

$$
n_e(\phi) = n_{e0}\left\{1 - \frac{4\alpha}{1+3\alpha}\left(\frac{e\phi}{T_e}\right) + \frac{4\alpha}{1+3\alpha}\left(\frac{e\phi}{T_e}\right)^2\right\}exp\left(\frac{e\phi}{T_e}\right). \tag{8.70}
$$

The dynamics of low phase velocity DA oscillations, whose phase speed is much less than the electron and ion thermal velocities, is governed by the following normalized equations:

$$
\frac{\partial n_d}{\partial t} + \frac{\partial(n_d u_d)}{\partial x} = 0, \tag{8.71}
$$

$$
\frac{\partial u_d}{\partial t} + u_d\frac{\partial u_d}{\partial x} + \frac{\sigma}{n_d}\frac{\partial p_d}{\partial x} = z_d\frac{\partial\phi}{\partial x}, \tag{8.72}
$$

$$
\frac{\partial p}{\partial t} + u_d\frac{\partial p}{\partial x} + 3p\frac{\partial u_d}{\partial x} = 0, \tag{8.73}
$$

$$
\frac{\partial^2\phi}{\partial x^2} = z_d n_d + n_e - n_{ic} - n_{ih}. \tag{8.74}
$$

$j = d$, e, ih, and ic stands for negative dust particle, high-temperature isothermal ion, low-temperature isothermal ion, and electron, respectively. n_j is the number density, u_j is the charged velocity, ϕ is the electric potential, and p_j is the charge fluid pressure.

Normalization: Here, the normalization is taken as

$$
x \to \frac{x}{\lambda_D}, \quad t \to \omega_{pd}t, \quad n_j \to \frac{n_j}{n_{j0}}, \quad u_d \to \frac{u_d}{C_d},
$$

$$
p_d \to \frac{p_d}{z_d n_{d0}T_d}, \quad \phi \to \frac{e\phi}{T_{eff}}
$$

where $\lambda_D = \left(\frac{T_{eff}}{4\pi z_d e^2 n_{d0}}\right)^{\frac{1}{2}}$, $\omega_{pd}^{-1} = (m_d/4\pi z_d^2 e^2 n_{d0})^{\frac{1}{2}}$, $p_{d0} = z_d n_{d0} T_d$, and $C_d = \sqrt{z_d T_{eff}/m_d}$. m_j, T_j, and e are mass, temperatures, and elementary charge. Moreover, we define $T_{eff} = (f/T_e + \mu/T_{ic} + \nu/T_{ih})^{-1}$ (the effective temperature), $\sigma = T_d/T_{eff}$, $f = n_{e0}/(z_d n_{d0})$, $\sigma_e = T_{eff}/T_e$, $\mu = n_{ic}/(z_d n_{d0})$, and $\nu = n_{ih}/(z_d n_{d0})$. Here, $\mu + \nu = 1$. The densities of nonthermal electrons feature Tsallis distribution [9] and the thermal two-temperature ions are given, respectively, by

$$n_e = f\left(1 + A\sigma_e\phi + B\sigma_e^2\phi^2\right)\left[1 + (q-1)\sigma_e\phi\right]^{(q+1)/2(q-1)}$$

$$n_{ic} = \mu\, exp\left(-\frac{\phi}{\mu + \nu\beta_1}\right),$$

$$n_{ih} = \nu\, exp\left(-\frac{\beta_1\phi}{\mu + \nu\beta_1}\right)$$

where $\beta_1 = T_c/T_h = $ (low-temperature)/(high-temperature), $A = -16q\alpha/(3 - 14q + 15q^2 + 12\alpha)$, $B = 16(2q-1)q\alpha/(3 - 14q + 15q^2 + 12\alpha)$, and α is the nonthermal parameter. In the extensive limiting case ($q \to 1$), density (8.70) reduces to the nonthermal electron density [8]

$$n_e = f\left(1 - \frac{4\alpha}{1 + 3\alpha}\sigma_e\phi + \frac{4\alpha}{1 + 3\alpha}\sigma_e^2\phi^2\right)exp(\sigma_e\phi). \qquad (8.75)$$

In contrast, for $\alpha = 0$, density (8.70) reduces to the nonextensive electron density $n_e = f[1 + (q-1)\sigma_e\phi]^{(q+1)/2(q-1)}$ [10].

Sagdeev potential: Using transformations (8.4) in Equations (8.71)–(8.74) and then integrating the transformed equation with the help of boundary condition $\phi \to 0$, $u_d \to u_{d0}$ (the equilibrium dust drift speed), $n_d \to 1$ as $|\xi| \to \infty$, we get

$$n_d = \frac{M - u_{d0}}{M - u_d}, \qquad (8.76)$$

$$z_d\phi = -Mu_d + \frac{u_d^2}{2} + \frac{3\sigma}{2}\left(\frac{M - u_{d0}}{M - u_d}\right)^2 + \frac{A}{2} \qquad (8.77)$$

where $A = 2Mu_{d0} - u_{d0}^2 - 3\sigma$. Equation (8.77) can be solved to find u_d as an explicit function of ϕ

$$u_d = M - \frac{1}{\sqrt{2}}\left[M^2 + 2z_d\phi - A + \sqrt{(M^2 + 2z_d\phi - A)^2 - 12\sigma(M - u_{d0})^2}\right]^{\frac{1}{2}}.$$
$$(8.78)$$

Integrating Equation (8.74) and using the above given boundary conditions, we get

$$\frac{d^2\phi}{d\xi^2} = -\frac{\partial\psi(\phi)}{\partial\phi},$$ (8.79)

where the pseudopotential is

$$\psi(\phi) = \left[-(M - u_{d0})u_{d0} + \sigma + (M - u_{d0})u_d - \sigma\left(\frac{M - u_{d0}}{M - u_d}\right)^3 \right]$$

$$+ f\left[-\frac{2(1 + A\sigma_e\phi + B\sigma_e^2\phi^2)}{(3q-1)\sigma_e}\left\{1 + (q-1)\sigma_e\phi\right\}^{\frac{3q-1}{2(q-1)}} \right.$$

$$+ \frac{4(A + 2B\sigma_e\phi)}{(3q-1)(5q-3)\sigma_e}\left\{1 + (q-1)\sigma_e\phi\right\}^{\frac{5q-3}{2(q-1)}}$$

$$+ \frac{16B}{(3q-1)(5q-3)(7q-5)\sigma_e}\left(1 - \left\{1 + (q-1)\sigma_e\phi\right\}^{\frac{7q-5}{2(q-1)}}\right)$$

$$\left. + \frac{2}{(3q-1)\sigma_e}\left\{1 - \frac{2A}{(5q-3)}\right\}\right]$$

$$+ \mu(\mu + \nu\beta_1)\left(1 - e^{-\frac{\phi}{\mu+\nu\beta_1}}\right)$$

$$+ \frac{\nu(\mu + \nu\beta_1)}{\beta_1}\left(1 - e^{-\frac{\beta_1\phi}{\mu+\nu\beta_1}}\right).$$ (8.80)

When we consider only dust particles and two-temperature isothermal ions without electron ($n_e = 0$), our result agrees with Tagare's result [11].

For the double layers, the Sagdeev potential $\psi(\phi)$ should be negative between $\phi = 0$ and ϕ_m, where ϕ_m is some double root of the pseudopotential corresponding to the maximum wave amplitude. Therefore, for the formation of double layers, $\psi(\phi)$ must satisfy conditions (8.20)–(8.22). To find the region of existence of the double layer, one has to study the nature of $\psi(\phi)$. In Figure 8.6, $\psi(\phi)$ is plotted against ϕ for $q = 0.61$ (solid line) and 0.65 (dashed line). It is seen that for $q = 0.61$, conditions (8.20)–(8.22) are both satisfied, and hence, a double layer exists. However, it is found that for $q = 0.65$, condition (8.20) is satisfied but $\psi(\phi) \neq 0$ at $\phi = \phi_m$, i.e., $V(\phi)$ does not cross the ϕ axis at any point other than 0. Hence, for $q = 0.62$, a double layer could not exist. It is, therefore, found that q has a significant role in the formation of the double layer.

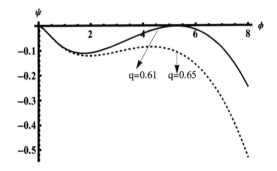

Fig. 8.6:   The pseudopotential $\psi(\phi)$ is plotted against ϕ for $q = 0.61$ (solid line) and 0.65 (dashed line). Other parameters are $M = 1.5$, $\sigma = 0.02$, $\mu = 0.282$, $\beta = 0.0224$, $u_{d0} = 0.001$, $\sigma_e = 0.05$, $z_d = 825$, $f = 0.0317$.

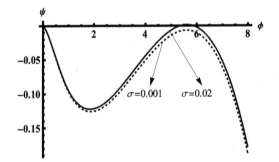

Fig. 8.7:   The effect of the finite dust temperature on the pseudopotential $\psi(\phi)$ for $\sigma = 0.02$ (solid line) and 0.001 (dashed line). Other parameters are the same as Figure 8.6.

In Figure 8.7, $\psi(\phi)$ is plotted against ϕ, for $\sigma = 0.02$ (solid line) and $\sigma = 0.001$ (dashed line). It can be seen that a double layer exists for $\sigma = 0.02$. So, it is found that a finite dust temperature has a significant role in the formation of the double layer.

8.6   Effect of Ion Kinematic Viscosity

The presence of dissipation effects in plasma plays an important role in the dynamics of nonlinear waves. The dissipation arises due to the Landau damping, kinematic viscosity, wave–particle interaction, and so on. Experimentally, the effects of dissipation caused by the kinematic viscosity on the propagation of solitary wave structures were observed and discussed in

Ref. [12]. Here, we consider the nonextensivity of electrons, which has been discussed in Chapter 1. The basic normalized equations are

$$\frac{\partial n_i}{\partial t} + \frac{\partial (n_i u_i)}{\partial x} = 0, \tag{8.81}$$

$$\frac{\partial u_i}{\partial t} + u_i \frac{\partial u_i}{\partial x} = -\frac{\partial \phi}{\partial x} - \eta \frac{\partial^2 u_i}{\partial x^2}, \tag{8.82}$$

$$\frac{\partial^2 \phi}{\partial x^2} = (n_e - n_i \delta_1 + z_d \delta_2) \tag{8.83}$$

where n_j, u_j, ϕ, T_j, η, C_s, and λ_{de} are the number density, the charged velocity, the plasma potential, the temperature, the kinematic viscosity, the ion acoustic speed, and the Debye length, respectively. Here, $j = i$, and e, which stands for ions, and electrons, respectively. $\eta = 1/C_s \lambda_{De}$, $C_s = \sqrt{T_e/m_i}$, $\omega_{pi}^{-1} = (m_i/4\pi n_{i0}e^2)^{1/2}$, $\lambda_i = (T_e/4\pi n_{i0}e^2)^{1/2}$ $\delta_1 = n_{i0}/n_{e0}$, $\delta_2 = n_{d0}/n_{e0}$, and $n_e = (1 + (q-1)\phi)^{\frac{q+1}{2(q-1)}}$. z_d is the dust charge number and the dust grains are assumed to be massive, immobile, and negatively charged.

Normalization: Here, the normalizations are taken as

$$n_i \to \frac{n_i}{n_{i0}}, \quad n_e \to \frac{n_e}{n_{e0}}, \quad u_i \to \frac{u_i}{C_s}, \quad \phi \to \frac{e\phi}{T_e}, \quad t \to \omega_{pi}t, \quad x \to \frac{x}{\lambda_i}.$$

By using transformation (8.4), Equations (8.81)–(8.83) are reduced to

$$-M \frac{dn_i}{d\xi} + \frac{d(n_i u_i)}{d\xi} = 0, \tag{8.84}$$

$$-M \frac{du_i}{d\xi} + u_i \frac{du_i}{d\xi} = -\frac{d\phi}{d\xi} - \eta \frac{d^2 u_i}{d\xi^2}, \tag{8.85}$$

$$\frac{d^2 \phi}{d\xi^2} = n_e - n_i \delta_1 + z_d \delta_2. \tag{8.86}$$

Using boundary conditions $n_i \to 1$, $u_i \to 0$, when $\xi \to \pm\infty$, we obtain from Equations (8.84)–(8.85)

$$n_i = \frac{M}{M - u_i} \tag{8.87}$$

$$\frac{(M - u_i)^2}{2} = \frac{M^2}{2} - \phi - \eta \frac{du_i}{d\xi}. \tag{8.88}$$

Let

$$F(\phi) = \int_0^\phi n_i d\phi. \tag{8.89}$$

Now using (8.87)–(8.89) in (8.86), we get

$$\frac{d^2\phi}{d\xi^2} = \frac{\partial\psi}{\partial\phi} \tag{8.90}$$

where

$$\psi(\phi) = \frac{2}{(3q-1)}[1 + (q-1)\phi]^{\frac{(3q-1)}{2(q-1)}} - \delta_1 F(\phi) + z_d\delta_2\phi - \frac{2}{(3q-1)}. \tag{8.91}$$

Small-amplitude approximation: To get the explicit expression of pseudopotential, one has to get the explicit expression for $F(\phi)$. From Equations (8.87) and (8.89), we have

$$F'(\phi) = \frac{M}{M - u_i}. \tag{8.92}$$

So,

$$\frac{du_i}{d\xi} = \frac{M}{[F'(\phi)]^2}F''(\phi)\frac{d\phi}{d\xi}. \tag{8.93}$$

Taking

$$w = f'(\phi) = n_i \tag{8.94}$$

and using the results of Equations (8.88) and (8.93), we get

$$w' = \frac{\frac{w^2 M^2}{2} - \phi w^2 - \frac{M^2}{2}}{\eta M \sqrt{\frac{4}{3q-1}[1 + (q-1)\phi]^{\frac{3q-1}{2(q-1)}} - 2\delta_1 F'(\phi) + 2z_d\delta_2\phi - \frac{4}{3q-1}}}. \tag{8.95}$$

It is seen from Equation (8.95) that the equation even holds when η is zero, provided one takes the appropriate limit. For $\eta = 0, w^2$ can be obtained from the following equation:

$$\frac{w^2 M^2}{2} - \phi w^2 - \frac{M^2}{2} = 0. \tag{8.96}$$

So,

$$n_i = w = \frac{M}{\sqrt{M^2 - 2\phi}}. \tag{8.97}$$

For nonzero but small η, we consider terms up to $O(\eta)$ and get from Equation (8.95)

$$w = \frac{M}{\sqrt{M^2 - 2\phi}} + \frac{\eta M \frac{d\phi}{d\xi}}{(M^2 - 2\phi)^2}. \tag{8.98}$$

Using (8.86) in Equation (8.98), we have

$$\frac{d^2\phi}{d\xi^2} = [1 + (q-1)\phi]^{\frac{(q+1)}{2(q-1)}} - \frac{\delta_1 M}{\sqrt{M^2 - 2\phi}} - \frac{M \delta_1 \eta \frac{d\phi}{d\xi}}{(M^2 - 2\phi)^2} + z_d \delta_2. \tag{8.99}$$

Considering the terms up to $O(\frac{\phi}{M^2})$ in Equation (8.99) and differentiating with respect to ξ, we get

$$\frac{d^3\phi}{d\xi^3} = \frac{d\phi}{d\xi}\left(\frac{q+1}{2} - \frac{\delta_1}{M^2}\right) + \frac{(q+1)(q-3)}{2}\phi\frac{d\phi}{d\xi} - \frac{\delta_1\eta}{M^3}\frac{d^2\phi}{d\xi^2}. \tag{8.100}$$

Equation (8.100) is the well-known KdVB equation written in terms of the single variable $\xi = x - Mt$. Using the boundary conditions $\phi = 0$, $\frac{d\phi}{d\xi} = 0$ and a particular solution of the above KdVB equation [13] is obtained as follows:

$$\phi = \frac{A^2 g^2}{(e^{-A\xi/2} - Bg)^2} \tag{8.101}$$

where $A = -\frac{2\eta\delta_1}{5M^3}$ and $B = \pm\sqrt{\frac{(q+1)(q-3)}{6}}$. g is the integration constant that depends on the initial condition and M is determined from the following equation:

$$25(q+1)M^6 - 50\delta_1 M^4 + 12\delta_1^2\eta^2 = 0. \tag{8.102}$$

When $Bg = -1$, the above solution is the same as the solution obtained by W. Malfliet [14] who used the tanh method. However, if η is not too small, one cannot derive Equation (8.101). For arbitrary η, one can get Sagdeev's potential up to any order in ϕ by the suitable expansion of $F(\phi)$. Now, considering $F(\phi)$ up to ϕ^4 terms, we have

$$F(\phi) = \phi + b\phi^2 + c\phi^3 + d\phi^4 \tag{8.103}$$

where b is determined from the following equation:

$$2bM^2 - 1 - 2b\eta M \sqrt{\frac{(q+1)}{2}} - 2\delta_1 b = 0.$$

c and d are given by

$$c = \frac{4b - 2b^2 M^2 - 2\eta M b(q+1)(q-3)}{[12(1+q) - 48\delta_1 b][3M^2 - 6\eta M\sqrt{(q+1)/2} - 2\delta_1 b]}$$

and

$$d\left[12\eta M \sqrt{\frac{q+1-4\delta_1 b}{2}} - \frac{4\delta_1 \eta M b}{\sqrt{2}\sqrt{q+1-4\delta_1 b}} - 4M^2\right]$$
$$= 6bcV^2 - (4b^2 + 6c) + d_1$$

where

$$d_1 = c\eta M \left[\frac{(q+1)(q-3) + 24\delta_1 c}{2\sqrt{2}\sqrt{q+1-4\delta_1 b}}\right] + \frac{\eta M b}{\sqrt{2}}\left[\frac{\{(q+1)(q-3) + 24\delta_1 c\}^2}{144(q+1-4\delta_1 b)^{3/2}}\right.$$
$$\left. - \frac{(q+1)(q-3)(3q-5)}{48\sqrt{q+1-4\delta_1 b}}\right].$$

One can also write

$$\psi = -\frac{1}{2}\left(\frac{d\phi}{d\xi}\right)^2. \tag{8.104}$$

We get from our previous equation

$$\psi = -\frac{2}{(3q-1)}[1 + (q-1)\phi]^{\frac{3q-1}{2(q-1)}} + \delta_1 F(\phi) - \delta_2 z_d \phi + \frac{2}{3q-1}. \tag{8.105}$$

Keeping terms up to ϕ^2, we get

$$\frac{d^2\phi}{d\xi^2} = A_1 \phi + A_2 \phi^2 \tag{8.106}$$

where $A_1 = -(q+1)/2 + 2b\delta_1$ and $A_2 = (q-3)(q+1)/8 + 3c\delta_1$. Integrating Equation (8.106), with the same boundary conditions, we obtain

$$\phi = -\frac{3A_1}{2A_2}\mathrm{sech}^2\left(\frac{\sqrt{A_1}\xi}{2}\right). \tag{8.107}$$

Now, keeping terms up to ϕ^3 of Equation (8.105), we have

$$\frac{d^2\phi}{d\xi^2} = A_1\phi + A_2\phi^2 + A_3\phi^3 \tag{8.108}$$

where $A_3 = -(q-3)(q+1)(3q-5)/48 + 4\delta_1 d$. Solving Equation (8.108), we obtain

$$\phi = \left[-\frac{A_2}{3A_1} + \sqrt{\left(\frac{A_2^2}{9A_1^2} - \frac{A_3}{2A_1} \right)} \cosh(\sqrt{A_1}\xi) \right]^{-1}. \tag{8.109}$$

If $A_2^2 = \frac{9}{2}A_1A_3$, then solution (8.109) would not be valid and a shock wave solution is obtained, which is given by

$$\phi = P(1 + \tanh\alpha(\xi + \xi_0)) \tag{8.110}$$

where ξ_0 is the integration constant and $P = -\frac{3A_1}{2A_2}$, $\alpha = \frac{A_2}{3\sqrt{2A_3}}$, $(A_0 > 0)$.

If $\delta_1 b = (q+1)/4$ and $\delta_1 c = (3-q)(q+1)/24$, it is seen from Equations (8.107) and (8.109) that the solution does not exist. For these values of parameters, one must take a higher-order term. When $A_1 < 0$, but $\delta_1 c \neq q(3-q)(q=1)/24$, both these solutions will show periodic behavior. Hence, for solitary wave solution, we assume $A_1 > 0$ and $A_3 \neq 0$.

Figure 8.8 shows the plot of ψ vs. ϕ for $\eta = 0.03$ (dotted line) and 0.05 (bold line) when $\delta_1 = 2.235$, $q = 1.1$. It is seen that as η increases, the amplitude of the soliton increases.

To show the effect of the nonextensivity of electrons, we use the q distribution function $f_e(v) = C_q\{1 + (q-1)[m_e v^2/2T_e - e\phi/T_e]\}^{1/(q-1)}$, where

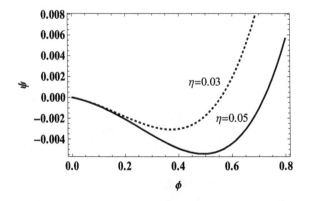

Fig. 8.8: The plot of ψ vs. ϕ for $\eta = 0.03$ (dotted line) and 0.05 (solid line).

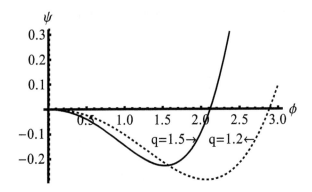

Fig. 8.9: The plot of ψ vs. ϕ for $q = 1.2$ (dotted line) and 1.5 (solid line).

$f_e(v)$ is the particular distribution that maximizes the Tsallis entropy and C_q is the normalization constant. To see the effect of nonextensive parameter q in Figure 8.9, ψ is plotted against ϕ for $q = 1.2$ (dotted line) and 1.5 (solid line). Other parameters are the same as those in Figure 8.8. We find from this figure that the amplitude of the soliton increases highly as q increases. Hence, both q and η play significant roles in the formation and shape of solitary waves in plasma.

For large-amplitude DIASWs, one has either to solve the coupled Equations (8.94) and (8.95) or has to include higher-order terms in the expansion. However, the solution given in Equation (8.109) is already a higher-order solution that cannot be obtained easily using the RPT method. For small amplitude, one can neglect the term of the order ϕ^4 in the pseudopotential, while for a shock wave solution, one has to include higher-order terms.

8.7 DIASWs in Magnetized Plasma

In a strong magnetic field, ion pressure has a significant effect on the formation of solitary waves. If the magnetized plasma is in a collisionless state and the magnetic field is strong, the pressure becomes anisotropic. The plasma then behaves differently in each of the parallel and perpendicular directions. The ion pressure obeys two different equations of state in both directions in the magnetic field. Chew–Goldberger–Low (CGl) theory [15] or a double adiabatic theory can be used when there is no coupling between the perpendicular and parallel pressure. Anisotropic pressure has a significant effect on the solitary waves. In anisotropic plasmas, the pressure tensor can be written in a matrix form as

$$\mathbf{P} = \begin{pmatrix} p_\perp & 0 & 0 \\ 0 & p_\perp & 0 \\ 0 & 0 & p_\parallel \end{pmatrix}.$$

If $p_\perp = p_\parallel$, this becomes isotropic pressure. According to the CGL theory, the scalar pressures $p_\perp$ and $p_\parallel$ can be written as

$$p_\perp = p_{\perp 0}\left(\frac{n_i}{n_{i0}}\right) \quad and \quad p_\parallel = p_{\parallel 0}\left(\frac{n_i}{n_{i0}}\right)^3$$

where $p_{\perp 0}$ and $p_{\parallel 0}$ are the perpendicular and parallel pressures at equilibrium. Subindex 0 denotes the value at the equilibrium. The Boltzmann relation gives the density of electrons as

$$n_e = n_{e0}e^{\frac{e\phi}{T_e}}. \tag{8.111}$$

The basic normalized equations are

$$\frac{\partial n}{\partial t} + \frac{\partial n v_x}{\partial x} + \frac{\partial n v_z}{\partial z} = 0, \tag{8.112}$$

$$\frac{\partial v_x}{\partial t} + \left(v_x\frac{\partial}{\partial x} + v_z\frac{\partial}{\partial z}\right)v_x = -\frac{\partial \phi}{\partial x} + v_y - \frac{p_{\perp 0}}{T_e n_{i0}}\frac{1}{n}\frac{\partial n}{\partial x}, \tag{8.113}$$

$$\frac{\partial v_y}{\partial t} + \left(v_x\frac{\partial}{\partial x} + v_z\frac{\partial}{\partial z}\right)v_y = -v_x, \tag{8.114}$$

$$\frac{\partial v_z}{\partial t} + \left(v_x\frac{\partial}{\partial x} + v_z\frac{\partial}{\partial z}\right)v_z = -\frac{\partial \phi}{\partial z} - \frac{3p_{\parallel 0}}{T_e n_{i0}}n\frac{\partial n}{\partial z}, \tag{8.115}$$

$$\left(\frac{\partial^2}{\partial x^2} + \frac{\partial^2}{\partial z^2}\right)\phi = \beta[e^\phi - \delta_1 n + \delta_2] \tag{8.116}$$

where n, ϕ, and z_d are the number density, the electrostatic potential, and the dust charge number, respectively. The charge of the dust is written as $q_d = -ez_d$, where e is the elementary charge. v_i and m_i are the velocity and the mass of ions. We assume that the wave is propagating in the xz plane. $\beta = \frac{r_g^2}{\lambda_e^2}$, $\delta_1 = \frac{n_{i0}}{n_{e0}}$, and $\delta_2 = \frac{n_d z_d}{n_{e0}}$. $r_g = \frac{C_s}{\Omega}$ is the ion gyroradius and $\lambda_e = \left(\frac{T_e}{4\pi n_{e0}e^2}\right)^{1/2}$ is the electron Debye length.

Normalizations: Normalizations are taken as

$$\Omega t \to t, \quad (C_s/\Omega)\nabla \to \nabla, \quad v_i/C_s \to v, \quad n_i/n_{i0} \to n, \quad e\phi/T_e \to \phi$$

where $C_s = (T_e/m_i)^{1/2}$ is the ion acoustic velocity, $\Omega = \frac{eB_0}{m_i c}$ is the ion gyrofrequency, and n_{j0} are equilibrium densities.

Sagdeev potential: To obtain the solutions for Equations (8.112)–(8.116), we introduce a variable defined in a moving coordinate given by

$$\xi = l_x x + l_z z - Mt \tag{8.117}$$

where l_x and l_z are directional cosines and M is the Mach number of the localized wave. Equations (8.112)–(8.116) can then be reduced to ordinary differential equations in terms of ξ.

$$M(1-n) + n(l_x v_x + l_z v_z) = 0, \tag{8.118}$$

$$-M\frac{dv_x}{d\xi} + \left(v_x l_x \frac{d}{d\xi} + v_z l_z \frac{d}{d\xi}\right) v_x = -l_x \frac{d\phi}{d\xi} + v_y - \frac{p_{\perp 0}}{T_e n_{i0}} \frac{1}{n} l_x \frac{dn}{d\xi}, \tag{8.119}$$

$$-M\frac{dv_y}{d\xi} + \left(v_x l_x \frac{d}{d\xi} + v_z l_z \frac{d}{d\xi}\right) v_y = -v_x, \tag{8.120}$$

$$-M\frac{dv_z}{d\xi} + \left(v_x l_x \frac{d}{d\xi} + v_z l_z \frac{d}{d\xi}\right) v_z = -l_z \frac{d\phi}{d\xi} - \frac{3p_{\parallel 0}}{T_e n_{i0}} n l_z \frac{dn}{d\xi}, \tag{8.121}$$

$$(l_x^2 + l_z^2)\frac{d^2\phi}{d\xi^2} = \beta[e^\phi - \delta_1 n + \delta_2]. \tag{8.122}$$

Using (8.118) in (8.119), we get

$$\frac{M}{n}\frac{dv_x}{d\xi} = l_x\left(\frac{d\phi}{d\xi} + \frac{p_{\perp 0}}{T_e n_{i0}} \frac{1}{n}\frac{dn}{d\xi}\right) - v_y. \tag{8.123}$$

Using (8.119), we get

$$\frac{M}{n}\frac{dv_y}{d\xi} = v_x. \tag{8.124}$$

Using (8.121), we have

$$\frac{M}{n}\frac{dv_z}{d\xi} = l_z\left(\frac{d\phi}{d\xi} + \frac{3p_{\parallel 0}}{T_e n_{i0}} n\frac{dn}{d\xi}\right). \tag{8.125}$$

Considering

$$F(\phi) = \int_0^\phi n\,d\phi, \tag{8.126}$$

we have

$$v_z = \frac{l_z}{M}\left(F(\phi) + \frac{p_{\|0}}{T_e n_{i0}}n^3\right). \tag{8.127}$$

Using (8.126) and (8.127) in (8.118), we obtain

$$l_x v_x + \frac{l_z^2}{M}\left\{F(\phi) + \frac{l_z^2}{M}\frac{p_{\|0}}{T_e n_{i0}}(n^3 - 1)\right\} = \left(1 - \frac{1}{F'(\phi)}\right)M. \tag{8.128}$$

From (8.122), we have

$$(l_x^2 + l_z^2)\frac{1}{2}\left(\frac{d\phi}{d\xi}\right)^2 = \beta[e^\phi - 1 - \delta_1 F(\phi) + \delta_2\phi]. \tag{8.129}$$

As can be seen in (8.129), Equation (8.122) can be integrated to the form

$$\frac{1}{2}\left(\frac{d\phi}{d\xi}\right)^2 + \psi(\phi) = 0 \tag{8.130}$$

where $\psi(\phi)$ is the Sagdeev potential.

In a small-amplitude approximation, $F(\phi)$ can be expanded in terms of ϕ such that

$$F(\phi) = \phi + a_1\phi^2 + a_2\phi^3 + a_3\phi^4 + a_4\phi^5 + \cdots \tag{8.131}$$

and from (8.128), we can get

$$v_x = A\phi + B\phi^2 + C\phi^3 + D\phi^4 \tag{8.132}$$

where

$$A = \frac{\left[-\frac{l_z^2}{M}\left(1 + 6a_1\frac{p_{\|0}}{T_e n_{i0}}\right) + 2a_1 M\right]}{l_x},$$

$$B = \frac{\left[-\frac{l_z^2}{M}\left(a_1 + \frac{p_{\|0}}{T_e n_{i0}}(9a_2 + 12a_1^2)\right) + 3a_2 M - 4a_1^2 M\right]}{l_x},$$

$$C = \frac{\left[-\frac{l_z^2}{M}\left(a_2 + \frac{p_{\|0}}{T_e n_{i0}}(8a_1^3 + 12a_3 + 36a_1 a_2)\right) + 4a_3 M - 12a_1 a_2 M + 8a_1^3 M\right]}{l_x},$$

$$D = \frac{-\frac{l_z^2}{M}\left(a_3 + \frac{p_{\|0}}{T_e n_{i0}}(15a_4 + 27a_2^2 + 48a_1 a_3) + 36a_1^2 a_2\right)}{l_x}$$

$$+ \frac{5a_4 M - 9a_2^2 M - 16a_1 a_3 M + 36a_1^2 a_2 M - 16a_1^4 M}{l_x}.$$

From (8.129), we get

$$\left(\frac{d\phi}{d\xi}\right)^2 = \frac{2\beta}{l_x^2 + l_z^2}\left[(1 + \delta_2 - \delta_1)\phi + \left(\frac{1}{2} - \delta_1 a_1\right)\phi^2 + \left(\frac{1}{6} - \delta_1 a_2\right)\phi^3 \right.$$
$$\left. + \left(\frac{1}{24} - \delta_1 a_3\right)\phi^4\right]. \tag{8.133}$$

Keeping terms up to ϕ^2 order, we can get Sagdeev's equation as

$$\frac{d^2\phi}{d\xi^2} = A_1\phi + A_2\phi^2 = -\frac{d\psi}{d\phi} \tag{8.134}$$

where $A_1 = \frac{\beta}{l_x^2 + l_z^2}(1 - 2\delta_1 a_1)$ and $A_2 = \frac{\beta}{l_x^2 + l_z^2}\left(\frac{1}{2} - 3\delta_1 a_2\right)$. From Equation (8.124), we get

$$M\frac{dv_y}{d\phi}\frac{d\phi}{d\xi} = v_x F'(\phi), \tag{8.135}$$

and from Equation (8.123), we get

$$v_y = \left(l_x + l_x\frac{p_{\perp 0}}{T_e n_{i0}}\frac{1}{F'(\phi)}\frac{dn}{d\phi} - \frac{M}{F'(\phi)}\frac{dv_x}{d\phi}\right)\frac{d\phi}{d\xi}. \tag{8.136}$$

Equating the terms of ϕ with equal powers in Equations (8.135) and (8.136), the values of a_1 and a_2 can be decided by the following equations:

$$A = Y_1(1 - 2\delta_1 a_1) \tag{8.137}$$

$$a_2\left[\frac{3MX_2}{l_x} + 3Y_1\delta_1 - 3\frac{p_{\perp 0}}{T_e n_{i0}}\frac{(X_2 - 1)}{M}\right]$$
$$= \frac{Y_1}{2} + Z_1 X_2 - 2a_1 A + (1 - 2\delta_1 a_1)a_1\left(\frac{l_x}{2M}X_1 - 2Y_1\right). \tag{8.138}$$

The expressions for $X_1, X_2, Y_1,$ and Z_1 are given as

$$X_1 = \frac{4M^2\beta}{l_x^2 + l_z^2}, \quad Y_1 = \frac{M\beta\left(l_x + 2a_1\frac{p_{\perp 0}l_x}{T_e n_{i0}} - MA\right)}{l_x^2 + l_z^2},$$

$$Z_1 = \frac{\left(\frac{l_x^2 a_1}{M} + 4a_1^2 M\right)}{l_x}, \quad X_2 = 1 + \frac{2M^2\beta(1 - 2\delta_1 a_1)}{l_x^2 + l_z^2}.$$

The solution for (8.133) is given by

$$\phi = -\frac{3(1 - 2\delta_1 a_1)}{1 - 6\delta_1 a_2}\operatorname{sech}^2\left(\frac{\sqrt{A_1}\xi}{2}\right). \tag{8.139}$$

Again, keeping terms up to ϕ^3, we have

$$\frac{d^2\phi}{d\xi^2} = A_1\phi + A_2\phi^2 + A_3\phi^3 \tag{8.140}$$

where $A_3 = \frac{\beta}{l_x^2 + l_z^2}\left(\frac{1}{6} - 4\delta_1 a_3\right)$. a_3 is obtained from the following equation:

$$a_3\left[4Y_1\delta_1 + 3X_1(1 - 2\delta_1 a_1)\left(\frac{M}{l_x} - \frac{p_\perp 0 l_x}{T_e n_{i0} M}\right) + \frac{4M}{l_x}\right]$$

$$= \frac{1}{l_x}\left[\frac{l_z^2}{M}\left(a_2 + \frac{p_{\parallel 0}}{T_e n_{i0}}\right) + 12 a_1 a_2 M - 8 a_1^3 M\right]$$

$$- 4A a_1^2 - 4B a_1 - 6A a_2 + \frac{Y_1}{6}$$

$$+ \frac{X_1}{2}\left(\frac{1}{2} - 3\delta_1 a_2\right)\left(\frac{a_1 l_x}{M} - B + 3\frac{p_\perp 0 l_x}{T_e n_{i0} M} a_2\right) + \frac{3X_1}{4l_x}(1 - 2\delta_1 a_1)$$

$$\times \left(\frac{l_x^2 a_2}{M} + \frac{l_z^2 a_2}{M} + \frac{l_z^2 p_{\parallel 0}}{M T_e n_{i0}} + 12 a_1 a_2 M - 8 a_1^3 M\right).$$

Solution for Equation (8.134) is given by

$$\phi = \left[-\frac{A_2}{3A_1} - \sqrt{\frac{A_2^2}{9A_1^2} - \frac{A_3}{2A_1}}\cosh(\sqrt{A_1}\xi)\right]^{-1}. \tag{8.141}$$

If $A_2^2 = \frac{9}{2}A_1 A_3$, then solution (8.141) would not be valid and a shock wave (double-layer) solution is obtained, which is given by

$$\phi = -\frac{3A_1}{2A_2}[1 + \tanh\alpha(\xi + \xi_0)] \tag{8.142}$$

where ξ_0 is the integration constant and $\alpha = -\frac{A_2}{3\sqrt{2A_3}}$, $A_3 > 0$.

In Equation (8.139), it can be seen that if $2\delta_1 a_1 = 1$, then the amplitude of the solitary wave will be 0 and if $6\delta_1 a_2 = 1$, then the amplitude will be infinite. Thus, the expansion of $V(\phi)$ up to $O(\phi^3)$ is valid, only if $\delta_1 a_1 \neq \frac{1}{2}$ or $\delta_1 a_2 \neq \frac{1}{6}$. If $\delta_1 a_1 = \frac{1}{2}$ or $\delta_1 a_2 = \frac{1}{6}$, then the expansion should be made up to $O(\phi^4)$ and in that case, the soliton solution will be given by Equation (8.141). Again, if $A_2^2 = \frac{9}{2}A_1 A_3$, then Equation (8.141) no longer admits a solitary solution. For that particular set of parameters, we get a shock wave solution, which is given by Equation (8.142). Furthermore, from Equations (8.139) and (8.141), one more condition is required, $A_1 > 0$, for the existence of soliton solution. From the discussions so far, it is clear that the amplitude of the solitary waves depends on a_1, a_2, a_3, which are functions of β. This means that the amplitude of the solitary wave changes with the change of the external magnetic field.

8.8 Solitary Kinetic Alfven Waves

We have already discussed Alfven waves in Chapter 1. We have seen that there are different types of Alfven waves. The kinetic Alfven waves grow from the perpendicular effects. These waves follow an electric field and propagate perpendicularly to the ambient magnetic field. It can be stimulated in plasma either by drift wave instability or resonant mode conversion of a surface magnetohydrodynamic wave. KAW involves an exact solution that springs from the balance between the perpendicular dispersion and the compressible nonlinearity of the waves. The electrons tend to follow the magnetic lines of force due to their small Larmor radii. It produces a charge separation and leads to what is known as the kinetic Alfven waves (KAWs). Ion drift, for example, contributes to the kinetic properties of Alfven waves. The KAW develops a longitudinal parallel electrostatic field due to the finite-Larmor radius (FLR) effect. They also have dispersive characteristics.

Solitary kinetic Alfven wave (SKAW) exists due to the interplay between the nonlinear steepening and their dispersive character [16]. They play an important role in the study of the coupling of the ionosphere and magnetosphere. The strong electromagnetic solitary spikes dominate the auroral low-frequency turbulence, according to the observation of the Freja satellite [17, 18]. These structures could be interpreted as hump-type and dip-type SKAWs. A recent observation from Freja and Fast satellites [19] showed the presence of SKAWs in Earth's ionosphere.

We will discuss the effect of ion temperature on the existence of large-amplitude solitary waves and double layers in the plasma model. Here, we consider a two-fluid homogeneous plasma model in a uniform ambient magnetic field.

$$\frac{\partial n_e}{\partial t} + \frac{\partial n_e v_{ez}}{\partial z} = 0 \tag{8.143}$$

$$\frac{\partial v_{ez}}{\partial t} + v_{ez}\frac{\partial v_{ez}}{\partial z} = \alpha\left(-E_z - \frac{1}{n_e}\frac{\partial n_e}{\partial z}\right) \tag{8.144}$$

$$\frac{\partial n_i}{\partial t} + \frac{\partial n_i v_{ix}}{\partial x} + \frac{\partial n_i v_{iz}}{\partial z} = 0 \tag{8.145}$$

$$\frac{\partial v_{ix}}{\partial t} + v_{ix}\frac{\partial v_{ix}}{\partial x} + v_{iz}\frac{\partial v_{ix}}{\partial z} = \alpha Q E_x + v_{iy} - \frac{\sigma}{n_i}\frac{\partial n_i}{\partial x} \qquad (8.146)$$

$$\frac{\partial v_{iy}}{\partial t} + v_{ix}\frac{\partial v_{iy}}{\partial x} + v_{iz}\frac{\partial v_{iy}}{\partial z} = -v_{ix} \qquad (8.147)$$

$$\frac{\partial v_{iz}}{\partial t} + v_{ix}\frac{\partial v_{iz}}{\partial x} + v_{iz}\frac{\partial v_{iz}}{\partial z} = \alpha Q E_z - \frac{\sigma}{n_i}\frac{\partial n_i}{\partial z} \qquad (8.148)$$

$$-\frac{\partial^3 E_x}{\partial z^2 \partial x} + \frac{\partial^3 E_z}{\partial x^2 \partial z} = \frac{1}{\alpha Q}\left[\frac{\partial^2 n_e}{\partial t^2} + \frac{\partial^2 (n_i v_{iz})}{\partial t \partial z}\right]. \qquad (8.149)$$

n_j ($j = i$ and e stand for ions and electrons, respectively) and ω_{pi} are the density and the ion plasma frequency, respectively. $Q = \frac{m_e}{m_i}$, $E_x = -\frac{\partial \phi_1}{\partial x}$, $E_z = -\frac{\partial \phi_2}{\partial z}$, $V_A = \frac{cB_0}{(4\pi n_0 m_i)^{\frac{1}{2}}}$, $\sigma = \frac{T_e}{T_i}$, and $\alpha = \frac{\beta}{2Q}$. Two potentials ϕ_1 and ϕ_2 are included to justify a low-β plasma model.

Normalization: Here, normalization is taken as follows:

$$n_j \to \frac{n_j}{n_0}, \quad t \to \Omega t, \quad v_i \to V_A, \quad x \to \frac{cx}{\omega_{pi}}.$$

Electric fields are normalized by $\frac{T_e \Omega_{ci}}{e v_A}$, and magnetic field is normalized by B_0.

Energy integral and the Sagdeev potential: We introduce a stationary independent variable $\eta = xk_x + zk_z - \omega t$, where $\omega = \frac{V}{V_A}$ is the phase velocity of the wave in the unit of the Alfven velocity V_A and $k_x^2 + k_z^2 = 1$. Here, it is assumed that a uniform ambient magnetic field B_0 acts along the z-direction on the plasma. Equations (8.143)–(8.149) can be expressed in the stationary frame, and the resulting ordinary differential equations are solved by taking the following boundary conditions: $v_{ix} = v_{iz} = v_{ez} = 0$ at $n_i = n_e = 1$ when $\eta \to \infty$. The electron velocity along the z-direction is

$$v_{ez} = \frac{\omega}{k_z}\left(1 - \frac{1}{n_e}\right). \qquad (8.150)$$

The electron density is

$$n_e = e^{-\frac{1}{k_z}\int E_z d\eta}\left[\exp A\left(1 - \frac{1}{n_e^2}\right)\right] \qquad (8.151)$$

where $A = \frac{\omega^2}{2\alpha k_z^2}$. The following relationship

$$k_x v_{ix} + k_z v_{iz} = \omega\left(1 - \frac{1}{n_i}\right) \qquad (8.152)$$

is obtained from Equation (8.145) and will be used later to obtain v_{ix} and v_{iy}. Maxwell Equation (8.149) in stationary frame is given by

$$-k_x k_z^2 \frac{d^3 E_x}{d\eta^3} + k_z k_x^2 \frac{d^3 E_z}{d\eta^3} = \frac{1}{\alpha Q}\left[\omega^2 \frac{d^2 n_e}{d\eta^2} - \omega k_z \frac{d^2(n_i v_{iz})}{d\eta^2}\right]. \quad (8.153)$$

Applying the charge neutrality condition $n_i = n_e = n$ and the boundary conditions as mentioned above, the electric field in the z-direction is calculated as

$$E_z = k_z\left(\frac{2A}{n^3} - \frac{1}{n}\right)\frac{dn}{d\eta}. \quad (8.154)$$

The components of the ion velocity are given as follows:

$$v_{iz} = \frac{k_z}{\omega}\left[\alpha Q\left(-\frac{2A}{n} - n + 2A + 1\right) - \sigma(n-1)\right], \quad (8.155)$$

$$v_{ix} = \frac{\omega}{k_x}\left(1 - \frac{1}{n}\right) - \frac{k_z^2}{\omega k_x}\left[\alpha Q\left(\frac{2A}{n} + n - 2A - 1\right) + \sigma(n-1)\right], \quad (8.156)$$

$$v_{iy} = \frac{1}{k_x}\left[\left(\frac{n^2}{2} - n + \frac{1}{2}\right) - \frac{k_z^2}{\omega^2}\left[\alpha Q\left(2An + \frac{n^3}{3} - An^2 - \frac{n^2}{2} - A + \frac{1}{6}\right) + \sigma\right.\right.$$
$$\left.\left.\times\left(\frac{n^3}{3} - \frac{n^2}{2} + \frac{1}{6}\right)\right]\right]\frac{d\eta}{dn}. \quad (8.157)$$

By substituting v_{ix}, v_{iy} in Equation (8.146) expressed in stationary frame, we have

$$E_x = \left[-\frac{\omega^2}{\alpha Q k_x n^3} + \frac{k_z^2}{\alpha Q k_x}\left[\alpha Q\left(-\frac{2A}{n^3} + \frac{1}{n}\right) + \frac{\sigma}{n}\right] + \frac{k_x \sigma}{n\alpha Q}\right]\left(\frac{dn}{d\eta}\right)$$
$$-\frac{1}{\alpha Q k_x}\left[\left(\frac{n^2}{2} - n + \frac{1}{2}\right) - \frac{k_z^2}{\omega^2}\left[\alpha Q\left(2An + \frac{n^3}{3} - An^2 - \frac{n^2}{2} - A + \frac{1}{6}\right)\right.\right.$$
$$\left.\left.+\sigma\left(\frac{n^3}{3} - \frac{n^2}{2} + \frac{1}{6}\right)\right]\right]\frac{d\eta}{dn}. \quad (8.158)$$

After successive integration of Equation (8.153) and using Equation (8.155) and the boundary conditions $\left(\frac{dn}{d\eta}\right) \to 0$ and $n \to 1$, we get

$$-k_x k_z^2 \frac{dE_x}{d\eta} + k_x^2 k_z \frac{dE_z}{d\eta} = \frac{1}{\alpha Q}[\omega^2 n - \omega k_z n v_{iz}] + c = \frac{1}{\alpha Q}\left[\omega^2(n-1)\right.$$
$$\left. - k_z^2 n\left[\alpha Q\left(\frac{2A}{n} + n - 2A - 1\right) + \sigma(n-1)\right]\right]. \quad (8.159)$$

Now, by substituting E_x and E_z from Equations (8.154) and (8.158) into Equation (8.159) and after some algebraic manipulations, we get

$$
\frac{\frac{1}{2}\left(\frac{dn}{d\eta}\right)^2 \frac{k_z^4}{n^6}\left[\frac{\omega^2}{\alpha Q} - (n^2 - 2A) - \frac{n^2\sigma}{\alpha Q}\right]^2}{k_z^2\left(1 - \frac{k_z^2}{\omega^2}\right)}
$$

$$
= -\frac{\omega^2\sigma}{\alpha^2 Q^2}(n - \log n) + \frac{k_z^2\sigma}{\alpha Q}\left(2A\log n + \frac{n^2}{2} - 2An - n\right)
$$

$$
+ \frac{k_z^2\sigma^2}{\alpha^2 Q^2}\left(\frac{n^2}{2} - n\right) + \frac{\omega^4}{\alpha^2 Q^2}\left(-\frac{1}{n} + \frac{1}{2n^2}\right)
$$

$$
- \frac{k_z^2\omega^2}{\alpha Q}\left(-\frac{A}{n^2} + \log n + \frac{2A}{n} + \frac{1}{n}\right)
$$

$$
- \frac{k_z^2\sigma\omega^2}{\alpha^2 Q^2}\left(\log n + \frac{1}{n}\right) - \frac{\omega^2}{\alpha Q}(n - \log n)
$$

$$
+ k_z^2\left(2A\log n + \frac{n^2}{2} - 2An - n\right) + \frac{k_z^2\sigma}{\alpha Q}\left(\frac{n^2}{2} - n\right)
$$

$$
+ \frac{2A\omega^2}{\alpha Q}\left(-\frac{1}{n} + \frac{1}{2n^2}\right) - 2Ak_z^2\left(-\frac{A}{n^2} + \log n + \frac{2A}{n} + \frac{1}{n}\right)
$$

$$
- \frac{2Ak_z^2\sigma}{\alpha Q}\left(\log n + \frac{1}{n}\right) + C \tag{8.160}
$$

where $C = \frac{k_z^2}{2}\left[(1 + 2A)^2 + 4A + \frac{\sigma^2}{\alpha^2 Q^2}\right] + \frac{k_z^2\sigma}{\alpha Q}(4A + 1) + \frac{\omega^2}{\alpha Q}\left[(A + 1)(1 + k_z^2) + \frac{\sigma}{\alpha Q} + \frac{\omega^2}{2\alpha Q} + \frac{k_z^2\sigma}{\alpha Q}\right]$.

Finally, we get

$$
\frac{1}{2}\left(\frac{dn}{d\eta}\right)^2 + \psi(n, \alpha, Q, \omega, k_z, \sigma) = 0 \tag{8.161}
$$

where Sagdeev's potential $\psi(n, \alpha, Q, \omega, k_z, \sigma)$ is given as

$$
\psi(n, \alpha, Q, \omega, k_z, \sigma)
$$

$$
= -\frac{n^4\left(1 - \frac{k_z^2}{\omega^2}\right)}{k_z^2\left[\frac{\omega^2}{\alpha Q} - (n^2 - 2A) - \frac{\sigma n^2}{\alpha Q}\right]^2}\left[\left(\frac{k_z^2}{2} + \frac{k_z^2\sigma}{\alpha Q} + \frac{k_z^2\sigma^2}{2\alpha^2 Q^2}\right)n^4\right.
$$

$$
\left. - \left[k_z^2(2A + 1) + \frac{\omega^2}{\alpha Q}\left(1 + \frac{\sigma}{\alpha Q}\right) + \frac{k_z^2\sigma}{\alpha Q}2(A + 1) + \frac{k_z^2\sigma^2}{\alpha^2 Q^2}\right]n^3\right.
$$

$$+\left[\frac{\omega^2}{\alpha Q}\left(1-k_z^2-\frac{k_z^2\sigma}{\alpha Q}+\frac{\sigma}{\alpha Q}\right)\right]n^2\log n$$

$$+\left[\frac{k_z^2}{2}\left[(1+2A)^2+4A+\frac{\sigma^2}{\alpha^2Q^2}\right]+\frac{k_z^2\sigma}{\alpha Q}(4A+1)\right.$$

$$+\frac{\omega^2}{\alpha Q}\left[(A+1)(1+k_z^2)+\frac{\sigma}{\alpha Q}+\frac{\omega^2}{2\alpha Q}+\frac{k_z^2\sigma}{\alpha Q}\right]\right]n^2$$

$$-\left[\frac{\omega^2}{\alpha Q}\left[\frac{\omega^2}{\alpha Q}+2A+(2A+1)k_z^2+\frac{k_z^2\sigma}{\alpha Q}\right]+2Ak_z^2\left(1+2A+\frac{\sigma}{\alpha Q}\right)\right]n$$

$$+\left[\frac{\omega^2}{\alpha Q}\left[\frac{\omega^2}{2\alpha Q}+A(1+k_z^2)\right]+2A^2k_z^2\right]\right].$$

Soliton and other types of solutions may be obtained similarly as discussed in the previous section.

8.9 Collapse of EA Solitary Waves

To study the speed and shape of electron acoustic solitary waves, we consider the basic equations in an *e-i* plasma, where ions and hot electrons are mobile in the back ground of Maxwell distribution.

$$\frac{\partial n_j}{\partial t}+\frac{\partial(n_ju_j)}{\partial x}=0, \tag{8.162}$$

$$\frac{\partial u_j}{\partial t}+u_j\frac{\partial u_j}{\partial x}+\frac{\mu_j}{n_j}\frac{\partial p_j}{\partial x}=-z_j\mu_j\frac{\partial\phi}{\partial x}, \tag{8.163}$$

$$\frac{\partial p_j}{\partial t}+u_j\frac{\partial p_j}{\partial x}+3p_j\frac{\partial u_j}{\partial x}=0, \tag{8.164}$$

$$\frac{\partial^2\phi}{\partial x^2}=n_{0h}e^{\phi}-\Sigma_jz_jn_j \tag{8.165}$$

where $\mu_j=m_j/m_i$, $z_j=q_j/e$, and $j=i,c$ represent ions and cold electrons, respectively. The subscript h denotes the hot electron.

Normalizations: The normalizations are taken as

$$n_j\to\frac{n_j}{n_{0e}},\quad u_j\to\sqrt{\frac{m_e}{T_h}}u_j,\quad p_j\to\frac{p_j}{n_{0e}T_h},\quad T_j\to\frac{T_j}{T_h},\quad \phi\to\frac{e\phi}{T_h},$$

$$x\to\frac{x}{\lambda_D},\quad t\to w_it.$$

n_j, p_j, T_j, and ϕ are the number density, the pressure, the temperatures, and electric potential, respectively. m_e is the mass of the electron. Also, λ_D and ω_i are the Debye length and the ion plasma frequency, respectively. $\lambda_D = \sqrt{\frac{K_B T_h}{4\pi n_{0e} e^2}}$ and $\omega_i = \sqrt{\frac{4\pi n_{e0} e^2}{m_i}}$.

Sagdeev potential and collapse of solitons: By using the traveling wave transformation (8.4), Equations (8.162)–(8.165) are reduced to

$$-M\frac{dn_j}{d\xi} + \frac{d(n_j u_j)}{d\xi} = 0, \tag{8.166}$$

$$-M\frac{du_j}{d\xi} + u_j\frac{du_j}{d\xi} + \frac{\mu_j}{n_j}\frac{dp_j}{d\xi} = -\frac{d\phi}{d\xi}, \tag{8.167}$$

$$-M\frac{dp_j}{d\xi} + u_j\frac{dp_j}{d\xi} + 3p_j\frac{du}{d\xi} = 0, \tag{8.168}$$

$$\frac{d^2\phi}{d\xi^2} = n_{0h}e^\phi + n_c - n_i. \tag{8.169}$$

Integrating the above equation and using the boundary condition ϕ, $\frac{d\phi}{d\xi}$, u_i, u_c, $u_h \to 0$, $n_i \to 1$, $n_c \to n_{0c}$, $p_i \to T_i$, $p_c \to n_{0c}T_c$ at $|\xi| \to \infty$, we get

$$n_c = \frac{M n_{0c}}{M - u_c}. \tag{8.170}$$

Now, eliminating ϕ, n_c, n_i, p_c, p_i in terms of u_c and keeping terms up to $O(\mu)$, we get

$$\frac{d^2 u_c}{d\xi^2} = \frac{\partial\psi}{\partial u} \tag{8.171}$$

where

$$\psi(u_c) = g(u_c)[\psi_h(u_c) + \psi_c(u_c) + \psi_i(u_c)]. \tag{8.172}$$

Here, $g(u_c) = -\frac{1}{\left[(M-u_c)\left(\frac{3T_c M^2}{(M-u_c)^4}-1\right)\right]^2}$, $\psi_h(u_c) = n_{0h}(1 - e^{v_1})$, $\psi_c(u_c) = n_{0c}\left[Mu_c + T_c\left(1 - \frac{M^3}{(M-u_c)^3}\right)\right]$, $\psi_i(u_c) = v_1 + \frac{\mu v_1^2}{2M^2} + \frac{3\mu T_i v_1}{4M^2}$, and $v_1 = \left(-Mu_c + \frac{u_c^2}{2}\right)\left(1 - \frac{3T_c}{(M-u_c)^2}\right)$. $\psi_h(u_c), \psi_c(u_c)$, and $\psi_i(u_c)$ manifest the effects of n_h, n_c, and n_i, respectively. All $\psi_h(u_c), \psi_c(u_c)$, and $\psi_i(u_c)$ are obtained from Equation (8.169) by using Equation (8.167). Calculations are done neglecting the terms of $O(\mu^2)$. Thus,

$$\frac{d^2 u_c}{d\xi^2} = g_1(u_c)\left[n_{0h}e^{v_1} + \frac{n_{0c}M}{M - u_c} - 1 - \frac{\mu v_1}{M^2} - \frac{3\mu T_i}{4M^2}\right]$$

$$+ g_2(u_c)\left[n_{0h}(1 - e^{v_1}) + n_{0c}\left[Mu_c + T_c\left(1 - \frac{M^3}{(M - u_c)^3}\right)\right]\right.$$

$$\left. + v_1 + \frac{\mu v_1{}^2}{2M^2} + \frac{3\mu T_i v_1}{4M^2}\right] \tag{8.173}$$

where $g_1(u_c) = \frac{1}{(M - u_c)^{-3}[3T_c M^2 - (M - u_c)^4]}$, $g_2(u_c) = 2\frac{(M - u_c)^9 + 9T_c M^2 (M - u_c)^5}{[3T_c M^2 - (M - u_c)^4]^3}$, and $\psi(u_c) = \frac{(u_c')^2}{2}$. To find the region of existence of solitary waves, one has to study the nature of the function $\psi(u_c)$, and $\phi_1(u_c)$ is defined as

$$\psi(u_c) = \frac{(u_c')^2}{2} \tag{8.174}$$

where

$$u_c'' = \frac{\partial \psi}{\partial u}$$

$$= \phi_1(u_c). \tag{8.175}$$

$\phi_1(u_c)$ has two roots: one being at $u_c = 0$ and the other at some point $u = u_{c1}(\geq 0)$. Also, $\phi_1(u_c)$ should be positive on the interval $(0, u_{c1})$ and negative on (u_{c1}, u_{max}). Here, u_{max} is obtained from the nonzero root of $\psi(u_c)$. To get the shape of the solitary wave, we have solved the differential equation numerically $u_c'' = \psi_1(u_c)$ with $u_{0c} = 0.423062, u_{0c}' = 0$, and Figure 8.10 depicts the soliton solution $u_c(\xi)$ plotted against ξ. It is seen that $u_{0c} = 0.423062$ is the critical value for u_c. For $u > u_{0c}$, the soliton solution ceases to exist as can be seen in Figure 8.11. In this figure, u_{0c} is

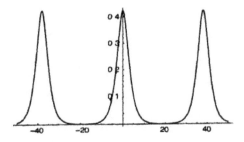

Fig. 8.10: The soliton solution $u_c(\xi)$ plotted against ξ.

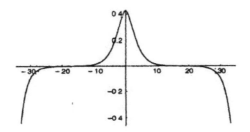

Fig. 8.11: The collapse of soliton $u_c(\xi)$ plotted against ξ.

taken as 0.423063 (all other parameters are the same as in Figure 8.10). Hence, it is seen that for an extremely small change of the value of u_{0c}, the periodic behavior of the wave as well as solitary wave is destroyed.

8.10 Collapse of DASWs in Presence of Trapped Ions

The ion and electron distribution functions are significantly modified in the presence of large-amplitude solitary waves, which are excited by the two-stream instability [19]. In this context, one may consider a vortex-like distribution for ions in the plasma. Accordingly, we consider the trapped or vortex-like ion distribution $f_i = f_{if} + f_{it}$, where

$$f_{if} = \frac{1}{\sqrt{2\pi}}e^{-\frac{1}{2}(v_i^2+2\phi)} \qquad for \ |v_i| > \sqrt{-2\phi} \tag{8.176}$$

$$f_{it} = \frac{1}{\sqrt{2\pi}}e^{-\frac{1}{2}\sigma_{it}(v_i^2+2\phi)} \quad for \ |v_i| \le \sqrt{-2\phi}. \tag{8.177}$$

The ion distribution function is continuous in velocity space and satisfies the regularity requirements for an admissible BGK solution. Here, the ion velocity v_i in Equations (8.176) and (8.177) is normalized by the ion thermal speed v_{Ti}; $\sigma_{it} = \frac{T_i}{T_{it}}$, where T_i is the free ion temperature and T_{it} is the trapped ion temperature. Integrating the ion distributions over velocity space, we get ion number density as

$$n_i = I(-\phi) + \frac{1}{\sqrt{\sigma_{it}}}e^{-\sigma_{it}\phi}erf(\sqrt{-\sigma_{it}\phi}), \quad for \ \sigma_{it} > 0 \tag{8.178}$$

$$n_i = I(-\phi) + \frac{1}{\sqrt{\pi|\sigma_{it}|}}W_D(\sqrt{\sigma_{it}\phi}) \qquad for \ \sigma_{it} < 0 \tag{8.179}$$

where

$$I(x) = [1 - erf(\sqrt{x})]e^x,$$

$$erf(x) = \frac{2}{\sqrt{\pi}} \int_0^x e^{-y^2} dy,$$

$$W_D(x) = e^{-x^2} \int_0^x e^{y^2} dy.$$

We consider a three-component dusty plasma system consisting of massive, micron-sized, negatively charged, inertial dust grains, Boltzmann distributed electron, and vortex-like ion distribution. The basic equations are

$$\frac{\partial n_d}{\partial t} + \frac{\partial (n_d u_d)}{\partial x} = 0, \tag{8.180}$$

$$\frac{\partial u_d}{\partial t} + u_d \frac{\partial u_d}{\partial x} = \frac{\partial \phi}{\partial x}, \tag{8.181}$$

$$\frac{\partial^2 \phi}{\partial x^2} = n_d - n_i + n_e \tag{8.182}$$

where $n_i = e^{-\phi} erfc\sqrt{-\phi} + \frac{1}{\sigma_{it}} e^{-\sigma_{it}\phi} erf\sqrt{-\sigma_{it}\phi}$ and $n_e = \mu_0 e^{\alpha\phi}$. n_j ($j = i, e,$ and d denote ion, electron, and dust particles, respectively), u_d, and ϕ are the number density, the dust fluid velocity, and the electrostatic potential, respectively. T_i, M_d, and e are the ion temperature, the dust mass, and the electron charge, respectively.

Normalizations: The normalizations are taken as

$$n_j \rightarrow \frac{n_j}{n_{j0}}, \quad u_d \rightarrow \frac{u_d}{C_d}, \quad \phi \rightarrow \frac{e\phi}{T_i}, \quad x \rightarrow \frac{x}{\lambda_D}, \quad t \rightarrow \omega_{pd}t.$$

λ_D and ω_{pd} are the Debye length and the dust plasma frequency, respectively. $\lambda_D = \sqrt{\frac{T_i}{4\pi z_d n_{d0}e^2}}$, $\omega_{pd} = \sqrt{\frac{4\pi z_d^2 n_{d0}e^2}{m_d}}$, $\mu_1 = \frac{1}{1-\beta}$, $\mu_0 = \frac{\beta}{1-\beta}$, $\beta = \frac{n_{e0}}{n_{i0}}$, and $\alpha = \frac{T_i}{T_e}$. T_e is the electron temperature.

Sagdeev potential and collapse of solitons: By using the traveling wave transformation (8.4), Equations (8.180)–(8.182) are reduced to

$$-M\frac{dn_d}{d\xi} + \frac{d(n_d u_d)}{d\xi} = 0, \tag{8.183}$$

$$-M\frac{du_d}{d\xi} + u_d \frac{du_d}{d\xi} = \frac{d\phi}{d\xi}, \tag{8.184}$$

$$\frac{d^2\phi}{d\xi^2} = n_d - n_i + n_e. \tag{8.185}$$

Integrating the above equation and using the boundary conditions ϕ, $\frac{d\phi}{d\xi} \to$ 0, $n_d \to 1$, $u_d \to u_{d0}$ at $|\xi| \to \infty$, we obtain

$$n_d = \frac{1}{\sqrt{1 + \frac{2\phi}{M^2}}}. \tag{8.186}$$

Using (8.186) in Equation (8.185), we get

$$\frac{\partial^2 u_d}{\partial \xi^2} = \frac{\partial \psi(u_d)}{\partial u_d} \tag{8.187}$$

where

$$\psi(u_d) = -\frac{\psi_i(u_d) + \psi_e(u_d) + \psi_d(u_d)}{(M - u_d)^2}, \quad \psi_d(u_d) = M u_d,$$

$$\psi_i(u_d) = -\left[e^{M u_d - \frac{u_d^2}{2}} \operatorname{erfc}\left(M u_d - \frac{u_d^2}{2}\right) + \frac{1}{\sigma_{it}\sqrt{\pi}} e^{M u_d - \frac{u_d^2}{2}} \operatorname{erf}\left(M u_d - \frac{u_d^2}{2}\right) \right.$$

$$\left. + \frac{1}{\sigma_{it}\sqrt{\pi}} \sqrt{M u_d - \frac{u_d^2}{2}} (\sigma_{it} - 1) \right] + 1,$$

$$\psi_e(u) = \frac{\mu_0}{\alpha} \left(1 - e^{\alpha\left(-M u_d + \frac{u_d^2}{2}\right)}\right).$$

Expanding *erf* and *erfc* functions and neglecting much higher-order terms $O(\phi^4)$, Equation (6.18) can be written as

$$\psi_i(u) = -\mu_1 \left[1 + v u_d - \frac{u_d^2}{2} - \frac{4(1 - \sigma_{it})}{3\sqrt{\pi}} \left(v u_d - \frac{u_d^2}{2}\right)^{\frac{3}{2}} + \frac{\left(-v u_d + \frac{u_d^2}{2}\right)^2}{2} \right.$$

$$- \frac{8(1 - \sigma_{it}^2)}{15\sqrt{\pi}} \left(v u_d - \frac{u_d^2}{2}\right)^{\frac{5}{2}} - \frac{\left(-v u_d + \frac{u_d^2}{2}\right)^3}{6}$$

$$\left. - \frac{16(1 - \sigma_{it}^3)}{105\sqrt{\pi}} \left(v u_d - \frac{u_d^2}{2}\right)^{\frac{7}{2}} + \frac{\left(-v u_d + \frac{u_d^2}{2}\right)^4}{24} \right]. \tag{8.188}$$

Hence, $\psi(u)$ and $\frac{d^2 u}{d\xi^2}$ can be obtained up to $O(\phi^4)$ from Equations (8.187) and (8.188).

We can also write

$$\psi(u_d) = \frac{(u_d')^2}{2}. \tag{8.189}$$

To find the region of existence of solitary waves, one has to study the nature of the functions $\psi(u_d)$, and $\phi_1(u_d)$ is defined by

$$u_d'' = \frac{\partial \psi_d}{\partial u_d} = \phi_1(u_d).$$

For solitary wave, $\phi_1(u_d)$ has two roots: one being at $u_d = 0$ and other at some point $u_d = u_{d1}(\geq 0)$. Also, $\phi_1(u_d)$ should be positive on the interval $(0, u_{d1})$ and negative on (u_{d1}, u_{dmax}). Here, u_{dmax} is obtained from the nonzero root of $\psi_d(u_d)$. To get the shape of the traveling solitary wave, one has to solve $\phi_1(u_d) = u_d''$ numerically with suitable boundary conditions.

To get the shape of the solitary wave, we have solved numerically $u_d'' = \phi_1(u_d)$ with $u_d = 0.324728, u_d' = 0$, and Figure 8.12 depicts the soliton solution $u_d(\xi)$ plotted against ξ. $u_{d1} = 0.324728$ is the critical value for u_d. For $u_d > u_{d1}$, the soliton solution ceases to exist, and it is shown in Figure 8.13. In this figure, u_{d1} is taken as 0.324729. Hence, it is seen that a small change of the value of u_d can destroy the periodic behavior of the wave as well as solitary wave. The divergent part of the wave for the negative

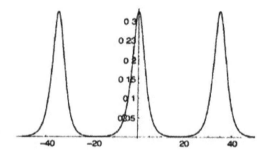

Fig. 8.12:   The soliton solution $u_d''(\xi)$ plotted against ξ for $u_{d1} = 0.324728$.

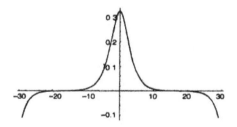

Fig. 8.13:   The collapse of soliton $u_d''(\xi)$ plotted against ξ for $u_{d1} = 0.324728$.

value of u_d cannot be shown because of the presence of the square root of u_d in the differential equation.

References

[1] R. Z. Sagdeev in, In M. A. Leontovich (eds.), *Reviews of Plasma Physics.* Vol. 4 , New York: Consultants Bureau (1966), p. 23.

[2] M. Remoissenet, *Waves called Solitons.* 3rd ed. Burlin: Springer verlag (1999).

[3] A. Das, A. Bandyopadhyay, and K. P. Das, *J. Plasma Phys.* 28, 149 (2012).

[4] F. Sayed and A. A. Mamun, *Phys. Plasmas* 14, 014501 (2007).

[5] K. Roy, T. K. Maji, M. K. Ghorui, P. Chatterjee, and R. Roychowdhury, *Astrophys. Space Sci.* 352, 151 (2014).

[6] U. N. Ghosh, P. Chatterjee, and M. Tribeche, *Phys. Plasmas* 79, 789 (2013).

[7] G. Williams, I. Kourakis, F. Verheest, and M. A. Hellberg, *Phys. Rev. E* 88, 023103 (2013).

[8] R. A. Cairns, A. A. Mamun, R. Bingham, R. Bostron, R. O. Dendy, C. M. C. Nair, and P. K. Shukla, *Geophys. Res. Lett.* 22, 2709 (1995).

[9] M. Tribeche, R. Amour, and P. K. Shukla, *Phys. Rev. E* 85, 037401 (2012).

[10] M. Tribeche, L. Djebani, and R. Amour, *Phys. Plasmas* 17, 042114 (2010).

[11] S. G. Tagare, *Phys. Plasmas* 4, 3167 (1977).

[12] Y. Nakamura and A. Sarma, *Phys. Plasmas* 8, 3921 (2001).

[13] S. Maitra and R. Roychoudhury, *Phys. Plasmas* 12, 054502 (2005).

[14] W. Malfliet, *Am. J. Phys.* 60, 650 (1992).

[15] G. F. Chew, M. L. Goldberger, and F. E. Low, *Proc. R. Soc. London, Ser. A* 236, 112 (1956).

[16] D. J. Wu, G. L. Huang, D. Y. Wang, and C. G. Falthammar, *Phys. Plasmas* 3, 2879 (1966).

[17] J. E. Wahlund, P. Louran, T. Chust, H. De Feraudy, A. Roux, B. Holback, P. O. Dovner, and G. Holmgren, *Geophys. Res. Lett.* 21, 1831. Doi: 10.1029/94GL01289.

[18] P. Louran, J. E. Wahlund, T. Chust, H. De Feraudy, A. Roux, B. Holback, P. O. Dovner, and G. Holmgren, *Geophys. Res. Lett.* 21, 1847. Doi: 10.1029/94GL00882.

[19] J. S. Makela, A. Malkki, H. Koskinen, B. Holback, and L. Elliason, *J. Geophys. Res. [Space Phys.]* 103, 9391 (1998). Doi: 10.1029/98JA00212; K. Stasiewicz, G. Holmgren, and L. Zanetti, *ibid* 103, 4251 (1998). Doi: 10.1029/97JA02007.

Chapter 9

Conclusion and Future Scopes

In this book, we have studied the linear and nonlinear waves in different plasma environments (classical plasma, dusty plasma, and quantum plasma). Moreover, the interaction of waves in various plasma models is also investigated. We have considered the fluid approach for this study. To study linear waves, the fluid equations are linearized in the neighborhood of an equilibrium point, and the first-order perturbed quantities are considered wavy (proportional to e^{kx-iwt}, where k is the wavenumber and w is the natural frequency). The relationship between the frequency and the wave number is obtained and is called the dispersion relation. This relation gives different wave modes in plasma. Several wave modes and their features are investigated in various unmagnetized and magnetized plasmas.

Nonlinear evolution equations (NLEEs) are becoming significant in modern research because of their wide range of applications. Today, the research of NLEEs is becoming very popular. It is applied in various fields such as mathematical physics, nonlinear mechanics, particle physics, plasma physics, nonlinear optics, marine science, atmospheric science, automation, and others. The trend originates from the fact that NLEEs may explain a wide range of natural phenomena that linear equations cannot do. Wave phenomena are significant in understanding natural phenomena, as it maintains a good relationship between the theory and experiment or observation. Naturally, as almost all physical phenomena are nonlinear (do not satisfy the principle of superposition), the derivation of the nonlinear evolution equation for such nonlinear phenomena is a must. After explaining the basic properties of plasma theory, we have focused on the basic properties of nonlinear waves. We have explained these in the first two chapters. Chapter 4 discusses the derivation of nonlinear waves in a plasma medium by using the famous reductive perturbation technique (RPT). The reductive perturbation technique is a special type of multiscale perturbation technique where two different timescales are incorporated into the coordinate frame by considering two different stretched coordinates. The perturbation parameter ϵ considered here depends upon ω and k, where ω is the frequency and k is the wave vector. This technique gives different information for different values of ϵ. The lowest order of ϵ gives the dispersion relation and phase speed. The next orders provide the desired evolution equation and evolution equation for dressed soliton, respectively.

Chapter 3 discusses different techniques to obtain the traveling wave solutions of different nonlinear evolution equations like solitary waves, shock waves, and change of shape of soliton to shocks and vice versa. In the presence of damping or forcing terms in the evolution equation, we get the solution from the conservation principles of KdV or KdV-type equations as and when required.

The plasma devices used in the plasma laboratory are spherical and cylindrical. So, the evolution equations required to model the situation should contain nonplaner terms. In Chapter 6, we derive evolution equations in nonplaner geometry. The equation contains a nonsingular term at $t = 0$. The solution of such an equation in the neighborhood of the singular point is obtained by numerical simulation.

Sometimes, the results observed in the laboratory do not match the theoretical results obtained from KdV-type equations. In those cases, a higher-order correction of KdV or similar equations is necessary. Considering the next higher-order terms in RPT, one can easily obtain the equation whose solution improves the result obtained from solitons. Such improved solitons are called dressed solitons. In Chapter 5, we consider the properties of dressed solitons in different plasma environments also.

Some nonperturbed methods are applied to understand the existence of solitons and to observe other important features like the dependence of parameters on the amplitude and width of a soliton. Sagdeev's pseudopotential approach is one such method by which one can understand the effect of plasma parameters' region where the solitons or shocks exist. It also explains how the plasma parameters affect the amplitude and width of the solitons. An improved technique has been developed to understand the speed and shape of solitons. It is also shown that the solitons are very sensitive to initial conditions, and the shape of the soliton is destroyed for a small change of initial speed.

Interactions of solitons are the main issue for soliton dynamics. Starting from the famous work of Zabusky and Kruskal, several theoretical and experimental investigations have been conducted to understand the interaction of solitary waves. Chapter 7 investigates all the interactions of solitons like head-on, overtaking, and oblique collision. Theoretically, the solitons should regain their shape after an infinite time. But it has been observed that the solitons regain their shape after a finite time. Moreover, in that finite time, the collision of multisoliton causes weak turbulence called soliton turbulence in the medium. Again, the head-on collision causes relatively strong turbulence than overtaking collision. The nonlinear medium plasmas show several nonlinear waves other than solitons. Those are cnoidal waves, envelop solitons, lump, breather, dromions, etc. Interactions of those waves may lead to new phenomena which may be discussed in the future and may be included in the next edition.

Possible development may be done in near future:

(1) Interaction between soliton and lump, lump–lump, lump–breather, and soliton–breather in plasmas can be investigated.
(2) Effect of damping and forcing on soliton turbulence is another important area that may be given emphasis.
(3) Chaos and hyperchaos in the presence of externally applied force may be investigated.
(4) Effect of noise may be incorporated in place of externally applied periodic force considered in all problems.

Index